# Using dBASE IV® 1.5

## Special Edition

DEVELOPED BY

QUE CORPORATION

Revised by

STEVE DAVIS

*Using dBASE IV 1.5*, Special Edition



Library of Congress Catalog No.: 92-60273

ISBN: 0-88022-968-3



94 93 5

Interpretation of the printing code: the rightmost double-digit number is the year of the book's printing; the rightmost single-digit number, the number of the book's printing. For example, a printing code of 92-1 shows that the first printing of the book occurred in 1992.

Screen reproductions in this book were created using Collage Plus from Inner Media, Inc., Hollis, NH.

*Using dBASE IV 1.5*, Special Edition, covers dBASE IV through Version 1.5.

*Publisher:* Lloyd J. Short

*Associate Publisher:* Rick Ranucci

*Product Development Manager:* Thomas H. Bennett

*Book Designers:* Scott Cook and Michele Laseau

*Production Team:* Scott Boucher, Paula Carroll, Michelle Cleary, Mark Enochs, Brook Farling, Kate Godfrey, Laurie Lee, Jay Lesandrini, Loren Malloy, Juli Pavey, Caroline Roop, Sandra Shay, Kevin Spear, Mary Beth Wakefield, Allan Wimmer

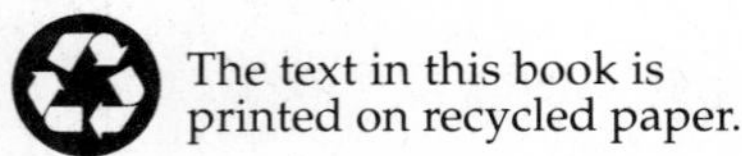

# CREDITS

**Product Director**
Timothy S. Stanley

**Acquisitions Editor**
Tim Ryan

**Production Editor**
Lori A. Lyons

**Editors**
Sara Allaei
Jo Anna Arnott
Don Eamon
Diana R. Moore
Colleen Totz

**Technical Editor**
Erik A. McBeth

*Composed in Cheltenham and MCPdigital by Que Corporation.*

# ABOUT THE AUTHORS

**Jim Bauman** specializes in the high end of PC training and support. He provides direct instruction in office software systems for managers and PC specialists, develops computer training delivery systems, and customizes user documentation and support tools. Besides dBASE, his software expertise includes WordPerfect, Paradox, Lotus 1-2-3, Ventura, PageMaker, and PC SAS, along with more than the usual number of utilities, organizers, and labor savers. Mr. Bauman came into computers with an educational background in biological and social science research. He holds a B.S. in Zoology and a Ph.D. in Linguistics. He works out of the Washington, D.C., area from a base of operations in the Blue Ridge "Country Roads" area of Martinsburg, West Virginia.

**Steve Davis** has been writing and editing books on dBASE and other computer-related subjects, as well as general non-fiction and reference works, for more than ten years. He revised Que's *dBASE IV Tips, Tricks, and Traps* and *dBASE IV Quick Reference*. Steve also has developed applications in dBASE IV. He is the president of Steve Davis Publishing in Dallas, Texas.

**Rick Hellewell** is a microcomputer specialist for the City of Sacramento, and is also a consultant to businesses and home users. He has served as president of the Sacramento PC Users Group, the fifth largest user group in the United States, and is the Associate Editor of *Sacra Blue*, their monthly newsletter. He was coauthor for Que's *MS-DOS 5 User's Guide*, Special Edition. Although his family is computer oriented, with three computers spread throughout the house (including one for his three children), he has been known to spend time away from a computer.

**Timothy S. Stanley** works as a product development specialist for Que. He has contributed to quite a number of Que books, including *Using Windows 3.1*, Special Edition, *Upgrading to Windows 3.1*, *Upgrading and Repairing PCs*, 2nd Edition, and *Introduction to Databases*. He also is the author of *Windows 3.1 Quick Reference*, *MS-DOS 5 Quick Reference*, and *Batch Files and Macros Quick Reference*.

**Peter Stephenson** is a well-known writer, consultant, and lecturer on local area networks, databases, and office automation. He has been involved in high technology for the last 27 years, 12 of which have been in personal computers. Mr. Stephenson has been programming in dBASE for the past 7 years, and coauthored Que's *dBXL and Quicksilver Programming: Beyond dBASE*. He has been an independent consultant for the past 9 years, operating out of Rochester Hills, Michigan.

**John Zumsteg** has worked with microcomputers and database management programs since their introduction to the computing world. Experienced on a range of computers, he prefers desktop computers and systems like dBASE IV because they bring computing power to everyone. Mr. Zumsteg has developed many PC database systems, primarily in the airline industry, and currently is the Director of Management Information Systems for Horizon Air, the regional airline of the Northwest United States. In this role, he is responsible for the design, development, and implementation of large and complex database programs, as well as conducting classes in all areas of PC applications.

# TRADEMARK ACKNOWLEDGMENTS

Que Corporation has made every effort to supply trademark information about company names, products, and services mentioned in this book. Trademarks indicated below were derived from various sources. Que Corporation cannot attest to the accuracy of this information.

dBASE II, dBASE III, and Framework are registered trademarks, and dBASE III Plus, dBASE IV, and RapidFile are trademarks of Borland International.

HP is a registered trademark and LaserJet is a trademark of Hewlett-Pakcard Co.

IBM and IBM PS/2 are registered trademarks of International Business Machines Corporation.

Lotus, 1-2-3, and VisiCalc are registered trademarks of Lotus Development Corporation.

MS-DOS and Multiplan are registered trademarks of Microsoft Corporation.

PC-Kwik is a registered trademark of Multisoft Corporation.

PostScript is a registered trademark of Adobe Systems.

WordPerfect is a registered trademark of WordPerfect Corporation.

WordStar is a registered trademark of WordStar International Incorporated.

Trademarks of other products mentioned in this book are held by the companies producing them.

# CONTENTS AT A GLANCE

# TABLE OF CONTENTS

## Part II: Getting Productive with dBASE IV

## Part III: Learning More about dBASE IV

## 11 Designing and Printing Labels .......... 269



## 12 Using Queries To Search Databases .......... 285

## Part IV: Solving Information Problems with dBASE IV Programming

## Part V: dBASE IV Reference Guide

## Using Functions .......... 775



## Using SET Commands .......... 845

# CONVENTIONS

The conventions used in this book have been established to help you learn to use the program quickly and easily.

Key combinations are represented with a hyphen separating the two keys. For example, Alt-F7 means to press and hold the Alt key, press the F7 key, and then release both keys. Keys separated by commas are to be pressed and released independently. For example, F,L means to press and release the F key, and then press and release the L key.

Menu options appear with first letter uppercase, such as "choose the Control Of Printer option from the Print menu."

*Italic* type emphasizes an important point, introduces a new term or concept, or indicates a word or phrase that you should type.

A `special typeface` denotes on-screen messages or text.

Special tips, notes, cautions, and warnings are included in the text to flag pieces of information that are especially worthy of note.

The mouse icon points out actions that can be performed using the mouse.

# Introduction

When MS-DOS was introduced for the IBM-PC in 1981, dBASE II database management software already had been providing information solutions for CP/M computer users for several years. Although spreadsheet software such as VisiCalc helped to establish the personal computer as a common desktop accessory, dBASE II brought the exciting power of database management to personal computer users. The ability to categorize, store, and report information through dBASE II's English-like commands enabled non-data processing people to take control of their own information needs. Those people who obtained and used dBASE had a "leg up" on those who didn't have access to it. If you could have polled a group of 1978 CP/M computer users for their ideal mix of software, you would have gotten a significant response for WordStar, VisiCalc, and dBASE II.

Many situations have changed in the world of personal computing since the late 1970s. Today's computers are vastly more powerful. The powerful new computers can run thousands of available program packages. MS-DOS has been improved through five major upgrades. dBASE II has evolved through dBASE III, dBASE III Plus, and dBASE IV to dBASE IV 1.5. Users and word processor preferences have changed, but dBASE remains the most popular database manager program. The features and benefits of dBASE IV 1.5 put mainframe computer capabilities at your fingertips.

Que's *Using dBASE IV 1.5*, Special Edition, is your resource for bridging your information management needs with dBASE IV's features and benefits. Hundreds of thousands of computer users have significantly upgraded their skills by learning from Que's *Using* titles. *Using dBASE IV 1.5*, Special Edition, represents a commitment to you. The commitment is to present to you the complex, powerful dBASE IV program in a logical and informative fashion. Using this book, you understand how to organize your information needs, master the user interface, and ultimately make your work more productive.

## Who Should Read This Book?

*Using dBASE IV 1.5*, Special Edition, is written for PC users who need a tutorial reference to dBASE IV. The book explains the key concepts of dBASE IV without being highly technical or intimidating. *Using dBASE IV 1.5*, Special Edition, recognizes that your learning time is limited. The book reflects the important consideration that you need to become productive immediately and then builds on practical skills as you learn intermediate and advanced concepts. If you are new to dBASE and are learning dBASE IV, this book is ideal for you. The text does not rush database concepts or presuppose that you are familiar with a topic. If you are upgrading to dBASE IV 1.5 from an earlier version, you find the inclusion and treatment of new features to be your fast track for taking advantage of the upgrade. Whether you are a relative beginner or you simply need to brush up on your dBASE skills, you will find this book to be an important addition to your computer library.

## What Hardware Do I Need?

This book assumes that you have, at the minimum, an IBM-PC XT or equivalent computer with 640K of RAM and 6M of available disk space before installing dBASE IV. If you have an IBM-PC AT, PS/2, or equivalent Intel 80286, 80386, or 80486 microprocessor-based computer, dBASE IV 1.5 operates more efficiently. Book discussions of *disk caching* assume that you have extended or expanded memory installed on your system. Discussions of *color screen control* assume that you have Color Graphics Adapter (CGA), an Enhanced Graphics Adapter (EGA), or Video Graphics Array (VGA) capability. Considering its power, dBASE IV 1.5 operates on nearly every personal computer compatible with the IBM PC standard. To take advantage of the discussions of producing printed reports, you should have a printer connected to your system.

# What's in This Book?

You can flip quickly through this book to get a feel for its organization. *Using dBASE IV 1.5*, Special Edition, divides the generous scope of dBASE IV into five distinct parts. Each part builds on your learning in the preceding part. Each part is designed to provide you with a level of practical capability. You need not proceed to a subsequent part to benefit from the capabilities of dBASE presented in an earlier part. You may, for example, stop reading after Part II to utilize what you learned. You may choose not to proceed to Part III for several weeks or more. Still, you can use dBASE and benefit from that use.

In addition to four tutorial parts, the book contains a detailed Reference Guide that includes the dBASE IV 1.5 commands and the menu item sequences used to access any particular function. As an additional feature, the Reference Guide includes a section containing several useful tables referencing functions, SET commands, and system variables. Take a moment to read about each part of the book.

**Part I: Understanding dBASE Fundamentals**

Part I is an introductory tutorial on dBASE IV and database management. In Part I, you discover that you can use database management techniques without having to learn complex or confusing concepts. You learn how to relate database management concepts to everyday information-keeping methods. Part I enables you to "think" database management.

Chapter 1, "Discovering Databases," presents the concept of a database as an information storage and retrieval mechanism. The emphasis of Chapter 1 is on thinking about and planning database solutions for information problems.

Chapter 2, "Designing a Database Application," gets right to the practical aspects of designing a simple database. You relate computer database management to the use of manual information systems. You learn about data types and why they are important. You develop an understanding of information reliability and how to control reliability. You gain an instinct for organizing data for effective database applications.

Chapter 3, "Managing Files and Disks," provides a clear understanding of DOS's file storage mechanisms and dBASE's provisions for utilizing files. dBASE IV makes extensive use of DOS's file services while storing and retrieving the numerous dBASE-specific files. If your knowledge of subdirectories, paths, directory listings, and files is lacking, this chapter brings you up to speed. You won't have to worry about bypassing dBASE's multidirectory capability because your DOS knowledge is in need of an upgrade. This chapter provides the information you need to be confident in using all dBASE's filing capabilities.

### Part II: Getting Productive with dBASE IV

Part II gets right to the dBASE IV program. Part II's chapters are basic and tutorial in nature, yet you get productive with dBASE IV right away. The information presented in this section is designed to help you learn the dBASE IV program's personality and begin to tap dBASE IV's information management power without having to master more advanced concepts. If you have been intimidated by the scope of fully featured database management programs, Part II demonstrates that you *can* be productive without an extensive investment in learning time.

Chapter 4, "Getting Started with dBASE IV," begins your hands-on use of the program by getting your dBASE IV installation off on the right foot. You use the DBSETUP program in an informed manner as you step through the configuration of the dBASE IV program and the printers. You learn to start dBASE IV and are introduced to the dBASE IV Control Center, the screen from which you start all your activities in dBASE. You learn how to use the menu system, what a *catalog* is to dBASE IV, and how to create a catalog for your own applications. Information on using a mouse with dBASE IV 1.5 also is included in this section.

Chapter 5, "Using Routine Commands," takes you on an informational tour of the well-designed Control Center and menu system. Working with dBASE IV and this chapter gives you an intuitive feel for the logic of the user interface. When you are comfortable with the "rhythm" of the user interface as presented in this chapter, you can concentrate more of your learning resources on database management issues presented in subsequent chapters.

Chapter 6, "Creating the Database Structure," takes you "hands-on" into the design of a database. This chapter introduces and demystifies database terminology. This chapter steps you through the database definition process, the saving of your definition, and the modification of existing definitions. Just as databases are at the core of database management software, this chapter is at the core of your dBASE IV learning.

Chapter 7, "Adding and Editing Data," shows you how to access your databases to add data. You see the distinction between adding *new* data and editing *existing* data. You see the dBASE IV word processor features as you learn about memo-field editing. You learn about the Browse screen as an alternative presentation for your database information. Finally, you learn techniques to locate a desired record from all your data.

Chapter 8, "Organizing the Database," introduces the versatility and power associated with creating indexes. You see how to organize the ordering of the information in your databases. Your knowledge of indexing is useful for viewing data, finding individual records, and categorizing information. This chapter provides the fundamental understanding of indexes that you need when you explore more advanced concepts in Part III.

**Part III: Learning More about dBASE IV**

Part III presents more advanced concepts when you are ready to move on from the knowledge you gained in Parts I and II. In Part III, you use the Control Center and the menu system to their maximum potential.

Chapter 9, "Creating and Using Custom Screen Forms," shows you how to add professional-looking polish to your editing screens. This chapter familiarizes you with methods of designing clear, informative editing forms that you or another user find pleasing to use. You learn how to create calculated fields in the form, and how to use picture functions, edit options, and templates to validate the data that is entered in a field in the form.

Chapter 10, "Writing Reports in dBASE IV," does for your printed view of database information what Chapter 9 does for your screen view. You use the dBASE report designer to produce professional-quality reports complete with headings and summaries.

Chapter 11, "Designing and Printing Labels," enables you to produce versatile labels in a variety of formats. You can use your database information to produce labels ranging from mailing labels to inventory shelf tags.

Chapter 12, "Using Queries To Search Databases," explains dBASE IV's powerful and user-oriented Query By Example feature. Incorporating queries into your information-searching activities increases your information selectivity significantly.

Chapter 13, "Using dBASE IV Expressions and Functions," teaches you how to incorporate dBASE's extensive expression and function capabilities. You learn what expressions and functions are, and how you can use them to add versatility to editing screens, report forms, indexes, and more.

Chapter 14, "Designing, Defining, and Creating Relational Databases," is an effective presentation concentrating on the extensive relational database provisions of dBASE IV. Through relations, your dBASE IV power increases an order of magnitude.

Chapter 15, "Managing dBASE IV Systems," provides more about the SET commands that you can use to customize dBASE's operating environment. You use CONFIG.DB to change the SET options. You also learn how to create macros, which can save you from keying in repetitious operations, and you are introduced to the dot prompt, of key importance in Part IV.

**Part IV: Solving Information Problems with dBASE IV Programming**

Part IV adds the power of programming to your dBASE skills. dBASE IV incorporates a pseudo-compiled programming language you can use to automate database management. The fact that thousands of professional program developers choose the dBASE language to do their work is a testament to the language's capabilities.

Chapter 16, "Getting Started with dBASE IV Programming," eases you into programming rationale and concepts. In this chapter, you see that you don't have to be a information management specialist to begin programming in the dBASE IV environment.

Chapter 17, "Understanding the Mechanics of Custom Applications," introduces you to many of the common commands you use when you program with dBASE IV. You learn the syntax of the commands as well as how to apply the commands in real-world situations. You learn practical programming skills by examples that you can generalize to your own applications. You see a "dot prompt" approach to accessing dBASE IV capabilities that you accessed earlier through the Control Center.

Chapter 18, "Using Menus, Procedures, and User-Defined Functions," arms your programming efforts with major program constructions, such as menus, procedures, and user-defined functions (UDFs). This chapter shows you how to incorporate these important programming considerations into your applications.

Chapter 19, "Planning and Producing Reports and Labels," enables you to get the most from your printer and printed reports. You learn to create ad hoc reports as well as customized reports.

Chapter 20, "Using the Applications Generator and the Compiler," highlights two of the dBASE IV programmer's most potent tools. You learn how to use the Applications Generator to reduce your program-coding responsibilities while retaining the features of dBASE IV programs. You see how your applications and code segments can be compiled into secure pseudo-code.

Chapter 21, "Using dBASE IV SQL," introduces dBASE's implementation of Structured Query Language (SQL). SQL promises to be the best solution for the inter-operation of data management environments. This chapter prepares you to make practical use of SQL. You even see how to embed SQL code in your dBASE applications.

**Part V: dBASE IV Reference Guide**

Part V is a rich dBASE IV reference source. Part V devotes sections to dot prompt and programming commands, built-in functions, SET commands, system variables, and SQL commands. The CONFIG.DB file is covered, and so is accessing command actions through the Control Center and menu system. Also included is information on using a mouse with dBASE IV 1.5. This complete reference section extends the usefulness of *Using dBASE IV 1.5*, Special Edition, beyond a learning tool to a reference tool.

# Understanding dBASE Fundamentals

CHAPTER 1

# Discovering Databases

In many ways, a database is like an expert consultant. A database stores a wealth of data about a particular topic, classifies and organizes data, updates this knowledge as new facts and figures are presented, and reports answers to questions you or others ask.

With all these points of similarity, however, one major difference exists between the database and a consultant: The database has no built-in intelligence. The range of functions the database can perform is determined by the database management system that created and set the database in motion. Furthermore, every operation a database performs must be directed by someone who understands how the database management system works and, equally important, the reasons why the database was originally set up.

This chapter highlights the database design process by illustrating the preparation and planning you must perform before you begin working with databases.

# Solving Problems with Databases

Every database originally is designed to solve some problem. This problem may be a business, home, or personal problem. It may be a complicated or simple problem, or it may be a problem that recurs regularly or happens only once. In all cases, resolving the problem requires organization of a body of knowledge. The database provides a way to organize facts pertaining to the problem in such a way that the solution suggests itself.

If you think about many common, daily activities, you probably will discover a database underlying them. Databases come into play in common business problems, such as getting out payroll, keeping track of expenditures and revenues, sending notices to customers, ordering supplies and managing inventory, paying taxes, and so on (see fig. 1.1). Success in handling these business problems depends on the effort—or lack of it—that goes into organizing the information each problem demands.

FIG. 1.1

Identifying the problem.

Consider, for example, maintaining payroll records. If you work for an organization with more than a few employees, the accountant who writes your check probably relies on a written base of data about you and all other employees (see fig. 1.2). The accountant has to have on hand the legal name, Social Security number, wage rate, and the number of hours an employee works during each pay period—all to solve the problem of how much money to include in the check. If the firm withholds taxes from your check, the accountant also has to know your tax rate and how many deductions you are claiming on the W-4 form.

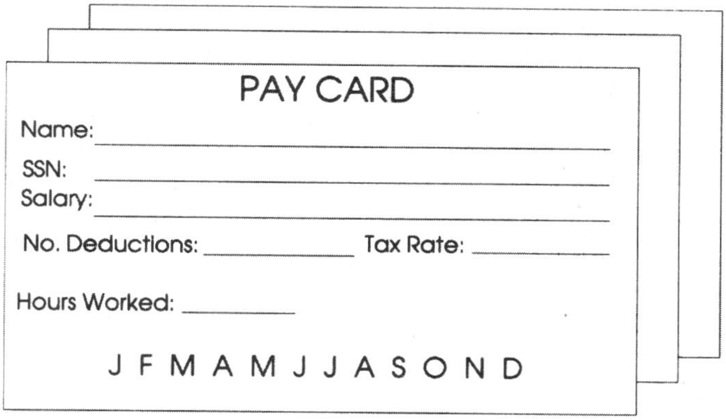

PAY CARD

Name: ____________________

SSN: ____________________

Salary: ____________________

No. Deductions: __________ Tax Rate: __________

Hours Worked: __________

J F M A M J J A S O N D

FIG. 1.2

A sample payroll card.

So far, the accountant needs at least six items of data about you and all other employees in the firm. Typically, this data gathering is only the start of the task. If solving the payroll problem also includes deducting for contributions to a pension program, accounting for overtime pay at a different pay rate, accommodating sick leave and vacations, or even the cost of mailing the checks to you, more items of data about you and the other employees must be gathered and recorded. This information is listed in table 1.1.

**Table 1.1 Additional Information for a Payroll Database**

| Problem | Information required |
|---|---|
| Pension program | Employee deduction<br>Employer deduction |
| Overtime | Overtime hours<br>Overtime rate(s) |
| Sick leave and vacation | Sick leave taken<br>Vacation leave taken<br>Earned sick leave<br>Earned vacation leave |
| Checks mailed | Employee address<br>City<br>State<br>ZIP code |

Databases can handle more than business problems. Databases also can help you send out Christmas cards, balance a checkbook, organize a music collection, or plan a garden. At the technical end of the spectrum, you also find databases involved in launching satellites, curing diseases, forecasting weather, and balancing national budgets.

As you can see, a *database* is a description of a set of objects, people, events, transactions, locations, and so on. A database is different from other kinds of descriptions because a database organizes what it describes into categories. These categories are chosen and defined specifically to address the problems the database is designed to solve, which may limit what the database can do. In database usage, informational categories are referred to as *fields*. You see fields used in the section, "Fine-Tuning a Database Design," later in this chapter.

Because database descriptions can range anywhere from the simple to the complex, and because the purposes for a database can range from one to many, also understand that a database management system needs the flexibility to handle many different situations. In dBASE IV, you have a program that can handle complex database management tasks, but also can manage even the smallest everyday problem.

## Thinking of a Database Solution

A database is set up in response to a problem. In and of itself, a database doesn't solve the problem but instead provides the means to find a solution. The problem embodies the purpose behind setting up the database. The database developer has to constantly keep this purpose in mind when setting up the system.

Recognizing the problem is an important step in determining how to proceed. Choosing a database management system, setting up the informational categories that make up the database, and formulating the questions that a database answers are important considerations. Stating the problem and outlining requirements for resolution are critical steps in ensuring that the resulting database system can answer the questions and perform the procedures needed to solve the problem.

In database parlance, the term *application* refers to the problem, the database set up to solve this problem, and even the solution itself. The accountant's database for handling the payroll problem can be called a *payroll application*. Notice that the name of the application explicitly describes its purpose.

Although a typical database is set up to address a particular problem, you aren't restricted to solving only this problem. Informational categories in the database often can serve other purposes (see fig. 1.3). If the payroll database includes the addresses of the firm's employees, for example, this database also can serve as the basis for other applications that require employee names and addresses, such as sending out notices about the company picnic. The financial information in the payroll database can be used as a partial record of company expenses, or to predict the coming year's expenses. In these cases, the same database serves a mailing list application, an accounting application, and a budgeting application.

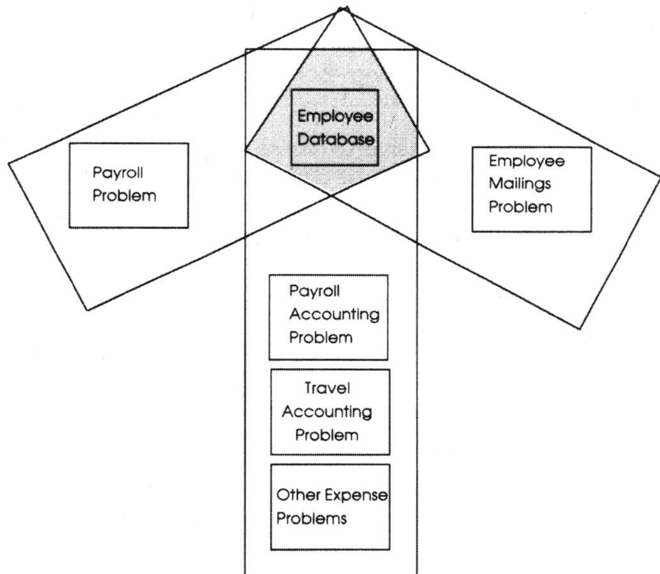


FIG. 1.3

A database serving multiple purposes.

By now, you probably begin to realize that some applications need more data than can be stored easily or effectively in a single database. An accounting application, for example, needs to record all the expenses and revenues for the firm during a certain time period.

The payroll database serves as an important component of an accounting application because one category of expenses is recorded. The payroll database, however, doesn't record other expenses, such as travel, utilities, rent, or taxes, and doesn't account for revenues, such as sales, dividends, or interest. Recording all these items is necessary to fulfilling the main purpose of the accounting application: to generate a balance sheet and income statement for the time period (see fig. 1.4).

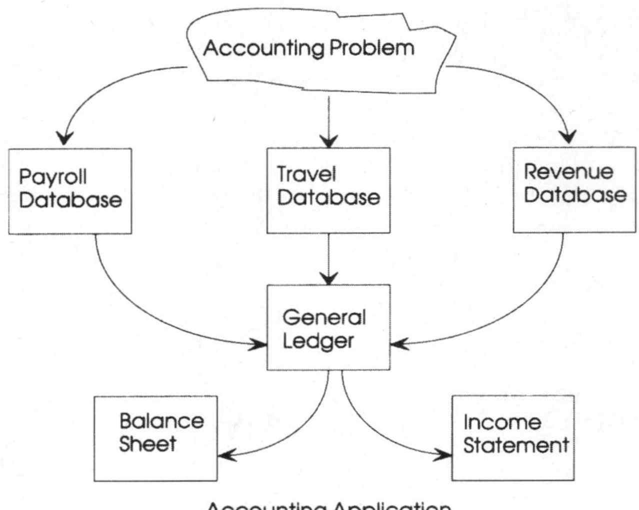


FIG. 1.4

A multidatabase application.

In theory, you can design a single, massive database to address every detail of the accounting application. In most database management systems, however, setting up a number of different databases that the full application uses to pull together the needed information may be a better method. In the context of dBASE IV, this kind of multidatabase application is known as a *relational database application*. The term *relational* refers to the fact that the component databases are logically related to one another.

You can set up the payroll database to calculate the net pay and the taxes withheld for each employee. This information is sufficient for cutting checks, but this payroll application can go further by recording check amounts as entries into a general ledger database that supports the accounting function. Here, the general ledger database doesn't end up with duplicate information; it just "feeds on" output from the payroll application. You also can set up other feeder databases to support other expense transactions—such as a travel database that records long-distance and local transportation charges, per diem charges, and miscellaneous charges for individual trips—and then sums these items and places the total for each trip into the ledger database.

# Planning a Database Application

In the world of business and government is a class of computer professionals known as *systems analysts*. The systems analyst is a problem solver who understands the needs of the organization and who commands a set of computerized problem-solving tools, particularly a database management system. Systems analysts take individual problems that can be solved with a computer, choose appropriate software tools, and set up applications structured around these tools.

When building applications, you can use the same reasoning process that a professional systems analyst uses. Imagine that you are an analyst brought in to help a small book seller get organized. Table 1.2 lists the steps you must take to approach the problem.

**Table 1.2 Major Steps in the Systems Analysis Process**

| Step | Description | Scenario |
|---|---|---|
| 1 | Assemble some indicators of a problem. | The company is taking mail orders for several best-sellers but doesn't have enough items in stock to fill the orders. The order clerks have to respond with a back-order note to the customer. Certain items are seriously overstocked, however, and even more of the items are in the purchasing pipeline. Both problems occur frequently. |
| 2 | Examine and analyze the underlying issues. | On inspection, you find that the store relies primarily on the memory of sales clerks to determine how many copies of a book are on the shelves at a given moment. Orders for current books may be placed in response to a clerk's suggestion or in response to customer requests, and no one checks whether an order for this item is already pending. |
| 3 | Synthesize the indicators and formulate the problem. | Proper controls over the store's inventory are lacking. Management of inventory relies too heavily on the memory and discretion of clerks. |
| 4 | Determine the solution. | Set up a computerized inventory application that reports accurate numbers of items in stock and on order. The application is to be built around a central database, which is updated daily with information contained in sales slips and purchase orders. |

After you plan the solution, how do you put the application together? As a guideline, you let the details of the problem determine the data requirements for both the database and the information output. Above all, you want to make sure that the building blocks of the database are sufficient to produce all the needed information.

**TIP** Databases solve problems. The more effort you put into understanding a problem, the more useful the database becomes.

To achieve this goal, you may want to plan backwards. Determine what results you want and how you want these results assembled and arranged. Lay out the reports you want the database to create and use the information requirements of the reports as the basis for deciding what building blocks to include in the database.

Consider the book seller example. You want the order clerk to be able to check current inventory before placing a new order. The clerk needs to see a report that lists each book by title and also shows, for each book, the number purchased, the number sold, and the difference between the number purchased and the number sold. The report can be simple, as shown in table 1.3.

**Table 1.3 Orders Report**

| Title | Purchased | Sold | Available/On order |
|---|---|---|---|
| Root Canals of Holland | 16 | 5 | 9 |
| Tongue in Cheek | 5 | 4 | 1 |
| Chinese Junks | 3 | 3 | 0 |

For sales clerks, you need a similar report that shows at a glance whether a book is available in the store and how many copies of this book are on hand. This report may resemble table 1.4.

Both reports are fed with data from purchase orders and sales slips. The database must include, at a minimum, the book title, the number of books purchased, and the number sold. Given this information, the database management system can calculate the difference between the number purchased and the number sold, and report the result as the number available. Because the purchase orders include books ordered but not yet received, you also need to instruct the database management system to break apart the number purchased into the number received and the number on order. The quantity on hand is the difference between the number received and the number sold.

**Table 1.4 Quantity on Hand Report**

| Title | Quantity on Hand |
|---|---|
| Root Canals of Holland | 2 |
| Tongue in Cheek | 1 |
| Chinese Junks | 0 |

The database requires only four items of information to create the necessary reports: book title, copies purchased, copies received, and copies sold (see fig. 1.5).

Book Inventory
Database

Title

Number Purchased

Number Received

Number Sold

---

Quantity on Hand = Purchased – (Received + Sold)

Quantity Available = Purchased – Sold

FIG. 1.5

Real and calculated fields for book inventory database.

After you understand the requirements, you can start dBASE IV and use the dBASE development tools to create the database. (You start creating databases in Chapter 6.) But before you begin working with a complex program like dBASE IV, you need to understand the program's purpose and overall working strategy.

# Using dBASE IV as a File Clerk

As a database management system, dBASE IV must control the fundamental operations needed to create, update, and *query*—or ask questions of—databases. Consider a database as no more than a glorified filing system—in its simplest form, no different from a paper-based filing system. Card catalogs, personnel folders, phone books, contract files, report cards, membership lists, ledger sheets, calendars, to-do lists, and train schedules are just some examples of paper-based filing systems.

Each of these paper-based systems must be continually maintained, updated, and invoked to answer questions, in the same way a database that resides on a computer must be maintained, updated, and invoked. With a paper-based system, a file clerk, bookkeeper, or some other person takes the responsibility for performing all these activities. The point is: *Anything a person does to, for, and with a database, the computer database management system also must be able to do.*

From this perspective, a database management system is the electronic equivalent of a file clerk. This system intermediates between you and the hardware of the computer, just as the file clerk intermediates between you and the pages or slips of paper that store data (see fig. 1.6). You simply request the desired information, and dBASE or the file clerk carries out your wishes. In both cases, you don't need to know precisely where the data is stored, whether on a disk or in a filing cabinet. You only have to know how to ask for the data.

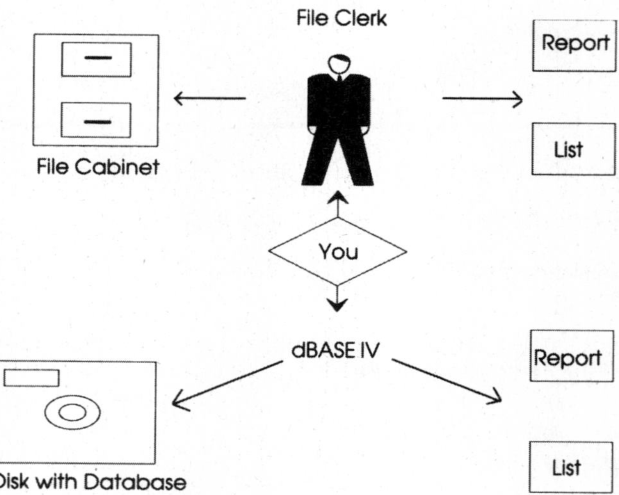


FIG. 1.6

Mirrored roles of dBASE and the file clerk.

If you imagine every kind of request you can make of a file clerk, you find that dBASE also has a way to make a similar request. Learning dBASE means that you learn how to make requests in a form that dBASE understands, with the command language and tools dBASE provides.

The language you use to communicate with dBASE is known as a *command language* because this tool consists of words and phrases that build what corresponds to imperative, or command, sentences in English. A command sentence is an instruction or order to do something: "Get me the Rogers folder! Reschedule the meeting for Wednesday. Fill out this personnel application form. Show me how much we have left in that budget. Calculate everyone's raise. Rearrange these items in alphabetical order." Given a database that contains the information to satisfy these requests, each of the preceding English commands can have a dBASE IV equivalent.

Table 1.5 shows examples of the kinds of requests you can make of a database management system.

**Table 1.5 Catalog of Database Commands**

| Type of Request | Examples |
|---|---|
| Update the database | Adding new data<br>Changing data that already exists<br>Removing obsolete items<br>Replacing one data value with another |
| Reorder the database | Arranging data alphabetically, numerically, or chronologically<br>Grouping data by common values for some category |
| Show information | Querying to verify data<br>Querying to extract similar data<br>Reporting and formatting similar data |
| Calculate new information | Calculating statistical data<br>Calculating new values based on old data<br>Calculating future or past dates |
| Maintain the database | Backing up database files<br>Adding or removing information categories<br>Designing data-entry and edit screens<br>Programming database function menus |

In following chapters, you explore each of these topics separately. For now, however, just appreciate the scope of what a database management system permits you to do.

# Fine-Tuning a Database Design

Anyone who regularly receives junk mail from dozens of mail order houses, political parties, special interest groups, or advertisers may think the purpose of a mailing list is to harass and annoy. From the mailer's perspective, however, the problem that underlies the creation of the mailing list database is communicating some message in a cost-effective way. A mailing list also can be used to perform a specific business or personal activity, such as to send you monthly bank statements, help you send holiday greeting cards, or send you a monthly copy of *Double Barreled Databases*.

When deciding what information to include in a mailing list database, try to keep focused on the problem at hand (as you do in designing any application). To solve a single, isolated problem, the mailing list database definition can include only the following fields:

- Last name of addressee
- First name of addressee
- Street address of addressee
- City of addressee
- State of addressee
- ZIP Code of addressee

Why bother with separate fields for the last and first names? You can get by with a single name field, but you soon learn that splitting—rather than lumping together—related sets of data into the smallest possible units tends to be a better solution. This kind of organization gives you more flexibility in reorganizing the data and in applying the split fields to different uses. Because the last name is separate from the first, you can use the database to generate a list of addressees alphabetized by last name. The separate name fields also enable you to build an application that drops either part of the name into a salutation on a letter: the first name drops into friendly letters (*Dear John*), and the last names drops into formal letters (*Dear Mr. Smith*).

In general, avoid lumping categories into single fields. You gain a great deal of flexibility with more specific categories. **TIP**

Now, consider a few variations on the basic mailing list. First, what must you do to the list if the addressees receive mail at a business address? You can add a field, such as COMPANY, which includes the name of the business, to avoid the problem of trying to reach Lotte Jones at 1 Rockefeller Plaza, New York City, an address with thousands of tenants. You also may have to include a suite, room, apartment number, or a department name to handle the possibility of five William Browns at the Department of Labor, Washington, DC. If the mailing list must be polite and respect protocol and etiquette, you can include a field for the addressee's title: Mr., Mrs., Dr., and so on.

So far, the database is set up to adequately handle the problem of getting all the information required of a mailing and also supplies all you need to print mailing labels. Now, consider some other problems you may want this database to handle. Imagine that you are a membership director for a charitable organization that collects dues from members. Membership renewal time has arrived, and you have to get out a mailing to all members who haven't yet paid dues for the current year. How does a database handle this problem?

As presently designed, the database cannot handle this problem efficiently because no record is currently included of who has paid and who hasn't. A good way to handle the problem is to add another field to the database that provides a simple Yes or No indicator of whether each person has paid. You can call this field PAID. You then can tell the database management system to pull out, or *extract*, the names of only members who haven't yet paid (all members whose PAID field says `No`). As you discover in Chapter 12, this kind of task is easy to set up in dBASE IV.

As the membership director, you have another problem—how to get personalized thank-you notes to individuals who sent in more than $500, mentioning in each note the exact amount of the addressee's contribution. In dBASE IV, this kind of application is known as a *mail-merge report layout.* You learn how to set up a mail-merge report in Chapter 10, but for now think about what information you have to include in the database to carry out the objective. Can the task be handled by modifying the PAID field you set up previously? Also consider what you have to do to the database definition to be able to telephone people on the list, to produce a list of employees in an organization, and to generate a magazine subscription list. Table 1.6 shows an example of modifying a database design to handle new problems.

**Table 1.6 Modifying Database Design**

| Problem areas | Database design modification |
|---|---|
| Mailing labels | Address data |
| Mail-merge letters | Personal/unique data<br>(depending on purpose of letter) |
| Membership list | Membership number<br>Enrollment dates<br>Dues paid<br>Contributions made<br>Skills inventory |
| Phone list | Phone numbers |

The point of these mental exercises is to get you to appreciate the importance of considering what you want the database to do *before* you set up the database. If you don't think through the requirements and plan carefully, you risk turning the database design process into an expensive and frustrating exercise in trial and error.

# Summary

In this chapter, you explored the database design process and how the process underlies the solution to business, home, or personal problems. The database design records the information required to solve the problem, from within the database. After you complete the design and add the data, you can manipulate the database to extract the information needed to address the problem. The full scope of the database—the problem, the database, and the extracted information—constitute the database application.

Applications can be relatively simple—a single problem can be solved through a single database. An application also can consist of numerous problems addressed by one or more databases. The job of a database management system, such as dBASE IV, is to maneuver through one or all of the databases in an application to process information needs. dBASE IV does this in much the same way a file clerk does; dBASE accepts commands and then pulls the information, based on knowledge of where the data is stored.

The job of analyzing application requirements can be simple or complex, depending on the type and the number of results you want the database management system to yield. The more complex the problem, the more effort you should put into carefully designing the application.

2

CHAPTER

# Designing a Database Application

In Chapter 1, you learned that a database is a model of a problem, set up and managed with a database management system. The design of the database, therefore, reflects both the problem the database is intended to solve and the features and limitations of the database management system used to create it. In this chapter, you examine some practical issues that surround this relationship.

## Designing Valid and Reliable Databases

A critical issue during the database design process is taking steps to ensure that the data in the database is always *valid* (true and factual). Data must accurately model the reality it describes. If not, you have a situation that computer folklore inelegantly describes as "garbage in, garbage out."

Put another way, the answers you get from an expert who derives his answers from defective data fall somewhere between simply misleading and downright destructive. Consider the implications of a payroll database that lists your salary incorrectly, a voter registration database that doesn't purge deceased voters, a navigation system that fails to record a sand shoal, or an inventory system that incorrectly records the quantity of an order. When data in a database is inaccurate, any questions that rely on this data are answered incorrectly. Wrong answers cause frustration and wasted time, and occasionally produce disastrous consequences.

Spend some time ensuring that the database is reliable. Every piece of data in the database may be accurate, but if the methods used by the database management system aren't reliable, you still may get wrong answers. Ask yourself two questions about the database: Is the data valid (is each piece of data correct)? Is the database reliable (are answers correct, and does the same question always yield the same answer)?

Consider an employee database that erroneously records entries twice. If an application relies on this database to count the number of employees, how accurate is the answer? What about a mailing list database that records values for states in an inconsistent way—sometimes as postal abbreviations (MT, MS, MN) and other times as word abbreviations (Mont, Miss, Minn). Is this kind of database useful for sorting entries logically by state? These examples illustrate the importance of consistency and care in entering data into the database. Remember both points during the design process and during the data-entry and editing processes.

# Giving Information a Type

Typically, the first step in designing a database is to lay out a list of the fields the database needs to answer the questions you designed the database to address. In Chapter 1, you explored how to use these questions as a guide in determining the fields to include. In this chapter, you take the process farther by considering the kind of information each field holds.

Virtually any computer-based application requires that you store on computer disk the data which supports the application. Without data storage, you must retype the data each time you switch on the computer. You learn more about how dBASE IV manages disk storage in Chapter 3. For now, however, understand the important role disk storage plays in determining the structure of a database.

Any data stored on computer disk must be of a specific *type*. You can have two fundamental types of data: *numeric* and *character*. You must choose a type for the data because the computer uses different processing routines for different data types—computers store numbers differently than text. Most programs that work with both kinds of data have a means for distinguishing between the two. As a user of these programs, you need to understand what you want the program to do with the data and then select the type accordingly.

Because dBASE IV works with both numeric and character data, you can use this system to perform arithmetic calculations. If you include in a home inventory database a field that records the cost of each of your possessions, for example, you can instruct dBASE to calculate the total value of all your possessions. The program does this in the same way you do it by hand or by calculator—by adding up the cost of individual items. dBASE, however, can add these numbers only if, during the database design process, you defined the COST field to store numeric data. Computer programs, including dBASE, cannot perform mathematical operations on character-type data—the data must be numeric type.

**TIP**

Decide whether you intend to do arithmetic with a field you are proposing for the database. If so, make this field numeric. If not, make the field a character field, even if you customarily call the field a "number" in English. Because you seldom need to add or subtract ZIP Codes, for example, you can make a ZIP_CODE field a character field. You also may want to make a ZIP_CODE field a character field because many ZIP Codes include leading zeros (01139, for example), and Canadian postal codes contain non-numeric characters (K2M 8R6, for example).

As you plan a database, consider whether the task you want the application to perform requires mathematical calculations on the data. If so, then during the database design process tell dBASE IV which fields to store as numeric data. Not all information that *looks* like a number should be stored as numeric data. Social Security numbers and telephone numbers, for example, needn't be stored as numeric data because these kinds of data are never used as numbers in a mathematical operation—unless you need to calculate the total of all Social Security numbers in the database, or to find the result when you divide a phone number by 6! In any case, such results are meaningless. In these two cases and others, defining the fields that hold these numbers as character-type fields, and storing the values as character data, makes more sense.

Dates require special consideration when you define database fields. On one hand, dates are clearly more than numbers—consider the month names. On the other hand, you may want to perform arithmetic on dates; for example, you may want to calculate someone's age from the difference between the date of birth and today, or you may want to calculate the date 75 days from today. Dates seem to be part character, part numeric.

To cope with the dual nature of dates, dBASE IV includes a separate data type called *date*. The date type stores dates as numbers on a Julian-based calendar system but displays these numbers on-screen and in reports in the common MM/DD/YY format. (*MM/DD/YY* refers to month/day/year, with two spaces allotted for each unit of time. In MM/DD/YY format, January 15, 1992 appears as 01/15/92.) When adding information for a field defined as a date, you enter date values in the normal MM/DD/YY format, and dBASE IV converts the values into Julian date numbers. In this way, you gain the benefits of both the character and numeric data types. Table 2.1 summarizes the most important points about the three principal types of data in dBASE databases.

**Table 2.1 Primary Data Types in dBASE IV**

| Type | Purpose |
|---|---|
| Character | Stores all data that contains letters, punctuation, or digits. Can store any character that you can type from the keyboard. |
| Numeric | Stores all data made up of numbers that may be used in an arithmetic calculation. |
| Date | Stores true and complete dates. Allows date arithmetic on stored dates. |
| Logical | Uses True or False; Yes or No. |

Table 2.2 shows examples of fields you may want to include in a personnel database and the data types you can assign to them.

## Using Data Types To Validate Data

An added benefit of specifying data types is that dBASE can help control the validity of data items. When you select the numeric data type for a field, for example, dBASE asks for the width of the largest entry you expect for the field. Indirectly, this width determines the largest number you can enter as a value for this field. If you specify a width of 6 places (and no decimal places), the largest number you can enter in this field is 999,999—dBASE will not permit a higher number. This example is a somewhat crude illustration of *validity checking*. In Chapter 9, you learn how to make a more precise validity check.

**Table 2.2 Data Types for a Personnel Database**

| Field | Type |
|---|---|
| Last name | Character |
| First name | Character |
| Social Security number | Character |
| Date of birth | Date |
| Date of hire | Date |
| Department name | Character |
| Office phone number | Character |
| Starting salary | Numeric |
| Current salary | Numeric |

**TIP** You can better ensure validity of data by trying to anticipate the kinds of errors you or someone else may make when entering data.

For date-type fields, dBASE IV performs more sophisticated checking. If you enter an impossible date, dBASE displays an error message and prompts you to enter a valid date. For example, dBASE does not accept July 62, 1992. The program understands and accounts for leap years and rejects February 29, 1990 but accepts February 29, 1992. dBASE IV also takes leap years into account when performing date calculations, such as counting the number of days between two dates.

With character data, dBASE is less restrictive. This data type is something of a catchall for information that cannot be classified as numeric, date, or one of the other special data types covered in Chapter 5. The program does no real validity checking on character data; you can enter virtually any data in a character field, as long as the data doesn't exceed the character length you specify for the field. (Although dBASE does no validation of character data, you can set up highly sensitive validation of character entries. You learn how to perform this procedure in Chapter 9.) If you specify a width of 12 for the LAST_NAME field, for example, you can enter *Jones* (5 characters), *Robinson* (8 characters), and *Morgenthaler* (12 characters), but not *Schlotterbecker* (15 characters—3 more than the limit). When defining a character field in a database, be sure that you make the field wide enough to accommodate the widest value you expect to enter in this field.

## Designing a Reliable Database

The reliability of a database results from applying care and consistency during the data entry and editing processes, but you can design some additional safeguards into the application to ensure that the database performs reliably.

One problem that jeopardizes reliability is duplicate entries in the database; that is, entries that record the same piece of information twice. Duplicate entries cause overcounting in summary operations, other inaccuracies if an attempt to delete the data removes only one of the entries, and still more problems if one entry is changed and the other entry is not. In the latter case, when the information appears on a report, you don't know which of the two entries represents the most current data.

Guarding against duplicate entries is something dBASE IV can do through the programming language, without much help from you (Part IV of this book describes the programming language). To prepare a database to take advantage of these programming features, however, you may need to set up a field that checks for duplicates. This kind of field is called a *key field.* A key field is designed to ensure that each entry in the field uniquely describes the field's object.

Some fields commonly used as key fields include Social Security numbers, area codes and phone numbers, inventory control numbers, credit card numbers, and product serial numbers. Each of these numbers uses a coding system, which ensures that no two objects or people can be described by the same number.

When you design a database, give yourself the same assurance. The more entries you have in a database, the more important are these safeguards. If you design a home inventory system, for example, include a field that serves as a unique product identification number (ID).

One way to do this is to set up an eight-position coding scheme. The first two positions categorize the item broadly. In an inventory database, for example, AR identifies art, CP identifies computer equipment,

FU specifies furniture, and so on. The next four positions can indicate the month and year of purchase—AP92 for April 1992, JN91 for June 1991, and so on. The last two positions can indicate price in hundreds of dollars; for example, a $210 item is coded as 02, a $1,250 item is coded as 12, and a $7,200 item is coded as 72 (see fig. 2.1).

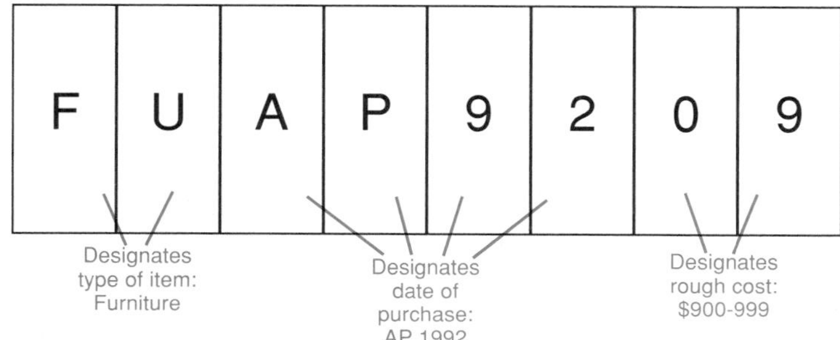


FIG. 2.1

A coding scheme for a home inventory database.

To test your understanding of this concept, think about what you can do to distinguish between legitimate duplicates, such as a pair of identical lamps or dual stereo speakers. If these items have the same price and were purchased at the same time, the coding system in figure 2.1 is inadequate. What are some other limitations of this coding system?

You can modify the definition of a field even after you set it up. A well-defined field can easily become inadequate over time as your needs grow and change. Although dBASE IV can accommodate changes, you still may need to put some effort into predicting what the application may need five years from now and design for the future. Consider the implications of having to redesign the Social Security numbering system if you need to be persuaded about the enormity of changing a system.

## Ensuring Reliability

Besides the coding scheme, another useful technique for ensuring reliability is to set up a means of automating—or partially automating—the data entry process. Although dBASE IV cannot do a great deal to help you with the actual typing of data, it can help you organize the data-entry process in a way that lessens the chance of errors. dBASE performs this procedure through a structure known as a *form,* also commonly known as a *data-entry form.*

A form is a visual guide to putting the right kind of information in the database. The fields of the database are displayed on the computer screen in a way that helps the person entering the data. Forms work best when the fields are arranged in a natural and logical way. Suppose that your firm uses a paper form to get the name and address of individuals interested in more information about your product. The fields on the form are arranged in logical groups (see fig. 2.2). You logically expect the last name to be close to the first name; finding the first name at the top of the form and the last name somewhere at the bottom of the form would be illogical and surprising.

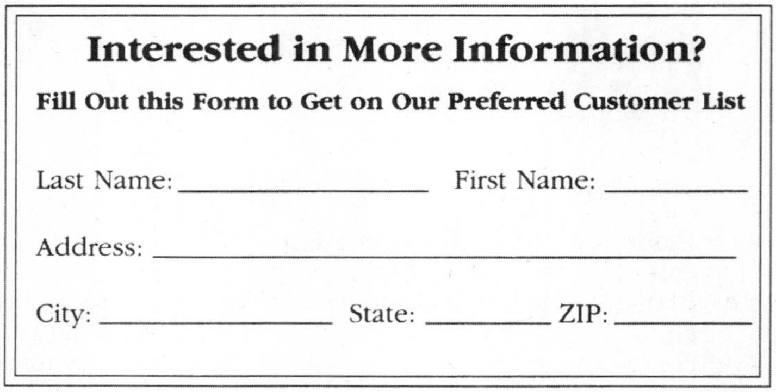

**Interested in More Information?**

**Fill Out this Form to Get on Our Preferred Customer List**

Last Name: ________________ First Name: __________

Address: ______________________________________

City: ________________ State: _________ ZIP: __________

FIG. 2.2

A paper-based data-entry form.

Remember that the main difference between dBASE IV and a consultant is that dBASE lacks intelligence. An example is dBASE IV's inability to see the logical connection between first names and last names. As far as dBASE knows, these two fields are unrelated. Unless you indicate otherwise, dBASE IV doesn't associate the two fields with each other.

One way to build logical organization within and between fields is to define the fields sequentially, in logical order. If you want the data-entry person to enter an employee's Social Security number before typing anything else about this employee, for example, make the Social Security number the first field in the database definition. If following the Social Security number with the employee's last name makes sense, set up the last name as the second field in the database definition.

When you finish, you have a form that matches the logical order in which you want to record the full set of information. You aren't required to set up a database this way, but doing so helps dBASE IV's forms-creation system set up the database right the first time. You may find that the order of the database is exactly the order someone may follow when writing down the information.

After you define all the fields of the database in the order in which you want them, dBASE IV constructs a default data-entry form. Every time you enter information for a new event or object, dBASE uses the default form as the guide for the data-entry process. Figure 2.3 shows a default data-entry form for a simple mailing list database. Notice that the fields are arranged vertically on-screen, in the order in which they were defined.

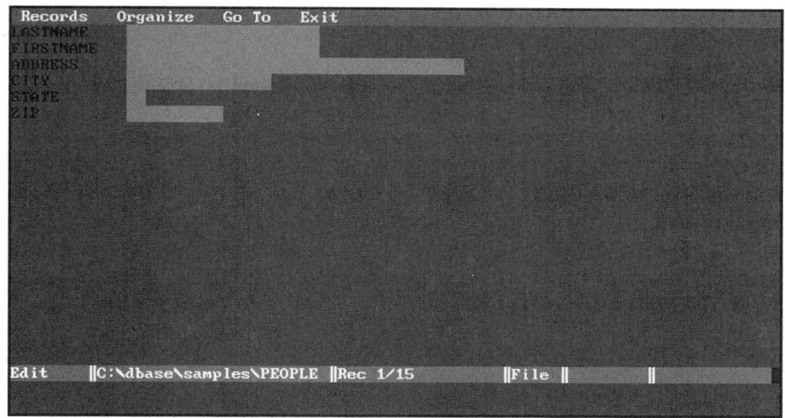


FIG. 2.3

A default data-entry screen.

Figure 2.4 represents a custom-designed form that contains the same fields as the default form but arranges these fields in a way that more closely matches the arrangement of fields as they may appear on a paper form. Think about a situation in which customers who come into a store fill out a paper form so that they are included on a mailing list, and the data-entry person uses these slips of paper to update the database. Which of the two forms—the default form shown in figure 2.3 or the customized form shown in 2.4—is likely to lead to fewer data-entry errors? Without question, the form organized in the same way as the paper form helps you get the right data in the right slot more often than the default form.

## Building Validity and Reliability Checks into a Form

Even when you use a custom form, you may enter invalid values for a field. dBASE IV offers several options, however, for validating input. If you want states always to be entered as two-letter postal abbreviations (VA, CA, WA), for example, your form can handle this for you.

```
Records  Organize  Go To  Exit

              Mailing List Data Entry Form

  Last Name:                    First Name:
    Address:
       City:              State:     Zip:

Edit  |C:\dbase\samples\PEOPLE |Rec EOF/15   |File |
```

FIG. 2.4

A custom-designed data-entry form.

One way you can restrict possible entries is through the field definition process. You already know that every field has to have a data type and a width. If you give the STATE field a width of 2, you effectively eliminate the possibility of entering any state abbreviation longer than two letters—no more Vir, Calif, Wash, and so on.

You also can set an option that converts all alphabetic characters typed to uppercase letters, so if the typist does not have Caps Lock on, the data still will be formatted properly.

If you are offering the user a short list of possible entries, you can provide a multiple-choice list. The typist merely presses the first letter of the choice desired or presses the space bar to cycle through the options available. These and other formatting options are discussed in Chapter 9.

FROM HERE...

**For Related Information...**

▸▸ "Validating Data and Formatting Fields," p. 205.

# Teaching dBASE New Tricks

Occasionally, you may want dBASE to do things for a single operation that you haven't programmed. You may want dBASE to find the average salary of employees in each division of a company, for example, and then rank the divisions from highest to lowest average. This example is a task that dBASE cannot perform completely in one operation. dBASE can calculate the averages for you easily but has no direct way to rank the results.

To get dBASE IV to perform the ranking, you use the dBASE IV programming language to create the instructions for dBASE. The programming language creates another component of a full application (the first component is a database), known as a *program file*. The program file stores the new set of instructions so that the instructions can be called up easily and used when needed.

You don't have to use program files exclusively to store custom-built instructions. You also can use these files to store a sequence of dBASE commands that must be carried out in a consistent order each time or that are too complex to execute one at a time.

An example of a task that calls for a complex set of commands is a lookup table with more possibilities than fit in the validity check of a form. To use this long lookup table, you can set up the table as a second database. The application then consists of a minimum of two databases: one that stores the data and one that holds the lookup table. You also have to set up a way for the two databases to communicate when you are entering or editing data (see fig. 2.5).

The commands you need in dBASE to set up a multicomponent application aren't necessarily this complex, but several commands exist, and these commands have to be repeated for each data-entry or editing session. You can save some effort and ensure greater reliability if you include these *environment setup* commands within a program file.

**WARNING:** You can easily write a program file that gives the wrong results. Make sure that you test all program files thoroughly.

Building program files can be challenging because the process demands that you understand the "mind" of dBASE and how it learns. Issuing a command to an assistant is one thing; teaching the assistant how to do something new, however, is quite another thing. Chapters 16 through 18 provide more information about programming in dBASE.

# Ensuring Consistent Answers

So far, you have seen dBASE IV applications from the vantage point of the central database. The database is the critical design element in the application—without the database, nothing else happens. You also saw how an application can include a second database that can feed specified information to the main database or support the database by holding auxiliary information. An example of a *feeder* database is a payroll database that calculates employee payroll checks and *feeds* the results to an accounting database. An example of a support role is a lookup table that supports the user in the data-entry process by validating entries.

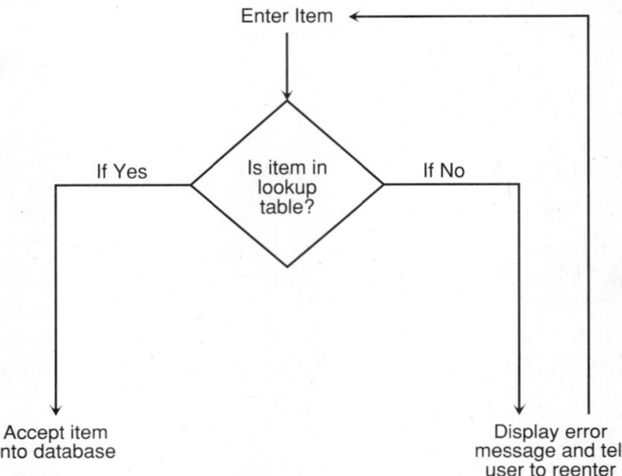


FIG. 2.5
How dBASE acts on a lookup request.

Databases, of course, have little importance outside the role they play as problem-solving tools. As you learned previously, the problem is solved by posing a question to the database or by requesting a listing of information in some acceptable format. In the next section, "Organizing the Database Application," you explore the kinds of questions you may ask the database, see how dBASE IV recognizes and stores questions for later use, and see how dBASE presents the answer.

dBASE IV uses the term *query* as an equivalent for *question*. You query a database to find the answer to a question. The query is written in a form known as a *query form*, which provides an example of the kind of information you want reported. For a model of how the query-by-example process works, think of a library in which you request books by filling out a slip asking for details (subject matter, author, or title) of the books you want to see.

In dBASE IV, you fill out a similar form, using a *file skeleton*, to indicate your interests in seeing different information in the database. Figure 2.6, for example, shows a query form asking for names of people in Chicago. The information is presented in a *view* of the database. When dBASE processes the query, dBASE filters the database to retain just the information that answers the query; dBASE also organizes the information into a special table that you can view but not change.

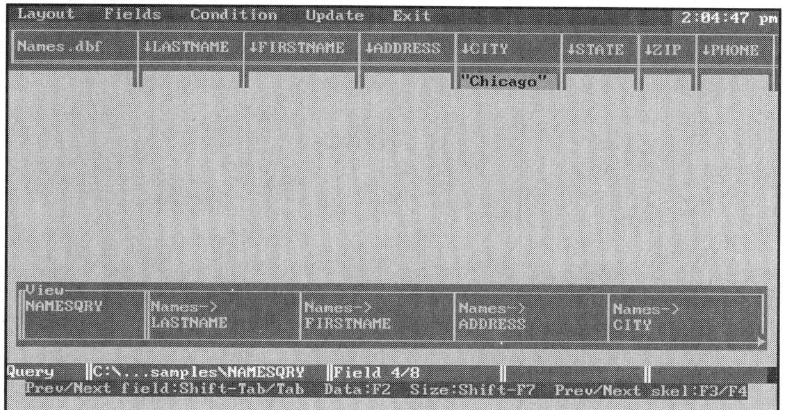


FIG. 2.6

A query form requesting information.

Because most people tend to ask the same questions at different times, dBASE IV can save these query forms for later reuse; you don't have to rewrite them. Queries, therefore, can become important components of an application. By ensuring consistency in the way you ask questions from one occasion to the next, query forms build reliability into an application. Query forms are covered in detail in Chapter 12.

You also can generate information from a database through a *report form* or a *label form*. These two application components are constructed by using the same principles as query forms; you specify what you want to appear on the report or label page. The difference is that you can format on the page the output of the report and label forms in a way that you cannot with a view form. Besides content, report and label forms also specify the arrangement and organization of information on the page. Figure 2.7 shows a report form listing names and addresses grouped by state.

Just as with query forms, dBASE IV can save the specifications for reports and labels for later reuse. Because dBASE can save these forms, you save time and effort when you have to redo the report every time the data changes. Report and label forms also confer greater reliability on the application. After you get the report or label specifications right, the specifications stay right from one use to the next.

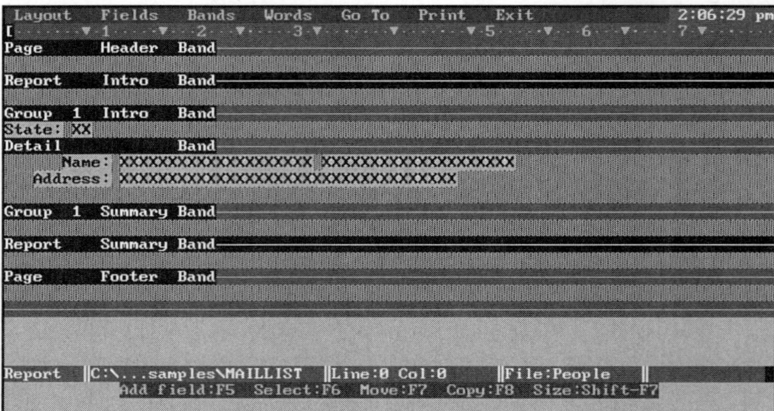


FIG. 2.7

A report form listing names and addresses grouped by state.

# Organizing the Database Application

An application can have a lot of pieces, and these pieces have to be created, stored, and tracked independently. Does dBASE IV help with the organization of these pieces, or do you have to rely on your memory and call up each piece as needed? Here, both you and dBASE do some of the work.

First, the easy part. Without help from you, dBASE IV can assemble all the pieces of the application into what is referred to as a *catalog*. The catalog is just a way to keep things that belong together in a logical heap. Catalogs are tremendously helpful in keeping the application desktop neat.

You can look at the contents of a catalog through a dBASE IV facility known as the *Control Center*. The Control Center, in part, displays the separate contents (the kinds of files) of the application in *panels* (see fig. 2.8). The Control Center has six panels, each named for the kind of file listed: Data, Queries, Forms, Reports, Labels, and Applications. Without knowing it, you already saw examples of the kinds of files stored in each of these panels, except for the Applications panel. Chapters 4 and 5 provide general information on using the Control Center.

If the Control Center lists files in the application, the Applications panel organizes particular tasks within the full application. A single task, such as checking an entry in a lookup table, can require two or more separate components. The Applications panel can organize these components into a single task and present this task and others to you in a menu of possibilities. Just selecting the task you want from the menu sets in motion all the machinery necessary to accomplish this task.

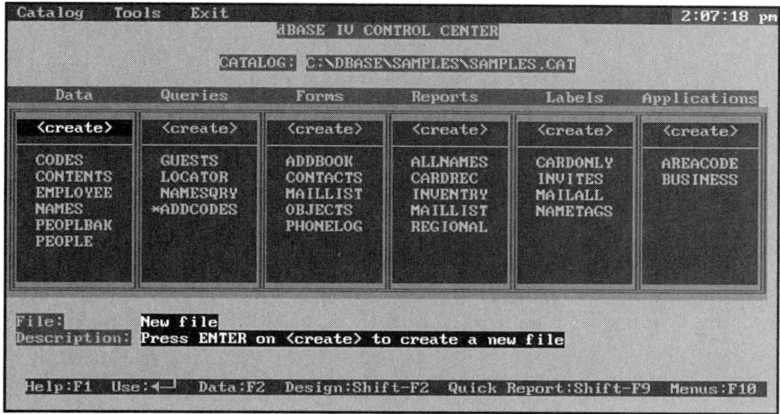


FIG. 2.8

The dBASE IV Control Center screen.

**NOTE** Although dBASE offers capabilities to expand applications with queries, forms, reports, and menus, an application can be as simple as a single database.

New users can use the Applications panel on a more basic level. With a little work, you can set up a menu-access system to help people with little knowledge of dBASE IV to work with an application that you design. The user doesn't have to know many dBASE IV procedures to use the application. The menu you design through the Applications panel restricts the user's activities to just the functions you want used. The user stays out of trouble, and so does the database. The Applications panel is described more fully in Chapter 20.

# Summary

In this chapter, you learned about the importance of keeping databases accurate in order to generate worthwhile information. Accuracy is defined in terms of the *validity* (correctness) of the database and the *reliability* (ability to generate correct results) of the database. You learned that dBASE IV offers many techniques for ensuring both validity and reliability, but that the burden of designing databases that support accuracy falls on you.

Probably the most important tool dBASE IV provides for checking accuracy is a customized data-entry form. With this tool, you can build in checks of the validity of the data values you enter in a field. Another set of tools comprises query, report, and label designs that encode and store specifications for information. These tools offer greater assurance that the reported information conforms exactly to your needs from one request to the next.

Finally, you learned that even with the wealth of features dBASE IV provides, you may occasionally ask the program to do something it wasn't programmed to do, and you may have to organize individual tasks for someone else's benefit. To help with these tasks, dBASE IV includes a programming language that enables you to design customized instructions.

3

CHAPTER

# Managing Files and Disks

You know that dBASE IV takes advantage of the hardware resources of a computer to work as a computerized database management system. In contrast, a paper-based database management system uses card catalogs, indexes, and filing cabinets to store material, typewriters, pencils, and preprinted forms to prepare reports and jot down requests for information. A computer-based system uses computer equivalents of these filing tools. The computer keyboard, for example, takes the place of the pencil and typewriter for entering data; disk drives take the place of the filing cabinets for storing data; and the printer and monitor take the place of forms and typewriters for presenting information in reports.

The filing clerk who carries out the management tasks needed to maintain a paper database has to understand the makeup of the system, where and how the data is stored and filed, how to make changes, and so on. The filing clerk also must abide by the rules and regulations of the office that controls access to the system. Office protocol, for example, may stipulate that only certain file cabinets are used, require that all reports be channeled through a typing pool, require permission to access certain kinds of files, and so on.

With dBASE IV as the computerized filing clerk, you can expect dBASE IV to know the rules of database operation and to abide by these rules consistently. dBASE IV knows where data is stored, how to access and change the data, and how to set up and present reports. Like a human filing clerk, however, dBASE IV also must conform to a higher authority to gain access to needed resources. This higher authority is the computer's operating system. The operating system functions in a way analogous to the office protocols by which the filing clerk must abide. The operating system sets the stage for all the work done on the computer and controls access to all the computer's important resources.

# Understanding What DOS Does

On an IBM or compatible computer, the operating system is a version of DOS (the disk operating system). DOS also is a program you must start—in popular terminology, *boot*—each time the computer is switched on. If the computer has a hard disk, necessary to run dBASE IV, the booting process takes place automatically when you flip on the switch. After you start DOS, you can run other software programs designed to work with DOS.

DOS programs, including dBASE IV, have to *invoke*, or call, DOS to "get permission" to carry out many operations. If dBASE wants to find data stored on disk, for example, dBASE first must ask DOS to make sure that the disk drive can be accessed. To print a report, dBASE must ask DOS to make sure that the printer is turned on and available. dBASE also relies on DOS to send data to the printer at a rate that the printer can manage.

Most of these calls to DOS are handled in the background; you aren't even aware of these activities. DOS, however, gives programs some flexibility to control the operating environment directly, particularly if multiple resources of the same kind are connected to the computer. Consider how dBASE IV handles multiple disk drives.

You can have several disk drives attached to the computer, but at any single moment, DOS permits access to only one drive. If, through dBASE, you have stored data on different disks, you must tell dBASE which drive you want the program to access. In theory, you can give the instruction directly to DOS; but you customarily give the instruction to dBASE, which in turn, transmits the instruction to DOS.

dBASE IV's command arsenal has a set of commands that enable the program to indirectly control the computer's hardware. To be fully at ease with dBASE, you need to understand how dBASE works with hardware and with DOS. Before reading about DOS's filing system, take a minute to review some aspects of the storage devices with which the filing system operates: the disk drives.

# Understanding Disk Drives and Disks

A *disk drive* is a piece of computer hardware that makes possible storing and retrieving data. This data is physically stored on the disks that reside temporarily or permanently in the drive. A temporary disk is known as a *floppy disk*. A permanent disk is known as a *fixed disk* or a *hard disk* (see fig. 3.1).

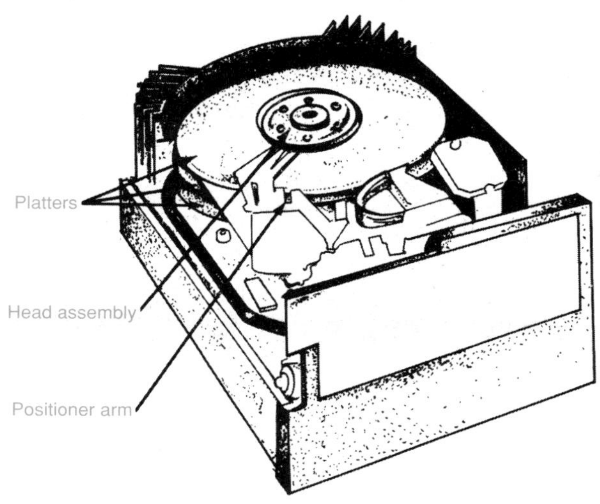


FIG. 3.1

The main components of a hard disk drive.

A typical system running dBASE IV has at least one floppy disk and one hard disk. The hard disk is a requirement.

Floppy disks come in two sizes: 5 1/4 inch and 3 1/2 inch. Each size also is available in two common densities: double and high. The combination of size and density affects the overall storage capacity of the disk (see table 3.1). Storage capacity of floppy disks is usually measured in thousands of bytes, or *kilobytes* (K). A kilobyte is actually 1024 bytes. Larger disks are measured in millions of kilobytes, or *megabytes* (M).

**Table 3.1 Floppy Disk Sizes and Capacities**

| Size and density of disk | Storage capacity |
|---|---|
| 5 1/4-inch double density | 360 K |
| 5 1/4-inch high density | 1.2 M |
| 3 1/2-inch double density | 720 K |
| 3 1/2-inch high density | 1.4 M |

Hard disks also come in different sizes and densities, although you can be less concerned with the details. You need to know only the overall capacity of the hard disk. A hard disk has far greater storage capacity than a floppy disk and therefore, capacity customarily is measured in megabytes (M). Hard disks in most computers today range from 20 megabytes up to hundreds of megabytes.

The surface of a disk is made up a number of concentric *tracks*, each of which is subdivided into a number of *sectors* (see fig. 3.2). The number of tracks and sectors is a factor of the size and density of the disk. Data is stored on the tracks and sectors as magnetically coded bits of information. Data is placed on and retrieved from the surface by the read and write heads of the drive mechanism. The drive heads are analogous to the read and write heads of a tape recorder and perform a similar function.

FIG. 3.2

The physical organization of a disk.

## Understanding How DOS Interacts with the Disk

When you give a command to save material on a disk, DOS determines where space is available on the disk, directs the read/write heads to this location, and alters the magnetic surface in a way that represents the data. When you give a command to retrieve data from disk, DOS determines where the information is located, sends the heads to the starting position, and reads the information by copying the data to the computer's memory. The details of these processes are more complicated than this brief outline, but the outline is accurate.

If dBASE IV gives a command to store part of a database, the data is stored wherever space is available on the disk surface. When you perform a database management operation, such as adding a record to a database, dBASE IV requests DOS to find room on the disk and to store the entry in the room found on disk. DOS works more efficiently if the disk has available space contiguous to the previously saved data, but having adjacent storage locations for a single file on the disk isn't critical. DOS can locate the data no matter where this information is placed on disk.

When you use a disk to store dBASE IV data, however, you must abide by the following few rules:

- The complete database must be on a single disk. The database cannot be split over two or more disks.
- You must tell dBASE in which drive the disk you want to store the data is located. If you do not specify a drive, dBASE assumes that you want to use the current drive.
- You must store the data under a file name. DOS uses file names to tag the location of the file on disk. File names are important because the same disk can store multiple files.

# Using DOS File Names

*File names* are the handles DOS uses to place and locate data on the disk surface. Anything placed on the disk must have a name. If the data doesn't have a name, DOS cannot find the information.

When you work with dBASE IV to create a database or application file, dBASE gives you the opportunity to save the work to disk. If you save the work, dBASE asks that you provide a file name. In this section, you look at how file names are constructed. As you may expect, you need to follow a set of rules when you assign file names.

File names must conform to a pattern acceptable to DOS. All programs that operate under DOS, including dBASE IV, must follow the same set of file-naming rules. File names consist of two parts: the file name and the file extension. The second part, the *extension*, is optional for some programs and required for other programs. In dBASE IV, you assign the first part of the file name; dBASE assigns the extension. dBASE IV uses the extension to distinguish between types of files, such as databases from data-entry forms from queries from reports.

The DOS file-naming rules further stipulate that the first part of the file name must use between one and eight keyboard characters; extensions, if present, use between one and three characters. Most characters—such as letters and digits—are acceptable, although most punctuation signs are unacceptable. File names, for example, cannot include a colon (:), semicolon (;), or comma (,). The period (.) separates the first name from the extension; the period can be used *only* for this purpose. You cannot use many special symbols, such as the asterisk (*) and greater-than sign (>), in file names. You also cannot use the space character, even to separate the first name and the extension.

Table 3.2 gives some acceptable and unacceptable file names; table 3.3 gives a list of the most important extensions used in dBASE IV.

**Table 3.2 Acceptable and Unacceptable File Names**

| File name | Acceptable? | Reason/comment |
|---|---|---|
| PAYROLL.DBF | Yes | |
| payroll dbf | No | Space separates name and extension |
| wilson | Yes | No extension |
| marchreport | No | More than 8 characters in name |
| jan_data.dbf | Yes | Underscore is acceptable character |
| feb;data.dbf | No | Semicolon is not acceptable character |

**Table 3.3 Common File Extensions Used in dBASE IV**

| dBASE file name | Type of file |
|---|---|
| payroll.dbf | Database file |
| payroll.frm | Report file |
| payroll.qbe | Query file |
| payroll.scr | Data-entry format file |
| payroll.lbl | Label file |
| payroll.app | Application file |

## Understanding Disk Directories and Subdirectories

If the filing system consisted of only file names, managing the system would be an easy task. DOS, however, imposes what new users of computers occasionally consider complicated nuisances known as disk directories. A *directory* is a logical organizational unit for a disk. If a disk is large and contains a great deal of surface area—as does a hard disk—using DOS to treat the surface as one large filing space becomes impractical.

If you had a filing room with no cabinets, you may be able to set up a filing system that enabled you to find information you needed; work becomes much easier, however, if you buy some filing cabinets. Directories are analogous to filing cabinets. Directories divide the enormous capacity of a hard disk into manageable areas. DOS also enables directories to contain other directories. Just as you can subdivide information in a filing cabinet into separate drawers, a directory can have one or more *subdirectories*. As you find when you work with DOS, directories usually have subdirectories.

**TIP**

If you work with a hard disk with which you are unfamiliar, do yourself a favor: become familiar with the hard disk's directory organization before you work with the disk.

The net result is that a disk can be apportioned into a whole maze of nooks and crannies, which take the overall look of an airport built on a hub concept. To find a particular flight, you go to a particular terminal, walk down a particular corridor, branch off to a subcorridor, and proceed to the particular gate where the plane is waiting (see fig. 3.3). Just like the airport, you follow disk directories along a series of paths to the specific flight, or file, you want to access. You can get to a particular directory only by making your way along its path. To go from one directory to another, you have to back down the path you are on and go up the other path.

The first time you use a disk, only one directory exists, the *root directory*. This directory serves as the main trunk line for all directories and subdirectories you put on the disk. How do you decide which directories you need for the disk? Your needs determine the answer to this question, but first, consider the following stipulations:

- The files that make up the programs, including dBASE IV, should be allocated to individual directories. In practice, when you install most programs on a hard disk, the installation instructions specify how to create a separate directory for the program, or by default, the install programs set up a separate directory for you.

- The files you create with programs (for example, the database files created with dBASE IV) should be grouped into one or more subdirectories located along the path from the directory that stores the program files. With dBASE IV, for example, create subdirectories that branch from the directory that stores the dBASE IV program files.

- Group similar files into subdirectories. If you create different applications in dBASE, for example, create a different subdirectory for each application. This organizational technique is helpful when you use a program like dBASE IV, which creates and stores many kinds of files.

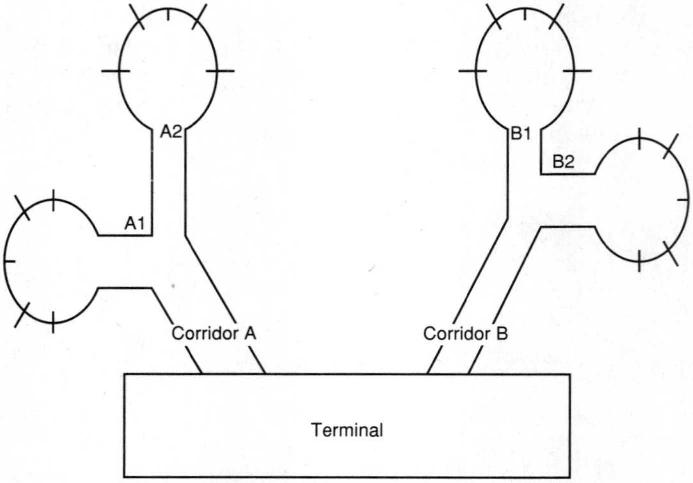

FIG. 3.3

An airport hub layout.

Figure 3.4 explains these principles by showing a hard disk directory *tree*, configured for a business that runs dBASE IV, a word processor, and a spreadsheet package.

As mentioned earlier in this chapter, the filing system is mostly transparent to you as the user. When you want to save data to disk, you use the Save command for the program you're working in and provide a file name. DOS takes over, finds room on the disk to store your work, and adds the name of this file to its list of all the files on the disk. This file listing is called a *directory*, not to be confused with the term of the same name which refers to a logical section of the disk. The directory referred to here is equivalent to a table of contents for the disk. In fact, you will find that each disk directory or subdirectory has its own directory listing. You can have as many directory listings on your disk as you have directories and subdirectories.

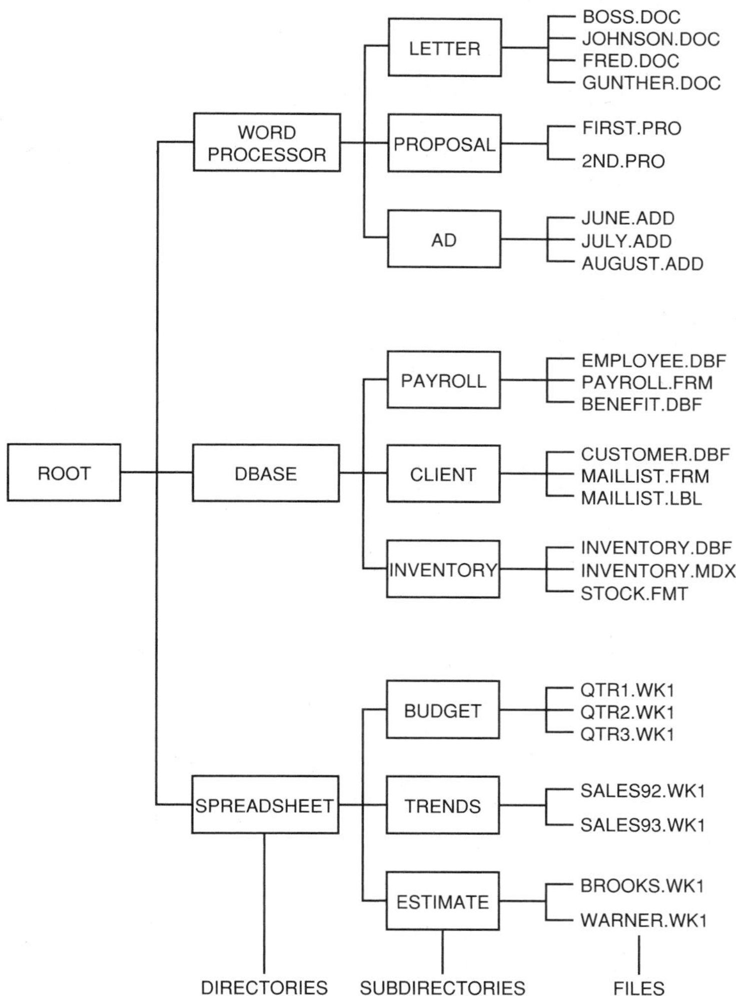


FIG. 3.4

A directory tree for a hypothetical business.

# Summarizing the DOS Filing System

The following list summarizes what you learned about the DOS filing system:

- The physical surface of a disk is divided into a series of tracks and sectors, each of which can store data.
- An area of the disk surface is designated by DOS to store the directory listing of the disk contents.

- Logical subdivisions of the disk, known as *subdirectories*, break up the full storage capacity of the disk into manageable segments.
- You can access a separate directory listing for each subdirectory on the disk.
- Files represent logical chunks of data stored on disk.
- A file name for each file on the disk consists of a first name and an optional extension.

In the following section, you examine the procedures needed to work effectively with DOS. This treatment of DOS isn't exhaustive but covers only what you need to know about DOS so that you can work more effectively with dBASE IV.

# Using DOS Filing Procedures

Now that you have a logical concept of what DOS does, you need to understand how to control the filing system. You also need to know that you control certain aspects of the system and that other aspects are handled by dBASE IV. Together with applicable DOS commands, the aspects you control are listed in table 3.4.

**Table 3.4 DOS Filing Procedures and Commands**

| DOS procedure | DOS command |
|---|---|
| Putting the filing system on a disk | FORMAT |
| Setting up subdirectories | MKDIR or MD (for MaKe DIRectory) |
| Changing from one subdirectory to another | CHDIR or CD (for CHange DIRectory) |
| Eliminating a directory | RMDIR or RD (for ReMove DIRectory) |
| Inspecting the full set of subdirectories on a disk | TREE |

# Understanding the Default Drive and Directory and the Prompt

Before you look at individual procedures, you have to learn about certain basics in giving DOS commands. First, you need to understand the concept of a *default drive and directory*. When you boot the operating system, DOS focuses its attention on the root directory of the drive from which DOS started. Usually, this drive is the hard disk. How do you know for sure? Look at the prompt that appears before the flashing cursor on-screen. DOS uses letters to designate the different drives on the computer. The letters A and B typically refer to floppy drives; letters C and higher refer to hard drives. The colon (:) always appears after the drive letter. If the on-screen prompt reads `C:>` or `C:\>`, you know that drive C, the hard disk, is the default drive. If the prompt reads `A:>` or `A:\>`, you know that drive A, a floppy disk, is the default drive.

**NOTE** If the computer uses a program-access menu, menu options you select typically change the directory. Be aware of which directory the menu system accesses for each option.

You can change the default drive by typing the letter (plus the colon) of the drive you want and pressing Enter. To change the default drive to drive A, type *A:* and press Enter. The prompt changes to reflect the new default.

In many computer setups, the default directory also can be discerned from the prompt. If the prompt is `C:\>`, for example, the backslash character (\) after the colon indicates that the root directory of drive C is the default. If you change the default directory by using the CHDIR command, the prompt changes to show the new subdirectory. If you change the default directory to DBASE (the directory that stores the dBASE program files), for example, the prompt may read `C:\DBASE>`. The prompt reflects the path the system took to go to the new directory; in other words, the path from the root directory (\) to the DBASE subdirectory. The drive and directory indicated by the prompt is the default drive and directory.

If the prompt doesn't reflect a change of directory, you can issue a DOS command so that the prompt does show the path. Type *PROMPT $P$G* at the DOS prompt and press Enter.

**NOTE** You can type DOS commands in upper- or lowercase.

# Understanding the DOS Path

DOS expects the programs you want to run, such as dBASE IV, and the data you want to retrieve, such as a database file, to be on the default drive and in the default directory. Likewise, if you create and then want to store a new file on disk, DOS assumes that, unless you specify otherwise, you want to store the file on the default drive and directory. If you request a program or data file without specifying the location of the desired information, DOS looks only on the default drive and directory. If DOS cannot find the file, you see the `Bad command or file name` error message.

DOS accepts one exception to the rule that you have to be located in the correct drive and directory to access a program file. You can instruct DOS to run a program, such as dBASE IV, from any directory if you have previously given a PATH command that references the DBASE subdirectory. Assuming that the directory in which the dBASE program is stored is named DBASE, you can type *PATH C:\DBASE* at the DOS prompt and press Enter. After you give this command, you can run dBASE IV from any directory.

You can run the PATH command automatically by embedding it in the AUTOEXEC.BAT file, located in the root directory of the boot disk. When you boot DOS, all commands in AUTOEXEC.BAT are carried out. When you are going through the dBASE IV installation procedure, you can choose to add the DBASE directory to the path (if you want), so you rarely have to type the PATH command. You also can embed the PROMPT $P$G command in the AUTOEXEC.BAT file. In Chapter 4, you learn the implications of the PATH command for starting dBASE IV.

## Understanding DOS External and Internal Commands

DOS commands must be accessible to you in the same way any other program file is accessible. This means that when you issue a DOS command, DOS returns a `Bad command or file name` message if the right program file isn't found in the default directory. Make sure that DOS can always find the DOS program files by including in the system path the directory that stores the DOS program files. To specify a system path that includes the DOS directory (the directory where the DOS program files are located) and the DBASE directory, include the following command in the AUTOEXEC.BAT file:

```
PATH C:\;C:\DOS;C:\DBASE
```

Notice that the path includes a reference to the root directory (C:\) and that each directory is separated from other directory names by a semicolon (;).

You can carry out a number of DOS commands known as *internal commands* from any disk location regardless of the path setting. Internal commands include the most commonly used DOS commands, such as the CHDIR and MKDIR commands. DOS commands that cannot be called from any directory regardless of the path setting are known as *external commands*. FORMAT and TREE are external commands. If you see a `Bad command or file name` message after you issue an external command, change to the directory that stores the DOS files and reissue the command. This error message indicates that the DOS directory isn't in the system path. You can correct this problem by including the directory in the PATH command (either from the C:\ prompt or in the AUTOEXEC.BAT file).

## Formatting Disks

When you first buy a disk, it usually doesn't come with a filing system embedded on it. This is because you may want to use the disk with an operating system other than DOS. To put the DOS filing system on the disk, you use the DOS command FORMAT to *format*, or prepare, the surface of the disk. This command lays out the area of the disk for the directory listing, subdivides the surface into the number of tracks and sectors appropriate for the size and capacity of the disk drive (and for the density of the disk's surface), and sets up the root directory.

To use the FORMAT command, specify the letter of the drive in which the disk is located. In practice, you typically format only floppy disks, so the command you type is *FORMAT A:* or *FORMAT B:*. In principle, however, you also can format a hard disk by typing *FORMAT C:*. Be extremely careful that you don't format the hard disk by mistake. In the process of formatting a disk, DOS wipes out all traces of files already on the disk, leaving you with a completely clean slate. You definitely will give yourself and your co-workers a major headache if you format the hard disk accidentally. Restoring millions of bytes of programs and data isn't a trivial task.

Recognize the implication of a default drive when you format. For example, assume that the prompt reads C:\> when you issue the FORMAT command. If you give the command without specifying the drive in which the disk you want to format is located, DOS assumes that you want to format the disk in the default drive. Because the default drive usually is the hard disk (drive C), you're in for the same trouble as if you typed *FORMAT C:*.

# Creating and Navigating Subdirectories

Earlier in this chapter, you learned the necessity of creating a system of subdirectories to better manage the storage capacity of a hard disk. You also can set up subdirectories on floppy disks, but the advantage of doing this is limited because the capacity of a floppy disk is already within manageable limits.

Subdirectories are created through one of two processes. The first method is when hard-disk installation routines for software create directories and copy program files to the hard disk. The second method is when you create the directories in anticipation of data-storage needs. Subdirectories are assigned names by using the same general rules that apply for file names. The directory name can contain eleven characters or less and can include no spaces or special punctuation signs.

When creating a subdirectory, remember that the subdirectory is created as a branch of the current directory. Consequently, you move first to the directory that is the *parent* of the *child* subdirectory you want to create. Change directories with the CHDIR or CD command followed by the path you take to travel to this directory. The sample scenarios given in table 3.5 assume that the hard disk has a DBASE directory and a PAYROLL subdirectory as a child of the DBASE directory.

**Table 3.5 Examples of Changing Directories**

| Current location | Destination | Command |
|---|---|---|
| Root directory | PAYROLL directory | CD \DBASE\PAYROLL *or* CD DBASE\PAYROLL |
| PAYROLL directory | Root directory | CD \ |
| DBASE directory | PAYROLL directory | CD PAYROLL |
| PAYROLL directory | DBASE directory | CD \DBASE *or* CD .. |
| PAYROLL directory | MAILLIST directory | CD \DBASE\MAILLIST *or* CD ..\MAILLIST |

Notice that the following conventions are used when changing directories:

- The root directory is indicated by an initial backslash (\) that follows the CD command.

- If the destination directory is a child of the current directory, you can move to the destination directory by typing the name of the subdirectory after the CD command.
- If the destination directory is the parent of the current directory, you can move to the destination directory by typing two periods (..) after the CD command.
- You can go to any directory by typing the full path to this directory from the root. This method is fail-safe, although doing so may necessitate typing a long path name.

**NOTE** Many current programs offer ways to manipulate and navigate directories without using DOS procedures. Check the documentation for your program for these shortcuts.

The child and parent relationships between directories are collectively organized into what DOS refers to as the *directory tree*. The structure is called a *tree* because you can diagram the full set of directories as a series of limbs, branches, and twigs off the central root (refer back to fig. 3.4).

To see the full set of directories on a disk, type *tree* and press Enter. (The type of display you see will depend on the version of DOS you have.) Each branch of the tree is separately accounted for. If a branch has subdirectories, they are listed; if a branch has no subdirectories, DOS reports this fact. If you have many directories, the list flashes by faster than you can read it. You can print out the full list by typing *TREE > PRN*. This command directs the output of the TREE command to the printer.

**TIP** If you type *TREE | MORE*, the display pauses when the screen is full until you press a key. This is helpful when viewing a long tree.

Assume that you now are at the desired level and branch of the tree for creating the new directory. To create the new directory, type *MKDIR* or *MD* followed by the name of the new directory. If DOS finds the name acceptable, the directory is created. You then can move to the new directory in the usual way (by typing *CD* or *CHDIR*).

What you create can be undone. If you no longer need a directory, you can delete the directory by using the RMDIR or RD command. You must give this command from the parent directory of the directory you want to remove. The directory you want to remove also must be empty; the directory must contain no files or subdirectories. If these conditions hold, type *RMDIR*, then the name of the directory you want to remove, and press Enter.

**For Related Information...**

▸▸ "Managing Files and Disks from dBASE IV," pp. 109.

# Understanding Other DOS Procedures

DOS carries out a great number of other tasks. Some tasks include commands to manipulate individual files or blocks of files. These commands include procedures for identifying the names of files, erasing or deleting files, copying files from one location to another, and renaming files. Chapter 5 explains the dBASE IV commands that perform the same operations.

# Summary

In this chapter, you looked at the foundations of DOS, the computer's operating system. You saw that DOS sets the rules by which all programs, including dBASE IV, must operate. These rules include ways to name files and organize the disk into logical segments called directories. You learned about some procedures that DOS provides for manipulating directories and for providing access to program files. These procedures are activated by commands that enable you to format the surface of a disk; to create, change, and remove directories; and to inspect the entire directory tree.

In Chapters 4 and 5, you start working with dBASE IV, using as a foundation the information in this and earlier chapters. Just as you were exposed to the logic of the computer system and the logic of databases in this and previous chapters, you begin the examination of dBASE IV by exploring the logic and *personality* of dBASE's organization—how you set up, command, and come to understand dBASE IV.

# Getting Productive with dBASE IV

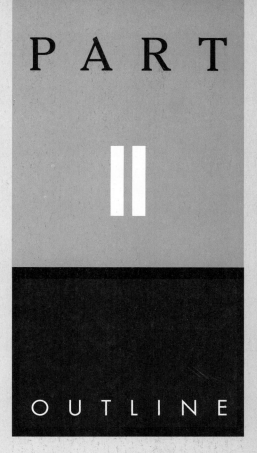

4

CHAPTER

# Getting Started with dBASE IV

Now that you have a conceptual foundation of database logic and DOS operation from the preceding chapters, you are ready to begin working with dBASE IV. This chapter begins by showing you how to install dBASE IV on your hard disk. dBASE IV does not run from the floppy disks on which you received the program; you install dBASE IV by using the Install program, located on the Install disk.

Next, you learn how to configure dBASE IV to run with your particular hardware arrangement, especially the printer and the monitor. You configure dBASE IV by using a program called DBSETUP.EXE, which is copied to the DBASE directory on your hard disk during the installation process.

This chapter then shows you how to begin creating database applications by issuing commands to dBASE IV. These commands are organized and accessed through a toolbox that dBASE IV refers to as the *Control Center*. You learn how to pick and choose command tools by using a menu of options that the Control Center makes available.

Finally, you learn how the Control Center works in conjunction with a special filing system called a *catalog*. The catalog collects and displays all the file components of a database application. You learn not only how to use the tools in the Control Center, but also how to set up catalogs for different applications.

# Installing dBASE IV

To work properly, dBASE IV must be installed on your computer's hard disk. Because dBASE IV is a pretty hefty program, you need a minimum of 4M of available space to store the core program and the *overlay files* necessary to run it. If you have less than that amount of space, dBASE IV displays a message saying it cannot install itself. You must free some space on the disk by deleting data or program files for some other software. To see how much room you have available on your disk, issue the DOS DIR command. The amount of available space is reported at the end of the file list.

In addition to sufficient disk space, dBASE IV requires a minimum of 640K of computer memory. Although dBASE uses only 450K, some of the rest of that memory is taken up by DOS and by various system drivers. The more memory dBASE IV has available, the more efficiently it can run.

If you have a 286, 386, or 486 class computer with more than 640K of memory, dBASE IV can take advantage of that memory whether it is configured as expanded or extended memory. dBASE uses a disk-caching program to do this; a disk-caching program tries to anticipate your next data request based on previous requests so that the data is available and ready without going to disk to get it. The dBASE IV caching program, called DBCACHE, can markedly improve search times and increase overall performance.

**NOTE** If you already are using another disk-caching program, such as Smartdrive or PC-Kwik, do not install DBCACHE.

During the installation process, you are asked whether you want to install a cache if you have expanded or extended memory. If you do, dBASE IV automatically loads the cache every time you load dBASE. If you intend to run any background or TSR (terminate-and-stay-resident) programs while running dBASE IV, the installation of the cache is a little more complex. Consult the dBASE IV installation instructions for details.

The following instructions assume that you are installing dBASE IV as your first version of dBASE. Begin by inserting the Install disk into the floppy drive; carry out the following steps from the DOS prompt:

1. Type *A:* and press Enter to change the default drive to A.
2. Type *INSTALL* and press Enter. This action loads and activates the installation program.

3. Respond to the prompt for the drive and directory on which you want to install dBASE IV. The default is C:\DBASE. You do not have to create this directory ahead of time.
4. You see a screen prompting for your name, company name, and the program's serial number. Fill out this screen and press Ctrl-End when you're finished.
5. At various points during the installation, you are prompted for information about your system or asked to change disks. Respond appropriately and complete the action by pressing Enter.
6. At some point during the installation, you are asked whether you want dBASE to update the AUTOEXEC.BAT file. If you respond Yes, the Install program adds or alters the PATH command to include the DBASE directory in the system path (see Chapter 3 for more information about the system path).
7. You also are asked whether you want the installation program to modify the CONFIG.SYS file. If you respond Yes, the Install program checks to see whether the FILES variable is set to at least 99 and the BUFFERS variable to at least 15. If you do not have a CONFIG.SYS file, Install adds it. If you have a CONFIG.SYS file, but it does not contain the FILES or BUFFERS variable, one or both are added.

After you finish the installation, configure dBASE for the particular hardware options on your system. If you want, you can begin to work with dBASE using the default configuration. The default configuration selects display characteristics for your monitor, selects start-up options, and gives you basic printer control.

# Configuring dBASE IV

During the installation procedure, the Install program creates a file in the DBASE directory called CONFIG.DB. This file contains all the configuration information dBASE IV needs to adapt itself to your hardware options and to your working preferences. You can control dozens of options with the CONFIG.DB file, but many of them pertain to highly specialized situations. Some of the more general options you can control include the color characteristics of your monitor, how dates are represented, and how currency values are represented. If you have a monochrome monitor, the color characteristics are irrelevant. Even though the CONFIG.DB file is set up by the Install program, you use the DBSETUP program to modify CONFIG.DB.

Strictly speaking, you don't have to run DBSETUP to configure dBASE. You probably can live happily with the choice of display characteristics dBASE gives you. The main advantage of running DBSETUP is to inform dBASE about the capabilities of your printer.

The DBSETUP program creates one or more printer drivers in your DBASE directory. Most printers behave in a "plain vanilla" way if you use dBASE IV's "generic" printer driver. To access the particular features of a printer, however, you must configure a driver for that printer. The printer's special features then become available to you as style options when you format reports.

dBASE IV enables you to configure up to four different printer drivers and make one of them the default driver. Any time you print a report, you can pick one of the four drivers. If you don't choose a driver, dBASE sends the report to the printer you set up as the default.

## Running the Configuration Program DBSETUP

After you successfully install dBASE IV, run the DBSETUP program to specify your configuration preferences. Start the program by moving to the DBASE directory and typing the program name, as detailed by these steps:

1. Type *CD C:\DBASE* and press Enter.
2. Type *DBSETUP* and press Enter.

The screen shown in figure 4.1 appears, listing the available commands in a pull-down menu. With these commands, you can modify an existing file or create a new CONFIG.DB file. Select an option from the pull-down menu by using the up- and down-arrow keys to highlight the option, and then pressing Enter. As you change options, a different message appears at the bottom of the screen, giving a short explanation of what that option does. Above the message line is the navigation line, which lists the instructions for maneuvering around the menu system. Above the navigation line is the status bar. The status bar identifies that you are working in DBSETUP mode and tells you the location of the CONFIG.DB file (in fig. 4.1, the CONFIG.DB file is located in C:\DBASE). The `Opt` indicator identifies the number of the highlighted command out of all the commands in the current menu (in fig. 4.1, the `Opt` indicator reads `1/2`, which is the first of two options highlighted in the current menu).

If you select the Modify Existing CONFIG.DB option and press Enter, the main menu bar for the setup program appears (see fig. 4.2). The menu bar groups the major setup options across the top of the screen. Each option has an associated pull-down menu from which you select options. If you want to change menu options, use the left- and right-arrow keys to close the current pull-down menu and open the adjacent one. In figure 4.2, the Printer pull-down menu is open.

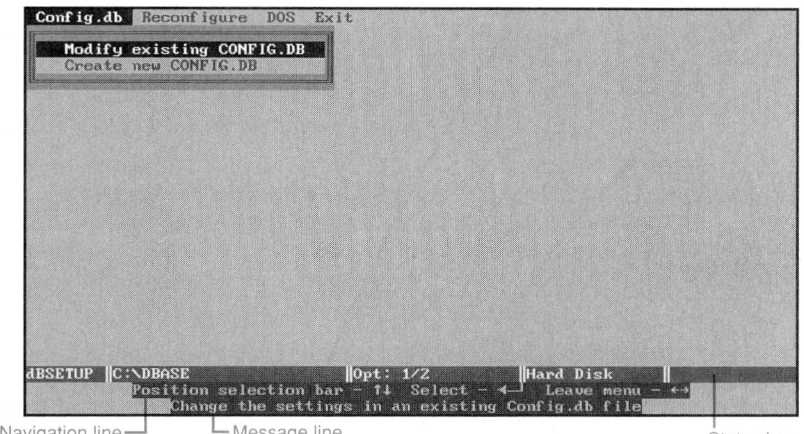


FIG. 4.1

The start-up screen for the DBSETUP program.

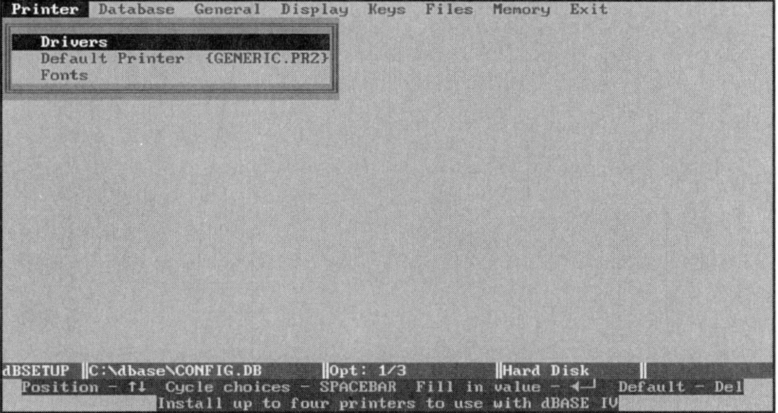


FIG. 4.2

The main menu bar for the DBSETUP program.

## Configuring Printers

The Printer menu contains the commands you use to set up printer drivers. If you want to set up a printer driver for the Hewlett-Packard LaserJet Series II printer, for example, follow these steps:

1. Highlight the Drivers option in the Printer menu and press Enter. You see a window with four empty slots, one for each of the printers you can configure. The cursor is located on the first slot.
2. Press Shift-F1 to see a list of the available printer drivers.
3. Use the down-arrow key to find the HP option on the list and press Enter. You see a second list of just Hewlett-Packard printers.
4. Highlight the LJII 6 lpi option and press Enter. This option name reflects the Series II printer operating at 6 lines per inch (lpi). Although the name doesn't specify, this option also sets up the printer in portrait orientation (that is, the page prints on the long dimension of the paper). If you want to print in landscape orientation (across the width of the paper), you must select a different driver.
5. With the cursor in the Device column, press Shift-F1 and select the computer port to which the printer is connected. Generally, this port is LPT1. Press Enter.

After completing this process, your screen should look the one in figure 4.3. If you have other printers to configure, repeat these steps for each printer. When you are finished, save all the drivers by pressing Ctrl-End.

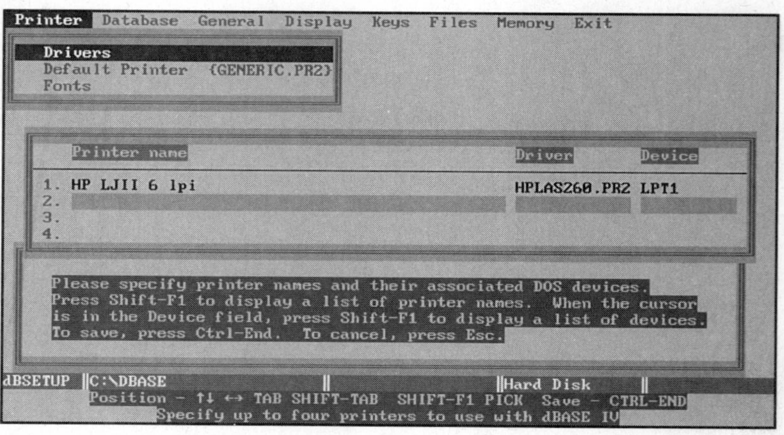


FIG. 4.3

Configuring a printer driver for the HP LaserJet II.

If you have configured multiple printer drivers, you may want to change the default printer assignment to reflect the printer you use most often. Follow these steps to change the default printer:

1. Select the Default Printer option from the Printer menu and press Enter.
2. From the list of printers you configured, select the printer you want to make the default and press Enter.

With the Fonts option on the Printer menu, you can specify alternative fonts from the list of fonts available for your printer. To use this option, you must know what the set-up or printer-control codes for the fonts are. Consult the documentation for your printer for this information. If you don't choose alternative fonts, dBASE IV uses the printer's default font. Consult the dBASE IV documentation for additional details on changing fonts.

## Configuring Settings

The other DBSETUP menu options—Database, General, Display, Keys, Files, and Memory—specify the values for all of dBASE IV's environmental settings. These settings are grouped logically according to overall purpose. At this point, you have little reason to change any of the default settings. If you work with dBASE in a country other than the United States, however, you may want to change the General settings, some of which are displayed in figure 4.4.

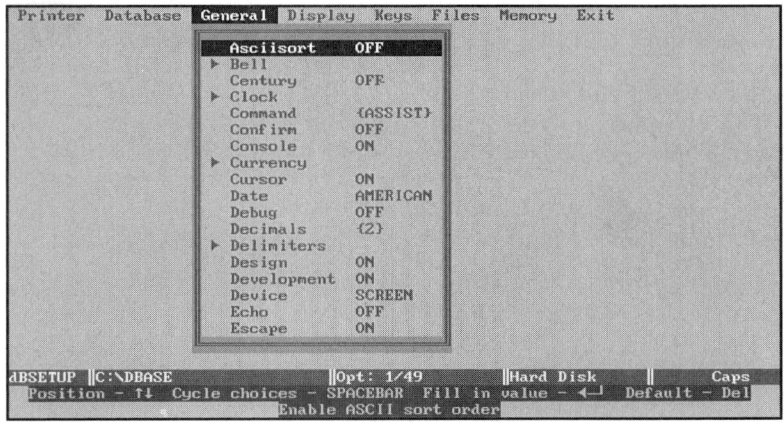


FIG. 4.4

A partial list of General menu settings.

Notice that some of the settings in figure 4.4 have arrowheads in front of their names. The arrowhead indicates that these settings have submenus in which the values are specified. Open the submenu by selecting the setting and pressing Enter. Other settings in the list have their values specified by the word ON or OFF or by another multiple-choice option. These settings have a fixed set of values from which you choose by selecting the setting and pressing the space bar to rotate through the available options. Finally, some settings have a value enclosed in curly brackets. To change the values for these settings, select the setting and type the new value.

## Changing the Date Format

The Date setting is set by default to AMERICAN, meaning that dates are expressed in dBASE IV in the standard American MM/DD/YY format. In other countries, dates are expressed in other notations; many European countries, for example, use the DD/MM/YY format. You may want to change this setting to agree with some other date convention. The full list of possibilities is shown in table 4.1.

**Table 4.1 Values for the Date Setting**

| Description | Format |
|---|---|
| American and USA and MDY | MM/DD/YY |
| ANSI | YY.MM.DD |
| British and French and DMY | DD/MM/YY |
| German | DD.MM.YY |
| Italian | DD-MM-YY |
| Japanese and YMD | YY/MM/DD |

To change the Date setting, highlight it and press the space bar until the option you want appears.

## Changing the Currency Format

Currency is another setting you may want to change if you need to express currency figures in some unit other than dollars. If you want to express currency in Deutsche Marks (DM), for example, change the Currency value by following these steps:

1. Select the Currency setting from the General menu and press Enter. A window appears with settings for Justification and Symbol (see fig. 4.5).
2. If the new currency symbol is to appear to the left of the number, leave the Justification setting alone. If the symbol is to appear to the right of the number, highlight the Justification setting and press the space bar to change the setting to `RIGHT`. In this example, leave the Justification setting as `LEFT`.
3. Place the cursor on the Symbol setting and press Enter.
4. Type the new currency symbol, in this case *DM*. If you want to separate the symbol from the number, press the space bar once (press the space bar either before or after you type the currency symbol, depending on whether the symbol is to precede or follow the number). Press Enter again to record the new symbol.
5. Press the Esc key to close the window. Your new settings are saved.

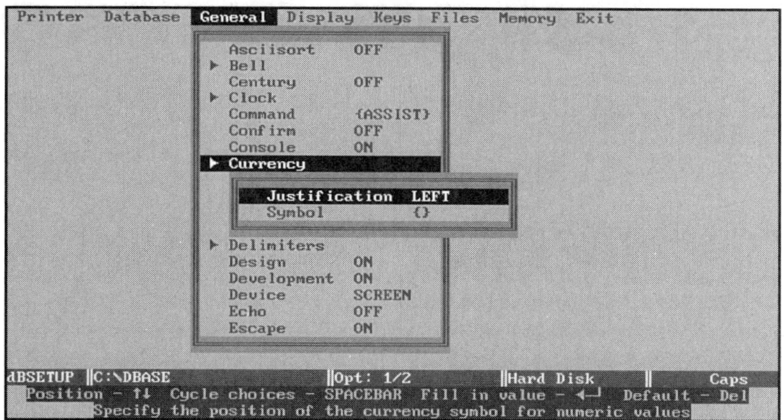


FIG. 4.5

The settings options for Currency configuration.

If you want to specify a currency symbol not found on your keyboard—for example, the British pound symbol (£)—enter the symbol by holding the Alt key and typing on the numeric keypad (make sure that Num Lock is on) the ASCII numeric code for this symbol. The ASCII code for the pound symbol is 156. In step 4 of the preceding instructions, press and hold the Alt key, and press 156 (use the numeric keypad to type these numbers); the pound symbol appears on-screen. Four common currency symbols are available using this method. Their codes are given in table 4.2.

**Table 4.2 International Currency Symbols**

| Currency | Symbol | ASCII code |
|---|---|---|
| British pound | £ | 156 |
| Japanese yen | ¥ | 157 |
| Spanish peseta | Pt | 158 |
| French franc | *f* | 159 |

In addition to using different currency symbols, some currencies use different punctuation. German currency, for example, uses periods where US convention uses commas, and commas where US convention uses periods. The figure $45,890.98, for example, is expressed in Deutsche Marks as DM 45.890,98.

To change these formatting conventions, change the Point setting to , (a comma) and the Separator setting to . (a period). These settings are found in the General menu of the DBSETUP main menu.

Any changes you make to the Currency setting are displayed only in form and report files in which you indicate that you want to use the Financial-format picture function to express a numeric value. See Chapter 9 for details on selecting picture functions.

# Changing Display Settings

The Display menu of the DBSETUP program controls the color settings of dBASE IV structures that appear on-screen. These structures include text, messages, boxes, titles, and so on. If you have a color monitor, you can change the color of each structure independently. Figure 4.6 shows settings for each structure for a color monitor. Each of the structures has a foreground color code (preceding the slash character) and a background color code (following the slash character). The codes identified by their common color names are included in the table 4.3.

The color codes followed by a plus sign (+) indicate intense variants of normal colors with noticeably different hues.

To change the display setting for a structure, select the structure from the Display menu and press Enter. The list of possible colors is arrayed in two columns, the first for foreground color, the second for background color. To change the foreground color, use the up- and down-arrow keys to move to your selection. To change the background color, press the right-arrow key and then use the up- and down-arrow keys to make your selection. To make text blink on the screen, press

Enter after selecting the appropriate color. (Be sensible with this feature; a little blinking goes a long way.) When you're finished, press Ctrl-End to save your selections.

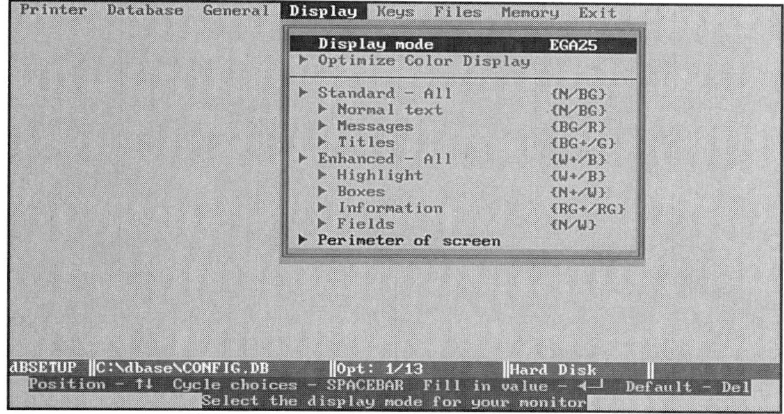


FIG. 4.6
The Display settings for a color monitor.

**Table 4.3 Color Names and Codes**

| Color name | Color code |
|---|---|
| White | W |
| Black | N (indicating no color) |
| Gray | N+ |
| Blue | B |
| Red | R |
| Green | G |
| Brown | GR (a mix of green and red) |
| Yellow | GR+ (a mix of intense green and red) |
| Cyan | BG (a mix of blue and green) |
| Magenta | RB (a mix of red and blue) |

# Ending the Configuration

The other menus on the DBSETUP main menu control aspects of the dBASE IV working environment that, in most cases, you will not have to use (refer to the dBASE documentation for information about these menus). The exception is the Keys menu, which enables you to set up special function keys to run specific commands or enter text sequences. These keys, however, can be reprogrammed for use only at the dot prompt, an operating mode described in more detail in Part IV of this book.

When you have made all the configuration changes you want, save the changes to the CONFIG.DB file by pulling down the Exit menu, selecting the Save and Exit option, and pressing Enter. You return to the original menu. Select the Exit option and press Enter.

FROM HERE...

**For Related Information...**

▸▸ "Customizing dBASE IV with SET Options," pp. 394.

▸▸ "Using SET Commands," pp. 845.

▸▸ "Using the System Configuration File," pp. 935.

# Starting dBASE IV

After reading through the purposes of dBASE IV and spending time getting it installed and configured, you are now ready to load the program and begin working. When you load dBASE IV, a copy of dBASE IV is taken from the hard disk and inserted into the computer's memory. Until you get the program into memory, you cannot do any work with it.

Loading dBASE IV is simple. If you followed the suggestions of the Install program and placed the C:\DBASE directory into the system path in the AUTOEXEC.BAT file, just type *DBASE* from the system prompt and press Enter. If dBASE IV is not in the system path, you first must change to the DBASE directory (type *CD C:\DBASE*) before you type *DBASE*.

You also can change directories after you're in dBASE. The steps for doing so are described in Chapter 5. You may have to change directories from within dBASE if your computer uses a program-access menu or a DOS shell that shields you from using DOS directly.

Naturally, you're going to want to put your data somewhere after you set it up, and you're going to want access to any data created in earlier sessions. If you followed the suggestions in Chapter 3, you already have set up a directory to store your data; this directory is a *child* of the DBASE directory. If you have not done this, you may want to set up a directory now as a practice area. Call the directory anything you want, but if you're stuck for a name, call it PRACTICE. To set up this directory, follow these steps from the DOS prompt:

1. Type *CD C:\DBASE* to change to the DBASE directory.
2. Type *MD PRACTICE.*

After you set up this directory, you can save yourself some time if you change to that directory before you load dBASE. If you're still in the DBASE directory, type *CD PRACTICE.* If you're at the root directory, type *CD\DBASE\PRACTICE.* After you're in the PRACTICE subdirectory, type *DBASE* to start the program.

The reason you start dBASE IV from the subdirectory where you want to store and retrieve your data files is that the PATH command in AUTOEXEC.BAT works only for program files, not for data files. Even if you put the PRACTICE data directory in the system path, DOS does not search for any data files in it.

To summarize, you usually take the following steps to work with an application you want to build or have already built:

1. Make sure that the directory of the dBASE program files is in the system path.
2. Change to the data directory that stores the application with which you want to work.
3. Load the program from that directory.

You may, for example, give the following commands for a dBASE IV payroll application:

| Command | Purpose |
|---|---|
| PATH C:\DBASE | Includes the DBASE subdirectory in the system path. This command usually is given by the AUTOEXEC.BAT file. |
| CD C:\DBASE\PAYROLL | Changes to the subdirectory storing the payroll application files. |
| DBASE | Loads the dBASE IV program into the computer's memory. |

# Using the Mouse

Before you start using dBASE IV 1.5, a brief discussion of the mouse is in order. When you start dBASE IV 1.5, the program automatically checks to see whether a mouse driver is loaded into memory. (Previous versions of dBASE do not support the mouse.) If you want to use the mouse, be sure that you have loaded the mouse driver (usually MOUSE.SYS in your CONFIG.SYS file, or MOUSE.COM in your AUTOEXEC.BAT file) before running dBASE IV. Consult the instructions that came with your mouse hardware for information on installing the proper driver.

When the mouse is active, dBASE IV displays a *mouse pointer* on the screen. The mouse pointer is a small rectangle (like a cursor) that can be moved around the screen by moving the mouse. This pointer is used to reposition the cursor or select items on the screen, similar to the way you use the arrow keys.

If you are unfamiliar with using a mouse, you should understand a few terms. When instructed to *click* an item, you should move the mouse to position the mouse pointer on the item, and then press and release the *mouse button*. If you have more than one button on your mouse, you normally use only the left button. To *double-click* an item, press the button twice very quickly. To *drag* an object with the mouse, hold down the button while moving the mouse. For more details about using the mouse with dBASE IV, refer to the section "Using the Mouse with dBASE IV 1.5" in Part V.

Don't worry if you don't have a mouse. Anything that can be done with the mouse in dBASE IV also can be accomplished using the keyboard.

**For Related Information...**

▸▸ "Using the Mouse with dBASE IV 1.5," p. 929.

# Using the Control Center and the Dot Prompt

After you load dBASE IV and acknowledge the sign-on screen, you see the Control Center (see fig. 4.7). The *Control Center* is a collection of command tools you access through a series of menus. You become more familiar with these menus in the remainder of this book; for now, you should understand the general strategy in manipulating the Control Center tools.

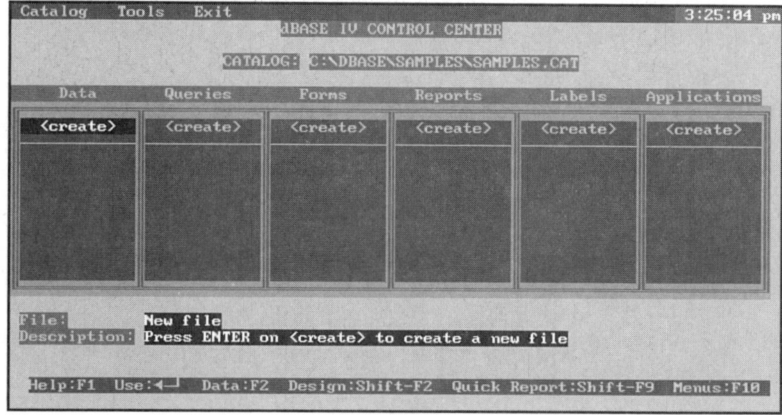


FIG. 4.7

The Control Center.

You can command dBASE IV with the Control Center or the dot prompt. The *dot prompt* represents a command-driven user interface; instead of choosing commands from a menu, you type them on a command line. The Control Center menus give you assistance at each step in generating a command by visually presenting all the options; the dot prompt requires you to memorize the commands and the way they are assembled (in addition to being an accurate typist). The dBASE dot prompts are mostly unforgiving of spelling and grammar errors; you get it right or you do it over.The error boxes that appear when you try to enter a command containing an error, however, give you the option to edit the command and correct the mistake.

**NOTE** If you're familiar with the dot prompt commands from an earlier version of dBASE, you will be happy to learn that these commands still work in largely the same way, although the dBASE command language has been enhanced greatly.

On the other hand, if you know what you're doing, the dot prompt provides more flexibility without being slowed by menu navigation. More importantly, learning dot prompt commands initiates you into programming dBASE IV. Many of the commands described in Chapters 16 through 19 can be used at the dot prompt.

You access the dot prompt from the Control Center by pressing the Esc key. You see a message asking whether you want to abandon the operation in progress (see fig. 4.8). (The current operation in this case is the Control Center.) If you respond Yes, you see the dot prompt (see fig. 4.9). To return to the Control Center from the dot prompt, type *assist* and press Enter; alternatively, press F2. Commands can be typed in uppercase or lowercase letters.

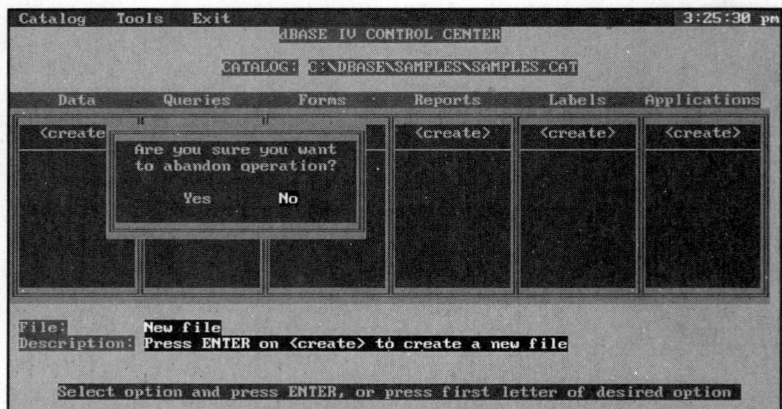


FIG. 4.8

The abandon operation prompt.

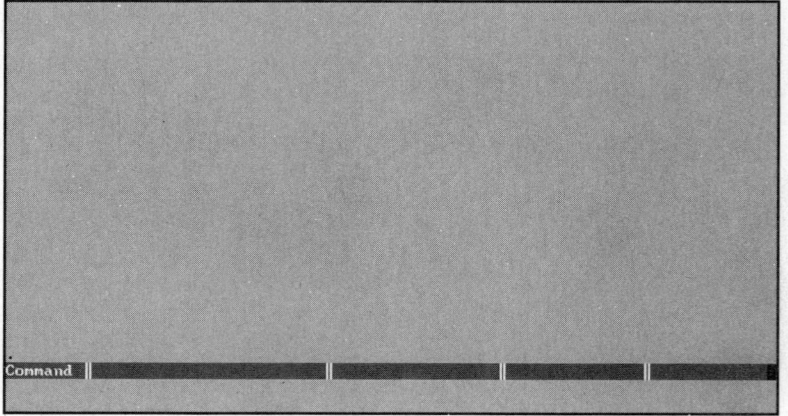


FIG. 4.9

The dBASE IV dot prompt.

Following is a summary of the methods you use to switch between the Control Center and the dot prompt:

- To leave the Control Center for the dot prompt, press Esc. At the abandon operation prompt, select Yes. You also can access the Exit menu and select Exit to Dot Prompt.

- To return to the Control Center from the dot prompt, type *assist* and press Enter. Alternatively, press F2.

## Understanding How the Control Center Works

The Control Center includes a number of components, each of which is intended to organize your database work and assist you in commanding dBASE IV. The most prominent components are the *panels* that take up the majority of the center of the screen. The panels are used to organize and list the different files that make up a database job.

In addition to the panels that organize access to the database and support files, the Control Center also includes a number of other features. Collectively, these features provide information, instructions, and access to commands.

Locate on the Control Center in figure 4.10 the features described in table 4.4.

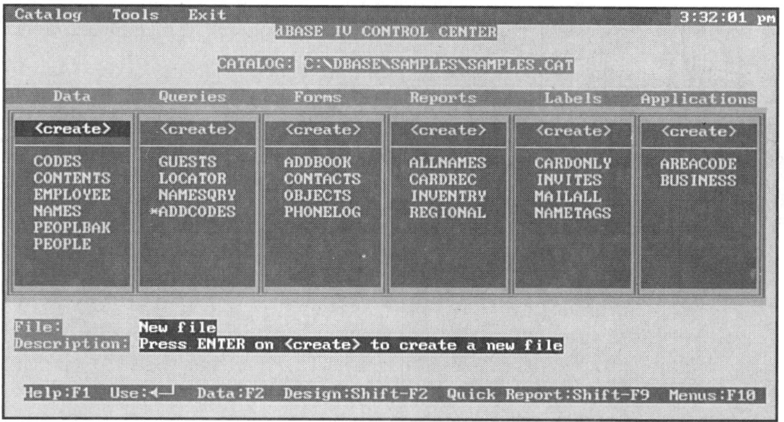


FIG. 4.10

Panels listing files for a database application.

Figure 4.10 shows a list of files created to handle a particular database application—one that manages a set of work projects for a home construction and remodeling firm. The application requires a number of different databases, queries, forms, and reports, each of which is listed under the appropriate panel.

**Table 4.4 Features of the Control Center**

| Feature and location | Description |
|---|---|
| The menu bar in the top left of the screen | Displays the command options you can select from the Control Center. |
| The clock in the upper right corner | Provides the current time. The clock is turned off by giving the command SET CLOCK OFF at the dot prompt. |
| The name of the current screen in the top center of the screen | Identifies this screen as the Control Center. |
| The path and name of the current catalog centered above the panels | Identifies the group of related dBASE IV files whose names appear in the panels. |
| The panels in the center of the screen | Organize and list the different files in the database. |
| The name and description of the currently selected file below the panels | Describes the currently selected file. The file description is optional. If the panel selector below the panels is on <create>, the file name reads `New File`. |
| The navigation line below the file identifier | Lists important command keys accessible from the current screen (described in Chapter 5). |
| The message line at the bottom of the screen | Reports a concise description of the command option when you select a menu command. |

In Chapter 2, you looked at the role each component of a database application plays in ensuring the accuracy of data or the reliability of information. The Control Center keeps tabs on each of these components through the panels. Table 4.5 summarizes these roles in reference to the panels and points you to the locations in the book where the topics are discussed in detail.

**Table 4.5 The Role of the Panels in the Control Center**

| Panel | Chapter | Purpose |
|---|---|---|
| Data | 14 | Lists all the databases associated with the application. Files grouped here have the DBF extension. |
| Queries | 12 | Lists all queries built on one or more of the databases. Files include view queries with QBE extensions and update queries with UPD extensions. Update queries are marked with an asterisk (*) preceding the file name. |
| Forms | 9 | Lists all the data-entry and editing forms built for a database or query. Source files have the SCR extension. |
| Reports | 10 | Lists all the reports issued for a database or query. Source files have the FRM extension. |
| Labels | 11 | Lists all the label files issued for a data base or query. Source files have the LBL extension. |
| Applications | 20 | Lists all the application menu and program files that organize, manipulate, or use any other file. Source files have the APP extension or the PRG extension. Other types of files also are implicitly organized here. |

The most common way of adding a file to the Control Center is to create it. You see that each panel includes a <create> button immediately below the panel name. Place the cursor on <create> and press Enter to signal that you want to create a file of that specific type. After you activate <create>, dBASE IV displays a design screen specific to that panel. Specify the requirements for the file you are creating and save the file under a name you give it; that name appears on the panel list.

## Accessing Files from the Panels

Notice that each panel has a horizontal line directly under <create>. This line is a guide that shows which files currently are open and which are closed. To run or modify a previously created file, you have to open it first. Opening a file makes the file available to the computer's memory. When you open a file in the Control Center, it appears above the horizontal line in its panel. You can tell at a glance which files are open by seeing which files are above the line. You can open a file in several ways, but using a prompt box makes the process clearest. Assume, for example, that you want to open the Employee database file. Place the *panel selector* (also called the *cursor*) on that file name and press Enter. The prompt box shown in figure 4.11 appears. With the selector on the Use File option, press Enter again. By selecting Use File, you open the file and place its name above the panel line (see fig. 4.12).

**NOTE**

The prompt box shown in figure 4.11 appears only if the Instruct setting is set to On. On is the system default, so it is probably set. If not, you can change it by following the procedure described in Chapter 15.

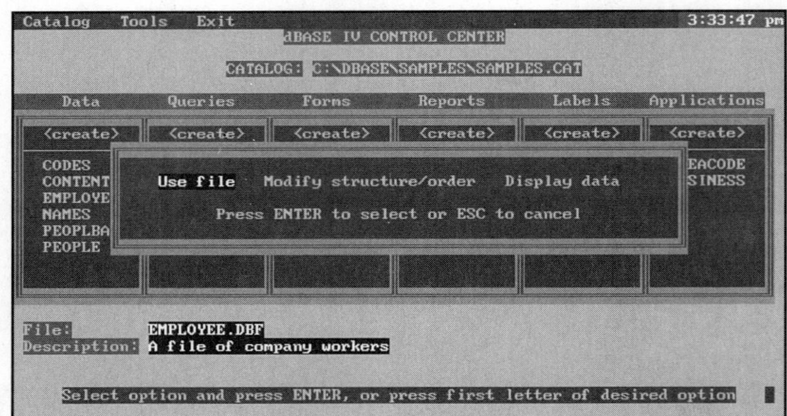


FIG. 4.11

The prompt box for the Data panel.

You should understand that all files other than database files depend on or grow out of a database file. When you create any other type of file, you typically have a database file in use before you create the new file. If you do not, when you enter the design screen, the first thing you must do is specify the name of the database for which you are designing the file.

*View queries* (one type of file listed in the Queries panel on the Control Center) operate in much the same way as databases. In fact, dBASE IV sometimes refers to databases and view queries with the common term *view*.

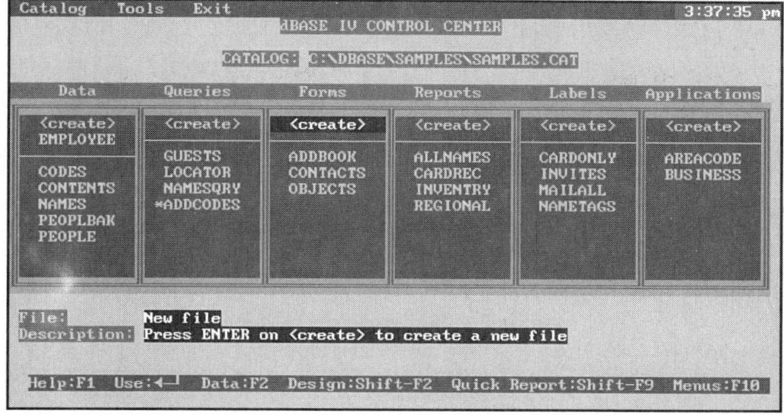


FIG. 4.12

Opening the Employee database.

dBASE IV “remembers” which files belong with which database. If you open a database file that has other files associated with it, for example, those files are brought above the horizontal lines in their respective panels. Figure 4.13 shows the effect of opening the Employee database. This database has associated query and form files, which are displayed above the horizontal lines simultaneously with the database.

```
Catalog  Tools  Exit                                          3:41:22 pm
                      dBASE IV CONTROL CENTER
                CATALOG: C:\DBASE\SAMPLES\SAMPLES.CAT
  Data       Queries     Forms      Reports     Labels     Applications
<create>    <create>    <create>    <create>    <create>    <create>
EMPLOYEE    *EMPLOY     PHONELOG
                                    ALLNAMES    CARDONLY    AREACODE
CODES       EMPLOY      ADDBOOK     CARDREC     INVITES     BUSINESS
CONTENTS    GUESTS      CONTACTS    INVENTRY    MAILALL
NAMES       LOCATOR     OBJECTS     REGIONAL    NAMETAGS
PEOPLBAK    NAMESQRY
PEOPLE      *ADDCODES

File:        EMPLOYEE.DBF
Description: A file of company workers

Help:F1  Use:◄┘  Data:F2  Design:Shift-F2  Quick Report:Shift-F9  Menus:F10
```

FIG. 4.13

Opening the Employee database with associated query and form files.

Even though you design a support file, say a report, for use with a specific database, you can use that support file with another database. To use a report file with a second database, the second database must use the same fields that the report uses. If it doesn't, dBASE can print only the fields that the second database uses. To use the support file with the second database, open the second database, and then open the support file. When you try to print, modify, or display the report, the dialog box in figure 4.14 appears, asking whether you want to use the current view or database, or the original view or database. The original database is named in the dialog box.

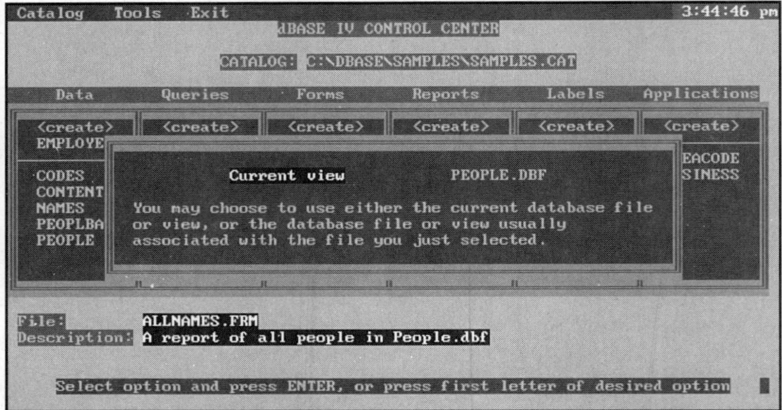


FIG. 4.14

Changing a report file to support a new database or query.

Following is a summary of how you manage the Control Center panels through the prompt box. Chapter 5 describes how you can open files more quickly using the F2 and Shift-F2 keys.

- To open a database file, move the panel selector to the Data panel and select the file you want. Press Enter to open the prompt box. Select the Use File option. Press Enter again.
- To close a database file, move the panel selector to the file you want to close. Press Enter to open the prompt box. Select the Close File option. Press Enter again.
- To open a support file (query, form, report, or label), open the correct database (or query) file. Move the panel selector to the panel and file you want. Press Enter to open the prompt box. Indicate what you want to do: print, modify, or display.

## Understanding the Conventions Used To Operate the Menu System

The menu bar at the top of the Control Center screen is one of many dBASE IV menus. A menu is associated with each distinct work surface and design screen in the program. All the menus operate in the same way. This section describes the general principles you apply when using any menu bar.

A *menu* in dBASE IV represents groups of commands. These command groups appear as options across the top of the screen. The Control Center menu has the options Catalog, Tools, and Exit. Each option is associated with a pull-down menu that lists individual commands from which you select.

The way you select menu items depends, of course, on whether you are using the keyboard or the mouse.

If you are using the mouse, simply click the mouse pointer on the name of the menu you want to pull down from the menu bar. Then click the item you want to select from that menu. To leave a menu, click an area outside the menu, or select another menu.

Using the keyboard, you can access the menu bar by pressing the F10 key, or press and hold the Alt key and press the first letter of the menu name you want. To access the Exit menu, for example, you can press Alt-E. If you use F10, the cursor appears at the menu option you used last. If you haven't used the menus in the current session, the cursor appears on the leftmost option. To change menu options, use the left- and right-arrow keys to close the current pull-down menu and open the adjacent one. To exit the menu bar, press Esc.

To select a command from a pull-down menu, use the up- and down-arrow keys to move the selector to the item you want; press Enter to activate that command. After you are familiar with the options, you can type the first letter of the command you want. Doing so moves the selector to that item and immediately opens it without you having to press Enter.

Depending on the circumstances, some commands in a pull-down menu may be dimmed. Dimmed commands are not currently available. If the panel selector is on <create>, for example, you cannot access the Remove Highlighted File From Catalog command from the Catalog menu. You can activate this command only if the panel selector is on a file name.

Some commands in a pull-down menu have arrowheads in front of them (see the Import command from the Tools menu, shown in fig. 4.15). The arrowhead indicates that the command has another pull-down menu associated with it, from which you make a second choice. Some second-level commands have pull-down menus of their own, from which you select third-level commands.

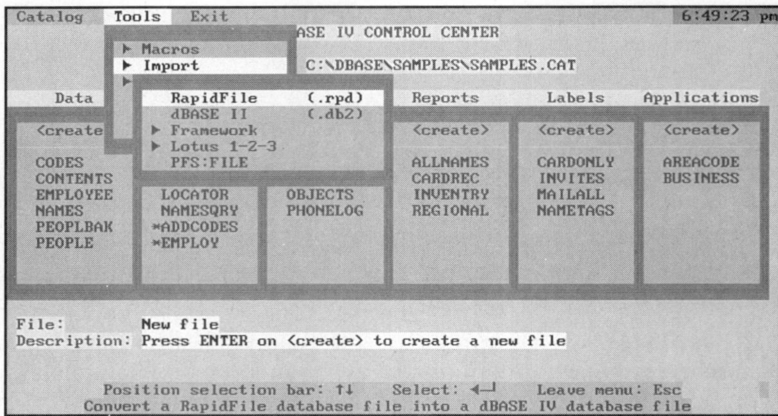


FIG. 4.15

Activating a pull-down command with an arrowhead.

Some commands in a menu may have other, deeper, levels. When you activate the DOS Utilities command from the Tools menu, for example, the Control Center screen is replaced with a file list from the current DOS directory. A new menu bar also appears (see fig. 4.16). This screen is described in detail in Chapter 5.

```
DOS   Files   Sort   Mark   Operations   Exit                    6:50:59 pm
                        C:\DBASE\SAMPLES
  Name/Extension      Size    Date & Time        Attrs     Space Used

  <parent>           <DIR>    Feb  5,1991  4:48p  ****
  ACCT_REC DBF       1,347    Jan 24,1992  1:50a  a***          2,048
  ACCT_REC FRG       6,231    Jan 24,1992  1:50a  a***          8,192
  ACCT_REC FRM       4,224    Jan 24,1992  1:50a  a***          6,144
  ACCT_REC MDX       8,192    Jan 24,1992  1:50a  a***         10,240
  ACCT_REC PRG       9,032    Jan 24,1992  1:50a  a***         10,240
  ADDBOOK  FMO       2,228    Jan 24,1992  1:50a  a***          4,096
  ADDBOOK  SCR       2,486    Jan 24,1992  1:50a  a***          4,096
  ADDCODES UPD       5,035    Jan 24,1992  1:50a  a***          6,144
  ALLNAMES FRM       1,912    Jan 24,1992  1:50a  a***          2,048
  AREACODE PRG       6,460    Jan 24,1992  1:50a  a***          8,192

Total  <marked>              0  (   0 files)                         0
Total  <displayed>     653,020  ( 132 files)                   815,104

Files:*.*                                          Sorted by:  Name
DOS util|C:\dbase\SAMPLES
      Position selection bar:↑↓  Mark file:◄┘  Directories:F9
```

FIG. 4.16

The DOS utilities command, activated from the Tools menu.

Typically, a pull-down menu command requires you to do one of two things: fill in a value the command needs to operate, or select a setting from a fixed list of possibilities (dBASE IV calls such lists a *pick list*). If you have to fill in a value, dBASE IV provides a space into which you type the value (see fig. 4.17). Press Enter when you finish typing the value.

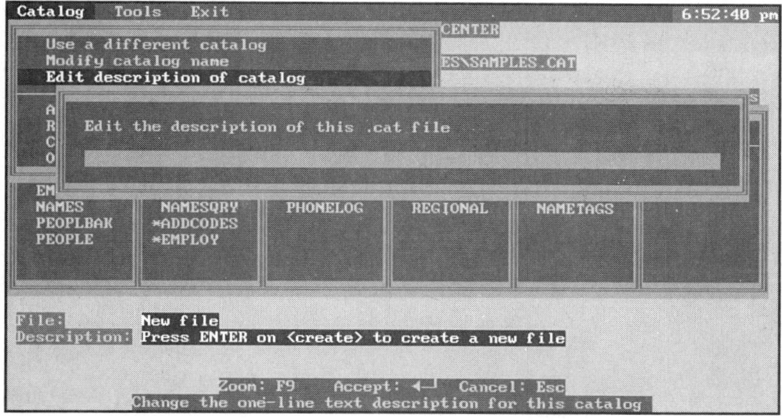


FIG. 4.17 A command requiring a fill-in response.

If the command generates a pick list, choose an item from the list by using the up- and down-arrow keys to move the selection bar to the item, and then press Enter; or you can simply type the first few letters of the item. In the pick list shown in figure 4.18, for example, the Employee item was selected by pressing the letter E.

MOUSE

You can use the mouse to select items from a pick list. Highlight the item by clicking on it. Click the highlighted item again to select it.

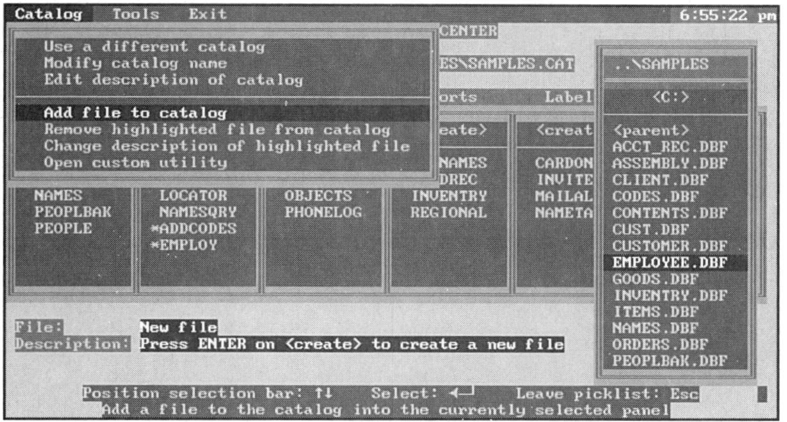


FIG. 4.18 A command using a pick list.

If the list of fixed possibilities for a command is limited (and particularly if one of the those options is a default value), you may be able to use a multiple-choice selection process instead of a pick list. When you select the Settings command from the Tools menu, for example, the screen shown in figure 4.19 appears. Notice that the Date Order command highlighted on the list is set to MDY. Access the other possibilities (DMY and YMD) by pressing Enter or the space bar to cycle through the possibilities. Commands with curly braces { } surrounding a value are variations of fill-in commands. Change these values by pressing Enter, typing a value, and pressing Enter again.

To cycle through multiple-choice fields by using the mouse, click on the input field until the value you want is displayed.

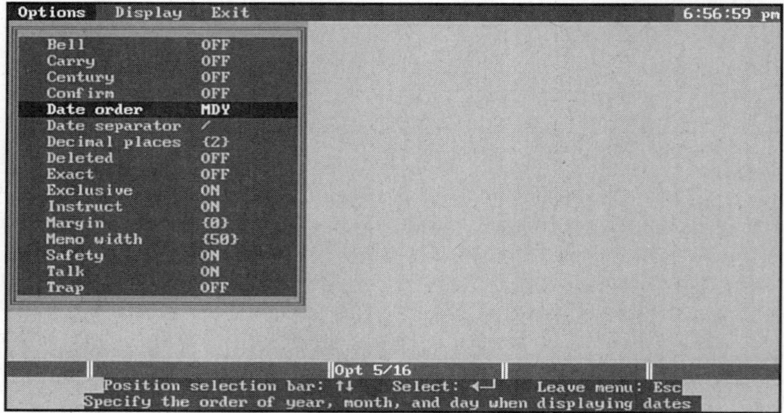


FIG. 4.19

Commands with multiple-choice items.

Table 4.6 summarizes menu navigation and command selection techniques.

**Table 4.6 Accessing Menu Options**

| Desired action | What to do |
|---|---|
| Access the menu bar for the current screen | Press F10 or press Alt-*letter*, where *letter* is the first letter of the menu option you want, or click the menu name with the mouse. |
| Change menu options | Press the left- or right-arrow key to move to adjacent options, or click another option. |
| Select commands from pull-down menus | Use the up- and down-arrow keys to move the selector to the item you want and press Enter, or click the item. Alternatively, type the first letter of the name of the command. The selector moves to that item and immediately activates it. You do not have to press Enter. |

| Desired action | What to do |
|---|---|
| Fill in a command response | Type the response in the blank provided and press Enter. |
| Select from a pick list | Use the up- and down-arrow keys to move to the item you want, or type enough of the name of the item to move the selector to that item, and press Enter. Or double-click the item. |
| Select from a small list of possible values | Use the Enter key or space bar, or click the mouse, to cycle through the values and select the one you want. |
| Leave the menu bar | Press the Esc key, or click outside the menu. Generally, dBASE exits automatically from the menu bar after you activate a command. |

The Control Center also makes available a number of commands through means other than the menu. You already have seen one example of the alternatives to the menu in the file access commands, which you activate by using the prompt box (see "Accessing Files from the Panels," earlier in this chapter). Another way to access files is to use the special function keys. Special function keys generally perform editing or selection tasks, which bypass or shortcut some menu-navigation processes. The Control Center makes only limited use of function keys, specifically using only the F1, F2, Shift-F2, Shift-F9, and F10 keys. The F1 (Help) and F10 (menu-bar access) keys are general-purpose keys used by all screens. Only F2, Shift-F2, and Shift-F9 have special purposes in the Control Center (see Chapter 5). In general, screens list the available function keys on the navigation line near the bottom of the screen. If all the available options do not fit on a single line, you must remember the options yourself.

When key labels, such as `Help:F1`, appear at the bottom of the screen, you can click on these key labels to simulate the key press.

# Understanding the Concept of a dBASE IV Catalog

If you read Chapter 3, you know how DOS organizes files into directories. You also know the advantages of setting up different directories for each of the applications you plan to build in dBASE IV. In this section, you refine that organizational plan by considering a dBASE IV filing structure called a *catalog*. A catalog works like a DOS directory, but also is able to cross directory boundaries when organizing the files of an application.

Earlier in this chapter, you were briefly introduced to a catalog as the structure that identifies the files clustered together on the panels. Although in a catalog you can put together files that have nothing in common with one another, you defeat the purpose of a catalog if you do. Files in a catalog belong together logically; the catalog implicitly recognizes the relationship between these files.

## Creating a Catalog

If you are starting dBASE IV fresh and are in a new data directory with no files in it, you must create a catalog to reflect the work you're going to store in this directory. dBASE IV does not allow you to work in the Control Center without a catalog. So, if you have the proverbial blank slate, dBASE IV initially assigns a blank catalog named UNTITLED. Every directory you use for the first time with dBASE IV is set up with an UNTITLED catalog. Assume that you are in a directory called PRACTICE, which you want to use for practicing the exercises in this book. If you start dBASE IV from this directory, you see the screen shown in figure 4.20.

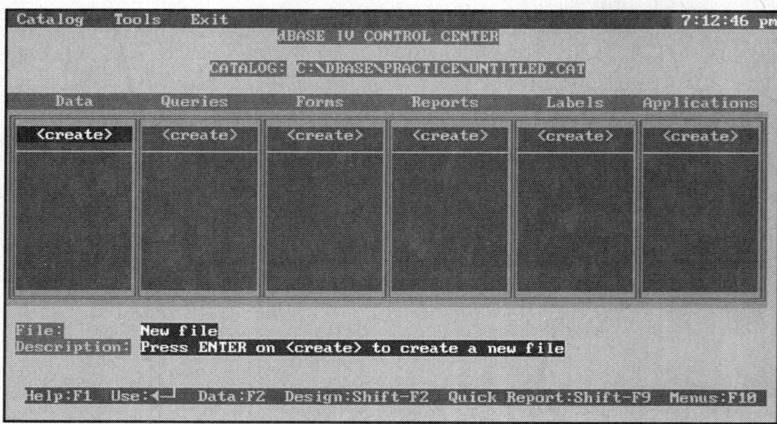


FIG. 4.20

Beginning work in a new directory with an UNTITLED catalog.

Unless you have some reason to keep the name UNTITLED, change the catalog name. Follow these steps to change the catalog name from UNTITLED to a name you specify:

1. Press Alt-C to pull down the Catalog menu.
2. Press M to select Modify Catalog Name. The current catalog is listed after the directory path.
3. Press Backspace to delete the name UNTITLED.CAT, type the new name (in this case *PRACTICE*, as shown in fig. 4.21), and press Enter. The CAT extension is added automatically.

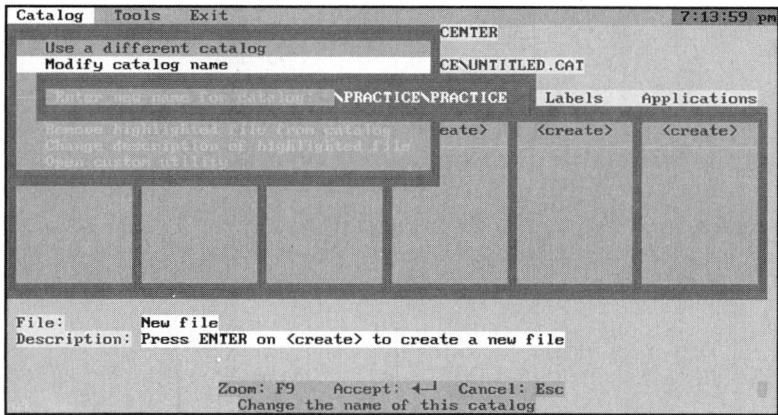


FIG. 4.21

Changing the name of the UNTITLED catalog to PRACTICE.

Catalog names must follow the file-naming rules described in Chapter 3. The catalog itself is a file that stores the names and vital statistics of all the member files. When you create a catalog, dBASE IV assigns it the name you specify and adds the extension CAT.

You may encounter situations in which you want to set up more than one catalog in the same directory (to subdivide a logical set of files into two sub-applications, for example). To create a second catalog for a directory, follow these steps:

1. Pull down the Catalog menu.
2. Select Use a Different Catalog. A pick list of existing catalogs for this directory appears (see fig. 4.22). Notice that a <create> option is in the pick list so that you can set up a new catalog.
3. Select <create> and press Enter.
4. On the fill-in line, enter the name of the new catalog. dBASE IV creates the new catalog and changes to that new catalog.

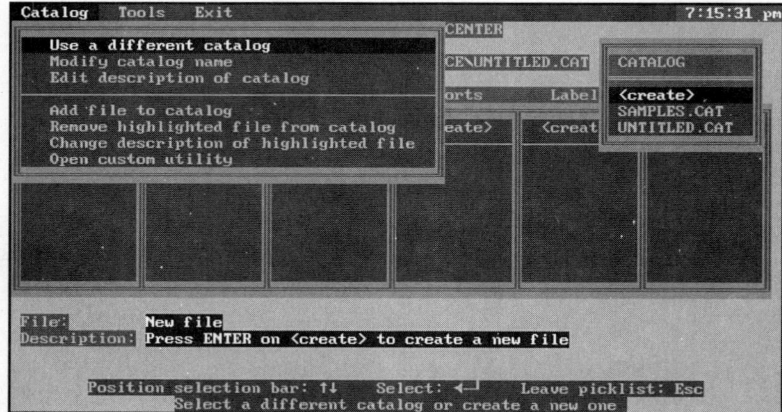


FIG. 4.22

Creating a new catalog in the current directory.

If you have multiple catalogs in a directory, dBASE IV keeps track of the one you used last and restores that one to the screen the next time you work in that directory. Any time you change to a new directory, however, dBASE IV also changes the catalog. Switching catalogs manually is covered in Chapter 5.

**NOTE** The information about the catalog you last used in a directory is stored in a file called CATALOG.CAT. This file also stores a master list of all the catalogs in the directory. Do not remove this file from your directory.

**WARNING:** If you run dBASE IV from one directory and try to access a catalog from another directory, the file listings in the catalog may be deleted if those files do not exist in the current directory. To be safe, create the catalog and files and start dBASE IV from the same directory.

## Adding an Existing File from Another Directory to a Catalog

You may think that putting related files together in the same directory is enough to indicate a relationship. But remember that a single database can logically serve two or more different applications. Consider an Employee database that supplies information to a payroll and a mailing-list application. If the two applications are in different directories, you can place the same database in both directories. This solution, however, wastes disk space. More importantly, it jeopardizes the integrity of the database because you have to make the same changes to both copies or remember to copy to the other directory the database to which you make a change.

The dBASE IV catalog provides an answer. You set up two catalogs to reflect each of the directories in which the applications reside. You may have called one directory PAYROLL and the other MAILLIST. Suppose that you intend to keep the Employee database in the PAYROLL directory. If you follow the steps in the preceding section, "Creating a Catalog," the Employee database is set up automatically in the PAYROLL catalog at the time you create the database.

When you switch to the MAILLIST directory, the MAILLIST catalog knows nothing about the Employee database file. You must add the database file to the catalog. But you don't want to add the Employee file to the catalog by re-creating the file. Instead, pull down the Catalog menu from the Control Center menu bar and select the Add File To Catalog command. This command enables you to add files to the catalog, even if they are located in other directories or even on other disks.

To add a file from another directory to the current catalog, follow these steps:

1. In the Control Center, place the panel selector in the Data panel if you want to add a database file (place the panel selector in another panel if you want to add a file of another type).
2. Access the Catalog menu.
3. Select the Add File To Catalog command. A pick list appears, showing files of the type appropriate for the panel you have selected.
4. If the file you want is in another directory, select the <parent> option (see fig. 4.23). A list of files in the next higher directory on the tree appears. Child directories of this directory are listed in angle brackets (see fig. 4.24).
5. If the file you want is in one of the child directories, select it and press Enter. If the file you want is in the PAYROLL directory, for example, select <PAYROLL> from the pick list.

   A list of all the database files in that directory appears.
6. Select the database you want to add. That database is added to the Data panel. To add the Employee file, for example, select that file from the pick list.

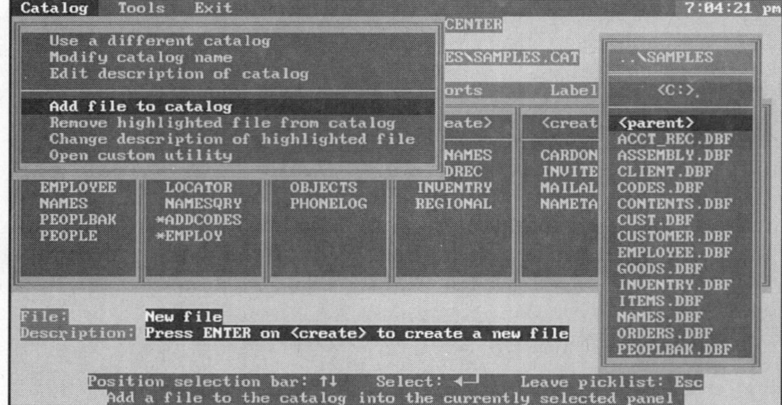


**FIG. 4.23**

Using the <parent> option to change the pick list.

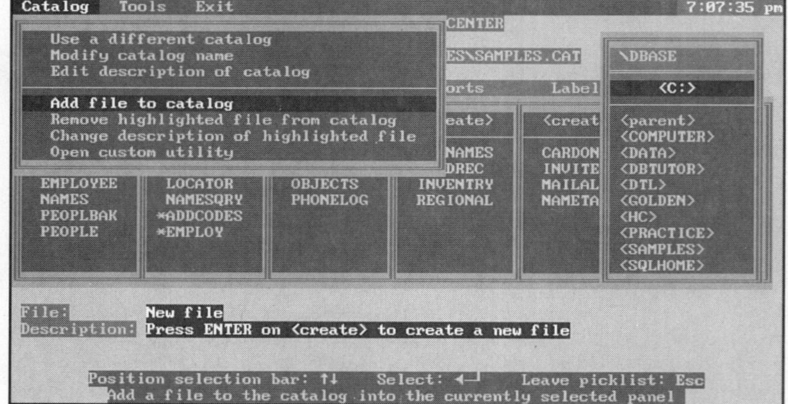


**FIG. 4.24**

Child directories listed in angle brackets in the pick list.

7. If the file you want is on another drive, select the drive identifier (usually <C:>) and select the drive you want from the pick list that appears. Continue with step 4.

You can use the mouse to select menu and pick list options. For example, click on Catalog in the menu bar, click on the Add File To Catalog option, and then double-click on the desired file name in the displayed pick list.

**For Related Information...**

▸▸ "Changing the Catalog," p. 92.

# Summary

This chapter focused on how to get started working with dBASE IV. In this chapter, you learned how to install and configure dBASE IV to your hardware and your preferences. You also learned how dBASE takes the concept of an application (a job that must be done or a problem that must be solved) and translates the concept into a solution that uses a number of different kinds of files: queries, forms, reports, labels, and applications, all of which depend on one or more underlying databases.

You learned about the Control Center, which is set up as a guide to the components of an application; a catalog organizes the particular set of files that form an application family. These files are listed in the panels of the Control Center.

You also learned that the Control Center provides direct or indirect access to all the commands that dBASE IV can carry out. You learned to use some of these commands in this chapter—those that control the creation and selection of a catalog. You use another set of basic commands in Chapter 5.

5

CHAPTER

# Using Routine Commands

You use certain dBASE commands more frequently than others; you will use some commands, in fact, every time you use the program. This chapter discusses those commands you use routinely.

This chapter also discusses the transition from one work area to another. Chapter 4 described the Control Center as a jumping-off place for all the work you do in setting up and using the files your applications require. When you select <create> from one of the panels, you see what dBASE IV calls a *design screen*. This chapter describes how to access those design screens. Although you don't do any actual design work at this time, you do get a feel for the workings of the system.

One of the most common tasks you perform with any database is to display it. You display a database to check your facts, to recall what the database does, to find out what's missing, and so on. Later chapters describe how you can restrict the view of the database through queries and reports so that you see just the data you want to see. In this chapter, you take the "grand tour" of a database, using cursor-movement commands to travel within the full set of data.

At times, you may not remember the correct command to use or which menu contains a specific option. For these occasions, dBASE IV provides an on-board help system sensitive to the points about which you need information. This chapter describes the help system in some detail.

Finally, you may want an easier or quicker path through the menus. If dBASE IV doesn't have a shortcut, you can devise one of your own by creating a macro. In this chapter, you take a brief look at dBASE IV's macro-generating capability.

# Working with Routine Commands

Every dBASE IV work session has to start and end. Chapter 4 described how to get going by making sure that dBASE IV is installed and configured properly for your computer. You learned that you change to the directory where your work is stored and type *dbase* at the DOS prompt to start dBASE. After dBASE is loaded, you routinely follow this sequence of steps to use the program:

1. Check the catalog. The catalog determines the list of files that appears in the Control Center panels. If you're not using the right catalog, change to it.
2. Open a database. Opening a database makes the database available for changes, additions, and updates.
3. Carry out your work. You activate the display and design screens available through the Control Center panels and use these screens as tools to perform your database work.
4. Close the database. Databases are not truly secure against the dark side of computers—power outages, voltage spikes, frozen keyboards, and the like—until they have been closed. You should be particularly careful to close files before leaving dBASE IV.
5. Back up the files. Always make backup copies of your work to another disk.
6. Quit dBASE IV. Quitting dBASE IV ensures that the program starts properly the next time.

In the next few sections, you look more closely at each of these actions and learn the procedures you need to carry them out.

# Changing the Catalog

Chapter 4 described how catalogs operate and how to set them up. Assuming that you have a number of catalogs on your disk directory, you need to know how to manipulate them. Choosing a catalog is the first step in manipulating catalogs.

When you start dBASE IV, the Control Center always shows an active catalog. If you haven't created one for the current directory, dBASE IV displays the UNTITLED catalog. If you have created one or more catalogs, dBASE starts with the last catalog you worked with in the previous work session. You can change to another catalog in the same directory by using the Catalog menu and selecting the Use A Different Catalog command. A pick list with all available catalogs appears (see fig. 5.1). As you move the selector among the catalogs, you may see a description window appear above the file identification line. Select the catalog you want.

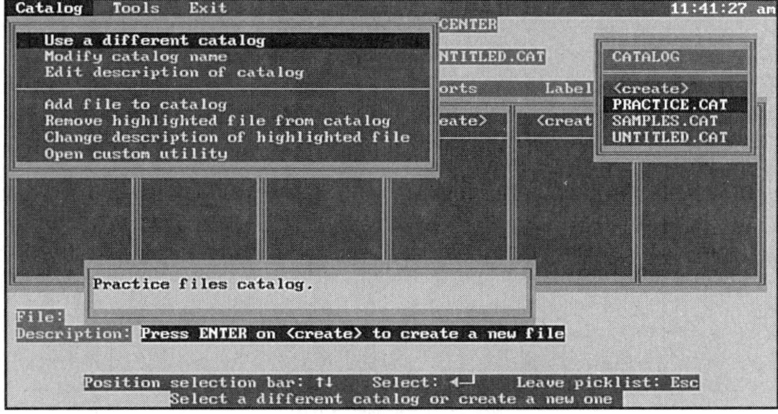


FIG. 5.1

Changing to a different catalog.

After you select a catalog, that catalog stays in effect until you choose another one. You can activate a catalog from the dot prompt by issuing the SET CATALOG TO <*name*> command.

> **WARNING:** Before you change to another catalog, close all open files. If you don't close the files, the open files are added to the catalog to which you change.

In addition to changing catalogs, you can modify the name of the catalog and edit a description of the catalog. A description can be useful if you use many catalogs (the description appears on-screen, as shown in fig. 5.1, to remind you of the contents of the catalog), but serves no other purpose. Selecting the Modify Catalog Name or Edit Description of Catalog command from the Catalog menu displays a window with the old name or description (see fig. 5.2). Use the Backspace key to erase the old name or description and type the new name or description. Press Enter to complete the process.

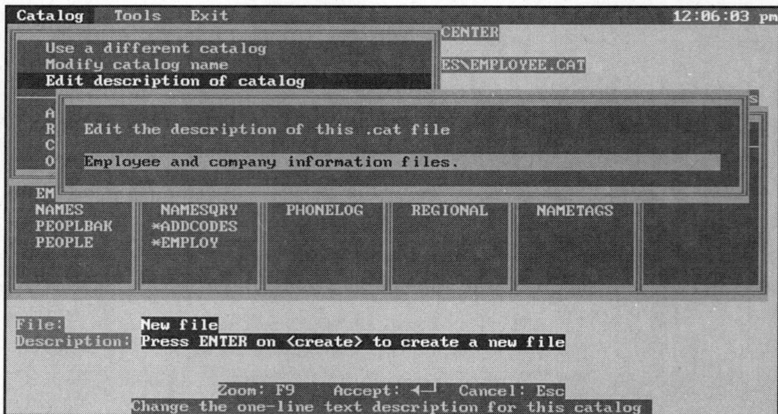


FIG. 5.2

Editing the description of a catalog.

Any file you create with the Control Center is added to the current catalog. If you no longer need a file, you can remove it from the catalog, and optionally remove it from disk, by using the Remove Highlighted File From Catalog command. You also can press Del as a shortcut around the menu. This option works only for the current file—the one highlighted by the panel selector. If the selector is located on a <create> option, you cannot access this command. You cannot remove a file if it is open (above the horizontal line).

After you activate the Remove Highlighted File From Catalog command, you are asked to verify the decision. If you respond Yes, the file is removed from the catalog and you are asked whether you want to remove the file from disk. If you respond Yes, the file is completely deleted and dBASE keeps no memory of it.

You also can add files to a catalog even if those files were created or modified without an open catalog. If you create a file at the dot prompt without having a catalog set, for example, the file is added to the disk but isn't recorded as a member of any catalog. If you later want to attach that file to a catalog, select Add File To Catalog from the Catalog menu. When you activate this option, dBASE IV displays a pick list of all the files of the same type as the panel in which the cursor is located. Choose the file you want to add. In Chapter 4, you learned how you can change the default drive and directory using other options available on a pick list. Change the drive and directory if necessary to locate the file you want to add.

The Change Description Of Highlighted File command from the Catalog menu enables you to make or change a description of a file. The description appears on the Control Center screen as part of the file identification. You must highlight in the Control Center panel the file you want to change before you can access the command. When you select the command, you see a fill-in window. Type a new description or edit an existing one.

# Opening Files from the Control Center

To use a file listed on the Control Center panels, you must open the file. You open most files for the sake of viewing or displaying them, for the purpose of changing their design, or, in the case of certain types of files, for printing them. Two or more of these options are listed in the prompt box that opens when you highlight a file name and press Enter. The options you see depend on the type of file with which you are working. For database files in the Data panel, for example, the prompt box looks like it does in figure 5.3. The Modify Structure/Order option accesses dBASE IV's database design screen; the Display Data option accesses the database information screen. The Use File option moves the selected file above the line, which opens the file.

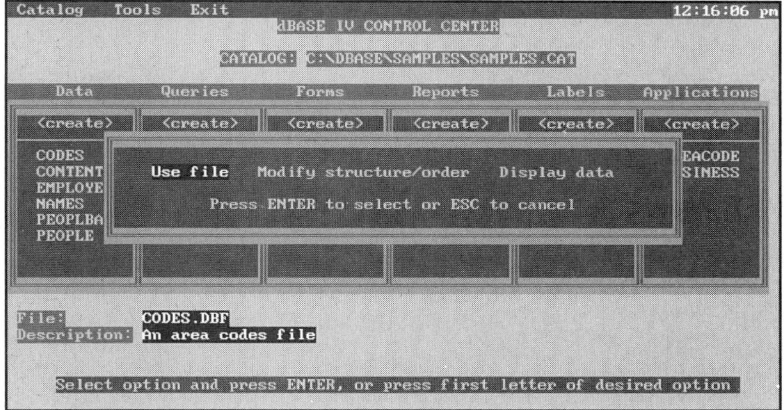


**FIG. 5.3**

The prompt box for the Data panel.

**NOTE** The prompt box appears only if the INSTRUCT setting is set to ON (the default setting). When INSTRUCT=ON, dBASE provides a good deal of on-screen assistance when you select commands and perform other operations. If you want to turn this setting OFF for some reason, you can do so by selecting the Tools menu, selecting Settings, and choosing the appropriate option from the submenu that appears. You can learn more about the INSTRUCT command in Chapter 15 and in Part V's "Using SET Commands."

The navigation line at the bottom of the Control Center screen lists several commands and corresponding function keys (refer back to fig. 5.2). The function keys offer shortcuts to accessing files for display, design, or printing purposes. Function keys act as shortcuts, or *hot keys*, for certain menu-based commands that appear in prompt boxes. Table 5.1 lists the function keys and the prompt box functions they perform.

**Table 5.1 Function-Key Equivalents of Prompt Box Options**

| Function key | Prompt box option |
|---|---|
| F2 (Data) | Display Data (works for all panels except Applications) |
| Shift-F2 (Design) | Modify Structure/Order (Data panel) |
| | Modify Query (Queries panel) |
| | Modify Layout (Forms, Reports, and Labels panels) |
| | Modify Application (Applications panel) |
| Shift-F9 (Quick Report) | Print Columnar Report (works for all panels except Applications) |

If you are using a mouse, you can click the key labels on the navigation line instead of pressing those keys. From the Control Center screen, for example, if you click `Help:F1`, you see a help screen, or you can click `Menus:F10` to access the pull-down menus. Similarly, you can click the key labels `Data:F2`, `Design:Shift-F2`, and `Quick Report:Shift-F9` to perform the functions listed in Table 5.1.

The prompt boxes for the Data, Queries, and Applications panels also include options to Use File (Data panel), Use View (Queries panel), and Run Application (Applications panel). The Use File and Use View commands move the highlighted file above the panel's horizontal line. The Run Application command places the application's custom-designed main menu on the screen or runs a program.

If you have turned the INSTRUCT setting OFF, highlighting a file name and pressing Enter places the file name above the line. If the file is already open, pressing Enter closes the file.

You open database files so that you can work with them. The Control Center organizes your work using the various tools available in its panels (see Chapter 2 for a review of problem-solving techniques). You explore the potential of these panels as problem-solving tools in later chapters of the book (the Forms panel is described in Chapter 9; the

Reports panel in Chapter 10; the Labels panel in Chapter 11; the Queries panel in Chapter 12). For now, however, you should understand the organization of the display and design screens you activate from the panels and how you work with these screens.

## Understanding dBASE IV Screens

The Shift-F2 (Design) and F2 (Data) keys display different screens in dBASE IV. The Shift-F2 (Design) key displays a different design screen for each panel: a Query design screen, Forms design screen, and so on. Each design screen has its own look, its own set of commands, and its own purpose. You learn to use each of these design screens in Chapters 9 through 12.

The F2 (Data) key presents one of two display screens for the particular range of data specified by the file: the Browse screen (shown in fig. 5.4) and the Edit screen (shown in fig. 5.5). Regardless of what panel the panel selector is in, F2 always displays the database that underlies the highlighted file. The exception is for files in the Applications panel, in which the F2 key has no effect at all.

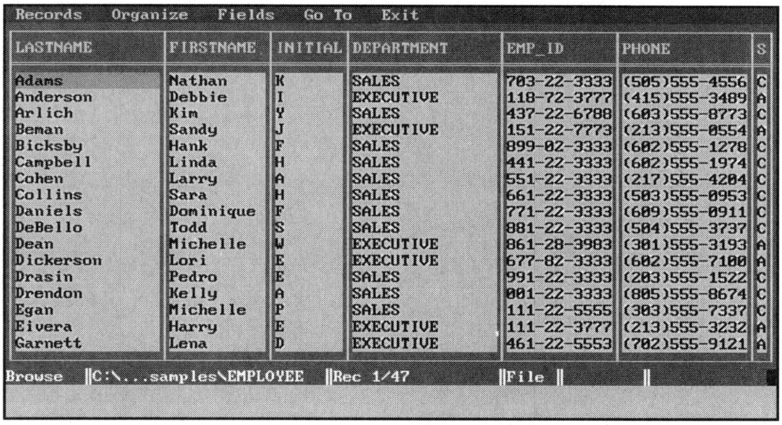

Records Organize Fields Go To Exit

| LASTNAME | FIRSTNAME | INITIAL | DEPARTMENT | EMP_ID | PHONE | S |
|---|---|---|---|---|---|---|
| Adams | Nathan | K | SALES | 703-22-3333 | (505)555-4556 | C |
| Anderson | Debbie | I | EXECUTIVE | 118-72-3777 | (415)555-3489 | A |
| Arlich | Kim | Y | SALES | 437-22-6788 | (603)555-8773 | C |
| Beman | Sandy | J | EXECUTIVE | 151-22-7773 | (213)555-0554 | A |
| Bicksby | Hank | F | SALES | 899-02-3333 | (602)555-1278 | C |
| Campbell | Linda | H | SALES | 441-22-3333 | (602)555-1974 | C |
| Cohen | Larry | A | SALES | 551-22-3333 | (217)555-4204 | C |
| Collins | Sara | H | SALES | 661-22-3333 | (503)555-0953 | C |
| Daniels | Dominique | F | SALES | 771-22-3333 | (609)555-0911 | C |
| DeBello | Todd | S | SALES | 881-22-3333 | (504)555-3737 | C |
| Dean | Michelle | W | EXECUTIVE | 861-28-3983 | (301)555-3193 | A |
| Dickerson | Lori | E | EXECUTIVE | 677-82-3333 | (602)555-7100 | A |
| Drasin | Pedro | E | SALES | 991-22-3333 | (203)555-1522 | C |
| Drendon | Kelly | A | SALES | 001-22-3333 | (805)555-8674 | C |
| Egan | Michelle | P | SALES | 111-22-5555 | (303)555-7337 | C |
| Eivera | Harry | E | EXECUTIVE | 111-22-3777 | (213)555-3232 | A |
| Garnett | Lena | D | EXECUTIVE | 461-22-5553 | (702)555-9121 | A |

Browse ‖C:\...samples\EMPLOYEE ‖Rec 1/47 ‖File ‖ ‖

FIG. 5.4

The Browse screen.

By default, dBASE IV displays the Browse screen when you first press F2 (Data). From the Browse screen, you can toggle to the Edit screen by pressing F2 again. Each time you press F2, you switch to the opposite display. When you leave the display screens, dBASE IV remembers the screen (Browse or Edit) you last used and displays that screen when you press F2 for another round.

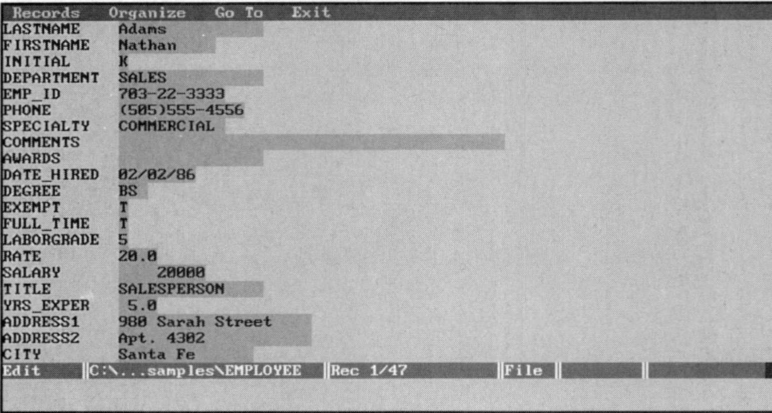


FIG. 5.5

The Edit screen.

You also can use F2 from a design screen to view data as you are constructing a design or to test the effect of the design on the underlying file. To return to the design screen, select the Return To Design option from the Exit menu of the display screen. The Shift-F2 (Design) key also takes on a different role when you use it from a design screen. From a design screen, Shift-F2 switches you to a Query design screen, as described in Chapter 12.

Table 5.2 summarizes the different uses of the F2 (Data) and Shift-F2 (Design) keys.

## Understanding the Screen Layout

The display and design screens share a common layout even though they differ in particulars. Each screen has a *menu bar* at the top that lists the menu options needed to carry out work in that screen. The menu bar operates the same way as the Control Center menu. To access the menu, press F10 or Alt-*letter*, where *letter* is the first character of the menu option you want.

At the bottom of the screen is a *status bar*, which is subdivided into a number of sections. Each section displays a different bit of information about the working environment for the screen. The number of sections in the status bar varies with the screen, but a typical status bar includes the sections shown in figure 5.6.

## Table 5.2 Uses of F2 (Data) and Shift-F2 (Design) Keys

| Pressed from | Result |
|---|---|
| *F2 (Data)* | |
| Control Center | Switches to a display screen |
| Display screen (Browse or Edit) | Switches to the other display screen |
| Query design screen | Tests design in a display screen |
| Form, Report, or Label design screen | Tests design in a display screen |
| Application design screen | No effect |
| *Shift-F2 (Design)* | |
| Control Center | Switches to the design screen for the current panel |
| Display screen (Browse or Edit) | Switches to the Query design screen |
| Query design screen | No effect |
| Form, Report, or Label design screen | Switches to the Query design screen |
| Application design screen | No effect |

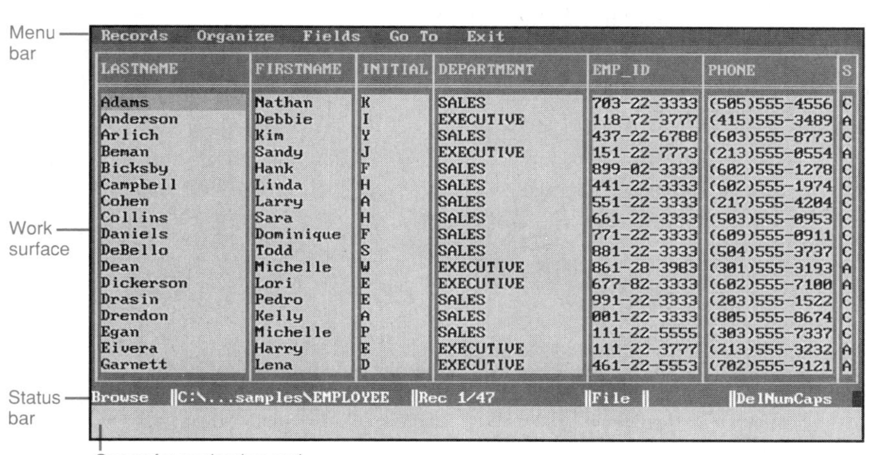


FIG. 5.6

A status bar for the Browse screen.

The leftmost section of the status bar identifies the screen by its function. The second section identifies the file you are displaying or designing in the screen. The third section identifies the position of the record selector in a display screen, or the position of the screen cursor in a design screen. The fourth and fifth sections provide information about the source of the data on the screen and its updatability. In a display screen, for example, the fourth section may display `File`, indicating that the data derives from a database file, or it may display `View`, indicating that the data derives from a view query. If the fourth section displays `View`, the fifth section may display `Read Only`, indicating that you can look at but not make changes to the data, although dBASE IV 1.5 does allow some views to be edited. If the fourth section displays `File`, the fifth section is blank.

The sixth section provides indicators of what toggle keys are engaged. If you press the Caps Lock key, for example, the `Caps` indicator appears in the sixth section. If you press the Insert key, the `Ins` indicator appears. If you press the Num Lock key, the `Num` indicator appears. The `Del` indicator appears in situations in which you have deleted a record (see Chapter 7 for more details).

Below the status bar, each screen reserves space for a *navigation line* and a *message line*. These lines contain the same kind of information they do in the Control Center screen. The navigation line specifies certain hot-key controls; the message line provides short descriptions of menu options and work-surface options.

The main part of a screen is occupied by the *work surface*. The work surface falls between the menu bar and the status bar. The appearance of the work surface varies, depending on the screen. You must learn how to control the work surface of each different screen and how to navigate within that work surface. How you control a screen depends largely on the purpose of the screen, although some common operating principles affect all screens. In addition, some general rules apply when you navigate within any screen. All screens make use of the same set of navigation keys, but the effect of a key varies with the screen.

## Controlling Screens

After you display a screen, you do your work and then exit back to the Control Center. If you work with a display screen, any changes you make are saved back to the database during the course of the session. If you work with a design screen, the work you do is not complete until you save it to a file name. You are prompted to save the work as you exit the screen.

Every screen has an Exit option on its menu bar. You can leave the screen at any time by pressing Alt-E or by clicking Exit and responding to the options in the Exit menu. Even when you exit a screen, the screens differ; some screens have more Exit options than others. Every screen always includes an Exit command, however, that returns you to the Control Center. Table 5.3 lists all the possible Exit menu options and the screens in which you encounter them.

**Table 5.3 Exit-Menu Options**

| Exit-Menu option | Control Center screen | Browse and Edit screens | Query Design screen | Form, Report, and Label screens |
|---|---|---|---|---|
| Exit | | ✓ | | |
| Save Changes and exit | | | ✓ | ✓ |
| Abandon Changes and exit | | | ✓ | ✓ |
| Transfer to query design | | ✓ | ✓ | |
| Return to design | | ✓ | ✓ | |
| Exit to dot prompt | ✓ | | | |
| Quit to DOS | ✓ | | | |

## Navigating within a Work Surface

Each work surface, whether in a display screen or a design screen, enables you to make changes to the data or to the specifications that the screen controls. To make these changes, you move the screen's cursor to where you want to record the change. The term *navigation* refers to the way you move the cursor around the screen.

The details of how you navigate a screen vary depending on the screen in which you're working. For now, just consider the keys you use to navigate the Browse and Edit display screens. Table 5.4 lists these keys and their functions in the two display screens. When you learn about the design screens, you see that most keys perform a screen-specific job in moving the cursor over the work surface.

Certain function keys can perform cursor-movement commands. For the Browse and Edit display screens, for example, you can use the F3 (Previous) and F4 (Next) keys to move between fields. These function keys duplicate the actions of the Shift-Tab and Tab keys, respectively.

**Table 5.4 Cursor-Navigation Keys in the Browse and Edit Screens**

| Key | Browse screen | Edit screen |
|---|---|---|
| → | Right one position | Right one position |
| ← | Left one position | Left one position |
| ↑ | Up one row | Up one field |
| ↓ | Down one row | Down one field |
| Ctrl-→ | End of field then start of next field | End of field then start of next field |
| Ctrl-← | Start of previous field | Start of previous field |
| PgDn | Next screen of table | Next screen of record or next record |
| PgUp | Previous screen of table | Previous screen of record or previous record |
| Ctrl-PgDn | Last record of table | Last record |
| Ctrl-PgUp | First record of table | First record |
| End | Last field in current record | End of current field |
| Home | First field in current record | Start of current field |
| Tab | Next field | Next field |
| Shift-Tab | Previous field | Previous field |
| Enter | Next field | Next field |
| F3 | Previous field | Previous field |
| F4 | Next field | Next field |

You also can use the mouse to navigate the Browse and Edit screens. If you place the mouse pointer on the top line of the Browse work area, for example, the pointer becomes an up arrow, indicating that if you click that line, the cursor will move up, just as if you had pressed the up-arrow key. Likewise, you can click the bottom line to move the cursor downward, or click the leftmost and rightmost vertical field borders to move the cursor to the next field or previous field.

## Exiting Screens

When you finish your work in a screen, you must return to the Control Center. You can return to the Control Center in a number of ways, the most foolproof being to use the Exit menu on the menu bar. Every screen has an Exit menu. Each screen differs in its particular Exit commands (as detailed in table 5.3), but all screens include one or more options to return to the Control Center. A display screen has a simple Exit command; a design screen has commands to Save Changes And Exit and Abandon Changes And Exit. Select Save Changes And Exit if you want to record into a file any work you have done in the screen; select Abandon Changes And Exit if you want to discard that work.

To leave a screen, pull down the Exit menu and select the command you want: Exit (press E), Save Changes And Exit (press S), or Abandon Changes And Exit (press A). The Query design screen or the Browse and Edit display screens sometimes show the Return To Design option, which permits you to return to a design screen. This option appears only if you have accessed these screens from a Forms, Report, or Label design screen. Another Exit menu option you may see is Transfer To Query Design. This option normally appears in the Browse and Edit display screens.

All the ways you can transfer between and get in and out of different screens make for a complicated set of procedures. Figure 5.7 puts the whole system into perspective by diagramming the various options. Entry routes are diagrammed with solid lines; exit routes are diagrammed using dashed lines. The Applications design screen is not considered in the figure because it does not have direct relations with display screens or Query design screens.

Notice that figure 5.7 also shows the Control Center Exit options. You can Exit to the dot prompt or you can Quit To DOS.

In addition to using the Exit menus to exit a screen, you also can exit screens more directly by using the Esc key and the Ctrl-End key combination. The Esc key functions more or less as a shortcut for the Abandon Changes And Exit option from the menu; the Ctrl-End combination functions as an equivalent for the Save Changes And Exit option. You learn in Chapter 7 that Ctrl-End also is used to exit from certain fill-in boxes and dialog boxes and from the word processor and memo writer.

When you use the Esc key to exit a screen, dBASE IV prompts you to verify that you want to abandon the operation in progress. If you respond Yes, you return to the Control Center; if you respond No, the Esc request is canceled. Remember that the Esc key always returns you to the Control Center if you respond Yes. Suppose that you are in the Browse screen, and then you transfer to the Query design screen. If you press Esc from the Query design screen, you do not return to the Browse screen; you return to the Control Center.

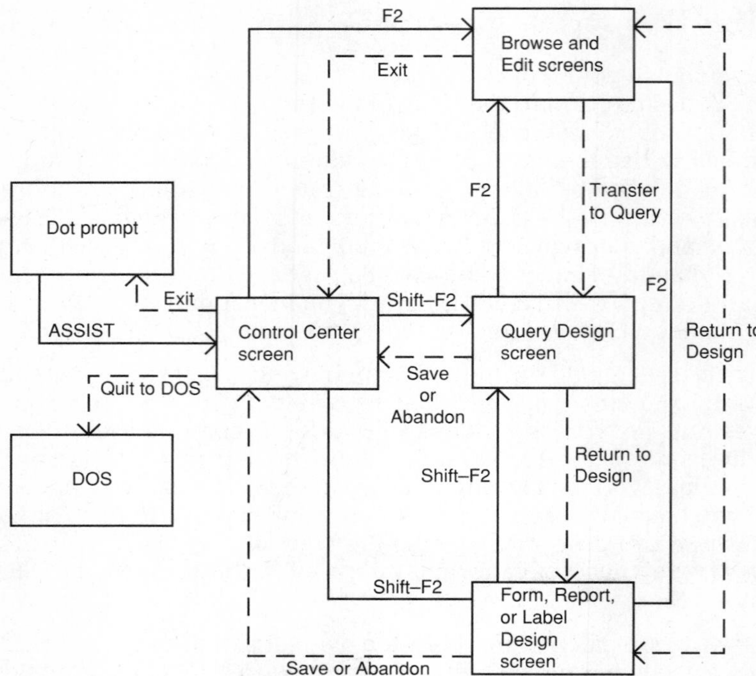


FIG. 5.7

The screen entry and exit options.

# Closing a Database

You have learned some basic techniques for performing some routine operations: opening and changing a catalog, opening a database or support file, and maneuvering within and between dBASE IV's system of screens. After you complete your work on a database, remember to close that database in preparation for doing work on another database or to end your working session and return to DOS. In general, leave databases open only as long as you are working on them. When you're finished, close them to protect them against unforeseen damage. Even though dBASE IV provides some safeguards against losing or damaging data accidentally, loss of power or a surge of electricity to the computer can damage your database. Closing the database eliminates the possibility of damage.

From the Control Center, you can close a database in one of two ways. The first way is to place the panel selector on the database name, press Enter to activate the prompt box (see fig. 5.8), select the Close File option, and press Enter again. (Notice that the Open File option in the prompt box changes to Close File if the database file is already open.)

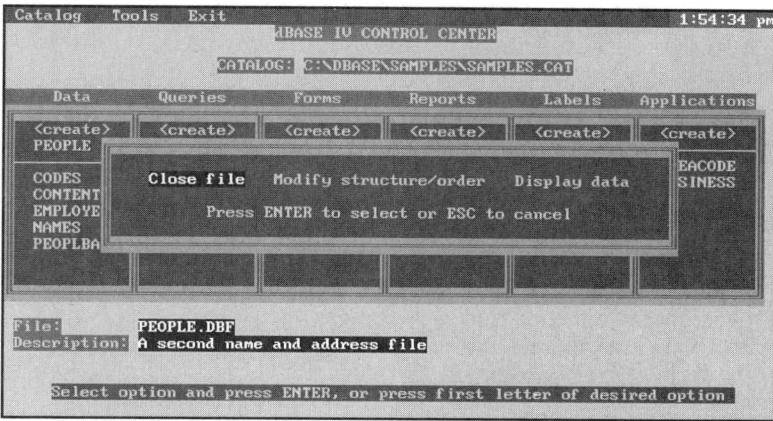


**FIG. 5.8**

Using a prompt box to close a database file.

The second way to close a database file is to simply open another file. dBASE IV can manipulate only one database at a time in each work area, although it can reference multiple databases simultaneously. (Referencing multiple databases is introduced in Chapter 1 and described in greater detail in Chapter 14.) When you open one file, dBASE IV closes another file that is already open.

**NOTE** When you exit to the dot prompt from the Control Center, any database that is open remains open.

# Backing Up Files

Understanding the need for careful backup of your work with dBASE IV is essential. All your files are important, but your databases, by virtue of the large investment of time and energy you put into them, are critical. Make sure that you back up these files after every change.

In "Displaying Only Specified Files in the File List," later in this chapter, you learn how to use the Files and Operations menus in the DOS Utilities screen to make copies of files. Refer to this section if you want detailed information about these menus. For now, however, you can follow these steps to make backup copies of your important files:

1. Starting at the Control Center, open the Tools menu.
2. Select the DOS Utilities option and open the DOS Utilities screen.
3. A list of files in the current directory is displayed. If you need to display files from another directory, highlight the <parent> directory marker and press Enter or click the mouse.

4. Mark the files you want to back up by highlighting the file name and pressing Enter or clicking the mouse. An arrowhead pointer appears before the file name to show it is marked.

   If you select a file by mistake, press Enter or click again to unselect it. You can scroll up and down the file list by using the arrow keys, or by clicking the top or bottom line of the file display box. Be sure that you have enough disk space available on the floppy disk to which to you will be copying the files.

5. Open the Organize menu.
6. Select the Copy option.
7. At the prompt box, select Marked Files.
8. Type the name of the destination drive and directory in the fill-in box; if you're copying to drive A, for example, type *A:*.
9. Press Ctrl-End to begin the copy process.

If you want to back up a particular DBF database file, copy over the associated DBT (memo file) and MDX (index) if they exist.

# Quitting dBASE IV

The last of the routine operations you perform during a work session with dBASE IV is to quit the program and return to the DOS prompt. Quitting is an important safeguard in ensuring that your files are properly closed before you exit. If, for some reason, you neglect to close your files (as described in "Closing a Database," earlier in this chapter), the quit operation closes them for you.

To quit the program and end your dBASE IV session, you can select Quit To DOS from the Exit menu at the Control Center. If you select Exit To Dot Prompt from the Exit menu, you go to the dot prompt screen, where you can type *Quit* to exit dBASE IV. In any case, you are returned to the operating system from which you began dBASE IV.

**For Related Information...**

▸▸ "Customizing dBASE IV with SET Options," p. 394.

# Using the dBASE IV Help System

For those times when your memory fails or when you encounter a strange menu item, you can take advantage of dBASE IV's on-screen help system. This system is sensitive to your current position in the menu system, a feature called *context sensitivity*. In practice, context sensitivity brings you information pertinent to the situation about which you called for help.

Suppose that in the Control Center Tools menu, you activate the Export command and find you don't understand the Character Delimited option. You can call up the help system and see a short explanation of what each item in the menu means. If the information is not sufficient or if it suggests another topic, you can access help on that other topic by using commands within the Help menu to bring up related information. You also can bring up a complete table of contents of help topics and navigate through the table to locate a particular topic. To suppress the help screens, refer to Chapter 15. If you need additional help, you're likely to find it in this book or in the dBASE IV documentation.

Activate the help system by pressing F1 (Help), or click the `Help:F1` label on the navigation line. Exit from the help system by pressing Esc. When you exit help, you resume your work at exactly the point from which you called for help.

After you're in the help system, any cursor movements and commands you activate affect the help system, not the Control Center or the display or design screen you were in when you accessed help. The help system includes two types of screens: contents screens and information screens. A *contents screen* lists topics about which you can get more detailed information (see fig. 5.9). Select a topic from the list to narrow the topic list or to go to an information screen. The message line for a contents screen displays the options `More General:F3` and `More Specific:F4`. Press F3 to display a more general contents screen than the current one; press F4 to display a more specific contents screen. If you are at the lowest level of specificity, pressing F4 displays the information screen for the highlighted topic.

If you are using the mouse to access Help, click on the `Help:F1` label in the navigation line. Click on the topic you want to choose or click on the `More General` or `More Specific` labels at the bottom of the screen. Click outside the help box to close it.

An *information screen* has some additional options (see fig. 5.10). The screen shown in figure 5.10 has the Previous Screen and Next Screen options, usually about closely related topics or extensions of the current topic. The F3 key is used to move to the previous screen; the F4 key moves to the next screen. Notice that the message line registers these different functions for the F3 and F4 keys.

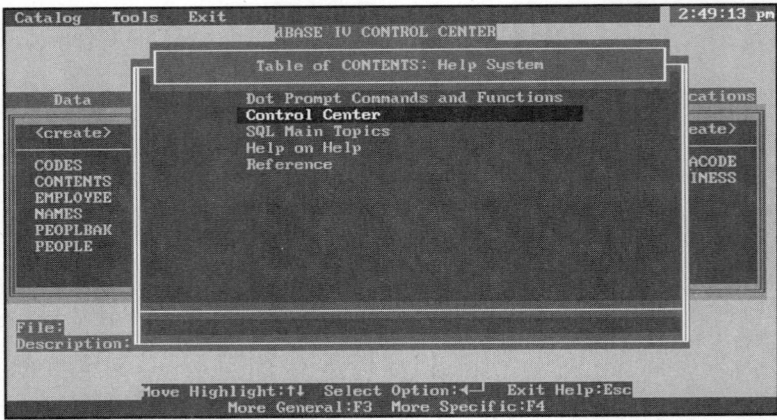


FIG. 5.9

A contents screen from the help system.

Instead of using the F3 and F4 keys, you can use the mouse and click on these function labels in the navigation line.

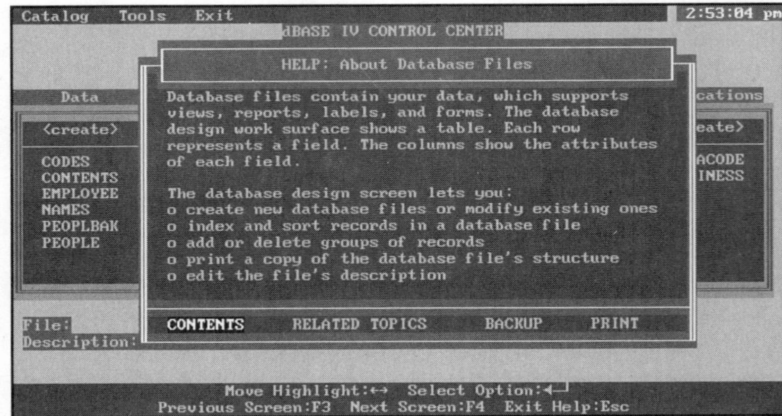


FIG. 5.10

An information screen from the help system.

Also notice that an information screen has a list of command buttons at the bottom of the window. The possible command buttons and their functions are as follows:

| Command button | Function |
|---|---|
| CONTENTS | Returns to the most specific contents screen about this information topic. |
| RELATED TOPICS | Presents a list of content topics closely related to the current topic. This list is presented in a separate window from the main help window. |

| Command button | Function |
|---|---|
| BACKUP | Moves to the previous topic in the same way as the F3 key. |
| PRINT | Prints the current information screen. |

To activate one of these command buttons, move the cursor to the button you want and press Enter. You also can press the first letter of the button or click the button. Remember that pressing Esc or clicking outside the help box closes the help system and returns you to your calling point.

# Managing Files and Disks from dBASE IV

With the exception of one group of important commands, the first part of this chapter explained the cycle of routine commands you use during a dBASE IV working session. The group of commands discussed in this section includes the commands you use to manage your disks and files in ways that the Control Center cannot handle. Some of the most common situations in which you use these commands are as follows:

- Changing data directories after you start dBASE IV
- Copying files from one disk to another, especially for backup purposes
- Deleting files that may not be part of a catalog

All the commands in question are included on the DOS Utilities submenu. You access this submenu from the Control Center Tools menu, and then press D to select the DOS Utilities option. The DOS Utilities screen with its work surface and menu appears (see fig. 5.11).

If you scan the list of files in figure 5.11, you see files with extensions such as FRG, MDX, and SCR. These extensions were not listed as possibilities in Chapter 3 when dBASE IV file types were discussed. You learn the significance of these file extensions in later chapters.

The DOS Utilities screen has as its work surface a list of files from the current drive and directory, identified in the top center of the work surface. The file list includes, from left to right, the following information on each file:

- The name of each file
- The file extension
- The actual size of the file
- The date and time the file was last modified
- A list of the file's attributes
- The amount of disk space required for the file

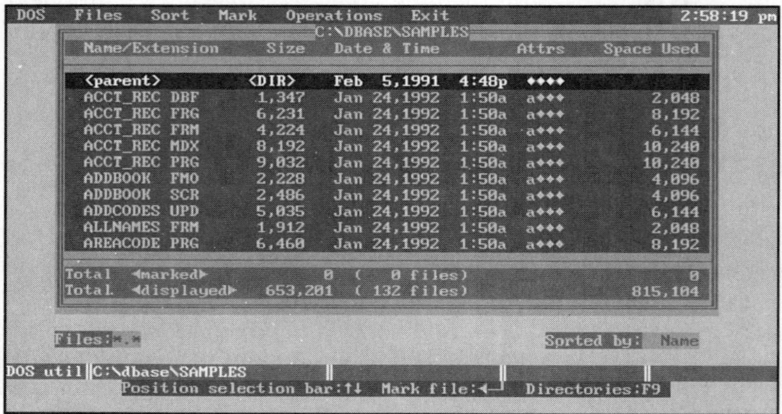


FIG. 5.11

The DOS Utilities screen.

At the bottom of the file list, the total sizes for all files listed and all files marked are reported. Marking files is discussed in the section, "Displaying Only Specified Files in the File List," later in this chapter.

Below the totals lines, the work surface reports the status of two indicators: `Files` and `Sorted by`. The `Files` indicator specifies which files in the directory are listed—the naming pattern used to list the files. The default naming pattern is *.*, indicating that files with any first name (the first *) and any extension (the second *) are included in the list.

The `Sorted by` indicator specifies the order in which the files appear in the list. The default value is `Name`, meaning that the files are sorted alphanumerically by letters and numbers in the first name.

## Changing and Displaying Directories

The file list in the DOS Utilities screen is controlled through the menu bar and certain function-key shortcuts. From the information in the preceding section, you may have surmised that you can change the file list by changing the directory, the pattern in the `Files` indicator, and the Sorted By order. In fact, all are possible; singly or together, these three options control the list and overall arrangement of the files you see.

The most important of the commands that affect the file list is the one that changes the DOS directory, because this command determines the list of available files. In Chapter 4, you learned that changing the directory is an important step in changing catalogs. dBASE IV derives its list of available catalogs from the list of files with the CAT extension found in a particular directory. If the catalog you want is in a disk directory different from the current one, you have to change to a new directory before changing the catalog.

You change directories for one of two reasons: to change the default for purposes of establishing a new catalog, and to view another directory for the sake of information. Each of these purposes is served by a different command from the menu bar.

To change the default directory and, by implication, the catalog, use the DOS menu and the Set Default Drive:Directory command (see fig. 5.12). To view the list of files in the directory to which you changed, use the Files menu and the Change Drive:Directory command (see fig. 5.13).

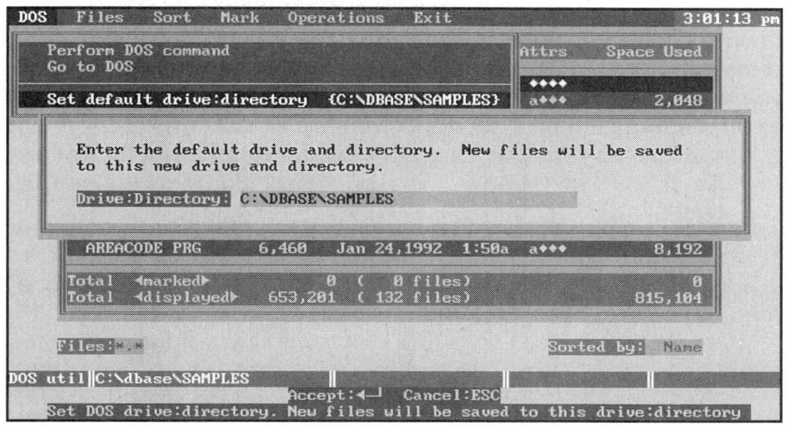


FIG. 5.12

Setting the default drive and directory.

When you activate either of these commands, dBASE IV presents a fill-in box into which you type the path of the new drive or directory. You can take advantage of several shortcuts in this process. You can generate a pick list consisting of all the directories on a particular drive, arranged in tree fashion. With the tree on-screen, "climb" through it with the selector, highlight the directory you want, and press Enter to select it. Using the mouse, you also can double-click the directory you want.

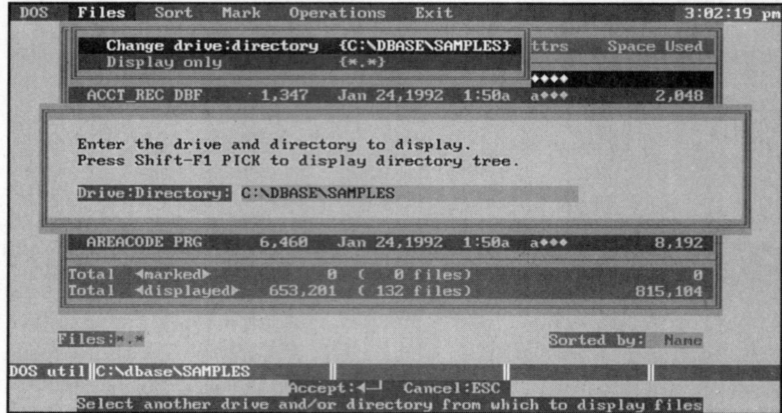


FIG. 5.13

Viewing a different drive and directory.

To generate a pick list, activate the Set Default Drive:Directory command. Instead of typing the new directory in the fill-in box, press Shift-F1 (Pick). dBASE IV generates a directory tree (see fig. 5.14). If you want to change to the DBTUTOR directory, for example, move the selector bar to that branch of the tree and press Enter, or double-click the mouse, to complete the change and return to the DOS Utilities work surface. You can use this same shortcut with the Change Drive:Directory command on the Files menu; however, you can use an even easier way. Instead of activating the menu bar, just press F9 (Zoom) directly from the DOS Utilities screen or click the Directories:F9 label. dBASE IV creates a directory tree, and you can select a directory in the same way as using the full command procedure. You can use the F9 (Zoom) method only to change the file view; you cannot use F9 to change the default directory.

To return to the files display, press F9 again, or click the `Files:F9` label in the navigation line.

If you want to change the drive and the directory with the directory-tree pick list, move the cursor to the top of the tree to the drive-designator letter; for example, C: (refer to fig. 5.14). If you highlight the drive letter and press Enter or click it, you see a pick list of drives for your computer. Select the desired drive and press Enter, or double-click with the mouse, to change to that drive. If the target drive also has directories, select a directory from the tree that appears.

You can change the directory of the file list in a final way: select the name of a directory in the list. If you are in the DBASE directory and you want to change to the PRACTICE directory, for example, select PRACTICE in the file list (see fig. 5.15). If you want to move backward along the tree, select the <parent> directory item in the list. This action takes you back one level in the tree. If the directory you want to move to is not directly adjacent to the current directory, repeat these steps until you find the correct directory.

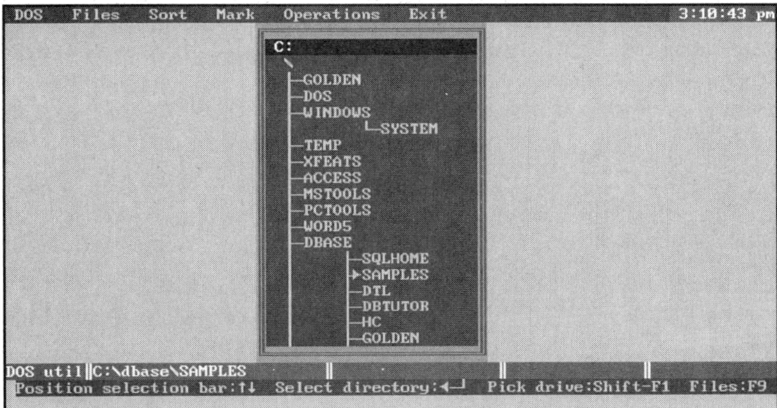

FIG. 5.14

Using the directory-tree pick list to change directories.

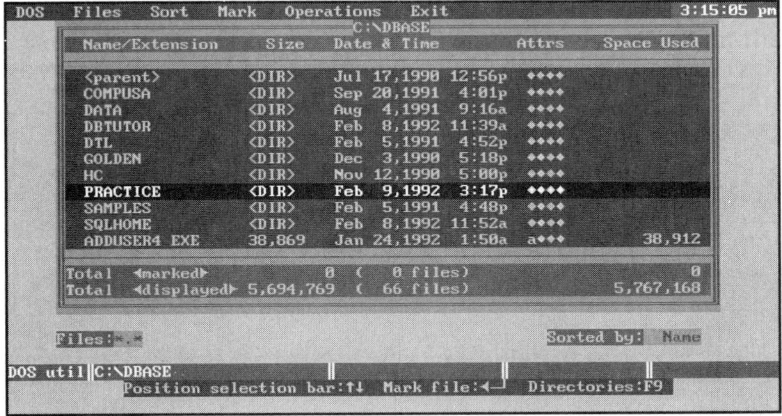

FIG. 5.15

Changing a directory through the file list.

## Controlling the Display of the File List

Changing the directory causes a different list of files to appear on the work surface, but the list still includes all the files in the directory. You may need only a portion of the complete list of files to address a particular question. You may, for example, want to inspect a list of "foreign" files, say Lotus 1-2-3 Release 2.2 worksheets, with the idea of importing the data into a dBASE IV file. Because Lotus 1-2-3 Release 2.2

files end with the extension WK1, you can save yourself some search time if you organize all the WK1 files together in the list or restrict the list to just WK1 files.

You can address this problem in two ways: sort the list by extension and move the selector to the items you are interested in, or extract the WK1 files from the list by filtering out other types of files. You use the Sort menu for the first approach; use the Operations menu for the second.

## Sorting the File List

By default, the file list you see on-screen is sorted by file name. Using the Sort menu, you can rearrange the list of files according to another file characteristic: Extension, Date & Time, or Size (see fig 5.16). Use these other sorting options to locate files by some feature you remember about the files. If you forgot the name of a file but remember that you created it last October, for example, you can arrange the list by Date & Time and focus easily on those files that meet your search criterion. To sort files by extension (for example, to locate all the WK1 files), select Extension.

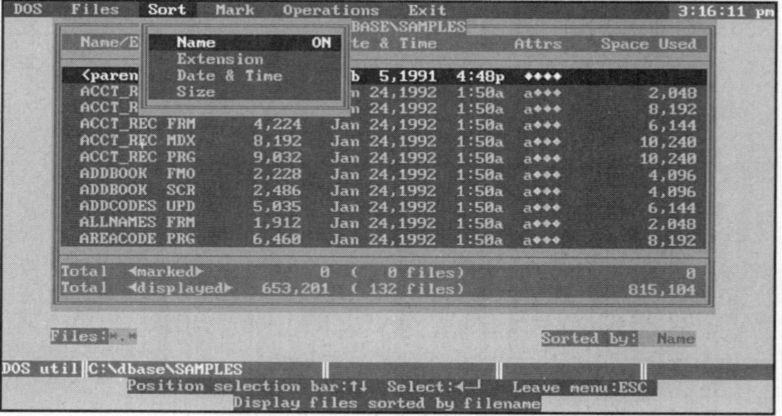


FIG. 5.16

The Sort menu.

To change the sort order, activate the Sort menu and select the sort option you want. The list of files is reordered immediately.

## Displaying Only Specified Files in the File List

The DOS Utilities Operations menu lists the filing operations you can perform on single or multiple files in the file list. This menu includes the most common types of filing activities, including deleting files, renaming files, and copying and moving files to other disks or directories.

To carry out a filing operation, start by marking the files on which you want to operate. Do this by moving the cursor to the file you want and pressing Enter. An arrowhead appears in front of the file to mark it. If the files you want to mark have a common element in their file names, you can mark them more quickly by using the Files menu to limit the display to only the target files, and then using the Mark menu to mark all the files in the display in a single step.

Suppose that you wanted to mark all the files with the extension WK1. Access the Files menu, and then select Display Only. A fill-in box appears, asking you to indicate the pattern for the files you want (see fig. 5.17). To list only the WK1 files, type **.WK1*. The leading asterisk indicates that you do not care what the first name of the file is, you only care that the file has the WK1 extension. Table 5.5 shows some other patterns you can specify using the asterisk wild card. The table also includes examples of patterns built using the question-mark (?) wild card. Use the question mark in place of a single character position in the file name or extension.

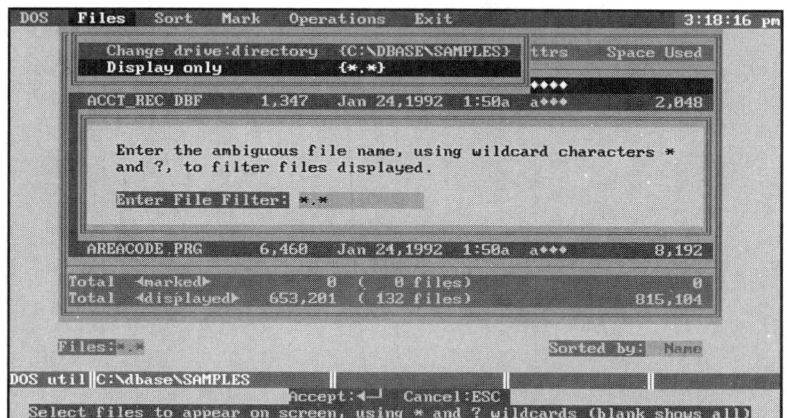


FIG. 5.17

Limiting the file display with the Display Only command.

After you mark the files, access the Operations menu; select the operation you want to perform (see fig. 5.18). Deleting files removes them permanently from disk; renaming files changes their names or extensions; copying files creates exact replicas on another disk or directory;

moving files copies files to a new location and deletes them from the original location.

**Table 5.5 Using Wild Cards To Limit File Displays**

| Pattern | Example of files selected |
|---|---|
| *.* | All files |
| *.SCR | All files with the SCR extension |
| ACCTS.* | All files with the name ACCTS, regardless of extension |
| ACCT?.DBF | All files with ACCT as the first four positions of the name and any other character in the fifth position, and the extension DBF; for example, ACCT2.DBF and ACCT8.DBF |
| ACCTS.D?? | All files with the name ACCTS, and an extension beginning with the letter D; for example, ACCTS.DBF, ACCTS.DBO, and ACCTS.DOC |

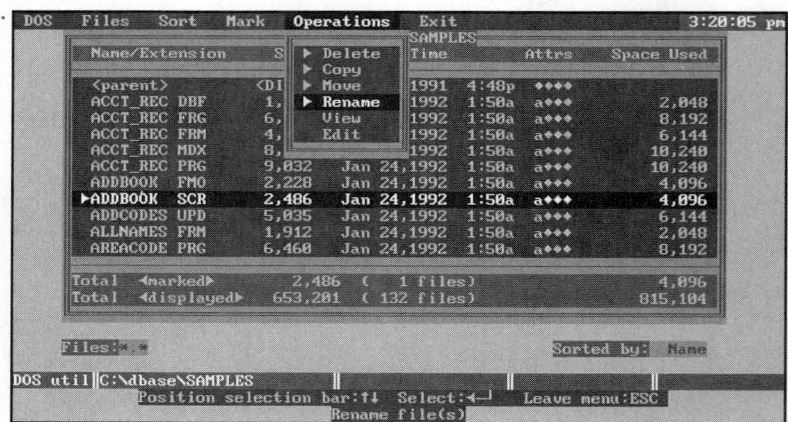


FIG. 5.18

The Operations menu of the DOS Utilities screen.

Before asking for the details of the operation you select, dBASE IV asks you to specify on which of the following groups of files you want to operate:

- A single file (the one highlighted by the selector)
- All the marked files
- All the displayed files

After indicating which files you want, the next step is to state the details of the operation you selected from the Operations menu. Table 5.6 lists the requirements for each operation. Choose the correct specifications to start the operation.

**Table 5.6 Requirements for Different Filing Operations**

| Option | Requirements |
|---|---|
| Delete | Verify that you want to proceed or cancel. |
| Copy or Move | Specify a destination drive and directory, and then specify a different file name or file name pattern. |
| Rename | Specify the new file name or file name pattern. |

The two other options on the Operations menu, View and Edit, are used only with what dBASE IV calls *text files*. Text files also are called *print files* or *ASCII files*. The View command shows the contents of the highlighted file; the Edit command switches to the dBASE IV word processor so that you can make changes to the highlighted file.

Use the View command if you need an instant refresher on what information a file holds and the file name alone doesn't jog your memory. You can use the command on nontext files, but the information may be garbled. For instance, compare figures 5.19 and 5.20. Figure 5.19 shows the view of a text file; figure 5.20 shows the view of a nontext file. You may be able to tell whether a file is a text file or a nontext file by examining the file's extension. The text file in figure 5.19 has the extension FRG; the nontext file in figure 5.20 has the extension FRM. You can better appreciate the distinctions between file extensions after reading the chapters about programming in Part IV of this book.

# Automating a Repetitive Process with Macros

As you learned earlier in this chapter, backing up files is important in ensuring the security of your data. You should not only back up your files; you should back up regularly. Although the steps in the process are not difficult (see "Backing Up Files," earlier in this chapter), they can take some time, and you may be tempted not to do them as you're racing to meet your car pool at 5 o'clock.

```
                                                        3:22:20 pm
* Program...........: E:acct_rec.FRG
* Date..............: 1-25-92
* Versions..........: dBASE IV, Report 1.5
*
* Notes:
* ------
* Prior to running this procedure with the DO command
* it is necessary use LOCATE because the CONTINUE
* statement is in the main loop.
*
*-- Parameters
PARAMETERS gl_noeject, gl_plain, gl_summary, gc_heading, gc_extra
** The first three parameters are of type Logical.
** The fourth parameter is a string.  The fifth is extra.
PRIVATE _peject, _wrap

*-- Test for no records found
IF EOF() .OR. .NOT. FOUND()
   RETURN
ENDIF

                        -- 8% --
   Display control: SPACEBAR:Next screenful,  RETURN:Start/stop scroll.
```

FIG. 5.19

Viewing a text file.

```
                                                        3:23:50 pm
dBASE IV Generic Design File Version 1.0~~#~report.prfC:\DB278\ACCT_RECp\X~p\q;
>p\14p\O;+p\4DATED}~          MM/DD/YY
PAGENON}~999INVOICE_NOC~}ACCT_RECXXXXXXXXXXTDAT_OF_BILD}ACCT_REC          MM/DD/Y
Y%CUST_IDC~}ACCT_RECXXXXXXT.AMT_LSTBILN,ACCT_REC          999,999.996DAT_LSTBILD5
ACCT_REC          MM/DD/YY?AMT_LST_PDN>ACCT_REC          999,999.99HOLDBALANCENGACC
T_REC          999,999.99QAMT_OF_CURNPACCT_REC          999,999.99ZAMT_OF_BILNYACCT
_REC          999,999.99cINVOIC_OLDCb~ACCT_RECXXXXXXXXXXTmCOMMENTSCk~ACCT_RECXXXX
XXXXXXXXXXXXXXXXXXXXXXXXTwNOTESCuP~ACCT_RECXXXXXXXXXXXXXXXXXXXXXXXXXXXXXXXXXTN;O
LDBALANCE999,9999.99TOTAL OLD BALANCESN;AMT_OF_BIL999,9999.99TOTAL CURRENT INVO
ICES (08@HPX`hpxX,L,#..>PAGE  q.,". A-T FURNITURE INDUSTRIES"ACCOUNTS RECEIVABL
E REPORT,m/,
c2,Z,Q,H,          ?,6,..,%,
,G,
..R*INVOICE NUMBER: 'DATE: CUSTOMER ID: -PREVIOUS INVOICE #: SENT: PREVIOUS INV
OICE: $ AMOUNT PAID:          ----------PREVIOUS BALANCE: $ 1CURRENT ORDERS:
COMMENTS: ==========.CURRENT INVOICE:  $ NOTES: O,&,w&..R.TOTAL AMOUNT OF PREVI
OUS BALANCES:  $ .TOTAL AMOUNT OF CURRENT INVOICES:   $ R4..%PREPARED BY FINANC
IAL DEPARTMENTdBASE IV Generic Design File Version 1.0

                        --100% --
                  Press any key to continue...
```

FIG. 5.20

Viewing a nontext file.

One way you can make the process go a little smoother is to create what dBASE IV calls a *macro* to record the steps. Then when you want to back up your files, you don't have to key in each step yourself; you can "play" the macro and have it carry out the steps automatically.

To set up a macro, you record the steps you want it to perform. To record a macro, follow these steps:

1. Press Shift-F10 (Macros), and then select Begin Recording.
2. Assign the macro to a function key (F1 through F9) or to a letter key.

When you assign a macro to a function key or to a letter key, you give the macro a name. You use this name to call the macro. If you assign the macro to the F9 key, for example, you can call it by pressing Alt-F9.

3. Perform all the steps you want the macro to do. dBASE IV records these steps to the macro as you perform them.

4. Press Shift-F10, and then select End Recording.

To play back a recorded macro, press Alt-*function key*, where *function key* is the one you assigned to the macro in step 2 of the preceding instructions. If you assigned the macro to a letter, press Alt-F10; at the prompt, type the letter of the macro you want to call.

Using Shift-F10 and Alt-F10 to record and play back macros is the simplest way to use macros. You also can control macro creation and playback by using the Control Center Tools menu and selecting the Macro command. From the Control Center, access the Tools menu, and then select the Macros command. The submenu shown in figure 5.21 appears.

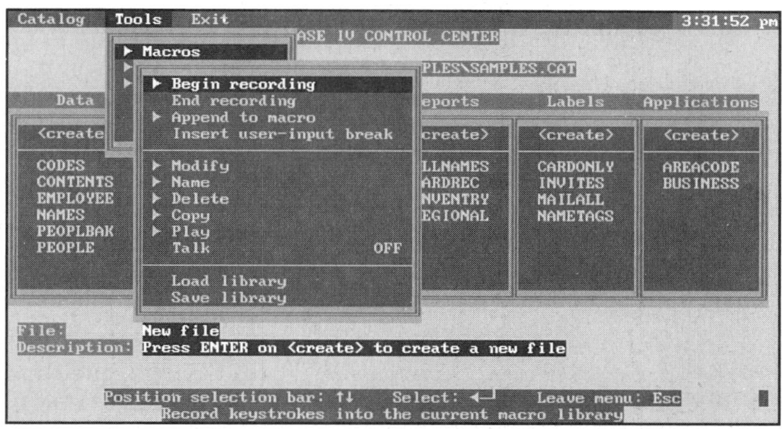


FIG. 5.21

The Macros submenu.

This menu has commands that enable you to begin recording and to play back the macro. These commands work the same way as Shift-F10 and Alt-F10, described in the preceding steps, but they ask you to provide the name for the macro by selecting it from a macro display table (see fig. 5.22). If you have not created any macros when you first inspect the table, the table is empty. If you select Begin Recording and then press a function key or a letter to name a macro, that slot on the table is occupied and you begin recording immediately. As you record a macro, the message line on all screens reads `Recording Macro; Press Shift-F10 E to end.`

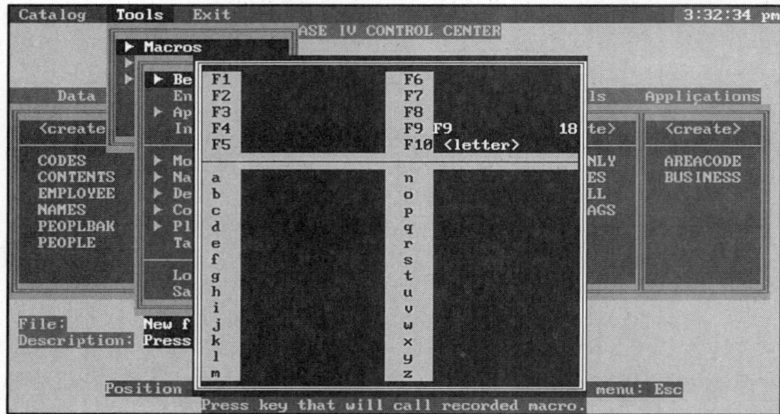


FIG. 5.22

The macro display table.

If you select Play from the Macros submenu, the display table reappears, listing the keys that have been assigned. Just press the key for the macro you want; dBASE IV begins to play back the macro immediately.

dBASE IV plays back the macro faster than you can follow with your eyes. If you want to slow down the process so that you can see what's happening, select the Talk command from the Macros menu so that the setting is ON rather than OFF. Now when you play the macro, dBASE IV reports each macro command on the message line, and you see the effect of the command on-screen. If the macro still runs too fast for you, you can slow it down further by pressing < (the less-than sign) one or more times while the macro is running. Likewise, if you want to speed up the playback, press > (the greater-than sign).

The macros you create stay around only for the length of your current work session. If you want to use the macro on subsequent days, you must save it. You use the Save Library command from the Macros menu for this purpose. When you activate this command, dBASE IV requests the name of the library in which you want to store the macros (see fig. 5.23). Fill in a regular file name (for example, GENERAL) and press Enter. dBASE IV saves the macro library under the name you give it and assigns it the extension KEY.

When you want to use the library in a later session, activate the Load Library command from the Macros menu. dBASE IV displays a pick list of all available libraries in the current directory. Select the library you want and press Enter to bring it to the macro display table. If the library is on another directory or disk, the pick list gives you the option of changing directories.

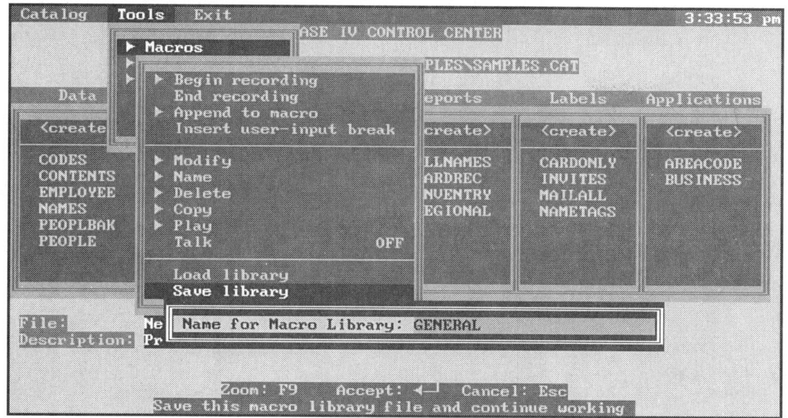


FIG. 5.23

Specifying the name for a macro library.

With the Name command on the Macros menu, you can place a short description of the macro on the macro display table in place of the single letter or function key. If you record the database-backup procedure to a macro with the F9 key, for example, select Name from the Macros menu, specify the letter of the macro you want to name, and type a more descriptive macro name. The name must be 10 characters or less and cannot contain a space (see fig. 5.24). The next time you use the macro display table, you see the name you assigned, rather than just a letter (see fig. 5.25).

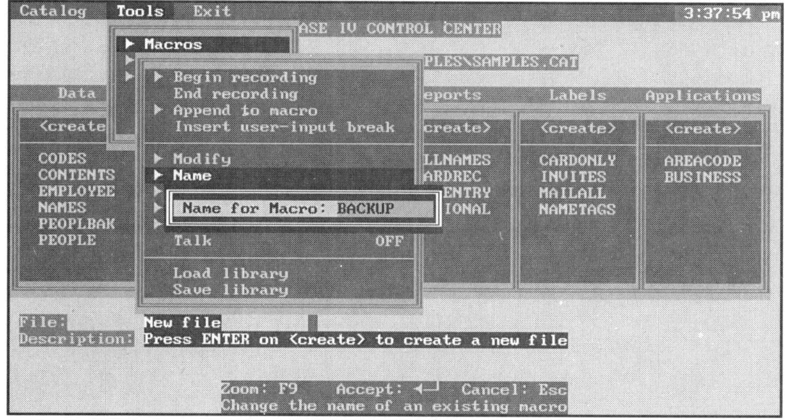


FIG. 5.24

Naming a macro.

In the macro display table, each macro name is followed by a number representing the number of keystrokes in the macro.

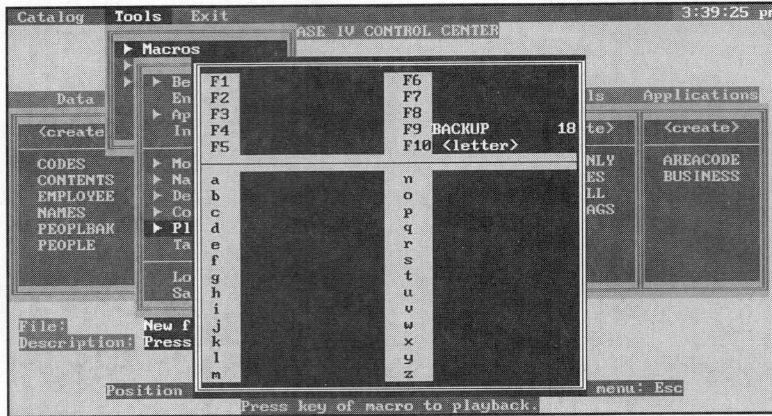


FIG. 5.25

A named macro in the macro display table.

Other commands on the Macros menu enable you to edit a macro without recording it again. One way to do this is to add or append commands to the end of a current macro. Use the Append To Macro command for this purpose. Select the macro you want to modify, and then carry out the necessary commands. As you perform the commands, they are recorded in the usual way.

A more flexible approach to changing a macro is to use the Modify command. This command displays an edit screen in which the individual commands and cursor controls you recorded are listed (see fig. 5.26). You can change any of these commands, add to them, delete them, and so on. After you make your changes, press F10 (Menu) to display the Exit menu for the edit screen, save the changes, and return to the Control Center.

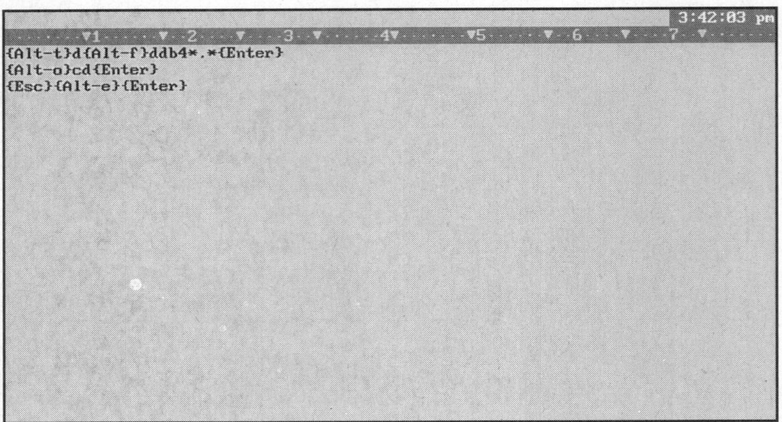


FIG. 5.26

Using the Modify command to edit a macro.

Notice that commands and cursor controls in the edit screen are specified by enclosing their names in curly braces { }. The names of the keys are the same as the names on the key caps, with the exception of the arrow keys. To indicate an arrow key, use the following names:

{rightarrow}
{leftarrow}
{uparrow}
{downarrow}

In addition, if you use a booster key such as Shift, Alt, or Ctrl, separate the booster key from the activated key by a hyphen; for example {Ctrl-End}, {Alt-T}, and so on. Letters and words you type to activate menu options and fill-in boxes are not enclosed in braces. They are typed directly.

**For Related Information...**

▸▸ "Using Keyboard Macros," p. 521.

▸▸ "Macro Commands," p. 647.

# Summary

This chapter took you on a tour of the Control Center and explored most of the options available through its menus. You learned how to use the DOS Utilities command from the Tools menu to control filing and disk-management operations, including changing the default disk and directory, sorting file lists, and backing up, deleting, and renaming files. You also learned to use the F1 (Help) command, which gives you access to an extensive set of information screens about every command in dBASE IV.

In addition, you looked at the Control Center as the gateway to creating and working with database and other types of files; you reviewed how dBASE IV uses catalogs to manage the types and names of files that appear in the Control Center panels. You worked with dBASE IV using screens made available through the Control Center panels. You learned about the two types of screens, display and design, and discovered the relationship these screens have through the F2 (Data) and the Shift-F2 (Design) keys. You also learned about the Exit options for each screen.

Finally, you looked at the Macros menu and how to use it to automate repetitive tasks. The commands available through the Macros menu enable you to record keystrokes into a macro, play back the macro, and modify the macro. The commands also give you the ability to save a collection of macros into a macro library and retrieve that library into other applications.

All the commands covered in this chapter constitute a basic or routine set of commands—commands you can use on a daily basis to complete most of the work you do with dBASE IV. Understanding these commands well prepares you to understand the workings of every screen, menu, and function-key list you encounter in later chapters.

6

CHAPTER

# Creating the Database Structure

Earlier in this book, you learned how databases are made up of sets of data about different objects, places, persons, events—any collection of "entities" that can be described. The problem is that you have to be able to describe all the entities in the collection in the same terms or categories. Even though your grandmother may not have had databases in mind, she intuitively understood the principle when she said, "You cannot mix apples and oranges."

You determine the categories you use by deciding what kinds of questions you want the database to answer and by uniquely distinguishing each entity in the database. In Chapter 2, you learned that databases often are set up with a single category, such as a Social Security number; a single category ensures the uniqueness of each entity.

A database, then, is a collection of informational categories about a similar group of entities and a collection of detailed facts and figures about each entity in the database. The collection of categories is referred to as the *structure* of the database; the collection of facts is referred to as the *data*. Even though both parts of the database are stored on disk in a single file, you should think of the process of creating the database as two separate tasks. The two tasks you perform to create a database are defining the structure and inputting or entering data.

In this chapter, you learn how to put the structure of the database together. In Chapter 7, you work on the data-entry and editing procedures involved in the creation of a database.

# Understanding Database Terminology

As you become acquainted with the dBASE IV procedures you use to put together a database, you should become comfortable with the terms dBASE IV uses to describe database structures and values. You encounter these terms in help screens, messages, and command prompts. To take full advantage of what dBASE is telling you, you have to understand dBASE's language.

The first term you should understand is *field*. A field is synonymous with a database *category*. A field stores a particular type of data. If you think of a database as a table, a field is identified at the top of a column of data and includes all the data in that column. In a personnel database, for example, you may have a Social Security number field, a last name field, a department field, and a salary field. Such a database has four fields and four columns. In common usage, saying that a database has four columns is the same as saying that it has four fields.

The next term to understand is *record*. A record is the set of details or facts that describe a single entity in the database. Because the description of an entity is limited by your choice of database fields, the record consists of the set of details across all fields. In the personnel database, for example, a record consists of one piece of information from each of the four fields. A personnel record consists of a Social Security number, a last name, a department, and a salary.

Again, if you think of a database as a table, a record can be represented by a single row of data—an item of data for each of the columns or fields in the table (see fig. 6.1).

Another important term you should know is *value*. A value is an individual item of data at the intersection of a row and a column. In the database table model in figure 6.1, a value is equivalent to what goes in a single slot of the table. To pinpoint a value in the table, you must describe it in terms of the record it belongs to and the field it occupies. It is Virgil's name, or Harry's Social Security number, or Dana's salary.

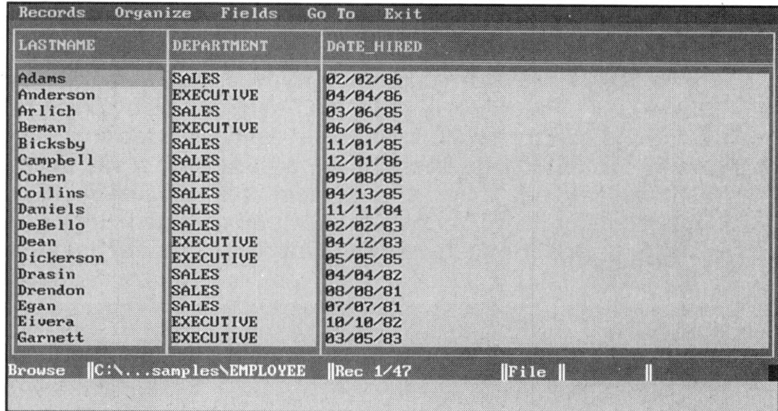

Records Organize Fields Go To Exit

| LASTNAME | DEPARTMENT | DATE_HIRED |
|---|---|---|
| Adams | SALES | 02/02/86 |
| Anderson | EXECUTIVE | 04/04/86 |
| Arlich | SALES | 03/06/85 |
| Beman | EXECUTIVE | 06/06/84 |
| Bicksby | SALES | 11/01/85 |
| Campbell | SALES | 12/01/86 |
| Cohen | SALES | 09/08/85 |
| Collins | SALES | 04/13/85 |
| Daniels | SALES | 11/11/84 |
| DeBello | SALES | 02/02/83 |
| Dean | EXECUTIVE | 04/12/83 |
| Dickerson | EXECUTIVE | 05/05/85 |
| Drasin | SALES | 04/04/82 |
| Drendon | SALES | 08/08/81 |
| Egan | SALES | 07/07/81 |
| Eivera | EXECUTIVE | 10/10/82 |
| Garnett | EXECUTIVE | 03/05/83 |

Browse ‖C:\...samples\EMPLOYEE ‖Rec 1/47 ‖File ‖

FIG. 6.1

A table model of a database.

# Establishing the Database Definition

Chapter 2 included a discussion about data types, or field types. As you may remember, a *data type* specifies the kind of data you intend to store in a field. You can use one of three basic data types: character, numeric, or date. Each type confers on its field certain properties that enable dBASE IV to check the validity of data entered in that field and to do certain kinds of processing on the data. Designating a field as numeric, for example, enables the data in the field to be calculated.

When you assign a field type to a field, you *define* that field within the structure of the database. In other words, the structure of the database consists of the list of fields you want to include in the database and the type you want to assign to each field. To complete the definition of the database, you also assign each field a width and indicate whether you want dBASE IV to maintain the database records by ordering the values for that field. This last feature of the definition is called the *index value* of the database.

The *width* of a field specifies the length of the longest data item that can be stored in the field. The maximum width is determined by the field type. A character field can be as wide as 254 positions and as small as 1 position. A date field, on the other hand, is always 8 positions wide, an indication that the field always stores values in the MM/DD/YY format.

Determining the width of a numeric field has one additional complexity. You must tell dBASE IV how many decimal places you want to store in that field. The width, then, has to account for these decimal places. To determine the width, count one position for each digit of the number, one position for each decimal place, and one position for the decimal point. If the largest number you want to store in a numeric field is 999,999.999, for example, the width of this field is 10; the field has 3 decimal places. Notice that you don't count a position for the comma. In fact, a true number cannot store a comma.

The index value for a field is probably the simplest part of the field definition: you specify Yes or No for each field. Yes signifies that you want dBASE IV to maintain an index which, if you choose to use it, displays your records alphabetically, numerically, or chronologically by the values in that field. A more detailed discussion of indexes appears in Chapter 8.

To summarize, a database description calls for the following information about each field in the database:

- Name
- Type
- Width
- Decimal places (for numeric fields only)
- Index value

## Using Logical and Float Field Types

In addition to the three primary field types—character, numeric, and date—dBASE IV permits three other field types that you use in special circumstances. The first of these is called a *logical* type. A logical field always has a width of 1 position and permits only four possible values: true (T or t), false (F or f), yes (Y or y), or no (N or n). Internally, a yes value is stored as true, and a no value is stored as false. A logical field is set up to handle information with only two possible values. You can think of a field that specifies whether someone is alive or not, for example, as a logical field type. Unless you admit to the possibility of zombies as some intermediate state, this field has only two alternatives.

You can set up certain categories in more than one way. If the database has a Sex field (which can have one of two possible answers), for example, you can set it up as a character field with a width 1 and with possible values *M*(ale) and *F*(emale); alternatively, you can set up the field as a logical field with possible values *T*(rue) and *F*(alse). What are the advantages of each approach? With a character field, the allowable values are closer to what the world recognizes as alternatives in the category. With a logical field, someone reading the table of values may not know whether T means male or female. On the other hand, a logical field has more built-in validity control. With a logical field, dBASE IV permits only the values true, false, yes, and no. If your finger slips and you press R instead of T, dBASE IV does not accept the entry into a logical field. If you make this typing error with a character field (unless you take some precautions by specifying validity checks, as discussed in Chapter 2 and detailed in Chapter 9), dBASE IV records the R as a correct value. A disadvantage of a logical field is that you cannot index on it directly. This can be awkward, though not impossible, if you want a list of names organized by sex.

The second new field type dBASE IV permits is the *float* type. The word *float* refers to a floating-point number, which is a number that stores a value to the full precision of the system rather than to a designated number of decimal places. In every respect, a float field is defined in the same way as a numeric field. You still specify the width and number of decimals in the same way. The only differences happen internally in how the number is stored on disk. Without getting involved in the technical details, you should understand how this difference affects you and your work.

If you store the result of a calculation as a floating-point number, dBASE IV stores the calculated value to the full precision of the system, even though the number displays only to the limits of the definition. For instance, what you see on-screen as 2 may be stored as 2.000000000001. If you perform calculations with this number, you may get results in which 2+2 does not exactly equal 4. In earlier versions of dBASE, columns of numbers sometimes did not add up correctly to the penny. The dBASE IV solution was to add the numeric field type to get around this difficulty with the float field type.

What guidelines should you follow in defining numbers? If you deal with scientific or technical applications that include very large or very small numbers, and you need high levels of precision in all your calculations, set your numbers up in float fields. For just about any other application, set your numbers up in numeric fields.

## Using Memo Field Types

The last field type you need to know about is the *memo* field, which most dBASE IV users find useful. The memo field accommodates data that is not clear-cut, that is larger than 254 characters, or that doesn't fit any particular pattern. If you need to keep track of miscellaneous details about people in your database—say, Joe's wife's name, Mabel's wedding anniversary, John's favorite restaurant, and so on—how do you handle this information? You certainly don't want to set up separate fields for spouse names, anniversaries, and likes and dislikes. The problem with this approach is that dBASE IV creates space for these fields in every record, whether you need to use the fields or not. Besides being wasteful of disk space, such an arrangement cripples the database design and makes the database inefficient.

You could set up a character field to use for stray facts. Because a character field can be as long as 254 positions, such a field can record a whole series of comments. The problem with this solution, however, is the same as setting up separate fields. dBASE IV sets aside the space for this field for each record in the database, whether you use the field or not.

The perfect solution is to use memo fields. If you designate a field as a memo type, dBASE IV reserves 10 positions in each record for the memo field. These 10 positions, however, are not used to store data. The data you type in the memo field is stored in a separate file. dBASE IV sets up this file automatically whenever you use a memo field. The memo-field file has the same name as the database, but it has the extension DBT instead of DBF. When you open a database file, dBASE IV automatically opens any associated DBT file.

dBASE uses the 10 positions reserved in the database record to store a *pointer* to where the data is actually stored in the DBT file. In other words, the memo field contains only a direction to the location of the data. You don't have to worry about setting up this pointer yourself. In fact, you never see the pointer. When you need to store or retrieve a memo, you make a special request to open the memo field by pressing Ctrl-Home; dBASE IV takes it from there (see Chapter 9 for details on entering memos).

For a single record, you can store up to 64 thousand bytes of data in a memo field. Storing memos of that size as a matter of course is not practical, but the potential exists.

You pay a price for the flexibility of memos, and you may want to consider these costs when you design your database systems. The contents of a memo field generally are hidden from view; they don't appear in a display view of the database. You must specifically request that the memo for a particular record appear, or you can design a "memo window" in a customized data-entry form to reveal the memos automatically. You also are limited in how you can search for information in a memo. The search process is slower for memos than for regular fields and cannot take advantage of the query-by-example method you can use for searching other types of fields. Even with these limitations, memo fields are a useful way to keep all your facts in order.

**For Related Information...**

▸▸ "Understanding the Concept of an Index," p. 165.

# Defining the Database Structure

Databases are created in dBASE IV with the database design screen (see fig. 6.2). From the Control Center, you access this screen by putting the panel selector on the Data panel's <create> button and pressing Enter or Shift-F2 (Design), or by clicking on <create> with the mouse.

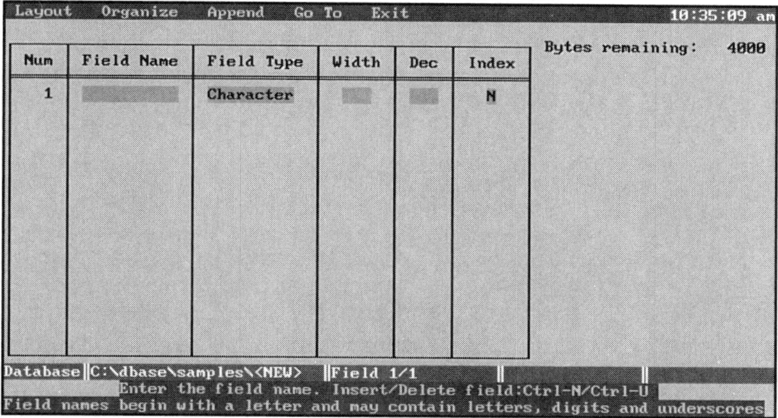


**FIG. 6.2**

A blank database design screen.

If you understand dBASE IV's requirements for setting up field definitions, the layout of the database design screen should present no surprises. Its work surface is a simple table format, in which columns are designated for the Field Name, Field Type, Width, number of decimal places (Dec), and the Index value.

The rest of the design screen is made up of the menu bar across the top of the screen, the status bar below the work surface, and the navigation and message lines at the bottom of the screen. Notice that the status bar displays the name of the design screen in the first section; the second section indicates by the word `<NEW>` that you are working on a new file—a file that has not been named yet. The third section lists the number of the field the selector currently is highlighting and the total number of fields in the structure. At start-up, this section reads `Field 1/1`. The fourth section is blank, and the fifth section lists key indicators, including `Ins` (if the Ins key is pressed) and `Caps` (if the Caps Lock key is pressed).

To define the structure of a new database, you fill out one row on the work surface for each field in the database. You start with the first field (Num 1). When you finish defining the first field, the cursor advances to Num 2.

Start defining a field by typing the name of the field. The field name can be up to 10 characters long. It can be made up of any combination of letters, digits, or the underscore (_) character, as long as the name begins with a letter. You may have a tendency to use spaces in names; the space, however, is an illegal character. If you try to use the space or any other illegal character, dBASE IV beeps and ignores the character.

After you enter the field name, press Enter or Tab to advance to the Field Type column. In this column, notice that dBASE IV uses the default Character type. If you want the field to be a character type, advance to the Width field by pressing Enter or Tab again. If you want to change the type, press the first letter of the type you want: **N**umeric, **F**loat, **D**ate, **L**ogical, or **M**emo (or **C**haracter to change back to the default). dBASE records that type and advances to the next column. If you forget what the choices are, you can press the space bar to cycle through the possibilities. When the correct type appears, press Enter to advance the cursor.

Selecting a field type determines where the cursor goes next. If you select the character, numeric, or float type, the cursor advances to the Width column. If you select date, the cursor automatically records a width of 8 and advances to the Index column. If you select a logical or memo type, the cursor records fixed widths (1 for logical and 10 for memo) and advances to the Field Name column for the next field. You cannot set an Index for logical or memo fields.

The navigation and message lines at the bottom of the screen provide information about your possibilities at the moment. In particular, these lines provide information about the limits you can set on field widths for character and numeric fields and on the number of decimal places you can set for numeric fields.

Chapter 2 described the structure of a hypothetical personnel database that consisted of a number of character, date, and numeric fields. This list is repeated here as table 6.1. The table also includes two new fields: Active, a logical field that records whether the employee is on active assignment or on leave without pay; and Comment, a memo field. Table 6.1 also lists an example of the largest or longest values that can be entered in each field. Look at those formats and decide on a width and decimal setting for each field. You can compare your answers to the completed design screen in figure 6.3. For practice, try entering the field definitions yourself. If you make a mistake during entry, back up the cursor to the mistake, erase it with the Del or Backspace key, and enter the correct setting. To correct the Field Type column, just press the letter for the new type; dBASE IV makes the correction automatically, including changing the width and index value if necessary.

**Table 6.1 Design Requirements for a Database Structure**

| Field | Type | Example |
|---|---|---|
| Last name | Character | Katzenellenbogen |
| First name | Character | Ann Margaret |
| Social Security | Character | 555-66-8970 |
| Date of birth | Date | 04/04/45 |
| Date of hire | Date | 06/08/89 |
| Department | Character | Engineering |
| Office phone number | Character | 555-9999 |
| Starting salary | Numeric | 999999.99 |
| Current salary | Numeric | 999999.99 |
| Active | Logical | T |
| Comment | Memo | On extended leave |

## For Related Information...

▸▸ "Working with the Data File," p. 434.

FROM HERE...

```
Layout  Organize  Append  Go To  Exit                              10:40:36 am

                                                        Bytes remaining:   3897
 Num   Field Name    Field Type   Width   Dec   Index

   1   LASTNAME      Character     16             N
   2   FIRSTNAME     Character     12             N
   3   SSN           Character     11             N
   4   BIRTH_DATE    Date           8             N
   5   HIRE_DATE     Date           8             N
   6   DEPT          Character     11             N
   7   PHONE         Character      8             N
   8   START_SAL     Numeric        9      2      N
   9   CURR_SAL      Numeric        9      2      N
  10   ACTIVE        Logical        1             N
  11   COMMENT       Memo          10             N

Database ║C:\dbase\samples\<NEW>  ║Field 6/11  ║
              Change option to index on this field:Spacebar
```

FIG. 6.3

A completed database structure.

# Saving the Database Structure

After you complete the definition and layout of your database fields, you must save the structure before you can start the second phase—entering your data. You can save the structure in one of two ways: by using the Layout menu or the Exit menu. Each of these menus has a save command. The Layout menu save command performs an interim save, meaning that the command saves the structure but returns to the database design screen. The Exit menu save command saves the database and returns to the Control Center. In either case, you are asked to provide a name for the new database during the save operation.

If you activate the Layout menu, the pull-down menu shown at the top left of figure 6.4 appears. If you then select Save This Database File Structure, a fill-in box appears that asks for the name of the database. Type the file name and press Enter. dBASE saves the database with the name you specify and adds the extension DBF. Remember that the file name cannot be longer than eight characters, not including the extension. After you complete the save, notice that the second section of the status bar shows the new file name.

After you save the database structure, you can add data (as explained in Chapter 7), reorganize it, or design queries (as explained in Chapter 8). You add data by using the Append menu or by pressing F2 (Data). You reorganize data by using the Organize menu. You design a query by pressing Shift-F2 (Design). Although you do not have to start these operations from the database design screen, you can use this screen as an access point.

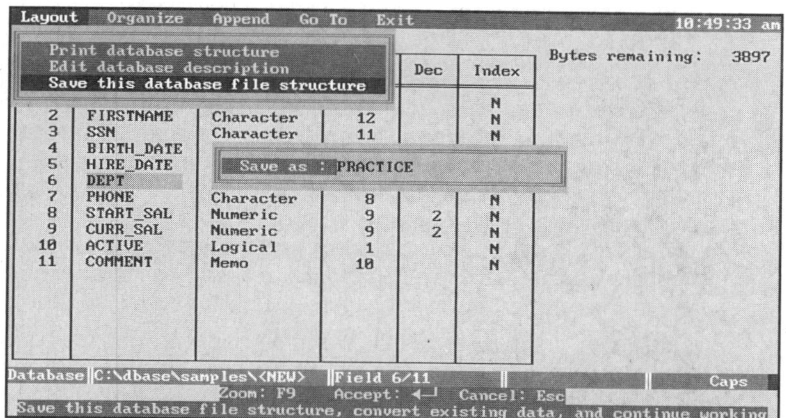


FIG. 6.4

Saving the completed database description.

**NOTE**

For your reference, you may want a paper copy of the structure of the database. A paper copy can be helpful when you need to cite the names of fields or work with the database from the dot prompt. To generate the printout from the database design screen, use the Layout menu and the Print Database Structure command. Assuming that the print settings are correct for your printer, select the Begin Printing option from the print menu that appears. The print menu is discussed in more detail in Chapter 10.

You may find that including a short description of the database is helpful. The description you type appears in the file identification section of the Control Center when you highlight the database file name in the Data panel. You assign the description by using the Layout menu Edit Database Description command. When dBASE presents a fill-in box asking for the description, type the description and press Enter (see fig. 6.5).

After you finish your work in the database design screen, exit back to the Control Center by using the Exit menu. This menu has two options: Save Changes And Exit and Abandon Changes And Exit. You can duplicate the function of the Save Changes And Exit option by pressing Ctrl-End; duplicate the Abandon Changes And Exit option by pressing Esc. If you abandon your work, only the changes you made since the last time you saved the database are lost.

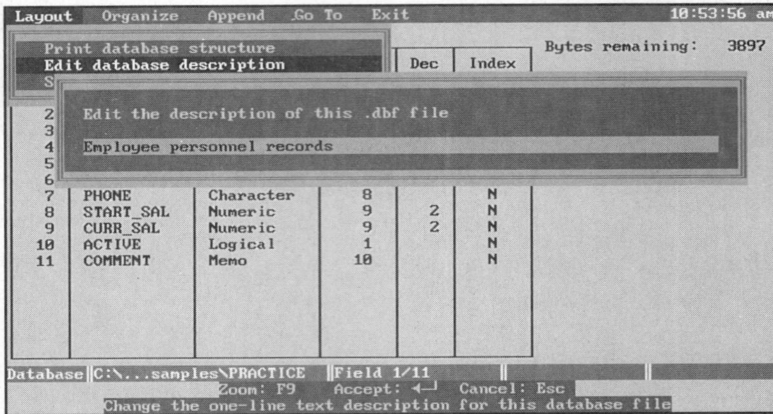


FIG. 6.5

Entering a description for the database file.

# Modifying a Database Structure

After you create a database structure, you may think that the structure is written in stone. With dBASE IV, however, your database can change as the world changes. If you want to make structural changes to a database, reactivate the database design screen. Highlight the database name in the Data panel of the Control Center and press Enter to display the prompt box. Select the Modify Structure/Order option (see fig. 6.6) to return to the database design screen. You then can make changes to each field in the structure. A shortcut that bypasses the prompt box is to highlight the database file name in the Control Panel and press Shift-F2 (Design).

To modify the structure of a database file with the mouse, click on the file name in the Data panel to highlight it, and then click on the `Design:Shift F2` label in the navigation line.

When you make changes to a database for which you have already entered some data, be careful about the kinds of changes you make to the structure. Eventually, dBASE IV pours the data back into the database structure. If you make too many changes or the wrong kinds of changes to your structure when you modify it, the data may no longer "fit" in the structure. If you make a drastic change, such as deleting a field from the structure, all the data that was in that field is lost when you save the structure. You cannot pour something back if you break the vessel.

You may think that changing the name of a field has the same effect because dBASE IV may not recognize the vessel. dBASE IV can recognize the vessel, however, by its name and by the other attributes that define its "shape" (the type and width of the field). Things get complicated and you lose data if you change the name *and* the shape in the same step. As a rule, don't change a field's name and make changes to the type or size of that field or any other field in the same modification. If you must change two attributes of a field, do so in two separate steps. Change the name first, save the structure, then change the type or width, and save the structure again. Being careful safeguards your data through the change.

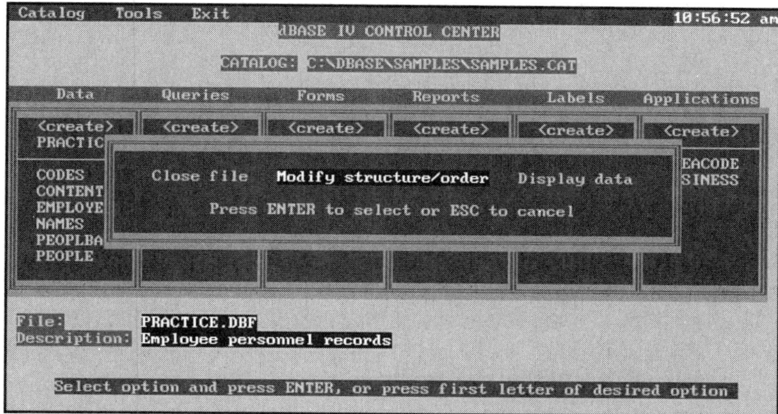


FIG. 6.6

Modifying a database structure.

To more easily modify the structure of a database that has a lot of fields, use the Go To menu from the database design screen (see fig. 6.7). This menu includes commands to move the selector to the top field in the list, the last field in the list, and to any particular field given its number in the list. Activate the Go To menu in the usual way, and then select a command.

```
Layout  Organize  Append  Go To  Exit                         10:58:17 am
                          Top field
                          Last field
                          Field number
Num  Field Name   Field Ty                  Index    Bytes remaining:  3897

 1   LASTNAME     Characte                    N
 2   FIRSTNAME    Character   12              N
 3   SSN          Character   11              N
 4   BIRTH_DATE   Date         8              N
 5   HIRE_DATE    Date         8              N
 6   DEPT         Character   11              N
 7   PHONE        Character    8              N
 8   START_SAL    Numeric      9      2       N
 9   CURR_SAL     Numeric      9      2       N
10   ACTIVE       Logical      1              N
11   COMMENT      Memo        10              N

Database C:\...samples\PRACTICE  Field 1/11
Position selection bar: ↑↓   Select: ◄┘   Leave menu: Esc
Move to the first field in the database file structure
```

FIG. 6.7

The Go To menu of the database design screen.

**For Related Information...**

▸▸ "Working with the Data File," p. 434.

# Summary

In this chapter, you learned how to build database structures. dBASE can handle any kind of data you want to include in the database, from character values to numbers to dates. You also learned about the special logical field type, which handles categories that have only two possible values, and the special memo field type, which handles data that cannot be categorized easily.

You learned how to define each field by using the database design screen. The definition of a field consists of a name, type, width, number of decimal places (if applicable), and index value.

Finally, you learned that you can make changes to the database structure. When saved, a database structure acts as a mold or framework for the data you will place in it. Although you try to define the database structure correctly the first time, dBASE IV is flexible enough to permit modifications to the structure. Be careful when you make changes to the structure so that you don't lose data when you resave the structure.

7

CHAPTER

# Adding and Editing Data

Chapter 6 explained how to create the database structure, which is half the job of putting a database together. In this chapter, you undertake the second half of the job: putting data into the database and making changes to the data. This part of the job is often referred to as *data entry* because you enter data into reserved slots in the database. If you think of the structure of the database as a paper form or information sheet, the job of entering data is similar to the task of filling out the form.

Data entry is obviously an important job, one on which the integrity of the database hinges. If you enter data properly, the questions you later ask of the database provide reliable answers. If you don't enter data carefully or consistently, the answers you get are likely to be wrong to some greater or lesser extent.

## Understanding the Data-Entry Process

In response to your giving a display-data command, such as pressing F2, on the current database (for example, the Practice database), dBASE IV displays a data-entry form on the screen (see fig. 7.1) or the Browse screen. (From the Browse screen, you can press F2 again to reach the data-entry form.) This form is equivalent to the work surface of the Edit screen; it shows all the fields in the database arranged vertically in the order you defined them. Each field name is followed by a "slot" into which you type the value for that field. The slot is as long as the width you defined for that field. In Chapter 2, you learned that dBASE IV applies validity checks to the entries you type based on the field type you assigned to a field. In Chapter 9, you learn that you can refine the validity checks to make them much more powerful. With this basic layout, you can add new records to the database and edit records already in the database.

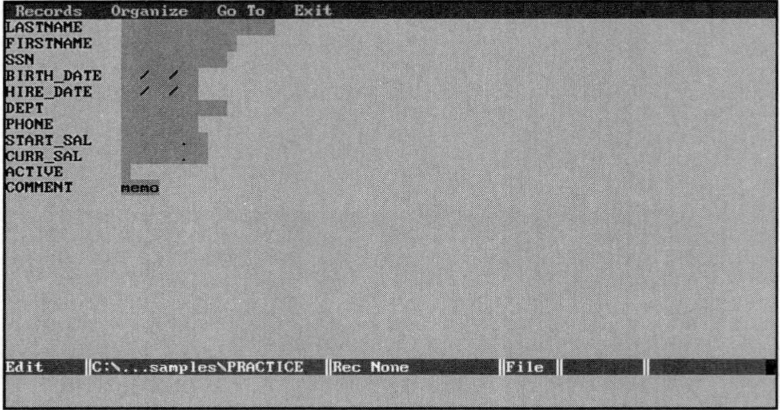


FIG. 7.1

A blank data-entry form for a database.

At any one time, the data-entry form gives you access to one record and to one field in the record. That record is called the *current record* and that field is called the *current field*. To add a new record to the database, you fill out the current field, advance to the next field, fill it out, and continue in this way until all the fields are filled out. If you continue to add records, dBASE IV displays another blank form for the next record you want to add.

**NOTE**

The record you just filled out is not necessarily added immediately to the disk file. The record is first added to a "record buffer" in the computer's memory. When the buffer is full, dBASE IV writes all the records in the buffer to disk. The buffer also is "flushed" when you close the database. To have dBASE IV save each record individually, issue the command SET AUTOSAVE ON from the dot prompt.

dBASE IV assigns each record in the database a *record number*. Each time you add a new record to the database, dBASE IV finds the record with the highest number, adds 1 to it, and assigns that number to the new record. The records you add, therefore, are assigned numbers in the order you enter them in the database. dBASE IV refers to this order as the *natural order* or the *order of entry*. When you display records, they appear in natural order. In Chapter 8, you learn how to alter the natural order to arrange and display records in other ways.

When you first open a database, dBASE IV automatically positions itself at the first record in the database. This location is also referred to as the *top* of the database. When you add records, dBASE goes to the bottom of the database and steps beyond the last record to an area called the *end of file*, or EOF for short. This area is identified on the status bar when you add records. The third section of the status bar reads `Rec EOF/#`, where # represents the total number of records in the database. The only exception to this notation is the case in which no records are in the database at all. In this case, the status bar reads `Rec None`.

# Calling Up Display Screens

The data-entry form is used for adding and editing records. Notice that the data-entry form appears as the work surface of the Edit screen.

In Chapter 5, you learned that the Edit and Browse screens provide two different, but related, views of the database. The Edit screen shows one record to a screen, using the format of a data-entry form; the Browse screen displays multiple records in table view, which is in an arrangement of columns and rows. Each column in the Browse screen represents a single category (field) in the database; each row represents a complete record of data in the database. The names of the fields are listed across the top row of the Browse screen. In the Edit screen, you see a single record with the fields arranged vertically. The names of the fields appear at the left edge of the screen.

You can add and edit records in either view, switching between the two views even within the same activity. The only exception is with a database that has no records. In this case, you cannot switch to Browse view (dBASE IV ignores your request if you try). Because you activate the add and edit record commands from a display screen, the first step in adding or editing records is to call up the display screen.

To access a display screen, follow these steps:

1. In the Control Center, highlight the database name in the Data panel and press Enter, or click on the database name with the mouse. The prompt box shown in figure 7.2 appears.

2. Select the Display Data command, or press F2 (Data). If you are using a mouse, click on `Data:F2`.

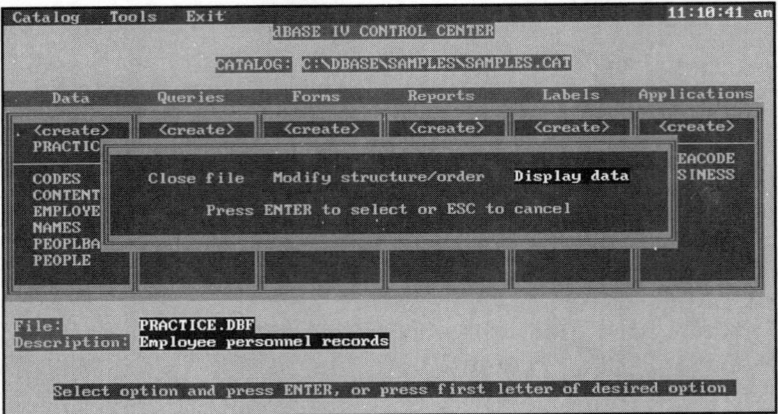


FIG. 7.2

Using the prompt box to display data.

One of the two display screens appears. If your database has no records, the Edit screen appears. If the database does have records, the screen you used for your last viewing appears. If this is your first viewing, dBASE puts you in the Browse screen.

When a particular view is displayed, you can easily switch to the other view by pressing F2 (Data). The only time pressing F2 doesn't work is when the database has no records.

**FROM HERE...**

**For Related Information...**

◂◂ "Understanding dBASE IV Screens," p. 97.

◂◂ "Understanding the Screen Layout," p. 98.

# Adding Records to the Database

If you have a new database, the only thing you can do is add a record. When you display the Edit screen, the data-entry form is placed on the work surface, and the cursor is positioned so that you can type the value for the first field of the first record.

If you are adding records to a database that already has some records, you must take another step after the display screen appears. When the display screen first appears, dBASE IV places the record pointer on the current record, usually the top record. Remember that you add new records past the bottom of the database. For this reason, you must bring the record pointer to the last record, and then signal your intent to add records. You can do this in one step by pulling down the Records menu from the menu bar and selecting the Add New Records command (see fig. 7.3).

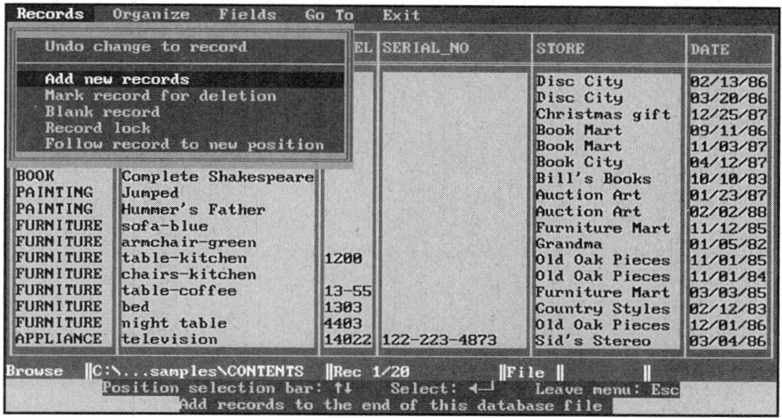


FIG. 7.3

Using the Records menu to add new records.

Another way to add records bypasses the Records menu. If you manually move the record pointer to the end of the database, and then attempt to go to the next record, dBASE IV displays a message asking whether you want to add new records (see fig. 7.4).

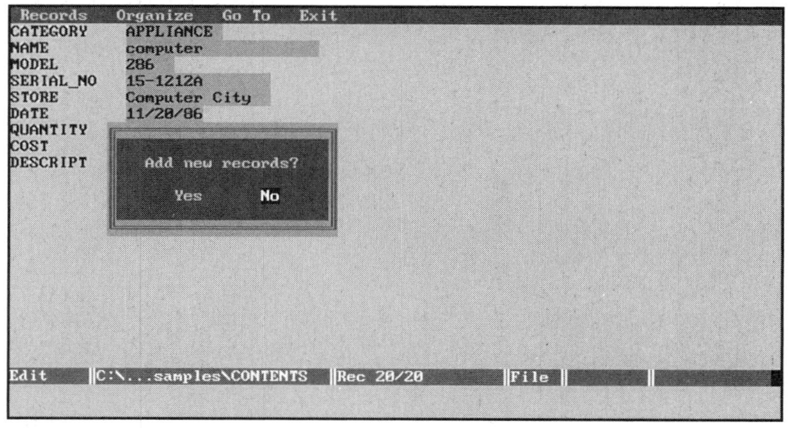


FIG. 7.4

Moving to the bottom of the database to add a new record.

After you signal your intention to add a new record, dBASE IV displays a blank data-entry form in the Edit screen or a blank row in the Browse screen. You fill out the record one field at a time. Depending on how much data you enter in the field, one of two things happens. If the data you enter completely fills the field, dBASE IV beeps and advances the cursor to the next field. If the data does not fill the field, you must signal that you're finished entering data for that field by pressing Enter. Pressing Enter advances the cursor to the next field. When you fill out the last field, dBASE IV advances out of the current record, displays a blank form for the next record, and positions the cursor in the first field of that new record.

**NOTE**

If you're working in a quiet area, you may find distracting the beep dBASE IV makes when you fill a field with data. If you want to turn the beep off for your current working session, you can do so before calling up the display screen from the Control Center. Activate the Tools menu and select the Settings option. From the Settings submenu, select the Bell option and change the setting to OFF by pressing the space bar or Enter, or by clicking with the mouse.

Likewise, if you don't want dBASE IV to automatically advance to the next field, you can turn the Confirm setting ON. If you do this, you must always press Enter (or use the mouse or arrow keys) to advance the cursor to the next field.

## Adding Data to Different Field Types

The type of field you enter data into makes some slight differences in how you enter that data and how it is displayed. In all fields, you enter the data from left to right. In a character field, the data is aligned or justified to the left side of the field. If you do not completely fill the field, you have some trailing blanks to the right of the last character. In some situations, you may want to get rid of those trailing blanks (see Chapter 12).

In a numeric field, the numbers are aligned or justified to the right side of the field. Right justification is helpful in displaying columns of numbers, because the numbers line up on their decimal point. When you enter a new number or replace an existing number, however, you type the digits for the number at the left side of the field. If the number contains decimals, when you press the decimal point the number aligns properly within the field slot. If the number does not contain decimals, it aligns properly when you press Enter to advance the cursor.

dBASE is set up initially to record dates in the form MM/DD/YY. Notice that any date fields in the data-entry form already have the slashes (/) in the field slot to separate the month, day, and year. You do not have to type these slashes when you enter a date, although you can if you want. If you don't type the slashes, you must type a leading zero for any month, day, or year less than 10. To enter the date January 1, 1909, for example, you can type *010109* or *1/1/9*. If you type a slash, dBASE takes that as a signal to end one unit and begin the next. If you make an error entering a date so that what you type is not a valid date, dBASE displays the message `Invalid date (Press space)`. Press the spacebar and edit the entry to make it a valid date.

**NOTE**

You may wonder how you indicate years from different centuries if you have only two year positions to work with in a date field. In fact, dBASE IV stores dates with a century indicator in the form YYYYMMDD. When you enter a date such as *01/01/92*, for example, dBASE stores it as 19920101. dBASE assumes that the date falls in the 20th century. For dates in other centuries, you must change the template to reflect the year with four positions rather than two. To change the template, access the Tools menu at the Control Center, select Settings, and then select Century (see fig. 7.5). By default, the Century setting is OFF. When you change the setting to ON by pressing Enter or the spacebar, or by clicking the mouse, dBASE displays all date templates as MM/DD/YYYY. You then can enter and display dates with a full century specification.

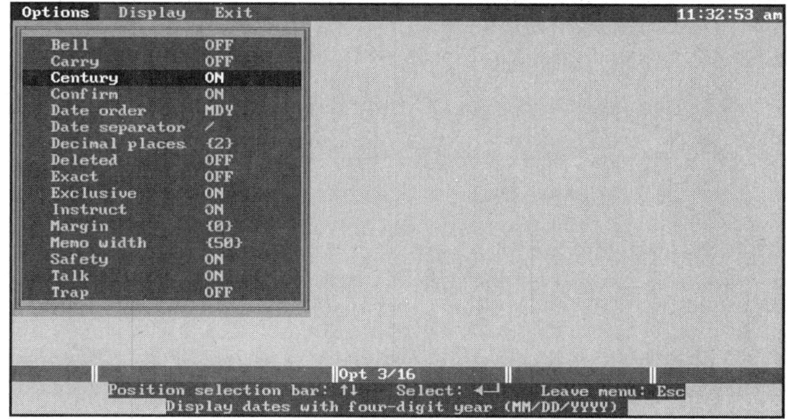


**FIG. 7.5**

Changing the Century setting to ON.

The situation with logical fields is simpler because your choices are limited to T, F, N, or Y in either uppercase or lowercase letters. Attempting to enter anything else causes dBASE to beep without advancing the cursor, although no error message appears.

# Adding Data to Memo Fields

Memo fields present more of a data-entry challenge than other fields because the data is stored in a separate file (see Chapter 6 for an explanation of memo fields). When you view a database with memo fields in Edit or Browse mode, you see only a marker in the field. The marker is simply the word `memo` or `MEMO`, displayed in uppercase or lowercase letters. In the database shown in figure 7.6, for example, the COMMENT field has memo markers in both uppercase and lowercase letters. By convention, dBASE IV uses `memo` to indicate that the record has no text in that memo field; `MEMO` indicates that the record does have text in the memo field.

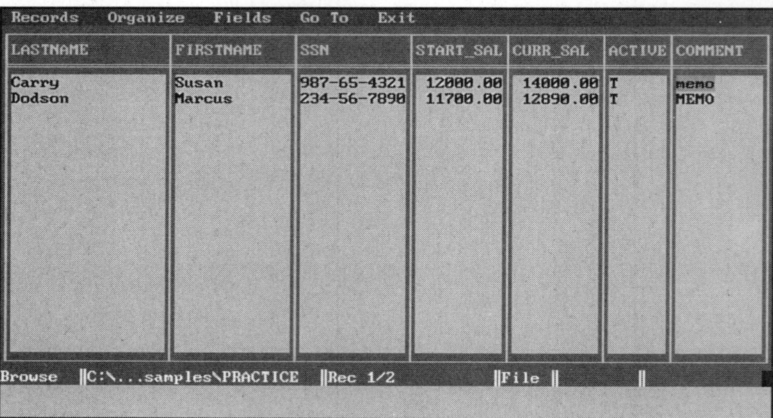


FIG. 7.6

The markers for a memo field.

If the record has text in the memo field, you don't see that text until you open the memo field. If you want to add text to a memo, you must open the field before you can add text. You can open a memo field in one of four ways:

- Place the cursor on the memo marker and press Ctrl-Home.
- Place the cursor on the memo marker and press F9 (Zoom).

- From the preceding field in the record press F4 (Next); from the following field press F3 (Previous). These keys advance the cursor and open the memo in one move.
- Double-click on the memo marker with the mouse.

## Using the dBASE Word Processor

After you open a memo field, the regular display disappears and dBASE IV gives you access to its built-in word processor (see fig. 7.7). As you type the text of the memo, dBASE word-wraps it to fit within the margins set by the ruler line, which appears below the word processor's menu bar. The ruler line marks the margins for the memo with the characters [ for the left margin and ] for the right margin. By default, the left margin is set at 0 and the right margin is set at 65, meaning that dBASE can put up to 65 characters on each line of the memo. Because dBASE IV word-wraps text, you don't have to press Enter at the end of each line of text. Press Enter only when you want to end a paragraph or override the word-wrapping feature for a particular line.

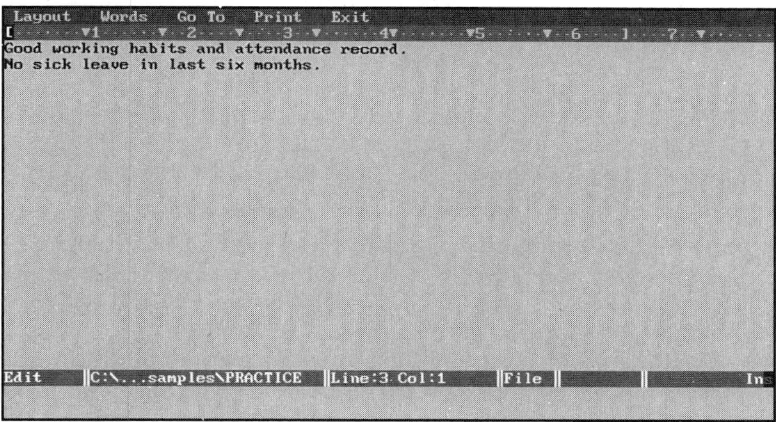


FIG. 7.7

An open memo field within the word processor.

After you type the memo, save it. When you save the memo, you exit from the word processor and return to the memo marker in the Edit or Browse screen. Save the memo in one of these ways:

- Press Ctrl-End.
- Press F3 (Previous) or F4 (Next). These keys also advance the cursor to the previous or next field in the display screen after leaving the word processor.

- Access the word processor's Exit menu, and then select the Save Changes And Exit option.

If you are writing a long memo, you can save it periodically as you work without exiting the word processor by using the word processor's Layout menu. This menu has only one command: Save This Memo Field.

If you change your mind after entering any new text and don't want to save the memo, press Esc to abandon the memo. You also can access the Exit menu, and then select Abandon Changes And Exit.

If you have previously saved the memo through the Save This Memo Field command, abandoning the word processor will not undo the previous save. You must delete all the memo text and then save changes and exit, or press Ctrl-End.

## Understanding More about the Word Processor

The word processor is used not just for writing memos, but for writing certain types of reports (see Chapter 10) and for writing program files (see Chapter 16). When you use the word processor in these situations, the menus look different from the menus you use when you write memos. See the referenced chapters for illustrations and explanations of the differences. Another use for the word processor is editing macros (see Chapter 5). When you edit macros, the word processor menus are the same as for editing memos.

The word processor menu bar has pull-down menus that enable you to make adjustments to the format of the text (the Words menu), to move the cursor to a specific word or phrase within the text (the Go To menu), and to print the text (the Print menu). Some of these same commands also are available through hot-key shortcuts. In addition, some key commands have no equivalents on the menus. Table 7.1 lists the possible commands in the word processor. These commands function the same way for all uses of the word processor.

**Table 7.1 Word Processing Commands**

| Function | Menu/Command | Key command | Details |
|---|---|---|---|
| Delete previous word | | Ctrl-Backspace | |
| Delete to end of current word | | Ctrl-T | |

| Function | Menu/Command | Key command | Details |
|---|---|---|---|
| Delete current line | Words/Remove Line | Ctrl-Y | |
| Insert new line | Words/Add Line | Ctrl-N | Forces text to the right of the cursor to a new line |
| Insert page break | Words/Insert Page Break | | Causes text following the page break to appear at the top of a new printed page |
| Go to specific line | GoTo/Go To Line Number | | Type the line number at the prompt |
| Search for specific text | GoTo/Forward Search or Backward Search | Shift-F5 | Type the text to search for at the prompt |
| Search for next occurrence of text | GoTo/Forward Search | Shift-F4 | |
| Search for previous occurrence of text | GoTo/Backward Search | Shift-F3 | |
| Replace searched text with specified text | GoTo/Replace | Shift-F6 | Indicate the search text and the replace text; acknowledge the replacement for each occurrence |
| Select text for copy, move, or deletion | | F6 | Move the cursor over the text to be selected and press Enter, or drag the mouse over the text and release the button. Press Esc to cancel the selection. |

*continues*

**Table 7.1 Continued**

| Function | Menu/Command | Key command | Details |
|---|---|---|---|
| Move text | | F7 | Select text, and then move the cursor to the target position using the arrow keys or the mouse |
| Copy text | | F8 | Select text, and then move the cursor to the target position by using the arrow keys or the mouse, and press F8 |
| Delete block | | Delete | Select text beforehand |

In addition to the editing commands, the word processor includes some special cursor-movement keys, listed in table 7.2.

**Table 7.2 Cursor-Movement Keys in the Word Processor**

| Action | Keys to press |
|---|---|
| Move to following word | Ctrl-→ |
| Move to previous word | Ctrl-← |
| Move down one screen | PgDn |
| Move up one screen | PgUp |
| Move to top of text | Ctrl-PgUp |
| Move to bottom of text | Ctrl-PgDn |
| Move to beginning of current line | Home |
| Move to end of current line | End |

You also can use the mouse to reposition the cursor by moving the mouse pointer to the appropriate location and clicking.

**TIP**

The Words menu has an interesting command that gives you control over the left margin of the memo. This command, called Enable Automatic Indent, determines how the Tab and Shift-Tab keys operate. If you set this command to YES and press the Ins key (the `Ins` indicator appears on the status bar), the next time you press Tab, the left margin is reset one tab stop to the right—eight positions. Any text on the line is pushed to the right. If the line is part of a paragraph, the rest of the paragraph is aligned at the new tab stop (see fig. 7.8).

Each time you press the Tab key, the text moves another tab position to the right. Reverse this effect by pressing Shift-Tab to reset the margin one tab setting to the left.

If Enable Automatic Indent is set to OFF and the `Ins` indicator is on, pressing the Tab key indents only the first line of the paragraph; the left margin isn't reset. If the `Ins` indicator is off, pressing the Tab key moves only the cursor; the text on the line doesn't move.

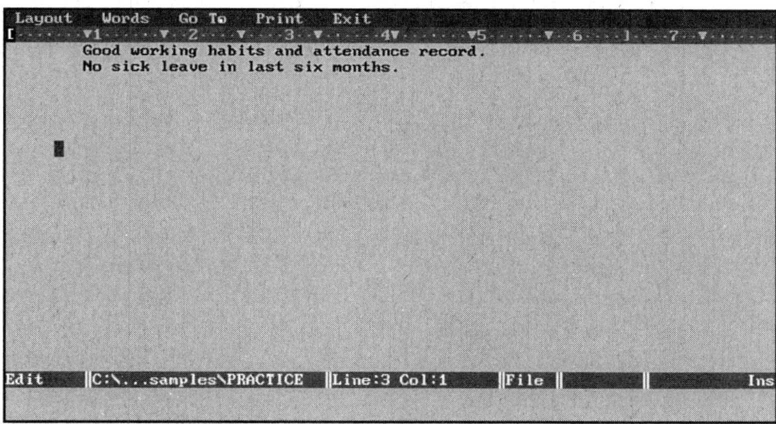


FIG. 7.8

Pressing Tab with the automatic indent enabled in the Words menu.

With the other commands available through the Words menu, you can turn the ruler line off (Hide Ruler) and read or write a memo from or to a text file (Write/Read Text File). If you have a document written in another word processor and that document has been saved as a text file or ASCII file, for example, you can incorporate that file into a dBASE IV memo by using the Read Text From File option. Using this option saves you the trouble of typing the text a second time. When you select the Write Selection To File option, you save an already typed memo as a text file (see fig. 7.9). The file is saved with the name you provide, along with the TXT extension.

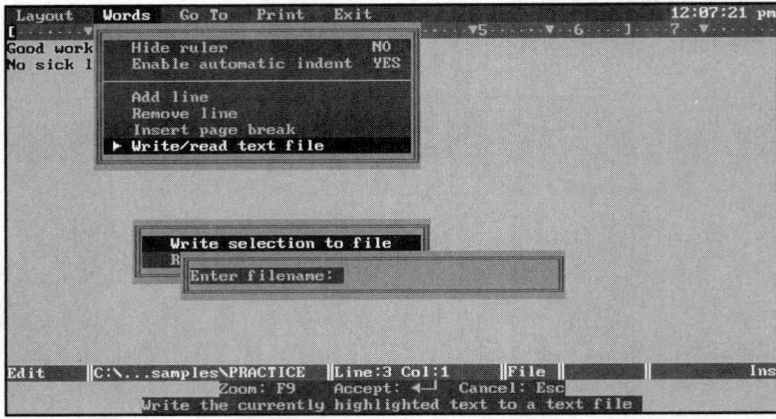


FIG. 7.9

Writing a memo to an external text file.

The Print menu enables you to print a copy of the memo currently on-screen. The word processor Print menu has options similar to those on other Print menus (see Chapters 10 and 11 for details).

# Editing a Record As You Add It

Before you move to the next blank record, you can correct the current record by bringing the cursor back to the item you want to change, erasing the error, and substituting the correction. How you move the cursor depends on the display screen you're using. If you are in the Edit screen, use the up- and down-arrow keys to move the cursor to the preceding and following fields. If you are in the Browse screen, use Tab instead of the up-arrow key and Shift-Tab instead of the down-arrow key to move between fields. The Tab and Shift-Tab keys also work in the Edit screen. In either screen, use the left- and right-arrow keys to move the cursor within a field. If you exceed the limits of a field, the left- and right-arrow keys advance the cursor to the adjacent field.

You also can use the mouse to move the cursor to the field you want to edit by repositioning the mouse pointer and clicking. Clicking the leftmost and rightmost vertical borders in the Browse screen moves the cursor one field to the left or right.

After you localize the error, erase it by using the Backspace key (if the cursor is to the right of the error) or the Delete key (if the cursor is directly on the error). If you want to erase the entire value in a field, use the Field menu Blank Field command in the Browse screen.

You also can erase a field partially or totally by using Ctrl-T or Ctrl-Y. These keys erase from the point of the cursor to the right. If you want to erase the entire field, the cursor should be at the left edge of the field.

Depending on the type of error you are correcting, you sometimes can type the correction right over the error instead of deleting the error first. If you want to insert new characters in the middle of a string, press the Ins key, position the cursor where the new characters are to be inserted, and type. When you press Ins, the `Ins` indicator appears in the status bar. Pressing Ins a second time turns the `Ins` indicator off and returns dBASE to overwrite mode.

# Editing Existing Records

In principle, editing an existing record presents no new challenges other than finding the record you want to edit. After you find the record, changing that record is a matter of following the instructions presented in the preceding section.

When you use the data-entry form to edit records, dBASE IV first must locate the record you want and make it the current record. You learn several ways to locate the record, but the important point to understand is that you can make changes only to the current record.

If you have made one or more changes to a record and then decide that the changes are incorrect and you want to restore the original data, undo all the changes you made by using the Record menu Undo Change To Record command.

**WARNING:** After you move the record pointer from the current record to a different record, dBASE IV records the changes to the current record. You no longer can undo the changes, even if you make that record current again.

# Deleting Records and Recovering Deleted Records

You make individual changes to records to update the status of fields whose values change. In cases in which all the values for a record have changed, erasing all the current values and typing new values from scratch may be easier. You can do this with the Blank Record command from the Records menu. Blanking a record leaves an *empty* record in the database; it does not *remove* the record from the database. If you want to eliminate the record totally to reflect an employee's resignation, for example, you must delete it.

Deleting records is a two-step process. First you place a mark on the record, indicating that you want to delete the record, and you eliminate all the marked records. The second step is called *packing the database*. dBASE IV has you delete in two steps so that you have the opportunity to reverse your decision and unmark a record. Up until you pack the database, any or all of the records you mark can be unmarked and spared deletion.

Marking a record is done in one of two ways. You can use the Records menu Mark Record For Deletion command. This command places a `Del` indicator on the current record; be sure that you select the correct record before issuing the command. The `Del` indicator appears in the sixth section of the status bar (see fig. 7.10). You also can mark the record by using the hot key Ctrl-U.

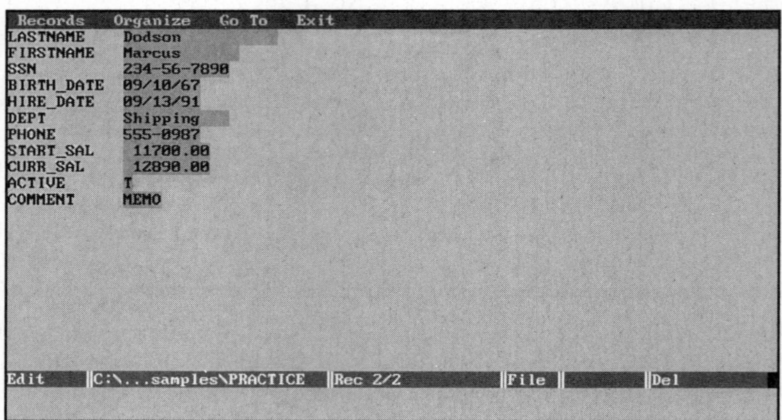


**FIG. 7.10**

A record marked for deletion with the `Del` indicator.

After you mark a record, you can remove the mark by using the Records menu again. For a marked record, the menu replaces Mark Record For Deletion with Clear Deletion Mark. Select Clear Deletion Mark to remove the mark from the current record. You also can remove the deletion mark for a record by pressing Ctrl-U a second time. If you want to remove the marks on all deleted records, use the Organize menu Unmark All Records command.

After you determine that you do want to pack the database, give the command to eliminate all the marked records: select Erase Marked Records from the Organize menu.

> **WARNING:** Erasing marked records permanently deletes the marked records and renumbers all the records in the database. You cannot recover the deleted records at this point.

# Altering the Browse Screen During Editing

If you prefer to make changes to the database in the Browse screen rather than the Edit screen, you have some additional controls over the appearance of the fields on the screen and the placement of the cursor. These controls are particularly useful with databases that have a lot of fields. As an example, assume that you are working with the database shown in figure 7.11. If you view this database in the Browse screen, you have too many fields to display in one screen width. In addition to the fields you can see in the current screen width, there are fields to the right hidden from view. Note that only the first three characters of the PHONE field are visible on the right of the screen.

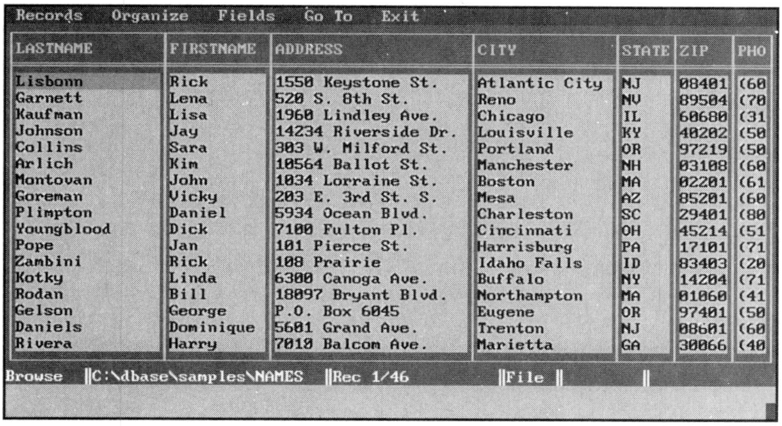

Records Organize Fields Go To Exit

| LASTNAME | FIRSTNAME | ADDRESS | CITY | STATE | ZIP | PHO |
|---|---|---|---|---|---|---|
| Lisbonn | Rick | 1550 Keystone St. | Atlantic City | NJ | 08401 | (60 |
| Garnett | Lena | 520 S. 8th St. | Reno | NV | 89504 | (70 |
| Kaufman | Lisa | 1960 Lindley Ave. | Chicago | IL | 60680 | (31 |
| Johnson | Jay | 14234 Riverside Dr. | Louisville | KY | 40202 | (50 |
| Collins | Sara | 303 W. Milford St. | Portland | OR | 97219 | (50 |
| Arlich | Kim | 10564 Ballot St. | Manchester | NH | 03108 | (60 |
| Montovan | John | 1034 Lorraine St. | Boston | MA | 02201 | (61 |
| Goreman | Vicky | 203 E. 3rd St. S. | Mesa | AZ | 85201 | (60 |
| Plimpton | Daniel | 5934 Ocean Blvd. | Charleston | SC | 29401 | (80 |
| Youngblood | Dick | 7100 Fulton Pl. | Cincinnati | OH | 45214 | (51 |
| Pope | Jan | 101 Pierce St. | Harrisburg | PA | 17101 | (71 |
| Zambini | Rick | 108 Prairie | Idaho Falls | ID | 83403 | (20 |
| Kotky | Linda | 6300 Canoga Ave. | Buffalo | NY | 14204 | (71 |
| Rodan | Bill | 18097 Bryant Blvd. | Northampton | MA | 01060 | (41 |
| Gelson | George | P.O. Box 6045 | Eugene | OR | 97401 | (50 |
| Daniels | Dominique | 5601 Grand Ave. | Trenton | NJ | 08601 | (60 |
| Rivera | Harry | 7010 Balcom Ave. | Marietta | GA | 30066 | (40 |

Browse ║C:\dbase\samples\NAMES ║Rec 1/46 ║File ║

FIG. 7.11

A sample Browse screen.

Arranging the Browse screen so that the LASTNAME, FIRSTNAME, and PHONE fields are visible on the screen simultaneously would be helpful. If you "pan" the screen to the right using the Tab key or the mouse, the first field disappears from the display. You can solve this problem by locking the first two fields on the screen with the Fields menu Lock Fields On Left command.

Specify the number of fields from the left side of the screen you want to lock. For this example, lock two fields (see fig. 7.12). Fields that are locked do not move when you pan the screen.

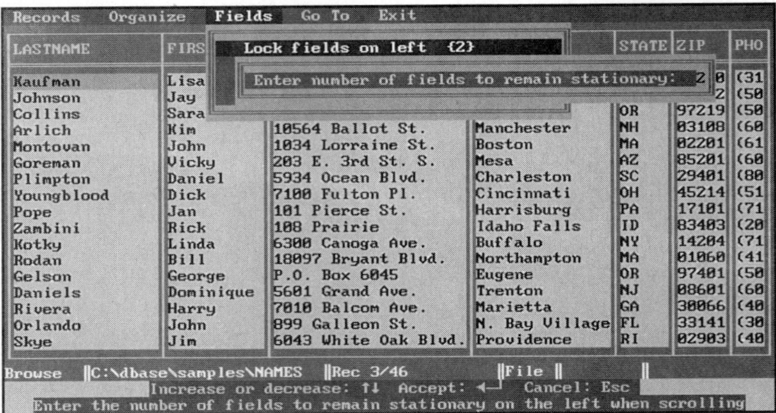


FIG. 7.12

Locking fields on the screen.

Another way to make room on the screen for more fields is to resize a field. If the CITY field normally is 14 characters wide, but you only need to see 10 characters, for example, you can narrow the width of the display for that field.

To squeeze the CITY field, put the cursor in the CITY field and use the Fields menu Size Field command (see fig. 7.13). The message line displays a prompt asking you to use the left- and right-arrow keys to resize the field. When you have resized the field, press Enter to end the operation.

You also can use the Shift-F7 (Size) key to change the width of the field.

Another Fields menu option you can use when you need to edit one field for a series of records is the Freeze Field command. This command asks you to specify the field you want to edit; dBASE restricts the cursor to just that field. You cannot move the cursor to any other field in the database unless you unfreeze the cursor. After selecting the Freeze Field command from the Fields menu, type the name of the field you want to freeze (see fig. 7.14). To undo the freeze, issue the command a second time and erase the target field.

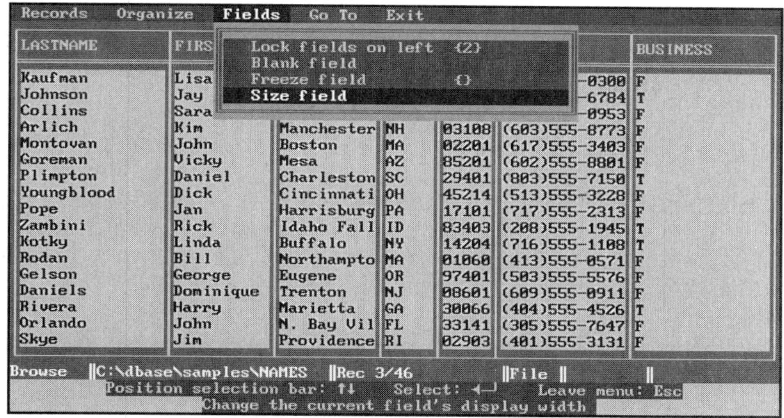


FIG. 7.13

Resizing a field with the Size field command.

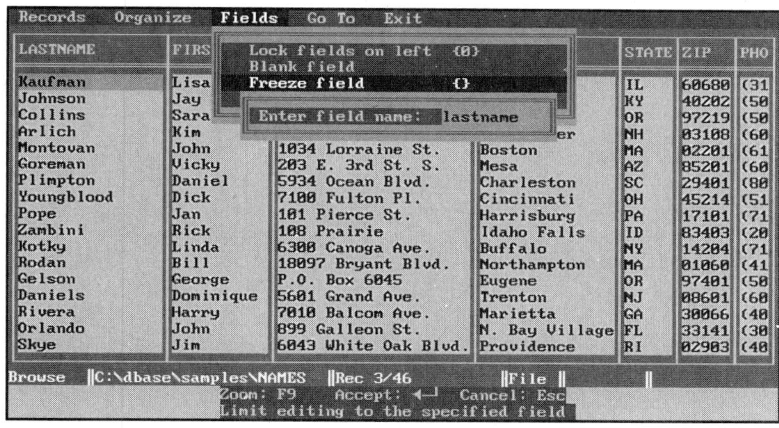


FIG. 7.14

Freezing a field on the screen.

# Searching for the Record To Edit

Now that you know the techniques you can use to edit a database, consider the set of tools dBASE IV provides for locating the records you need to edit. If you're dealing with a database that has a lot of records, using the cursor keys to search for the one record you want to edit out of thousands is inconvenient. If you use the cursor keys to search for a record, you must check the values in the search field for each record until you find the one you want. If you start at the top and go down through the database, and the record you want is near the top, the search is over quickly. If the record is near the bottom, however, your patience wears thin long before you find the record. Fortunately, dBASE IV can search the database in a fraction of the time it takes you to search manually.

You can use the Go To menu of the Edit or Browse screen to search a database quickly (see fig. 7.15). The menu works the same for both screens. The two commands you use to search are Forward Search and Backward Search. Before you issue either of these commands, however, position the cursor in the field you want to search; then specify the value in that field for which you are searching.

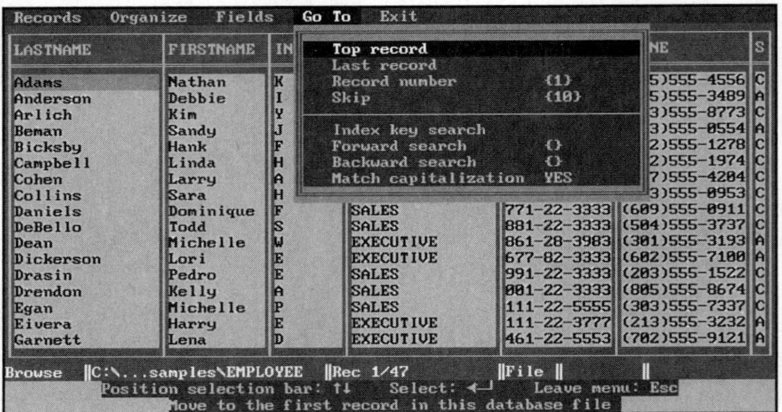


FIG. 7.15

The Go To menu of the Edit and Browse screens.

If you are interested in finding the name of the regional representative in Buffalo, NY, for example, place the cursor in the CITY field, access the GoTo menu, select Forward Search, type *Buffalo* at the `Enter search string:` prompt, and press Enter (see fig. 7.16). dBASE IV looks forward through the database from the current record and stops when it encounters a city value equal to *Buffalo*. dBASE then makes this record the current one and places it at the top of the screen. If dBASE doesn't find a match before reaching the end of the database, it cycles to the top of the database and continues the search from there. If it cannot find *Buffalo*, dBASE displays a `Not found` message and ends the search.

**TIP** dBASE enters your search value in the Forward Search and Backward Search slots when you enter the value in either slot, which enables you to shift the search forward or backward without retyping the value.

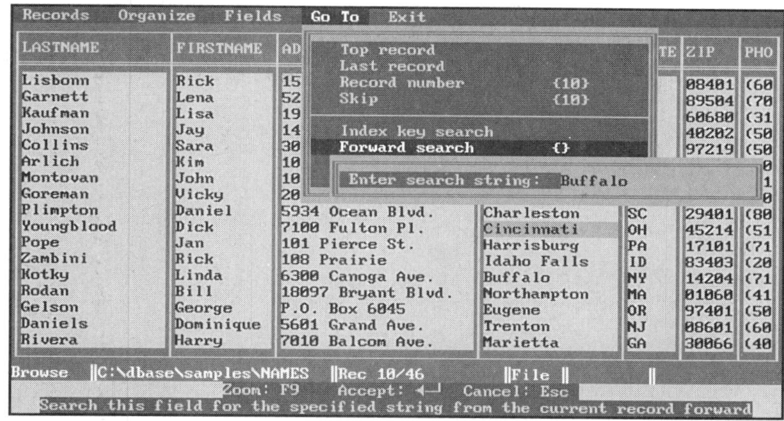


FIG. 7.16

Specifying the search value.

If the database contains more than one *Buffalo* in the CITY field, you can search for additional occurrences by reissuing the Forward Search command or by pressing Shift-F4 (Find Next). If you want to go back to a previous occurrence, issue the Backward Search command or press Shift-F3 (Find Previous).

dBASE IV locates only exact matches; you must type the search value exactly as it appears in the database. One exception to this rule applies to uppercase and lowercase matches. dBASE ignores the case of the characters as it searches if you set the Match Capitalization option in the GoTo menu to NO.

You can use wild-card characters in the search string. A *wild card* can be an asterisk (*) or a question mark (?). An asterisk signifies that you don't care what precedes or follows the literal characters in the search string. If you're looking for New York and you type *New** as the search string, for example, dBASE finds New York as well as New Orleans, New Brighton, and any other city beginning with New.

The question mark takes the place of a single position in the search string. If you are looking for cities with names of four letters, for example, use the search string ????. Four question marks limit the search to those cities with four letters. If the first character of the city name has to be M, for example, modify the search string by typing *M???*.

If you want to move randomly through the database, you can take advantage of the other commands in the Go To menu. The Top Record and Last Record commands take you to the first and last records in the database. The Record Number command moves to the record with the number you specify. The Skip command designates a number of records you jump between. The default is set to 10, but you can change it to jump in larger or smaller increments. You have to repeat the command to keep skipping, although dBASE returns your skip setting from one command to the next. The last option, Index Key Search, requires an index. This command is discussed in Chapter 8.

FROM HERE...

**For Related Information...**

▸▸ "Finding What You're Looking For," p. 448.

# Generating a Quick Report

As you have seen, dBASE enables you to easily enter and edit information in your database. At times, you need a hard copy of your database information. This hard copy, or *report*, enables you to view all the data so that you can, ahead of time, determine which records need editing. You also can take a hard copy of data with you, if your computer is not one that travels easily.

Although dBASE gives you the capability of creating professional-looking reports, you also can easily print quick reports. A *quick report* is a columnar report that provides necessary information, such as a page number for each page, the date the report is printed, the name of each field as a heading, and all the data in the database. Each field is represented in a column. Figure 7.17 shows a quick report of the Project database generated by dBASE IV. This database was introduced earlier in this chapter.

Creating a quick report is easy. From the Control Center, use the arrow keys to highlight in the Data panel the database for which you want to create a quick report (see fig. 7.18). To create the quick report, press Shift-F9 (Quick Report). A menu appears on the screen (see fig. 7.19). This is the same menu you see when you open the Print menu when creating a custom report (as described in Chapter 10).

The following chart lists the options on the menu in figure 7.19:

| Option | Purpose |
|---|---|
| Begin Printing | Send the report to the selected destination (printer or file) |
| Eject Page Now | Use for form-feed paper |

| Option | Purpose |
|---|---|
| View Report On Screen | Print report to screen |
| Use Print Form { } | Use custom printer settings |
| Save Settings To Print Form | Save custom printer settings |
| Destination | Display a menu to select printer or file as the destination |
| Control of Printer | Display menu to select text quality and page-advance options |
| Output Options | Display menu to select pages to print, starting page number, and number of copies |
| Page Dimensions | Display menu to select page length, offset, and line spacing |

Page No. 1
07/25/92

| PROJID | CUSTOMER | ACT_DATE | REVENUE | CLOSED | COMMENT |
|---|---|---|---|---|---|
| ST8810 | Stacey Toons | 02/03/91 | 450.00 | Y | This project was billed at a premium rate because of customer rush order. |
| DR8811 | Drexel Ranger | 11/06/91 | 1250.00 | Y | |
| FK8901 | Frank Kisser | 01/22/92 | 2675.00 | Y | This project was billed at a premium rate because of customer rush order. |
| MT8902 | Matt Tunney | 02/12/92 | 1025.00 | N | |
| BR8812 | Ben Radcliffe | 12/18/91 | 925.00 | Y | Follow up with customer in two years for addition to this project. |
| MR8903 | Molly Richards | 03/04/91 | 8750.00 | N | |
| ST8812A | Stacey Toons | 10/01/91 | 1200.00 | Y | |
| ST8902 | Stacey Toons | 12/15/91 | 3465.00 | Y | Next project in 1992. |
| BR8902B | Ben Radcliffe | 02/17/92 | 4320.00 | N | Customer testing project with company internally before completion of the project. |
| BR8902C | Ben Radcliffe | 02/25/92 | 2500.00 | N | |
| ST8812B | Stacey Toons | 12/16/91 | 560.00 | Y | |
| MR8902 | Molly Richards | 02/23/92 | 800.00 | N | |
| DD8809 | Dede Diamond | 09/28/91 | 2600.00 | Y | |
| WT8811 | Wayne Tibbets | 11/11/91 | 125.00 | Y | Worked on small project hoping to get larger projects. |
| BR8902D | Ben Radcliffe | 02/27/91 | 795.00 | N | Perfoming this work at minimal fee as a promo for this customer. |
| BR8902A | Ben Radcliffe | 02/12/91 | 795.00 | Y | |
| | | | 32235.00 | | |

FIG. 7.17

A quick report.

To print the quick report to the printer, highlight Begin Printing on the Print menu and press Enter. The quick report prints to the printer and looks like the report shown in figure 7.17. Notice in the quick report that any numeric fields are totaled and the total is printed at the bottom of the report. For more information about writing reports in dBASE IV, see Chapter 10.

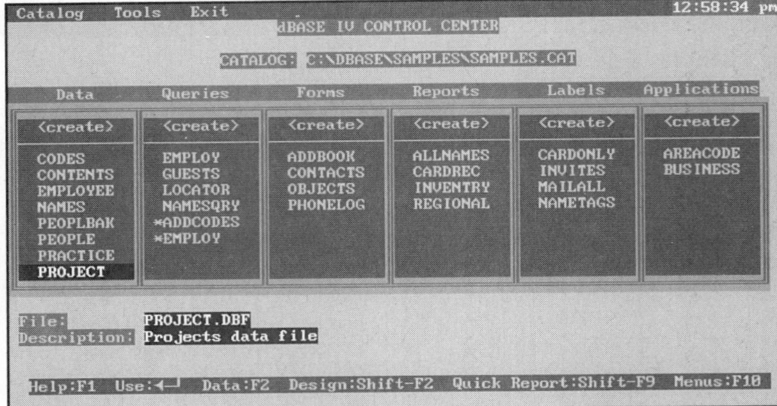


FIG. 7.18

Highlighting the database for which you want a quick report.

```
Catalog  Tools  Exit                                   12:59:07 pm
                    dBASE IV CONTROL CENTER
          CATALOG: C:\DBASE\SAMPLES\SAMPLES.CAT
    Begin printing              Reports   Labels    Applications
    Eject page now
    View report on screen       <create>  <create>  <create>

    Use print form  {}          ALLNAMES  CARDONLY  AREACODE
    Save settings to print form CARDREC   INVITES   BUSINESS
                                INVENTRY  MAILALL
  ► Destination                 REGIONAL  NAMETAGS
  ► Control of printer
  ► Output options
  ► Page dimensions

File:        PROJECT.DBF
Description: Projects data file
     Position selection bar: ↑↓   Select: ↵   Leave menu: Esc
            Start printing, using current print settings
```

FIG. 7.19

The menu that appears after you press Shift-F9.

# Summary

In this chapter, you learned the general strategy used to add new records to a database and alter values after you enter a record. Adding records is a simple procedure that requires you to choose the view you want to use: Edit or Browse. The Edit screen presents records one at a time; the Browse screen displays as many records as fit on the screen.

The disadvantage of the Browse screen is that you see a limited number of fields on-screen at any one time. dBASE IV includes some commands in the Fields menu, however, that partially compensate for this limitation. These commands enable you to freeze a field on-screen, lock certain fields on the display, and resize fields.

You also learned that dBASE includes numerous editing commands to control insertion, deletion, and substitution operations. You can use the delete commands to mark entire records for deletion, recover the record, and finally pack the database.

Finally, you learned how to use dBASE to perform routine searches for specific values in the database for the purpose of locating the records you want to edit. These searches can be exact or can include wild cards to specify a less exact match. You also learned how to obtain a quick report of the database so that you can have a hard copy of your data.

8

CHAPTER

# Organizing the Database

A database is set up to solve problems. The kinds of problems you can solve depend on the fields you put in the database and how you define those fields in the database structure. At times, however, you may want to view or output the database's records in an order other than the one in which you put the records into the database. Assume that you have to get out a mailing to your customers as cheaply as possible. If you send the mailing bulk rate, you save a lot on postage. The post office, however, requires that bulk mail be presorted by ZIP code. The problem is to organize the list numerically by ZIP code.

To solve the organization problem, dBASE IV provides indexing and sorting tools, both of which are available on the Organize menus of the Edit, Browse, and Database design screens.

## Understanding the Concept of an Index

The most efficient way to organize a database is to establish an *index* for the field on which you want the records ordered. An index directs the display screen to show the records in a particular order. Instead of showing records in the order they were entered in the database, the index imposes a new display order on the database. You should understand that the index does not actually rearrange the records in the disk file; the index only causes them to *appear* rearranged on-screen.

Suppose that you have the following database:

| Record # | Name | ZIP Code |
|---|---|---|
| 1 | Jones | 25149 |
| 2 | Smith | 31511 |
| 3 | Jefferson | 21691 |
| 4 | Pauly | 31972 |
| 5 | Richmond | 21101 |

If you organize this database so that the ZIP codes are in numerical order, the database appears on-screen in the following order:

| Index # | Name | ZIP Code |
|---|---|---|
| 1 | Richmond | 21101 |
| 2 | Jefferson | 21691 |
| 3 | Jones | 25149 |
| 4 | Smith | 31511 |
| 5 | Pauly | 31972 |

If you think about it, an index is equivalent in function and purpose to an author catalog in a library. The author catalog contains an alphabetized list of entries by author, in which each entry points to the location of the book on the shelves. A dBASE IV index does the same thing: it provides a list in alphabetical (or numerical or chronological) order, in which each entry points to the location of the full record in the database. When you display data by using an index, the records appear rearranged in the Browse and Edit screens; if you look at the status bar, however, you see that the record pointer still refers to the record by its original record number.

dBASE IV recognizes two types of indexes: a *multiple index* or *MDX index*, and an *NDX index*. The NDX index is really a carryover from earlier versions of dBASE and is included in dBASE IV for the purpose of maintaining compatibility with earlier versions. If you have never worked with dBASE

or if you are starting new applications in dBASE IV, you may never have to use NDX indexes. At times, however, you may want to create a separate index file for special purposes, so dBASE IV 1.5 enables you to have both MDX files and NDX files. The advantage to using the MDX multiple index file is that dBASE IV automatically updates all the indexes in the file without you having to open several different index files.

The letters *MDX* and *NDX* refer to the file extension assigned to the index. (Indexes are stored on the disk under a file name.) If you work with an MDX index, dBASE IV stores the index on disk under the same name as the database but distinguishes the index from the database by assigning the extension MDX. Remember that the database file has the extension DBF.

You may have to index on more than one field. With a customer database, for example, you may want to solve some problems with a list of customers alphabetized by last name; you may want to solve other problems with a list alphabetized by city. If dBASE IV provided only one index, you would have to re-create whatever index you needed every time you wanted to use it.

Instead, dBASE IV uses the MDX file as a repository for all the indexes you need for the database, up to a total of 47. If you need more than one index, you create each separately and supply each a name. dBASE IV stores each index in the MDX file and references the indexes by the names you assigned. dBASE refers to the name of the index as the *index tag*.

## Creating an Index

You can create an index in two ways. The first way is simple, requiring only that you mark a field in the Database design screen. Chapter 6 explained that the structure of the database includes an option for each field called Index. For this option, you can specify Yes or No; the default is No. If you change the value of the Index setting to Yes during database design or modification, dBASE IV creates an index with a tag of the same name as the field name. Creating the index is that simple. Figure 8.1 shows the Database design screen. Notice that the LASTNAME, CITY, and ZIP fields are marked Y in the Index column.

**NOTE** The index that dBASE creates through the Index field in the structure table is *ascending*; that is, the index is organized from the lowest value to the highest value. For character fields, the index also is organized in ASCII sorting sequence. To understand the distinction between ASCII and dictionary sorting sequences, see the section "Reorganizing the Database by Sorting," later in this chapter.

Layout Organize Append Go To Exit 4:57:44 pm

Bytes remaining: 3920

| Num | Field Name | Field Type | Width | Dec | Index |
|---|---|---|---|---|---|
| 1 | LASTNAME | Character | 15 | | Y |
| 2 | FIRSTNAME | Character | 10 | | N |
| 3 | ADDRESS | Character | 20 | | N |
| 4 | CITY | Character | 14 | | Y |
| 5 | STATE | Character | 2 | | N |
| 6 | ZIP | Character | 5 | | Y |
| 7 | PHONE | Character | 13 | | N |
| 8 | BUSINESS | Logical | 1 | | N |

Database C:\dbase\samples\NAMES Field 8/8

Enter the field name. Insert/Delete field:Ctrl-N/Ctrl-U

Field names begin with a letter and may contain letters, digits and underscores

FIG. 8.1

The Index column of the Database design screen.

The second way to create an index relies on the Organize menu. This menu is available from the Database design screen and the Browse or Edit screen (see fig. 8.2). With the Create New Index option from the Organize menu, you can create a simple index on a single field. You also can create more complex indexes that use more than one field.

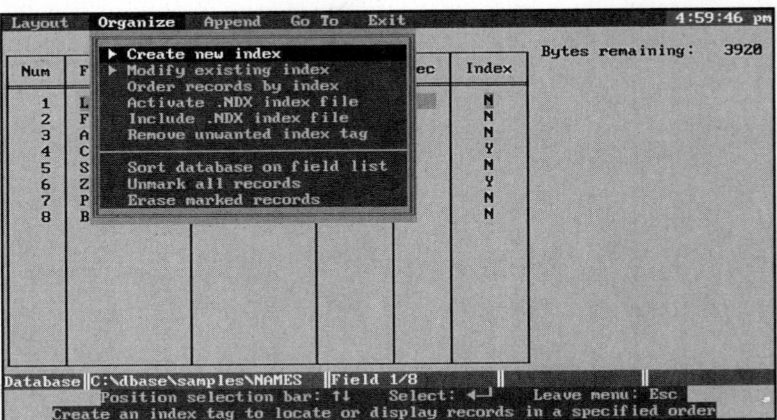


FIG. 8.2

The Organize menu.

Suppose that you want to create an index that organizes employees by last name. If you have a large database, some last names are likely to be duplicated. (Think about the likelihood of finding more than one Smith in an organization of a thousand employees.) To handle this ambiguity, you also organize by first name within last name. If last names are duplicated, records are secondarily organized by first name. The index you need to manage this situation must reference two fields simultaneously; you cannot do that by entering Y in the Index column of the Database design screen. Instead, use the Create New Index command in the Organize menu and specify an index that combines both fields.

When you activate the Create New Index command, you display a fill-in box that asks you for the name you want to give the index and the expression on which you want to construct the index (see fig. 8.3). The fields you want in this example must be combined, or in technical terms, *concatenated*. In the example, the LASTNAME field is added to the FIRSTNAME field (`lastname+firstname`) to form the index. If necessary, you can concatenate more than two fields. You may, for example, want to include the employee's middle initial in the index to organize names in which the last and first names are the same. To include the INITIAL field in the index, use the index expression `lastname+firstname+initial`. dBASE more succinctly refers to an index expression as a *key*.

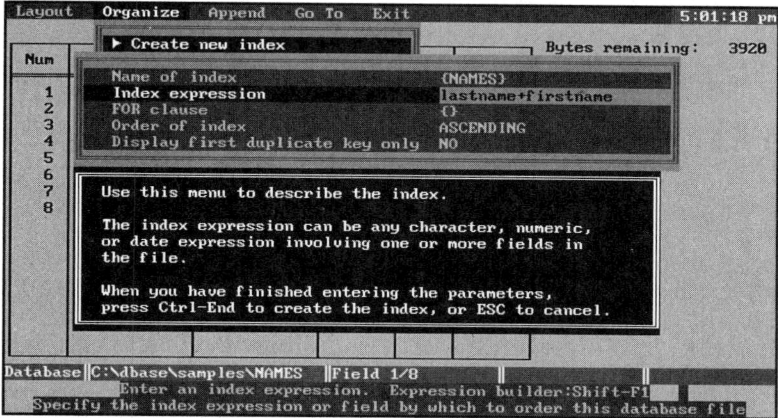
Layout Organize Append Go To Exit 5:01:18 pm
Create new index
Bytes remaining: 3920
Num
Name of index {NAMES}
Index expression lastname+firstname
FOR clause {}
Order of index ASCENDING
Display first duplicate key only NO
Use this menu to describe the index.
The index expression can be any character, numeric, or date expression involving one or more fields in the file.
When you have finished entering the parameters, press Ctrl-End to create the index, or ESC to cancel.
Database C:\dbase\samples\NAMES Field 1/8
Enter an index expression. Expression builder:Shift-F1
Specify the index expression or field by which to order this database file

FIG. 8.3

Creating an index on multiple fields.

TIP

When you include a field name in an expression, you can type the name in upper- or lowercase or any combination of the two.

The rules for creating indexes specify that you can concatenate fields of only the same type. You can concatenate character fields with character fields, but not with numeric or date fields. For example, you cannot create an index on `lastname+date_hired` or `lastname+salary`. Fortunately, you can convert incompatible fields to the character field type for purposes of indexing, as explained in Chapter 12.

## Understanding the Options in Creating an Index

dBASE IV requires a name and an index expression for any index, but you also have available some options that vary the "normal" index. One of these options controls how the index is ordered: lowest to highest or highest to lowest within the range of values. The lowest-to-highest alternative is referred to as an *ascending* index; the highest-to-lowest, as a *descending* index. In a character field, an ascending index progresses from the letter A to the letter Z. To put your index in descending order, choose Create New Index from the Organize menu, highlight the Order Of Index option in the fill-in box, and press the space bar or Enter to change the setting from ASCENDING to DESCENDING.

Another option available in the fill-in box that appears when you select Create New Index is Display First Duplicate Key Only. This option is set to NO by default; it controls whether records with duplicate index values are displayed once per record (when set to NO) or displayed only once (when set to YES). When this option is set to YES, dBASE displays a unique list, where each index value appears only once in the list. If you want to see a list of all the cities in which your customers live, but you don't want the cities to be repeated in the list, set Display First Duplicate Key Only to YES.

The FOR Clause option in the fill-in box determines whether the index applies to the full database or only to selected records. If the database lists customers from all of New England, but you want to list only those customers in Massachusetts, for example, you can restrict the index to just those people (see fig. 8.4). Restricting the index in this fashion speeds up the indexing procedure, which slows as the size of the database grows. Restricting the index also has the effect of hiding records that do not meet the condition you specify. When the index is active, you see only the records that meet the condition.

You set the conditions in the FOR Clause option by referencing the name of the field on which you want to set the restriction (in fig. 8.4, the field is STATE), providing a logical operator (in this case, the equal sign), and specifying the condition (in this case, "MA"). Quotation marks are used to enclose the condition only when the field being restricted is a character field. If you are working with a numeric field, don't use punctuation around the number condition (for example, SALARY = 25000). If you are working with a date field, enclose the date in braces (for example, HIRE_DATE = {01/01/89}). For more information about specifying conditions, refer to Chapter 13.

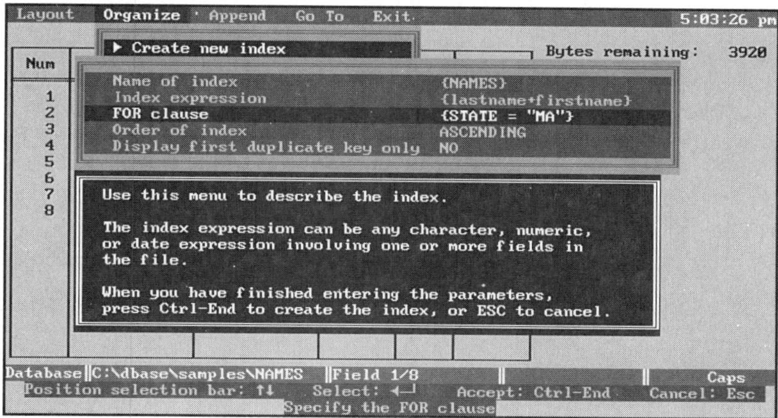


FIG. 8.4

Restricting the index to selected records.

# Using Indexes

After you create one or more indexes, you should know what to do with them. An index is like a helpful friend you call on only when you need something special done. Until you do call, the index sits in the background absorbing what's happening to the database. When you update the database by adding, deleting, or changing records, the index notes the changes and updates itself automatically. When you need the index, it's ready to give you the correct answer.

To use an index, select the Organize menu from a display screen or the Database design screen and select the Order Records By Index option. dBASE displays a pick list of all the index tags in the production index file. Choose an item from the list by highlighting it and pressing Enter. Notice that when you highlight a tag, the key (or index expression) for that tag is revealed to the left of the tag name (see fig. 8.5); use this information as a reminder of what the index is set up to do.

**NOTE**

The default indexes set up for databases by dBASE IV can contain up to 47 index tags. These are known as multiple-index files (MDX files), or *production indexes*. Separate index files can be created, called NDX files, but these are used primarily for compatibility with dBASE III files or for temporary indexes.

If you want to revert to the original order of the database, you can select the Natural Order option at the top of the pick list.

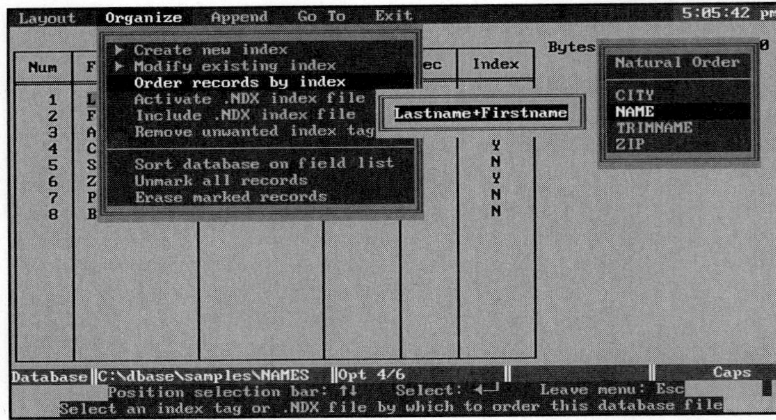


FIG. 8.5

Choosing an index to use.

The pick list of tag names also appears if you select Remove Unwanted Index Tag or Modify Existing Index from the Organize menu. If you select Remove Unwanted Index Tag and choose a tag from the list, the tag is deleted. If you select Modify Existing Index, you can modify the definition of the selected tag. Modifying a tag involves the same choices you make when you create a tag.

After you select an index tag to use, that index stays in effect for any work you do with the database until you select another tag or close the database. When you close the database, dBASE IV loses its memory for which index, if any, you may have set. If you want to reorder the database later, you must select that index tag again from the Organize menu.

**FROM HERE...**

**For Related Information...**

▸▸ "Putting Your Database in Order," p. 443.

# Reorganizing the Database by Sorting

Indexing definitely is the most important tool dBASE IV provides for reorganizing the database, but it's not the only one. You also can reorder the database by using a sorting procedure available through the Organize menu's Sort Database On Field List option.

In contrast to indexing, *sorting* a database causes a physical rearrangement of records on disk; in other words, the record numbers are reassigned. To sort, dBASE IV requires another database file name; it cannot sort the database within the same file. The consequence of sorting is that you have two copies of the same data: the original database and the sorted database. You can get rid of the original after the sort, but you have a period of time in which both copies are on disk. If the database is large, you may not have enough room on disk to store both copies, particularly if you are using a floppy disk.

Even if you abandon the original database, you find that the sorted database doesn't remember that it is sorted or how to maintain itself in sorted order. If you sort a database and then add records to it, for example, the new records are not added in sorted order; they are added at the bottom of the database. If you want to keep the database sorted, you must take it through another sorting procedure. You have to sort the database after each major modification. Needless to say, this process can be tedious and time-consuming.

If you overlook the disadvantages of sorting, you can see one major advantage. A sort enables you to arrange records in dictionary order. *Dictionary order* follows the conventions used in arranging entries in a standard English dictionary; uppercase and lowercase versions of the same letter are considered the same letter. Indexing, on the other hand, uses ASCII order to arrange entries. *ASCII order* sorts capital letters (A through Z) before lowercase letters (a through z). In ASCII sequence, for instance, the name *daVinci* is sorted after the name *Zola*. Chapter 13 explains how you can simulate this sorting advantage by building a sort operator into a query.

**TIP**

You can perform dictionary sorting with indexes by using the UPPER function. UPPER(lastname) will simulate a dictionary sort on the LASTNAME field, for example.

To sort on one or more fields, activate the Organize menu, select Sort Database On Field List, and fill out a sort form that specifies what fields you want to sort and in what order you want the values sorted (see fig. 8.6). The first field named in the list determines the highest level of the sort; other fields named below it are secondary sorts. You don't have to select the same sort type for each field in the list. You can make one field sort ascending dictionary and the next descending ASCII.

**NOTE** To select the name of a field in the Sort menu, you can type the name of the field or press Shift-F1 (Pick List) to bring up a list of fields. Highlight the field you want and press Enter to place it. To change the type of sort, press Enter from the Field order column and use the space bar to rotate to the sort order you want. All fields—character, numeric, and date—have the same possibilities. You cannot sort on a logical or memo field.

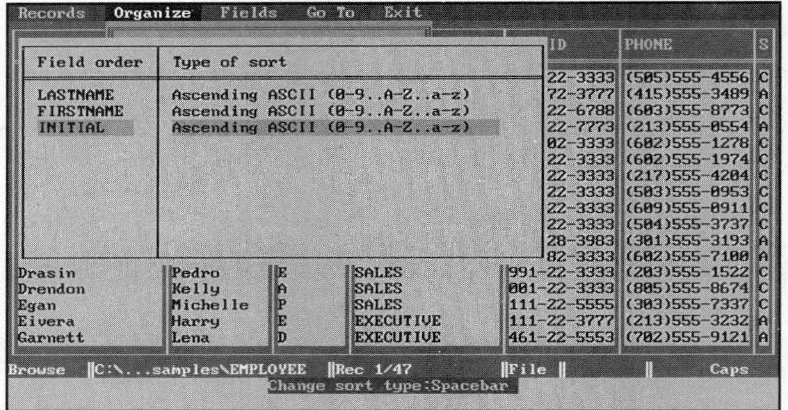


FIG. 8.6

Sorting a database.

When you finish specifying the sort conditions, press Ctrl-End. dBASE IV asks for the name of the file in which you want to store the sorted records. Type a name and press Enter. If the name is already in use, you are asked to verify that you want to overwrite that file. Finally, you are asked whether you want to supply a description for the file. If you provide a description, the description appears on the file identification line of the Control Center whenever you highlight the file in the Data panel.

FROM HERE...

**For Related Information...**

▸▸ "Putting Your Database in Order," p. 443.

# Applying Indexes

Indexes bridge the gap between database design and database work. On the design side, indexes help keep your database organized by the categories you need to report database information. Indexes save you time and effort in reordering records each time you need a different arrangement. On the work side, indexes and sorted database files can achieve ends in themselves. The problem you want to solve may be adequately answered simply by rearranging records.

Indexes are important to two menu commands within the Browse and Edit screens. One of these commands, Index Key Search in the Go To menu, provides the same search capability as the Forward Search and Backward Search commands. The difference is that the Index Key Search command restricts the search to the key field or fields; you don't have to locate the cursor in a particular field before you conduct the search, and you can search on values that span two or more fields, assuming that the index expression you set up was based on more than one field. If you set up an index on the expression STATE+CITY, for example, you could enter a search value, such as `DCWashington` for Washington, DC (see fig. 8.7), and locate the cursor at the correct matching record.

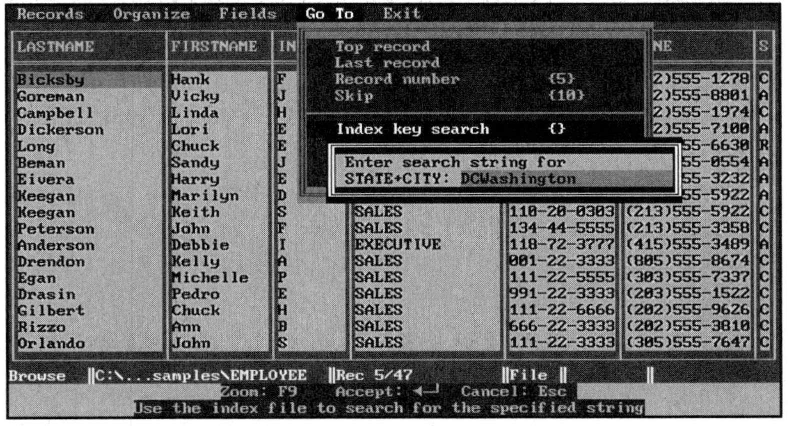


FIG. 8.7

Entering a search condition on a complex index expression.

**NOTE** When you enter a search value for a complex index expression, dBASE does a literal search for the value. If you are searching an index built on the fields LASTNAME+FIRSTNAME, and the LASTNAME field is 12 characters wide, you would have to account for the full width of the field in specifying a search expression. To locate the record for Richard Mather, for example, you would have to type *Mather Richard*, making sure to follow the last name with enough blanks or spaces—6 in this case—to fill out 12 character positions. To get around this difficulty, index on LASTNAME–FIRSTNAME. With this index, you can specify the search value as MatherRichard.

Assuming that you are working in the Browse or the Edit screen, you set up an index key search by accessing the Go To menu and then choosing the Index Key Search command. In the fill-in slot, you type the search value with no surrounding quotes and press Enter. dBASE IV searches the database on the index and, if the program finds a matching value, moves the cursor to that record. If more than one record in the database meets the search condition, dBASE moves the record pointer to the first record in the list.

Because the database has been rearranged by the key fields, all the other records that meet the condition are immediately below. If you are working in the Browse screen, you can see these records on the same screen (see fig. 8.8); if you are working in the Edit screen, you can press PgDn to reveal the records. Using Shift-F3 (Find Previous) and Shift-F4 (Find Next) isn't necessary. In fact, these keys do not work with Index Key Search.

Records Organize Fields Go To Exit

| LASTNAME | FIRSTNAME | INITIAL | DEPARTMENT | CITY | STATE | ZIP |
|---|---|---|---|---|---|---|
| Gilbert | Chuck | H | SALES | Washington | DC | 20002 |
| Rizzo | Ann | B | SALES | Washington | DC | 20002 |
| Orlando | John | S | SALES | N. Bay Village | FL | 33141 |
| Zambini | Rick | J | EXECUTIVE | Idaho Falls | ID | 83403 |
| Kaufman | Lisa | C | SALES | Chicago | IL | 60680 |
| Cohen | Larry | A | SALES | Decatur | IL | 62526 |
| Johnson | Jay | O | SALES | Louisville | KY | 40202 |
| DeBello | Todd | S | SALES | New Orleans | LA | 70175 |
| Montovan | John | U | SALES | Boston | MA | 02201 |
| Rodan | Bill | H | SALES | Northampton | MA | 01060 |
| Dean | Michelle | W | EXECUTIVE | Baltimore | MD | 21201 |
| London | Eric | S | SALES | Minneapolis | MN | 55415 |
| Lucas | John | M | SALES | Durham | NC | 27701 |
| Larson | Jill | O | SALES | Lincoln | NE | 68506 |
| Arlich | Kim | Y | SALES | Manchester | NH | 03108 |
| Lisbonn | Rick | R | SALES | Atlantic City | NJ | 08401 |
| Daniels | Dominique | F | SALES | Trenton | NJ | 08601 |

Browse ║C:\...samples\EMPLOYEE ║Rec 19/47 ║File ║ ║

FIG. 8.8

The result of carrying out an indexed search for Washington, DC.

One other command that becomes available to you when you order records by an index is Follow Record To New Position in the Records menu (see fig. 8.9). This command controls how the record pointer moves after you make a change to the database that involves a key field. When you order records by an index, dBASE IV maintains that order throughout any changes you make. If you edit a record and change its key value, the record immediately assumes its proper place in the order based on the new key value. The setting for the Follow Record To New Position command determines whether the screen cursor goes with the new record or stays in the position where it was initially. If the command is set to YES, the cursor moves; if the command is set to NO, the cursor moves to the record that previously followed the changed record. YES is the default setting.

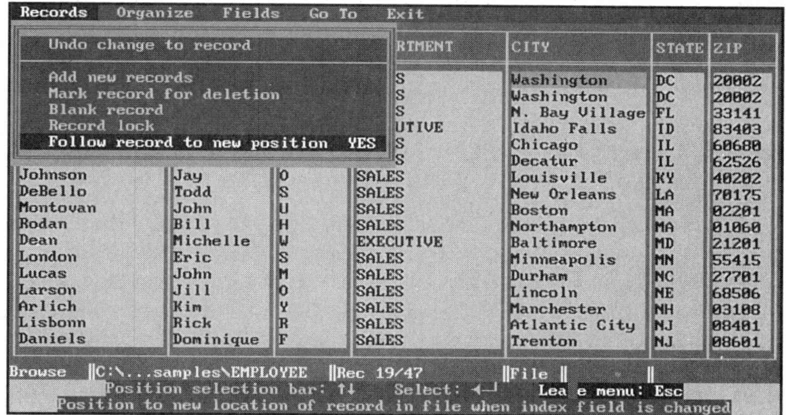


FIG. 8.9

The Follow Record To New Position command.

In normal practice, you change the setting to NO if you have to change a whole series of records. If you need to relocate 10 employees from Washington, DC, to 10 different areas, for example, you would order the records by an index on STATE+CITY, do an index search for Washington, DC (type *DCWashington*), and then edit the city and state for each Washington entry. When you press the down arrow (in Browse) or PgDn key (in Edit) to move to the next Washington record, the record you just changed moves to its new location.

To ensure that the cursor moved to the next Washington record, rather than moving with the changed record, you need to change the Follow Record To New Position setting before you start your edits. Access the Records menu, and then select Follow Record To New Position. dBASE changes the setting to the opposite value without prompting you and returns to the work surface.

**For Related Information...**

▸▸ "Finding What You're Looking For," p. 448.

# Summary

In this chapter, you took the first step in getting dBASE IV to address the kinds of problems you set up the database to handle. In particular, you looked at one important type of problem—reorganization of data in the database.

The techniques that dBASE IV provides to reorder the database include indexing and sorting, with indexing being the more general-purpose tool. You can create an index when you need to rearrange records based on the values in one or more fields. Using options in the Organize menu, you can write an expression that specifies the indexing order; then you can use that index as the guide to displaying records.

Sorting achieves the same purpose as indexing. Sorting, however, physically rearranges records in the database file and stores them in a second file on disk. Because the sorted information resides in a second database file, making changes to the original file does not automatically update the sorted database.

# Learning More about dBASE IV

Creating and Using Custom Screen Forms

Writing Reports in dBASE IV

Designing and Printing Labels

Using Queries To Search Databases

Using dBASE IV Expressions and Functions

Designing, Defining, and Creating Relational Databases

Managing dBASE IV Systems

9

CHAPTER

# Creating and Using Custom Screen Forms

Although you can use dBASE's default data-entry screens to enter, edit, and view data, a custom form makes entering and editing data easier and more accurate. A custom data-entry form ensures that entered data is formatted correctly and is of the correct type: characters go into a character field, numbers go into a numeric field, and so on.

You can design custom forms for all important dBASE functions. You can use the same form to input data, edit existing data, and simply view data. You also can design different forms for each of these purposes, changing the formatting and editing options. You can design one form that displays data without allowing any changes, for example, and another that displays only certain parts of a database's information.

In this chapter, you learn how to create a custom form by using the dBASE Forms design screen. You learn how to place fields on the form and move them around to make the form pleasing to the eye. dBASE provides a wide array of formatting and editing options that give you full control over the data you enter and how that data is displayed on-screen. Custom forms make a huge difference in how easy and productive dBASE can be. With the information in this chapter, you can create elegant and easy-to-use forms for your dBASE systems.

# Designing Forms

Before you start creating forms, think about the design of the form. Although dBASE makes changing the design of a form easy, you will find it quicker and simpler to create a complete and elegant form if you think about the design before you start. Follow these simple tips about form design:

- Don't crowd data fields and text onto a form. You can use as many pages as you want for a form. Two uncrowded, easy-to-read-and-use pages are better than one hard-to-understand page.
- Group data logically. If you're designing an order-entry form, for example, group customer information in one area, order information in another, and shipping information in a third. You can use boxes and lines to define the areas more clearly.
- Make the data-entry flow logical. dBASE accesses fields on the form from top to bottom, and—if you have more than one field on a line—from left to right. If you're going to enter customer data, for example, place the fields so that you enter the customer name, then address, then telephone number. Imagine the frustration of using a form in which you enter the telephone number after the city but before the state!
- Use the capabilities of the Forms design screen as much as possible. The Forms design screen includes editing functions to ensure that valid data is entered, messages to prompt the user, and colors to emphasize important data.

Designing and creating custom data-entry and viewing forms once required tedious programs that placed the text and data fields on the form by row and column. dBASE IV's Forms design screen makes creating and modifying forms a breeze. Planning the design, however, still saves you time and frustration.

# Creating Forms with the Forms Design Screen

You design forms by using the Forms design screen, which you access from the Control Center. You place fields that accept and display database information on the Forms design work surface. Then you add text, lines, and boxes to make the form more readable and easier to use. This chapter explains how to create a custom form you can use to input data into a database.

## Accessing the Forms Design Work Surface

To begin the creation of a new form, you must access the Forms design screen. To access this screen, start from the Control Center and follow these steps:

1. In the Data panel, highlight the database file for which you want to create a custom form, and press Enter. When the selection box appears, choose Use File. That file is now the active file in the catalog. (Active files appear above the horizontal line in the Data panel.)

2. Move the cursor to the Forms panel, highlight <create>, and press Enter. This action tells the Control Center you want to create a new form. If you want to modify an existing form, highlight the name of the form in the Forms panel and press Enter. When the selection box appears, choose Modify Layout.

   If you have set INSTRUCT to OFF (using the Settings option on the Tools menu), you must highlight an existing form and press Shift-F2 to modify that form. With INSTRUCT set to OFF, highlighting a form name and pressing Enter causes dBASE to activate that form, placing it on the screen.

3. When the Forms design screen appears, the Layout menu is displayed. Press Esc to close the Layout pull-down menu. The Forms design screen appears (see fig. 9.1). You design the Customer database form on the work surface of this screen.

When selecting files from the Control Center, you can use the mouse to select the file by double-clicking it. To create a new form file, for example, double-click on <create> in the Forms panel. To exit a menu by

using the mouse, click outside of the menu. Click on the work surface of the Forms design screen to close the Layout menu.

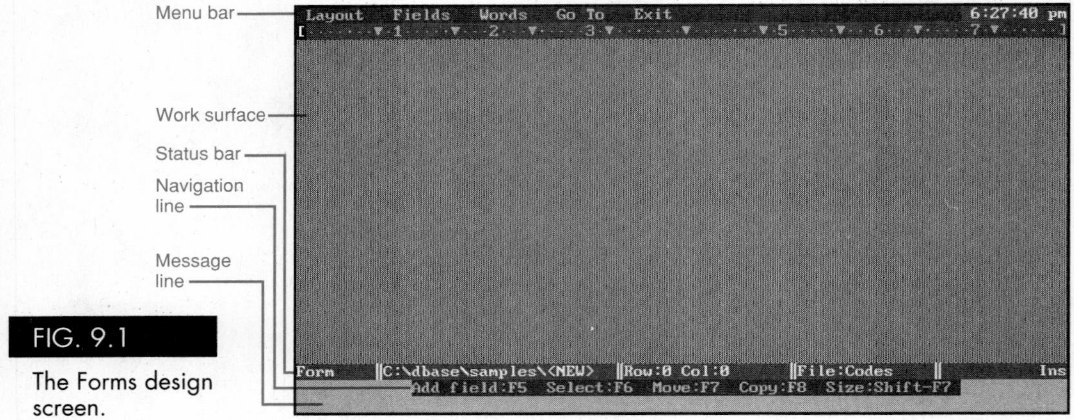


FIG. 9.1

The Forms design screen.

The Forms design screen is basically a work table on which you arrange form elements to make a presentable, easy-to-read form you can use to display and enter data. Before you start to create a form, take a quick tour of the Forms design screen.

Across the top of the screen is the familiar dBASE menu bar, modified to fit the Forms design screen functions. Each item on the menu bar contains options that apply to the process of designing and creating forms. As with other dBASE menus, you access the menu bar by pressing F10, using the arrow keys to highlight the menu item wanted, and then pressing Enter to activate the pull-down menu with the options. You also can activate a pull-down menu by pressing Alt+*letter*, where *letter* is the first letter of the menu selection. After you pull down a menu, you can move to other pull-down menus by moving to the right or left with the right- or left-arrow keys.

Moving from one pull-down menu to another is quick and easy using the mouse. Just click on the new menu name in the menu bar.

You may want to take a moment to explore the menus available in the design surface screen: Layout, Fields, Words, Go To, and Exit. Pull down each menu and look at the options available. These options will be discussed in more detail in the exercises that follow.

The status bar appears below the work surface, showing information about the form. The leftmost section of the status bar shows the word `Form` to remind you that you are in the Forms design screen. The next section shows the name of the current form, with a complete DOS path. If you haven't yet named the current form by saving it, the name of the form is `<NEW>`. The next section of the status bar shows the row and column of the cursor's position. To the right of the `Row:Col:` display is the name of the database file for which you're building this form. The rightmost section of the status bar shows the state of the Num Lock key, the Caps Lock key, and the Ins key. When any of these keys are in effect, an indicator appears in the last section of the status bar.

The work surface takes up most of the screen. On the work surface, you add data fields, text, lines, and boxes to make the form readable and usable.

The next-to-last line of the screen is the dBASE navigation line, showing "hot-key" assignments. The display on the navigation line changes, depending on what you're doing on the Forms design work surface. The navigation line always provides appropriate assistance.

As usual, the last line of the screen is the message line, which provides helpful messages about what you are doing at any given time. Error messages also appear here.

## Adding Fields to the Form

The first thing you do with a blank Forms design work surface is add the necessary database fields. dBASE gives you two ways to do this. The Quick Layout option of the Layout menu places all the fields of the active database on the surface at once, ready to be moved and formatted. The Add Fields option of the Fields menu enables you to place the fields on the work surface one at a time, at the location you choose. You use both methods at different times.

### Using Quick Layout To Add Fields

With the Quick Layout option, you put all the fields of a database on the Forms design work surface at once. If you know your form is to include all of a database's fields, Quick Layout is a quick and easy way to put all the fields on the work surface. To put all the fields on the work surface, simply choose Quick Layout from the Layout menu. When the work surface reappears, all the fields are on the form, much like a default input/display screen. Figure 9.2 shows the Forms design work surface after using Quick Layout.

The rest of this chapter uses this layout as the basis for creating a custom form for the Customer database.

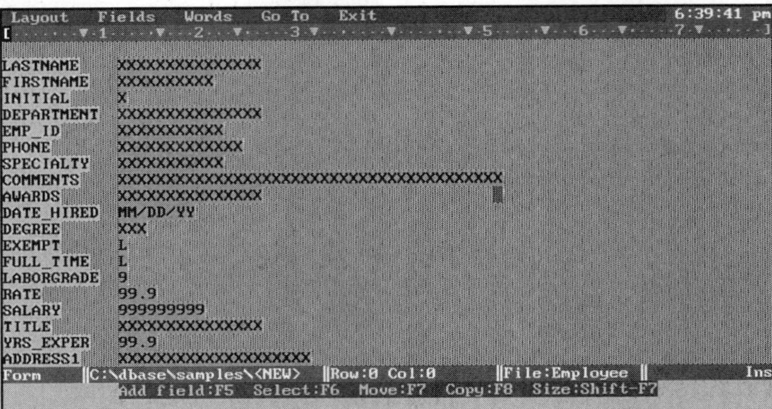


FIG. 9.2

Adding all the database fields to the Forms design work surface with the Quick layout option.

After all the fields are on the work surface, you can use the F7 (Move) and Shift-F7 (Size) keys to move the fields to their proper places and size the fields. You also can add text, lines, and boxes as necessary and attach formatting options. When designing a form, you can specify validity checks to help ensure that data entered into the form is valid. A *validity check* can ensure that numeric digits only are entered into a database field, even if that field is of character type. All these processes are detailed later in this chapter.

## Using Add Fields To Place Fields on the Form

You may want to design a form that does not include all the fields of a database. Such forms are useful particularly for displaying or editing data when you may not want to display or edit all the fields of a database. Forms that don't include all the database fields sometimes can be created most easily by adding the fields to the work surface one at a time.

To add individual fields to the work surface, follow these steps:

1. Position the cursor on the Forms design work surface where you want the field to appear.
2. Choose Add Field from the Fields menu, or press F5 (Add Field). A Field List menu appears (see fig. 9.3). The left column of the Field List menu shows all the fields of the active database—the name of the database is at the top of the left column.

The right column of the menu is titled CALCULATED. This column lists fields that have values calculated from other database fields or other form fields. When you first create a form, this column is empty, except for the <create> option. You learn about calculated fields in the section "Adding Calculated Fields to the Form," later in this chapter.

3. Choose the field you want to add by highlighting it and pressing Enter.

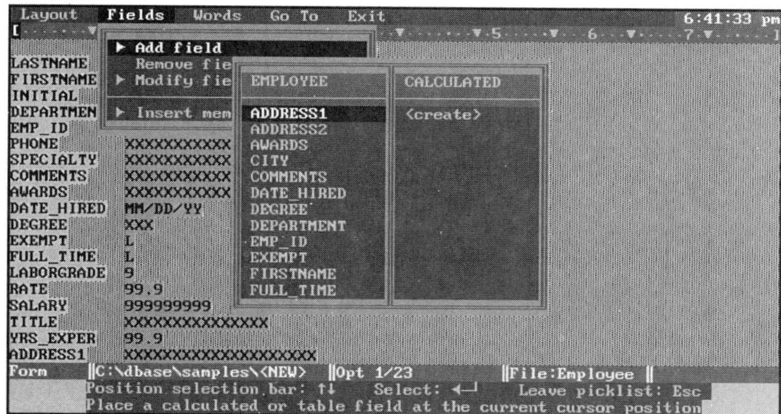


FIG. 9.3

The Field List menu.

When the Forms design screen reappears, the selected field is on the work surface at the cursor's location. Just as with fields placed with the Quick Layout option, fields placed individually with Add Fields can be moved or sized. You also can use editing and display functions on these fields, as described later in this chapter.

> **WARNING:** When adding fields to the work surface manually, do not place fields or text in the top row of the Forms design work surface. When you use the form for data entry or viewing, dBASE uses this row for the menus. If you put fields or text in the first line, the menus are overwritten.

## Saving the Form

As you design your form, save it often. Few things are more frustrating than being near the completion of a complicated form and having the power go out, causing you to lose all your work. Saving a form is simple and can be done often.

To save a form, follow these steps:

1. Select Save This Form from the Layout menu.
2. The first time you save a form, dBASE IV asks you for the name of the form. Names must conform to the DOS file-naming conventions: the name can be a maximum of 8 characters, have no spaces, and include only digits, characters, and the underscore or dash character. Use a name that represents the form in some way.
3. If you have already saved the form, the form name box has the name in it. Press Enter to accept the name and save the form. If you want to give the form a new name, enter the new name in the box. This renaming feature is useful if you want to modify a form and save both the original and the modified versions of the form. Give the modified version a new name; the original version remains unchanged.

## Moving, Copying, and Sizing Fields

To move or copy work-surface elements—such as fields, text, boxes, or lines—start with the same process; select the elements to be moved or copied. The technique of selecting elements differs for the different types of elements, but after an element is selected, the moving process is the same.

*To select a single field:* Place the cursor in the field you want to select, press F6 (Select), and complete the selection by pressing Enter.

*To select multiple fields:* Place the cursor at the beginning of the first field you want to select and press F6 (Select). Use the arrow keys to highlight the area that contains all the fields you want to select and move. As you do this, a *ghost* appears, showing you the area selected. When the ghost covers the fields you want to select, press Enter to complete the selection.

*To select a box:* Move the cursor to any location on the box. Press F6 (Select) and press Enter.

*To select text:* Move the cursor to the beginning of the text you want to select. Press F6 (Select). Use the arrow keys to move to the end of the text and press Enter to complete the selection.

*To select lines:* Lines on the form resemble text more than boxes, so you select them like text.

*To select an area of the form:* This technique works for selecting text, fields, or both. Place the cursor at one corner of the area you want to select and press F6 (Select). Move the cursor to the opposite corner of the area you want to select; notice the ghost that shows you what has been selected. When the ghost covers the area you want to select, press Enter to complete the selection.

You can use the mouse to select fields or text. Position the mouse pointer at the corner of the area to be selected. Holding down the mouse button, drag the mouse over the selection, and then release the button.

Figure 9.4 shows the Forms design work surface with a selected area.

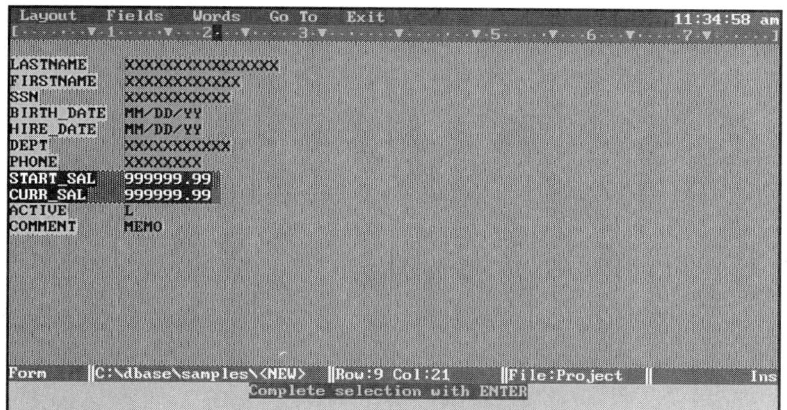


FIG. 9.4

A selected area, ready to be moved or copied.

After you select the area you want to move or copy, the next step is to press F7 (Move) or F8 (Copy). Then use the arrow keys to move the selected area on the work surface. The ghost of the selected area moves to show you where you are moving the area. After you position the ghost where you want it, press Enter to tell dBASE to move or copy the selected area. Figure 9.5 shows the ghost in its new position.

To move a block using the mouse, drag the mouse over the block to select it, click on `Move:F7` in the navigation line, position the mouse pointer to the new location, and click the mouse button.

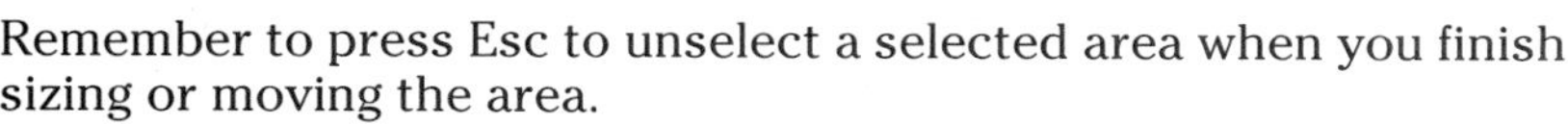

Remember to press Esc to unselect a selected area when you finish sizing or moving the area.

If you position the ghost on top of other fields, dBASE asks whether you want to delete the fields underneath the ghost. Make sure that you position the selected area correctly before you say Yes. When you confirm the deletion, the move or copy takes place, and anything under the ghost is gone permanently.

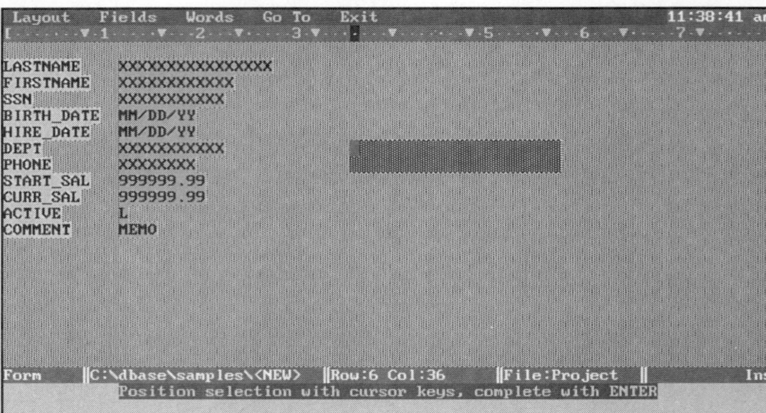


FIG. 9.5

Moving the ghost of the selected area to its new location.

The only difference between using F7 (Move) and F8 (Copy) is in the results. With Move, everything in the original selected area is removed from the screen; with Copy, the original selected area remains, as does the copy.

With Move and Copy, you can arrange the fields in a pleasing layout. Rearranging fields in this way is particularly handy if you used Quick Layout to place the fields on the work surface.

One easy way to rearrange the fields on the screen is to take the default Quick Layout and then center all the fields on the screen. To do this, select all the fields using F6 and the arrow keys, or by dragging the mouse. After you complete the selection, press F7 and move the entire box to the center of the screen and press Enter (see fig. 9.6). To cancel the selection, press Esc.

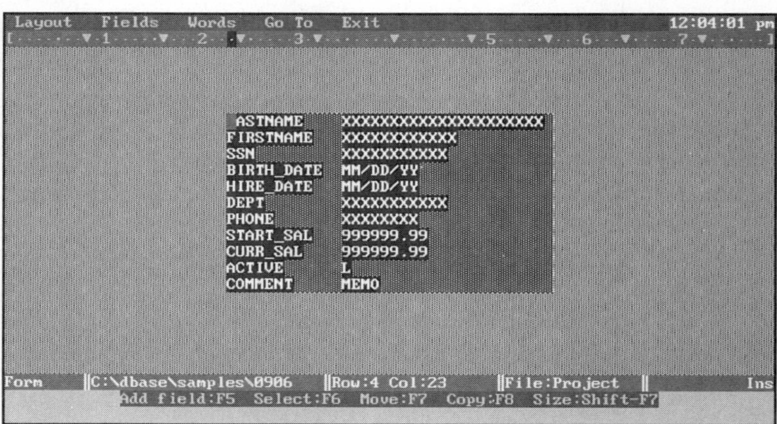


FIG. 9.6

Centering field layout on the screen.

To change the size of a field, select it as described earlier in this section and press Shift-F7 (Size). Now press the left-arrow key to decrease the size of the field, or press the right-arrow key to increase the size. The original size remains on-screen for reference, and a ghost appears to show the modified size. Press Enter when you have resized the field to your satisfaction. If the new size of the field extends on top of other fields on-screen, dBASE asks you to confirm that you want to delete the old, underlying field or text. Changing the size of a field on the form does not affect the size of the field in the database.

# Adding and Changing Text on the Form

Adding text to a form is a simple task. If you want to add text in an area that has no data fields, just place the cursor where you want the text to start and type the text. You can use the Position option on the Words menu to position the text, or you can use F6 (Select) and F7 (Move) to move the text. (See "Moving, Copying, and Sizing Fields," earlier in this chapter.)

To add a title to the form, follow these steps:

1. Place the cursor in Column 0 of Row 0. `Row:0 Col:0` appears in the status bar.
2. Choose Add Line from the Words menu or, with the `Ins` indicator in the status bar on, press Enter. (Turn on the `Ins` indicator by pressing the Ins key.) Either action adds a new blank line at the top of the form.
3. Move to the second blank row of the form; `Row:1 Col:0` appears on the status bar. (dBASE starts numbering rows and columns at 0, so the second row is Row:1.) Type a title for the form—for example, *Employee Information Data Entry Screen*.
4. Select the title you just entered by pressing F6 (Select) and then Home to move the cursor to the left margin. Press Enter to complete the selection.
5. Move the title to the center of the form. You can do this by pressing F7 (Move) and using the arrow keys to position the title; or you can use the Position option on the Words menu.

   To use the Position option, choose Position from the Words menu. A submenu offers you the choices Left, Center, and Right. Choose Center to place the title in the middle of the screen. When you return to the Forms design screen, the title is centered correctly.

If you used the Quick Layout option, the database fields were placed on the form with the field names to the left of the fields. As the database designer, these names make sense to you, but others using your database may need more understandable field descriptions. You can modify these descriptions easily.

If you have a database file that contains a field named LASTNAME, for example, and you want your form to display the prompt `Last Name:`, follow these steps:

1. Move the cursor to the *L* of *LASTNAME*.
2. Make sure the `Ins` indicator in the status bar is off. If the `Ins` indicator appears in the status bar, press the Ins key to remove it. Now as you enter text, you overwrite the characters under the cursor.
3. Type the text *Last Name:*. Notice that the new text overwrites the existing text.

   To delete existing text, position the cursor over the text to be deleted and press the Del key to remove it.

You can reposition a field on the screen by selecting the field and pressing F7 (Move). Use the arrow keys to move the field to the new location and press Enter. If the ghost of the field covers up part of the original field location, dBASE displays the prompt `Delete covered text and fields?` Answer Yes to accept the move.

Use these techniques to move the fields and text on the form until the form design is pleasing and easy to use. Figure 9.7 shows a modified version of the form, with more descriptive text and rearranged fields.

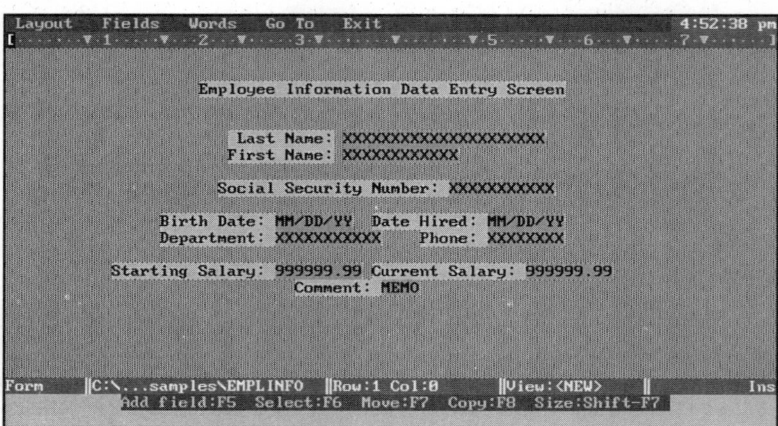


FIG. 9.7

The form with rearranged fields and text.

# Modifying the Appearance of a Memo Field

When you place a memo field on the form—using either the Quick Layout or Add Field option—the memo field appears as a "marker" with the word `MEMO` in it, just as it appears in default data-entry forms. You can leave the memo field this way or improve its appearance by having the memo field text appear in a box, or *window*, on the screen.

If you decide to leave a memo field in its default configuration, use it on the form just as you would a memo field in a default data-entry form. To access the contents of the memo field, press Ctrl-Home. To close the memo field, press Ctrl-W or Ctrl-End. When you place text in a memo field, the memo-field marker reads `MEMO` (in uppercase letters). An empty memo field shows the marker `memo` (in lowercase letters).

To change the memo field's appearance, follow these steps:

1. Move the cursor to the memo-field marker (the word MEMO) and choose Modify Field from the Fields menu.
2. Move to the Display option and press Enter. The setting changes from MARKER to WINDOW (see fig. 9.8).
3. Press Ctrl-End to accept the new field configuration.
4. The memo window marker appears on the screen as an `X` inside a box. Highlight this window marker and press Shift-F7 (Resize). Use the arrow keys to make the window the size you want, as in figure 9.9. Press Enter to accept the new size.
5. If you want to reposition the window, highlight it and press F7 (Move). Use the arrow keys to move the window to a new position, then press Enter. If you overwrite the Comments field description on the form, retype this text onto the form. Figure 9.10 shows the memo window moved to its new location.

   Use the mouse to move or size an object quickly, such as a memo window. Click on the object, then click on the `Move:F7` or `Size:Shift-F7` key labels at the bottom of the screen. Drag the mouse to size or reposition the object as desired, then click on it.

Notice in figure 9.10 that the memo-field marker is replaced by the window. When you use this form, as much of the memo-field contents as fit into the window are displayed.

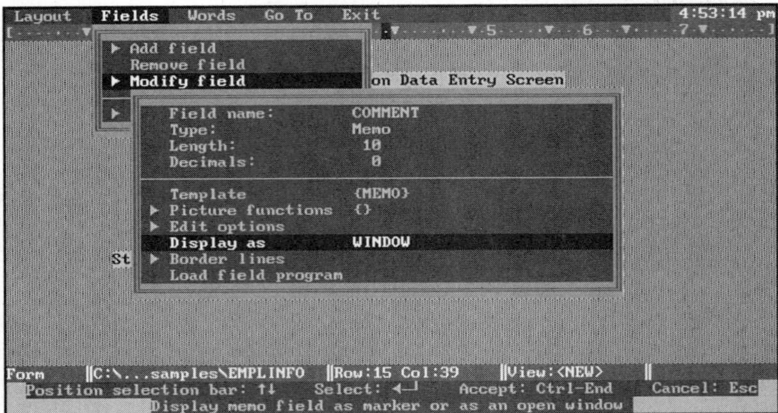


FIG. 9.8

Changing the display of a memo field.

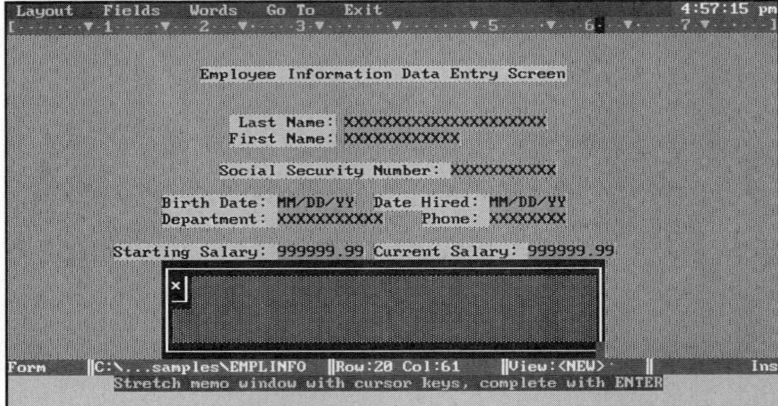


FIG. 9.9

Resizing the memo-field window.

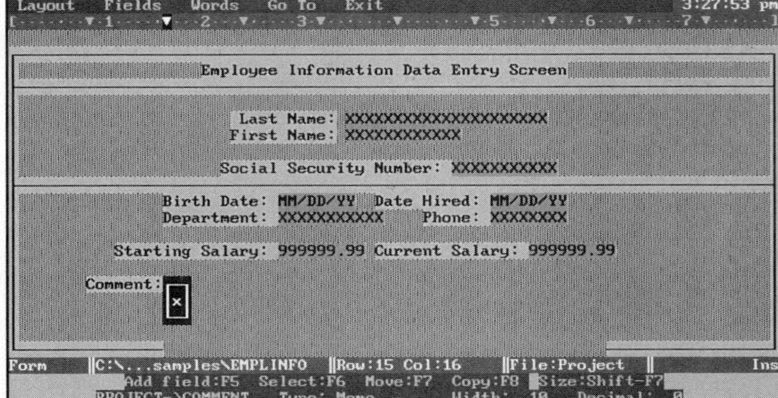


FIG. 9.10

The resized and repositioned memo-field window.

To access the memo-field window so that you can enter or edit data, use the same procedure as with the default marker: move the cursor to the memo-field window and press Ctrl-Home. The word processor is invoked inside the window. Exit from the memo-field window in the same way as with the marker: press Ctrl-End to save any changes and exit; press Esc to exit without saving the changes.

To open the memo window using the mouse, just double-click inside the window. Pull down the word processor menus from the top of the screen by clicking on the menu name and option you need. Click on the Exit menu and the Save Changes And Exit option, for example, to exit the window and save the information you have entered.

## Adding Boxes to the Form

Adding boxes to a form often improves the form's readability and the user's comprehension of the data. Boxes can more clearly define the relationship of groups of information on the form.

To add a box to the form, follow these steps:

1. Choose Box from the Layout menu. When the Box menu appears, choose the border style you want for the box (see fig. 9.11).

   The Using Specified Character option enables you to specify what character is to be used as the border. If you want a box made out of asterisks, for example, choose Using Specified Character, press *, and press Enter. The box is drawn out of asterisks.

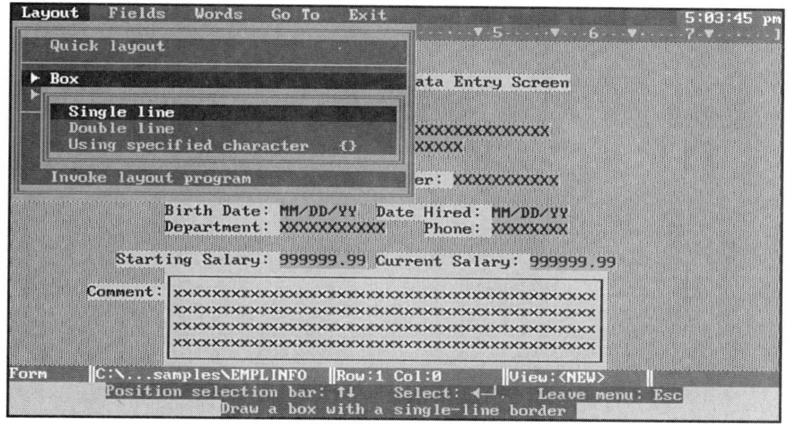


FIG. 9.11

Choosing the border style for a box.

2. When the work surface reappears, use the arrow keys to position the cursor at the upper left corner of the planned box, and press Enter.

3. Use the arrow keys to move the cursor to the lower right corner of the box. You can see the box change shape as you move this corner. As you move the cursor, the box extends over text and fields. When the box is the correct size and shape, press Enter to accept it.

To position a box using the mouse, first click on the location for the upper left corner of the box. Position the mouse pointer on the location for the lower right corner of the box, then click again.

The box in figure 9.12 serves as a border for the title of the form. You can move the box by selecting it (use F6 and Enter, as described earlier in this chapter), pressing F7 (Move), and then using the arrow keys to move the box. Only the box moves; any text in the box remains in its original position.

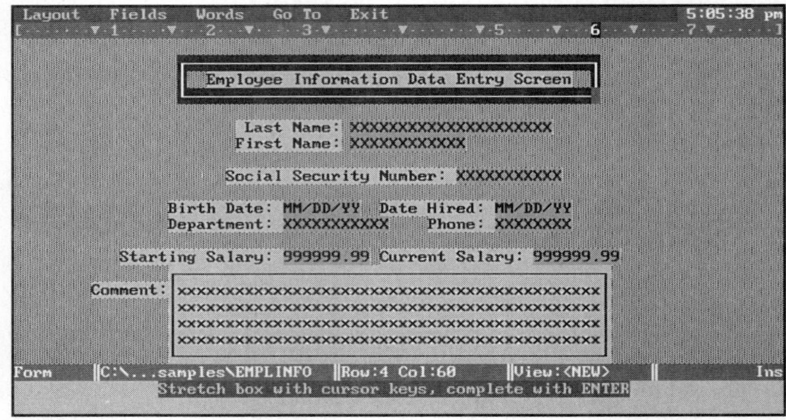


FIG. 9.12

Placing a box on the form.

To resize a box, select it and press Shift-F7 (Size). Use the arrow keys to move the lower right corner, changing the size of the box. With the F7 (Move) and Shift-F7 (Size) keys, you can completely change the appearance of the box on the form.

You may want to use several lines to divide the form into logical parts. Figure 9.13 shows the form divided into three parts: title, customer information, and purchase information.

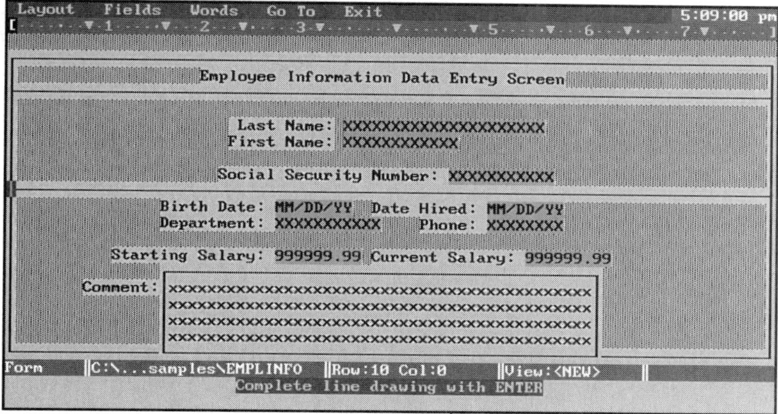


FIG. 9.13

Outlining parts of the form with lines.

**NOTE** When you use the Lines option, you use the arrow keys to "draw" the line. This means that lines don't have to be straight horizontal or vertical lines; they can "weave" between the text and fields on the form.

To place lines on the form (as shown in fig. 9.13), follow these steps:

1. Delete the box around the title on the form by moving the cursor to the box. Press F6 (Select), and then press Enter to complete the selection of the box. Press Del to remove the box from the title.
2. Select Line from the Layout menu.
3. Choose Single Line or Double Line from the submenu that appears. If you want to draw the line with characters (asterisks, for example), select Using Specified Character and type the character you want to use.
4. Move the cursor where you want the line to start and press Enter to start the line-drawing process.
5. Use the right-arrow key to draw the line across the form. When you reach the right edge of the form, use the down-arrow key to draw the line down.
6. Use the left-arrow key to draw the line to the left margin of the form. When you reach the left margin, use the up-arrow key to draw the line upward to the starting point. Use the right-arrow key to complete the upper left corner. You have drawn a complete box around the title.

7. Don't press Enter yet; use the arrow keys to continue drawing all the lines shown in figure 9.13. As you press the arrow keys, dBASE draws the line, correctly adding intersection characters where necessary. When you have drawn all the lines, press Enter.

You can use the mouse to draw lines by clicking instead of pressing Enter. Be sure to hold the mouse steady; otherwise, you could end of up with some squiggly lines that you have to delete one character at a time. To make your lines straight, use the arrow keys.

Unlike boxes, which can be selected and moved, lines are drawn on the page as if they were text. To delete lines, position the cursor on the line and press Del. You must delete each individual line character separately. You cannot move a line by using F6 (Select) and F7 (Move). You must delete each line character and redraw the line in its new location.

# Adding Color to the Form

Using colors on a custom form can make a significant contribution to the readability and usefulness of a form. You can use colors to identify important fields and to draw the user's eye to certain parts of the form.

To apply color to the form, select the area you want to color and then apply the new color to that area. Each row-and-column position on the form has two colors associated with it: a foreground color and a background color. The *foreground* refers to the character that is displayed in that position; the *background* refers to the area behind the character. The default form has a blue background with a white foreground, which means that the characters (foreground) are white on a field of blue (background). Table 9.1 shows the available foreground and background colors for a color monitor.

Monochrome monitors are much more limited. Monochrome monitors can display white, bright white, or black in the foreground, and white or black in the background. Monochrome monitors also can display an underline on foreground characters.

## Changing the Colors of a Field

To change the color of a field, follow these steps:

1. Select the field whose color you want to change by moving the cursor into the field. You do not have to press F6 (Select) if you want to add color to a single field. For this example, move the cursor to the Customer Number field.

2. Choose Display from the Words menu. A menu showing all of the foreground and background colors appears. A cursor appears to the left of the first choice in the Foreground column. Notice that the background color of the Foreground column is the current background color of the selected field, and the foreground color of the Background column is that of the selected field.

   To see how different foreground and background combinations look, use the up- and down-arrow keys to move the cursor up and down the Foreground column. As you move the cursor, the foreground colors of the Background column change, showing what the field looks like with this color combination.

   For this example, use the arrow keys to move the cursor to the Yellow foreground color.

3. To look at different background colors, press the right-arrow key to move the cursor to the Background column. Then use the up- and down-arrow keys to select different background colors. As you move the cursor, the background colors of the Foreground column change, again showing you what the field looks like with different backgrounds.

   For this example, move the cursor to the Red background color.

4. Press Ctrl-End to accept this combination.

**Table 9.1 Colors Available on a Color Monitor**

| Foreground | Background |
|---|---|
| Black | Black |
| Blue | Blue |
| Green | Green |
| Cyan | Cyan |
| Red | Red |
| Magenta | Magenta |
| Brown | Brown |
| White | White |
| Gray | |
| Light Blue | Blinking |
| Light Green | |
| Light Red | |
| Light Magenta | |
| Yellow | |
| Bright White | |

To select display colors with the mouse, click on the Words menu and the Display option, then click on the foreground and background colors you want to use. Click on the `Select & Exit:Ctrl-End` label in the navigation line to save your choices.

When the Forms design screen reappears, the field is shown in the new colors you selected.

## Changing the Colors of an Area on the Form

You may want to change the colors of an area of the screen—to draw attention to it, for example, or simply to make a more pleasing contrast on-screen. The process is not much different from changing a field's colors.

To change the colors of an area on-screen, follow these steps:

1. Select the area you want to color. In this exercise, you change the color of the form's title block. Move the cursor to position Row:0 Col:0, the upper left corner of the line box around the title.
2. Press F6 (Select), then move the cursor to Row:2 Col:79, the lower right corner of the title block. Press Enter to accept the selection.
3. Choose Display from the Word menu. When the color selection menu appears, make Blue the foreground color and White the background color.
4. Press Ctrl-End to accept this color selection.

When you return to the Forms design screen, press Esc to remove the highlighting from the selected area. Notice that the area is in the newly selected color scheme. Not all the area, however, may have the selected background color. Areas of the surface that have no characters—which appear as shaded positions—are not affected by the foreground and background colors and therefore take the default form background color of blue.

To fill in the title block with the new color, move the cursor to the shaded areas, make sure that the `Ins` indicator on the status bar is off (press Ins until the indicator disappears), and press the space bar. The spaces take on the color you set for the area, and the entire block appears as you planned.

Thoughtful use of colors can make the form easier to use. If the form contains fields that must be filled to maintain the database's integrity, for example, you can make those fields a different color from other fields. The user of the form then knows that he or she cannot skip past that field. (Make sure that the field is not left blank by using a validation check on the field.) A distinct field color visually reminds the user about why the field must be filled.

For forms used to view data, add color to emphasize the most important data. You can color an entire area with a different background color and change the field colors to emphasize these areas.

Use some caution when you design with color, however. Too many colors can confuse the screen. As a general rule, don't use more than two colors for the form's background and not more than two other colors for fields' backgrounds.

**For Related Information...**

◂◂ "Changing Display Settings," p. 66.

▸▸ "SET COLOR," p. 858.

# Adding Calculated Fields to the Form

You may want information on the form that must be calculated. Add a calculated field to give you this flexibility and power. You may have a Customer database, for example, that includes a field for the date of each customer's last purchase. You may want the form to display how many days from the current date that purchase was made.

To add a calculated field that subtracts the last purchase date from the current date, follow these steps:

1. On the work surface, type the prompt *Number of days since last purchase:*, as shown in fig. 9.14. Then position the cursor after the prompt in the location where the new field will appear. This text describes the calculated field you are going to add.

2. From the Fields menu, select Add Field, or press F5 (Add Field). The Field List menu appears.

3. Move the cursor to the <create> button of the CALCULATED column and press Enter. The Field Definition menu appears.

4. Give the field a name. Highlight the Name option, press Enter, and type the field name—for example, *SINCE_LST*. Do the same for a description—for example, *Days since last purchase* (see fig. 9.15).

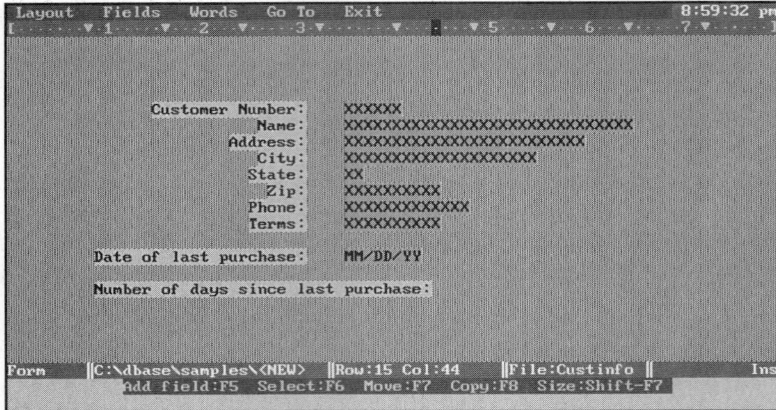


FIG. 9.14

Entering a prompt for a calculated field.

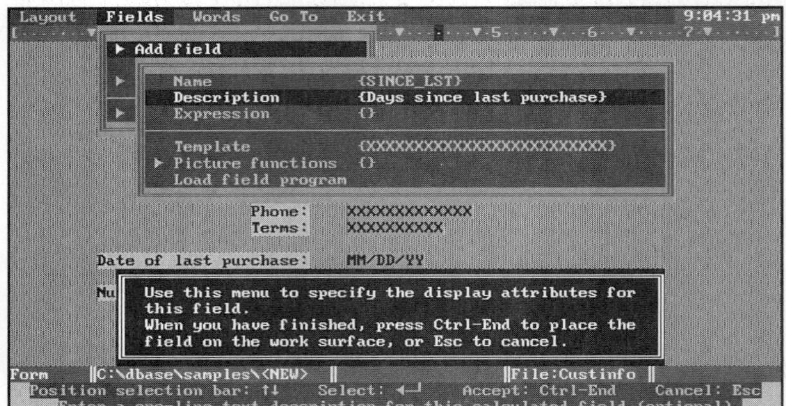


FIG. 9.15

The Field Definition menu.

5. Highlight the Expression option and press Enter. If you know the precise expression you want to use for the calculated field, simply type it. For this field, the expression is DATE() – LAST_PUR.

   Create the DATE() – LAST_PUR expression from the expression-builder menu. After you highlight the Expression option and press Enter, you can press Shift-F1 to display a menu with all database fields available, all the operators, and all the dBASE functions you can use in a calculated field expression. Move the highlight to the Function column, and then use the down-arrow key to highlight the DATE function. Press Enter to select that function. Figure 9.16 shows this expression-builder menu.

The Field Definition menu reappears, with DATE() in the Expression field. Press Shift-F1 again to display the expression-builder menu again. This time, move the cursor to the Operator column and highlight –. Press Enter. When the Field Definition menu reappears, the – is added to the Expression field.

Press Shift-F1 once more to display the expression-builder menu. Move the cursor to the Fieldname column and highlight LAST_PUR. Press Enter. When the Field Definition menu reappears, the entire expression DATE() - LAST_PUR is constructed in the Expression field.

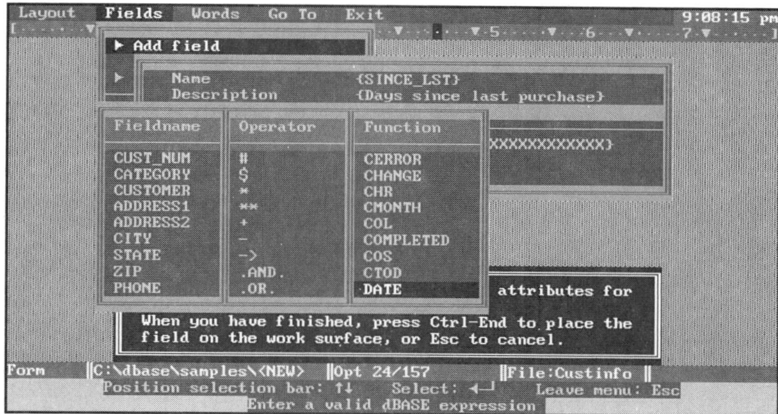


FIG. 9.16

The expression-builder menu.

6. Alter the Template option to read 9,999; the field will show up to 9,999 days since the last purchase.

   You alter the template by highlighting the Template option and pressing Enter. Use standard dBASE editing techniques to change the default template to 9,999. Press Ctrl-End to accept the new template. Detailed information about templates is found in "Validating Data and Formatting Fields," later in this chapter.

7. Highlight the Picture Functions option and press Enter. A menu of formatting options appears. Picture Function options are explained fully in "Validating Data and Formatting Fields," later in this chapter. For now, just use the down-arrow key to highlight the Trim option and press Enter to change the OFF setting to ON. Do the same with the Left Align option. Press Ctrl-End to accept these picture functions for the calculated field.

   Figure 9.17 shows the Field Definition menu for the calculated field. The field has a name, description, and an expression to calculate the value that will appear. The new template appears. The characters `TB` in the Picture Function field are the symbols for the Trim and Left align settings you defined in the Picture Functions menu.

8. Press Ctrl-End to accept this definition of the calculated field. The Forms design screen reappears, with the calculated field included.

With the mouse, you can easily select from options in menus and lists. To pick an item from the Expression Builder lists, for example, just double-click on the field name, operator, or function you want. To select a Picture function, click on the function from the Picture Functions submenu, then click on the `Accept: Ctrl-End` label in the navigation line. To cancel a menu choice, click on the `Cancel:Esc` label or click outside the menu area.

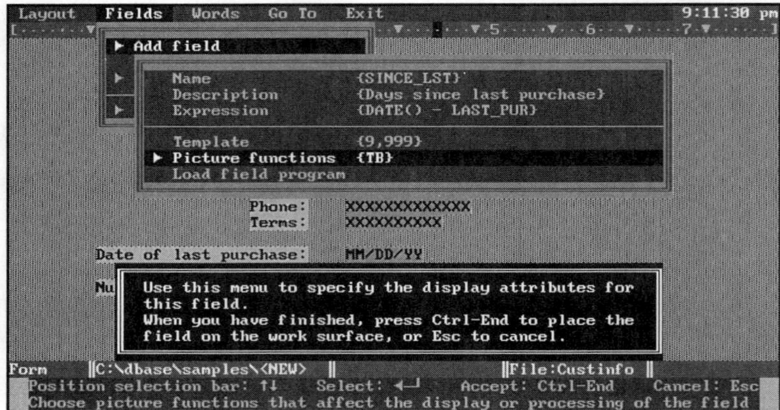


FIG. 9.17

The completed Field Definition menu for a calculated field.

When the form is placed on-screen with information from the database, dBASE calculates the number of days from the last purchase to the current date and displays it in this calculated field.

Now you are ready to move into another phase of form design—formatting the fields to accept only certain types of data. This type of formatting, often called *validity checking*, can help ensure that the data entered into the form is the right type of data.

**For Related Information...**

▸▸ "Working with Operators," p. 638.

▸▸ "Using Functions," p. 775.

# Validating Data and Formatting Fields

Databases require accurate data. Although no database system can assure complete accuracy of entered information, dBASE provides some powerful capabilities that help you avoid many "garbage-in, garbage-out" problems. Using dBASE forms, you can make sure that database fields receive information consistent with their field types. You can ensure that a field which must contain only numbers—whether that field is a numeric or character field—gets only numbers from the user. You also can set high and low limits on numeric fields, enabling character fields to receive only uppercase or lowercase letters.

The first way to validate data entered into a field is to use *templates* or *picture functions*. A field template enables you to specify valid input characters for each position of the field. Picture functions provide editing and validation capabilities that apply to the field as a whole.

A second way to validate data entered into a field is to use *edit options*. Edit options enable you to specify a range within which entered data must fall. You also can use edit options to make a field read-only and to set default values for a field.

Much of this chapter refers to using dBASE Forms design screen capabilities to validate data. You also can use template symbols and picture functions with forms you design to view the database on-screen. The rules of validation and formatting for data entered into a custom form also apply to data placed into a custom form from the database. Formatting fields with template symbols and picture functions makes data-viewing screens more readable and easy-to-use.

# Using Templates

A template enables you to specify character-by-character what type of data can be entered into a data-entry field. You can, for instance, tell dBASE you want all characters in a field to be numeric; if the user enters something other than a numeric, dBASE beeps impolitely and does not accept the entry.

If the field is 10 characters wide, the template for that field should contain 10 symbols, specifying what type of character can be entered into each position. To specify the template symbols, place the cursor on the field you want to modify and choose Modify Field from the Fields menu.

Then highlight Template on the Field Definition menu and press Enter. A help screen showing all the template symbols appears (see fig. 9.18). Use the help screen to assist you in finding the correct symbols for the template you enter in the input field.

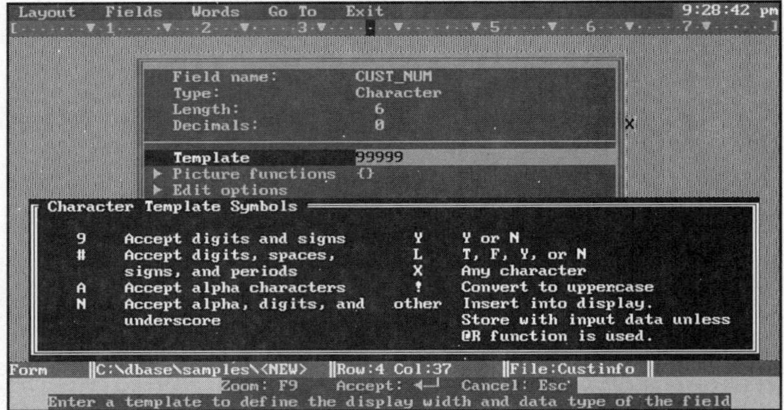


FIG. 9.18

The Template help screen for character fields.

Consider these two template symbols: A specifies that an alphabetic character must be entered at the position; 9 specifies a numeric entry (including a plus or minus sign). The following table shows some examples of different templates and their editing effects when you apply these symbols to a character field with a width of 5.

| Template | Data entered | Data displayed | Comment |
|---|---|---|---|
| 99999 | 12345 | 12345 | |
| AAAAA | 12345 | nothing | The template requires alphabetic characters, but only numerics were entered; dBASE rejects all the characters, beeping when the invalid characters are entered. |
| AAAAA | abcde | abcde | The template requires alphabetic characters, so it accepts the entry *abcde*. |
| 9A9A9A | abcde | nothing | dBASE rejects the entry because alphabetic characters are in the first position, which accepts only numeric data. |

As you can see, the template specifies what type of character can be entered and displayed at each position of the data field. If an invalid character is entered, dBASE beeps and rejects the extra character.

dBASE rejects the first invalid character entered. If you enter one or more valid characters before typing an invalid one, the valid characters are entered into the field.

The template characters you can use for a field differ with the type of field. Template characters for the different types of fields, with their validation effect, are listed in tables 9.2, 9.3, and 9.4.

**Table 9.2 Character-Field Template Symbols**

| Template | Effect |
|---|---|
| 9 | Accepts only digits (0 through 9) and signs (+, –). Does not accept a decimal point. |
| # | Accepts spaces, digits, signs, and a decimal point. Note that you can use the template characters *9* and *#* for character fields as well as numeric fields. |
| A | Accepts alphabetic characters only. |
| N | Accepts alphabetic characters, numeric digits, and the underscore character. |
| X | Accepts any character. |
| ! | Accepts any alphabetic character and forces it to uppercase. Other characters are unaffected. |
| other | Displays in the field any other character that you put in the template. When the user enters data into the field, the cursor skips these template characters, which become part of the input data. For example, you can specify a template of (999)999-9999 for phone numbers; users can enter numbers where the *9* template symbols are specified, but the parentheses and dash become part of the data stored for this field. (You can prevent these characters from becoming part of the input data by specifying the R picture function with the template.)<br>These "other" characters are referred to as *literals*; they are placed in the field exactly as you type them in the template. |

**Table 9.3 Numeric-Field and Float-Field Template Symbols**

| Template | Effect |
|---|---|
| 9 | Accepts only digits (0 through 9) and signs (+, –). Does not accept a decimal point. |
| # | Accepts spaces, digits, signs, and a decimal point. |
| . | Specifies the decimal point location. |
| , | Displays a comma at this position if the number is large enough. |
| * | Displays leading zeros as asterisks (*). Frequently used for check protection because this symbol fills the left side of the field with asterisks. |
| $ | Displays leading zeros as dollar signs ($). Also used for check protection. |
| other | Displays literal characters in the field display as you type them. |

**Table 9.4 Logical-Field Template Symbols**

| Template | Effect |
|---|---|
| L | Allows T (True), F (False), Y (Yes) or N (No). |
| Y | Allows only Y (Yes) or N (No). |
| other | Displays literal characters in the field display as you type them. |

No template symbols are available for date fields. You can modify the date-field formats by changing the way dBASE displays dates—use the Settings option of the Tools menu on the Control Center. Memo fields also have no template symbols available.

The following table shows some examples of template symbols applied to character fields:

| Value | Template | Result | Explanation |
|---|---|---|---|
| 123 | 99,999 | 123 | The comma template symbol has no effect if the number is not large enough to require the comma in this position. |
| 12345 | 99,999 | 12,345 | The comma template symbol takes effect here because the number is large enough to require a comma in that position. |
| 12345 | AAAAA | | The A template symbol allows only alphabetic data entry and display. During entry, dBASE beeps and rejects each digit as it is entered; during display, nothing appears. |
| 123ab | 999!! | 123AB | The 9 template symbol allows digits to be entered or displayed in the first three positions; the last two positions are changed to uppercase letters by the ! template symbol. |
| 12345 | NN,NNN | 12,345 | The N template symbol allows alphabetic and numeric input. |
| abcde | NN,NNN | ab,cde | The N template symbol allows alphabetic input; the comma literal puts the comma in the specified position. |

Template symbols used for numeric data fields are similar, but oriented more toward display of numeric values.

| Value | Template | Result | Explanation |
|---|---|---|---|
| 123<br>1234 | $9,999<br>$9,999 | $$$123<br>$1,234 | The $ template symbol replaces all leading zeros to the left of the first digit in the field with dollar signs. The * template symbol has the same effect, replacing leading zeroes with asterisks. |

| Value | Template | Result | Explanation |
|---|---|---|---|
| 123 | 999.99 | 123.00 | The . (decimal) template symbol determines the decimal position in the field. dBASE fills in positions after the decimal if the value does not have the same or more decimal positions. |

Template symbols are invaluable when you want to specify what can be entered into a field on a character-by-character basis. Picture functions offer validation and editing control for the field as a whole.

## Using Picture Functions

Use picture functions to validate characters entered into the field as a whole. You may want all characters entered in a field converted to uppercase. Rather than specifying a string of ! template symbols, you can simply specify the ! picture function, which forces all characters in the field to uppercase. The picture functions available differ depending on the type of data field being defined.

When creating a field, highlight the Picture Functions option on the Field Definition menu and press Enter. The Picture Functions menu appropriate to the type of field you are creating appears. To modify the picture functions for a field, place the cursor in that field and select Modify Field from the Fields menu or press F5 (Add field). The Picture Functions menu appropriate to the type of field you are modifying appears.

When you select Picture Functions for a character field, the menu shown in figure 9.19 appears. Move the highlight to the picture function you want to apply to the field and press Enter. Pressing Enter toggles the ON/OFF status of that function. If you select Scroll Within Display Width or Multiple Choice, additional menus appear to get more information from you.

Select or toggle the setting for a picture function by clicking on the option with the mouse. Click on the `Accept: Ctrl-End` label on the navigation line to save your choices.

If you are working with character fields, you can use the picture functions listed in table 9.5.

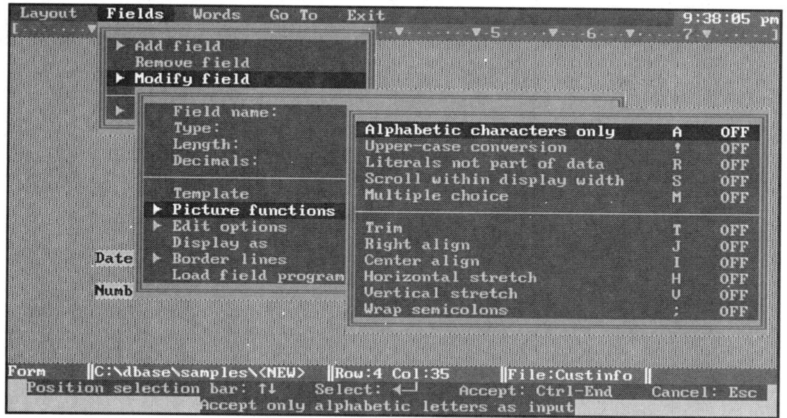


FIG. 9.19

The picture function help screen for character fields.

## Table 9.5 Character-Field Picture Functions

| Menu description | Picture function | Effect |
|---|---|---|
| Alphabetic Characters Only | A | All characters in the field must be alphabetic. |
| Upper-Case Conversion | ! | All characters entered into the field are forced to uppercase. Nonalphabetic characters are not affected. |
| Literals Not Part of Data | R | Literals are not stored as part of the data. Use this function in conjunction with a template using literal characters. A template like `(999)999-9999`, for example, accepts digits in the positions marked by *9* and includes the parentheses and dash in the data put into the database field. If you use the same template and add the R picture function, the data-entry effect is the same, but the parentheses and dash are not entered into the database. |

*continues*

**Table 9.5 Continued**

| Menu description | Picture function | Effect |
|---|---|---|
| Scroll Within Display Width | S | Scrolls entry within the display width. Use this function with a character field too wide to fit easily on the form. You can, for example, define a scroll width of 10 for a database field 15 characters wide. On the form, the field is 10 characters wide, but the field scrolls right and left to allow entry of up to 15 characters. When you select this option, you are asked to specify the scroll width. |
| Multiple Choice | M | Enables multiple choice for the field. You specify a list of acceptable inputs for this field. When you choose this option, an input box appears in which you list acceptable entries, separated by commas. If you use this function with a STATE field, for example, you can identify as acceptable the entries AL, AK, CA, and so on. |

When using a multiple-choice field on a form, you make a selection by pressing the space bar to scroll through the list; when the desired choice is highlighted, press Enter to select it. Alternatively, enter the first character of the desired choice; dBASE highlights the first choice that starts with that character in the multiple-choice list. Pressing the character again causes dBASE to highlight the next choice starting with that letter. When the desired choice is highlighted, press Enter to accept it.

The Picture Function help screen for character fields is divided by a horizontal line; below this line are six choices not available if you use the field for data entry. These six functions apply to fields that display data, rather than to fields that accept input. Several of these functions apply specifically to the display of memo fields, as shown in table 9.6.

**Table 9.6 Display-Field Picture Functions**

| Menu description | Picture function | Effect |
|---|---|---|
| Trim | T | Trims leading and trailing blanks off the value displayed in the field |
| Right Align | J | Aligns the value so that the last character is on the right margin of the field |
| Center Align | I | Centers the value in the field |

The picture functions available for numeric fields differ from those available for character fields. Table 9.7 lists the numeric-field picture functions.

## Using Edit Options To Control the Fields

In addition to using template symbols and picture functions to control data entry and presentation, you can use a series of edit options for each field. Edit options control actions that take place when the user enters the field.

To apply edit options to a form field, place the cursor on the field and choose Modify Field from the Fields menu or press F5 (Add Field). The Field Definition menu appears. Choose Edit Options from this menu. The Edit Options menu appears (see fig. 9.20). Now choose the options you want to apply to the field. Most edit options require you to provide additional information, although some options are activated simply by turning the setting ON or OFF. The edit options are described in the following paragraphs.

When you create a custom form, all fields can be edited. The Editing Allowed option can prevent editing in a field. When Editing Allowed is set to NO, data is displayed, but the cursor does not enter the field when the user accesses the form. These “read-only” fields are used when the database contains information you want to display but do not want someone to change.

## Table 9.7 Numeric-Field and Float-Field Picture Functions

| Menu description | Picture function | Effect |
|---|---|---|
| Positive credits followed by CR | C | Displays the characters CR (for credit) after positive numbers; a favorite of accountants. |
| Negative debits followed by DB | X | Displays the characters DB (for debit) after negative numbers; another accountant special. |
| Use ( ) around negative numbers | ( | Places parentheses around negative numbers. |
| Show leading zeros | L | Shows leading zeros; otherwise blanks are used. |
| Blanks for zero values | Z | Puts all blanks in a field that has a zero value. If you don't use this function, a database field that has a value of zero prints zeroes in each place on the field—for example, a field template of 99.9 shows a zero value as `0.0`. |
| Financial format | $ | Displays numbers in financial format: a leading dollar sign, commas in the number, and two decimal places. The dollar sign floats, occupying the position to the left of the first digit of the field value. |
| Exponential format | ^ | Uses the scientific form of a number: for example, 2.3E4 for 23,000. |

Sometimes, you may want a field to allow editing (Editing Allowed is set to YES) and sometimes you want the field to disallow editing. The Permit Edit If option enables you to set a condition under which the field can be edited. If the condition is not met, the user cannot access information in the field.

When you choose Permit Edit If, the {} entry field changes to enable you to enter a dBASE expression. Type the dBASE expression that determines whether dBASE is to allow the user to edit the field. You also can press Shift-F1 to display the expression-builder menu for help in creating the expression. The expression-builder menu is described in "Adding Calculated Fields to the Form," earlier in this chapter. dBASE expressions are covered in detail in Chapter 12. An *expression* essentially is a formula that dBASE evaluates to True or False. In this case, if the expression evaluates to True, the user can edit the field's information; if it evaluates to False, the field is skipped.

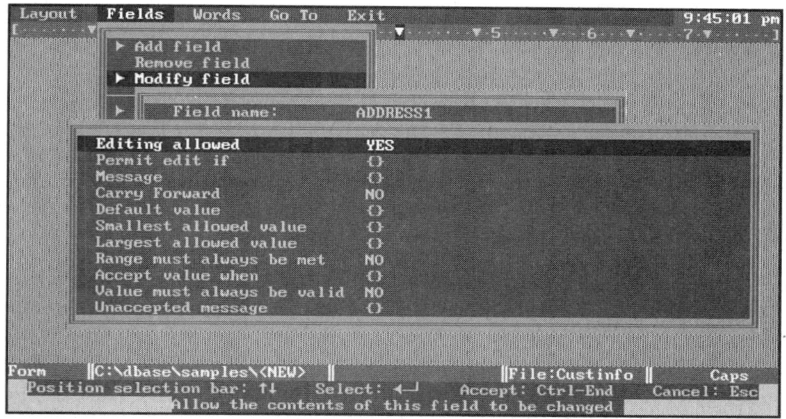


FIG. 9.20

The Edit Options menu.

In a customer database, for example, you can disallow the user from entering an address if no name is entered, because the customer name is a key information field. For each field, you can select Permit Edit If and enter the expression *CUST_NAME* <> "", which means "permit this field to be edited only if the CUST_NAME field is not blank."

**NOTE** When setting up forms that use Permit Edit If fields, remember that the fields in a dBASE form are processed from top to bottom and from left to right on the same line. If you want to permit an edit based on a field in the form, make sure that field is processed before the Permit Edit If field. Consider the CUST_NAME <> "" example. If you position the address field containing this condition on the form before the user has the chance to enter something in the CUST_NAME field, the expression always evaluates to False, and the user never can enter anything in the address field.

dBASE expressions can be simple or complex. When you specify a Permit Edit If expression, you are not limited to values in other fields on the form. You can have a field that uses the expression `CDOW(DATE())="Monday"`. (This expression allows entries on Mondays only.) The wisdom of such an expression is dubious, but this shows that you can permit data entry and editing for a wide variety of conditions.

The Message option enables you to specify a message (up to 79 characters) that is printed on the 25th line of the form when the cursor is in the associated field. This option enables you to provide context-sensitive help, which is a help message appropriate to the field being edited.

To add a message to a field, highlight the Message option and press Enter. Now type the message. When you finish typing the message, press Enter to accept the message and return to the Edit Options menu.

When the form is in use, the message appears when the cursor enters the field. Unfortunately, you cannot display a message on the 25th line of the screen for a field that was skipped because of a failed Permit Edit If test.

You can specify where you want the message to appear on the form by changing the Set Message To location. Change this setting in the Settings option of the Tools menu, located in the Control Center. This change applies to all messages in all forms that normally appear on the 25th line. Exercise caution when changing the message location; make sure that the new location you specify suits all the forms.

> **WARNING:** Do not include double quotation marks (" ") in the message you specify for the Message option. dBASE cannot interpret double quotation marks in a message correctly. When you save the form, dBASE reports a compile error, and the form is not usable.

When you enter new records into a database, dBASE normally blanks out all the fields in the new record. Sometimes, however, you may want a new record to contain a value entered in the preceding record; set the Carry Forward option to YES provide this capability.

If you are entering data sorted by date, for example, you want to be able to enter the date only when it changes from the preceding record; just set Carry Forward to YES for the date field. The date field for a new record displays the date entered in that field for the preceding record. The user accepts the date by pressing Enter when the cursor reaches that field. If the user wants to change the date, the user can do so with normal dBASE editing techniques.

You can have a field display a certain value whenever the field is used to enter a new record by specifying that value in the Default Value option. When the form appears, the default value appears in the field. The user can accept the default value by pressing Enter when the cursor enters the field or can change the value simply by typing a new value.

Suppose that you have an order-entry form with a date field, and you always want today's date to appear in the field when the form is used for data entry. You can have dBASE insert the current date in that field by typing *DATE()* for the Default value option. When the user accesses the form, the current date appears in the field; the user can change the date simply by entering a new date.

You can use any value as a default value, as long as it matches the field type. Character values must be enclosed in double quotation marks (" "). If you want to use the abbreviation for *Washington* as the default in a character field, for example, type *"WA"* for the Default Value option. If you want a specific date to appear as the default in a date field, type *{01/01/92}*.

Use the Smallest Allowed Value and Largest Allowed Value options to specify a range of acceptable values for the field. Specifying a range of acceptable values is most useful when used with date or numeric fields, but you also can do so with character fields.

You may have a form with a date field that you want to accept values for the year 1992 only. To set the range of acceptable values, highlight Smallest Value Allowed and type *{01/01/92}*; highlight Largest Value Allowed and type *{12/31/92}*—make sure that you include the curly braces. If you enter a date outside this range when you use the form, dBASE beeps and displays the following message:

```
Range is 01/01/92 to 12/31/92 (press SPACE)
```

Although less common, you also can specify ranges of acceptable values for character fields; in the case of character fields, the test is made alphabetically. Suppose that you have a database with a five-character PART_NUM field, and all the part numbers are prefixed with the letters A through D. You can specify the smallest value to be "A0000" and the largest value to be "D9999". Any value not starting with the letters A, B, C, or D causes an error: dBASE beeps and displays this message on the message line:

```
Range is "A0000" to "D9999" (press SPACE)
```

The Accept Value When option enables you to specify a dBASE expression that tests the value entered into the field. If the value passes the test (the expression evaluates to True), the value is accepted. If the value does not pass the test, the entry is rejected and must be reentered. The Accept Value When option is a powerful tool for making sure that the data going into a database is valid.

Suppose that you have a customer database, for example, and your company has decreed that customer numbers are five characters long. You can define a CUST_NUM field of character type with a length of five. To make sure that the entered customer number is a full five characters long, define an Accept Value When expression of LEN(LTRIM(TRIM(CUST_NUM)))=5. That expression says "the length of the CUST_NUM when leading and trailing blanks spaces are trimmed off must be 5." If you enter *A323* in the CUST_NUM field, the expression LEN(TRIM(CUST_NUM)) evaluates to 4, and the value entered is rejected.

Because dBASE expressions can be very complex, you can use the Accept Value When option to perform complex validation tests.

Use the Unaccepted Message option in conjunction with the Accept Value When option to specify a message to appear on the 25th line of the screen when the value entered into a field does not pass the Accept Value When expression. The Unaccepted Message option enables you to customize the error message for the field.

For example, if you define an Accept Value When expression of LEN(LTRIM(TRIM(CUST_NUM)))=5 (as described in the preceding example), you can define the Unaccepted Message as `Customer Numbers must be exactly 5 characters long`. If the user enters a customer number less than five characters long, this message appears. You also can use the Unaccepted Message option to give specific directions to the user in the event of a data-entry error. Unaccepted messages can be up to 79 characters long.

You can use the mouse to select Edit options. To toggle Yes/No values, click on the option. For options requiring data entry, type in the required information, then click on the `Accept` label on the navigation line. To expand the data-entry area for long expressions, click on the `Zoom:F9` label, enter the data, then click `Zoom:F9` again to return to the Edit options menu. To open the Expression Builder list, click on the `Pick Operators/Fields:Shift-F1` label.

In the Edit options menu, dBASE IV 1.5 offers two useful options. The Range Must Always Be Met option checks to see if the data falls within the specified range every time you exit the field if this option is set to Yes. Otherwise, data is checked only after it has been changed. The Value Must Always Be Valid option checks the validity of data every time you exit the field if set to Yes. Otherwise, validity is checked only when data is changed.

**For Related Information...**

▸▸ "Accepting User Input," p. 478.

▸▸ "@ Say...Get," p. 664.

# Creating Multiple-Page Forms

Some database designs have more fields than can fit onto one screen. Custom forms are easier to read and use if the data fields are not crowded onto the screen. You can design custom forms with up to 16 pages, although you seldom need more than two or three pages.

To design a custom form with more than one page, simply design the first page of the form, move the cursor to the bottom of the first page, and press PgDn. A second, blank page appears. Follow this same procedure to add subsequent pages. Scroll back to the first page by pressing PgUp; scroll to the last page by pressing PgDn.

When using a multiple-page form, use PgUp and PgDn to move forward and backward through the pages. When you reach the last page, pressing PgDn displays the first page of the next record. Similarly, pressing PgUp while on the first page of a multiple-page form displays the last page of the preceding record.

Multiple-page forms are useful even when you can fit all database fields on one screen. If your data falls into logical groups, putting those groups on separate pages may make the form easier to use. If you are entering data into a customer-information database, for example, you can use one screen for information about the customer's name, address, and telephone number, and another screen for information about the customer's business and purchasing guidelines. Each page takes and presents information about a different logical type of information about the customer.

**TIP**

When you use multiple-page forms, consider repeating one or two fields on each page so that the user has no doubt about which record he or she is working with. In the customer-information form example, you could include the customer name on each page of the multiple-page form. The user then can easily identify the customer with the information being entered. The values the user enters into the fields in the first page appear in these repeating fields on each subsequent page. Make these repeating fields "read-only" (set Editing Allowed on the Edit Option menu to NO). Doing so ensures that the cursor never enters these fields.

You can put a field on a form any number of times simply by positioning the cursor where you want the field to appear and choosing Add Field from the Fields menu.

# Saving and Using Forms

If you have come this far in this chapter, the hard part of designing and using custom forms is completed. After the form is designed, be sure to save it. To use the form, you access it from the Control Center.

After the form is complete, save it by choosing Save Changes And Exit from the Form design screen Exit menu. The first time you save a form—either by using Save Changes And Exit from the Form design screen Exit menu or by using Save This Form from the Layout menu—dBASE asks you for the name of the form. Enter a standard dBASE name of up to eight characters.

When you exit from the Forms design screen, notice that the form you just created is in the current catalog, ready to be used.

To use the form, move the cursor in the Control Center to the Forms panel, highlight the form name you want to use, and press Enter. You see the menu shown in figure 9.21, asking whether you want to display data or modify the layout. Choose Display Data.

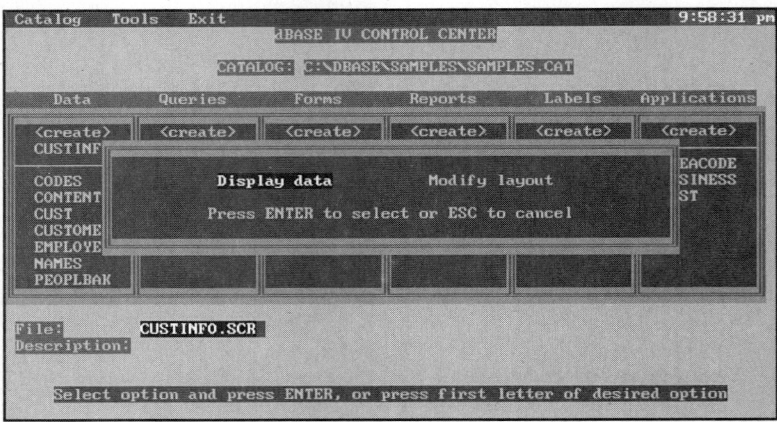


FIG. 9.21

Selecting the custom form to use.

The form appears on-screen, showing the information in the first record of the database, if the database contains records. Figure 9.22 shows a completed form in use. You can use the dBASE menu bar with a custom form just as you do with default forms to add records, edit existing records, and find the records you want to view or edit. Chapter 7, "Adding and Editing Data," describes the use of this menu bar when you enter data.

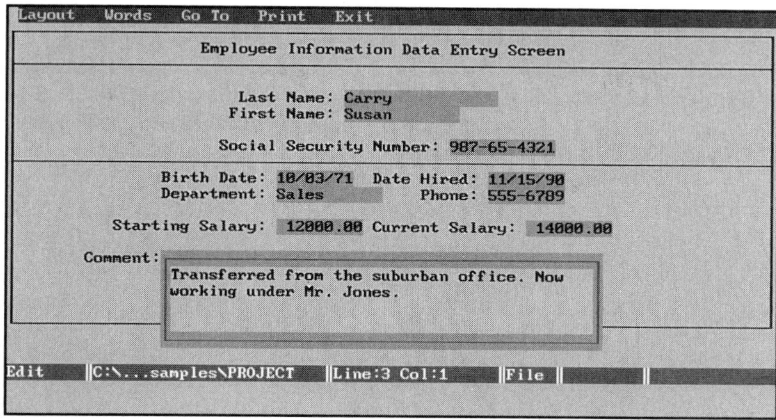
Layout Words Go To Print Exit

Employee Information Data Entry Screen

Last Name: Carry
First Name: Susan

Social Security Number: 987-65-4321

Birth Date: 10/03/71 Date Hired: 11/15/90
Department: Sales Phone: 555-6789

Starting Salary: 12000.00 Current Salary: 14000.00

Comment: Transferred from the suburban office. Now working under Mr. Jones.

Edit ||C:\...samples\PROJECT ||Line:3 Col:1 ||File ||

**FIG. 9.22**

A custom data-entry form.

**For Related Information...**

▸▸ "Set Format To," p. 873.

**FROM HERE...**

# Summary

Custom forms make dBASE easier to use, for you and for anyone who uses the system you design. This chapter has thoroughly introduced form design, including ways to format, edit, and validate the data entered and displayed on a custom form. The time you spend learning about and using custom forms is repaid many times over as you use the forms to modify and access the database.

CHAPTER 10

# Writing Reports in dBASE IV

Reports are the most visible evidence of a dBASE IV database application. You may have the most sophisticated database design, wonderful input screens, and a wealth of informative data in the system, but if your reports are difficult to read and understand, your database is less than successful. dBASE IV offers an extremely sophisticated, easy-to-use capability for creating excellent reports. The Report design work surface enables you to create reports simply by placing database fields on-screen. You then can add summary fields, text, boxes, and lines to make the report more informative and readable.

In this chapter, you move beyond the default quick reports you learned how to generate in Part II. You see how to define your report with database fields, how to create fields calculated from database fields, and how to summarize information from the entire report. You also learn how to group data so that the user of the report has better comprehension of the data. You may find that report writing is enjoyable and rewarding in dBASE IV.

# Using Quick Report

The fastest way to create a report in dBASE is to use Quick Report. The Quick Report feature generates a plain and simple report by printing—with little formatting—the data from a database. Although you usually want to generate elegant, customized reports with the dBASE Report Generator, you also may find times when Quick Report serves your purposes perfectly.

To create a Quick Report on the Customer database, follow these steps from the Control Center:

1. In the Data column, highlight CUSTOMER and press Enter to make Customer the active database.
2. Press Shift-F9 to activate Quick Report.
3. A menu appears, through which you specify printing information. If you want to view the report on-screen, choose that option. To print the report, simply press Enter—the option Begin Printing is highlighted when the menu first appears. Other options on the menu are discussed later in this chapter.
4. dBASE generates a report program, which takes a few seconds. Then the report prints. It is quite simple, containing just a page number, a date, basic column headings, and the information (see fig. 10.1).

```
Page No.    1
02/20/92

CUST_NUM   CUSTOMER                        CITY                STATE  ZIP

A00001     SMITH AND ASSOCIATES            Los Angeles         CA     90055
A10025     ALPHA ENTERPRISES               Los Angeles         CA     95075
B12345     JIM SMITH                       Santa Monica        CA     97090
C00001     L.G. BLUM AND ASSOCIATES        Los Angeles         CA     98007
C00002     TIMMONS AND CASEY LTD.          Los Angeles         CA     97207
L00001     BAILEY AND BAILEY               Los Angeles         CA     90022
L00002     SAWYER, LONG AND PETERS         Dallas              TX     75002

                Cancel viewing: ESC,  Continue viewing: SPACEBAR
```

FIG. 10.1

Viewing a Quick Report on the Screen.

To run a Quick Report from the Control Center using the mouse, click on the appropriate database file or query name. Then click on the `Quick report:Shift-F9` label on the navigation line to bring up the Print menu. Click on Begin Printing to start printing the report.

If you have created a query that limits the fields with the view skeleton or sorts the output, make that query active by highlighting it in the Queries column. Press Shift-F9 (Quick Report). The query then controls the output of the report.

Quick Report works fine when you need a fast report or when you want to have the output of a query printed. You quickly find, however, that most of your reports need more extensive formatting to present the database information clearly and elegantly.

**For Related Information...**

◂◂ "Generating a Quick Report," ch. 7.

▸▸ "Creating a Quick Report with LIST," ch. 19.

# Using the Report Design Screen

To create a dBASE IV report without using Quick Report, first make sure that you select the desired database from the Data panel of the Control Center. Then move the cursor to the Reports panel. If the <create> option in the Reports panel is not highlighted, use the arrow keys to highlight it and press Enter. The Report design screen appears (see fig. 10.2). Press Esc to remove the Layout pull-down menu and make the work surface visible. This surface is like a designer's table, on which you add, edit, and move around the many elements that make up a successful report. The following sections take you on a tour of the Report design screen.

## The Menus on the Report Design Screen

The dBASE IV Report menu appears at the top of the design screen. As with other menus, you access the Report design screen menu by pressing F10 and using the left- and right-arrow keys to highlight the menu option wanted. Alternatively, you can press and hold Alt as you type the first letter of the menu option you want—for example, press Alt-L to access the Layout menu. Each menu option has an associated pull-down menu from which you choose desired dBASE IV commands. To return to the work surface without taking any action from the menus, press the Esc key.

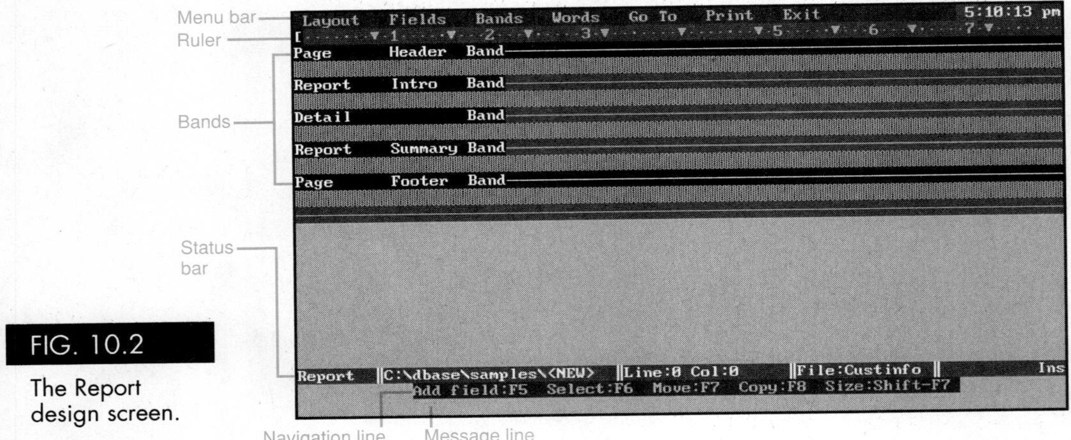


FIG. 10.2

The Report design screen.

To access menus with the mouse, click on the menu name in the menu bar, then click on a menu option. To close a menu, click outside the menu area.

## The Bands on the Report Design Screen

Figure 10.2 shows that the Report design work surface has five bands: the Page Header, Report Intro, Detail, Report Summary, and Page Footer bands. Below the title of each band is a shaded blank line. Text and fields placed in the blank line of the band print out in specific areas of the report. In this chapter, you use the Customer database to see how a report is created. Table 10.1 shows the structure of the Customer database.

Table 10.2 lists the bands on the Report design work surface and provides a description of each.

**Table 10.1 The Customer Database**

| Field | Field name | Type | Width | Dec | Index |
|---|---|---|---|---|---|
| 1 | CUST_NUM | Numeric | 5 | | Y |
| 2 | CUST_NAME | Character | 25 | | Y |
| 3 | STATE | Character | 2 | | Y |
| 4 | ZIP | Character | 5 | | Y |
| 5 | CURR_BAL | Numeric | 8 | 2 | N |
| 6 | CREDIT_LMT | Numeric | 8 | 2 | N |

**Table 10.2 Bands on the Report Design Work Surface**

| Band | Description |
|---|---|
| Page Header | Contains fields and text that print at the top of each page. A report title, a date and time stamp, and column headings are good examples of fields to put into the Page Header band, if you want them printed on each page. |
| Report Intro | Prints only on the first page of the report, after the Page Header band. A complete title and comments about the report are good candidates for the Report Intro band. |
| Detail | Prints once for each record in the database. As dBASE IV proceeds through the active database, it prints the fields in the Detail band once for each record. |
| Report Summary | Prints at the end of the report, after the last record printed in the Detail band. Use the Report Summary band to summarize data printed in the Detail bands. This summary can include totals and averages of numeric fields or counts of how many records were printed. |
| Page Footer | Prints at the bottom of each page of the report. This band is good for printing page numbers. |

# The Ruler on the Report Design Screen

The ruler appears across the top of the Report design screen, just under the menu bar. As the cursor moves in the work surface, a highlight moves on the ruler so that you can always see in what column the cursor is located. The numbers on the ruler represent tens position markers; instead of 10, 20, 30, you see 1, 2, 3. The down-facing arrows locate the tabs.

The ruler controls the left and right margins of the report, as well as the tab settings. To modify these report settings, choose Modify Ruler from the Words menu. The cursor moves into the ruler. Use the left and right arrows to move the cursor left and right along the ruler. Pressing the space bar is the same as pressing the right arrow.

To set a new tab, place the cursor at the desired location and press the ! key. A down-facing triangle appears to represent the tab. To remove a tab, place the cursor over the down-facing arrow and press Del or Backspace.

You can modify the margins of the report by using the ruler. The left margin is indicated by a left bracket ( [ ) in the ruler. The right margin is indicated by a right bracket ( ] ). Reset the margins by typing on the ruler a right or left bracket where you want the right or left margin to be.

After you modify the ruler to your liking, press Enter to return to the Report design work surface.

# The Status Bar on the Report Design Screen

The Report design screen uses the standard dBASE IV status bar, which shows information about the work surface. The leftmost section of the status bar reads `Report`, indicating that you are in the Report design screen. The next section shows the name of the report you are designing. If this is a new report, the path ends with `<NEW>`. The next section of the status bar relates information about the cursor location. If the cursor is in a band's title bar, this section reads `BAND`, followed by a fraction indicating which band. If the cursor is in the third of five bands, for example, the cursor location is `BAND 3/5`. If the cursor is in the lines of a band, the line and column numbers within that band are shown. The `File:` indicator specifies the currently active database file. The last section of the status bar shows the status of the Num Lock, Caps Lock, and Ins keys. If the `Num`, `Caps`, or `Ins` indicator appears in this section of the status bar, the related key is active. Press that key to deactivate it.

## The Navigation Line on the Report Design Screen

At the bottom of the Report design screen is the navigation line, which reminds you of the available function keys. Press F5 (Add Field) to place a new field on the work surface. Press F6 (Select) to select an existing field to be moved, copied, or resized. Press F7 (Move) to move a field. Press F8 (Copy) to copy a field. Press Shift-F7 (Size) to change the size of a field. Each of these selections is explained in more detail in this chapter.

Remember that you can click on the key labels (such as `Add field:F5`, `Move:F7`, and so on) on the navigation line with the mouse instead of pressing the function keys.

As with other work surfaces in dBASE, the last line is the message line, on which dBASE displays messages explaining what actions it expects.

# Designing Reports

To design a report with the Report design screen, simply place database fields where you want them to appear. Format them as necessary, add text where appropriate to improve the understanding of your report, and finish by placing lines and boxes to improve readability. As you add these elements, the report takes form on the work surface. To make a change to the report, simply change the elements on the work surface.

## Using Quick Layouts To Create a Default Report

When you first see the Report design screen, you have the proverbial "clean slate." Only the bands are on the work surface. First, place on the work surface the fields from the database that you want the report to use. Because you want these fields printed for each record in your database (you can limit which records are printed), place the fields in the Detail band. Choose Quick Layouts from the Layout menu to place all the fields from the database in the Detail band. You also can place selected fields in the Detail band one by one.

The quickest way to place fields on the Report design work surface is to choose Quick Layouts from the Layout menu. After you select this option, dBASE asks whether you want the layout in Column, Form, or Mailmerge format. Ignore Mailmerge for now. Figure 10.3 shows the work surface with Column layout; figure 10.4 shows the work surface with Form layout. The example developed in this chapter uses the Column layout because that is the layout used most commonly.

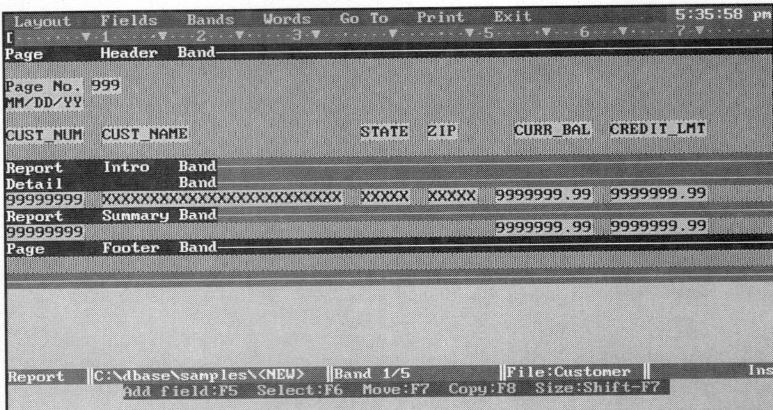


**FIG. 10.3**

The Column layout.

```
Layout   Fields   Bands   Words   Go To   Print   Exit         5:36:51 pm
Page        Header  Band
Page No. 999
MM/DD/YY
Report      Intro   Band
Detail              Band
CUST_NUM     99999
CUST_NAME    XXXXXXXXXXXXXXXXXXXXXXXXX
STATE        XX
ZIP          XXXXX
CURR_BAL     99999.99
CREDIT_LMT   99999.99
Report      Summary Band
Page        Footer  Band
Report  C:\dbase\samples\<NEW>  Band 1/5  File:Customer  Ins
        Add field:F5  Select:F6  Move:F7  Copy:F8  Size:Shift-F7
```

**FIG. 10.4**

The Form layout.

To use Quick Layouts to create a default report, follow these steps:

1. Choose Quick Layouts from the Layout menu. The cursor can be anywhere on the work surface.
2. The Quick Report menu appears, asking whether you want a Column layout, a Form layout, or a Mailmerge layout. If you want your report to have a column for each database field, choose

Column; if you want the report to print each database field on a separate line, choose Form. You mostly use Column layouts, so choose that and press Enter.

3. dBASE responds by creating a default report. In this report, all database fields are positioned in the Detail band, which prints once for each database record. The Quick Layout also places column headings—usually the database field names—at the top of the page, with a page number and report date.

In Column layout, dBASE places the database fields side by side in the Detail band, with two spaces between each field. The widths of the fields in the report are actually the same as the widths of the fields in the database. Figure 10.3 shows the design surface after a Column Quick Layout.

In Form layout, dBASE places database fields in the Detail band, putting one field on each line of the band. Figure 10.4 shows Form layout for the Customer database. The Column headings are replaced by a title to the left of each database field; the page number and report date remain in the Page Header band.

In the Column layout, note that the Quick Report totals all numeric fields in the Report Summary band. Delete any totals you do not want to appear in the report. In this report, for example, you would not want a total on the CUST_NUM field. Move the cursor to that field—the first one in the Report Summary band—and press Del to remove it.

## Testing the Report

The Print menu provides a quick and easy way to test your report. To see whether your report is doing what you want it to do, follow these steps:

1. Choose the Print menu from the Report design screen by pressing Alt-P. You also can press F10, use the arrow keys to highlight the Print option, and then press Enter.
2. Select View Report On Screen by using the arrow keys to highlight the selection and pressing Enter; or just press V.

   To access the Print options with the mouse, click on Print on the menu bar, and then click on the option you need.

dBASE IV creates the report file and runs the report, printing the output on-screen. dBASE pauses after displaying each page so that you can press Esc to exit from the report or press the space bar to continue viewing. If the report is more than 80 columns wide, longer lines wrap around to the next line on the screen. A single line of a 128-column report, for example, takes two lines on-screen. Figure 10.5 shows the report of the Customer database as it appears on-screen.

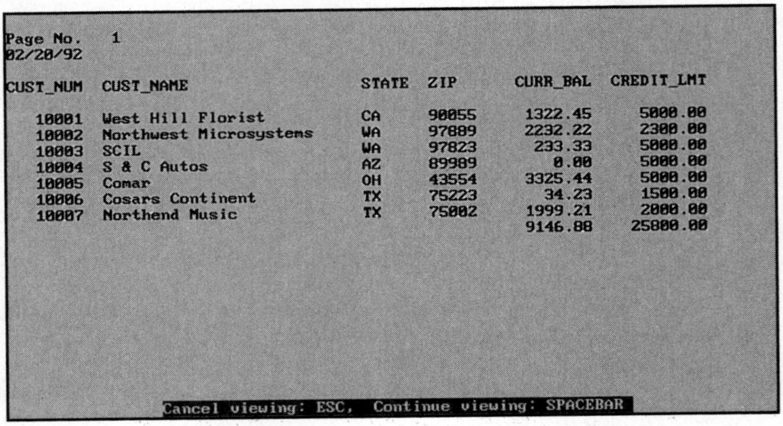

```
Page No.    1
02/20/92

CUST_NUM  CUST_NAME                    STATE  ZIP       CURR_BAL  CREDIT_LMT

   10001  West Hill Florist            CA     90055      1322.45     5000.00
   10002  Northwest Microsystems       WA     97889      2232.22     2300.00
   10003  SCIL                         WA     97823       233.33     5000.00
   10004  S & C Autos                  AZ     89989         0.00     5000.00
   10005  Comar                        OH     43554      3325.44     5000.00
   10006  Cosars Continent             TX     75223        34.23     1500.00
   10007  Northend Music               TX     75002      1999.21     2000.00
                                                         9146.88    25800.00

          Cancel viewing: ESC,  Continue viewing: SPACEBAR
```

FIG. 10.5

The view screen for the default Column report.

## Adding Fields to the Bands

You don't have to use the Quick Layouts option to put fields on the bands of the work surface; you can add them one at a time. Add individual fields to the bands when you are not going to include all the fields of a database in the report.

First, clear the Quick Layout report design from the screen by selecting Abandon Changes And Exit from the Exit menu, taking you back to the Control Center. Once again, select <create> from the Reports panel to create a new report form. Press Esc to close the Layouts menu that appears. To add fields individually, follow these steps:

1. Place the cursor where you want to insert a field. You normally place database fields in the Detail band. To place CUST_NUM, a field in the Customer database, place the cursor in column 0 of the Detail band. You can put a field in any column.

2. Choose the Fields menu and select Add Field or press F5. The field selection box appears (see fig. 10.6). All of the fields in the database appear in the leftmost column of the field selection box, where the name of the database is used as a heading. Choose a database field to add to the report by highlighting it and pressing Enter—for example, select the CUST_NUM field from the first column and press Enter.

You use the columns labeled Calculated, Predefined, and Summary to create specialized fields. These columns are covered later in this chapter.

3. After you select the field, the field format box appears (see fig. 10.7). This box presents information about the field—its name, type, length, and number of decimal places—along with options to alter the field's appearance on the report. Choose the default values by pressing Ctrl-End. The formatting options are covered later in this chapter, in "Changing the Way a Field Presents Data."

To place a field on the work surface using the mouse, just click on the location to reposition the cursor, click on Fields in the menu bar, and then click on Add Field. You can pick fields from the field selection box by double-clicking on the field name.

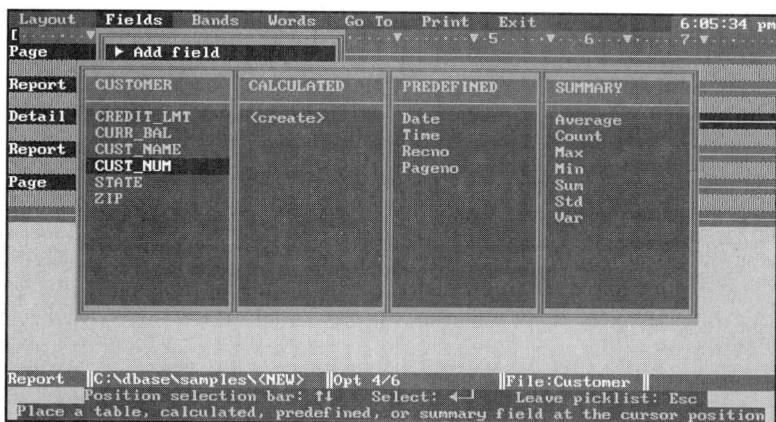


FIG. 10.6

The Add Field field selection box.

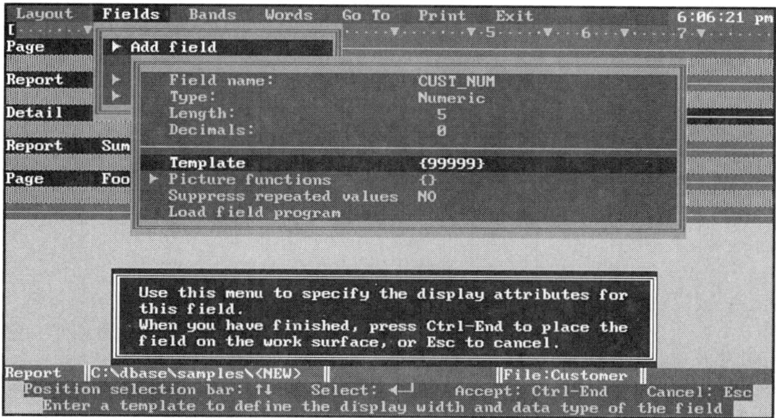


FIG. 10.7

The field format box.

After you press Ctrl-End, you return to the Report design work surface, which shows the newly added field. Repeat these three steps until all the fields you want to appear on the report are on the work surface. You can add fields to any band on the surface. Note that database fields, however, usually are in the Detail band, where they are printed once for each record. If you want to place fields in other bands, follow the same process.

## Moving Fields on the Bands

After you add fields to the bands of the Report design work surface, you may want to move them to make your report more readable. You can move a field anywhere on the band.

To move a field within a band, follow these steps:

1. Position the cursor on the field you want to move and press F6 (Select). Press Enter to select the field, preparing it to be moved.
2. Press F7 (Move). Using the arrow keys, position the cursor on the band where you want to move the field. You cannot move a field from one band to another band by using the arrow keys; if you need to do this, see the next set of steps.
3. After you move the field to its new position, press Enter. If you moved the field on top of another field or some text, dBASE asks whether you want to delete the covered field or text. If you reply Yes, the old field is deleted and replaced by the moved field. If you reply No, the move does not occur, and all fields remain in their original positions.

To move fields from one band to another, you follow a slightly different process:

1. Select the field you want to move by pressing F6 (Select), and then press Enter.
2. Before pressing F7 (Move), use the arrow keys to move the cursor to the band into which you want to move the field.
3. Press F7 (Move). A ghost of the field appears at the cursor location. You now can use the arrow keys to place the ghost at the new field's location.
4. Press Enter to complete the move.

To move a field with the mouse, select it by dragging the mouse over the field area, then release the mouse button. Click on the new location to reposition the cursor, then double-click on the `Move:F7` label in the navigation line.

Remember to press Esc to deselect a selected field after you have moved it.

If you move a field slightly so that its new position covers any part of its old position, you see the message `Delete covered text and fields? (Y/N)`. In this case, the covered field is the original position of the field you're moving. When you respond Yes, the field assumes its new position.

## Deleting Fields from the Bands

Deleting a field is even simpler than moving one. Simply place the cursor on the field and press Del. The field disappears from the band.

## Changing a Field's Size

Changing the size of a field—its length on the report—is simple. Move the cursor to the field you want to change and press Shift-F7 (Size). The entire field is highlighted. Press the arrow keys to make the field larger or smaller. The highlight shrinks or grows as you reduce or enlarge the field's length, although the `X`s that mark the size of the original field remain until you press Enter to accept the new size. If you decide not to resize the field, cancel the action by pressing Esc instead of Enter.

To resize a field with the mouse, click on the field, click on the `Size:Shift-F7` label in the navigation line, move the mouse pointer to resize the field, then click again.

## Changing the Way a Field Presents Data

When you first put a field on a band in the Report design screen, the field displays its data on the report just as the data appears in the database. You may want to modify the appearance of the data, however, to make your report look better and be more understandable. Suppose that the report uses a field which displays dollar amounts. The default presentation of the field is as follows:

```
134329.33
```

This format presents the information correctly, but in a less-than-readable format. With dBASE IV, you can change the format of the field so that the report information appears like this:

```
$134,329.33
```

This format has a nicer appearance and makes your report much more readable. To change the way a field presents its data, select the field you want to change and select Modify Field from the Field menu, or press F5. The field format box appears.

The top half of the field format box contains information about the field you are modifying: its name, type, length, and the number of decimal places it uses. The bottom half lists three options you can use to alter the presentation of the data in this field: Template, Picture Functions, and Suppress Repeated Values. The following sections explain how to use each of these options.

## Using the Template Option

A *template* is a string of formatting symbols, one for each position in a field. The *template symbol* controls what will be displayed in a particular position in the field. You use a template to alter the presentation of the field on the report.

For example, the template symbol 9 says, "Display only a numeric digit at this position." The template symbol comma (,) says, "Display a comma at this position." If you have a database field with a length of 5 that stores numeric data (even though the field type might be numeric, float, or character), and you want the report field to have a comma in the appropriate place if the database value is greater than 999, you can specify the template as follows:

    99,999

When the report is printed, dBASE fits the database value into the template, inserting the comma at the right place. A database value of 1324 appears in the report as 1,324.

Similarly, you can specify a decimal position for a numeric field with the template symbol for the decimal position, the period (.). Regardless of the length of the database numeric field, you can specify how many decimal places are printed on the report. If you want two decimal places and commas where appropriate, define the template as 99,999.99. Now the number 1324 appears as 1,324.00 on the report.

To define templates, choose the Template option in the field format box. The braces surrounding the default template disappear, and you can edit the template. If you add symbols that increase the length of the field—such as commas or decimal places—the field automatically increases in size. This increase may cause other fields on the line to shift right to accommodate the larger field.

Following is a list of the template symbols you can use in a dBASE IV report for numeric fields:

| Symbol | Function |
|---|---|
| 9 | Presents only digits, or a positive (+) or negative (–) sign. |
| # | Presents only digits, spaces, and the positive or negative signs. |
| . | Specifies the decimal point location in the field. |
| , | Displays a comma at this location if the number is large enough to require it. |
| * | Displays leading zeros as asterisks. Placed to the left of the first numeric template symbol, this symbol causes * to appear in all positions to the left of the first digit printed. For example, *999 prints the value 1 as **1. |
| $ | Displays the same as the *, except that a dollar sign is used instead. |
| other | Any other character you type in the template is inserted into the display. Use this feature to insert dashes or slashes into a numeric field. |

The best way to learn how to use template symbols is to look at examples and use the samples as the basis for new templates. The following table shows several useful examples of templates in a nine-character field.

| Data value | Template | Report presentation |
|---|---|---|
| 12345.67 | 99,999.99 | 12,345.67 |
| 12.34 | *99.99 | ****12.34 |
| 12.34 | $99,999.99 | $$$$12.34 |
| 5551212 | 999-9999 | 555-1212 |

With character fields, you use a different set of template symbols. Following is a list of the template symbols you use in a dBASE IV report for character fields:

| Symbol | Function |
|---|---|
| 9 | Displays digits and signs |
| # | Displays digits, signs, spaces, and periods |

*continues*

| Symbol | Function |
|---|---|
| A | Displays alphabetic characters only |
| N | Displays alphabetic characters, digits, and the underscore |
| X | Displays any character |
| ! | Converts the database value to uppercase in this position |
| other | Any other character you type in the template is inserted into the display at this position |

Again, some examples of the use of the character template symbols are helpful:

| Data value | Template | Report presentation |
|---|---|---|
| abcdefg | !!!!!!! | ABCDEFG |
| abcdefg | !AAAAAA | Abcdefg |
| 555443333 | 999-99-9999 | 555-44-3333 |

## Using the Picture Functions Option

You also can alter the presentation of data in a report field by using the Picture Functions option from the field format box. Using this option is similar to using template symbols, except that a picture function applies to the entire field, and a template symbol applies to only a single position in the field. To modify a field's presentation by using the picture method, choose Picture Functions from the field format box. Depending on the type of field you are changing, you see either the Character Picture Function menu (see fig. 10.8) or the Numeric Picture Function menu (see fig. 10.9).

To apply a picture function, highlight the function you want to apply to the field and press Enter. The function setting changes from OFF to ON. Press Enter again to change the setting back to OFF.

Picture functions apply to the entire field. If you select the Upper-Case Conversion function, for example, all characters in the field are converted to uppercase, regardless of their position. Compare this to using a template, in which you place the uppercase-conversion character (!) in each position where you want the conversion to occur.

Most character picture functions are self-explanatory. You will encounter the Vertical Stretch and Horizontal Stretch options when working with memo fields later in this chapter. Following is a description of the character picture functions.

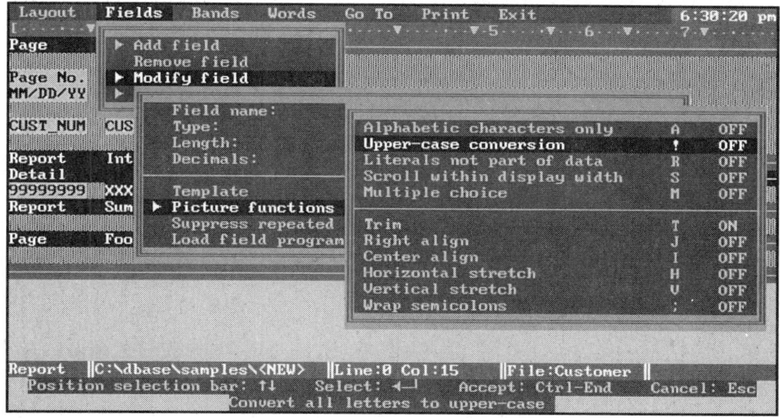


FIG. 10.8

The Character Picture Function menu.

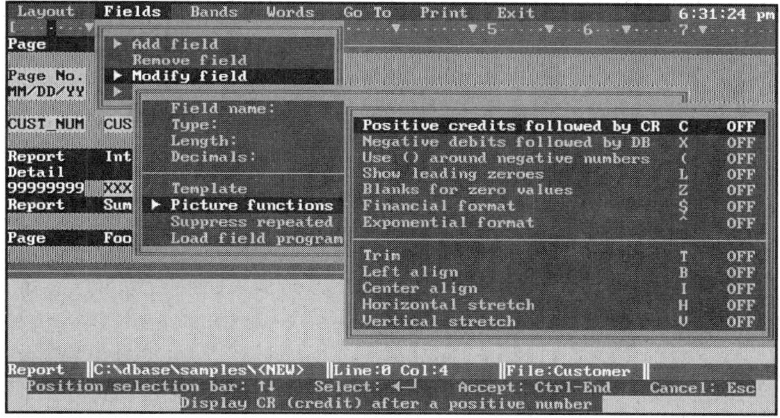


FIG. 10.9

The Numeric Picture Function menu.

| Function | Description |
|---|---|
| Alphabetic Characters Only | Displays alphabetic characters only. |
| Upper-Case Conversion | Converts all characters to uppercase (numbers are unaffected). |
| Literals Not Part Of Data | Literal characters in a field consist of nontemplate symbols that you want to appear in a field, such as the hyphen (-) in a phone number field that contains the string 999-9999. If you set Literals Not Part Of Data to OFF, the literal character is counted as one of the characters in the database field. If you set Literals Not Part Of Data to ON, the literal is inserted in the value but is not counted as one of the characters in the field. |

*continues*

| Function | Description |
|---|---|
| Scroll Within Display Width | Enables viewing data that is wider than the screen width. |
| Multiple Choice | Enables you to select among different choices for a field entry. |
| Trim | Removes leading-edge blanks from a value. If the database value has leading-edge blanks, this option causes the field to be left-justified in the report field because the option strips those blanks off. |
| Right Align | Moves the value to the right of the field. |
| Center Align | Centers the value in the field. Because dBASE defaults to left alignment for character fields, there is no option for left alignment. |
| Horizontal Stretch | Used for mail-merge reports, this option causes a long field or text from a memo field to extend to the left and right margins of the report, rather than be confined to the template width. |
| Vertical Stretch | Used for column or form reports, this option causes the field to take up as many lines as necessary—each line as wide as the field—to print the value. If you have a database character field length of 25, for example, you can specify a field width of 5 and toggle Vertical Stretch ON. If the field is completely full, dBASE uses 5 lines to print the field. |
| Wrap Semicolons | Tells dBASE to start a new line when the program encounters a semicolon in the database value for this field. |

Numeric picture functions also apply to the entire field, but they duplicate template symbols less than character picture functions do. Numeric picture functions enable you to bracket negative numbers—use parentheses ( ) around negative numbers. With numeric picture functions, you also can use a dollar sign, suppress printing when the field has a value of zero, or print `CR` or `DB` for positive and negative numbers in true accounting fashion.

You also can combine picture functions. If you want a field in financial format (a leading dollar sign, commas, and two decimal places) with a DB following negative numbers, for example, toggle Financial Format and Negative Debits Followed By DB to ON. Then define a template to place commas and decimals in the field. An important caution: putting DB or CR after a field does not increase the field's length on the surface.

The DB and CR overwrite anything that usually prints in the three spaces to the right of the field. If you use these picture functions, make sure that you leave space for them to the right of the field.

Use the mouse to select options from the Picture Functions menu. Just click on the option you want to use to toggle the ON/OFF settings, then click on the `Accept:Ctrl-End` label on the navigation line to save your settings.

Good use of template symbols and picture functions can turn an acceptable report into an excellent one. Well-presented data is easier to read and understand and makes a report look professional.

## Using the Suppress Repeated Values Option

Reports often have fields with values that repeat line after line and make the reports "busier" than necessary. A report of sales by customer number, for example, may have the customer number field in the Detail band. If the report is sorted on that field, the report could show many detail lines, each with the same customer number. To make the report easier to read, use the Suppress Repeated Values option on the customer number field.

When you use the Suppress Repeated Values option on a field, the field prints out only when the value of that field differs from the value of the field in the previous line. In the preceding example, therefore, the customer number field prints out only when the customer number changes. This arrangement makes the report much easier to understand.

**For Related Information...**

▸▸ "CREATE/MODIFY REPORT," p. 694.

# Adding to the Report

Although data printed from a database forms the heart of most reports, you may find it helpful to calculate data from the database and present that data on the report or to summarize fields from the report. You also may want to add fields to the Page Header and Page Footer bands to print out the report date or time and the page number of the report. dBASE provides you with the tools to add these powerful features to your reports. This section outlines how to add these specialized fields.

## Adding Calculated Fields

You may want to show information calculated from the fields of your database. The Customer report, for instance, may require a field showing the amount of credit remaining for each customer—a figure that dBASE can calculate by subtracting the current balance from the credit limit (CREDIT_LMT – CURR_BAL). To add such a calculated field, follow these steps:

1. Place the cursor on the bands of the work surface where you want the calculated field to appear. Choose Add Field from the Layout menu, or press F5. The Add Field field selection box appears (see fig. 10.10).

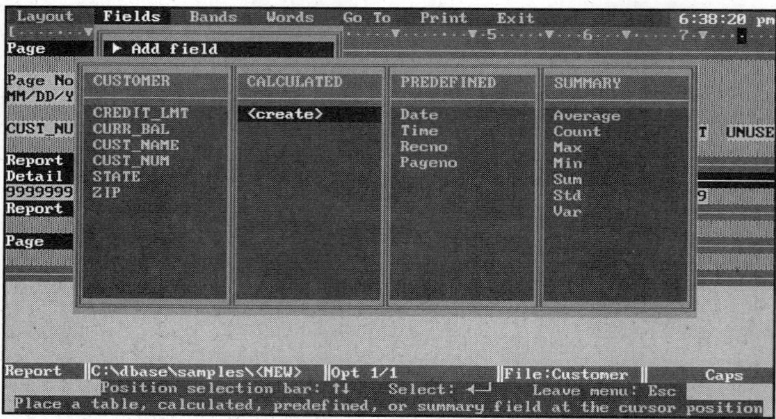


FIG. 10.10 The Add Field field selection box.

2. Move the highlight to the <create> option in the Calculated column. Press Enter to select this choice and to display the Field Definition menu (see fig. 10.11). Give the field a name and a description, and then move the highlight to the Expression option.
3. Press Enter to open the Expression field so that you can enter an expression. You can enter any valid dBASE IV expression (for more information on dBASE IV expressions, see Chapter 13). For this example, enter an expression that shows the amount each customer is over or under his or her credit limit. The formula for this is CREDIT_LMT – CURR_BAL (see fig. 10.12).

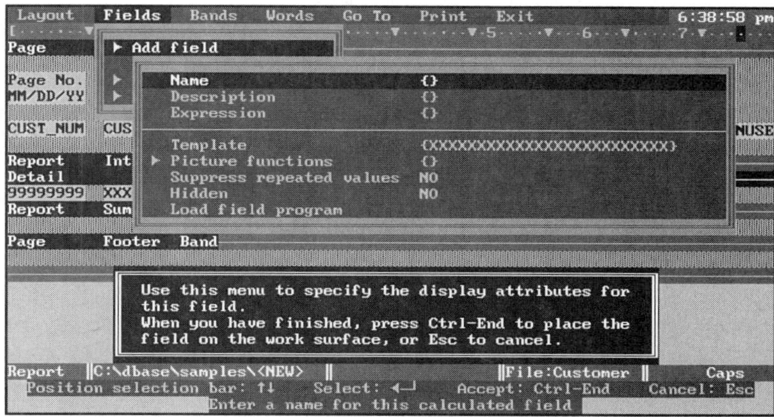


FIG. 10.11

The Field Definition menu.

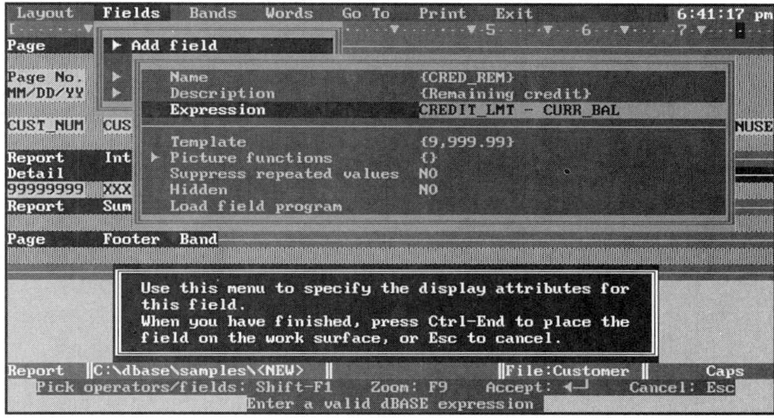


FIG. 10.12

Entering the expression for a calculated field.

4. Use the Template and Picture Functions menu selections to format the field as desired. Press Ctrl-End to finish the process and to return to the design screen, where you can see the newly created field.

Calculated fields can be as complicated as a dBASE IV expression allows them to be. They can contain multiple database fields—if the report is on multiple databases, fields can be from different databases—as well as any of the built-in dBASE IV expressions. The only limit on an expression defining a calculated field is that the expression cannot exceed 255 characters.

## Adding Summary Fields

Even though the Detail band reports on each record of the database, you also may want to see the totals of numeric database fields, the count of records in the report, or some other summary of the report's information. Summary fields appear in the Report Summary band that prints at the end of the report. To add a Summary field, move the cursor into the Report Summary band, position the cursor where you want the field to appear, and follow these steps:

1. Choose Add Field from the Fields menu. The right column of the field selection box (shown in fig. 10.10) lists the seven types of Summary fields available. Six of these types calculate a value based on a numeric field in the report. In each case, only values printed on the report are summarized. This arrangement is helpful when you use filters to print only a subset of an entire database. The types of Summary fields are as follows:

| Summary field | Description |
|---|---|
| Average | Calculates and displays the average value for the chosen numeric field |
| Max | Prints the highest value reported for a numeric field |
| Min | Prints the lowest value reported for the numeric field |
| Sum | Sums all the values for a particular field |
| Std | Prints the standard deviation of all values reported for the numeric field (standard deviation is a statistical measurement) |
| Var | Prints the variation (another statistical measurement) of all values reported for the numeric field |
| Count | Prints how many records are printed in the report |

2. Choose the type of Summary field you want by highlighting it and pressing Enter. The Summary Field Description menu appears (see fig. 10.13). As with other fields, give the Summary field a name and a description. Don't use a dBASE IV reserved word—such as *Count* or *Sum*—for the field name.

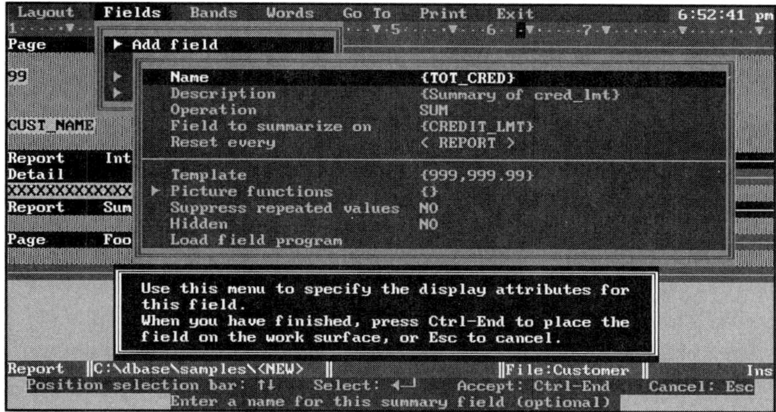


FIG. 10.13

The Summary Field Description menu.

The Operation option on the Summary Field Description menu is set to the Summary field type you choose in step 2, although you can change this value. (Press Enter to bring up a summary field list, from which you can make your choice.)

3. Tell dBASE IV what field in the report you want the Summary field to summarize or count. Highlight the Field To Summarize On option and press Enter. A pop-up menu showing all the fields in the current view appears (see fig. 10.14). Choose the field you want to summarize by highlighting it with the arrow keys and pressing Enter. Note that non-numeric fields appear dimmed, meaning that you cannot choose them.

   If you are using a mouse, double-click on a field name from the pop-up fields list to select a field to summarize.

4. The Reset Every option enables you to define when you want to reset the Summary field to zero. You may want to reset summary fields for reports only once, at the beginning of the report. In this case, the REPORT default is acceptable. You may want to reset a Summary field on each page. To change the setting, highlight Reset Every and press Enter to display the resetting options; then choose the PAGE setting.

5. Use the Template and Picture Functions options to format the appearance of the Summary field. When you're finished, press Ctrl-End to return to the Report design screen, which now shows the newly added Summary field in the Report Summary band.

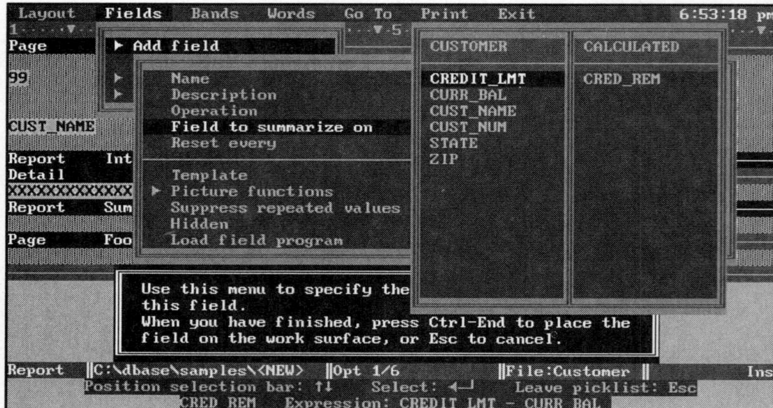


FIG. 10.14

The Field List menu.

# Adding Text Fields

Adding text to the Report design screen is simple. You move the cursor to the desired location and start typing. If you want to add a line, place the cursor in the line *above* where you want the new line and choose Add Line from the Words menu. If you have only one line in a band, you cannot insert a line above it by using Add Line. To add a line at the top of the band, turn Insert on, place the cursor at the beginning of the top line of the band, and press Enter. A new blank line appears.

# Adding Page Headers and Page Footers

The Page Header and Page Footer bands appear at the top and bottom of each report page. If you include a Report Intro band and a Report Summary band, the Page Header and Page Footer bands print before and after the Intro and Summary bands.

Page Headers and Page Footers are excellent for including information you want to appear on every page of the report. You may want to include at the top of each report page a short title of the report and a date and time stamp so that the reader doesn't have to turn back to the first page to determine this information. You also may want to put column headers in the Page Header band so that they print at the top of each page.

To add a Page Header, follow these steps:

1. Place the cursor in the Page Header band of the Report design work surface. Choose Add Line from the Words menu as many

times as necessary to increase the size of the Page Header band so that it accepts all the fields you plan to add.

The size of the Page Header band varies, depending on how you want to format the header and how many rows the column headers take.

2. In the top line of the Page Header band, type the report title. From the Words menu, choose Position and then choose Center. Press Enter to return to the Report design screen; notice that the title is centered on the page.

   The default width of the report is 255 columns. Unless you change that width, the title probably disappears off-screen to the right. Scroll to the right to see the title properly centered on the 255-column-wide report. If you want the report to be less than 255 columns wide, change the right margin on the ruler as discussed in "The Ruler on the Report Design Screen," earlier in this chapter.

3. On the next two lines of the Page Header band, the Quick Layouts option places the page number text and field, as well as a date stamp. Move the cursor to the line below the date stamp. Choose Add Field from the Fields menu. When the Add Field menu appears, move the cursor to the Predefined column. In this column are the following dBASE IV variables, already defined for you:

| Variable | Description |
|---|---|
| Date | Prints the date when the report is printed, in the format MM/DD/YY |
| Time | Prints the time when the report is printed, in the format HH:MM:SS |
| Recno | Prints the record number of the database record being printed. Although this predefined variable isn't useful in the Page Header or Page Footer band, you may want to use it in the Detail band. |
| Pageno | Prints the current page number of the report |

4. Choose the Time predefined variable and press Enter. The variable appears on the Page Header band below the date stamp.

5. Add column headings by typing text-field names above the data fields of the Detail band. Figure 10.15 shows the report with column headings in the Page Header band.

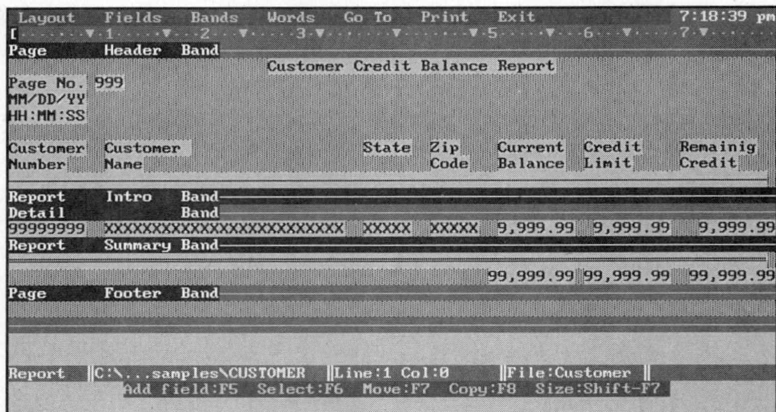


FIG. 10.15

The report with column headings in the Page Header band.

Now add solid lines to the report to set off the column headings from the Detail band, as shown in figure 10.16, by following these steps:

1. Choose Line from the Layout menu. In the Line Definition menu that appears, choose Single Line, Double Line, or Using Specified Character. With the Using Specified Character option, you can specify a character you want to use to draw the line. Press Enter to make your choice.

2. On the Report design screen, use the arrow keys to place the cursor where you want the line to start, and press Enter. You can draw a line on any line of any band.

   As you use the right- and left-arrow keys, the cursor moves and the line is drawn. When you finish drawing the line with the arrow keys, press Enter to stop drawing.

3. If you want to draw a box, repeat step 1, except choose Box from the Layout menu. When you return to the Report design screen, you can use the right- and left-arrow keys to extend the width of the box (just as you do for lines). Use the up-and down-arrow keys to extend the depth of the box.

You also can draw lines with the mouse. After selecting the type of line from the Layout menu, move the mouse pointer to the location where you want the line to begin. Drag the mouse to the location where you want the line to end and then release the mouse button. Click the mouse to end line drawing.

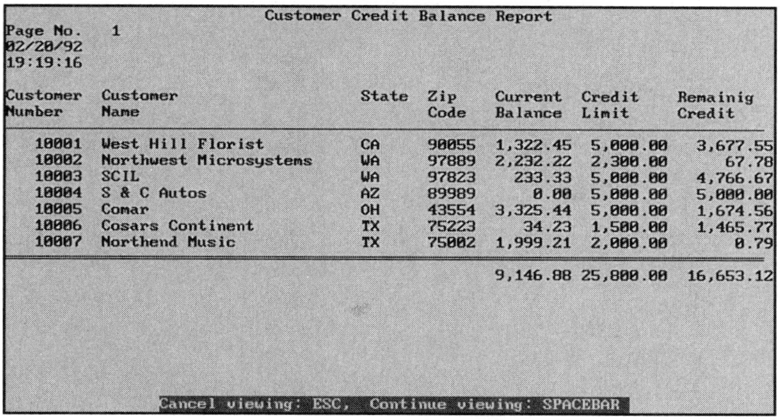

Customer Credit Balance Report

Page No. 1
02/20/92
19:19:16

| Customer Number | Customer Name | State | Zip Code | Current Balance | Credit Limit | Remainig Credit |
|---|---|---|---|---|---|---|
| 10001 | West Hill Florist | CA | 90055 | 1,322.45 | 5,000.00 | 3,677.55 |
| 10002 | Northwest Microsystems | WA | 97889 | 2,232.22 | 2,300.00 | 67.78 |
| 10003 | SCIL | WA | 97823 | 233.33 | 5,000.00 | 4,766.67 |
| 10004 | S & C Autos | AZ | 89989 | 0.00 | 5,000.00 | 5,000.00 |
| 10005 | Comar | OH | 43554 | 3,325.44 | 5,000.00 | 1,674.56 |
| 10006 | Cosars Continent | TX | 75223 | 34.23 | 1,500.00 | 1,465.77 |
| 10007 | Northend Music | TX | 75002 | 1,999.21 | 2,000.00 | 0.79 |
| | | | | 9,146.88 | 25,800.00 | 16,653.12 |

Cancel viewing: ESC, Continue viewing: SPACEBAR

FIG. 10.16

The report with column headings and solid lines.

## Adding Groups

When you print a report, dBASE IV processes and prints the records one after another. If the database is not indexed or sorted, the records appear as they were entered. If you index or sort the database, the records appear in the indexed or sorted order. Often, however, you want the report to group records—to put all the records of one customer, for example, on the report. In addition, you can group records and then include fields that summarize data for the group. You can group all the orders for one customer on a report, for example, and then print the total of each customer's orders. Grouping records can make a report much more readable.

The first step in grouping report data is to decide how you want it grouped. How you group your data depends on your database and what you want the report to accomplish. If you work with a database of customer orders, for example, you may want to group all orders for one customer together on the report and then summarize each customer's order total at the end of the group. For another report, you may want to group all the orders of one product together and then summarize the product's sales total at the end of the group. If your database contains information on each customer's address, you may want to group on ZIP Code so that the report provides information about where your sales are being made.

After you decide how to group your report, tell dBASE IV when to end one group and start a new one. If you're grouping on customer name, for example, tell dBASE IV to watch the field that contains the customer name. When the value of that field changes, dBASE IV starts a new group. You can specify any valid dBASE expression as the trigger for a new group, which is called the *group expression*.

Suppose that you want to create a report that groups records by State to create a geographical report. To create this group on your report, follow these steps:

1. Make sure that the database is sorted or indexed on the group expression. If the database is not sorted or indexed on the group expression, you get nonsense groupings because the records of one group (a customer name, for instance) are not together in the database.

   To sort the database on the group expression, press Shift-F2 (Design) to display the Query design work surface. There you can specify a sort on the group expression. For detailed information on doing this, see Chapter 12.

   You can create an index by pressing F2 (Data), which opens a Browse/Edit screen. There you can use the Organize menu to create or select an index. You then can select Return To Report Design from the Exit menu.

2. Make sure that the cursor is in a band above the Detail band and not in the Detail band, and then choose Add A Group Band from the Bands menu. The Group Definition menu appears (see fig. 10.17).

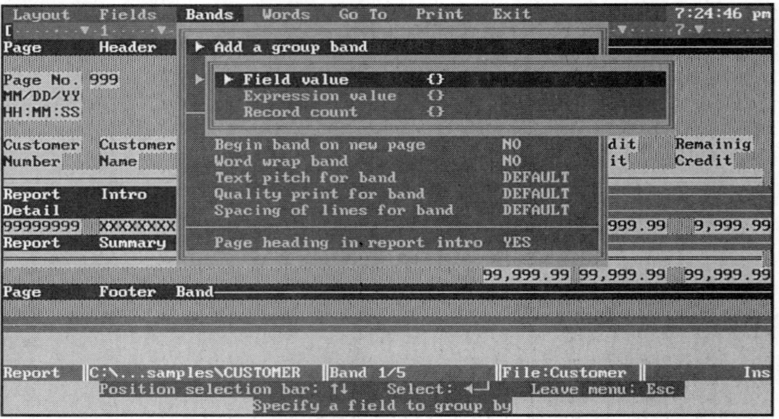


**FIG. 10.17**

The Group Definition menu.

3. If you want to group the report on one of the database fields, highlight Field Value and press Enter. A pop-up menu showing the database fields in the current view appears (see fig. 10.18). From this list, choose the field on which you want to group the report. For this example, highlight STATE and press Enter.

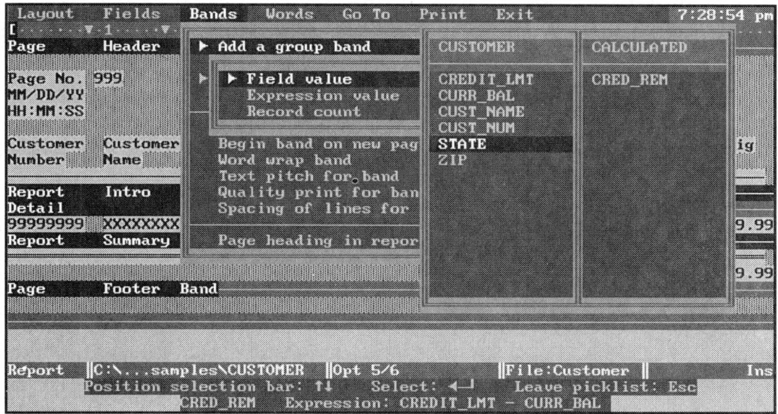

FIG. 10.18
Choosing the field on which the report is to be grouped.

You also can group a report on any standard dBASE IV expression. To do this, highlight Expression Value in the Group Definition menu and press Enter. Now enter any valid dBASE IV expression. Use this option, for example, if you want to group the report on a character field that may contain uppercase and lowercase letters. By entering the expression *UPPER(customer)*, you ensure that no group break occurs if the Customer field contains *ACME COMPANY* in one record and *Acme Company* in the next, assuming the current index is sorted on UPPER(customer).

Long reports without groups can be difficult to read. You can use the Record Count option to insert a blank line after a specified number of Detail band records are printed. Highlight Record Count in the Group Definition menu and press Enter. Type the number of records you want to print before a group break. When the Report design screen reappears, the Group 1 Intro and Group 1 Summary bands are on the surface. These bands cause a blank line to be printed after the specified number of detail band records are printed. You can use only one of these three types of group breaks in a group.

4. When the Report design screen reappears, you see that two more bands are added: the Group 1 Intro and Group 1 Summary bands (see fig. 10.19). These bands are similar to the Report Intro and Report Summary bands, except that they print at the beginning and end of each group. For clarity, enter something in at least one of these new bands so that the report clearly shows that a grouping has occurred.

```
Layout  Fields  Bands  Words  Go To  Print  Exit                7:33:38 pm
Page         Header  Band
                        Customer Credit Balance Report
Page No. 999
MM/DD/YY
HH:MM:SS

Customer  Customer                      State  Zip    Current   Credit     Remainig
Number    Name                                 Code   Balance   Limit      Credit
Report       Intro   Band
Group  1     Intro   Band

Detail               Band
99999999  XXXXXXXXXXXXXXXXXXXXXXXXX  XXXXX  XXXXX  9,999.99  9,999.99   9,999.99
Group  1     Summary Band

Report       Summary Band

                                            99,999.99 99,999.99  99,999.99
Page         Footer  Band
Report  ||C:\...samples\CUSTOMER  ||Line:0 Col:0    ||File:Customer ||      Ins
              Add field:F5  Select:F6  Move:F7  Copy:F8  Size:Shift-F7
```

**FIG. 10.19**

The Report design screen with Group bands added.

In the Group 1 Intro band, add text to explain which group is being printed. You can add the text *State:*, for example, and then add a field to show the STATE field value for that group. Figure 10.20 shows the addition of the *State:* text and the XX characters that represent the STATE field values. Figure 10.21 shows the report with the groupings.

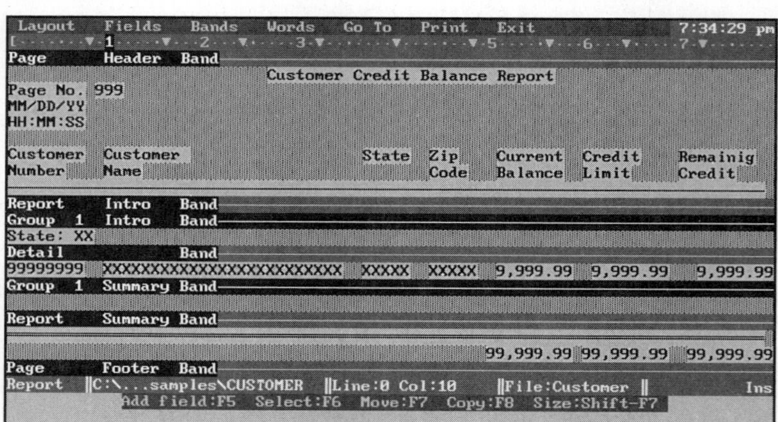


**FIG. 10.20**

Adding a field in the Group 1 Intro band.

```
Page No.   1
02/20/92
19:35:33

Customer  Customer                    State  Zip    Current   Credit     Remainig
Number    Name                               Code   Balance   Limit      Credit

State: AZ
   10004  S & C Autos                 AZ     89989      0.00  5,000.00   5,000.00

State: CA
   10001  West Hill Florist           CA     90055  1,322.45  5,000.00   3,677.55

State: OH
   10005  Comar                       OH     43554  3,325.44  5,000.00   1,674.56

State: TX
   10007  Northend Music              TX     75002  1,999.21  2,000.00       0.79
   10006  Cosars Continent            TX     75223     34.23  1,500.00   1,465.77

State: WA
   10002  Northwest Microsystems      WA     97889  2,232.22  2,300.00      67.78
   10003  SCIL                        WA     97823    233.33  5,000.00   4,766.67
                Cancel viewing: ESC,  Continue viewing: SPACEBAR
```

FIG. 10.21

The report with STATE code groups.

# Adding Group Summary Fields

You can add Summary fields for a group just as you do for a report. Place these fields in the Group Summary band. When a group ends, dBASE IV prints the Summary fields with information for the group. Report totals are not affected.

The following is an example in which fields are added to the Group Summary band. The first field is a STATE field, with some text to explain what STATE code the summary refers to. Another field summarizes the values of the CURR_BAL fields of the group.

To add fields to the Group Summary band, follow these steps:

1. Place the cursor in line 0, column 0 of the Group 1 Summary band. Enter the text *Summaries for State:*.
2. Choose Add Field from the Fields menu. The Field List appears.
3. Choose what type of field you want to put in the Group 1 Summary band. Move the cursor to the Customer column, which contains fields for the Customer database. Choose STATE and press Enter; then press Ctrl-End.
4. When you return to the Report design screen, a field for STATE is on the surface. Move the cursor to a position under the Current Balance heading and choose Add Field again.
5. The field list reappears. Move the cursor to the Summary column and select Sum. Press Enter to bring up the Field Definition box. Name the field (BAL_SUM), give it a description (Summary of Group CURR_BAL), and enter *CURR_BAL* in the field to summarize on.

6. Choose the Reset Every option. In the list menu that appears, you see that the group expression, STATE, is included. Choosing the Reset Every option means that the Summary field resets to zero whenever the group expression, STATE, changes. Because that change also triggers a new group, that's the choice you make. Rarely will you want a group Summary field to reset on anything but the group expression.

7. When you return to the Report design screen, the Summary field is in the Group 1 Summary band. Repeat this procedure for any other summary fields you want to add. Figure 10.22 shows the Report design screen with the summary fields added to the Group 1 Summary band. Figure 10.23 shows the report.

```
 Layout  Fields  Bands  Words  Go To  Print  Exit                 7:47:39 pm
Page        Header  Band
                                 Customer Credit Balance Report
Page No. 999
MM/DD/YY
HH:MM:SS

Customer  Customer                            State  Zip    Current   Credit     Remainig
Number    Name                                       Code   Balance   Limit      Credit

Report      Intro   Band
Group   1   Intro   Band
State: XX
Detail              Band
99999999  XXXXXXXXXXXXXXXXXXXXXXXXX  XXXXX  XXXXX  9,999.99  9,999.99   9,999.99
Group   1   Summary Band
Summaries for State: XX                           99,999.99 99,999.99  99,999.99
Report      Summary Band

                                                  99,999.99 99,999.99  99,999.99
Page        Footer  Band
Report   ║C:\...samples\CUSTOMER  ║Line:0 Col:0      ║File:Customer ║
       Add field:F5  Select:F6  Move:F7  Copy:F8  Size:Shift-F7
```

FIG. 10.22

The Report design screen showing with a Group Summary field.

```
Page No.   1
02/20/92
19:48:12

Customer  Customer                     State  Zip    Current   Credit     Remainig
Number    Name                                Code   Balance   Limit      Credit

State: AZ
   10004  S & C Autos                  AZ     89989      0.00  5,000.00   5,000.00
Summaries for State: AZ                                  0.00  5,000.00   5,000.00
State: CA
   10001  West Hill Florist            CA     90055  1,322.45  5,000.00   3,677.55
Summaries for State: CA                              1,322.45  5,000.00   3,677.55
State: OH
   10005  Comar                        OH     43554  3,325.44  5,000.00   1,674.56
Summaries for State: OH                              3,325.44  5,000.00   1,674.56
State: TX
   10007  Northend Music               TX     75002  1,999.21  2,000.00       0.79
   10006  Cosars Continent             TX     75223     34.23  1,500.00   1,465.77
Summaries for State: TX                              2,033.44  3,500.00   1,466.56
State: WA
   10002  Northwest Microsystems       WA     97889  2,232.22  2,300.00      67.78
   10003  SCIL                         WA     97823    233.33  5,000.00   4,766.67
Summaries for State: WA                              2,465.55  7,300.00   4,834.45
            Cancel viewing: ESC,  Continue viewing: SPACEBAR
```

FIG. 10.23

The report grouped by STATE and showing summary fields.

**For Related Information...**

▸▸ "Sorting the Query Output," p. 317.

# Printing the Report

You can print your report directly from the Report design screen by using the Print menu. You also can print from the Control Center by highlighting the name of the report in the Reports panel and pressing Enter. In both cases, dBASE IV displays the Print menu (see fig. 10.24). The Print menu gives you control over the report. Before actually printing the report, look at the four options for controlling the report printing: Destination, Control of Printer, Output Options, and Page Dimensions. Each of these options is discussed in the following sections.

FIG. 10.24

The Print menu.

# Defining Where the Report Will Print

If you choose Destination from the Print menu, the Destination menu appears (see fig. 10.25). Initially, the default setting in the Write To option is PRINTER. When you print with this setting selected, the report is sent to the printer currently defined. If you want to create a DOS file instead of a printed report, press Enter to change the Write To setting to DOS FILE. The default file name CUSTOMER.PRT appears in the Name of DOS File option.

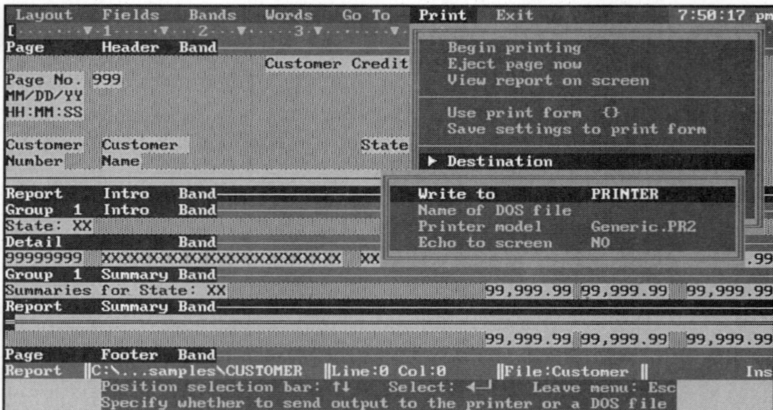


FIG. 10.25

The Destination menu.

You also can tell dBASE IV that you're using a different type of printer than you defined when you installed dBASE IV. To do so, highlight the Printer Model option in the Destination menu. Press Enter to cycle through the printer drivers defined during installation.

You also can tell dBASE IV to print the report to the screen at the same time the report is sent to the specified destination. Highlight the Echo to screen option and press Enter to change the setting from NO to YES.

## Controlling the Printer

You can control how the printer prints the report with the Control of Printer option on the Print menu. When you choose this option, the Printer Control menu appears (see fig. 10.26). You use options on this menu to customize the report.

The Text Pitch option defines the number of characters per inch that the printer uses for the report. Press Enter to cycle through the available pitches, which are a function of the printer driver selected from the Destination menu. ELITE (12 characters per inch), PICA (10 characters per inch), and CONDENSED (which varies by printer type, but usually is 15 to 18 characters per inch) generally are available settings for this option. The DEFAULT selection, though a function of the printer type, is usually 10 characters per inch.

The Quality Print option defines whether the report is to be printed in the standard print or a higher-quality print. Standard print is faster and generally acceptable for report purposes. You can change the Quality Print option to YES when you want the report to look better. Quality print also is called *letter quality* or *near-letter quality* in printer manuals. As with text pitch, the availability of quality print depends on the printer.

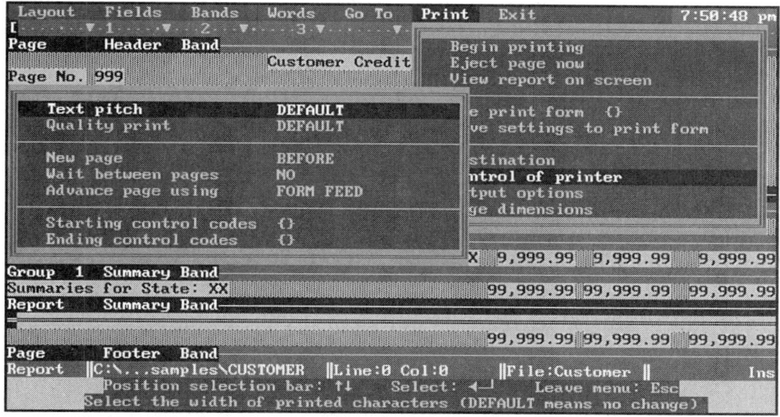


FIG. 10.26

The Printer Control menu.

Some printers default to standard print, and others default to quality print. For this reason, you have three choices: DEFAULT, YES, and NO. You can specify NO to override the quality print on a printer that defaults to quality.

The New Page option tells dBASE IV when to move the paper to the top of a new page. Press Enter to cycle through the choices. BEFORE moves the paper to a new page at the start of the report. BOTH issues a page eject before the report starts and when it's done. NONE causes no page ejects, either before or after the report is printed. AFTER causes the printer to go to a new page only when the report is completed.

The Wait Between Pages option has two choices. If you're printing a report on individual sheets of paper that must be fed into the printer manually, choose YES. dBASE IV pauses at the end of each page and waits until you tell it to continue printing. For continuous-feed computer paper, choose NO so that the report prints from start to finish without pausing.

The Advance Page Using option tells dBASE IV whether to send a form-feed command to the printer or to send a series of line-feed commands when the report has to go to the top of a new page. Some older printers cannot handle form-feeds; in these cases, press Enter to select the LINE FEED setting.

The Starting Control Codes and Ending Control Codes options enable you to enter strings of codes that the printer understands and uses to modify its actions. Although you may not need this capability, it does exist; codes are great for selecting fonts. Refer to your printer manual for a list of the codes the printer understands.

Use the mouse to select options from the Print menus. Just click on a menu item to cycle through the available options.

# Choosing Output Options

If you choose Output Options from the Print menu, the Output Options menu appears (see fig. 10.27). You use the four options on this menu to control specifics about the report you are printing.

The Begin On Page option enables you to skip pages of a report. Enter an integer from 1 to 32767, and the report starts on the page you specify.

The End After Page option is the opposite of the first option. You can specify which page of the report is the last page printed.

The First Page Number option tells dBASE IV what page number to use when it starts numbering pages. If you used the Begin On Page option to start printing the report at page 50, you can use the First Page Number option to start the page numbering at 50.

The Number Of Copies option specifies how many times the report is to print. The report is printed, from the Begin On Page setting to the End After Page setting, the number of times specified here.

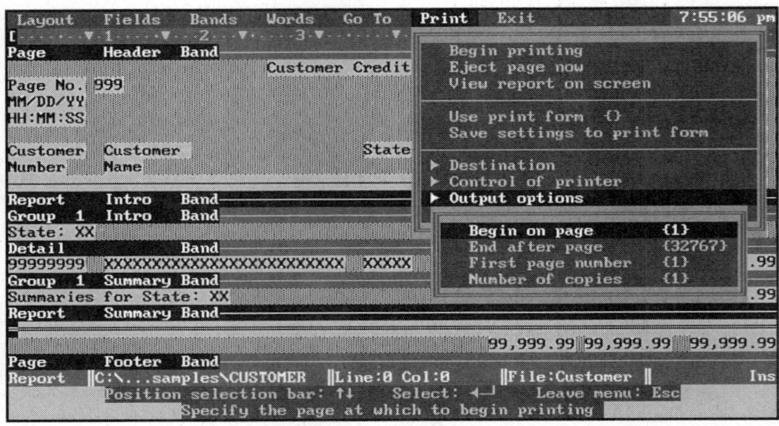


FIG. 10.27

The Output Options menu.

# Altering Page Dimensions

You can alter the dimensions of the printed page by using the Page Dimensions option from the Print menu. When you select this option, the Page Dimensions menu appears (see fig. 10.28).

The Length Of Page option defines how long the page is in terms of lines. A standard 11-by-14 7/8-inch computer page is 66 lines long, as is an 8 1/2-by-11-inch page. If you use nonstandard-sized paper, remember that the printer prints 6 lines per inch; use the Length Of Page option to set the page length accordingly.

For the Offset From Left option, specify an integer that represents the number of inches of extra margin added to the left edge of the page. Setting a left offset is helpful, for example, when you print the report on paper that has holes punched on the left edge. Without modifying the design of the report, you can add an extra half or three-quarters of an inch to clear the punch holes.

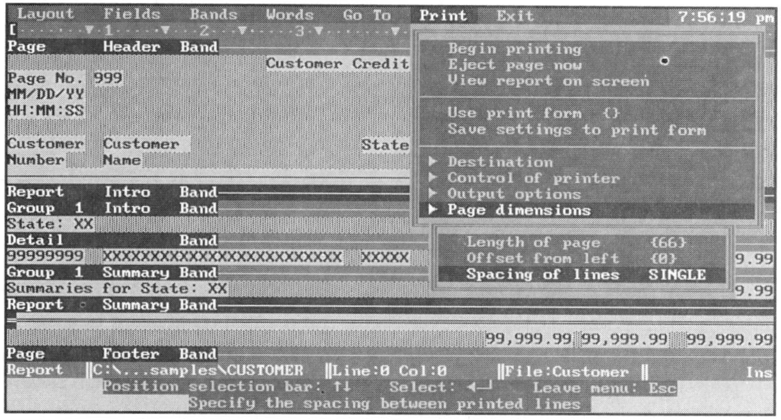


FIG. 10.28

The Page Dimensions menu.

The Spacing Of Lines option has three settings. Cycle through the settings by pressing Enter or clicking the mouse. You can choose SINGLE, DOUBLE, or TRIPLE spacing.

## Creating and Using Print Forms

After you specify the desired printer settings, you can save them to a print form with the Save Settings To Print Form option on the Print menu. A *print form* contains all the specifications you made for a report: the destination, page dimensions, and other settings made in the Print menu. When you choose Save Settings To Print Form, dBASE IV asks for a print file name. The default file name is the report name with the extension PRF.

After you save print settings, you can reestablish them for this or any other report by using the Use Print Form Option from the Print menu.

After you select this option, type the name of the print form that stores the specifications you want to use; dBASE IV reads those settings from the file and uses them. You can use a print form for any report you create, not just the report for which you originally set the specifications. Note that when you save your report design, the print form you have selected is automatically associated with the report as the default print form.

Choose a print form with the mouse by clicking on the Use Print Form option. When a pick list menu of available print form files appears, double-click on the file you want to use.

## Using Other Print Menu Options

After all the preparation you have done, you're ready to print the report. In practice, you may find that you seldom change the output options (Destination, Control Of Printer, and so on). The first option you select from the Print menu may be Begin Printing. When you choose Begin Printing, dBASE IV sends the report to the printer (or to the DOS file, if you made that specification), using the current default settings or the settings in the retrieved print form. If you want the printer to go to a new page before printing the report, choose Eject Page Now, and then select Begin Printing.

You can have the report print on-screen rather than on your printer by selecting the View Report On Screen option. Use this option when you want to review a report quickly to check its format, or just to see information.

**For Related Information...**

▸▸ "Working with Printers and Printing," p. 530.

# Using dBASE IV To Perform Mail-Merge Operations

Another feature of the Report design work surface is its capability to create mail-merge letters. *Mail merging* enables you to write a standard letter and then "plug" information from a database into the letter at specified locations. You can find many uses for mail-merge letters; this section describes one use.

## Getting Ready for the Mail Merge

This section uses as an example a letter to be sent to customers when they have overrun their credit limit. You use Mailmerge Layout to create the report, and then you write the form letter and merge information from the database into the letter.

Because you don't want to send the letter to every customer in the database, you don't merge information directly from the database. You create a query to limit the records in the database to those customers who have a current balance greater than their credit limit.

Suppose that you have a Customer database that includes an address and city name. The structure of the database looks like the following:

| Field | Field name | Type | Width | Dec | Index |
|---|---|---|---|---|---|
| 1 | CUST_NUM | Numeric | 5 | | Y |
| 2 | CUST_NAME | Character | 25 | | Y |
| 3 | ADDRESS | Character | 25 | | Y |
| 4 | CITY | Character | 15 | | N |
| 5 | STATE | Character | 2 | | Y |
| 6 | ZIP | Character | 5 | | Y |
| 7 | CURR_BAL | Numeric | 8 | 2 | N |
| 8 | CREDIT_LMT | Numeric | 8 | 2 | N |

## Creating the Query

You sometimes create a mail-merge document to send to all your customers. More often, however, you need to send information to only a select group of customers. In this example, you want to send a reminder to customers who have exceeded their credit limit. You must create a query to filter out those customers who have not exceeded their limit.

From the Control Center, select the database for which you want to create the query—in this case, the Customer database. Move the cursor to the Data panel, highlight the Customer database, press Enter, and select Use File from the menu that appears. Next, move the cursor to the Queries panel and select <create>. The Query design screen appears.

Press Tab or use the mouse to move the cursor to the CURR_BAL field. In the input area, type the following expression:

> CREDIT_LMT

This condition specifies that only those records in which the current balance (CURR_BAL) is greater that the credit limit (CREDIT_LMT) are to be selected (see fig. 10.29).

To save the query, select Save Changes And Exit from the Exit menu. When the `Save As:` prompt appears, type the name *OVERLMT* and press Enter. You return to the Control Center.

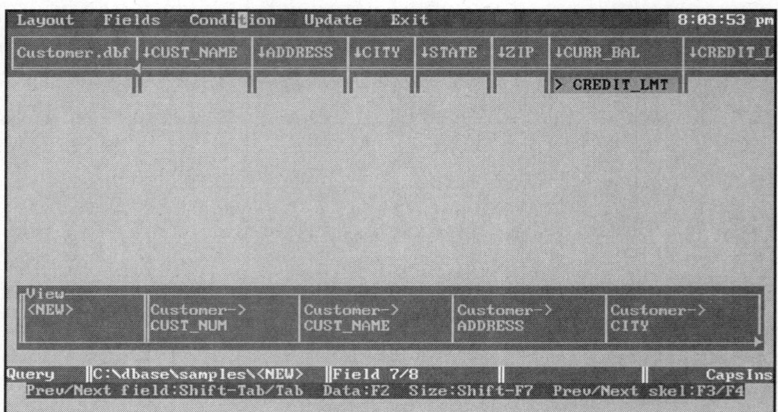


FIG. 10.29 The query to filter out customers who have exceeded their credit limit.

# Preparing the Mail-Merge Document

Creating a mail-merge report is similar to creating a column or form report. First, select the database or query that is to supply the data for the report. Because you created a query to control the records in the database used in the report, move the cursor to the Queries panel and highlight the OVERLMT query. Press Enter and select Use View from the menu that appears.

Move the cursor to the Reports panel, highlight <create>, and press Enter. When the Report design screen appears, the Layout menu is active. Select Quick Layouts from this menu, and then select Mailmerge Layout from the Quick Layouts menu.

When you select Mailmerge Layout, the screen and the settings in the Bands menu change (see fig. 10.30). All bands are now closed, except the Detail band. The Detail band increases in size so that you can start typing the text of the letter you want to use for the mail-merge operation.

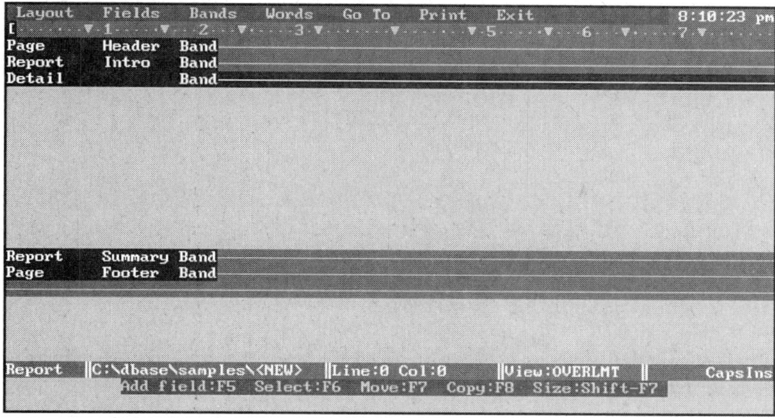


FIG. 10.30

The report screen for Mailmerge Layout.

The Bands menu differs from the standard report version of the menu when you select Mailmerge Layout. The options Begin Band On New Page and Word Wrap Band are both set to YES (see fig. 10.31). These options start each document on a new page—you usually want each letter on a separate page. The word-wrap option enables you to type in the Detail band just as you type in a word processor. When the cursor gets to the right margin, it automatically returns to the left margin of the next line. In other words, the Detail band has become a word processor.

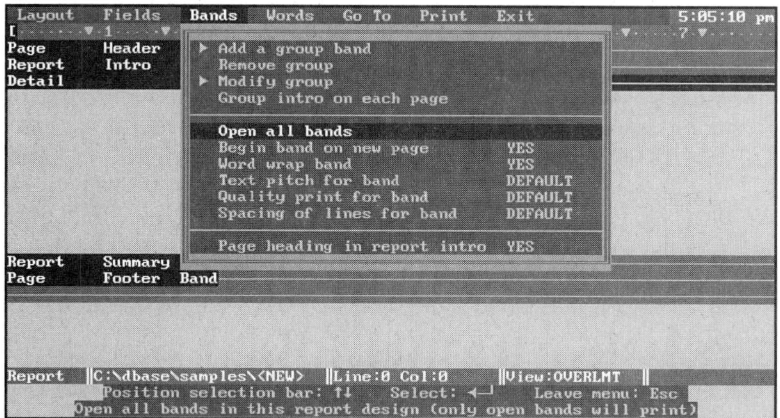


FIG. 10.31

The Bands menu.

Notice, too, that the Bands menu contains the following options:

Text Pitch For Band

Quality Print For Band

Although these options are set to the printer's default, you can change these options. You may want to set the Text Pitch For Band option to Pica, Elite, or Condensed, for example, to force the printer to print in a different pitch. You can set the Quality Print For Band option to YES so that if your printer has a letter-quality print mode, the document prints in letter quality.

You can cycle through available options in the Bands menu by clicking on the menu item. Click on Text Pitch For Band, for example, to select from Pica, Elite, or Condensed type.

Before you start typing information in the Detail band, set the margins. In this example, you are creating a letter, so you want the margins wide enough to accommodate a letter. From the Words menu, select Modify Ruler. Use the right-arrow key to move the cursor to column 65; press the right bracket ( ] ) to set the right margin and press Enter. You now have 65-character line width in which to type the document.

## Adding Fields and Text to the Mail-Merge Document

Although the Quick Layout option for the column and form layout sets up the bands and places fields in the report, the Quick Layout option for the mail-merge layout sets up the bands only. You have to place the fields on the form.

You add fields to a mail-merge document in the same way you add fields to a column or form report. From the Fields menu, select Add Field, or press F5 (Add Field). Then select the field you want to add.

Creating a mail-merge document is nothing more than adding fields and typing the text you want to become the document. For example, you will use the following template of the document you want to create in this example:

```
CUST_NAME

ADDRESS

CITY, STATE ZIP

Date

Accounts Payable:

Just as a reminder, we have extended a credit limit to
you of CREDIT_LMT. However, our records show that your
account has increased to CURR_BAL. Please send us at
```

```
least CURR_BAL - CREDIT_LMT to bring your balance to
the CREDIT_LMT credit limit.

Thank you for your prompt attention.
```

Notice that the letter uses field names. When you type the letter in the Detail band, you use field names where you want the information from the database to appear. Notice in the last sentence the expression CURR_BAL – CREDIT_LMT. This expression is replaced by a calculated field in the final version of the letter. When you create a calculated field, you must give it a name. For this example, call the calculated field REMIT. When you add the numeric fields (CURR_BAL, CREDIT_LMT, and REMIT), format the fields with Financial Format. Select Picture Function from the menu after you add the field, highlight the selection Financial Format, and press Enter to change the OFF setting to ON.

As you type the body of the letter and want to add a field to the text, remember to leave proper spacing between the text and the field. When typing the first sentence, for example, be sure to leave one space after the word *of* and before the field CREDIT_LMT.

To include the current date in your letter, use the predefined Date field, available through the Fields menu. Position the cursor where you want the date to appear, pull down the Fields menu, and select Add Field. From the selection box, choose Date from the Predefined column (see fig. 10.32). Press Ctrl-End to confirm your selection. A Date field appears as MM/DD/YY on the work surface.

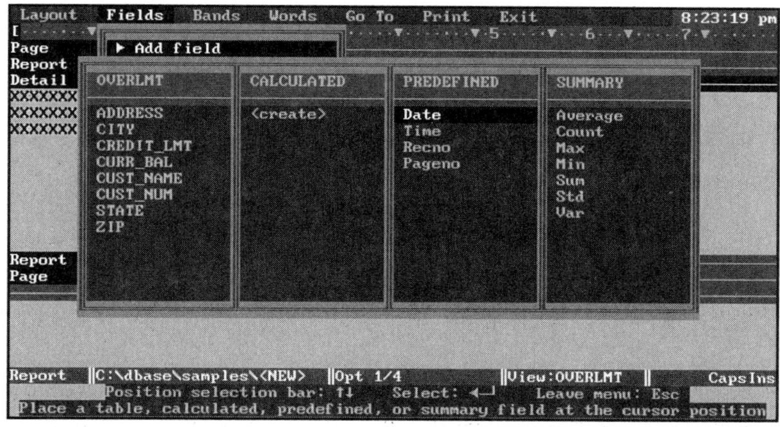


FIG. 10.32

Selecting the predefined Date field.

After you type the letter in the Detail band, move the cursor to the Page Header band and press Enter three times. This action places a top margin in the document so that the letter does not begin printing at the very top of the page. When you finish creating the mail-merge letter, it should look like figure 10.33.

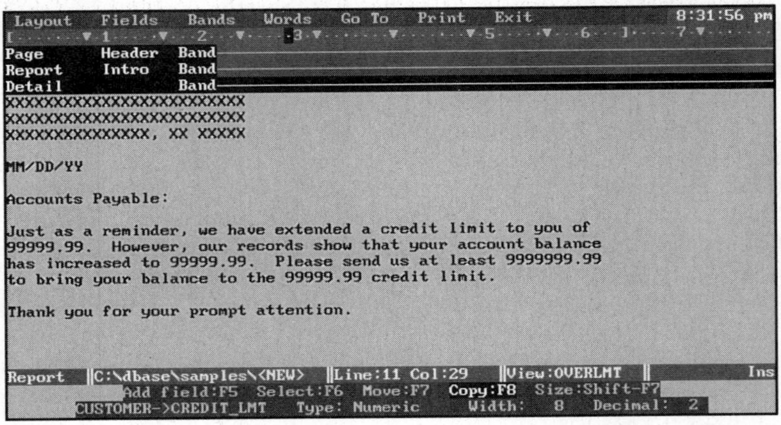

```
Layout  Fields  Bands  Words  Go To  Print  Exit                 8:31:56 pm
[.......▼.1.....▼...2...▼.....3.▼.........▼.........▼.5.....▼...6...]....7.▼.......
Page      Header  Band
Report    Intro   Band
Detail            Band
XXXXXXXXXXXXXXXXXXXXXXXXX
XXXXXXXXXXXXXXXXXXXXXXXXX
XXXXXXXXXXXXXXX, XX XXXXX

MM/DD/YY

Accounts Payable:

Just as a reminder, we have extended a credit limit to you of
99999.99.  However, our records show that your account balance
has increased to 99999.99.  Please send us at least 9999999.99
to bring your balance to the 99999.99 credit limit.

Thank you for your prompt attention.

Report  ||C:\dbase\samples\<NEW>  ||Line:11 Col:29   ||View:OVERLMT  ||        Ins
          Add field:F5  Select:F6  Move:F7  Copy:F8  Size:Shift-F7
       CUSTOMER->CREDIT_LMT   Type: Numeric      Width:   8   Decimal:  2
```

FIG. 10.33

The completed mail-merge letter.

Notice that when the cursor is on one of the field names, specifics about the field appear at the bottom of the screen. By moving the cursor through the text, you can verify that you added the correct fields in the correct places.

After you complete the mail-merge document, be sure to save it. From the Layout menu, select Save Report. When asked for a name, give this sample report the name CRED_MRG and press Enter. The report is saved to the disk.

## Printing the Merged Document

You can test the report before leaving the Report design screen. From the Print menu, select View Report On Screen to print the report to the screen. If you want to test the report on the printer, select Begin Printing from the Print menu. Your report should look like the one shown in figure 10.34.

In the Customer database, the customer SCIL was the only customer whose current balance exceeds the credit limit.

You may want to make changes in the Print menu, such as changing the number of copies that print or resetting the printer offset so that the document prints farther from the left edge of the page. If you do make these changes, save the changes to a print form file, as described earlier in this chapter.

Exit from the Report screen by selecting Save Changes And Exit from the Exit menu. The report is saved if you have made any changes since the last time you saved it. You then return to the Control Center.

```
SCIL
8484 Tech Dr.
Adams, WA 33423
June 9, 1992

Accounts Payable:
Just a reminder, we have extended a credit limit to you of
$5000.00. However, our records show that your account has
increased to $6533.33. Please sent us at least $1533.33 to bring
your balance to the $5000.00 credit limit.

Thank you for your prompt attention.
```

FIG. 10.34

A printed mail-merged letter.

Whenever you want to print this mail-merge file, highlight the report name (CRED_MRG) in the Reports panel, press Enter or click the mouse, and select Print Report. The Print menu appears, from which you can select a print form and then begin printing.

# Summary

With dBASE IV, you can create sophisticated reports for your databases. The Report design screen enables you to design and test your reports quickly by placing fields on-screen, moving and modifying them to make the report more readable. You then can view the results while still in the Report design work surface.

Reports are a visible result of your database. Good reports enable you to view and understand the information in the database. More important, good reports give others access to the information in your database. Reporting can make or break the success of a database system. With dBASE IV, your reports can shine.

11

CHAPTER

# Designing and Printing Labels

One of the first uses of PC database programs was to produce mailing labels from a database. Even with the sophistication of today's databases, this function is widely used. dBASE IV provides you with excellent tools for designing and producing your own mailing labels.

You can purchase sheets of labels from a stationery or office supply source. Labels are available in all shapes and sizes for computerized printing. For example, you can buy labels on paper that work in a pin-feed printer (a printer that pulls paper through by the perforations at the edges of the paper). Sheets of labels for pin-feed printers are available with one, two, or three rows of labels per sheet. Labels also are available for laser printers. Labels usually are 15/16-inch high by 3 1/2-inches wide. dBASE uses this size as a default but has many other common sizes available. You also can define a custom label size.

When defining labels, you must have the necessary address fields in your database. These fields should include a name and street address along with city, state, and ZIP code fields. Your database can have other fields, too. As with reports, you can use queries to limit which records are printed on labels.

In this chapter, you learn about the tools for and the techniques of creating labels from your dBASE IV databases. The basic tool is the

Label design screen, which is much like the Report design screen you learned about in Chapter 10. On the Label design work surface, you design the fields and formats for your labels. You then can save each design and recall it from the Control Center menu. You also can limit the output of the label by using a query, just as you do with a report.

# Designing Labels

You start creating your label design in the Control Center by selecting the catalog that contains the database from which your labels are generated. If that catalog is not the current one, choose Use a Different Catalog from the Catalog menu and then select the catalog you want to make the current one. When the right catalog is current, select the database from the Data panel and press Enter to make it the current database.

You now can create the label design. Move the cursor to the Labels panel of the Control Center and choose <create>. The Label design screen appears, as shown in figure 11.1. You create your label designs on the work surface of this screen.

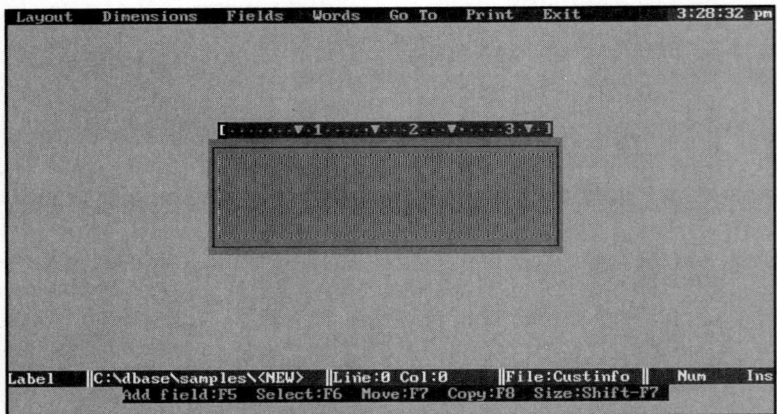


FIG. 11.1

The Label design screen.

# Understanding the Label Design Screen

The Label design work surface is much like the Report design work surface, but much smaller. The size of the work surface is smaller because a mailing label is usually tiny. Other than that, the only difference between the Report design screen and the Label design screen is that on the Label design screen menu, Dimensions is added and Bands is removed. Because the Dimensions menu is important for designing labels, you should take some time to review it.

Just as you create reports with the Report design work surface, you create labels by placing fields on the Label design work surface. These fields present information from the database selected from the Control Center. You can format these fields in different ways, move them around to position them in the most readable arrangement, and add whatever text fields you want.

The Dimensions menu shown in figure 11.2 enables you to define the sizes and types of labels that dBASE IV prints. This menu is divided into two parts: predefined sizes and other options. The Predefined Size option is a set of common label sizes and page formats; the options below the line enable you to design custom-sized labels.

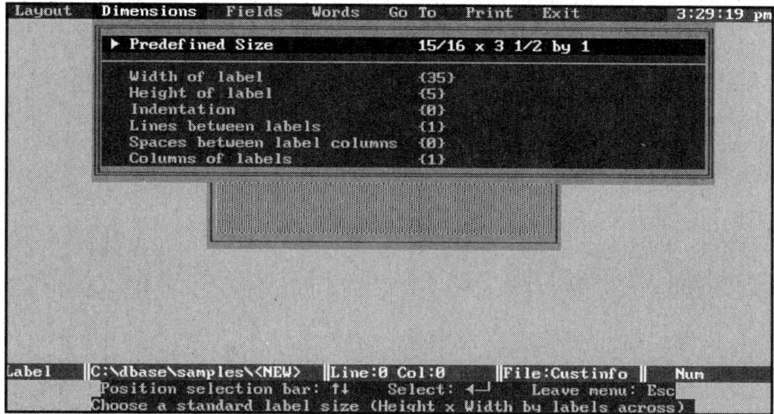


FIG. 11.2

The Dimensions menu.

## Choosing a Predefined Size

Choosing Predefined Size from the Dimensions menu opens a size menu (see fig. 11.3). The sizes listed in this menu are commonly used label sizes. Choose a size by highlighting it and pressing Enter. When the Label design screen reappears, notice that the Label work surface is adjusted to the correct size for your selected format.

You can use the mouse to select a label format. Click on the Dimensions menu label, click on Predefined Size, and then click on the size option you want.

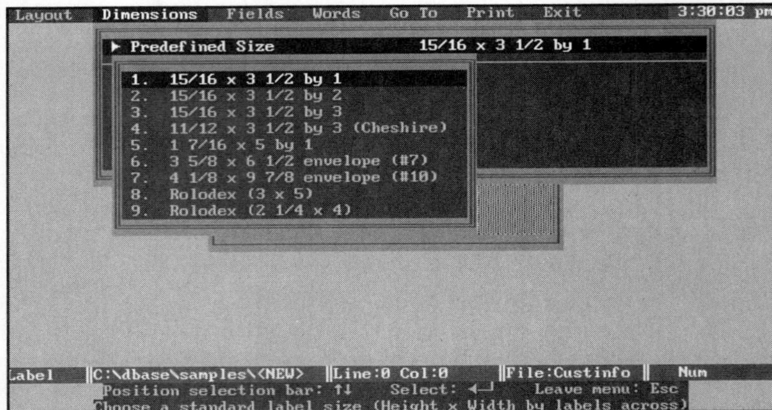


FIG. 11.3

The Predefined Size menu with predefined label formats.

## Choosing a Custom Size

Below the Predefined Size option on the Dimensions menu is a series of options for creating custom-sized labels. Figure 11.4 shows the meaning of these options (and several other useful measurements) on a sheet of mailing labels. You can use these options to customize the way your labels print. You can even use the Label design work surface to create a report that lists database information in columns—a feat impossible to accomplish with the Report design screen. Figure 11.5 shows an example of a two-column report created with the Label design screen.

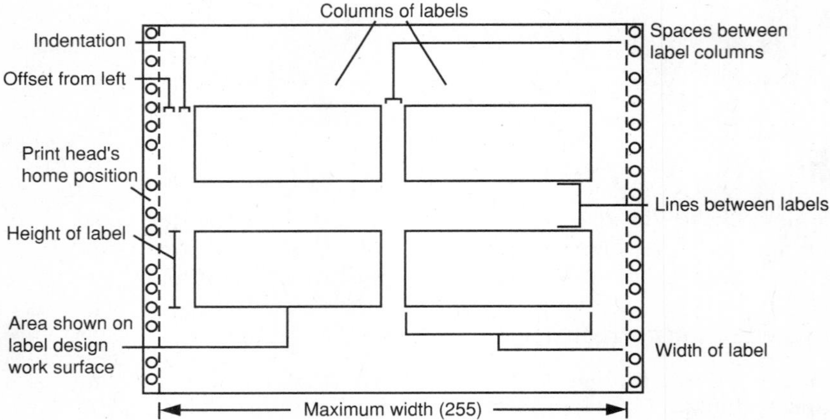


FIG. 11.4

Label design and printing options.

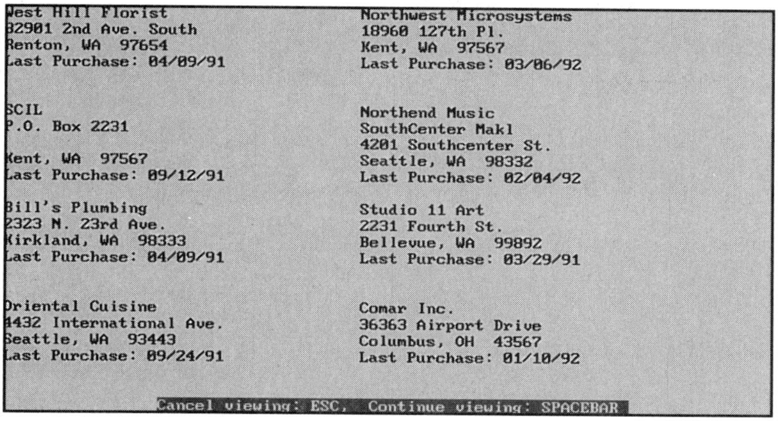

```
Jest Hill Florist                    Northwest Microsystems
32901 2nd Ave. South                 18960 127th Pl.
Renton, WA  97654                    Kent, WA  97567
Last Purchase: 04/09/91              Last Purchase: 03/06/92

SCIL                                 Northend Music
P.O. Box 2231                        SouthCenter Makl
                                     4201 Southcenter St.
Kent, WA  97567                      Seattle, WA  98332
Last Purchase: 09/12/91              Last Purchase: 02/04/92

Bill's Plumbing                      Studio 11 Art
2323 N. 23rd Ave.                    2231 Fourth St.
Kirkland, WA  98333                  Bellevue, WA  99892
Last Purchase: 04/09/91              Last Purchase: 03/29/91

Oriental Cuisine                     Comar Inc.
1432 International Ave.              36363 Airport Drive
Seattle, WA  93443                   Columbus, OH  43567
Last Purchase: 09/24/91              Last Purchase: 01/10/92

          Cancel viewing: ESC,  Continue viewing: SPACEBAR
```

FIG. 11.5

A two-column report created with the Label design screen.

This report shows database records listed side by side rather than one per row. Putting records side by side cannot be done with a dBASE report, yet this arrangement gives you a more condensed report.

The following options are available on the Dimensions menu:

| Option | Default | Description |
|---|---|---|
| Width of label | 35 | The number of characters on the label surface from the left edge to the right edge. The equivalent value in inches depends on the pitch you select in the Print menu. If you use Pica type, which is 10 characters per inch, 35 characters would equal 3.5 inches. If your printer is set for a different pitch, adjust this number. If your printer is set for 12 characters per inch, for example, it can print 42 characters on a 3 1/2-inch-wide label. |
| Height of label | 5 | The number of rows in the label, from top to bottom. Most printers use a spacing of 6 lines per inch; if your printer is set for a different figure, recalculate how many lines print on the label. |

| Option | Default | Description |
|---|---|---|
| Indentation | 0 | The number of characters from the left margin where the first character begins printing. |
| Lines between labels | 1 | The number of lines between the bottom of one label and the top of the next. |
| Spaces between label columns | 0 | The number of spaces between the right and left edges of labels on the same line. This value is 2 or 3 because labels generally have some space between them. |
| Columns of labels | 1 | Labels usually are laid out with 1, 2, or 3 columns on each sheet. As with any dimension, you can change this setting for custom applications. |

If you have a label format that isn't on dBASE's list of predefined sizes, you have to change the dimensions on the Dimensions menu to create the new format. To change the dimensions, follow these steps:

1. Take a sheet of labels and measure each of the dimensions listed in figure 11.4. Use 6 lines per inch for vertical measurements and 10 characters per inch for horizontal measurements.
2. Open the Dimensions menu by pressing Alt-D.
3. Move the highlight to the first dimension you need to alter. Press Enter and then type the new dimension. Press Enter again to accept the new dimension.

   To select label dimension options with the mouse, click on the Dimensions menu in the menu bar, then click on the option you want, type in the new dimension, and press Enter. Click the mouse outside the menu area to cancel the change.
4. Continue this process until you change all the dimensions that need to be altered. Press Esc to return to the Label design screen.
5. To save this label format, choose Save This Label Design from the Layout menu. Give the format a name and press Enter to save the design. The name appears in the Labels panel on the Control Center.

**TIP**

Creating a custom label design often requires some trial and error, no matter how carefully you measure the label sheet. Remember, too, that the alignment of the label sheet in the printer is critical. Aligning the sheet also may require some experimentation. When you print labels, you can print sample labels (one line of labels). You can use this option to align the paper correctly before starting to print a whole run of labels.

To illustrate the creation of a label design, this chapter creates labels from a CUSTINFO database that has the following structure:

| Field | Field name | Type | Width | Dec | Index |
|---|---|---|---|---|---|
| 1 | CUST_NUM | Character | 6 | | N |
| 2 | CUST_NAME | Character | 25 | | N |
| 3 | ADDR_1 | Character | 25 | | N |
| 4 | ADDR_2 | Character | 25 | | N |
| 5 | CITY | Character | 15 | | N |
| 6 | STATE | Character | 2 | | N |
| 7 | ZIP | Character | 9 | | Y |
| 8 | PHONE | Character | 10 | | N |
| 9 | CONTACT | Character | 10 | | N |
| 10 | CREDIT | Numeric | 8 | 2 | N |
| 11 | LAST_PUR | Date | 8 | | N |
| 12 | LAST_AMT | Numeric | 8 | 2 | N |
| 13 | PREFERD | Logical | 1 | | N |
| 14 | COMMENT | Memo | 10 | | N |

## Adding Fields to the Label Design

To place fields from your database onto the Label design work surface, follow these steps:

1. Move the cursor to the place where you want the name to print on the label. This position usually is Row:0, Col:0, but your design may place it elsewhere. The status line at the bottom of the Label design screen identifies the row and column position of the cursor.

2. Select Add Field from the Fields menu, or press F5 (Add Field).
3. From the list of fields shown in figure 11.6, choose CUST_NAME. The Field Definition menu appears. In this menu you can change the template for the field and specify picture functions, just as for a report field (see Chapter 10). Press Ctrl-End to accept the field when the template and picture functions are acceptable.

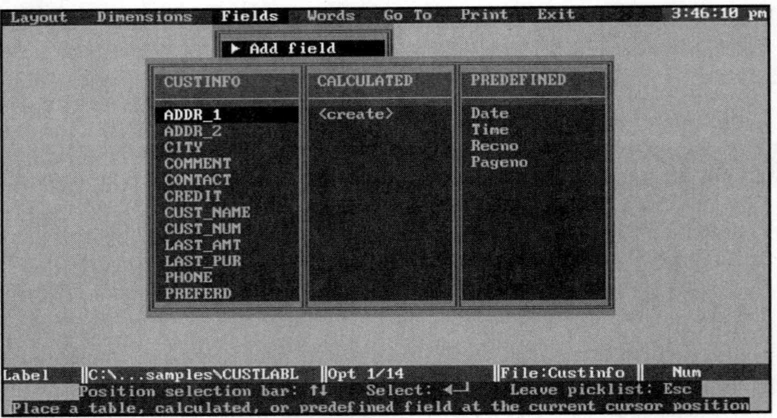


FIG. 11.6

The Field List menu.

4. When you return to the Label design screen, the field you just defined is on the Label design work surface. The Xs indicate the default template, just as in a report design.
5. Continue this process by placing each field on the work surface. As with reports, you can create calculated fields and use the four types of predefined fields: Date, Time, Recno (the record number of the field being printed), and Pageno (the page number currently being printed). Note that any predefined fields you add appear on each label on the sheet because the Label design is for one label.

Use the mouse to position fields on the label form. Click on the spot where you want to place a field. Click on the Fields menu label in the menu bar and then click on Add Field. From the fields list, select a field to add by clicking on the field name and then click again to accept your choice. To accept the template, click on the `Accept:Ctrl-End` key label in the navigation line.

You also can add literal text fields to a label design by moving the cursor to where you want the text to start and typing the text. In the example, the text `Thanks for your order!` was added to the bottom line of the design; this text prints out on each label.

Moving, copying, and deleting fields on the Label design screen is the same as moving, copying, and deleting fields on a report. For detailed information on these procedures, see Chapter 10.

When your design is completed, the Label design screen may look like figure 11.7. The fields are in place, and the literal text has been placed at the bottom of the label.

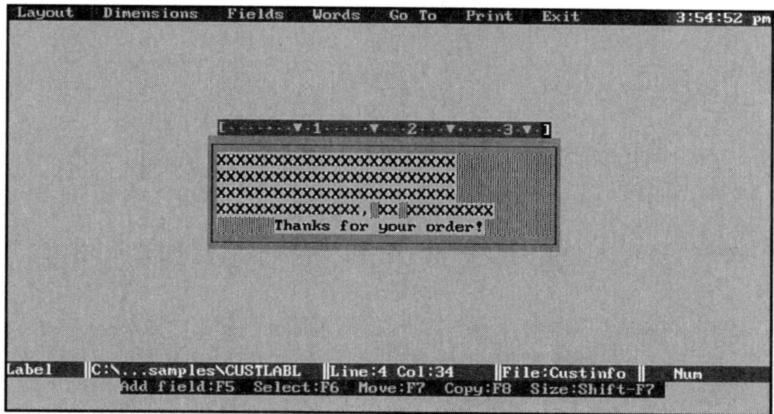


FIG. 11.7

A completed label design.

You can test your label design by choosing View Labels On Screen from the Print menu. dBASE compiles and executes the label design, and then puts the results on-screen. Figure 11.8 shows the label design in an on-screen test.

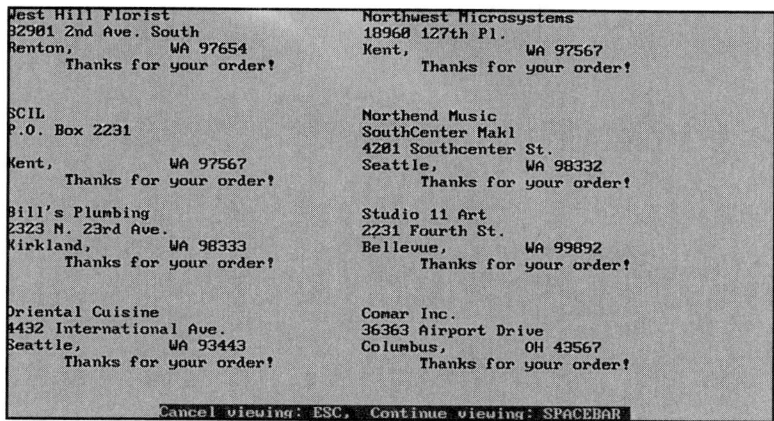


FIG. 11.8

The complete label design tested on-screen.

When dBASE prints your label design, it uses the full length of each field—whether or not the value in that field actually needs the full length. As a result, the line with the CITY, STATE, and ZIP fields looks awkward; in many labels, a large space appears between the end of the city name and the start of the state abbreviation. dBASE provides a way for you to eliminate this extra space.

On your label design, you can see a shaded column position between the CITY and STATE fields and another between the STATE and ZIP fields. This shaded position tells dBASE that you put nothing there. dBASE therefore places the fields on the label exactly as you placed them on the design. If you change that shaded position to a space or a character, dBASE interprets the design differently. To change the shaded position, follow these steps:

1. Move the cursor to the shaded position between the CITY and STATE fields.
2. Toggle the Ins key OFF and press the space bar. Your label design now appears as in figure 11.9.

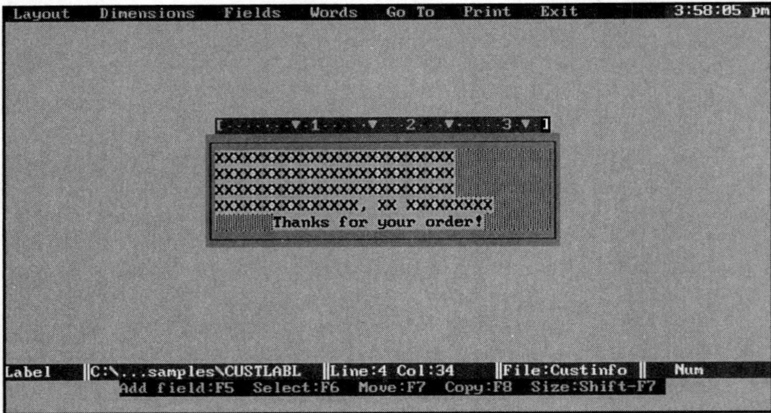


FIG. 11.9

The modified label design.

dBASE interprets the CITY, STATE, and ZIP fields as one field with a comma and one space between the CITY and STATE fields, and one space between the STATE and ZIP fields. Figure 11.10 shows the new design printed out. Notice that the line with the city, state, and ZIP Code differs from the standard design. The new design produces a much more professional-looking label.

```
West Hill Florist                      Northwest Microsystems
32901 2nd Ave. South                   18960 127th Pl.
Renton, WA 97654                       Kent, WA 97567
      Thanks for your order!                 Thanks for your order!


SCIL                                   Northend Music
P.O. Box 2231                          SouthCenter Makl
                                       4201 Southcenter St.
Kent, WA 97567                         Seattle, WA 98332
      Thanks for your order!                 Thanks for your order!

Bill's Plumbing                        Studio 11 Art
2323 N. 23rd Ave.                      2231 Fourth St.
Kirkland, WA 98333                     Bellevue, WA 99892
      Thanks for your order!                 Thanks for your order!


Oriental Cuisine                       Comar Inc.
4432 International Ave.                36363 Airport Drive
Seattle, WA 93443                      Columbus, OH 43567
      Thanks for your order!                 Thanks for your order!

                Cancel viewing: ESC,  Continue viewing: SPACEBAR
```

FIG. 11.10

Testing the improved design.

# Testing Your Label Design

With dBASE IV, you can quickly test your label design. Choose View Labels On Screen from the Print menu. dBASE compiles your design and then executes the label design and places the labels on-screen. You can see whether your fields appear as you want them to appear and that any calculated and predefined fields are working correctly.

Viewing labels on-screen is little help in making sure that the labels line up and print correctly on the label sheet. To make sure that the labels print correctly, select Generate Sample Labels from the Print menu. To test labels with this feature, follow these steps:

1. Load the label sheet into your printer. Position the top of the label sheet so that the first line prints in the first row of the labels. Because every printer is different, you probably will have to guess the first time. Make sure that the left edge of the labels is at the 0 column mark on the printer.

2. Choose Generate Sample Labels from the Print menu. dBASE prints one row of labels. Adjust the paper in the printer if the sample labels didn't print correctly.

3. Choose Generate Sample Labels again to see whether your adjustment is right. Continue adjusting and generating sample labels until the labels print correctly. Choose Print Label from the Print menu. dBASE starts printing all the labels from the database.

## Saving the Design

Saving the label form is the same as saving information produced on other work surfaces. Choose Save This Label Design from the Layout menu. dBASE IV compiles the label design. For this exercise, save the design as CUST. This process may take up to a minute. The Label design screen reappears so that you can continue to make changes and test them.

If you choose Save Changes And Exit from the Exit menu, dBASE asks whether you want to save the design if you made changes since the last time you selected Save This Label Design. You also can use the Exit menu if you saved a good design and then made changes you don't want to keep: choose Abandon Changes And Exit from the Exit menu. The program returns to the Control Center, where you see the name of your label design in the Labels panel. The name of the label design that appears in the Labels panel contains the last version you saved before selecting Abandon Changes And Exit.

To modify the label design, highlight the label name in the Labels panel of the Control Center and press Enter. In the selection box that appears, choose Modify Layout. You also can highlight the label name and press Shift-F2. You return to the Label design screen with your design ready for modification.

To modify a label format from the Control Center with the mouse, click on the file name in the Labels panel and then click on the `Design: Shift-F2` key label in the navigation line.

**For Related Information...**

◂◂ "Designing Reports," p. 229.

# Using Queries To Limit the Label Output

As with printing reports, you can use queries to limit the database records printed as labels. For example, you can use a query to limit the labels to records that have a specific state in the STATE field or to a range of ZIP Codes. The following steps show you how to use a query to print labels.

To limit printed labels to those records that have WA in the STATE field in the CUSTINFO database, follow these steps:

1. In the Control Center, choose the CUSTINFO database in the Data panel by highlighting it, pressing Enter, and then choosing Use File.

2. Move the highlight to the Queries panel and select <create>. The Query design screen appears (see fig. 11.11).

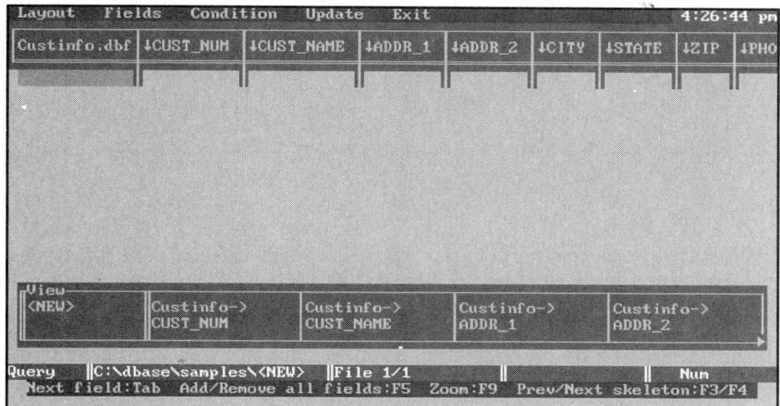

**FIG. 11.11**

The Query design screen with a database for labels in place.

3. Press Tab until the highlight is under the STATE field. Type *"WA"* (be sure to include the double quotation marks) to limit processing of the database to only those records with the value WA in the STATE field.

   Use the mouse to position the cursor under a field by clicking in the area under the field name. Click under the STATE field to place the highlight there, for example, and then type *"WA"* to specify records for the state of Washington.

4. Test the query by pressing F2 (Data). A table that shows the records with WA in the STATE field appears. Only these records will be printed as labels when this query is active.

   To test the query using the mouse, click on the `Data:F2` label in the navigation line. From the Browse screen that appears, click on the Exit menu name in the menu bar and then click on Transfer to Query Design to return to the Query design screen.

5. Save the query by choosing Save This Query from the Layout menu. You are asked to give the query a name. Enter *WA_STATE* to identify this query as one that limits the labels to those records with WA in the STATE field (see fig. 11.12).

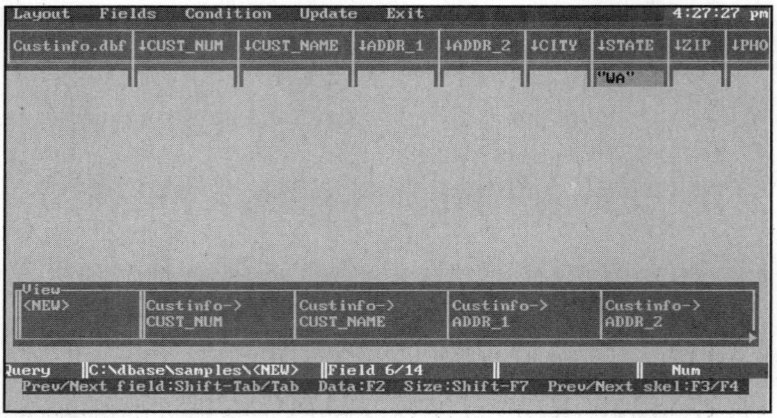

FIG. 11.12

Limiting the labels to those records with WA in the STATE field.

You also can save the query by choosing Save Query And Exit from the Exit menu. You are asked for a name to assign to this query.

6. To exit the Query design screen, select the Exit menu. If you made changes after the last save and want to save them, choose Save Query And Exit and press Enter. If you made changes you want to discard, choose Abandon Changes And Exit. You return to the Control Center, where your query is now in the Queries panel.

7. In the Control Center, the newly created query, WA_STATE, is shown above a line in the Queries panel, indicating that this query is the active query and controls database processing. Move the highlight to the Labels column and make the CUST label design active by highlighting it and pressing Enter.

8. From the selection box that appears, choose Print Label.

   A box will pop up asking if you want to use the current view or the original database. Select Current View to use the active query.

9. Follow the procedures for adjusting the label sheets in the printer and printing out the labels. Only database records that satisfy the condition you entered into the WA_STATE query are processed; only records with the value WA in the STATE field are printed.

Queries give you tremendous power over which labels are printed from your databases. Designing and using queries is discussed fully in Chapter 12.

# Printing Labels

After you complete the label design and test it on the Label design screen, you can return to the Control Center. There your label design is part of the current catalog, under the Labels panel.

To print your labels, follow these steps:

1. Make the correct database current by highlighting it in the Data panel of the Control Center, pressing Enter, and choosing Use File from the options presented.
2. If you're using a query to limit the label output, make the query active by highlighting it in the Queries panel and pressing Enter.
3. Move the highlight to the Labels panel, highlight the label design you want to use with this database, and press Enter.
4. From the options presented, choose Print Label; the Print screen appears as it does for a report.

   One important difference in printing labels and reports is the Generate Sample Labels option that appears on the Print menu when printing labels. For more information about using this option to align the label paper in the printer, see "Testing Your Label Design," earlier in this chapter.

To print labels from the Control Center with the mouse, click on the label format file in the Labels panel and then click on Print Labels in the instruction box that appears. (If Instruct is set to OFF, double-click on the file name.) When the Print menu appears, click on Generate Sample Labels or Begin Printing.

# Summary

With dBASE IV's Label design screen, you can quickly and easily create a wide variety of labels. Predefined sizes are available for all common label formats. With dBASE IV, you also can customize label formats.

You can use queries with labels to produce labels for mailing lists. Creating labels is one of dBASE IV's strongest features.

12

CHAPTER

# Using Queries To Search Databases

Even with small databases, you rarely want to look at every record in the database when you need some information. More likely, you want to look at a subset of the database. You can have dBASE IV display only the information you need and only from records that meet your criteria. In a database of customer information, for example, you can tell dBASE IV to show you only records that have a certain ZIP code range or that have a specific state. In large databases, you almost always want dBASE IV to limit to certain records what it displays and what it searches.

The tool you use to limit what dBASE IV searches and presents to you from your database is query by example (QBE). QBE is a Control Center operation, shown there as the Queries panel. You can refine your searches to the point where you can find one record out of thousands in the database. QBE also enables you to restructure fields, sort the database, perform calculations, and aggregate data. This chapter teaches you how to use QBE to limit dBASE IV searches and data presentations.

# Understanding Query By Example

To explain query by example, this chapter uses a customer database as an example. The structure of this database is shown in figure 12.1. This database is simple, but it serves to explain many facets of QBE.

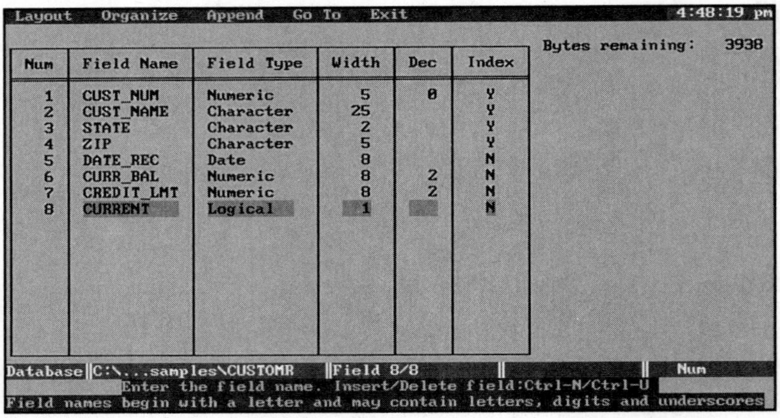

Layout Organize Append Go To Exit 4:48:19 pm

Bytes remaining: 3938

| Num | Field Name | Field Type | Width | Dec | Index |
|---|---|---|---|---|---|
| 1 | CUST_NUM | Numeric | 5 | 0 | Y |
| 2 | CUST_NAME | Character | 25 | | Y |
| 3 | STATE | Character | 2 | | Y |
| 4 | ZIP | Character | 5 | | Y |
| 5 | DATE_REC | Date | 8 | | N |
| 6 | CURR_BAL | Numeric | 8 | 2 | N |
| 7 | CREDIT_LMT | Numeric | 8 | 2 | N |
| 8 | CURRENT | Logical | 1 | | N |

Database C:\...samples\CUSTOMR Field 8/8 Num

Enter the field name. Insert/Delete field:Ctrl-N/Ctrl-U

Field names begin with a letter and may contain letters, digits and underscores

FIG. 12.1

The structure of the customer database example.

To see data from only certain records in your database, you *query*, or ask, dBASE IV to search the entire database but present only the records that meet your requirements. You use a query to view specific data and to create a specific report.

You can use a query to see data in the database that meets some limiting criteria. To query a dBASE database, you specify one or more conditions; when dBASE searches the active database, it ignores any record that does not meet those conditions. Records that meet the conditions are displayed on-screen. You can define the fields displayed by a query. (You don't have to display all the fields.) You also can sort or index the order in which the records are presented.

You can use a query to see only the summation of certain fields that meet your criteria instead of viewing each record. Queries are mini-reports that enable you to see the database information quickly.

If you want your reports to cover only records that meet certain conditions, use queries. You can query dBASE IV to limit a search to only those records that meet the conditions, to test and make sure that the conditions you specify retrieve the records you want, and to create a report to format the information for clarity and readability and send it to the printer. The records that appear in the report are limited by the query you make active.

# Creating a Query

The process of creating and using a query is simple and straightforward. From the Control Center, make active the database you want to query. Move the highlight to the Queries panel and select <create>. The Query design screen appears (see fig. 12.2). As with other work surfaces in dBASE IV, the Query work surface has a menu that offers choices appropriate for the creation of a query. At the bottom of the screen are the status bar and navigation line. As with other work surfaces, messages appear on the bottom line of the screen. A *file skeleton* for the Customer database file appears at the top of the screen; the *view skeleton* appears at the bottom of the screen.

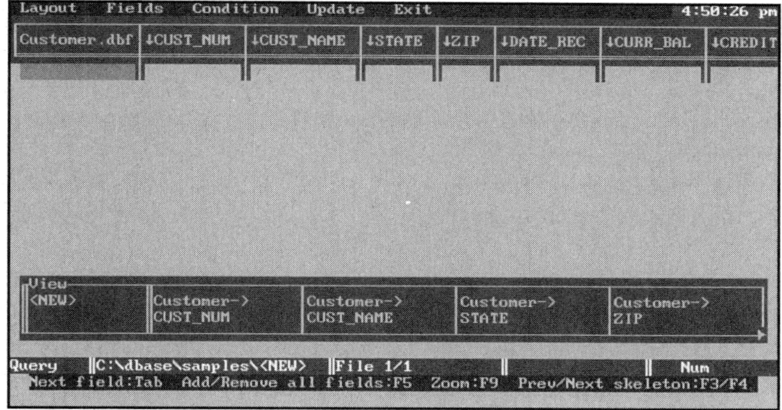


**FIG. 12.2**

The Query design screen.

Notice that the file skeleton lists the name of the current database (CUSTOMER.DBF) and the field names (CUST_NUM, CUST_NAME, and so on) in that database. You may not be able to see all of the fields, but pressing Tab scrolls the file skeleton to the right and enables you to see and access all fields in the database.

The view skeleton specifies which fields are displayed when a query is processed and the results displayed on-screen. Initially, all fields in the file skeleton are in the view skeleton, in the same order as in the file skeleton, but you can remove fields from the view skeleton or move them to different locations to change the appearance of the data when the query is processed. As with the file skeleton, not all fields appear on the view skeleton initially, but you can scroll to them by using Tab and Shift-Tab.

Using a mouse, you can move the highlight to a field on the file skeleton by clicking in the input area under the field name. Select a field in the view skeleton by clicking on the top line of the field box. To scroll through fields in the view skeleton that do not appear on-screen, click on the arrow located on the bottom line of the view skeleton.

You use the query by example technique in the Query design work surface. You see, on the work surface, the format of the database or databases you want to query. On the work surface, you type examples for which you want dBASE IV to search. If you want to see all the records in the Customer database that have WA in the STATE field, for example, you type *"WA"* in the STATE field in the file skeleton section of the design screen.

When you create a query, you specify the conditions you want dBASE IV to use to search the database. To specify a query condition, use the Tab, Shift-Tab, and the appropriate arrow keys to position the cursor in the field for which you want to specify a condition. Type the condition for which you want dBASE to search. If you want to search for records in which the ZIP Code is 48192, for example, move the cursor to the ZIP field and type *"48192"*. If the field is a character type field and you are searching for a literal character expression, enclose the expression in quotes.

After you specify this condition, press F2 (Data). dBASE IV searches the database and presents a new screen of information that matches the criteria for you to browse through. If you press Shift-F2 (Design), you return to the Query design screen, where you can change any condition to further refine the database search, or you can completely change all the conditions.

To see how a query works, activate a database from the Control Center. Move the cursor to <create> in the Queries panel and press Enter. When the Query design work surface appears, press F2 (Data). The query is processed, and dBASE IV places the data that matches the conditions on-screen. Because you didn't place any conditions on the data or change which fields will be presented, this query results in a screen essentially the same as the one that appears when you highlight a database name and press F2 (Data) from the Control Center. Figure 12.3 shows the data view for the Customer database that results from the default query.

Press Shift-F2 (Design) to return from the view screen to the Query design screen.

To get back to the Query design screen from the Browse (view) screen by using the mouse, you can click on the Exit menu name and then click on Transfer To Query Design.

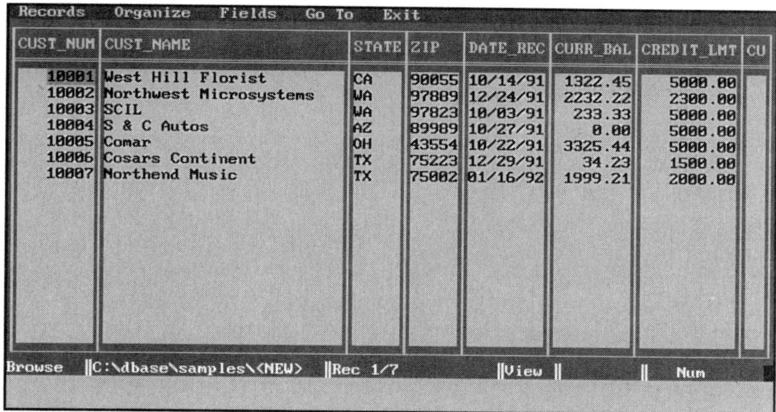


FIG. 12.3

The view of a database presented by the default query.

To create an effective and useful query, you must become familiar with the file and view skeleton areas of the Query design screen. You use these areas to modify the selected data and the presentation of that data on-screen.

## Understanding the File Skeleton

The file skeleton area of the Query design screen shows all the fields of the active database. If the database has more fields than can fit on-screen, they extend off the right side of the screen. To see the fields that are off the screen, press Tab to move right one field at a time, or press Shift-Tab to move left. If a field has a downward-pointing arrow to the left of the first character of the field name, that field is included in the view skeleton area of the screen. The data for a field marked with such an arrow appears when the query is processed.

You use the file skeleton to specify the conditions dBASE IV uses to search the database. You also can use the file skeleton to sort or index the data presented, to create summary fields, and to group the data in ways that you choose.

Refer to "Refining Database Searches," later in this chapter, for information about using the file skeleton to create queries.

## Understanding the View Skeleton

The view skeleton area of the Query design screen defines which of the database fields are presented in the view screen. Initially, all fields of the active database are included in the view skeleton; but you can add, delete, or move fields to customize the way data is presented in the view screen.

## Deleting Fields from the View Skeleton

When you first see the Query design screen, all fields of the active database are included in the file skeleton. All the fields of the records displayed in the view screen are included in the view. You may not want to display all the fields in the view screen. To modify what appears in the view screen, modify the view skeleton.

To remove fields from the view skeleton, follow these steps:

1. Move the cursor to the view skeleton area of the Query design screen by pressing F4 (Next). The highlight moves to the top border of the first field in the view skeleton.
2. Use Tab and Shift-Tab to move right and left in the view skeleton until the field you want to delete is highlighted.
3. Choose Remove Field From View from the Fields menu or press F5 (Remove From View) to remove the selected field from the view skeleton. The other fields move left in the skeleton to fill up the space left by the deleted field.

Using the mouse, you can remove a field from the view skeleton by clicking on that field and then clicking on the `Remove from view:F5` label on the navigation line. You also can click on the Remove Field From View option in the Fields menu.

## Adding Fields to the View Skeleton

You may want to return a field to the view skeleton after you remove it. To return such a field to the view skeleton, follow these steps:

1. Move the highlight to the file skeleton area of the Query design screen by pressing F4 (Next). The field under the database name is highlighted.
2. Press Tab and Shift-Tab to highlight the field you want to add to the view skeleton.
3. Select Add Field To View from the Fields menu or press F5 (Add Field). The selected field is added to the view skeleton, and a down arrow appears next to the field name in the file skeleton area of the screen.

With the mouse, you can add a field to the view skeleton by clicking on that field in the file skeleton and then clicking on the Add Field To View option in the Fields menu.

When dBASE IV processes a query, data in this field appears in the view screen.

## Moving Fields in the View Skeleton

You may want to rearrange the order of the fields in the view skeleton so that the most important fields appear on-screen when the query is processed. You may want less important fields to the far right of the display, where you can reach them with the Tab key.

To move fields in the view skeleton, follow these steps:

1. Move the cursor to the view skeleton area of the Query design screen by pressing F4 (Next).
2. Use Tab and Shift-Tab to highlight the field you want to move. Press F6 (Extend Select) to select that field. To move more than one field, use Tab and Shift-Tab to extend the selected fields to the right or left. After you select all the fields you want to move, press Enter.
3. Use Tab and Shift-Tab to move the selected fields to their new location. The selected fields move to new positions when you press the Tab and Shift-Tab keys. When the fields are where you want them, press Enter.

The fields are now in their new location.

Test the new arrangement of the view skeleton by pressing F2 (Data). dBASE processes the query and displays the data in a view screen. You can see whether the current format of the view skeleton is what you want. Press Shift-F2 (Design) to return to the Query design work surface. Continue making changes to the view skeleton until you are satisfied with the format.

# Refining Database Searches

When you process the default query, dBASE IV presents all the records in the database. You usually want to see only certain records, however. In a database of customer information, for example, you may want to see records of customers living in a certain geographical area. In an inventory database, you may want to look only at records in a certain part-number range. A database program is designed to organize and present data in different ways so that it serves different user purposes.

By using the Query design work surface, you can refine the searches that dBASE IV uses in your databases, making them as broad or as narrow as you want.

## Searching for Records with a Specific Value

To look at all the database records that have a specific value in one of the fields, place the search value below that field name in the file skeleton.

Follow these steps to specify a value in one of the fields:

1. Using the F3 (Previous) and F4 (Next) keys, move the highlight to the file skeleton.
2. Using Tab and Shift-Tab, move the cursor highlight to the field for which you want to define a search value.
3. Enter the search value in the field. Character search values must be enclosed in double quotation marks. If you want dBASE to present only records with WA in the STATE field, for example, enter *"WA"* in the STATE field of the file skeleton.
4. Press F2 (Data). dBASE IV searches the database and presents in a view screen the records that contain the search value.
5. To remove a search value from a field, highlight the field on the Query design work surface and press Ctrl-Y. The field blanks out, and that search criterion is removed.

You can use the mouse to position the cursor in the file skeleton by clicking the mouse pointer under the field name. Type in the search criteria and then click on the `Data:F2` label in the navigation line to execute the query.

The details of entering search values differ for different field types. The following sections provide details for entering criteria in character fields, numeric fields, date fields, and logical fields.

### Searching in Character Fields

In character fields, you must enclose the value for which you want dBASE to search in quotation marks, unless you are using a variable name or field name as the search criterion. Figure 12.4 shows the value "WA" under the STATE field of the Customer database Query design screen. This query asks dBASE IV to present only records that have the value WA in the STATE field. Figure 12.5 shows the view resulting from this query. Every record presented meets this condition. Press Shift-F2 (Design) to return to the Query design work surface.

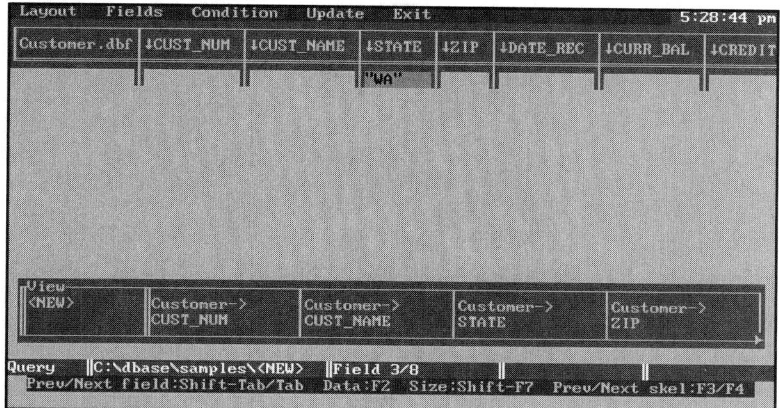


FIG. 12.4

Querying for records with "WA" in the STATE field.

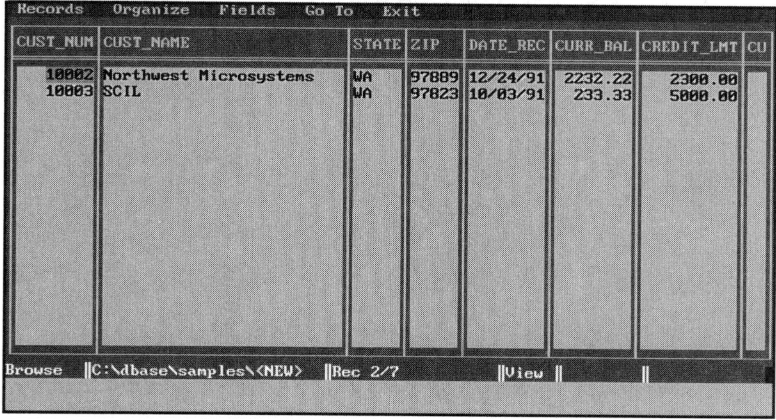


FIG. 12.5

The result of a search on a character field.

## Searching in Numeric Fields

Querying a numeric field is a matter of placing the search value below the search field. Figure 12.6 shows a Query search for all records with a credit limit of $5,000. Figure 12.7 shows a view screen of records from the Customer database that meet this criterion.

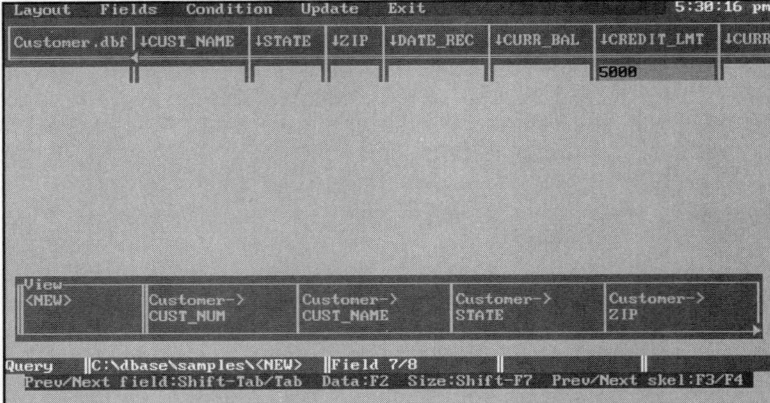


FIG. 12.6

Querying for records with a credit limit of $5,000.

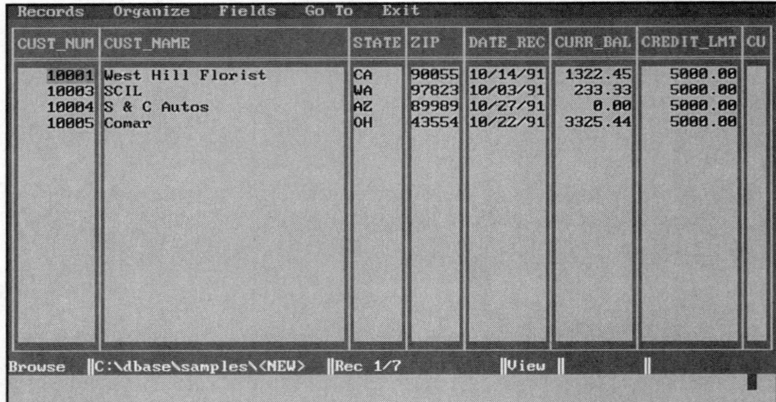


FIG. 12.7

The result of the search on a numeric field.

## Searching in Date Fields

Unless you use another date field name or variable as the search criterion, date fields require that you enclose the search data in braces ({ and }). To search for records with a date later than December 12, 1990, for example, enter this criterion as > *{12/12/90}*. Figure 12.8 shows the Query design work surface with this search data in the DATE_REC field. The result of this search is shown in figure 12.9.

## Searching in Logical Fields

Searches on logical fields require that you enter the search value as *.T.* for True or *.F.* for False. The periods before and after the logical value tell dBASE that this entry is not just the character *T* or *F*, but a logical value. Figure 12.10 shows the specification of a search on the logical field CURRENT; figure 12.11 shows the results of this query.

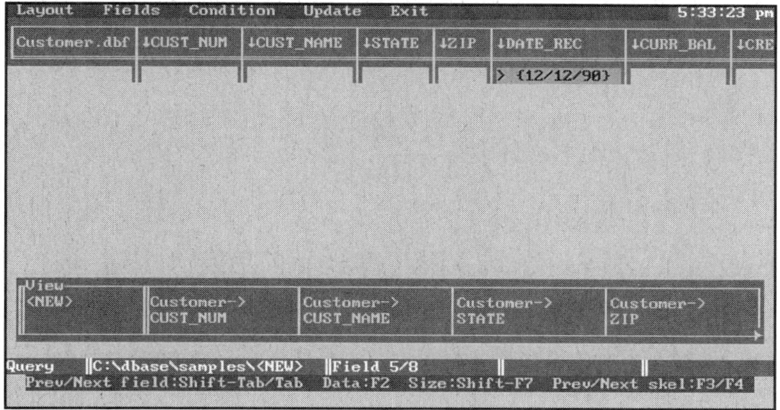


FIG. 12.8

Specifying a search on a date field.

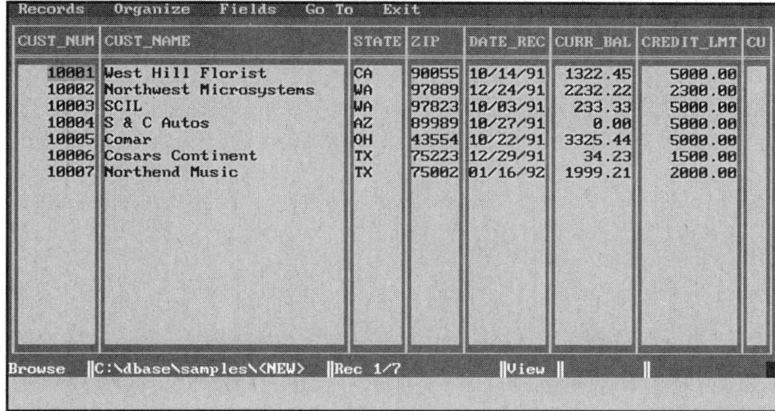


| CUST_NUM | CUST_NAME | STATE | ZIP | DATE_REC | CURR_BAL | CREDIT_LMT | CU |
|---|---|---|---|---|---|---|---|
| 10001 | West Hill Florist | CA | 90055 | 10/14/91 | 1322.45 | 5000.00 | |
| 10002 | Northwest Microsystems | WA | 97889 | 12/24/91 | 2232.22 | 2300.00 | |
| 10003 | SCIL | WA | 97823 | 10/03/91 | 233.33 | 5000.00 | |
| 10004 | S & C Autos | AZ | 89989 | 10/27/91 | 0.00 | 5000.00 | |
| 10005 | Comar | OH | 43554 | 10/22/91 | 3325.44 | 5000.00 | |
| 10006 | Cosars Continent | TX | 75223 | 12/29/91 | 34.23 | 1500.00 | |
| 10007 | Northend Music | TX | 75002 | 01/16/92 | 1999.21 | 2000.00 | |



FIG. 12.9

The result of a search on a date field.

Memo fields provide powerful capabilities, but their unique nature prevents their use in query by example. If you place a search criterion in a memo field in the file skeleton, dBASE rejects your query with the error message `Operation with memo field invalid`.

## Using Relational Operators in Searches

Most of the searches described in the preceding sections looked for a specific value. You may want to search for values above a certain value or below another value. For these searches, you need to specify the search with a *relational operator*. Figure 12.12 shows a query for records with a value in the CREDIT_LMT field greater than 2000.

Layout Fields Condition Update Exit 5:52:40 pm
Customer.dbf ↓STATE ↓ZIP ↓DATE_REC ↓CURR_BAL ↓CREDIT_LMT ↓CURRENT
.F.
View <NEW>
Customer-> CUST_NUM
Customer-> CUST_NAME
Customer-> STATE
Customer-> ZIP
Query C:\dbase\samples\<NEW> Field 8/8
Prev/Next field:Shift-Tab/Tab Data:F2 Size:Shift-F7 Prev/Next skel:F3/F4

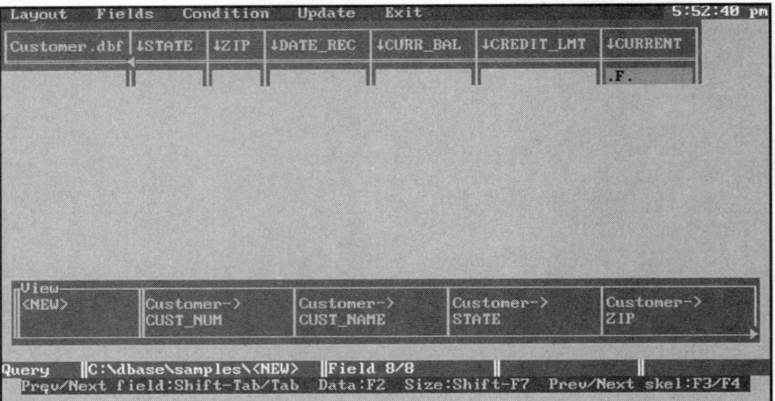

FIG. 12.10

Specifying a search on a logical field.

Records Organize Fields Go To Exit
CUST_NUM CUST_NAME STATE ZIP DATE_REC CURR_BAL CREDIT_LMT CU
10001 West Hill Florist CA 90055 10/14/91 1322.45 5000.00 F
10004 S & C Autos AZ 89989 10/27/91 0.00 5000.00 F
10005 Comar OH 43554 10/22/91 3325.44 5000.00 F
10006 Cosars Continent TX 75223 12/29/91 34.23 1500.00 F
10007 Northend Music TX 75002 01/16/92 1999.21 2000.00 F
Browse C:\dbase\samples\<NEW> Rec 1/7 View

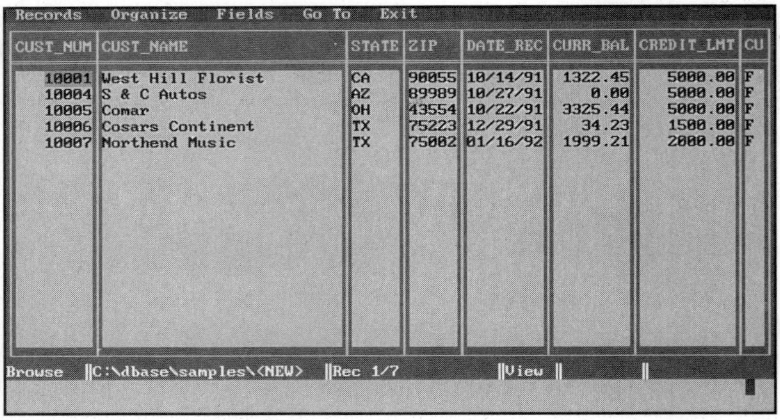

FIG. 12.11

The result of a search on a logical field.

**TIP**

Press Shift-F1 to pull up the Expression Builder menu to choose an operator when specifying search criteria. Select a relational operator from the second column (see fig. 12.13) by highlighting it with the mouse or the arrow keys, and then press Enter or click the mouse to include the operator in your expression.

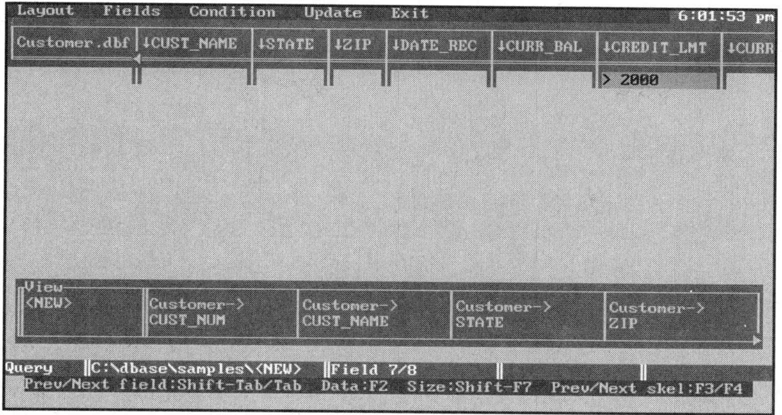


FIG. 12.12

Specifying a search with a relational operator.

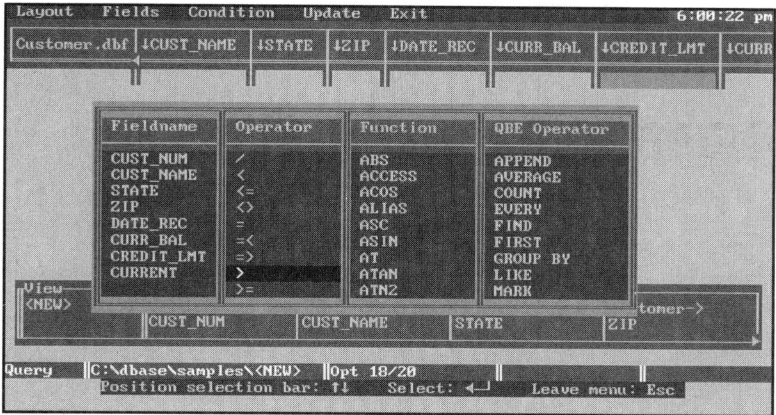


FIG. 12.13

Selecting a relational operator from the Expression Builder menu.

Table 12.1 lists the relational operators you can use in query searches.

## Searching with Wild Cards

The *like* relational operator enables you to find records that have character-field values matching a template you specify. To find all records that have the character W in the first position of the STATE field, for example, specify a search value of `like "W*"`. The * character is a wild card that matches any values. Figure 12.14 shows this search criterion in the Query design work surface; figure 12.15 shows the view result. If you enter *"W*"*, the query looks for STATE fields with exactly that string: an uppercase W followed by an asterisk (*). The like operator tells dBASE to interpret the * and ? characters as wild cards.

**Table 12.1 Relational Operators**

| Operator | Operator name | Description |
|---|---|---|
| > | greater than | All records whose field value is greater than the specified search value |
| < | less than | All records whose field value is less than the search value |
| = | equal | Only records whose field value is equal to the search value |
| <> or # | not equal | Records whose field value is not equal to the specified value |
| => | greater than or equal | Records whose field value is greater than or equal to the search value |
| => | less than or equal | Records whose field value is less than or equal to the search value |
| $ | included | Used in character fields, "$ AB" means "process records whose field includes the letters AB." See "Searching for Embedded Values" later in this chapter for information on using this operator. |
| Like | pattern match | Like the DOS wild-card search, allows wild-card characters. See the next section, "Searching with Wild Cards," for information on using this operator. |
| Sounds like | | A soundex match, which often finds words that "sound like" the search value |

You can use one of two wild-card characters with the like operator. The asterisk (*) means "all characters in all positions"; the question mark (?) means "any character in only this position." A search string of "W*", for example, can result in values of *Washington*, *Warhol*, and *Westerdale* (notice that the length of the result is irrelevant; only the first character must match the search criterion). A search string of "W?" results in values of *WA*, *WI*, and *WY* (the question mark holds the place of any single character).

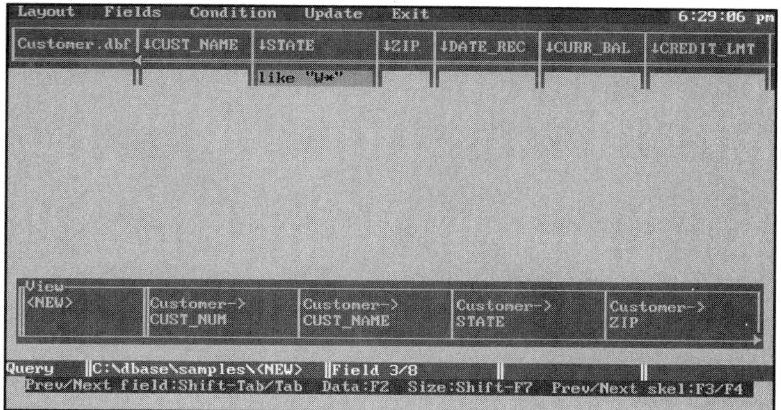


**FIG. 12.14**

A like search variable with the wild card.

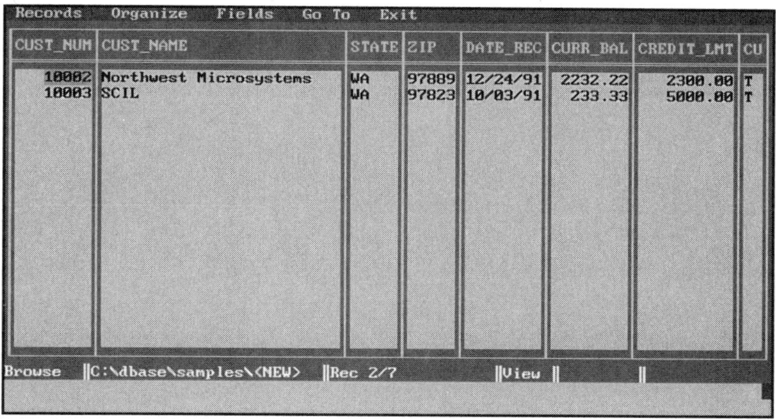


**FIG. 12.15**

The result of a like search.

## Searching for Embedded Values

Use the $ relational operator to search for values embedded in a character field. If you want to find all records in the Customer database that have the letters *Co* in the CUST_NAME field, for example, type *$ "Co"* in the CUST_NAME field in the file skeleton, as shown in figure 12.16. The result of this search is shown in figure 12.17. Notice that the search locates any record where the letters *Co* appear adjacent to one another in the CUST_NAME field. Notice that the letter *C* is capitalized and that the records that match this criterion also show a capital letter *C*.

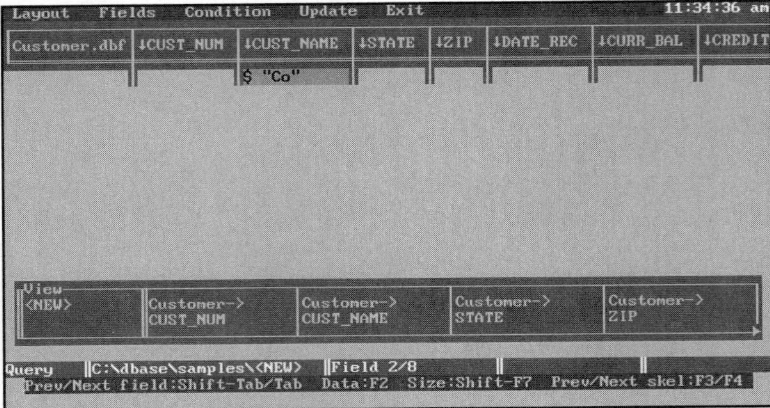


FIG. 12.16

Searching for embedded characters.

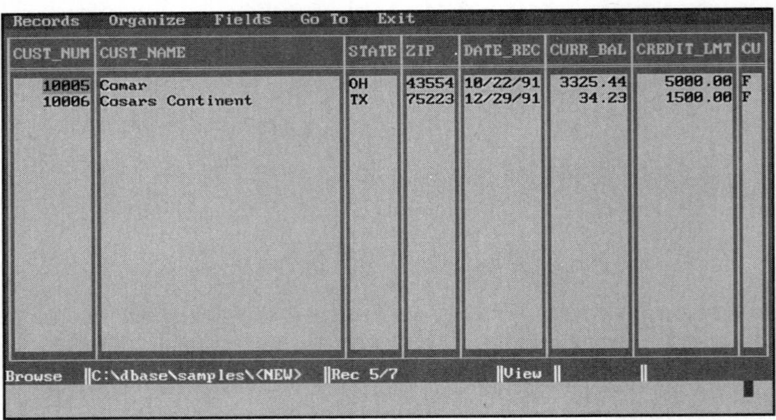


FIG. 12.17

The result of the search for embedded characters.

# Searching for Values in a Range

You may want the view screen to display records whose search field value falls between a range of values. In the appropriate field, use a statement that dictates the lower end of the range and a separate statement dictating the higher end of the range. Separate these two statements with a comma. When you press F2 (Data) to initiate the query, dBASE searches for records that meet both conditions and fall within your specified range.

Figure 12.18 shows the file skeleton with such a range specified in the CURR_BAL field. This query asks for all records between 1000 and 3000—those records with values greater than 1000 and less than 3000. Figure 12.19 shows the resulting view screen.

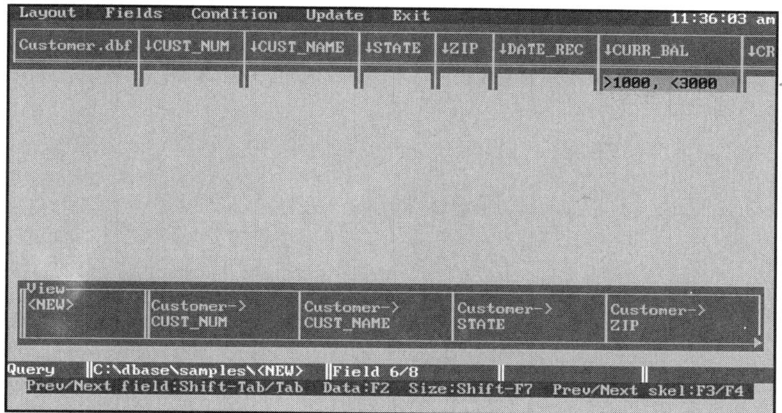


FIG. 12.18

Specifying a range search in a numeric field.

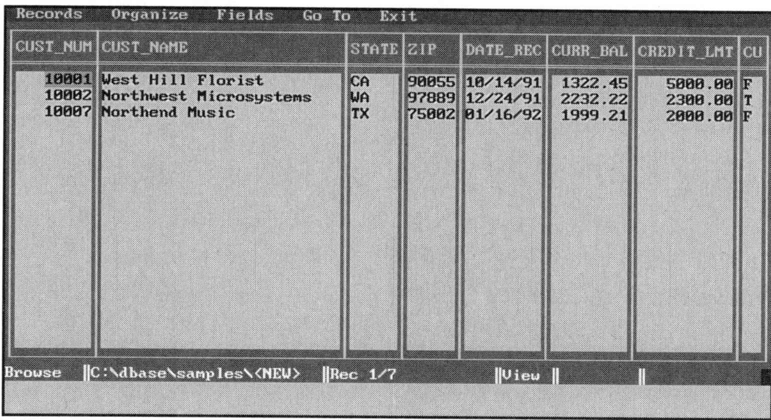


FIG. 12.19

The result of a range search.

When you work with a range specification, be sure that the first expression really does form the lower boundary, that the second forms the upper boundary, and that the two together indicate a range. A common mistake is to specify a range like <1000, >3000. This range asks for all records that are less than 1000 and greater than 3000. If dBASE IV finds any records that meet this criteria, something is seriously wrong!

## Searching for Records Meeting Multiple Conditions

dBASE IV provides several ways to combine searches in a query. You may want to search for more than one value in a field, or you may want to require that the processed records meet conditions in more than one field. Combining search conditions enables you to continue refining your database searches. The following sections explain how to conduct queries that meet multiple conditions.

## Searching for One Value in One Field and One Value in Another Field

When you want a search to find records that meet search values in two different fields, enter each search value in the appropriate field in the file skeleton. The query treats values in the same line in the file skeleton as AND searches. dBASE tests each database record to see whether it matches the first value *and* the second value. Suppose that you want to search the Customer database for all records with *WA* in the STATE field and with a value in the CURR_BAL field greater than $2000.00.

To create this query, follow these directions:

1. Remove any existing conditions or expressions by highlighting them one at a time and pressing Ctrl-Y. The field clears when you press Ctrl-Y.
2. Move the cursor to the STATE field and type *"WA"*. Make sure that you include the double quotation marks.
3. Move the cursor to the CURR_BAL field and type >*2000*. The Query design screen should look like figure 12.20.

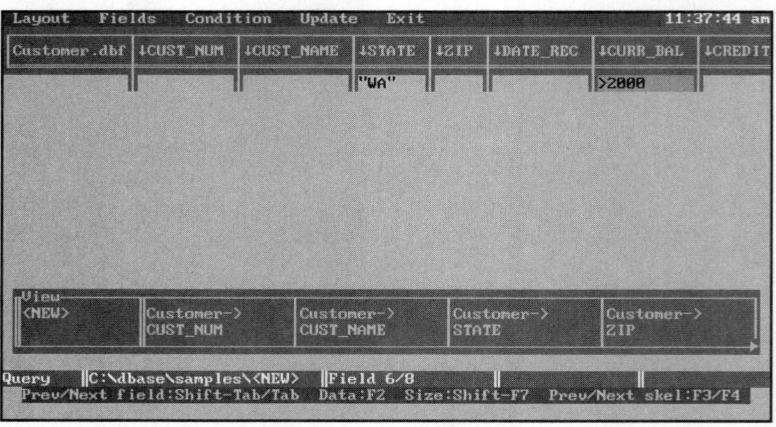


FIG. 12.20

An AND search on two fields.

4. Press F2 (Data) to process the query. dBASE searches the Customer database, looking for records that meet both criteria (records that have *WA* in the STATE field and that also have a CURR_BAL value greater than 2000). Figure 12.21 shows the result of this search.

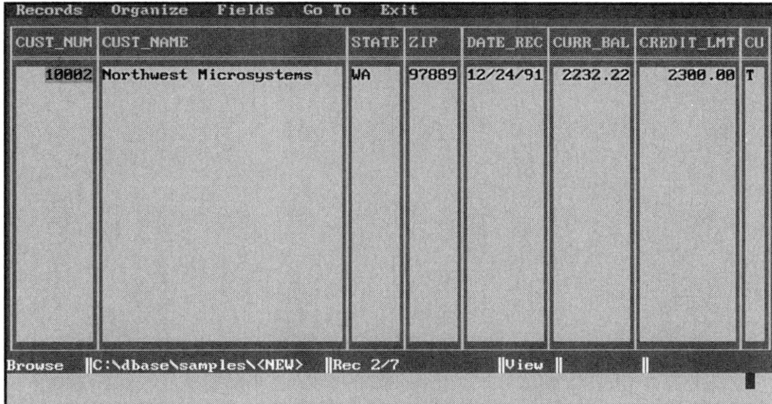


FIG. 12.21

The result of an AND search on two fields.

You can specify search values in as many of the file skeleton fields as you want, because dBASE IV treats each criterion on the same line as an AND condition. If the first match is made AND the second match is made AND the third match is made and so on, the record is included in the view screen.

## Searching for One Value or Another in the Same Field

As often as you want to give dBASE IV AND searches, you also may want to search for one value OR another value in a field. To search for one value OR another, place the first search value in the appropriate field in the file skeleton. Press the down-arrow key to add another line to the file skeleton. Place the second search value in the field on this second line. When you place search conditions on different lines in the file skeleton, dBASE treats each condition as an OR condition. (The search has to match one condition *or* the other to appear in the view screen.)

To try this out, remove the search criterion from the CURR_BAL field. Now, move the cursor to the STATE field and type in the criteria for this field as shown in figure 12.22.

Note that figure 12.22 shows a file skeleton that specifies a search for *WA* or *TX* in the STATE field. When you press F2 (Data) to start the search, dBASE searches for records in the Customer database. If the STATE field contains WA or TX, dBASE includes that record in the view screen. Figure 12.23 shows the results of this OR query.

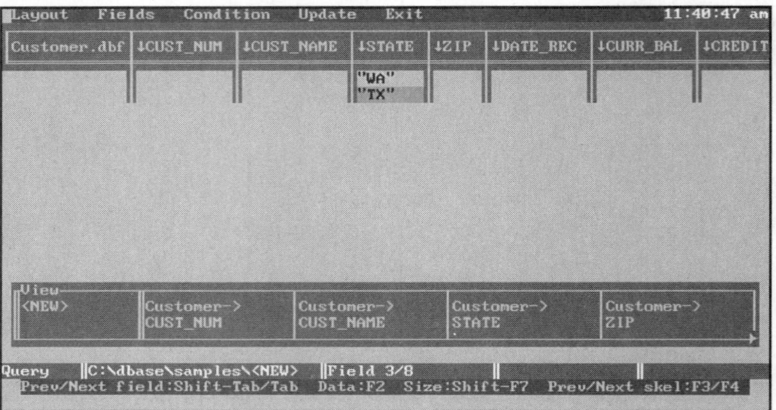


FIG. 12.22

An OR search on the same field.

Records Organize Fields Go To Exit

| CUST_NUM | CUST_NAME | STATE | ZIP | DATE_REC | CURR_BAL | CREDIT_LMT | CU |
|---|---|---|---|---|---|---|---|
| 10002 | Northwest Microsystems | WA | 97889 | 12/24/91 | 2232.22 | 2300.00 | T |
| 10003 | SCIL | WA | 97823 | 10/03/91 | 233.33 | 5000.00 | T |
| 10006 | Cosars Continent | TX | 75223 | 12/29/91 | 34.23 | 1500.00 | F |
| 10007 | Northend Music | TX | 75002 | 01/16/92 | 1999.21 | 2000.00 | F |

Browse ||C:\dbase\samples\<NEW> ||Rec 2/7 ||View ||

FIG. 12.23

The results of the OR search on the same field.

## Combining AND and OR Conditions

You can combine AND and OR queries. Search values on the same line of the file skeleton are treated as AND queries; values on separate lines are treated as OR queries. As an example, enter the values that define this query: Search for all records that have *WA* in the STATE field and that have less than $3,000 in CURR_BAL field, or that have *TX* in the

STATE field and more than $1,000 in the CURR_BAL field. Figure 12.24 shows this query constructed in the file skeleton; figure 12.25 shows the resulting view screen.

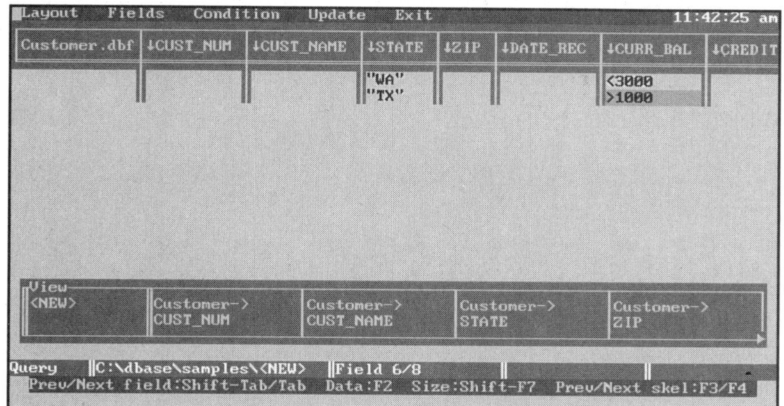


FIG. 12.24

Two AND searches combined into an OR search.

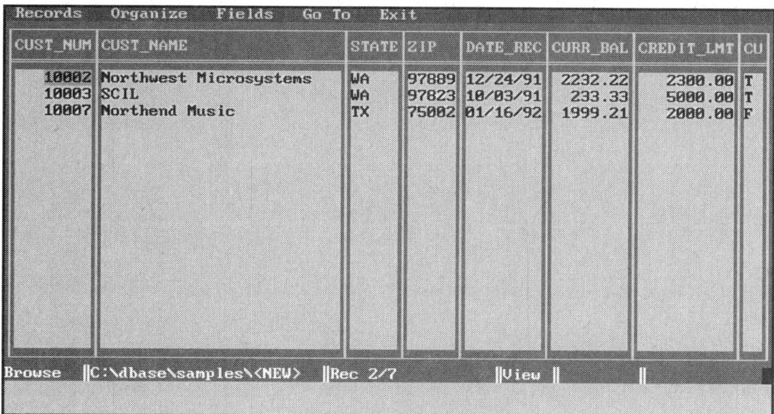


FIG. 12.25

The result of the combined AND and OR search.

You also can create a query in which you specify OR conditions on different fields. You place the OR conditions on different lines of the file skeleton. Figure 12.26 shows a search for records that have WA in the STATE field or that have more than $1,000 in the CURR_BAL field. Figure 12.27 shows the result of this query. Each record in the view screen meets the search criteria.

Queries can become quite complex. Theoretically, you can construct a query with 12 rows of OR conditions, and each query can contain any number of AND conditions. In practice, such a query is incomprehensible and takes a long time to process on a large database.

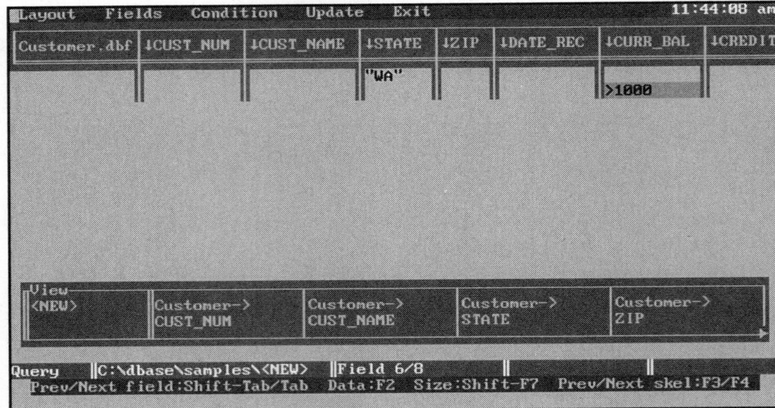


FIG. 12.26

An OR search on two different fields.

Records Organize Fields Go To Exit

| CUST_NUM | CUST_NAME | STATE | ZIP | DATE_REC | CURR_BAL | CREDIT_LMT | CU |
|---|---|---|---|---|---|---|---|
| 10001 | West Hill Florist | CA | 90055 | 10/14/91 | 1322.45 | 5000.00 | F |
| 10002 | Northwest Microsystems | WA | 97889 | 12/24/91 | 2232.22 | 2300.00 | T |
| 10003 | SCIL | WA | 97823 | 10/03/91 | 233.33 | 5000.00 | T |
| 10005 | Comar | OH | 43554 | 10/22/91 | 3325.44 | 5000.00 | F |
| 10007 | Northend Music | TX | 75002 | 01/16/92 | 1999.21 | 2000.00 | F |

Browse C:\dbase\samples\<NEW> Rec 1/7 View

FIG. 12.27

The result of an OR search on two different fields.

Generally, you find yourself using queries with one or two OR conditions and one or two AND conditions. Sometimes, you construct a simple query and then add more AND and OR conditions to refine the search until the view screen contains one or two very specific records.

## Using the Condition Box To Filter Records

Although applying filters to the fields in a file skeleton enables you to search and evaluate your database in a sophisticated manner, occasionally you use the condition box to filter records in the query. The *condition box* enables you to test each record as a whole instead of testing individual fields in the file skeleton. The condition box also enables you to "look inside" memo fields for certain conditions.

To open and use the condition box from the Query design screen, choose Add Condition Box from the Condition menu. An empty condition box appears on the Query design screen. The following sections explain how to use the condition box to test whether a record has been marked for deletion and how to search through a memo field for particular information.

## Using the Condition Box To Test for Deleted Records

You can use the condition box to test each record to see whether it was marked for deletion by following these steps:

1. In the Control Center, make the Customer database active by highlighting it in the Data panel and pressing Enter.
2. Press F2 (Data) to open a Browse or Edit screen for the Customer database. Mark several records for deletion by highlighting them and pressing Ctrl-U. (For this example, mark the records for deletion with CUST_NUM 4, 6, and 8.) When you mark the records, notice that the `Del` indicator appears in the status bar, indicating that each record was marked for deletion.
3. After you mark the records for deletion, press Shift-F2 (Design) to open a Query design screen for the Customer database.
4. Choose Add Condition Box from the Condition menu.
5. In the condition box, type *DELETED()*. This dBASE function returns TRUE if the record is marked for deletion and FALSE if the record is not marked for deletion. Figure 12.28 shows the condition box with this expression entered.

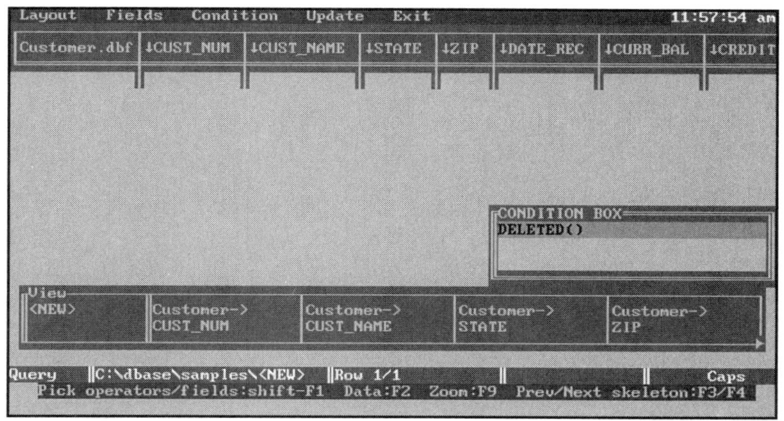


FIG. 12.28

The condition box set up to search for deleted records.

6. Press F2 (Data). Each record is evaluated by the expression in the condition box. Those records that meet the condition are included in the query processing; those records that fail are excluded. Figure 12.29 shows the results of this query. Only those records marked for deletion in step 2 are included in the view.

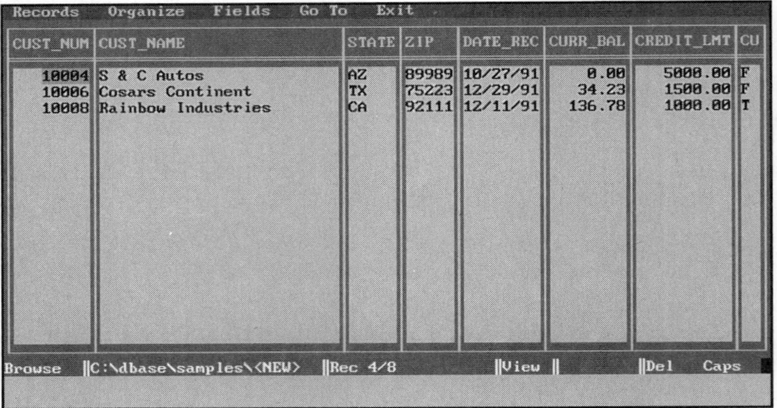


FIG. 12.29

The results of searching for records marked for deletion.

7. To unmark the records for deletion, highlight each one and press Ctrl-U. Unmark each record in the view and return to the Query design screen by pressing Shift-F2 (Design).

8. To make sure that you unmarked all the records, press F2 (Data) again. If you unmarked all the records, you see the No Records Selected warning box. If you forgot to unmark one or more of the records, they appear in the view screen.

Using the mouse, you can select menu options, such as Add Condition Box in the Fields menu, by clicking on the menu name and option. You can see the result of your query by clicking on the `Data:F2` label on the navigation line. Return to the Query design screen from the Browse screen by clicking on the Transfer To Query Design option in the Exit menu.

## Using the Condition Box To Search a Memo Field

To filter records based on values in a memo field, you must use the condition box. If your database has a memo field named COMMENT, for example, and you want to select records in which COMMENT contains the words *Call later*, you use a condition box. Follow these steps to perform this type of search:

1. Make the Customer database active by highlighting it in the Control Center and pressing Enter.
2. Move the cursor to <create> in the Queries panel and press Enter. A Query design screen appears with the CUSTOMER.DBF file skeleton.
3. Choose Add Condition Box from the Condition menu.
4. In the condition box, type the dBASE expression *"Call later" $ comment*. The $ (included in) operator tells dBASE to look at each memo field. If the character string *Call later* is in the memo field, the record is placed in the view. Figure 12.30 shows the Query design screen with this condition in place. Note that this is a case-sensitive search; for example, *call LATER* will not be found.

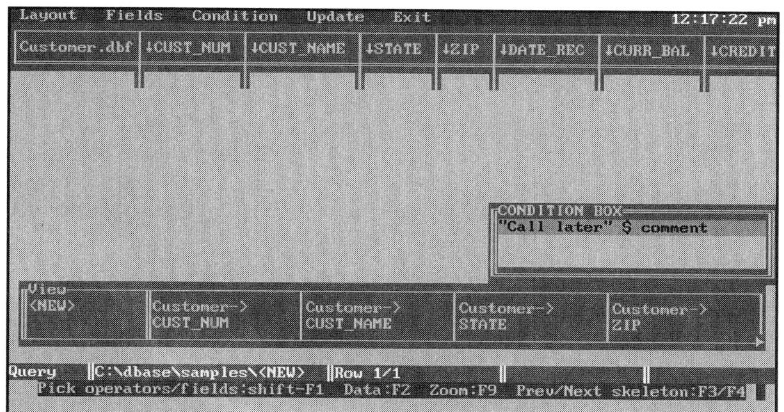


FIG. 12.30

The condition box set to search for text in a memo field.

5. Press F2 (Data). The view screen shows the records whose memo field contains the string *Call later*. To read the memo, place the cursor in the field marked MEMO and press Ctrl-Home. To exit the memo field, press Ctrl-End.

**TIP**

To type a complex condition statement, click on `Zoom:F9` in the navigation line when the condition box appears to expand the size of the box. Click on `Zoom:F9` again to shrink the box to its original size.

You can remove the condition box from the screen by choosing Remove Condition Box from the Condition menu. To hide the condition box (so that you can see the file skeleton, for example), choose Show

Condition Box from the Condition menu to change the full condition box to a marker. When you change the condition box to a marker, the words `CONDITION BOX` appear above the view skeleton to remind you that a condition is in effect. Choose Show Condition Box from the Condition menu again to display the full condition box again. If the box was hidden, it reappears when you move the highlight to the condition box.

Select YES or NO for Show Condition Box by clicking on the option in the Condition menu.

# Summarizing Values in the Query

In the preceding examples, you ask dBASE to display all records that meet the search criteria. Sometimes, however, you don't want to see every record; you only want to know information about the totals of these records. You can easily ask the query to display only summary information.

You can use five summary operators in a query: SUM, AVG (or AVERAGE), MIN, MAX, and CNT (or COUNT). To apply one of these summary operators to a field, place the operator in the appropriate field. Figure 12.31 shows a query that asks for the average value (AVG) of the values in the CURR_BAL field.

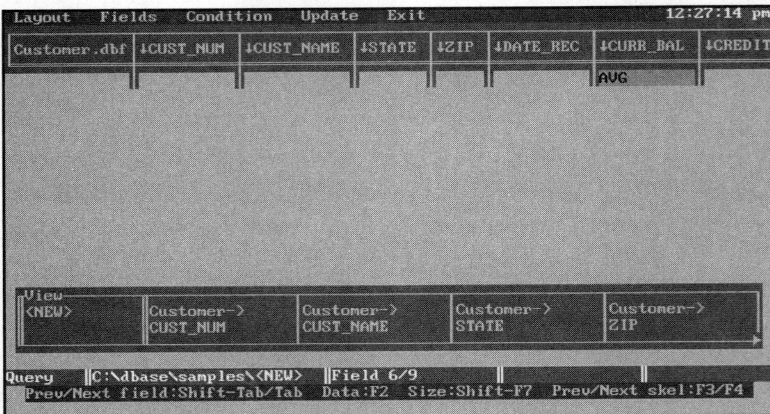


FIG. 12.31

The AVG summary operator in the CURR_BAL field.

Figure 12.32 shows the result of this query. The only field that shows a value is the field in which you specify the summary operator. The other fields are blank, which makes sense because dBASE IV cannot enter anything in the other fields.

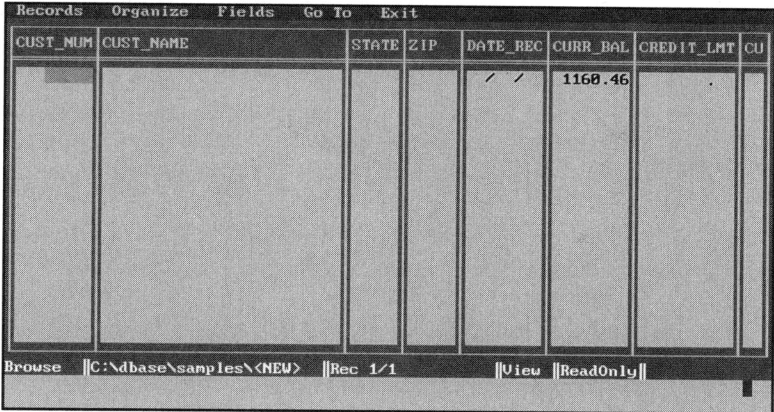


FIG. 12.32

The result of the search with the AVG summary operator.

You can include *summary operators* in AND combinations (see table 12.2). By placing AVG in the CURR_BAL field and "WA" in the STATE field, for example, you can find the average value of the CURR_BAL fields of records that also have WA in the STATE field.

**Table 12.2 Summary Operators**

| Operator | Description |
|---|---|
| SUM | Adds all the values in the field and returns the total |
| AVG (or AVERAGE) | Adds all the values in the field, and divides by the number of records, and returns the average value in that field |
| MIN | Returns the smallest value in that field |
| MAX | Returns the largest value in that field |
| CNT (or COUNT) | Counts the number of records that meet the specified conditions |

In all summary operations, if a condition is specified, the value returned is only for records that meet any specified search condition. If you specify no condition, all records are summed, or averaged, and so on.

## Grouping Records for Summary

In the preceding example, only records for one value of the STATE field are averaged. You can group records so that all records with the same value are summarized. The resulting view screen shows all the possible values of the STATE field, for example, with the average of the CURR_BAL field for each state.

To group records for summaries, enter the words *GROUP BY* in the field you want to group. This operation works the most efficiently if you have created an index for the GROUP BY field and have selected Include Indexes from the Fields menu. In figure 12.33, for example, the query is constructed so that all records for each state are grouped together and the average of the CURR_BAL field for that group is reported. The result of this grouped query is shown in figure 12.34.

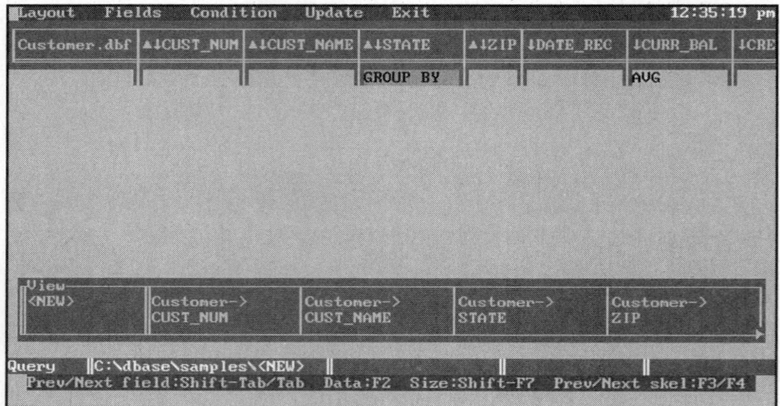


FIG. 12.33

Specifying a group view of a summary query.

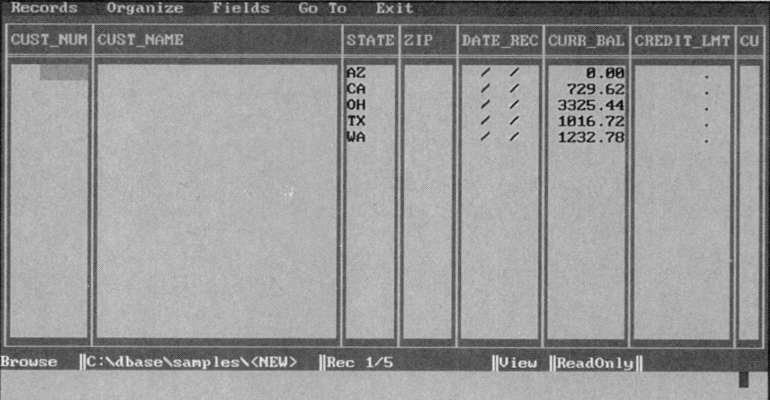


FIG. 12.34

The result of a grouped summary-operator query.

TIP

When you add operators (such as AVERAGE or GROUP BY) to the query, click on a field in a file skeleton where you will use the operator and then press Shift-F1 to open the Expression Builder menu (see fig. 12.35). Select the operator you want to use and click on it to place it in the field.

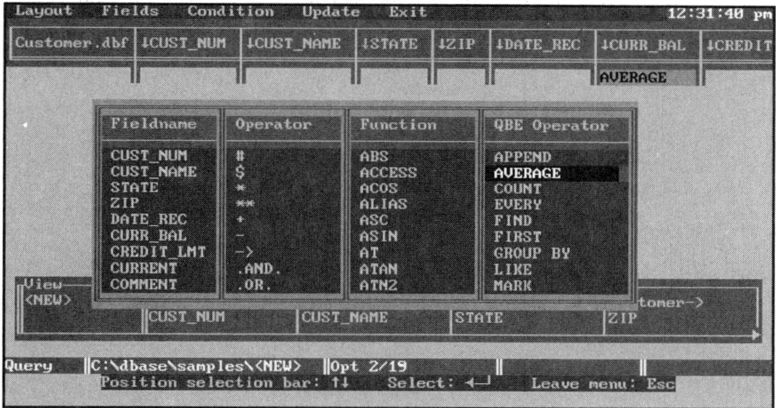


FIG. 12.35

Selecting an operator from the Expression Builder menu.

# Finding a Specific Record with a Query

You also can use queries to locate specific records in the database. This capability is much like the Forward Search option of the Go To menu, but it enables you to use the highly sophisticated conditions of a query. When you use a query to find a record, all applicable database records are shown in the view screen, with the first record that meets your query conditions highlighted.

To use queries to find a record, enter the query conditions as you normally do, but also enter the word *find* below the database file name in the file skeleton. Figure 12.36 shows an example of a FIND query that searches for the first record in the Customer database with a current balance value greater than 100.

Figure 12.37 shows the results of the FIND query. All the records in the database are shown in the view screen; the first record that meets the search criteria is highlighted in the top row. You can see the records that do not meet the search criteria above the top row by pressing the up-arrow key.

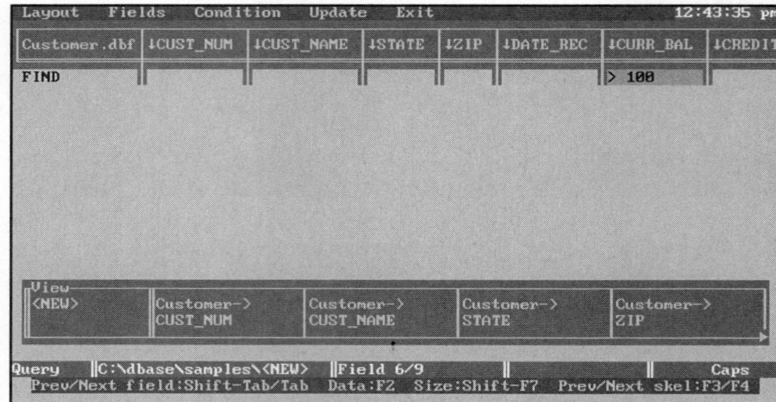


FIG. 12.36

Using FIND to locate the first record of a query.

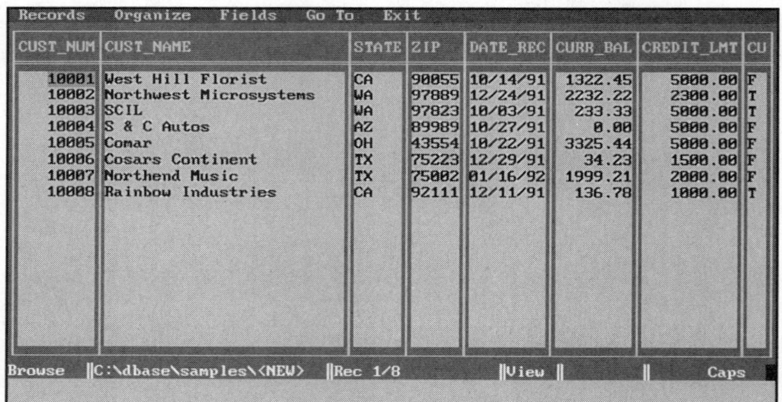


| CUST_NUM | CUST_NAME | STATE | ZIP | DATE_REC | CURR_BAL | CREDIT_LMT | CU |
|---|---|---|---|---|---|---|---|
| 10001 | West Hill Florist | CA | 90055 | 10/14/91 | 1322.45 | 5000.00 | F |
| 10002 | Northwest Microsystems | WA | 97889 | 12/24/91 | 2232.22 | 2300.00 | T |
| 10003 | SCIL | WA | 97823 | 10/03/91 | 233.33 | 5000.00 | T |
| 10004 | S & C Autos | AZ | 89989 | 10/27/91 | 0.00 | 5000.00 | F |
| 10005 | Comar | OH | 43554 | 10/22/91 | 3325.44 | 5000.00 | F |
| 10006 | Cosars Continent | TX | 75223 | 12/29/91 | 34.23 | 1500.00 | F |
| 10007 | Northend Music | TX | 75002 | 01/16/92 | 1999.21 | 2000.00 | F |
| 10008 | Rainbow Industries | CA | 92111 | 12/11/91 | 136.78 | 1000.00 | T |

FIG. 12.37

The result of a FIND query.

**For Related Information...**

▸▸ "SET FILTER TO," p. 872.

▸▸ "LOCATE," p. 731.

# Creating and Using Calculated Fields

Sometimes the database fields don't provide all the information you need in the view screen. If you need to calculate a value for each field in the view screen, for example, you can do so and then add that field to the view skeleton and use it as if it were a database field.

To add to the Customer database view screen a field that calculates how much credit each customer has remaining, follow these steps:

1. From the Query design screen, open the Fields menu and select Create Calculated Field. When the Query design screen reappears, you see a new skeleton: the *calculated fields skeleton*. In this skeleton, you create a field that calculates how much remaining credit each customer has.
2. The highlight is in the top box of the calculated fields skeleton, ready for you to create the formula for the field. For this example, type the formula *CREDIT_LMT–CURR_BAL*.
3. Add this calculated field to the view skeleton by pressing F5 and typing a name (in this example, type the field name *CRED_REM*). The field is added to the far right side of the view skeleton. You can move the field to another position in the view skeleton as outlined in "Moving Fields in the View Skeleton," earlier in this chapter.

You can use the calculated field to limit searches as if it were an official database field. Move the highlight to the calculated field by pressing F4 (Next) and then press the down-arrow key to highlight the box below the calculated field. Enter the search value. Figure 12.38 shows the calculated field CRED_REM with a search value of <1000. Figure 12.39 shows the result of this query. Notice in figure 12.38 that the CRED_REM calculated field was moved in the view skeleton so that you can see it without using the Tab key.

**For Related Information...**

◂◂ "Adding Calculated Fields to the Form," p. 201.

◂◂ "Adding Calculated Fields," p. 242.

▸▸ "Creating Calculated Field Values with Expressions," p. 357.

FROM HERE...

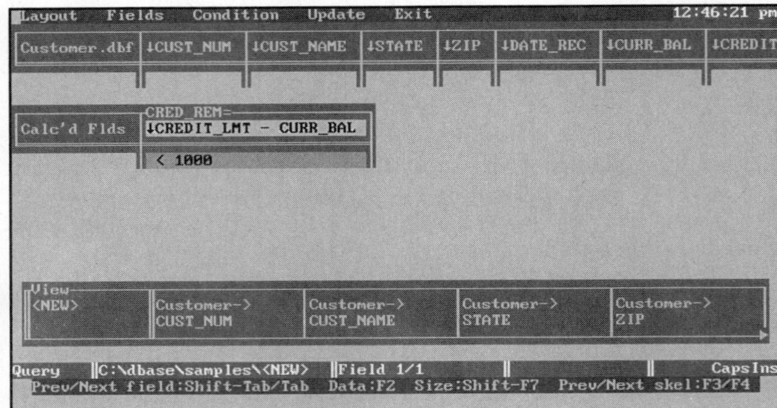


FIG. 12.38

Adding a search value to a calculated field.

Records Organize Fields Go To Exit

| CUST_NUM | CUST_NAME | STATE | ZIP | DATE_REC | CURR_BAL | CREDIT_LMT | CU |
|---|---|---|---|---|---|---|---|
| 10002 | Northwest Microsystems | WA | 97889 | 12/24/91 | 2232.22 | 2300.00 | T |
| 10007 | Northend Music | TX | 75002 | 01/16/92 | 1999.21 | 2000.00 | F |
| 10008 | Rainbow Industries | CA | 92111 | 12/11/91 | 136.78 | 1000.00 | T |

Browse C:\dbase\samples\<NEW> Rec 2/8 View Caps

FIG. 12.39

The result of a calculated field search.

# Ordering the Information in the View Screen

In all the previous examples, the view screen presented selected records in the order they were entered in the database. You may want to see these records in some other specified order. The Query design work surface provides two ways to order the view records: You can sort them, or you can tell the query to use an existing index and present them in indexed order.

## Sorting the Query Output

To sort the output of a query, specify your query conditions as you usually do and then move the highlight in the file skeleton to the field by which you want to sort. Select the Fields menu and choose Sort On This Field. The sort definition submenu appears, as shown in figure 12.40. Choose the type of sort you want and press Enter to return to the Query design screen. If you highlight the STATE field and select Ascending Dictionary as the type of sort, the entry `AscDict1` appears in the STATE field of the file skeleton. Press F2 (Data) to execute the query; figure 12.41 shows the resulting view screen. The records are sorted by the value in the STATE field.

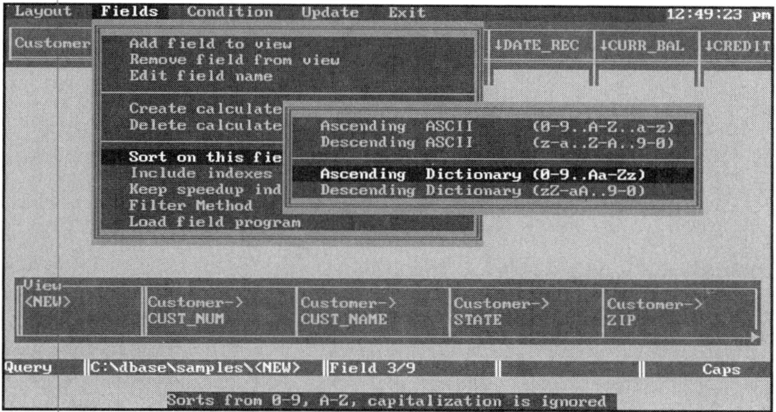


FIG. 12.40

The sort definition menu.

Records Organize Fields Go To Exit

| CUST_NUM | CUST_NAME | STATE | ZIP | DATE_REC | CURR_BAL | CREDIT_LMT | CU |
|---|---|---|---|---|---|---|---|
| 10004 | S & C Autos | AZ | 89989 | 10/27/91 | 0.00 | 5000.00 | F |
| 10001 | West Hill Florist | CA | 90055 | 10/14/91 | 1322.45 | 5000.00 | F |
| 10008 | Rainbow Industries | CA | 92111 | 12/11/91 | 136.78 | 1000.00 | T |
| 10005 | Comar | OH | 43554 | 10/22/91 | 3325.44 | 5000.00 | F |
| 10006 | Cosars Continent | TX | 75223 | 12/29/91 | 34.23 | 1500.00 | F |
| 10007 | Northend Music | TX | 75002 | 01/16/92 | 1999.21 | 2000.00 | F |
| 10002 | Northwest Microsystems | WA | 97889 | 12/24/91 | 2232.22 | 2300.00 | T |
| 10003 | SCIL | WA | 97823 | 10/03/91 | 233.33 | 5000.00 | T |

Browse C:\dbase\samples\<NEW> Rec 1/8 View ReadOnly Caps

FIG. 12.41

The result of the sorted query.

Notice that the message `ReadOnly` appears on the status line. When dBASE executes a sort, it creates a new database in a way similar to sorting a database from the Control Center. The ReadOnly message reminds you that you cannot access this database to change values in it.

dBASE offers four options for sorting your views. In Ascending ASCII, entries beginning with numbers appear first, then entries beginning with uppercase letters appear, in alphabetical order, followed by entries beginning with lowercase letters. Entries beginning with special characters, such as commas, semicolons, asterisks, and so on, are ordered by where the character appears in the ASCII sequence. Refer to the ASCII table in the "dBASE IV Reference Guide" for the ordering sequence. (ASCII refers to how characters are stored in a computer.) Descending ASCII is the reverse of Ascending ASCII.

Dictionary sorts treat uppercase and lowercase characters the same. The Ascending Dictionary sort follows the pattern Aa, Bb, Cc, and so on. Descending Dictionary reverses Ascending Dictionary.

The following table shows examples of the four types of sorts dBASE provides:

*Ascending ASCII*

8888888888
9999999999
AAAAAAAAAA
BBBBBBBBBB
CCCCCCCCCC
aaaaaaaaaa
bbbbbbbbbb
cccccccccc

*Descending ASCII*

cccccccccc
bbbbbbbbbb
aaaaaaaaaa
CCCCCCCCCC
BBBBBBBBBB
AAAAAAAAAA
9999999999
8888888888

*Ascending Dictionary*

8888888888
9999999999
AAAAAAAAAA
aaaaaaaaaa

BBBBBBBBBB
bbbbbbbbbb
CCCCCCCCCC
cccccccccc

*Descending Dictionary*

CCCCCCCCCC
cccccccccc
BBBBBBBBBB
bbbbbbbbbb
AAAAAAAAAA
aaaaaaaaaa
9999999999
8888888888

## Sorting on Multiple Fields

Sorting on multiple fields is simple. You just have to remember to specify the sorts in the order you want them sorted. If you want to sort on the STATE field first and then on the CUST_NAME field (so that the records appear alphabetized by customer name in each state), for example, define the STATE sort first and the CUST_NAME sort second.

When you define additional sorts, dBASE IV appends a number to each sort in the file skeleton. The sort process follows this numerical sequence: the lowest number indicates the major sort, the next lowest number is the next sort, and so on. Because dBASE assigns the appended sort numbers throughout the query session, you may have a query with a major sort defined as `AscDict9`, if you specified eight sorts previously in the session—even though none of those eight sorts are in effect at the time.

When you work with a query repeatedly, you may try nine different sorts; dBASE does not accept a tenth. If you used all nine sorts, you must save the query, return to the Control Center, select the query you just saved, and return to the Query design work surface. dBASE resets the sort counter, enabling you to continue with more sorts.

Figure 12.42 shows the file skeleton with a major sort by STATE and a secondary sort by CUST_NAME. Figure 12.43 shows the result of this multiple-field sort.

## Combining Sorts and Searches in the Same Field

You can put a search value and a sort in the same field. Enter the search value first and then choose Sort On This Field from the Fields menu. After you finish defining the sort, the search value and the sort definition appear in the file skeleton field, separated by a comma.

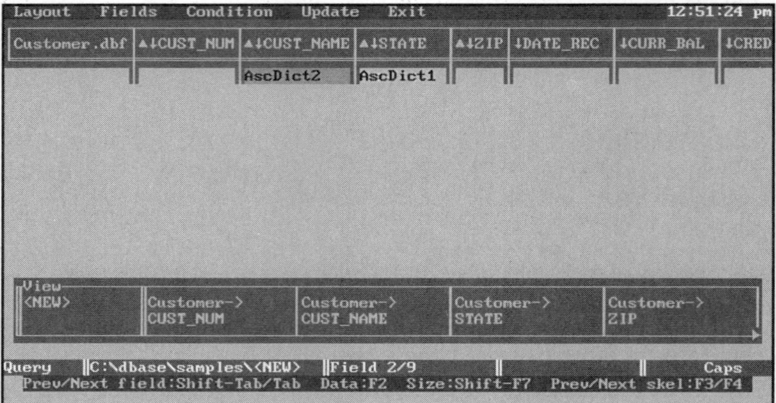


FIG. 12.42

A multiple-field sort defined in the file skeleton.

Records Organize Fields Go To Exit

| CUST_NUM | CUST_NAME | STATE | ZIP | DATE_REC | CURR_BAL | CREDIT_LMT | CU |
|---|---|---|---|---|---|---|---|
| 10004 | S & C Autos | AZ | 89989 | 10/27/91 | 0.00 | 5000.00 | F |
| 10008 | Rainbow Industries | CA | 92111 | 12/11/91 | 136.78 | 1000.00 | T |
| 10001 | West Hill Florist | CA | 90055 | 10/14/91 | 1322.45 | 5000.00 | F |
| 10005 | Comar | OH | 43554 | 10/22/91 | 3325.44 | 5000.00 | F |
| 10006 | Cosars Continent | TX | 75223 | 12/29/91 | 34.23 | 1500.00 | F |
| 10007 | Northend Music | TX | 75002 | 01/16/92 | 1999.21 | 2000.00 | F |
| 10002 | Northwest Microsystems | WA | 97889 | 12/24/91 | 2232.22 | 2300.00 | T |
| 10003 | SCIL | WA | 97823 | 10/03/91 | 233.33 | 5000.00 | T |

Browse C:\dbase\samples\<NEW> Rec 1/8 View ReadOnly Caps

FIG. 12.43

The result of a multiple-field sort.

If you want to sort the records by ZIP but you want to view only records in which ZIP>"60001", for example, the entry in the field skeleton could be >"60001", Asc1.

## Indexing the Query Output

Sorting the view screen usually can accomplish your query goals. In large databases, however, sorting can be slow. Sorting the database also requires additional disk space and eliminates your ability to change the data in the sorted database. To get around these limitations, you can use indexes on a database when you reorganize the contents of the view screen.

The drawback to indexes is that you cannot create them "on the fly" in the Query design work surface. If your database has the necessary indexes created before you enter the Query design work surface, you can access them. If you need an index you haven't created, however, you must return to the Control Center to create the index.

## Specifying an Index for the View

To reorganize a view by using an existing index, follow these steps:

1. In the Query design work surface, open the Fields menu and select Include Indexes so that the setting changes to Yes. Now all the indexes you have set for this database in the production index file are available. When you close the Queries Fields menu, symbols are displayed next to each indexed field.

   The symbol indicates the type of index order used:

   ▲ Up arrowhead, ascending ASCII.

   ▼ Down arrowhead, descending ASCII.

   # Pound sign (number symbol), field used in two index tags, one ascending ASCII and one descending ASCII.

   Choose YES or NO from the Include Indexes option in the Fields menu by clicking on the option.

2. Move the cursor to the field on which you want to index the view screen. Choose the Fields menu again and select the Sort On This Field option. Choose the type of sort you want. Note that the type of sort you choose must be the same type you used when you indexed the file. If you choose another type, the query is processed like a sort, and you gain nothing by using indexes.

3. Press F2 (Data) to process the sort. When the view screen appears (much faster now, particularly if you work with a large database), you can change the data because the `ReadOnly` message in the status line no longer is displayed.

## Using Complex Indexes in a Query

You may have created a complex index in the Control Center, such as CUST_NAME+STATE. After you specify Include Indexes, you can use complex indexes in a query. Complex indexes appear in the file skeleton to the far right, after all the database fields. You can use complex index fields for indexing and selecting as if they were regular database fields.

## Optimizing Queries

dBASE IV 1.5 provides options that enable you to speed up the search operation of a query. First, you can choose the filtering method to be used by the query by selecting Filter Method from the Fields menu. Four filter options are available:

| Option | Function |
| --- | --- |
| INDEX...FOR | Creates new index that includes only the records selected |
| OPTIMIZED | Selects the fastest filtering method for you |
| SET FILTER | Filters records to meet the query conditions |
| SET KEY | Selects records within a range if the key field is indexed |

The default method is OPTIMIZED, so you normally will not need to select a method. You should keep in mind, however, that you can determine whether the indexes created by your query are retained for future use. If you are going to use the query again, to avoid having the query re-create an index each time you execute it, select Keep Speedup Indexes from the Fields menu and set it to YES. If this selection is set to NO, indexes created by your query are discarded after you execute the query.

FROM HERE...

### For Related Information...

▸▸ See "SET FILTER," "SET KEY," "SET INDEX," and "SET ORDER," in "Using SET Commands," p. 845.

▸▸ "Index Functions," p. 778.

▸▸ "Putting Your Database in Order," p. 443.

# Changing a Database with an Update Query

You also can use the Query design work surface to update your database. With an *update query*, you can replace values in database fields, append records to the database from another database, and mark records for deletion (you also can unmark records previously marked for deletion).

To create and use an update query, start just as you do for a query by example. Open the desired database by highlighting it in the Data panel of the Control Center and pressing Enter. Next, move the cursor to the Queries panel, highlight <create>, and press Enter to display a Query design screen. To define this query as an update query, choose Specify Update Operation from the Update menu. The Update menu appears (see fig. 12.44).

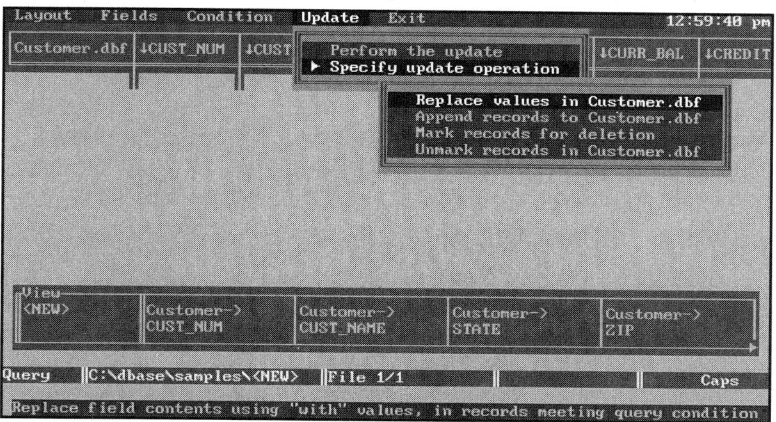


FIG. 12.44

The Update menu.

You can carry out four update operations: replace, append, mark, and unmark. The following sections explain how to use an update query to replace database values, append data, and mark and unmark records for deletion.

# Replacing Database Values with an Update Query

The Replace Values option enables you to replace the values of all or a subset of database records with another value. The replacement value can be any valid dBASE expression. For example, if the CUST_NUM values in the database start at 1 and you decide you want them to start at 10000 to match those shown in figure 12.25, you would follow these steps to replace the values in that field:

1. Choose Replace Values In Customer.dbf from the Update menu. Notice that the option includes the name of the currently active database.
2. Choose Proceed when dBASE tells you that the view skeleton will be deleted. Because update queries do not put data on-screen, you don't need a view skeleton.
3. The word `Replace` appears under the name of the database in the file skeleton to remind you that this query is an update query. (This portion of the skeleton is commonly known as the *pothandle*.)
4. Press Tab to move the highlight to the CUST_NUM field of the file skeleton. Type the dBASE expression *with CUST_NUM + 10000*. Figure 12.45 shows the update query with this replacement expression in place. This expression tells dBASE to replace all CUST_NUM values with the old CUST_NUM value plus 10000.

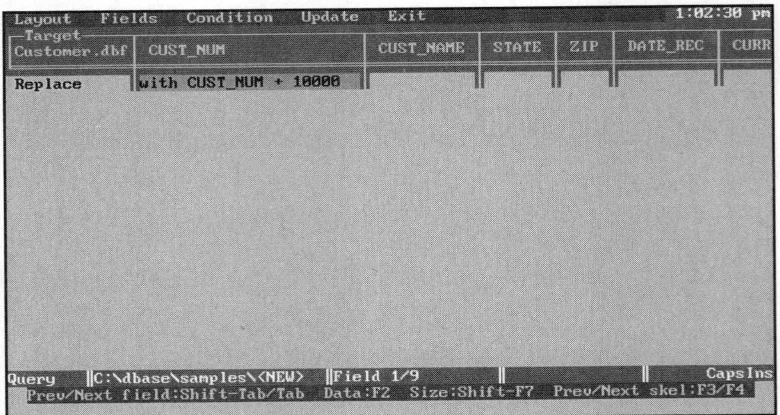


FIG. 12.45

Replacing a value in a database with an update query.

5. Choose Perform The Update from the Update menu. When the update is completed, dBASE displays a message that asks you to

press any key to continue. Do so to return to the Query design screen.

6. Press F2 to display the database with the CUST_NUM fields changed (see fig. 12.46).

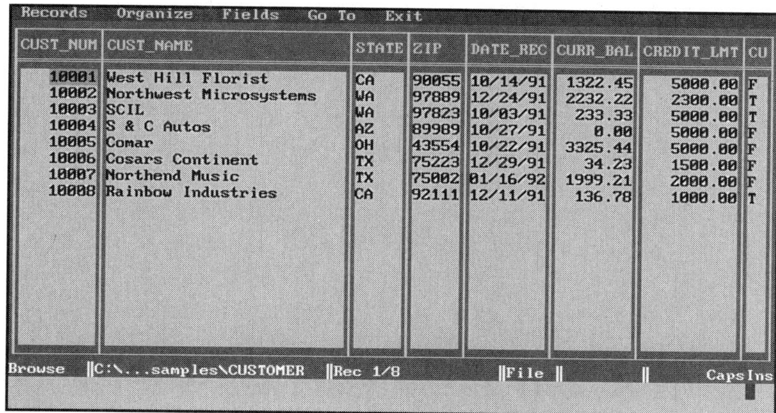


| CUST_NUM | CUST_NAME | STATE | ZIP | DATE_REC | CURR_BAL | CREDIT_LMT | CU |
|---|---|---|---|---|---|---|---|
| 10001 | West Hill Florist | CA | 90055 | 10/14/91 | 1322.45 | 5000.00 | F |
| 10002 | Northwest Microsystems | WA | 97889 | 12/24/91 | 2232.22 | 2300.00 | T |
| 10003 | SCIL | WA | 97823 | 10/03/91 | 233.33 | 5000.00 | T |
| 10004 | S & C Autos | AZ | 89989 | 10/27/91 | 0.00 | 5000.00 | F |
| 10005 | Comar | OH | 43554 | 10/22/91 | 3325.44 | 5000.00 | F |
| 10006 | Cosars Continent | TX | 75223 | 12/29/91 | 34.23 | 1500.00 | F |
| 10007 | Northend Music | TX | 75002 | 01/16/92 | 1999.21 | 2000.00 | F |
| 10008 | Rainbow Industries | CA | 92111 | 12/11/91 | 136.78 | 1000.00 | T |

FIG. 12.46

The results of updating a database field with an update query.

You can limit the records that are replaced by including search conditions in the update query. If you want to replace CUST_NUM values in records only for the state of WA, for example, type *"WA"* in the STATE field and *CUST_NUM+1000* in the CUST_NUM field. Only records meeting the specified condition are updated. As with query by example, you also can use AND and OR conditions to limit the replacement.

# Appending Data with an Update Query

You can use an update query to add records from one database to another when the structures of the two databases are not identical. (If the databases are identical, use the Append Records from dBASE File option of the Append menu in the Database design screen.) Suppose that you want to append records to the Customer database (called the *target* database) from a database named Oldcust (called the *source* database). To use an update query to append records from the Oldcust database, follow these steps:

1. Before you start dBASE IV, be sure that the source database—in this case, Oldcust—is in the current directory. Use the DOS COPY command to copy the source database into this directory, if necessary.

**NOTE** When you use the DOS COPY command to copy a database from one directory to another, make sure that you also copy the production index file and—if there is one—the memo field file associated with the database. Use the DOS * wild card to copy these files. To copy the Oldcust database from the C:\DBASE\OLDFILES directory to the C:\DBASE\CUSTOMER directory, for example, use the following DOS command:

```
COPY C:\DBASE\OLDFILES\OLDCUST.* C:\DBASE\CUSTOMER
```

This command ensures that all necessary files are copied.

2. Start dBASE IV; if necessary, open the catalog containing the target database by using the Use a Different Catalog option of the Catalog menu.
3. In the Data panel of the Control Center, select the target database file (in this case, the Customer database). Make the target database file the active database by highlighting it and pressing Enter. If the selection box appears, choose Use File.
4. Choose Add File To Catalog from the Catalog menu. When the file list appears, choose the source database (in this case, Oldcust) and press Enter. The Oldcust database is added to the catalog.
5. Highlight <create> in the Queries panel and press Enter. A new Query design screen appears with the CUSTOMER.DBF file skeleton in place.
6. Choose Add File To Query from the Layout menu. When the file list appears, choose the source database (in this case, Oldcust) by highlighting it and pressing Enter. A file skeleton for OLDCUST.DBF is added to the Query design screen (see fig. 12.47).
7. To start the append update, open the Update menu and choose Specify Update Operation. From the submenu that appears, choose Append Records To Customer.dbf and press Enter.
8. A warning box appears to tell you that changing the view query to an update query deletes the view skeleton. Choose Proceed to continue. Notice that when you return to the Query design screen, the word `Target` appears above the CUSTOMER.DBF file skeleton.
9. Define for the query the match-up of the fields in the two databases. Values in the NAME field of OLDCUST.DBF, for example, will be transferred to the CUST_NAME field in CUSTOMER.DBF. Even when the field names of the source database and target database are the same, you must tell the query how to match the fields.

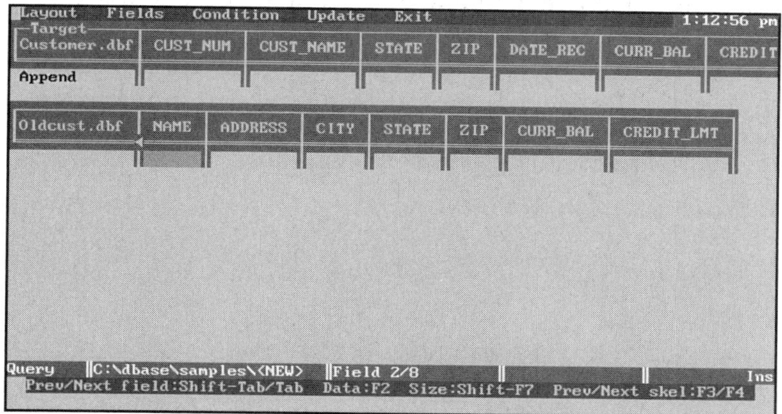


FIG. 12.47

Adding another file skeleton to the Query design screen.

Place a *variable pair* in the fields of the source database and the target database. Move the cursor to CUST_NAME in the CUSTOMER.DBF file skeleton and then enter a variable name in that field (for example, *NAME*). Press F4 (Next Skeleton) and Tab to move the cursor to the NAME field of the OLDCUST.DBF file skeleton and type the same variable name in that field. The variable names tell the query to match these two fields during the update and to transfer values from the NAME field in OLDCUST.DBF to the CUST_NAME field in CUSTOMER.DBF.

Place variable pairs in each of the fields that match up. Figure 12.48 shows the update query with variable pairs in place. Each variable pair tells the query where to put data from the source database into the target database.

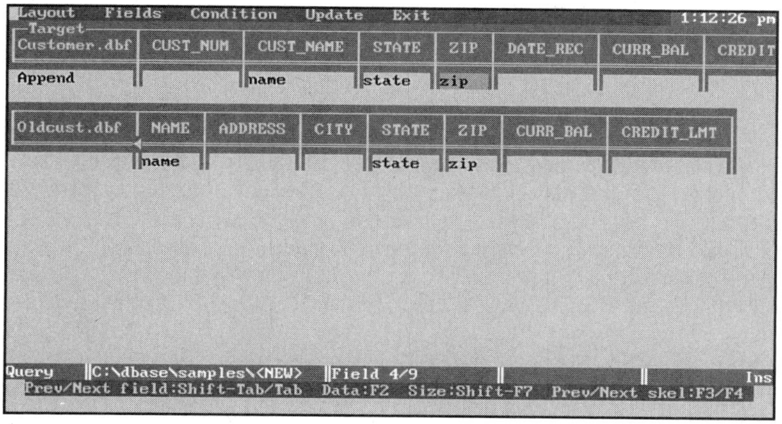

FIG. 12.48

Adding variable pairs to the file skeletons of the two databases.

10. Choose Perform the Update from the Update menu. dBASE executes the query, adding one record to the target database (CUSTOMER.DBF) for each record in the source database (OLDCUST.DBF). When the update is done, a note box appears with the message `Press any key to continue`. When you press a key, you return to the Query design screen.
11. To see the results of the query, press F2 (Data). A display of the database with the appended records appears.
12. To save this query, choose Save Changes And Exit from the Exit menu.
13. When you return to the Control Center, remove the source database (OLDCUST) from the Data panel by highlighting it and choosing Remove File From Catalog from the Catalog menu. Remove the source database if the append process is a one-time action. If you plan to append from the source database again, leave the source database in the catalog.

An append update can be complicated, but it gives you great flexibility in appending data from a source database with a structure different from that of the target database.

## Marking and Unmarking Records for Deletion with an Update Query

You can mark a record for deletion by highlighting it in a Browse or Edit window and pressing Ctrl-U. Choosing Erase Marked Records from the Organize menu of the Browse screen actually *packs*, or removes the records from, the database. To mark a large number of records for deletion, you can use an update query to mark them. The records can be isolated by a query condition.

To create an update query to mark records for deletion, follow the same steps you do for a replace update but choose Mark Records For Deletion from the Specify Update Operation menu (refer back to figure 12.44). In the file skeleton, specify the condition a record must meet to be marked. When you choose Perform The Update from the Update menu, those records meeting the search criteria are marked for deletion. Delete the records by pressing F2 (Data) from the Query design screen to display the Browse window and then selecting Erase Marked Records.

Similarly, you can unmark records with an update query. Select the Unmark Records option from the Specify Update Operation menu. The process is the same, but records that meet the search criteria and were marked for deletion are unmarked. Records not previously marked are not affected.

Update queries provide a tool for quick and easy modification of an entire database or of subsets of the database, which are specified by search criteria in the Query design screen.

# Saving a Query

After you construct a query that presents only the records you want in the order and format you want them, you may want to save the query for future use. Choose Save This Query from the Layout menu. dBASE IV prompts you for a name. Type a file name and press Enter. dBASE appends the extension QBE to the file name and saves the query in the current directory. dBASE also adds the query to the current catalog, in the Queries column. This query becomes a part of the current catalog and is available to use.

You can save a query and then use it as the basis for other queries. After you save the first query, choose it from the Control Center, make changes as necessary, and save it with a new name. The new query is added to the catalog; your original query is unaltered.

To save a query design and return to the Control Center using the mouse, click on the Exit menu name in the menu bar and then click on Save Changes And Exit. When you are prompted, type in a file name for the query and press Enter. If it was an Update query, an asterisk (*) is displayed before the file name in the Queries panel in the Control Center.

# Summary

The primary purpose of a database is to present data in organized ways and enable you to see the same data from different perspectives. The query by example feature of dBASE IV uses the Query design screen to provide an almost unlimited capability for viewing your database information. With the Query design work surface, you can construct simple queries to look at your data and then refine them step-by-step until you see only the records you want in the order you want them. You can summarize groups of records and do calculations on any field. In short, the Query design work surface has extraordinary capabilities that you can use to analyze the information in your database.

13

CHAPTER

# Using dBASE IV Expressions and Functions

In this chapter, you explore the intricacies of dBASE IV expressions and functions. You learn how to use them to sort and index data in ways that best suit your purposes. You see how to improve reporting capabilities by using expressions. You also learn how to use important dBASE IV functions as part of the expressions to develop even greater power over your data and its presentation.

## Understanding Expressions

A dBASE *expression* is a combination of database field names, value operators, dBASE functions, and constants that dBASE evaluates as a formula. dBASE uses the result of that evaluation for a variety of purposes: complex indexes; calculated fields in forms, labels, and reports; and test conditions in queries. dBASE expressions range from simple to complex. An example of a simple expression is a database field name used as an index key: if you want to index on one field, you specify that field name. Figure 13.1 shows a database index defined on the field CUST_NUM.

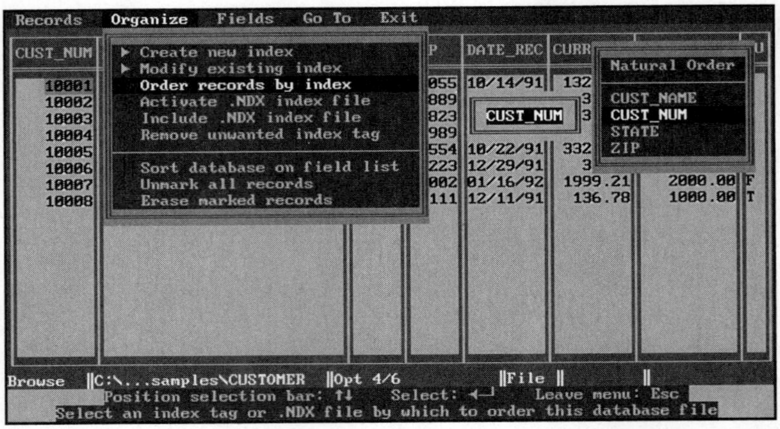

FIG. 13.1

A database index defined on CUST_NUM.

A dBASE IV expression is basically a formula. dBASE evaluates the formula for each record and then determines the value, which then can be used in indexes, in grouping data for views and reports, or in many other ways. You can enter expressions in an update query to edit a database, and you can use expressions to provide more sophisticated sorts and indexes. As always with dBASE IV, the best way to learn about expressions is to use them.

Expressions fall into two categories. One category evaluates to a value, which is then used to index a database or replace values in a database. The following are examples of expressions that evaluate to a value:

| Expression | Evaluation |
|---|---|
| LAST_NAME | This is the simplest type of expression: a single database field name. In a database sorted on the LAST_NAME field, the values in that field appear in alphabetical order. |
| LAST_NAME + FIRST_NAME | This expression uses two database field names: LAST_NAME and FIRST_NAME. The + operator *concatenates* the two values, creating a single value made up of the value in the LAST_NAME field followed by the value in the FIRST_NAME field. Used in an index, this expression presents the database records alphabetically by LAST_NAME and, where the LAST_NAME values are the same, alphabetically by FIRST_NAME. |

| Expression | Evaluation |
|---|---|
| DATE() – DUE_DATE | This expression uses the database field DUE_DATE and the dBASE function DATE(). When dBASE evaluates this expression, the program replaces the DATE() portion of the expression with the current date from the computer's clock. Subtracting the value in the DUE_DATE field of the database produces the number of days a payment is past due. (A positive number indicates past due; a negative indicates days until due.) This expression can be used in a report or form to define a calculated field. |

The second category of dBASE expressions is *logical expressions*, which evaluate to a true or false value. Logical expressions are often used to "filter" a database; dBASE evaluates the expression for each record in the database. Records that evaluate to true are included in processing; records that evaluate to false are excluded.

A logical expression is really two expressions separated by a logical operator, such as = (does the first expression equal the second?), > (is the first expression greater than the second?), or < (is the first expression less than the second?). When you learned about queries in Chapter 12, you created a logical expression by placing a state abbreviation under the STATE field in the file skeleton. Placing "WA" under the STATE field creates the logical expression STATE = "WA"; records that evaluate to true are included in the processing. The following are examples of logical expressions:

| Expression | Evaluation |
|---|---|
| LAST_NAME = "Jones" | For each database record, dBASE asks, "Is the value in the LAST_NAME field equal to (=) 'Jones'?" If the answer is true, the expression evaluates to true, and dBASE includes the record in the processing. |
| DUE_DATE > DATE() | For each database record, dBASE asks, "Is the value in the DUE_DATE field greater than (>) the current date, which is returned by dBASE function DATE()?" If DUE_DATE is greater, the expression evaluates to true, and dBASE includes the record in the processing. |

*continues*

| Expression | Evaluation |
| --- | --- |
| DATE() – DUE_DATE > 30 | This expression uses the minus (–) mathematical operator to determine the number of days between the current date and the value in the field DUE_DATE. If the calculated value is greater than 30, the expression evaluates to true, and dBASE includes the record in the processing. |

## Using Expressions in Indexes

You define a dBASE expression when telling dBASE how to index a database. The simplest expression for an index is a single database field name. When that index is controlling the database, the records are processed and presented as if the database were sorted on that field.

You can use expressions to create more sophisticated indexes on your databases. You can create an index with a primary field and a secondary field. The database appears to be sorted on the primary field; when more than one record exists with the same primary field value, those records are arranged on the values in the secondary field.

In the following example, use the Customer database to create an index on the state (STATE) and customer name (CUST_NAME) fields, making the STATE field the primary index key and CUST_NAME the secondary. This index orders the records by state and, within each state, by customer name.

1. Highlight the Customer database in the Data panel of the Control Center and press Enter. Choose Use File to make the database active.
2. Press F2 (Data) to open a Browse window for the database (see fig. 13.2). You can see that the database is ordered by CUST_NUM, just as the records were entered. Actually, no index is controlling the database in this figure; the Browse window presents the database in natural order.
3. Open the Organize pull-down menu and select Create New Index. The Create New Index menu appears, as shown in figure 13.3.

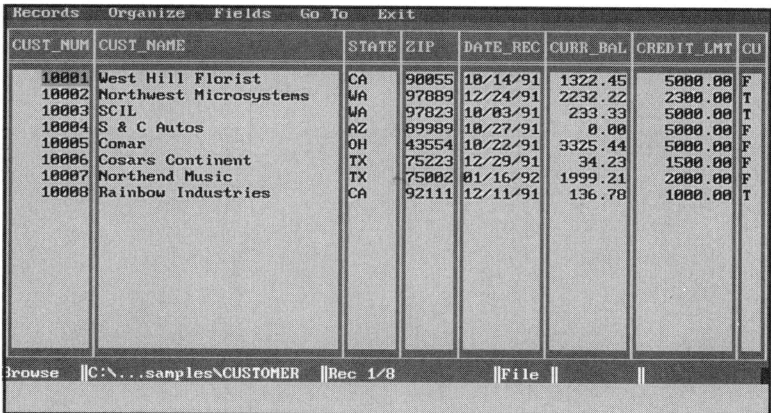


FIG. 13.2

The Customer database in natural order.

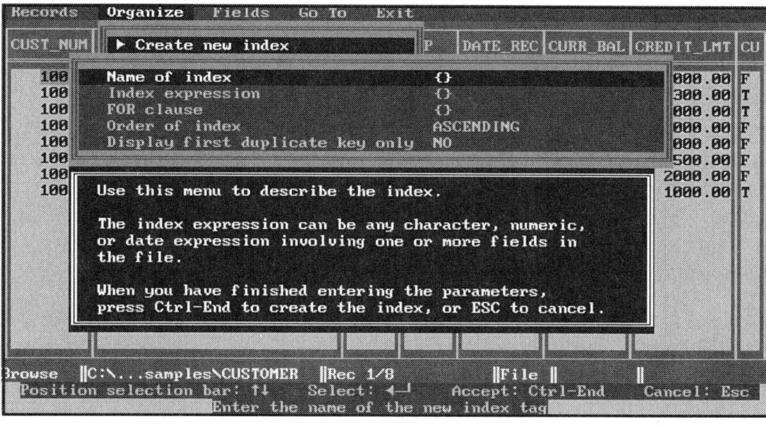


FIG. 13.3

The Create New Index menu.

4. Press Enter to remove the braces in the Name of Index row so that you can enter a name for this index. Type *ST_NAME* and press Enter.

5. Press the down-arrow key once to move the highlight to Index Expression. Press Enter to remove the braces so that you can enter an index expression.

**TIP** You can use the expression builder to help create an expression.

6. You now may type *STATE+CUST_NAME*, but with the expression builder, dBASE offers you help in creating an expression. Press Shift-F1 to activate the expression builder (see fig. 13.4).

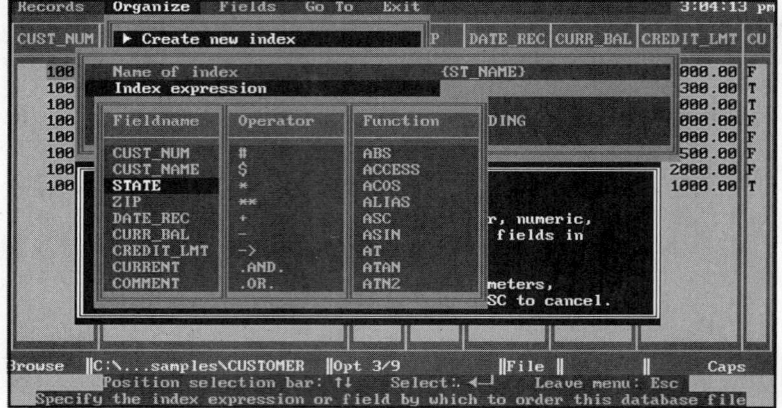


FIG. 13.4

The expression builder.

7. The expression builder shows you what you can include in the expression: the database field names for CUSTOMER.DBF, the operators you can include, and the dBASE functions. To select the STATE field, highlight STATE (use the arrow keys or press S), and then press Enter. When you return to the Create New Index menu, `STATE` appears in the Index Expression field.

8. Press Shift-F1 to return to the expression builder. Now press the right-arrow key to move to the Operator column and the down-arrow key to highlight the concatenate operator (+). Press Enter. You return to the Create New Index menu, which now displays the expression `STATE+` in the Index Expression field.

9. Press Shift-F1 again to return to the expression builder. Select the database field CUST_NAME and press Enter. This time when you return to the Create New Index menu, the expression `STATE+CUST_NAME` is in the Index Expression field. Your expression is complete.

10. Press Ctrl-End to accept the index definition. You return to the Browse screen, which is indexed and presented in the STATE+CUST_NAME order defined in the index. Figure 13.5 shows the Customer database indexed on this expression. You have successfully used a dBASE expression to create a complex index.

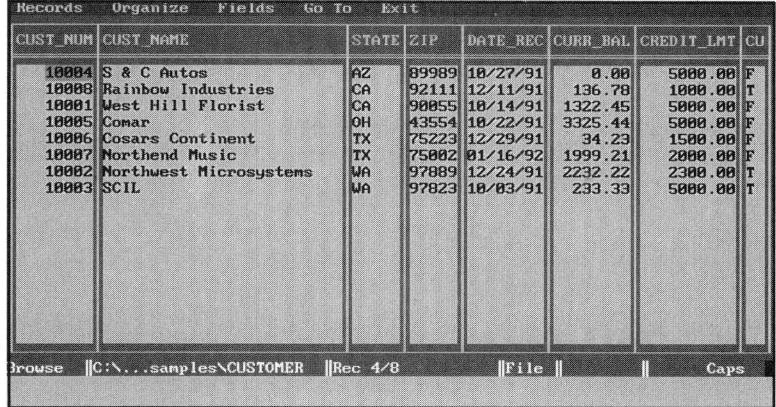
Records Organize Fields Go To Exit

| CUST_NUM | CUST_NAME | STATE | ZIP | DATE_REC | CURR_BAL | CREDIT_LMT | CU |
|---|---|---|---|---|---|---|---|
| 10004 | S & C Autos | AZ | 89989 | 10/27/91 | 0.00 | 5000.00 | F |
| 10008 | Rainbow Industries | CA | 92111 | 12/11/91 | 136.78 | 1000.00 | T |
| 10001 | West Hill Florist | CA | 90055 | 10/14/91 | 1322.45 | 5000.00 | F |
| 10005 | Comar | OH | 43554 | 10/22/91 | 3325.44 | 5000.00 | F |
| 10006 | Cosars Continent | TX | 75223 | 12/29/91 | 34.23 | 1500.00 | F |
| 10007 | Northend Music | TX | 75002 | 01/16/92 | 1999.21 | 2000.00 | F |
| 10002 | Northwest Microsystems | WA | 97889 | 12/24/91 | 2232.22 | 2300.00 | T |
| 10003 | SCIL | WA | 97823 | 10/03/91 | 233.33 | 5000.00 | T |

Browse ||C:\...samples\CUSTOMER ||Rec 4/8 ||File || || Caps

FIG. 13.5

The Customer database indexed on STATE+CUST_NUM.

By pressing Shift-F1 from a variety of menu locations, you can access the expression builder any time you need to define an expression. As you become more experienced with dBASE, you may simply type the expression you want, but the expression builder is a great help as you are learning.

You can use the mouse to select field names, operators, and functions from the Expression Builder menu. Click an item to select it; then click again to accept your choice and add it to the current expression.

## Using Expressions To Edit Databases

You can use dBASE expressions to edit the data in a database with an update query. Suppose that you decide to increase the credit limit of each of your customers by 25 percent. Complete the following steps to perform this task:

1. Highlight Customer in the Data panel and press Enter to make the Customer database active. Choose Use File from the selection menu that follows.
2. Move the highlight to the Queries column, where <create> is highlighted. Press Enter to create a new query.

> **WARNING:** When you change from a view query to an update query, dBASE deletes the view skeleton.

3. In the CUSTOMER.DBF file skeleton, type *replace*, or select Replace from the Update menu. This action tells dBASE that you want to create an update query to replace one (or more) database field values with new values. You see a warning that changing this view query to an update query deletes the view skeleton. This result is fine, so choose Proceed. When you return to the Query Design screen, the view skeleton is gone.

4. Press Tab to move the highlight to the CREDIT_LMT column. Enter *WITH CREDIT_LMT*1.25*. (Multiplying a value by 1.25 increases it by the desired 25 percent.)

   Alternatively, you can type *WITH* and then press Shift-F1 to activate the expression builder. Choose the CREDIT_LMT field and press Enter. Press Shift-F1 to reactivate the expression builder, and choose the multiplication operator (*) from the Operator column. When you return to the Query Design form, the replacement expression is `WITH CREDIT_LMT*`; you must enter the 1.25 from the keyboard.

5. The Query design screen now looks like figure 13.6. From the Update menu, choose Perform the Update. dBASE executes the update and presents a message box that reads `Press any key to continue....` Press a key, and you return to the Query design screen.

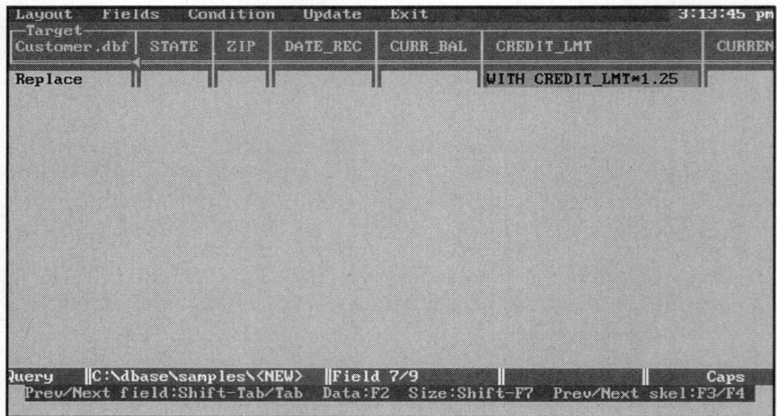


FIG. 13.6

The Query design screen with an update query in place.

6. Press F2 (Data) to show the Browse screen, and press the up-arrow key to return to the top of the database. If you compare the database now in figure 13.7 to figure 13.5, you can see that each value in the CREDIT_LMT field has been increased by 25 percent (ignore the sort order).

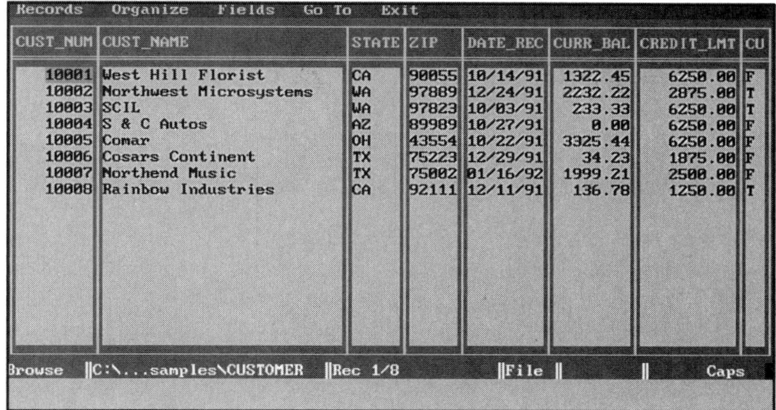

Records Organize Fields Go To Exit

| CUST_NUM | CUST_NAME | STATE | ZIP | DATE_REC | CURR_BAL | CREDIT_LMT | CU |
|---|---|---|---|---|---|---|---|
| 10001 | West Hill Florist | CA | 90055 | 10/14/91 | 1322.45 | 6250.00 | F |
| 10002 | Northwest Microsystems | WA | 97889 | 12/24/91 | 2232.22 | 2875.00 | T |
| 10003 | SCIL | WA | 97823 | 10/03/91 | 233.33 | 6250.00 | T |
| 10004 | S & C Autos | AZ | 89989 | 10/27/91 | 0.00 | 6250.00 | F |
| 10005 | Comar | OH | 43554 | 10/22/91 | 3325.44 | 6250.00 | F |
| 10006 | Cosars Continent | TX | 75223 | 12/29/91 | 34.23 | 1875.00 | F |
| 10007 | Northend Music | TX | 75002 | 01/16/92 | 1999.21 | 2500.00 | F |
| 10008 | Rainbow Industries | CA | 92111 | 12/11/91 | 136.78 | 1250.00 | T |

Browse ||C:\...samples\CUSTOMER ||Rec 1/8 ||File || || Caps

FIG. 13.7

The CUSTOMER database after an update query.

**For Related Information...**

▸▸ "Index Functions," p. 778.

**FROM HERE...**

# Including dBASE IV Functions in Expressions

The word *function* comes from programming languages: a function is a small program that returns a value of some sort. In dBASE IV, this definition holds true, but you don't have to know anything about programming to use functions. A function is like an electronic "black box." When you include a function in an expression, dBASE IV activates the black box, which returns a value. You also don't need to know anything about how the black box does its job; you need to know only what data you have to send to it and what type of value the black box returns.

Functions in dBASE IV return a value that you can use in a variety of ways. The easiest way to learn about functions is to experiment with them from the dot prompt. To get to the dot prompt from the Control Center, choose Exit to Dot Prompt from the Exit menu. The screen shown in figure 13.8 appears.

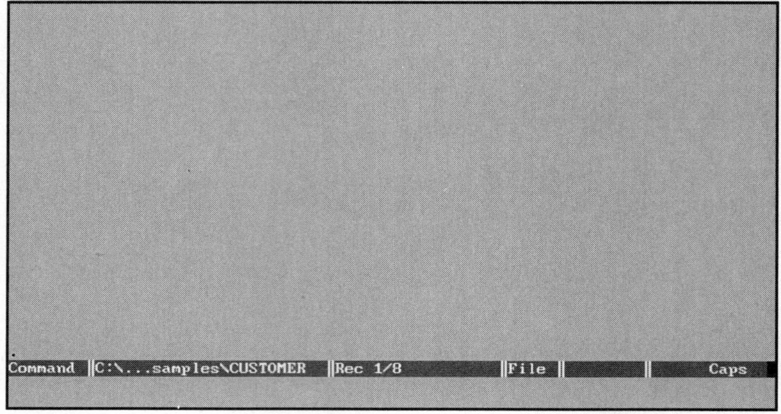


FIG. 13.8

The dot prompt screen, showing the command line to the right of the dot on the bottom line.

When you want to return to the Control Center, type *ASSIST* on the command line and press Enter, or simply press F2.

Working from the dot prompt is different from working in the Control Center; it is more like working from the DOS command line. You type a command and press Enter, and dBASE IV executes the command. The advantage of working from the dot prompt to test functions is that dBASE IV executes the function and outputs the result on the next line, giving you an immediate response to your command.

Functions have a set format: one word followed by parentheses. The function name can be in upper- or lowercase. Function names are dBASE-reserved words and should not be used for field names or index names. Some functions even have *arguments* within the parentheses; arguments are values that the function uses to calculate its return value. You enter these arguments based on the syntax of the functions. This section introduces you to some frequently used dBASE IV functions. For full details on these and other dBASE IV functions, see the "Quick Reference Guide" at the end of this book.

You can use the DATE() function to display the current system date. To see this function in action, type *? DATE()* at the dot prompt and press Enter. dBASE IV displays the current date and another dot prompt. The ? in front of the function tells dBASE IV to display on-screen the value of any expressions that follow the ?. The ? DATE() command tells dBASE IV to display the value returned by the DATE() function. When dBASE IV sees the DATE() function, the program gets the current date from the computer's system clock. That date is the *return value* of the function. You can use the return value like any other value for indexes, sorts, and calculations.

dBASE IV provides over 150 built-in functions, although many of them are used only while you are programming in the dBASE IV programming language. This chapter concentrates on functions you may find useful in sorting, indexing, querying, and reporting.

# Understanding the Types of Functions

dBASE IV functions fall into several categories. Some functions work with character values, whereas other functions work with numeric fields and values. A number of functions enable you to manipulate date fields. Another category of functions enables you to convert values from one type to another—a necessity whenever you construct expressions from different types of values.

> By using functions, you can convert values from one type to another. **TIP**

With many functions, you can best learn about them and what they do by experimenting with them from the dot prompt. In the following sections, the description of each function is accompanied by several examples you can run from the dot prompt.

Some functions require *arguments*, or values that the function uses to calculate the return value. These arguments are shown in the definition of the function; they are given names that define what they are and what types of data they must be.

## Using String Functions

String functions enable you to manipulate values stored as character data types. With these functions, you can search a character data value for another character data value or copy parts of strings. *Strings* are characters enclosed in single or double quotes, much the same as character data types in databases. The following are some of the more useful string functions, along with examples you can try from the dot prompt.

## AT( )

```
AT(<character string 1>, <character string 2> / <memo
field name>)
```

The AT( ) function returns the starting position of one character string (*<character string 1>*) within a second character string (*<character string 2>*). This function is useful when you need to know whether a value contains a certain string. The AT( ) function returns 0 if the value is not found in the string. In place of the second character string, you can specify a memo field name. The AT( ) function then searches the memo field for the search string.

Type the following at the dot prompt and observe the results:

```
? AT('Zum', 'John W. Zumsteg')
9
? AT('Zum', 'Amy Cook')
0
```

## LEFT( )

```
LEFT(<string>/<memo field name>, <number>)
```

LEFT( ) returns a string consisting of the number of characters specified, starting from the leftmost character of the string. LEFT( ) is useful when you are sorting or indexing on only the first character of a database field.

Type the following at the dot prompt and observe the results:

```
? LEFT('Smoke on the water',5)
Smoke
```

## RIGHT( )

```
RIGHT(<string> / <memo field name> , <number>)
```

The RIGHT( ) function is the converse of LEFT( ). RIGHT( ) returns a character value, starting from the rightmost character of a string.

Type the following at the dot prompt and observe the results:

```
? RIGHT('Smoke on the water',5)
water
```

## TRIM( ), RTRIM( ), LTRIM( )

```
TRIM(<string>)
RTRIM(<string>)
LTRIM(<string>)
```

RTRIM( ) removes trailing blanks from a string (blanks to the right of the last character); LTRIM( ) removes blanks to the left of the first character. TRIM( ) duplicates the action of RTRIM( ). These functions are useful when you are combining character values, which frequently have trailing blanks and occasionally have leading blanks.

Type the following at the dot prompt and observe the results:

```
?
LTRIM("<space><space><space><space><space><space>Works!")

Works!

?
RTRIM("Works!<space><space><space><space><space><space>")

Works!

? RTRIM("First
String<space><space><space><space><space><space>") +
LTRIM("<space><space><space><space><space><space>Second
String")

First StringSecond String
```

## UPPER( ), LOWER( )

```
UPPER(<string>)
LOWER(<string>)
```

The UPPER( ) and LOWER( ) functions change all the letters of a string to upper- or lowercase. You can use these functions when you want a sort to be a true dictionary sort, in which each upper- and lowercase letter is treated the same within the sort. In a nondictionary (ASCII) sort, *B* comes before *a* because uppercase letters sort before lowercase letters.

Type the following at the dot prompt and observe the results:

```
? UPPER("Banana Cream Pie")
BANANA CREAM PIE
? LOWER("DEREK and CRAIG")
derek and craig
```

## SUBSTR( )

```
SUBSTR(<string> / <memo field name>, <start position>,
[<number of characters>])
```

SUBSTR( ) returns a character value that is a part of the string passed as an argument. <*start position*> specifies the starting position from which characters are copied. The optional <*number of characters*> specifies how many characters to copy. If <*number of characters*> is omitted, all characters to the end of the input string are copied to the returned value.

Type the following at the dot prompt and observe the results:

```
? SUBSTR('John Zumsteg',6,3)
Zum
? SUBSTR('John Zumsteg',6)
Zumsteg
```

## Using Numeric Functions

Many numeric functions have specialized purposes. You may frequently use several numeric functions of basic or intermediate complexity in dBASE IV applications. All numeric functions return a numeric result.

### INT( )

```
INT(<numeric expression>)
```

INT( ) returns the integer value of a number. The integer value of a number is that number with any digits to the right of the decimal removed.

Type the following at the dot prompt and observe the results:

```
? INT(4.33234)
4
? INT(-4.33234)
-4
```

### MAX( ), MIN( )

```
MAX(<expression 1>, <expression 2>)
MIN(<expression 1>, <expression 2>)
```

MAX( ) and MIN( ) return the highest and lowest values of the two arguments. As with any function, you can use database fields as arguments for MAX( ) and MIN( ); therefore, you can use these functions to compare the values of two fields.

Type the following at the dot prompt and observe the results:

```
? MAX(100.232, 200)
200
? MIN(100.232, 200)
100.232
```

Suppose that a database record has the following values:

| | |
|---|---|
| CREDIT_LMT | 5000.00 |
| CURR_BAL | 3433.10 |

Then MAX and MIN work as follows:

```
? MAX(CREDIT_LMT, CURR_BAL)
5000.00
? MIN(CREDIT_LMT, CURR_BAL)
3433.10
```

## ROUND( )

ROUND(<*numeric expression*>, <*number of decimal places*>)

ROUND( ) returns the value of the first numeric argument, rounded off to the number of decimal places specified by the second argument. If the second argument is zero, the number is rounded off to an integer value.

Type the following at the dot prompt and observe the results:

```
? ROUND(4.433234, 2)
4.43
? ROUND(-4.433234,2)
-4.43
? ROUND(4.5,0)
5
? ROUND(-4.5,0)
-5
```

Notice that when you round 4.5, dBASE IV rounds to the next higher integer, the whole number 5. Negative numbers round as if they were positive.

You also can use ROUND( ) to round numbers to the nearest 10, 100, or so on. Specify the number of decimal places as a negative number. The number –1 rounds *numeric expression* to the nearest 10; –2 rounds to the nearest 100; –3 rounds to the nearest 1,000. Consider these examples:

```
? ROUND(32683, -1)
33680
? ROUND(32683 ,-3)
33000
? ROUND( -32683, -1)
-32680
? ROUND( -32683, -3)
-33000
```

## SIGN( )

```
SIGN(<numeric expression>)
```

SIGN( ) returns –1 if *<numeric expression>* is negative, 1 if the argument is positive, and 0 if the argument is zero. This function is useful for limiting database searches to records with one of these three possibilities (positive, negative, or zero) in a specific field.

Type the following at the dot prompt and observe the results:

```
? SIGN(22321)
1
? SIGN(-22321)
-1
? SIGN(0)
0
```

# Using Date Functions

Because dBASE IV has extensive date-handling capabilities, date functions are provided to extend the use of these capabilities. Remember that dBASE IV requires a date expression to be enclosed in braces: May 1, 1992, must be represented as {05/01/92}.

## CDOW( )

```
CDOW(<date variable>)
```

CDOW( ) returns the day of the week as a character string for the *<date variable>* you specify.

Type the following at the dot prompt and observe the results:

```
? CDOW({05/01/92})
Tuesday
```

## CMONTH( )

```
CMONTH(<date variable>)
```

CMONTH( ) returns the month as a character string for the *<date variable>* you specify.

Type the following at the dot prompt and observe the results:

```
? CMONTH({05/01/92})
May
```

## DATE( )

```
DATE( )
```

DATE( ) returns the current system date from the computer's internal clock. No argument is required.

Type the following at the dot prompt and observe the results:

```
? DATE( )
05/01/92
```

## DAY( )

```
DAY(<date variable>)
```

The DAY( ) function returns the day of the month as a numeric value for the *<date variable>* you specify.

Type the following at the dot prompt and observe the results:

```
? DAY({05/01/92})
1
? DAY({05/30/92})
30
```

## DMY( )

```
DMY(<date variable>)
```

DMY( ) returns the date argument in the format day, month, year for the *<date variable>* you specify.

Type the following at the dot prompt and observe the results:

```
? DMY({05/01/92})
1 May 92
```

## CTOD( )

```
CTOD(<character expression>)
```

CTOD( ) returns a date expression equivalent to the *<character expression>* argument. You use this function when importing data from other programs because dates always transfer as character strings. Note, however, that dBASE IV does not check the character string for validity when it converts the string to a date. In the examples that follow, the second example uses a nonsense string that dBASE IV converts to a valid date.

> **WARNING:** dBASE IV does not check the character string for validity when it converts the string to a date.

Type the following at the dot prompt and observe the results:

```
? CTOD("05/01/92")
05/01/92
? CTOD("99/88/77")
06/12/85
```

This conversion occurs because dBASE stores dates internally as the number of days from a base date; CTOD( ) converts the nonsense date string in the example to the number of days from the base date represented by 88 days, 99 months, and 77 years. The result is converted back to a date value that appears as 06/12/85.

The functions listed in this and the preceding sections are the most commonly used functions in dBASE IV. Other functions address financial and mathematical applications but generally are used in more advanced dBASE IV applications. Many other functions are used only when you work in the dBASE IV programming language. The "dBase IV Reference Guide" at the end of this book lists all the functions available in dBASE IV.

# Using Functions To Combine Data Types in Expressions

As mentioned earlier in this chapter, you can *concatenate*, or combine, character fields. If LAST_NAME and FIRST_NAME are both character fields, you can use the expression LAST_NAME + FIRST_NAME to concatenate FIRST_NAME to the end of LAST_NAME, resulting in a new expression. Concatenation works only for character fields, but several functions enable you to create expressions that mix different data types.

The following are functions that enable you to combine different data types by converting them to string types, which then can be combined.

## DTOS( )

```
DTOS(<date variable>)
```

DTOS( ) returns a character string in the format YYYYMMDD, representing the *<date variable>* argument you specified.

Type the following at the dot prompt and observe the results:

```
? DTOS({05/01/92})
19900501
```

## DTOC( )

```
DTOC(<date variable>)
```

DTOC( ) returns a string value in the standard MM/DD/YY format (or whatever date format you set with the SET DATE command) that represents the *<date variable>* you specify.

Type the following at the dot prompt and observe the results:

```
? DTOC({05/01/92})
05/01/92
```

The difference between DTOS( ) and DTOC( ) is that you can use DTOS( ) to index date fields. DTOS( ) returns dates in YYYYMMDD order so that dates can be ordered correctly. DTOC( ) uses the MM/DD/YY order; when you sort these values, months are sorted first, then days, then years. If you use DTOC( ) to convert dates to characters, 03/24/78 comes after 03/22/88, an inaccurate date sort. For reporting purposes, DTOC( ) is often the better choice; for indexing and sorting on date fields, however, DTOS( ) is the only choice.

## STR( )

```
STR(<numeric expression> [,<length>] [,<decimals>]
```

STR( ) returns a character representation of the *<numeric expression>* argument. Use STR( ) to convert a numeric value to a character value when you want to combine a numeric field with a character field in a dBASE IV expression. Optionally, you can specify how long the resulting string will be (*<length>*) and how many decimal positions it will contain (*<decimals>*).

## Using Nesting Functions

So far, the functions described in this chapter use data values as arguments. Remember that you can enter these arguments directly. The function CDOW({05/01/92}), for example, returns the character string `Friday`. Instead of a data value, you can use a field name as an argument. CDOW(FLT_DATE), for example, returns as a character string the day of the week whose date expression is in the FLT_DATE field. If the value of FLT_DATE is {05/01/92}, this function also returns `Friday`.

The arguments for a function don't have to be actual values; you can specify them as database fields, or they can be the return values from functions. This feature enables you to *nest* values for greater versatility.

Suppose that you want a report field to print the day on which the report is printed. You know that the DATE( ) function returns a date value of the current date, and that the CDOW(*date_expr*) function returns the name of the day as a character string for the specified argument. You can combine these two functions by *nesting* the DATE( ) function as the argument for the CDAY( ) function:

```
CDOW(DATE( ))
```

Because a function returns a data value, you can substitute the function anywhere you can place the data value—even as an argument to another function. This capability enables you to create functions that combine the capabilities of many functions.

Suppose that you have the character field LAST_NAME with a length of 15 in your database, and you want to take the middle five characters of that field and convert them to uppercase. You can do so using the following expression:

```
UPPER(SUBSTR(LAST_NAME,5,5))
```

The SUBSTR(LAST_NAME,5,5) function extracts the middle five characters. The result of this function becomes the argument for the UPPER(*char_expr*) function, which converts all letters to uppercase.

> **WARNING:** Avoid the common error of mismatching function types, such as nesting a numeric function in which the outer function requires a character argument.

You have almost no limit to the number of nests possible with dBASE IV functions. The more complex an expression becomes, however, the more difficult it is to debug. Remember to match opening and closing parentheses, because each function requires one set. Also, avoid the common error of mismatched function types, such as nesting a numeric function within an outer function that requires a character argument.

Given this introduction to the way functions work, you are ready to put them to work in your expressions, tapping some powerful capabilities of dBASE IV to organize and sort your data. The following section explains how to use functions in your expressions.

# Using Functions and Expressions To Create Indexes

Earlier in this chapter, you were introduced to dBASE IV expressions, which gave you the basis for understanding functions. With your knowledge of functions, you can delve more deeply into the uses of expressions. Expressions enable you to create sophisticated indexes, in which you can index first on one primary field and then on one or more secondary fields. Expressions also provide valuable ways to format data on-screen and in reports.

## Creating Dictionary and ASCII Sorts

When you first create an index expression, you may be perplexed at the results of an alphabetical sort. For example, *BAKER* comes before *abercrombie*. dBASE's default sort order is based on the ASCII character set. ASCII is an acronym for American Standard Code for Information Interchange and refers to a standard way computers store data internally. ASCII order arranges all uppercase letters before lowercase letters, which means uppercase *B* comes before lowercase *a*.

Functions placed within the indexing expression can correct this problem, however. You can convert the field you are indexing to upper- or lowercase before indexing. If you want to index on the LAST_NAME field and then on the FIRST_NAME field, for example, you can use the following expression:

```
UPPER(LAST_NAME + FIRST_NAME)
```

The actual values of the field in the database do not change when you index with this expression. Rather, dBASE IV concatenates the LAST_NAME and FIRST_NAME fields into one field, converts all characters to uppercase, and then stores that value in the index file as the key for that record. The database appears the same, but the displayed order changes: *abercrombie* comes before *BAKER*. This sort order is the order a dictionary follows when alphabetizing and is easier for the user to comprehend.

## Combining Functions for Indexes

When you create index expressions as explained in Part II, you can combine character fields to create a multifield index. In a database with FIRST_NAME and LAST_NAME fields, for example, you can create an index with the key LAST_NAME + FIRST_NAME to sort the database by last name, and then by first name within the same last name. Trying to combine noncharacter fields generates the message Data type mismatch. Functions, however, enable you to overcome these limitations and create sophisticated multilevel indexes.

**TIP** When you combine different fields to create multilevel indexes, you can combine only character data types. To combine other data types, you first must convert them to character data types.

### Converting Dates to Strings

Figure 13.9 shows a database that tracks information about an airline's advanced bookings. The database contains two character fields (FLT_NUM and SEGMENT), one date field (FLT_DATE), and three numeric fields (AUTH_LVL, SEAT_AVAIL, and GROUP_PAX).

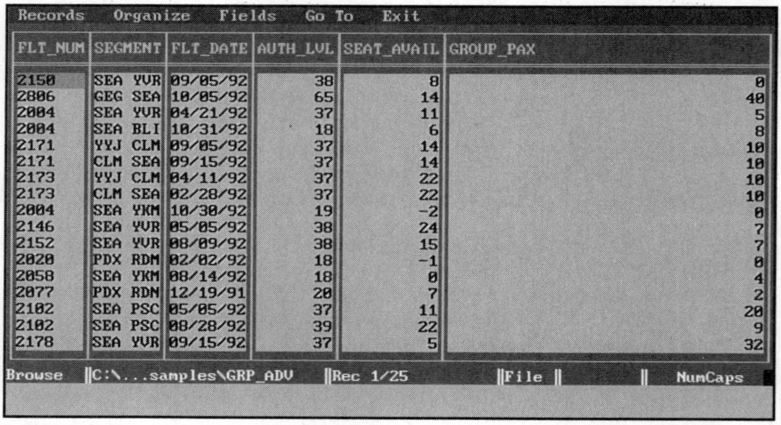

Records Organize Fields Go To Exit

| FLT_NUM | SEGMENT | FLT_DATE | AUTH_LVL | SEAT_AVAIL | GROUP_PAX |
|---|---|---|---|---|---|
| 2150 | SEA YVR | 09/05/92 | 38 | 8 | 0 |
| 2806 | GEG SEA | 10/05/92 | 65 | 14 | 40 |
| 2004 | SEA YVR | 04/21/92 | 37 | 11 | 5 |
| 2004 | SEA BLI | 10/31/92 | 18 | 6 | 8 |
| 2171 | YYJ CLM | 09/05/92 | 37 | 14 | 10 |
| 2171 | CLM SEA | 09/15/92 | 37 | 14 | 10 |
| 2173 | YYJ CLM | 04/11/92 | 37 | 22 | 10 |
| 2173 | CLM SEA | 02/28/92 | 37 | 22 | 10 |
| 2004 | SEA YKM | 10/30/92 | 19 | -2 | 0 |
| 2146 | SEA YVR | 05/05/92 | 38 | 24 | 7 |
| 2152 | SEA YVR | 08/09/92 | 38 | 15 | 7 |
| 2020 | PDX RDM | 02/02/92 | 18 | -1 | 0 |
| 2058 | SEA YKM | 08/14/92 | 18 | 0 | 4 |
| 2077 | PDX RDN | 12/19/91 | 20 | 7 | 2 |
| 2102 | SEA PSC | 05/05/92 | 37 | 11 | 20 |
| 2102 | SEA PSC | 08/28/92 | 39 | 22 | 9 |
| 2178 | SEA YVR | 09/15/92 | 37 | 5 | 32 |

Browse ‖C:\...samples\GRP_ADV ‖Rec 1/25 ‖File ‖ ‖ NumCaps

FIG. 13.9

The Advance Booking database.

An airline uses this database to manage its seat inventory. The following is an explanation of the fields in the database:

| Field name | Field contents description |
|---|---|
| FLT_NUM | A character field containing the flight number of a specific flight. |
| SEGMENT | Two cities served by a portion of the flight. A flight may go from Seattle (SEA) to Spokane (GEG) to Boise (BOI); the segments are SEA-GEG and GEG-BOI. |
| FLT_DATE | The date of the flight. |
| AUTH_LVL | The number of seats that can be sold on a segment. This number is usually about 10 percent greater than the number of seats on the airplane, to account for passengers who reserve seats but don't show up for the flight. |
| SEAT_AVAIL | The number of seats remaining to be sold on a segment. This is the number of seats available on the airplane less the number of seats sold. If the value of SEAT_AVAIL is negative, the flight has been overbooked. |
| GROUP_PAX | The number of passengers on this flight who are part of a group. This is important because group passengers always show up for a flight, so the airline cannot plan on a 10 percent no-show rate. |

As shown in figure 13.9, the Advanced Booking database is not ordered by any index. However, you may want to sort the database by flight number first, and then by date within flight number. To combine a character field with a date field in a single index expression, you must convert the date to a character using an expression such as the following:

```
FLT_NUM + DTOS(FLT_DATE)
```

The DTOS( ) function returns a character string in the format YYYYMMDD for the FLT_DATE value. This string is concatenated to the FLT_NUM character field value. The database is indexed then on that expression.

For example, one record in the database has a FLT_NUM value of 2150 and a FLT_DATE value of {09/05/92}. The index value for this field is 215019920905 (the flight date in YYYYMMDD format added to the flight number). Figure 13.10 shows the Create New Index menu with this index expression specified. (Notice that the index expression is truncated when displayed in the menu.)

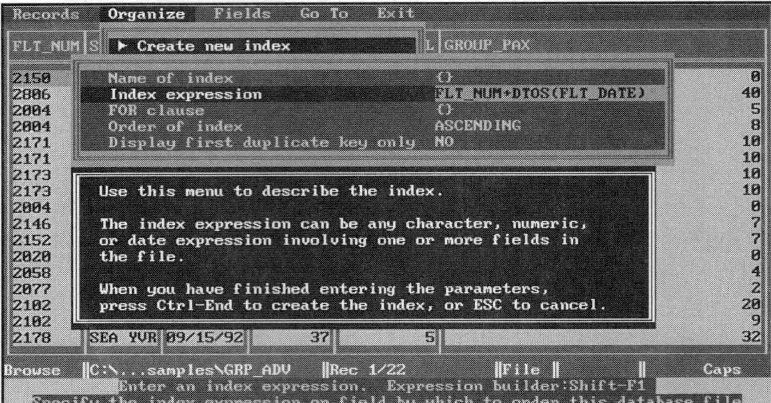


FIG. 13.10

Creating a new index for the Advance Booking database.

Figure 13.11 shows the database sorted by this index. The records are sorted first by FLT_NUM. Where more than one record exists for a specific FLT_NUM value, the records are sorted by FLT_DATE within the FLT_NUM. For example, notice the three records for FLT_NUM 2004; the records are sorted by FLT_DATE.

Records Organize Fields Go To Exit

| FLT_NUM | SEGMENT | FLT_DATE | AUTH_LVL | SEAT_AVAIL | GROUP_PAX |
|---|---|---|---|---|---|
| 2004 | SEA YVR | 04/21/92 | 37 | 11 | 5 |
| 2004 | SEA YKM | 10/30/92 | 19 | -2 | 0 |
| 2004 | SEA BLI | 10/31/92 | 18 | 6 | 8 |
| 2020 | PDX RDM | 02/02/92 | 18 | -1 | 0 |
| 2058 | SEA YKM | 08/14/92 | 18 | 0 | 4 |
| 2077 | PDX RDM | 12/19/91 | 20 | 7 | 2 |
| 2102 | SEA PSC | 05/05/92 | 37 | 11 | 20 |
| 2102 | SEA PSC | 08/28/92 | 39 | 22 | 9 |
| 2146 | SEA YVR | 05/05/92 | 38 | 24 | 7 |
| 2150 | SEA YVR | 09/05/92 | 38 | 8 | 0 |
| 2152 | SEA YVR | 08/09/92 | 38 | 15 | 7 |
| 2171 | YYJ CLM | 09/05/92 | 37 | 14 | 10 |
| 2171 | CLM SEA | 09/15/92 | 37 | 14 | 10 |
| 2173 | CLM SEA | 02/28/92 | 37 | 22 | 10 |
| 2173 | YYJ CLM | 04/11/92 | 37 | 22 | 10 |
| 2178 | SEA YVR | 09/15/92 | 37 | 5 | 32 |
| 2222 | YVR SEA | 02/24/92 | 15 | 2 | 13 |

Browse C:\...samples\GRP_ADV Rec 3/22 File NumCaps

FIG. 13.11

The view of the database indexed on FLT_NUM + DTOS(FLT_DATE).

## Converting Numeric Values to Strings

In much the same way that you combine dates and strings, you can combine strings and numerics. Instead of the DTOS( ) function, you use the STR( ) function to convert numerics to strings. In the Advance Booking database, you may want to see the records sorted by FLT_NUM and then by the SEAT_AVAIL value. To do so, index the database with the following expression:

```
FLT_NUM + STR(SEAT_AVAIL)
```

Figure 13.12 shows the database indexed on this expression.

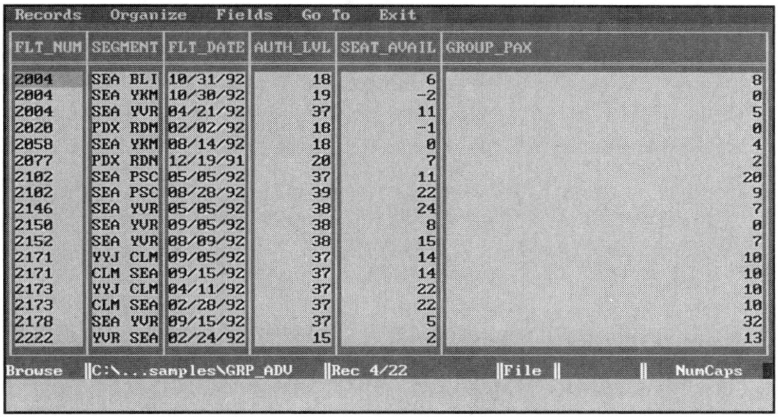

Records Organize Fields Go To Exit

| FLT_NUM | SEGMENT | FLT_DATE | AUTH_LVL | SEAT_AVAIL | GROUP_PAX |
|---|---|---|---|---|---|
| 2004 | SEA BLI | 10/31/92 | 18 | 6 | 8 |
| 2004 | SEA YKM | 10/30/92 | 19 | -2 | 0 |
| 2004 | SEA YVR | 04/21/92 | 37 | 11 | 5 |
| 2020 | PDX RDM | 02/02/92 | 18 | -1 | 0 |
| 2058 | SEA YKM | 08/14/92 | 18 | 0 | 4 |
| 2077 | PDX RDM | 12/19/91 | 20 | 7 | 2 |
| 2102 | SEA PSC | 05/05/92 | 37 | 11 | 20 |
| 2102 | SEA PSC | 08/28/92 | 39 | 22 | 9 |
| 2146 | SEA YVR | 05/05/92 | 38 | 24 | 7 |
| 2150 | SEA YVR | 09/05/92 | 38 | 8 | 0 |
| 2152 | SEA YVR | 08/09/92 | 38 | 15 | 7 |
| 2171 | YYJ CLM | 09/05/92 | 37 | 14 | 10 |
| 2171 | CLM SEA | 09/15/92 | 37 | 14 | 10 |
| 2173 | YYJ CLM | 04/11/92 | 37 | 22 | 10 |
| 2173 | CLM SEA | 02/28/92 | 37 | 22 | 10 |
| 2178 | SEA YVR | 09/15/92 | 37 | 5 | 32 |
| 2222 | YVR SEA | 02/24/92 | 15 | 2 | 13 |

Browse ‖C:\...samples\GRP_ADV ‖Rec 4/22 ‖File ‖ ‖ NumCaps

FIG. 13.12

A view of the database indexed on FLT_NUM + STR(SEAT_AVAIL).

One problem with this index expression is that negative values do not sort correctly because the minus (–) character appears late in both ASCII and dictionary sort order. You can correct this problem by adding the SEAT_AVAIL value to the highest value that SEAT_AVAIL can reach. If you assume that the value of SEAT_AVAIL may never exceed 1000, you can specify an index expression such as the following:

```
FLT_NUM + STR(1000+SEAT_AVAIL)
```

This function makes all the numbers positive so that the database sorts correctly, with negative numbers appearing before positive ones. Figure 13.13 shows the Browse window for the corrected database. Just as in creating dictionary indexes, the actual values of the database do not change by adding 1000; only the key values that dBASE IV stores as part of the index are modified.

Records Organize Fields Go To Exit

| FLT_NUM | SEGMENT | FLT_DATE | AUTH_LVL | SEAT_AVAIL | GROUP_PAX |
|---|---|---|---|---|---|
| 2004 | SEA YKM | 10/30/92 | 19 | -2 | 0 |
| 2004 | SEA BLI | 10/31/92 | 18 | 6 | 8 |
| 2004 | SEA YVR | 04/21/92 | 37 | 11 | 5 |
| 2020 | PDX RDM | 02/02/92 | 18 | -1 | 0 |
| 2058 | SEA YKM | 08/14/92 | 18 | 0 | 4 |
| 2077 | PDX RDN | 12/19/91 | 20 | 7 | 2 |
| 2102 | SEA PSC | 05/05/92 | 37 | 11 | 20 |
| 2102 | SEA PSC | 08/28/92 | 39 | 22 | 9 |
| 2146 | SEA YVR | 05/05/92 | 38 | 24 | 7 |
| 2150 | SEA YVR | 09/05/92 | 38 | 8 | 0 |
| 2152 | SEA YVR | 08/09/92 | 38 | 15 | 7 |
| 2171 | YYJ CLM | 09/05/92 | 37 | 14 | 10 |
| 2171 | CLM SEA | 09/15/92 | 37 | 14 | 10 |
| 2173 | YYJ CLM | 04/11/92 | 37 | 22 | 10 |
| 2173 | CLM SEA | 02/28/92 | 37 | 22 | 10 |
| 2178 | SEA YVR | 09/15/92 | 37 | 5 | 32 |
| 2222 | YVR SEA | 02/24/92 | 15 | 2 | 13 |

Browse ‖C:\...samples\GRP_ADV ‖Rec 9/22 ‖File ‖ ‖ NumCaps

FIG. 13.13

The index corrected to handle negative numbers.

## Converting Dates and Numerics to Strings

Combining an index on a date type and a numeric type requires you to convert both types to strings using the appropriate functions. If you want to index the database on the FLT_DATE field first and then the SEAT_AVAIL field, you specify an index expression such as the following:

```
DTOS(FLT_DATE) + STR(1000+SEAT_AVAIL)
```

Again, you can use the technique explained in the preceding section to index negative and positive numbers correctly. Figure 13.14 shows the Advance Booking database indexed by this function.

Records Organize Fields Go To Exit

| FLT_NUM | SEGMENT | FLT_DATE | AUTH_LVL | SEAT_AVAIL | GROUP_PAX |
|---|---|---|---|---|---|
| 2323 | PDX YVR | 12/07/91 | 11 | 6 | 5 |
| 2077 | PDX RDN | 12/19/91 | 20 | 7 | 2 |
| 2020 | PDX RDM | 02/02/92 | 18 | -1 | 0 |
| 2222 | YVR SEA | 02/24/92 | 15 | 2 | 13 |
| 2173 | CLM SEA | 02/28/92 | 37 | 22 | 10 |
| 2226 | PSC PDX | 03/16/92 | 15 | 10 | 5 |
| 2173 | YYJ CLM | 04/11/92 | 37 | 22 | 10 |
| 2324 | PSC YVR | 04/18/92 | 40 | 20 | 20 |
| 2224 | YVR PSC | 04/19/92 | 10 | 5 | 5 |
| 2004 | SEA YVR | 04/21/92 | 37 | 11 | 5 |
| 2102 | SEA PSC | 05/05/92 | 37 | 11 | 20 |
| 2146 | SEA YVR | 05/05/92 | 38 | 24 | 7 |
| 2152 | SEA YVR | 08/09/92 | 38 | 15 | 7 |
| 2058 | SEA YKM | 08/14/92 | 18 | 0 | 4 |
| 2102 | SEA PSC | 08/28/92 | 39 | 22 | 9 |
| 2150 | SEA YVR | 09/05/92 | 38 | 8 | 0 |
| 2171 | YYJ CLM | 09/05/92 | 37 | 14 | 10 |

Browse ‖C:\...samples\GRP_ADV ‖Rec 21/22 ‖File ‖ ‖ NumCaps

FIG. 13.14

The Advance Booking database indexed on DTOS(FLT_DATE) + STR(1000+ SEAT_AVAIL).

# Using Functions and Expressions To Format Reports

Expressions and functions have powerful features you can use in dBASE IV reports. Although the Report Design screen provides flexibility in formatting individual fields, you can increase this flexibility by using expressions and functions. For example, you can use expressions to group data in more sophisticated ways. Functions also expand the power of calculated fields. This section describes how to use expressions in formatted reports.

## Creating Calculated Field Values with Expressions

In Chapter 9, you learned how to create a calculated field by entering a dBASE expression, such as CREDIT_LMT – CURR_BAL. You also can use dBASE functions in calculated fields. You may want to include a field in a customer information form that calculates the number of days since the last order placed by a customer. If your database includes a field that shows the date of the last order (LAST_PUR, for example), you can create such a calculated field by following these steps:

1. If the customer information form already exists, highlight it on the Forms panel of the Control Center and press Enter. In this example, the form is named CUSTINFO. Choose Modify Layout from the selection box that appears.

2. Move the cursor on the Forms design work surface to where you want the calculated field to appear. You may want to add text to describe the field first.

3. Choose Add Field or press F5 (Add Field). Select <create> from the Calculated column in the fields list. In the Field Definition menu, give the field a name (*ELAPSED*), and a description (*Days since last order*).

4. Move the highlight to the Expression field. You can press Shift-F1 to activate the expression builder, or you can enter the following expression to calculate the days since the last order:

   ```
   DATE( ) - LAST_PUR
   ```

Change the Template field to 9,999. Because the value in this calculated field is always an integer (with no decimal places), you can remove the decimal places from the template (see fig. 13.15.)

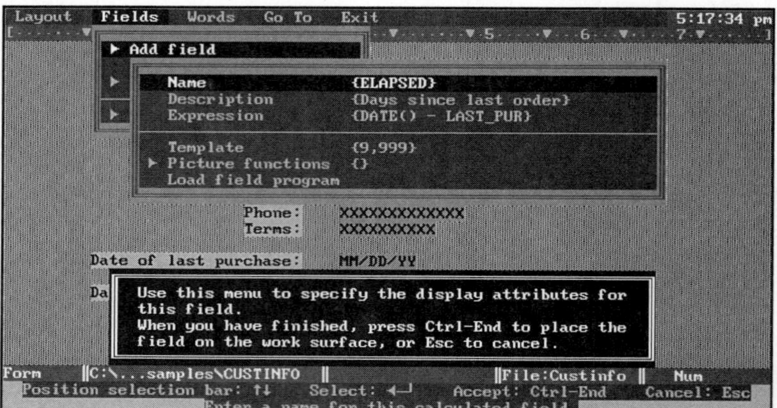


**FIG. 13.15**

Adding a calculated field to the Form design.

5. Press Ctrl-End to accept the new field, which is added to the Form design work surface. Add the text, *Days since last order:*. Figure 13.16 shows that the record now shows the number of days since the customer last placed an order.

Use the mouse to access the Fields menu by clicking the menu name; then click Add Field, and click on <create> in the Calculated column of the Fields list. To expand the input area for the field expression, click the `Zoom:F9` label in the navigation line; then click `Zoom:F9` again to return to the expression input prompt and press Enter to accept the expression. Click the `Accept:Ctrl-End` label to complete the operation and add the field to the work surface.

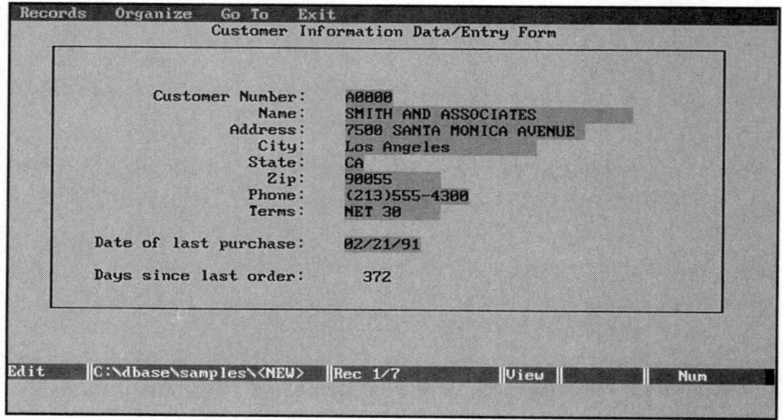


**FIG. 13.16**

The form in use, with a calculated field.

# Formatting Report Fields

One of the most important uses of expressions and functions in reports is formatting fields in ways not possible with the standard picture functions and template symbols. Using expressions in these ways can improve the looks and clarity of your reports.

Expressions and functions are extremely useful when formatting date fields on a report or form. Using the DATE() function in a date field results in the standard DD/MM/YY format, which does the job but is certainly less than elegant. You can use some date-formatting functions as part of an expression to create a variety of readable dates.

To display a date field with the format `Friday, March 6, 1992`, use the following four functions:

| | |
|---|---|
| CMONTH( ) | Returns a character string with the calendar month |
| CDOW( ) | Returns a character string with the day's name |
| DAY( ) | Returns the day component of the date, as a number |
| YEAR( ) | Returns a numeric year |

To change a date field of the standard MM/DD/YY format to a field that reads day, month, date, year (Friday, March 6, 1992), perform the following steps:

1. Delete the date field by placing the cursor on it and pressing Del.
2. Choose Add Field from the Fields menu, or press F5 (Add Field). You create an expression by using functions to display the date in the desired format.
3. In the Fields list that appears, move the highlight to the CALCULATED column, highlight <create>, and press Enter.
4. In the Field Definition menu, give the field a name (*CURR_DATE*) and a description (*Today's date*). Move the highlight to Expression and press Enter.
5. Enter the expression (or press Shift-F1 and use the expression builder) to format the field as follows:

   ```
   CDOW(DATE()) + ", " + MDY(DATE())
   ```

   Press Ctrl-End to accept this expression, and Ctrl-End again to accept the field definition. The field appears on the Report design work surface. Figure 13.17 shows the report, displayed on-screen with the View Report On-Screen option of the Print menu. You can see how the date field has been formatted.

```
                             Customer Credit Balance Report
Page No.    1
Friday, March 6, 1992
17:34:05

Customer  Customer                      State  Zip    Current   Credit     Remainig
Number    Name                                 Code   Balance   Limit      Credit
-----------------------------------------------------------------------------------
State: CA
   10001  West Hill Florist             CA     90055  1,322.45  6,250.00   4,927.55
Summaries for State: CA                               1,322.45  6,250.00   4,927.55
State: WA
   10002  Northwest Microsystems        WA     97889  2,232.22  2,875.00     642.78
   10003  SCIL                          WA     97823    233.33  6,250.00   6,016.67
Summaries for State: WA                               2,465.55  9,125.00   6,659.45
State: AZ
   10004  S & C Autos                   AZ     89989      0.00  6,250.00   6,250.00
Summaries for State: AZ                                   0.00  6,250.00   6,250.00
State: OH
   10005  Comar                         OH     43554  3,325.44  6,250.00   2,924.56
Summaries for State: OH                               3,325.44  6,250.00   2,924.56
State: TX
                Cancel viewing: ESC,  Continue viewing: SPACEBAR
```

FIG. 13.17

A report with the date formatted with dBASE IV functions.

This procedure is a more elegant way to present a date than the standard DD/MM/YY and improves the readability of your reports.

## Creating Query Filters

You can use expressions in many areas of a query, but they are primarily used in creating calculated fields and filter conditions. (Calculated fields are discussed in Chapter 9.) Your use of expressions and functions to create calculated fields for queries parallels the way you create such fields for reports (as discussed in Chapter 10).

*Filter conditions* enable you to exclude from query processing any records that do not pass the filter test defined by those conditions.

To create a filter in a query, follow these steps:

1. Open the Query design screen from the Control Center. If you are creating a new query, make sure that the appropriate database is current (highlight it in the Data panel, press Enter, and choose Use File), move the highlight to <create> in the Queries panel, and press Enter. If you are modifying an existing query, highlight that query in the Queries panel, press Enter, and choose Modify Query.

2. From the Query design screen, open the filter skeleton by choosing Add Condition from the Conditions menu.

3. In the Condition Box, enter an expression that dBASE IV tests against every record in the database. If the record passes the test, it is included in the view; if not, the record is excluded. Figure 13.18 shows the Condition Box with an expression using the function LEFT(CUST_NAME,1) on the left side of the logical test.

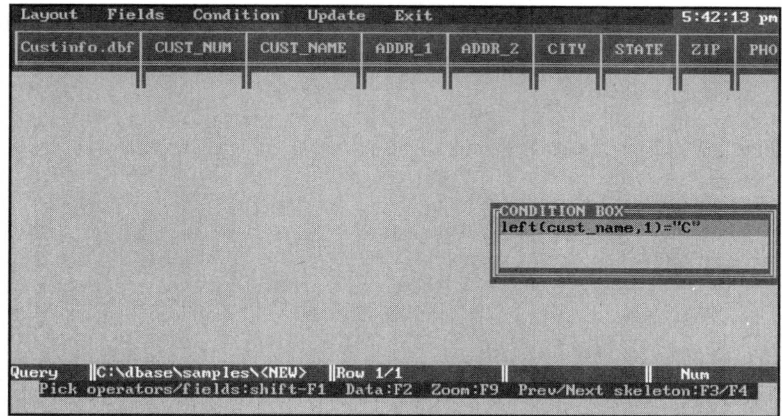


FIG. 13.18

The condition box with a function used as a filtering expression.

4. To view the database as filtered by the expression in the Condition Box, press F2 (Data).

Using expressions in filter conditions helps you refine your database searches. Using functions in these expressions gives you the capability to limit searches to narrow subsets of the database.

For more information on using queries, see Chapter 12, “Using Queries To Search Databases.”

**For Related Information...**

▸▸ “Using Functions,” p. 775.

**FROM HERE...**

# Summary

Expressions and functions are essential parts of your dBASE “tool kit.” Expressions enable you to combine two or more database fields for sophisticated indexing capabilities. Expressions also enable you to refine queries. dBASE functions give you the capability to create indexes combining different field types; you can now create an index with a primary sort on a character field and a secondary sort on a date field or a numeric field—an impossible task without dBASE functions. Expressions and functions also enable you to create more elegant form fields.

Understanding dBASE expressions and functions is a big step toward using dBASE IV's power and flexibility. Using these tools can unlock new ways of looking at the information in your database and presenting that information in reports and screens.

14

CHAPTER

# Designing, Defining, and Creating Relational Databases

Although you may work with database projects that require only one database, most dBASE applications require two, three, or more databases to represent the different types of data in the application. dBASE IV can create sophisticated database applications with multiple databases and tie those databases together in productive ways.

In this chapter, you learn the essentials of working with multiple-file databases. Defining the databases and how they work together is the most important aspect of creating these applications. The first part of this chapter discusses, in as simple terms as possible, the theory of relational databases. When you finish this section, you will not be an expert, but you will know enough to design and develop good multiple-file databases.

The rest of this chapter focuses on defining a multiple-file database system, including the files and the relationships you must tell dBASE about. You also learn to test the databases to make sure the file structures and relations work the way you want them to work. Finally, you learn the techniques of reporting on multiple-file, relational databases. The real strength of dBASE is its capability to create complex databases and relate them together; this chapter gives you the tools to make full use of these capabilities.

# Understanding Relational Databases

If you keep up with news from the computer world, you know that the buzz word in database systems is *relational*. All the latest and greatest database systems are relational—including dBASE and its competitors. If you haven't heard about relational database systems, trust the experts: relational databases are great. But what is this relational stuff and why is it so great?

Rather than trying to define the whys and wherefores of relational database systems, consider an example of how data in the "real world" falls together. From this example, you can see how a relational database can represent real-world data in a computer, making it easier for you to create database systems.

In just about every application you computerize, the data falls into logical groups. For example, a wholesaler computerizing her operation finds that the operation has information about each inventory part, each customer, and each order. In "database-ese," each of these logical groups of information is called a *data entity*. In a database system developed for this company, each entity has its own database file to hold that information.

The *relational* aspect of this system comes into play because a relationship exists between the data entities, and you want the database to represent those relationships. In this example, a relationship exists between the customer and the orders: a customer places each order. Similarly, a relationship exists between the order database and the inventory database: each order is for some part in inventory. Figure 14.1 graphically shows the data entities and the relationships between them.

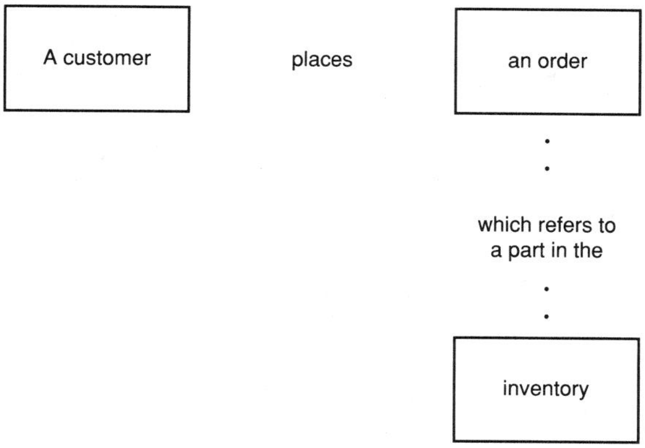

A customer places an order which refers to a part in the inventory

FIG. 14.1
A graphical representation of related databases.

In pre-relational database times, you could define databases and relationships in a database system, but once defined, they were extremely difficult to change. If a user wanted to add more types of information and new relationships to the database structure after the system was finished, that user usually was greeted with gales of laughter, tears, or enormous bills for the redesign and restructuring of the database—not to mention the recoding of many routines. Flexibility was not the name of the pre-relational database game.

Another problem with pre-relational databases is that they often didn't reflect reality, particularly in the business world in which constant changes are taking place. Today you may want the customer information tied to the ordering system; tomorrow you also may want the customer information tied to a customer contact system; the next day you may want the customer information tied to something entirely different. Real relational databases enable you to define these relationships "on the fly," as you need them. In fact, the relationships often change many times in a single database application.

A relational database system, then, can relate two or more database files to each other, enabling you to draw information from all files based on these relationships. When using a relational database system, you can quickly and easily change the relationships between the files.

Relational database systems such as dBASE have advantages over other types of systems. dBASE enables you to represent the real world more realistically in your computerized database system. Relational databases also make your system more consistent and reliable because you have almost no duplication of information in different database files. And because you have no duplication, a relational database system such as dBASE saves disk space and reduces the effort required for data entry and editing.

Consider this real-world situation: a company has a database of customer information that contains names, addresses, telephone numbers, and other important information about each customer. The company needs to track the orders it receives from its customers; the information for each order should contain the name, address, and telephone number of the customer, and information on the items the customer ordered. Storing the customer information for the order takes up a great deal of space in the computer and requires that the order-entry people enter the customer information for each order. But why reenter customer information when that data is already stored in the customer database?

Instead of entering the customer information for each order, the database can simply assign a customer number to each customer in the customer database. When entering an order, you enter that customer number rather than the name and address of the customer. You then tell dBASE that the customer database and the order database are related to each other by the customer number that exists in each database structure. When you access an order record, dBASE looks up and retrieves the customer information for the customer placing the order, based on the customer number that exists in both databases. This is the relational aspect of dBASE; you relate two files based on a field common to both files.

# Designing a Relational Database

In Part II of this book, you learned to design a database system with only one file. Designing, defining, and creating a multiple-file, relational database is not much different, but it requires more thought at the beginning and more testing along the way to ensure the results you want. You must ensure that the fields necessary to define the relation exist in the related database files. The next sections explain the steps you take to design a relational database:

1. Define the data entities for the system.
2. Decide what databases and fields to include in the system.
3. Determine how the data is related.
4. Refine the database design.

## Defining the Data Entities

When designing a relational database system in dBASE, start as you do when designing a single-file system, with a clear idea of the output you need from the system. In nearly all cases, you do not create a system from thin air; you usually automate a manual system or improve on an existing computerized system. This gives you a head start on what the system must do. You might begin by thinking about the way in which you want the system to present the results of data inquiries and the kinds of reports and screen output that will be produced.

Looking at the output you need from the system, you can identify information you must have in the databases. For example, you may need information for Customer and Inventory reports that can be taken from the CUSTOMER and INVNTRY databases. One other database file is necessary—the ORDER file. This database file must contain information about the customer placing the order, the date of the order, the salesperson who took the order, and what was ordered (for simplicity's sake, assume that an order contains only one item from inventory). The ORDER database file must be related to the other two files.

You can design the ORDER database to contain the customer information—name, address, city, state—and information about what was ordered—the part number, description, and price—but doing so is not efficient. The customer information is already in the CUSTOMER database, and the inventory information is in the INVNTRY database. If you duplicate the customer and inventory information in each ORDER record, you must enter it each time you take an order, and you must make sure that you enter it correctly each time. With its relational capabilities, dBASE can tie the ORDER database with the CUSTOMER and INVNTRY databases so that you can access the data in those two databases without having to store it in the ORDER database.

## Deciding What To Include in the Databases

When you start to design a database, don't worry about the relationships that may exist; concentrate only on the data the system needs. After you design the individual database structures, you can easily define the relationships and how to implement them in dBASE. Tables 14.1 through 14.3 show the three databases for the example system and the data you need (note that the field names given in the first column are not what you would type in dBASE):

**Table 14.1 Structure for CUSTOMER Database**

| Field name | Type | Width | Dec | Index |
|---|---|---|---|---|
| Customer Name | Character | 25 | | Y |
| Address 1 | Character | 25 | | N |
| Address 2 | Character | 25 | | N |
| City | Character | 15 | | N |
| State | Character | 2 | | Y |
| ZIP Code | Character | 9 | | Y |
| Phone | Character | 10 | | N |
| Contact | Character | 10 | | N |
| Credit limit | Numeric | 8 | 2 | N |
| Last purchase date | Date | 8 | | N |
| Last purchase amount | Numeric | 8 | 2 | N |
| Preferred Customer | Logical | 1 | | N |

**Table 14.2 Structure for INVENTORY Database**

| Field name | Type | Width | Dec | Index |
|---|---|---|---|---|
| Part Number | Character | 15 | | Y |
| Keyword | Character | 10 | | Y |
| Description | Character | 25 | | N |
| Supplier | Character | 25 | | Y |
| Qty On Hand | Numeric | 5 | 0 | N |
| Reorder point | Numeric | 5 | 0 | N |
| Price | Numeric | 8 | 2 | N |
| Cost | Numeric | 8 | 2 | N |
| Auto Reorder? | Logical | 1 | | N |

**Table 14.3 Structure for ORDER Database**

| Field name | Type | Width | Dec | Index |
|---|---|---|---|---|
| Customer Name | Character | 25 | | Y |
| Address 1 | Character | 25 | | N |
| Address 2 | Character | 25 | | N |
| City | Character | 15 | | N |
| State | Character | 2 | | Y |
| ZIP Code | Character | 9 | | Y |
| Phone | Character | 10 | | N |
| Order Date | Date | 8 | | N |
| Part Number | Character | 15 | | Y |
| Quantity | Numeric | 8 | 0 | N |
| Price | Numeric | 8 | 2 | N |
| Salesperson | Character | 3 | | N |

Although this chapter introduces the concept of including a CUST_NUM field in the CUSTOMER and ORDER databases, that field is not included in these database designs. At this point in the design process, concentrate on the data you need in the system; you don't *need* a customer number in the CUSTOMER or the ORDER database. In each of these databases, however, you do need the customer's name and address.

After you are sure that the database design incorporates the information you need to generate the reports and query screens, you are ready to figure out the relationships between the database files.

## Determining How Data Is Related

Computer system designers have long relied on graphical techniques (that is, scribblings on paper) to define computer systems. This section describes a graphical technique for figuring out the relationships you should include in the dBASE system you are designing.

First, draw a small box and put into it the name of one of the databases—for example, the CUSTOMER database. If you think about how CUSTOMER relates to other databases in the dBASE system, you know that a relationship exists between the customers and the orders of the company: customers place orders. Draw another box to the left of the CUSTOMER box and name it ORDER. Now draw a diamond between the two boxes (diamonds represent a relation) and draw lines between the boxes and the diamond. Figure 14.2 shows the diagram.

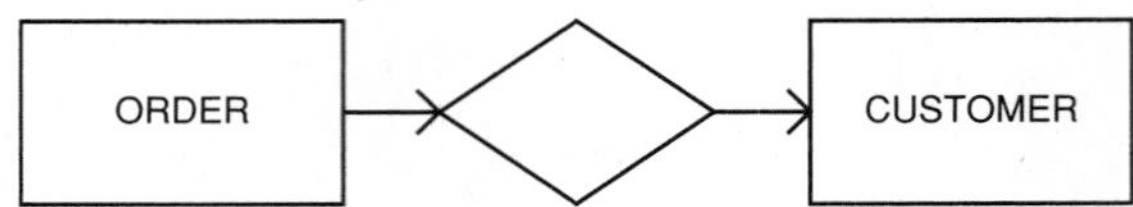


FIG. 14.2

The ORDER and CUSTOMER databases with a relationship between them.

You should give the relationship a name, for the sake of clarity (in this example, the relationship can be called *is placed by*; that is, ORDER is placed by CUSTOMER). You also should define how you want to implement this relationship; in other words, how you want to define the relationship to dBASE.

dBASE relates databases through a common field. Each database on either side of the relation must have a field that contains the same information. In the *controlling* database, you tell dBASE what the field is. In the *controlled* database, you can give the field a different name (although the field must be of the same data type and size), but the database must be indexed on that field if the relationship is to work.

In this example, the common information between the ORDER and CUSTOMER databases is the customer's name. If the ORDER database has the customer's name, dBASE can relate each record in ORDER with the proper record in CUSTOMER, providing you with access to CUSTOMER fields (such as the address, city, and state). You can use the NAME field in both ORDER and CUSTOMER to relate the two databases. However, you can use a trick that saves storage space, makes dBASE more efficient in using the relationship, and helps you be more accurate.

Instead of storing the entire customer's name in the ORDER database (which requires a large field and—because of spelling errors—increases the possibility that dBASE will not find the right record in the CUSTOMER database), replace the long NAME field in the ORDER database with a shorter field in which you store a customer number; name this field CUST_NUM. Then modify the CUSTOMER database to add a CUST_NUM field, making sure that you index on that field.

dBASE uses the two CUST_NUM fields to match records in the ORDER database to the customer information in the CUSTOMER database.

Wherever possible, use this technique to reduce redundant storage of large fields and to decrease the possibility of mistakes. Errors when entering a 1-to-6 digit customer number are much less likely than when entering up to 25 characters of a customer name. Now the database diagram looks like figure 14.3.

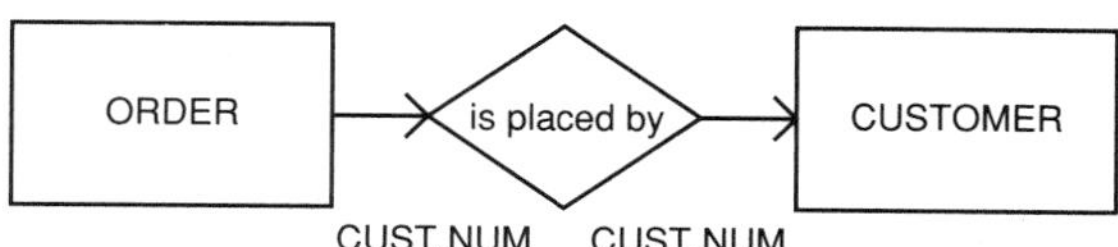


FIG. 14.3

The ORDER and CUSTOMER databases related by common fields.

A concept essential to your understanding of relational databases is *controlling database* and *controlled database*. When you use a relation in a dBASE database to access data in different files, one database file is the controlling database; the other is the controlled database. If you print a report from the ORDER database using the CUST_NUM relation to get information about the customer from the CUSTOMER database, ORDER is the controlling database and CUSTOMER is the controlled database. Because dBASE ties a record in CUSTOMER to a record in ORDER, ORDER controls which record in CUSTOMER is accessed. The controlled database must be indexed on the related field (in this case, CUSTOMER must be indexed on the CUST_NUM field). Make sure that your diagram makes a note of the need to index that field.

Now do the same thing with the INVNTRY database, drawing and defining the relationship between it and the ORDER database (see fig. 14.4). This diagram is called an *entity-relation diagram*. The diagram presents the entities (the database files) and the relationships (the way they are tied together) in a graphical, easy-to-understand format.

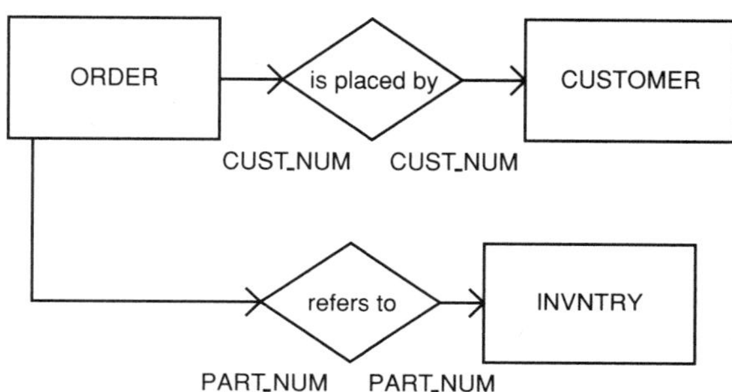


FIG. 14.4

A completed entity-relation diagram.

You can make changes to dBASE databases with incredible ease; flexibility is essential in designing and creating dBASE databases. Still, diagramming the database as described in this section really helps to ensure that the databases have the fields needed to tie them together, and that you have a good idea of the structure of the system you are designing.

## Refining the Database Design

After you have created the entity-relation diagram for your system, you can refine the database structures to include the necessary relational fields. Tables 14.4 through 14.6 show the refined structures of the three files (again, the field names given in the first columns are *not* what you type in dBASE):

**Table 14.4 Refined Structure for CUSTOMER Database**

| Field name | Type | Width | Dec | Index |
|---|---|---|---|---|
| Customer Number | Numeric | 6 | 0 | Y |
| Customer Name | Character | 25 | | Y |
| Address 1 | Character | 25 | | N |
| Address 2 | Character | 25 | | N |
| City | Character | 15 | | N |
| State | Character | 2 | | Y |
| ZIP Code | Character | 9 | | Y |
| Phone | Character | 10 | | N |
| Contact | Character | 10 | | N |
| Credit limit | Numeric | 8 | 2 | N |
| Last purchase date | Date | | 8 | N |
| Last purchase amount | Numeric | 8 | 2 | N |
| Preferred Customer | Logical | 1 | | N |

**Table 14.5 Refined Structure for INVNTRY Database**

| Field name | Type | Width | Dec | Index |
|---|---|---|---|---|
| Part Number | Character | 15 | | Y |
| Keyword | Character | 10 | | Y |
| Description | Character | 25 | | N |
| Supplier | Character | 25 | | Y |
| Qty On Hand | Numeric | 5 | 0 | N |
| Reorder point | Numeric | 5 | 0 | N |
| Price | Numeric | 8 | 2 | N |
| Cost | Numeric | 8 | 2 | N |
| Auto Reorder? | Logical | 1 | | N |

**Table 14.6 Refined Structure for ORDR Database**

| Field name | Type | Width | Dec | Index |
|---|---|---|---|---|
| Customer Number | Numeric | 6 | 0 | Y |
| Order Date | Date | 8 | | N |
| Salesperson | Character | 3 | | N |
| Part Number | Character | 15 | | Y |
| Quantity | Numeric | 5 | 0 | N |

Note that because the word *order* is a reserved word in dBASE, the name of the ORDER database is changed to ORDR. The second change is the addition of a CUST_NUM (Customer Number) field in the CUSTOMER.DBF file and the replacement of the customer information in ORDR.DBF file with the same CUST_NUM field. Finally, the INVENTORY database has been renamed INVNTRY, to meet the DOS restriction of eight-character file names.

Now the relational database design is complete. You know what data the files must contain, what indexes must be created, and how to relate the database files together. The next step is to transfer the paper design into dBASE.

**For Related Information...**

◂◂ "Designing Valid and Reliable Databases," p. 23.

# Creating Multiple-File Relational Databases in dBASE IV

After you define the database system on paper, you must define it to dBASE. Doing so is no different from defining single-file databases; in fact, the process is simply defining single-file databases one at a time until all the related databases are complete.

Entering data into related databases is also the same as entering data into single-file databases. You can create custom data-entry screens as described in Chapter 9. Remember, though, that the data you enter in the common, relational field must be identical in both databases. Customer numbers of 1 for a record in the ORDR database and 00001 in the related CUSTOMER database do not relate to each other.

The following steps summarize how to define this multiple-file database to dBASE IV and how to enter information into these databases:

1. Open a new catalog by choosing Use a Different Catalog from the Catalog menu in the Control Center. When the Catalog list menu appears, choose <create>. Enter the name for this catalog, *ORD_RPT*, when prompted. dBASE appends the CAT extension and opens a new, blank catalog in the Control Center.
2. With the highlight on <create> in the Data panel, press Enter to define the first database. The Database definition screen appears. Enter the fields in the ORDR database, as shown in table 14.6. When you are finished, the Database definition screen looks like figure 14.5.
3. After you define ORDR.DBF, press Ctrl-End to save the design. When you see the prompt `Save as:`, type *ORDR*. dBASE adds the DBF extension.
4. Although you can enter records now, you first should define the CUSTOMER and INVNTRY databases. Reply NO to the question: `Input data records now?`
5. Repeat steps 2 through 4 for the CUSTOMER and INVNTRY databases.

```
Layout   Organize   Append   Go To   Exit                          1:43:08 pm

 Num | Field Name | Field Type | Width | Dec | Index     Bytes remaining:   3963

  1    CUST_NUM     Numeric        6      0      Y
  2    ORDR_DATE    Date           8             N
  3    SALESPERS    Character      3             N
  4    PART_NUM     Character     15             Y
  5    QTY          Numeric        5      0      N

Database ║C:\dbase\samples\ORDR   ║Field 1/5   ║         ║      CapsIns
           Enter the field name.  Insert/Delete field:Ctrl-N/Ctrl-U
Field names begin with a letter and may contain letters, digits and underscores
```

FIG. 14.5

The ORDR.DBF file defined in the Database definition screen.

Use the mouse to access the Database design screen by double-clicking the <create> label in the Data column in the Control Center. When you have finished defining the database structure, click Exit; then click Save Changes And Exit.

You now have defined the three necessary databases, which appear in the Data panel of the Control Center. Now you can enter data into the databases. If you want to design custom data-entry screens, as you learned to do in Chapter 9, you should do that now.

Because the ORDR database uses its CUST_NUM field to relate to the CUSTOMER database and PART_NUM to relate to the INVNTRY database, the values you enter into these two fields also must exist in the related files. If you enter a record into the ORDR database with a customer number of 5, for example, you must be sure that a record with a customer number of 5 exists in the CUSTOMER database; otherwise, when you later try to relate the two databases, dBASE will not be able to find a CUSTOMER record to relate to the ORDR record. The same holds true for values entered into the PART_NUM field of ORDR. If that value is not in a PART_NUM field of the INVNTRY database, dBASE cannot relate an INVNTRY record with the ORDR record.

Enter the data into the two related databases first. Then you can print out the databases and have a reference when you enter information into ORDR, making sure that each value you enter into the related fields actually exists in the related databases.

To complete and print your report, perform the following steps:

1. Highlight CUSTOMER in the Data panel and press F2.

   If you have designed a custom form for this database, highlight that form in the Forms panel and press F2.

2. When you have entered all the customer records, press Ctrl-End to return to the Control Center.
3. Press Shift-F9 (Quick Report) to bring up the Print menu.
4. Make sure that your printer is plugged in, turned on, and hooked up to your computer. Choose Begin Printing from the Print menu.

This procedure gives you a printout of your CUSTOMER database, which you can use later to ensure the validity of the CUST_NUM values entered into the ORDR database.

Repeat steps 1 through 3 for the INVNTRY database, adding the inventory information you have. Again, print out the database to check PART_NUM values when entering information into the ORDR database. To enter your information into the ORDR database, perform the following steps:

1. Highlight the ORDR database in the Data panel and press F2.

   If you have created a custom entry form for ORDR, highlight the name of that form in the Forms panel and press F2.

2. When you enter a value into the CUST_NUM field, check the CUSTOMER database printout to make sure that the entered value exists in that database. This check ensures that you do not enter CUST_NUM values that don't exist, causing problems when you later try to relate the two databases.
3. When you enter a value into the PART_NUM field, check the value in the PART_NUM database printout. Again, this helps you make sure that you enter only valid part numbers.

Entering data into a relational database system is no different from entering data into a single database system, except that you must ensure that the values in the relational fields, such as CUST_NUM and PART_NUM, are valid. If you enter a value that doesn't exist in the related database, dBASE cannot draw information from the related database for your reports and queries.

FROM HERE...

**For Related Information...**

◂◂ "Adding Records to the Database," p. 142.

# Working with Multiple-File Relational Databases

When you want to view or obtain a report on a relational database system, you first set up a query that defines the files in the relational system and the way they are related. Next, you put into the query View skeleton the fields you want to include in the report, making these fields available on the Report design work surface. You then can use the query to test the database design and the relationships, ensuring that the proper indexes are in place and that links between the files work properly. Finally, you can move to the Report design screen and actually design the report.

The remainder of this chapter explains how to define the relational database you designed in the first part of the chapter. You set up the catalog and use the Query design screen to define the system to dBASE IV. Finally, you create a report that draws information from all three databases.

## Setting Up the Catalog and Query

After you define the databases to dBASE, you should create a catalog that contains the related files. Although you can just add the files to one big catalog, large dBASE systems with many different files and relations are more understandable when you maintain a catalog of database files for specific purposes. Suppose that the database system has the following files:

| File | Description |
|---|---|
| CUSTOMER | A customer information database |
| ORDR | A database of orders, related to CUSTOMER |
| INVNTRY | An inventory database, related to ORDR |

In this example, only three database files are related; all three are required for the queries and reports of the chapter. In real dBASE IV systems, however, you may have many database files (20 or more is common), many queries relating these files in different ways, and different reports. Each report may require a different combination of database files and a different query to control the report output. Although dBASE remembers which files and queries are required for each report, you may find your system easier to work with if you create catalogs for subsets of the data.

In an accounting system, for example, you may create a catalog that contains files and reports for working with the General Ledger. Another catalog may be for Accounts Payable, a third for Accounts Receivable, another for Inventory, and yet another for Payroll. Each catalog contains database files, queries, forms, reports, and labels used by that part of the system. This approach keeps your system more understandable and workable.

You already have created a catalog for this example called ORD_RPT. If you have designed queries, forms, reports, or labels that you want to add to this catalog, move to the appropriate panel and choose Add File to Catalog from the Catalog menu. A file list with the appropriate files (queries if you are in the Queries panel, forms if in the Forms panel, and so on) appears. Choose the file you want to add and press Enter. Continue this process until the catalog contains all the files you need.

When adding a file to the catalog, use the mouse to select the file. Click the file name in the selection list, and then click theSelectlabel in the navigation line. Click Accept to add the file to the catalog.

Figure 14.6 shows the ORD_RPT catalog. For the report you are creating, you want ORDR to be the controlling database; make it the active one by highlighting it in the Data panel and pressing Enter. After making ORDR the active database, move to the Queries panel, highlight <create>, and press Enter. dBASE presents the Query design screen, ready to define the relationships between the three database files.

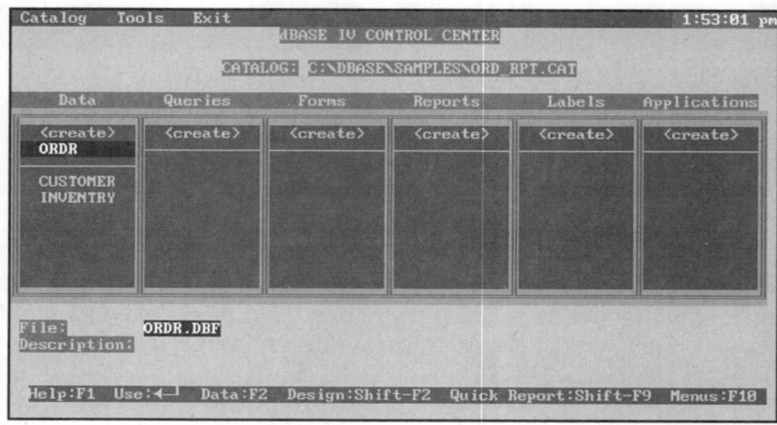


FIG. 14.6

The ORD_RPT catalog, with the three databases included.

# Using Queries To Set Up the Relationships

Now you have databases that are related: ORDR and CUSTOMER through the CUST_NUM fields, and ORDR and INVNTRY through the PART_NUM fields. To tell dBASE IV how these databases are related, you use a Query. Place the databases in the Query (the controlling ORDR database first), and then relate them by telling dBASE, in the file skeletons, what fields connect the databases. (See Chapter 12 for a detailed explanation of file skeletons.)

After you set up the query properly, you can test the relational aspects of the database system from the Query design screen and make changes as necessary. When you are confident that the query ties the databases together properly, you can save the query and use it later to create reports on the relational database system.

For the following examples, you use the relational database system designed in the first part of this chapter. The system uses three databases: ORDR, CUSTOMER, and INVNTRY. The object is to obtain a report that prints out the orders placed by each customer, with the part description and the customer's address.

# Defining the Relational Databases To Query

When dBASE displays the Query design screen, you see a file skeleton for the controlling database (the currently active database). You also see a View skeleton of all the fields in that database. The first step in defining a relational database system is to add the necessary files and indexes to the Query design screen.

Follow these steps to add the CUSTOMER database file to the query for the ORDR database and to specify the CUST_NUM field as the common field:

1. From the Control Center, move the cursor to the Queries panel and highlight <create>. Press Enter to display the Query design screen, with a file skeleton for the ORDR database.
2. Add the indexes you created to the controlling file, ORDR, by setting Include Indexes to YES in the Fields menu. Notice the symbols that appear next to each indexed field. Figure 14.7 shows the Query design screen with the indexes in place.

Toggle the Include Indexes settings from NO to YES by clicking the option in the Fields menu with the mouse.

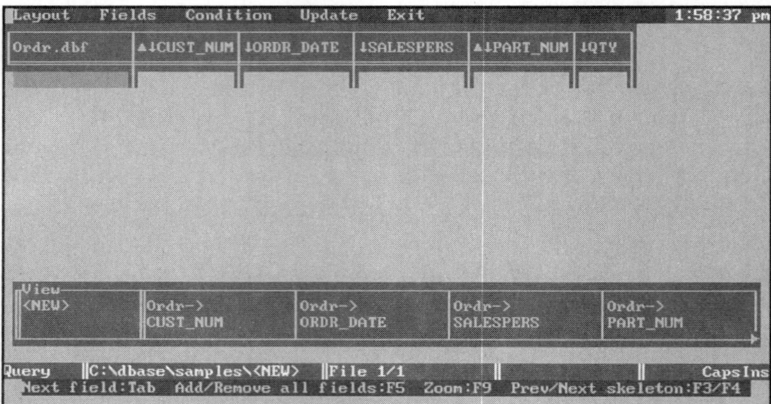


FIG. 14.7

The Query design screen with indexes attached.

3. Add the first related database, CUSTOMER, to the query by choosing Add File To Query from the Layout menu. When the list of database files appears, highlight CUSTOMER.DBF and press Enter (see fig. 14.8).



FIG. 14.8

Selecting CUSTOMER.DBF from the file list.

4. When the Query design screen reappears, a file skeleton for CUSTOMER.DBF is on the work surface. You should include the indexes of this database by placing the cursor in the

CUSTOMER.DBF file skeleton and then setting Include Indexes on the Fields menu to YES.

If you do not include indexes, dBASE creates them when it processes the query. These indexes are temporary and must be created each time the query is processed, however, which can take a great deal of time in a large database. For efficiency, make sure that the controlled database is indexed on the relational field and that Include Indexes is set to YES. Figure 14.9 shows the Query design screen with the two database file skeletons.

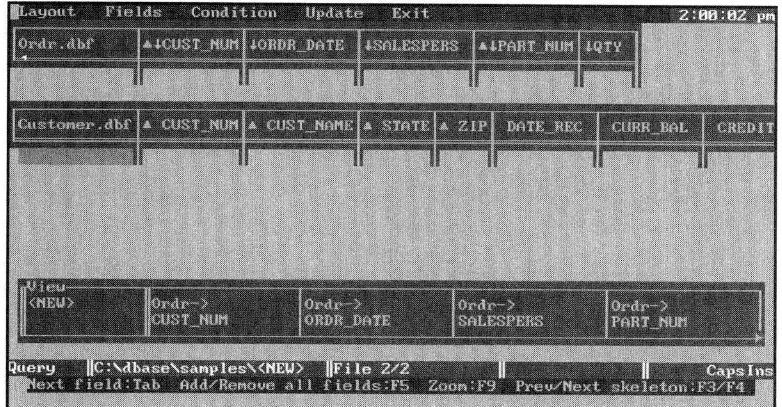


FIG. 14.9

The Query design work surface with two file skeletons.

5. Now tell the query to link the two database files. You know that the CUST_NUM field relates ORDR.DBF and CUSTOMER.DBF together. Highlight the CUST_NUM field in the ORDR.DBF file skeleton. From the Layout menu, choose Create Link By Pointing. With this option, you can “point” to the two fields that establish the relation and have the query set up the link. After you select Create Link By Pointing, `LINK1` appears on the Query design work surface, below CUST_NUM in the ORDR.DBF file skeleton, identifying the CUST_NUM field as one-half of the link between the two files.

6. In the message bar at the bottom of the screen, dBASE prompts you to move the cursor to the file skeleton of another file—in this case, the CUSTOMER.DBF file skeleton. Move the cursor to the CUST_NUM field in that file skeleton and press Enter. `LINK1` appears under this field, telling you that the two files are now linked, or *related*, based on the values in those two fields. Figure 14.10 shows the Query design work surface with the two files linked.

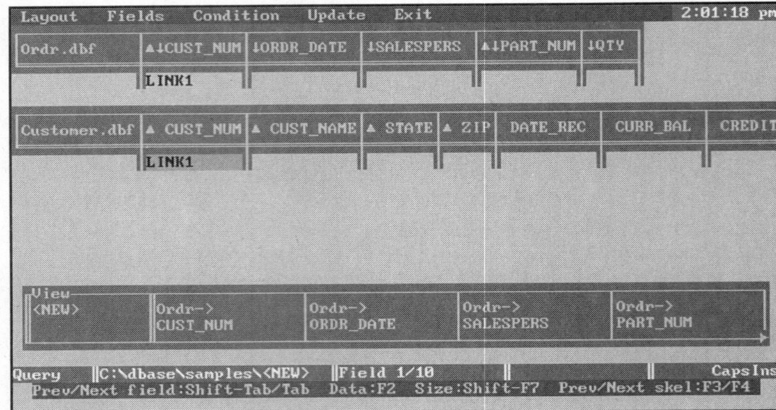


FIG. 14.10

Linking the ORDR and CUSTOMER databases.

7. Move the highlight to the CUSTOMER.DBF file skeleton and from the database, select a field you want to add to the View skeleton to test the relation. Add the field CUST_NAME to the View skeleton by highlighting it and pressing F5 (Add). The work surface now appears as shown in figure 14.11.

```
Layout  Fields  Condition  Update  Exit                        2:04:14 pm
Ordr.dbf      ▲↓CUST_NUM ↓ORDR_DATE ↓SALESPERS ▲↓PART_NUM ↓QTY
              LINK1
Customer.dbf  ▲ CUST_NUM ▲↓CUST_NAME ▲ STATE ▲ ZIP  DATE_REC  CURR_BAL  CREDIT
              LINK1
View
<NEW>         Ordr->      Ordr->      Ordr->      Ordr->
              CUST_NUM    ORDR_DATE   SALESPERS   PART_NUM
                 R/O
Query  C:\dbase\samples\<NEW>  Field 2/10                         CapsIns
  Prev/Next field:Shift-Tab/Tab  Data:F2  Size:Shift-F7  Prev/Next skel:F3/F4
```

FIG. 14.11

Preparing to test the relationship between two database files.

8. Test the query by pressing F2 (Data). The view of the data looks like figure 14.12.

Figure 14.12 shows that the query presents information about each order (the PART_NUM and QTY fields) from the ORDR database and about each customer (the CUST_NAME field) from the CUSTOMER database. If you want to check this relation, look at the printout of the

CUSTOMER database you generated earlier. dBASE looks at the value in the CUST_NUM field in the ORDR database and, through the LINK1 link specified on the Query design screen, retrieves the correct CUST_NAME from the CUSTOMER database.

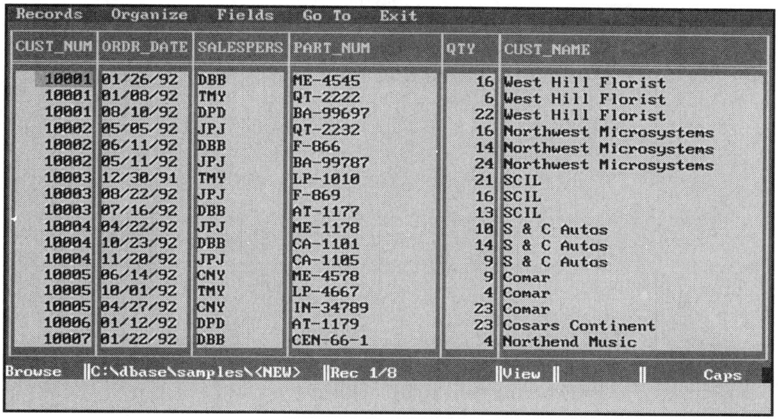

Records Organize Fields Go To Exit

| CUST_NUM | ORDR_DATE | SALESPERS | PART_NUM | QTY | CUST_NAME |
|---|---|---|---|---|---|
| 10001 | 01/26/92 | DBB | ME-4545 | 16 | West Hill Florist |
| 10001 | 01/08/92 | TMY | QT-2222 | 6 | West Hill Florist |
| 10001 | 08/10/92 | DPD | BA-99697 | 22 | West Hill Florist |
| 10002 | 05/05/92 | JPJ | QT-2232 | 16 | Northwest Microsystems |
| 10002 | 06/11/92 | DBB | F-866 | 14 | Northwest Microsystems |
| 10002 | 05/11/92 | JPJ | BA-99787 | 24 | Northwest Microsystems |
| 10003 | 12/30/91 | TMY | LP-1010 | 21 | SCIL |
| 10003 | 08/22/92 | JPJ | F-869 | 16 | SCIL |
| 10003 | 07/16/92 | DBB | AT-1177 | 13 | SCIL |
| 10004 | 04/22/92 | JPJ | ME-1178 | 10 | S & C Autos |
| 10004 | 10/23/92 | DBB | CA-1101 | 14 | S & C Autos |
| 10004 | 11/20/92 | JPJ | CA-1105 | 9 | S & C Autos |
| 10005 | 06/14/92 | CNY | ME-4578 | 9 | Comar |
| 10005 | 10/01/92 | TMY | LP-4667 | 4 | Comar |
| 10005 | 04/27/92 | CNY | IN-34789 | 23 | Comar |
| 10006 | 01/12/92 | DPD | AT-1179 | 23 | Cosars Continent |
| 10007 | 01/22/92 | DBB | CEN-66-1 | 4 | Northend Music |

Browse ‖C:\dbase\samples\<NEW> ‖Rec 1/8 ‖View ‖ ‖ Caps

FIG. 14.12

The view of a query for two related databases.

Now add and test another link. The ease with which you can add the third database reveals a strong point of dBASE's query by example feature: you can add and test one database file to the query at a time, making sure that the design is sound before moving on.

To add the third database file of this system to the query, return from the View screen to the Query design screen by pressing Shift-F2. (If you are on the Control Center screen, highlight in the Queries panel the query you just saved, and press Enter to return to the Query design screen.) Follow these steps to add the INVNTRY database to the query:

1. Choose Add File To Query from the Layout menu. When the file list appears, highlight the INVNTRY.DBF file and press Enter.

2. Add the indexes to the INVNTRY.DBF file skeleton by setting Include Indexes to YES on the Fields menu. The Query design work surface looks like figure 14.13.

3. Set the relation between the ORDR database and the INVNTRY database. Instead of using the Create Link By Pointing technique, you can set the links manually by moving to the ORDR.DBF file skeleton and selecting the PART_NUM field. (Remember that PART_NUM ties the ORDR and INVNTRY databases together.) Type *LINK2*. Press F4 (Next) twice to move to the INVNTRY.DBF file skeleton and then press Tab to highlight the PART_NUM field in that skeleton. Type *LINK2* in this field. These actions have the same effect as using the Create Link By Pointing process.

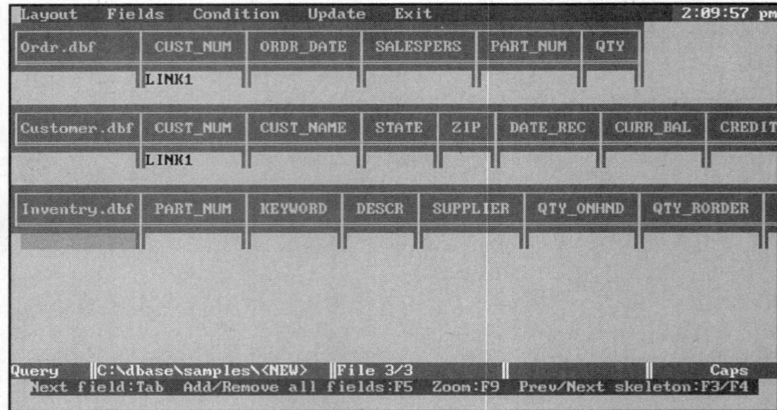


**FIG. 14.13**

Adding the third database to the query.

> **NOTE** You can use almost any word to establish the link between two databases; you don't have to use *LINK1* or *LINK2* (but don't use dBASE reserved words, such as COUNT, SUM or DO). You must type the same word in each of the relational fields, however, or dBASE becomes confused and rejects the query. For example, if you try to establish a link between ORDER.DBF and CUSTOMER.DBF by placing the word *ORDLINK* in the CUSTOMER file skeleton and *CUSTLINK* in the ORDER file skeleton, dBASE reports `File not linked`.

4. Return to the INVNTRY.DBF file skeleton and highlight the KEYWORD field; press F5 (Add) to add this field to the View skeleton. Adding this field enables you to test whether the ORDR and INVNTRY database relation is working. The Query design screen now appears as shown in figure 14.14.

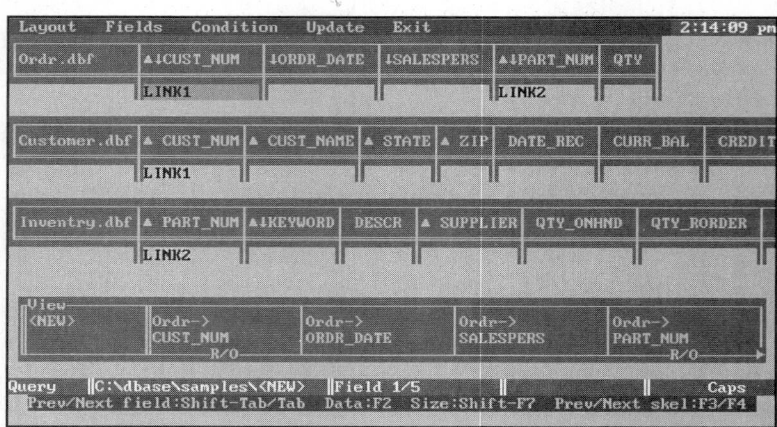


**FIG. 14.14**

Including fields from all three databases in the View skeleton.

5. Press F2 (Data) to test the query and the relational design of the database system. Figure 14.15 shows the KEYWORD field from the INVNTRY database, proving that the relation works. If you want, return to the Control Center and check the INVNTRY database to see whether the PART_NUM and KEYWORD fields are correct. dBASE is now getting information from the CUSTOMER database through the LINK1 link, and from the INVNTRY database through the LINK2 link. The relational database system works!

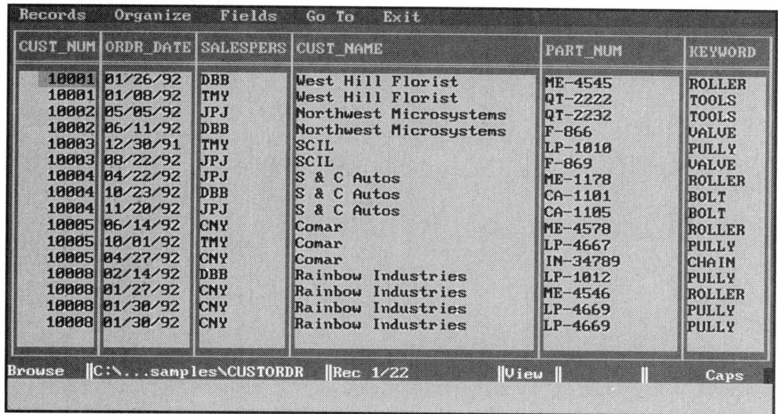

Records Organize Fields Go To Exit
CUST_NUM ORDR_DATE SALESPERS CUST_NAME PART_NUM KEYWORD
10001 01/26/92 DBB West Hill Florist ME-4545 ROLLER
10001 01/08/92 TMY West Hill Florist QT-2222 TOOLS
10002 05/05/92 JPJ Northwest Microsystems QT-2232 TOOLS
10002 06/11/92 DBB Northwest Microsystems F-866 VALVE
10003 12/30/91 TMY SCIL LP-1010 PULLY
10003 08/22/92 JPJ SCIL F-869 VALVE
10004 04/22/92 JPJ S & C Autos ME-1178 ROLLER
10004 10/23/92 DBB S & C Autos CA-1101 BOLT
10004 11/20/92 JPJ S & C Autos CA-1105 BOLT
10005 06/14/92 CNY Comar ME-4578 ROLLER
10005 10/01/92 TMY Comar LP-4667 PULLY
10005 04/27/92 CNY Comar IN-34789 CHAIN
10008 02/14/92 DBB Rainbow Industries LP-1012 PULLY
10008 01/27/92 CNY Rainbow Industries ME-4546 ROLLER
10008 01/30/92 CNY Rainbow Industries LP-4669 PULLY
10008 01/30/92 CNY Rainbow Industries LP-4669 PULLY
Browse C:\...samples\CUSTORDR Rec 1/22 View Caps


FIG. 14.15

The view of three linked databases.

**NOTE** Notice that as you add more database files and relations, the speed of query processing slows down. dBASE does a great deal of work when you ask it to tie multiple files together and display a report. Strangely enough, sorting the view as described in the following section can speed up the query-processing time.

Now you know that the database design works. The relational fields and indexes do their jobs, tying together three different databases and enabling you to retrieve data from one database based on the value in another. This is the heart of a relational database system, and you know how to create and use one.

# Sorting and Indexing a Query

You can add sorts or indexes to a query for a relational database system just as you can for a single-database query. Although the ORDR database controls what records are processed and placed in the View screen, you can sort on any field present in the View skeleton. This capability enables you to present the view sorted on CUST_NAME, for example.

To sort the View screen on the CUST_NAME field, follow these steps:

1. Press Shift-F2 to return to the Query design screen from the View screen.
2. Move the cursor to the field on which you want to sort the view—in this case, CUST_NAME in the CUSTOMER.DBF file skeleton.
3. Choose Sort On This Field from the Fields menu and choose Ascending Dictionary or type *AscDict1* (indicating that this is the first dictionary-order sort in the query). Figure 14.16 shows the Query design screen at this point.

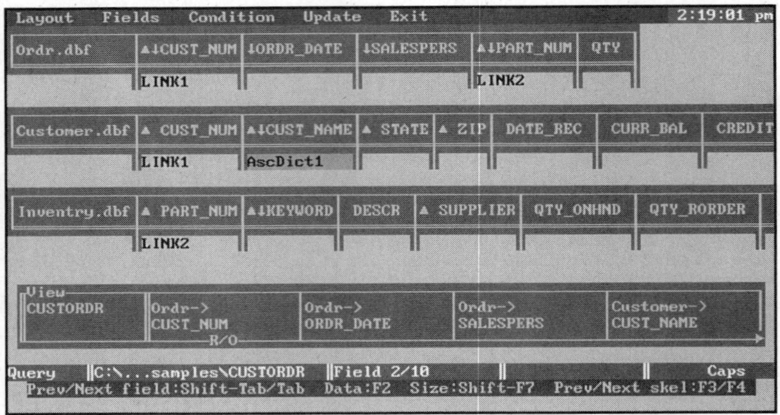


FIG. 14.16

Sorting the query on the CUST_NAME field.

4. Press F2 (Data) to see the view. Figure 14.17 shows that the view has been sorted on the CUST_NAME field. This extremely powerful capability gives you the flexibility to create reports sorted on any field you want.

**NOTE**

You can sort on a field that is not in the View skeleton. However, because the reason for sorting is to put the View records in some kind of order, this is not recommended. The View records sort correctly, but the sort order is not apparent, because the sorted field is not visible. You should always include the sort field in the view for clarity.

As with single-database queries, you can use indexes to increase the speed of the view processing. After you test the query and know that the database design accomplishes your goals, save the query by choosing Save This Query from the Layout menu, or Save Changes And Exit from the Exit menu. If you have not saved this query previously, you are prompted for a file name. You then can put this query into action when you want to report on the relational system.

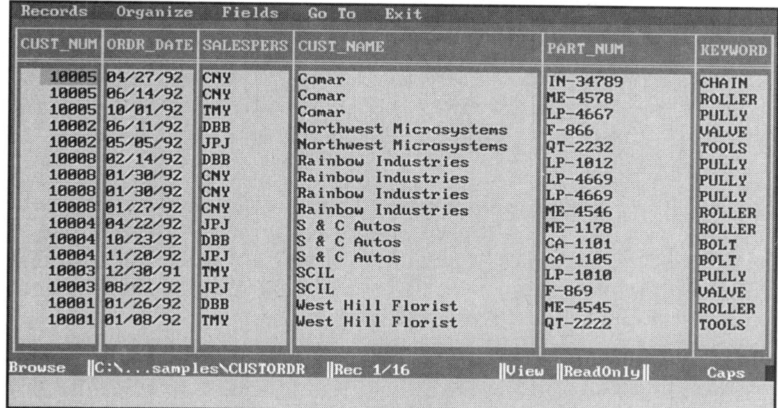


| CUST_NUM | ORDR_DATE | SALESPERS | CUST_NAME | PART_NUM | KEYWORD |
|---|---|---|---|---|---|
| 10005 | 04/27/92 | CNY | Comar | IN-34789 | CHAIN |
| 10005 | 06/14/92 | CNY | Comar | ME-4578 | ROLLER |
| 10005 | 10/01/92 | TMY | Comar | LP-4667 | PULLY |
| 10002 | 06/11/92 | DBB | Northwest Microsystems | F-866 | VALVE |
| 10002 | 05/05/92 | JPJ | Northwest Microsystems | QT-2232 | TOOLS |
| 10008 | 02/14/92 | DBB | Rainbow Industries | LP-1012 | PULLY |
| 10008 | 01/30/92 | CNY | Rainbow Industries | LP-4669 | PULLY |
| 10008 | 01/30/92 | CNY | Rainbow Industries | LP-4669 | PULLY |
| 10008 | 01/27/92 | CNY | Rainbow Industries | ME-4546 | ROLLER |
| 10004 | 04/22/92 | JPJ | S & C Autos | ME-1178 | ROLLER |
| 10004 | 10/23/92 | DBB | S & C Autos | CA-1101 | BOLT |
| 10004 | 11/20/92 | JPJ | S & C Autos | CA-1105 | BOLT |
| 10003 | 12/30/91 | TMY | SCIL | LP-1010 | PULLY |
| 10003 | 08/22/92 | JPJ | SCIL | F-869 | VALVE |
| 10001 | 01/26/92 | DBB | West Hill Florist | ME-4545 | ROLLER |
| 10001 | 01/08/92 | TMY | West Hill Florist | QT-2222 | TOOLS |



FIG. 14.17

The view sorted on the CUST_NAME field.

**For Related Information...**

▸▸ "SET RELATION TO," p. 888.

▸▸ "SET VIEW TO," p. 895.

**FROM HERE...**

# Reporting on Multiple-File Database Systems

Reporting on multiple-file, relational database systems is not much different from reporting on single-file systems. As with a single-file report, you set up a query to define the required files and fields within those files. Then you design and test the report on the Report design screen. When the design is the way you want it, save it with a name. The following sections explain the steps in creating a report for a relational database system.

## Designing the Report

Because reports on multiple-file, related databases are more complex than those for single-file reports, you should invest more time in planning the report. Time you spend planning is more than repaid when you move to the Query design screen to define the files and relationships and to the Report design screen to lay out the report.

To design a report, follow these steps:

1. Make sure that the query you create is active. If it is not active, highlight the query in the Queries panel and press Enter to make it the active query.
2. Move to the Report panel in the Control Center, choose <create>, and press Enter. The Report design screen appears. Choose Modify Ruler from the Words menu. Move the cursor in the ruler to column 80 and type a right square bracket (]) to mark the right margin of the report, and then press Enter.
3. Move the cursor to the Detail band and add the text *Order date:*. Then choose Add Field from the Fields menu, or press F5 (Add Field). The field list appears, containing only those fields in the View skeleton of the active query. Choose ORDR_DATE from the field list and press Enter. At this point, you don't need to know which database ORDR_DATE is from because it comes from the View skeleton of the active query. The Field Definition menu appears. Accept the defaults by pressing Ctrl-End.
4. Repeat step 3 for the SALESPERS field on the first line of the Detail band (add the literal text *Salesperson:* before the field).
5. Add a blank line to the Detail band by choosing Add Line from the Words menu, or by pressing Enter at the end of the line if Insert is on.
6. Repeat step 3 for the following fields on the second line of the Detail band: PART_NUM, QTY, KEYWORD, and DESC. Your detail band now contains all the necessary fields defined in the report. Figure 14.18 shows the Report design screen with Detail band fields in place.
7. Test the partial report by choosing View Report On Screen from the Print menu. Figure 14.19 shows the tested report. You can see that the Detail band contains the information you need.
8. Because you want the report to group orders together by customer, you must add a group, based on CUST_NUM. Move the cursor out of the Detail band and choose Add a Group Band from the Bands menu. For the Field Value option, specify the field CUST_NUM (see fig. 14.20).

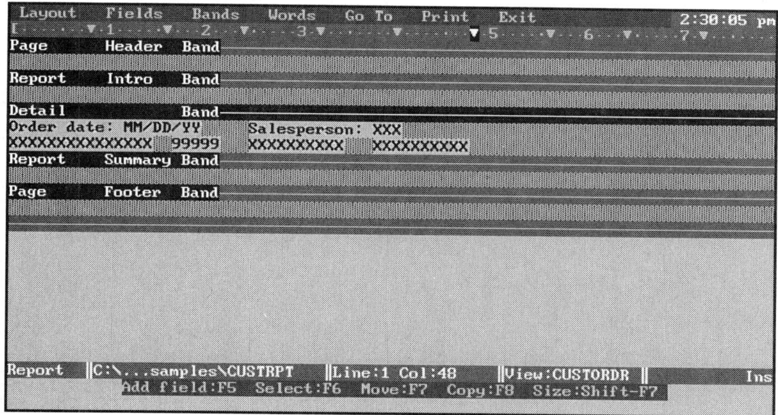


FIG. 14.18

The Report design work surface with fields in the Detail band.

```
Order date: 04/27/92      Salesperson: CNY
IN-34789              23  CHAIN        SM. CHAIN
Order date: 06/14/92      Salesperson: CNY
ME-4578                9  ROLLER       LG ROLLER
Order date: 10/01/92      Salesperson: TMY
LP-4667                4  PULLY        MED PULLY
Order date: 06/11/92      Salesperson: DBB
F-866                 14  VALVE        VALVES
Order date: 05/05/92      Salesperson: JPJ
QT-2232               16  TOOLS        HAND TOOL
Order date: 02/14/92      Salesperson: DBB
LP-1012               24  PULLY        MED PULLY
Order date: 01/30/92      Salesperson: CNY
LP-4669               19  PULLY        MED PULLY
Order date: 01/30/92      Salesperson: CNY
LP-4669               19  PULLY        MED PULLY
Order date: 01/27/92      Salesperson: CNY
ME-4546                2  ROLLER       LG ROLLER
Order date: 04/22/92      Salesperson: JPJ
ME-1178               10  ROLLER       LG ROLLER
Order date: 10/23/92      Salesperson: DBB
CA-1101               14  BOLT         NUTS/BOLTS
          Cancel viewing: ESC,  Continue viewing: SPACEBAR
```

FIG. 14.19

A view of the example report, testing the Detail band fields.

To add a group band using the mouse, click a band outside the Detail band, and then click the option in the Bands menu. Click Field Value, then the field name in the list that is presented (see fig. 14.20). Select the field by clicking Select in the navigation line.

9. On the Report design screen, move the cursor into the Group 1 Intro band and press Enter five times (make sure that the `Ins` indicator is on) to open up the band and provide enough lines to list the name and address of each customer.

10. In Row:0 Col:0 of the Group 1 Intro band, add the text *Customer Information*. Move to the next row and add the text *Customer Number :*. Press F5 (Add Field) or choose Add Field from the Fields menu to add the customer number field. When the field list appears, choose CUST_NUM from the list and press Enter. When you

return to the Report design screen, a field for CUST_NUM is in place.

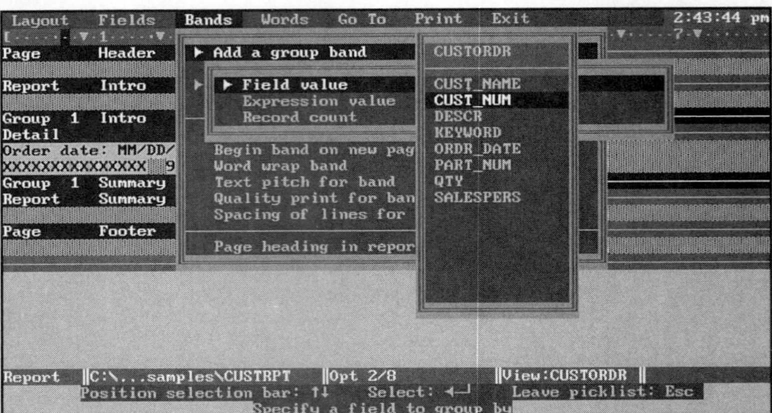


**FIG. 14.20**

Selecting a field for a group band.

11. Repeat step 10 to add the CUST_NAME field to the report, preceded by the literal text `Name:`. Your Report design screen should look like figure 14.21.

```
Layout  Fields  Bands  Words  Go To  Print  Exit          2:45:53 pm
Page     Header  Band
Report   Intro   Band
Group  1 Intro   Band
Customer information
  Customer Number : 999999
             Name : XXXXXXXXXXXXXXXXXXXXXXXXX
Detail           Band
Order date: MM/DD/YY       Salesperson: XXX
XXXXXXXXXXXXXXX 99999      XXXXXXXXXX   XXXXXXXXXX
Group  1 Summary Band
Report   Summary Band
Page     Footer  Band
Report  C:\...samples\CUSTRPT  Line:1 Col:50  View:CUSTORDR   Ins
   Add field:F5 Select:F6 Move:F7 Copy:F8 Size:Shift-F7
```

**FIG. 14.21**

Adding a CUST_NUM group to the report.

12. To make the report more readable, place a line in the Group 1 Intro band below the name.

    To add a line below the name, move the cursor to that line and choose Line from the Layout menu by highlighting that option and pressing Enter. Select Single from the line choices to make this a single line. Move the cursor to Column 0 of the line and press Enter to anchor the start of the line. Use the right-arrow key to draw the line across the page. When you reach the right margin, press Enter to anchor the right end of the line.

To separate customer records on the report more clearly, add a double line in the Group 1 Summary band, following the same procedure, but choosing Double from the line choices. Your Report design screen now appears as shown in figure 14.22.

```
                              Customer Order Report
Customer information
   Customer Number :  10005
              Name : Comar
-------------------------------------------------------------------------------
Order date: 04/27/92        Salesperson: CNY
IN-34789                23  CHAIN        SM. CHAIN
Order date: 06/14/92        Salesperson: CNY
ME-4578                  9  ROLLER       LG ROLLER
Order date: 10/01/92        Salesperson: TMY
LP-4667                  4  PULLY        MED PULLY
===============================================================================
Customer information
   Customer Number :  10002
              Name : Northwest Microsystems
-------------------------------------------------------------------------------
Order date: 06/11/92        Salesperson: DBB
F-866                   14  VALVE        VALVES
Order date: 05/05/92        Salesperson: JPJ
QT-2232                 16  TOOLS        HAND TOOL
===============================================================================
Customer information
   Customer Number :  10008
                Cancel viewing: ESC,  Continue viewing: SPACEBAR
```

**FIG. 14.22**

The example report with Customer information added.

13. Test the report by choosing View Report on Screen from the Print menu.
14. Finally, add a title to the report in the Page Header band. Add two blank lines to the Page Header band and move the cursor to Row:0 Col:0 of that band. Enter the first line of the title: *Customer Order Report*. Highlight the text you just entered and choose Position from the Words menu. Select Center by pressing C. The text moves to the center of the page.
15. Save the report by choosing Save This Report from the Layout menu, or by choosing Save Changes And Exit from the Exit menu if you are finished designing the report. When you return to the Control Center, your newly designed report is the Report panel.

## For Related Information...

◂◂ "Designing Reports," p. 229.

**FROM HERE...**

## Summary

Multiple-file, related databases are the heart of dBASE's power. In this chapter, you learned how to design multiple-file relational database systems based on the data of a planned system and the relational aspects of that data. The entity-relation diagram gives you an excellent tool for designing relational databases.

You then learned to use dBASE's excellent query capabilities to define and test the relationships between the database files. Finally, you learned to create reports from the relational database system, using the Query and Report design screens to access the related files. dBASE gives you an extraordinary amount of database power to design and implement complex, sophisticated database systems.

15

CHAPTER

# Managing dBASE IV Systems

In this chapter you learn about the SET commands, which set up dBASE IV's environment. SET commands affect many areas of from deciding whether the warning bell should operate or stay silent, to determining the number of decimal places that should show in data-display screens.

You also learn how to speed up your database operations with keyboard macros. Macros record what you do on the keyboard and enable you to "replay" the recorded keystrokes whenever you want to repeat that action. Finally, you learn how to work from dBASE IV's dot prompt, which also can speed up database work for more-experienced dBASE IV users.

# Customizing dBASE IV with SET Options

As you use dBASE IV, you may find that you want certain settings to be different from dBASE IV's defaults. You may, for example, dislike having dBASE beep when you finish filling a data-entry field; or you may prefer to press Enter to leave a field when entering data; or you may want to turn to the instruction screens you get with many dBASE actions. Such environmental settings can be changed through SET commands.

This section lists some of the SET commands you can change through the Settings option on the Control Center Tools menu. These settings also can be altered in the CONFIG.DB file. How to create this file is outlined later in the chapter. To change any setting, choose Settings from the Tools menu in the Control Center. Use the up- and down-arrow keys to highlight the setting. When you have changed the settings, press Esc to exit from the menu.

From the Settings Options menu, click an item with the mouse to cycle through the available options or to toggle the setting on or off. Choose Exit To Control Center in the Exit menu when you are finished.

You also can change all SET commands from the dot prompt. To reach the dot prompt from the Control Center, choose Exit To Dot Prompt from the Exit menu.

From the dot prompt, the syntax for changing ON/OFF SET commands is SET *<command>* *<setting>*, as you can see in the following examples:

```
SET BELL ON
SET EXACT OFF
```

For SET commands that require a value, the syntax is SET *<command>* TO *<value>*, as follows:

```
SET DATE TO MDY
SET DECIMALS TO 3
```

To return to the Control Center from the dot prompt, type the command *assist* at the dot prompt or press F2. Table 15.1 lists the SET commands and their functions (the default is shown in all uppercase letters):

**Table 15.1 SET Commands**

| Command | Purpose |
|---|---|
| BELL ON/Off | Sets the bell on or off for error conditions or when you fill an input field. If you dislike dBASE IV beeping at you, turn this setting off. |
| CARRY On/OFF | Carries information from the current record forward to a new record during append operations. When CARRY is set to OFF, the new record appears with all blank fields. |
| CENTURY On/OFF | Determines whether dates are shown with two-digit years (05/01/92) or four-digit years (05/01/1992). CENTURY ON defines four-digit years and OFF defines two-digit years. |
| CONFIRM On/OFF | Determines whether you must press Enter to exit a data-entry field. If CONFIRM is ON, you must press Enter to exit a data-entry field. If CONFIRM is OFF, the cursor moves to the next field when the current one is full. Setting CONFIRM to ON makes data entry consistent, because you always press Enter. If CONFIRM is OFF, sometimes you may press Enter (for example, when you enter a name smaller than the size of the character field) and sometimes you may not (for example, when you fill the field or enter a logical value). |
| DATE ORDER | Changes the order of month, day, and year values of a date. The options are MDY (05/20/92), DMY (20/05/92), or YMD (92/05/20). To see these alternatives, press the space bar. Each press of the space bar cycles to the next choice. To select a choice, move the highlight with the up- or down-arrow keys. |
| DATE SEPARATOR | Specifies what character is used to separate the numeric parts of a date. The default is the slash character (/), but you can change to a dash or a period by pressing the space bar to cycle through the choices. Use the dash (–) and period (.) when working with international systems that use these characters instead of the slash. |
| DECIMAL PLACES | Changes the default number of decimal places displayed as the result of calculations. The default is 2, but you can change it to any value between 0 and 18, inclusive. To change this value, press Enter or the space bar. You are prompted to enter the new decimal value. |

*continues*

**Table 15.1 Continued**

| Command | Purpose |
|---|---|
| DELETED On/OFF | Determines whether records marked for deletion are displayed in Browse and Edit windows and in reports. If DELETED is ON, marked records are ignored for display and calculation purposes. If DELETED is OFF, records are included whether or not they're marked for deletion. |
| EXACT On/OFF | Determines whether dBASE matches strings of different lengths. When EXACT is OFF, dBASE matches strings of differing lengths. When EXACT is ON, strings must match character-for-character as well as for length. When EXACT is OFF, a search for *Osh*, for example finds a record with *Oshkosh Cow Company*; if EXACT is ON, that record is not found because *Osh* is not exactly the same as *Oshkosh Cow Company*. |
| EXCLUSIVE On/OFF | Useful only if you're working on a network. If EXCLUSIVE is ON, other users cannot access any file you currently are working with. If EXCLUSIVE is OFF, other users can access your file. If applicable, a network administrator should set policy about the EXCLUSIVE setting. |
| INSTRUCT On/OFF | Determines whether dBASE presents information boxes. When INSTRUCT is ON, dBASE IV presents an information box when you select features. When INSTRUCT is OFF, the information boxes do not appear. INSTRUCT also affects actions in the Control Center. With INSTRUCT ON, choosing a database file from the Data panel by highlighting it and pressing Enter, for example, displays a selection box with the options Use File, Modify Structure/Order, and Display Data. You choose which option you want by highlighting it and pressing Enter. If INSTRUCT is OFF, this selection box never appears. Highlighting a database file and pressing Enter simply makes the file active. To modify the structure or order, highlight the file and press Shift-F2 (Design); to display the data, press F2 (Data). Other panels have similar selection boxes when INSTRUCT is ON; these also do not appear when you set INSTRUCT to OFF.<br><br>Setting INSTRUCT to ON is helpful as you learn dBASE IV; but, as your familiarity with dBASE increases, you may find you can work faster with INSTRUCT OFF. |

| Command | Purpose |
|---|---|
| MARGIN | Sets the left margin of printed reports. Adjusts the printer offset of the left margin for all printed output. The default value is 0, which means that each line starts at the printer's leftmost position, column 0. To adjust where dBASE starts each line, set MARGIN to the number of columns from the printer's column 0 you want the line to start. Note that the size of the margin depends on your printer's type size. If you're using Pica type (10 characters per inch), specify 10 to move the left margin 1 inch to the right; if you're using Elite type (12 characters per inch) and want a 1-inch margin, set MARGIN to 12. |
| MEMOWIDTH | Determines width, in characters, of the memo field when displayed on-screen. The default is 50; you can set MEMO WIDTH from 5 to 250 characters wide. This setting also determines the default width of memo fields that appear when creating reports with the Report design screen. |
| SAFETY ON/Off | Determines whether dBASE displays a warning about overwriting files. If SAFETY is ON, dBASE always displays a warning message and asks for confirmation if an action is about to overwrite an existing file. If SAFETY is OFF, the file is overwritten without confirmation. |
| TALK ON/Off | Determines whether results of various dBASE IV operations appear on-screen. When TALK is ON, the results are shown on-screen. This setting is applicable mostly when you work from the dot prompt or with custom programming. |
| TRAP On/OFF | Determines whether a dBASE IV debugger is activated when a program error occurs. This setting is another programming capability. |

## Changing the Actions of the Function Keys

You can assign character strings to the function keys (except F1). If you want F3 to execute the command DO TEST, for example, put into the CONFIG.DB file the following line:

F3="DO TEST;"

The ; acts as a carriage return, telling dBASE IV to execute the command. If you leave the semicolon out of the string, you must press Enter after you press F3. Now when you use dBASE IV, you can execute the command DO TEST simply by pressing the F3 function key.

Other possibilities for function-key assignments may be to open specific files or views, set format files, or carry out longer strings of commands. If you want to string two or more commands together, separate them with the ; carriage-return character. The following line executes three commands:

```
F4="SET VIEW TO AMMS; SET FORMAT TO AMMSCRN; APPEND;"
```

This single line works the same as if you entered the following three commands from the dBASE IV dot prompt:

```
SET VIEW TO AMMS

SET FORMAT TO AMMSCRN

APPEND
```

If you have a favorite text editor, such as BRIEF by Solution Systems, you can use that program instead of the built-in dBASE IV editor. To tell dBASE IV what editor to use, place the following line in the CONFIG.DB file:

```
TEDIT=\BRIEF\B
```

This line tells dBASE what editing program to execute when you want to modify command files (choosing dBASE program from the Applications panel). B.EXE, in the BRIEF directory, executes in this example. Place the following line in the CONFIG.DB file to define the word processor you use for editing memo fields:

```
WP=\BRIEF\B
```

By entering these commands in the CONFIG.DB file, dBASE uses your editor when you want to enter text in a memo field, or edit a program file). Note that if your text editor doesn't load, it may require more memory than your particular system provides.

## Using CONFIG.DB To Change SET Options

The CONFIG.DB file can contain settings for many of the SET commands that change the dBASE IV environment: settings to change the actions of function keys, different color settings, and the initial catalog that dBASE IV uses, and so on. When you start dBASE IV, the program looks for a CONFIG.DB file in the current directory. If the file isn't there, dBASE IV looks for this file in the directory in which the dBASE IV program resides (usually C:\DBASE).

Because dBASE IV searches the current directory first, you can have a different CONFIG.DB file for each dBASE IV application you create—as long as you keep each application in a separate subdirectory, as recommended earlier in this book. You also can have a custom CONFIG.DB in the DBASE directory for times when you don't need an application-specific configuration file.

Creating a CONFIG.DB file is simple. From the Control Center, perform the following steps:

1. Move the highlight to the Applications panel, choose <create>, and press Enter.
2. In the selection box that appears, choose dBASE Program.
3. The text-editing window appears. Enter the commands you want included in the CONFIG.DB file. Figure 15.1 shows a CONFIG.DB file entered in the text-editing window.

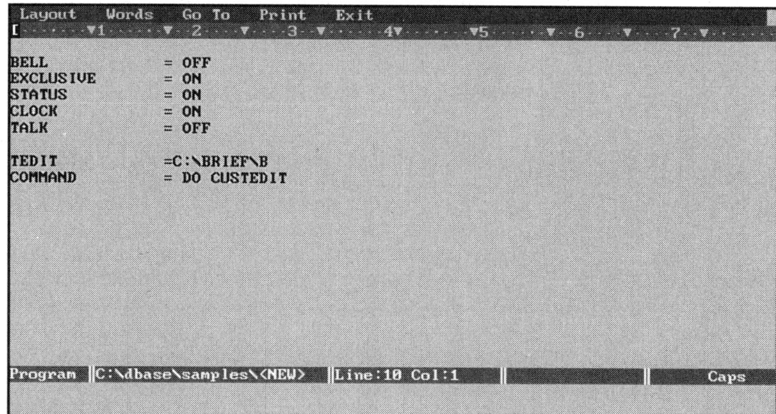


FIG. 15.1

Creating a CONFIG.DB file in the text-editing window.

4. Press Ctrl-End to save the file. When you see the prompt `Save as:`, enter *CONFIG.DB*. If you want the CONFIG.DB file to be in a directory other than the one from which you started dBASE, enter the full path. If you want this CONFIG.DB file to be in the C:\DBASE\GL directory and you started dBASE from another directory, for example, enter *C:\DBASE\GL\CONFIG.DB* to place this CONFIG.DB in the correct directory. Of course, dBASE looks only in the default directory for CONFIG.DB. It does not follow the path set by the PATH command.

5. When you return to the Control Center, CONFIG.DB appears in the Applications panel. Highlight the file name and choose the Remove Highlighted File From Catalog option from the Catalog menu. This CONFIG.DB file doesn't need to appear in the catalog.

6. Choose Yes when asked for confirmation to remove this file from the catalog, and No when asked whether you want to delete this file from the disk.

This process creates a CONFIG.DB, which is executed each time dBASE IV starts from the directory in which you placed the file.

The CONFIG.DB file can help you customize dBASE IV to your liking, or to the preference of those who use a system that you create. You can include in your CONFIG.DB file commands to set all the settings available in the Settings option of the Tools menu. Also, several options not on that menu can be set in the CONFIG.DB, as follows:

| SET command | Purpose |
|---|---|
| CATALOG TO *<catalog name>* | Enables you to define the catalog that appears in the Control Center when you start dBASE IV |
| CLOCK On/OFF | Determines whether or not the clock in the upper right corner on-screen is displayed |
| HEADINGS ON/Off | Tells dBASE IV whether to display field names at the top of LIST and DISPLAY commands |
| HELP ON/Off | Determines whether dBASE IV displays a help box when you make an error. After you are comfortable with dBASE IV, you can speed up your work by setting HELP to OFF. |

# Creating a CONFIG.DB File with DBSETUP

Included with dBASE IV is a utility named DBSETUP, which eases the task of creating a CONFIG.DB file. DBSETUP is a DOS command, so you must run DBSETUP from the DOS command line. To create a CONFIG.DB file with DBSETUP, follow these steps:

1. Use the DOS CD command to change to the directory for which you want to create a CONFIG.DB file. When you start dBASE IV, it looks first in the current directory for a CONFIG.DB file; if one is not found, it looks in the path directories. You can create a customized CONFIG.DB file for a specific directory.

2. If the directory containing dBASE IV and DBSETUP is not in the DOS path, set a path that points to this directory with the DOS path command, as follows:

   PATH=C:\DBASE

3. At the DOS prompt, type *DBSETUP* and press Enter. The DBSETUP work surface appears (see fig. 15.2).

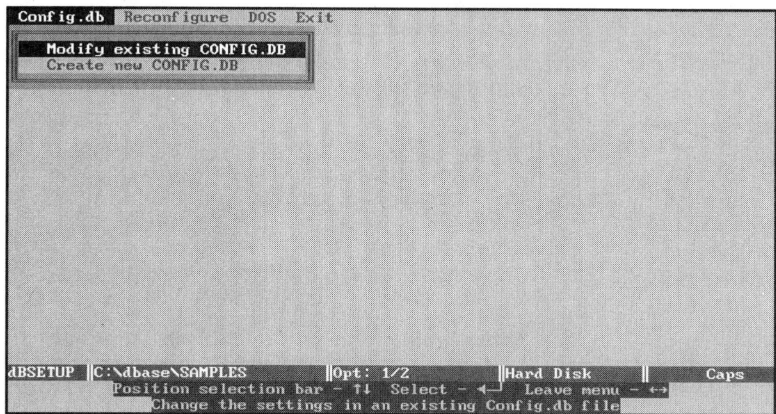


FIG. 15.2

The DBSETUP screen.

4. Move the highlight to the CONFIG.DB menu option and choose Create New CONFIG.DB from the pull-down menu. DBSETUP presents the CONFIG.DB menu, with the Printer pull-down menu open, as shown in figure 15.3.

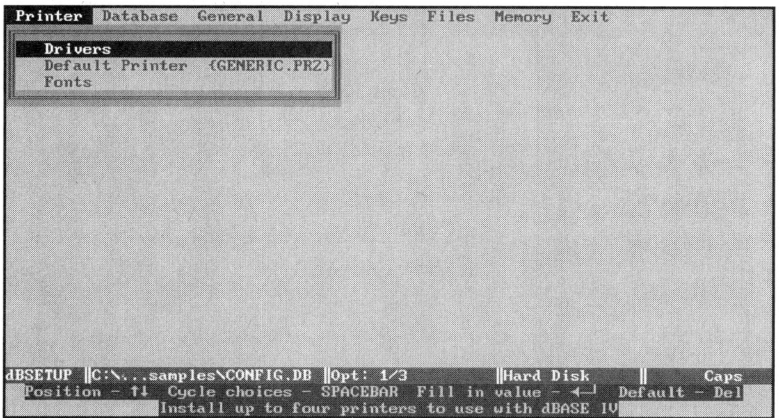


FIG. 15.3

The Printer pull-down menu.

You can change the CONFIG.DB options in seven areas: Printer, Database, General, Display, Keys, Files, and Memory. By moving through the pull-down menus, you can see what can be changed. Table 15.2 lists these menus with a summary of the options that appear on each:

**Table 15.2 DBSETUP Menus**

| Menu | Description |
|---|---|
| Printer | Enables you to install printer drivers, specify the default printer, and specify fonts to be used for each printer |
| Database | Enables you to set dBASE IV parameters that apply to database operations. Generally, you don't need to change these. |
| General | Contains most of the SET commands and other commands that affect dBASE IV's display, such as the Delimiters and Date options |
| Display | Enables you to change the CRT display mode. (Available options vary with the type of display.) Other options in the Display menu refer to colors used for screens and fields. |
| Keys | Enables you to change the command strings bound to the function keys. With these options, you can create mini-macros. |
| Files | Enables you to set (among other things) the catalog that is on-screen when dBASE IV starts, the default drive on which new files are saved, the directory path for file searches, and several directory paths that dBASE requires to operate |
| Memory | Contains options that "fine-tune" dBASE IV. Before changing these, read the dBASE IV manual thoroughly. You should not have to change any of these options; but if you do, be sure that you understand what you're doing. |

Each menu on the CONFIG.DB menu bar has several options for you to set. The menu has two types of options: those with the setting in brackets ({ }), which require you to enter the setting; and those that have a limited number of settings you can see by pressing the space bar or Enter. In either case, after the option is set, moving the highlight to another option or another menu accepts your choice.

For example, move the highlight to the General menu. Among the options on this menu are Command and Date. Command is an option that tells dBASE what command to execute when it starts up. The default setting for this option is ASSIST, which is seen in brackets. To change this default, move the highlight to Command and press Enter. An input box appears with the prompt `Enter command to run at start-up:`. If you want dBASE to start a dBASE program named INITIAL, you enter the command *DO INITIAL*. When you press Enter, you return to the General menu and see your command in brackets on the Command option line.

To change Date, move the highlight to Date. Pressing Enter or the space bar cycles through the choices available. When you reach the choice you want to use, moving the highlight off Date accepts that choice. You also can move to other menus.

When you finish setting the dBASE IV environment options, choose Save Changes And Exit from the Exit menu. If you have made any changes from the default settings, DBSETUP asks for a drive and directory in which to save the CONFIG.DB file. Press Enter to save the file in the current directory. If you want to create the CONFIG.DB file in another directory, include the drive designator and directory path. Figure 15.4 shows that DBSETUP is to store the CONFIG.DB file in the \DBASE\CUST directory of drive C. The directory you specify must be valid, or DBSETUP does not save the CONFIG.DB file.

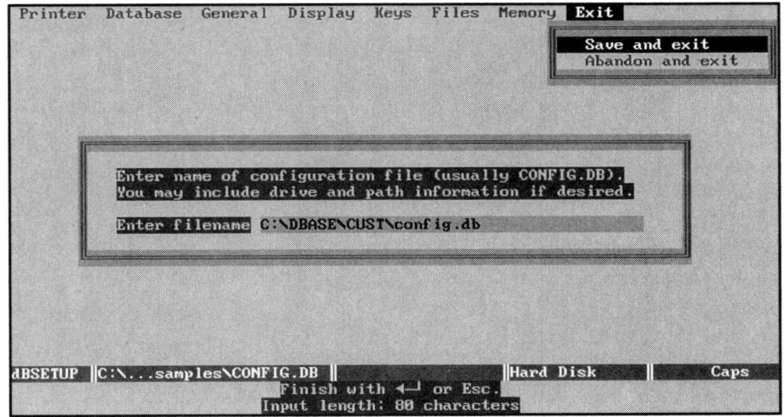


FIG. 15.4

Defining the directory in which to save the CONFIG.DB file.

**For Related Information...**

▸▸ "Using the System Configuration File," p. 935.

◂◂ "Configuring dBASE IV," p. 59.

▸▸ "Setting Up Your Environment," p. 425.

FROM HERE...

# Using Macros

A *macro* assigns a string of text to a specific key or combination of keys. When you press that particular key or key combination, dBASE IV "plays back" the string of text as if you typed it from the keyboard. Macros can save you much time and typing if you find yourself entering the same sequence of keystrokes over and over.

## Creating a Macro from the Keyboard

To record and save a macro from the keyboard, follow these steps (this example macro prints out a report that has been designed previously):

1. Move the highlight to <create> in the Data panel. Because macros record and play back all keystrokes, you should always start recording from <create> in the Data panel for macros you execute from the Control Center. By doing this, you know to place the highlight in this same place before you play back any Control Center macro.

2. Choose the Macros option from the Tools menu in the Control Center. The Macros menu appears, as shown in figure 15.5.

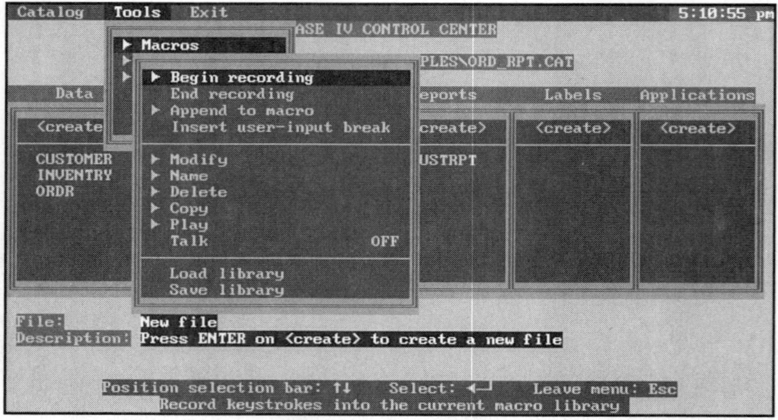


FIG. 15.5

The Macros menu.

3. Choose Begin Recording from the Macros menu. The Macro list appears (see fig. 15.6). This list shows the keys to which you can assign macros. You can assign a macro to any function key except F10, or to any letter of the alphabet. You see how to play back the macros later in this example.

4. Press C to assign the macro you're creating to the C key.
5. Return to the Control Center. Every keystroke you make now is recorded in the macro.

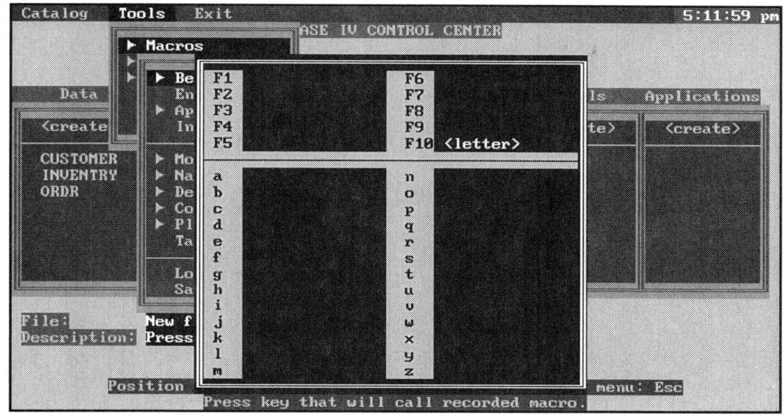


FIG. 15.6

The Macro list.

To print out the report named CUSTOMER, perform the following steps:

1. Move the highlight to CUSTOMER in the Report panel.
2. Choose the CUSTOMER report by pressing Enter.
3. If INSTRUCT is ON, choose Print Report from the selection box that appears.
4. From the Print menu, choose Begin Printing by pressing Enter, or choose View Report On-screen if you first want to view the report.
5. When the report is finished printing, press Shift-F10 and choose End Recording from the selection box that appears. dBASE IV quits recording keystrokes to your macro.

**NOTE** When you are asked to press the key to which the macro is to be assigned, and while you are recording the macro, the mouse is inactive. Use the keyboard for recording macros.

A quicker method of creating macros is to simply press Shift-F10, select Begin Recording, and then press the letter to which the macro will be assigned. Press Shift-F10 to stop recording.

## Playing Back a Macro from the Keyboard

To play back the macro, perform the following steps:

1. Place the highlight on <create> in the Data panel. If you start all Control Center macros from this point, you will always know to start from this position.
2. Choose Macros from the Tools menu. The Macro menu appears.
3. Choose Play from the Macro menu. The Macro list appears.
4. Press C to play back the macro, which you assigned to C in step 4 of the recording procedure. If you had assigned the macro to a function key, you would press the function key here.

   The macro will "play back," printing your report just as if you had gone through the steps outlined previously.

**T I P** A quick way to play back a macro is to press Alt-F10 followed by the letter representing the macro.

If you want to save this macro permanently, you must save it as part of a macro library. A *macro library* saves all macros defined to a named macro library file. This process enables you to create many macros, each assigned to different keys, and then save all of them to a file. To save a macro library, choose Macro from the Tools menu and Save Library from the Macro menu. You are prompted for a name for this macro library. Enter a DOS name (up to eight characters long).

To load a saved macro library, choose Macro from the Tools menu and Load Library from the Macro menu. You are prompted for the name of the library. Enter the name and press Enter. dBASE loads the macro library and all the macros in it appear in the Macro list.

You don't want a separate macro library for each macro you create, because you have to load a new library every time you want to use a different macro. The best macro-management technique is to create one library for all your macros and load that library once each time you start dBASE IV. You may want to create individualized libraries for each application. You can create one library containing macros that all applications use, load that library, add to it macros specific to an application, and then save that expanded library with a new library name.

**WARNING:** Macros execute just as you record them. If you do something major to the dBASE IV environment—such as changing catalogs—the macro may be unable to find files or make the proper choices that were available with the catalog for which the macro was created. Take care that you execute a macro with dBASE IV set up exactly as it was when you created the macro.

**For Related Information...**

▸▸ "Macro Commands," p. 647.

# Using the Dot Prompt

So far in this book, you have learned to tap dBASE IV's power from the Control Center. For many applications and dBASE IV users, the Control Center is more than adequate to meet all needs. Sometimes, however, especially as you become more proficient with dBASE IV, you find that you want to do things faster. Moving through the Control Center to set up and run applications sometimes requires excessive keystrokes. For more advanced (and adventurous) users, dBASE IV provides the dot prompt method of using dBASE IV.

## Reaching the Dot Prompt

To reach the dot prompt from the Control Center, choose Exit To Dot Prompt from the Exit menu. The dBASE IV dot prompt screen appears (see fig. 15.7). The cursor is on the bottom line, next to a dot (hence the name *dot prompt*), and dBASE IV is waiting for you to enter a command string.

## Understanding a Command String

*Command strings* essentially are sentences; they contain a verb and an object. A command string also may contain one or more *modifiers* or *arguments* (things that tell dBASE IV how to do something). Consider the following command:

USE *customer* ORDER *cust_num*

USE is the verb, telling dBASE IV what action to take. The USE command tells dBASE IV to open a database into the current work area. *Customer* is the object, telling dBASE IV what database to associate with the USE command. ORDER is a modifier, which tells dBASE IV to order the records by the index tag *cust_num*.

**FIG. 15.7**

The dBASE IV dot prompt screen.

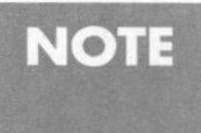


When you use dot prompt commands, uppercase or lowercase has no effect on the command. *USE*, *Use*, *use*, or even *uSe* are all the same thing to dBASE IV.

Many dBASE IV commands can have more than one modifier. Commands also can have optional phrases. The only way to learn the nuances of the many dBASE IV commands is to spend some time with the "dBase IV Reference Guide" in Part V of this book, which lists every command along with its modifiers and options. Keep this guide handy as you work with the dot prompt so that you can consult it quickly to learn about the commands.

To start using the dot prompt and its command line, you may find useful the following list of simple command verbs:

| Dot prompt command | Description |
|---|---|
| USE *database_name* | Tells dBASE IV to use *database_name* as the current, active database |
| SET *parameter* | Sets the *parameter*, as described in "Customizing dBASE IV with SET Options," earlier in this chapter. For example, SET BELL OFF, SET CONFIRM ON, SET SAFETY OFF. |
| SET ORDER TO *index_name* | Makes *index_name* the controlling index for the active database |

## Reusing a Previous Command

The dot prompt screen has several features you should know about if you want to use the screen to its best advantage. You can use the up-arrow key to move back to a previous command that has scrolled up the screen. With the cursor on the command you want, press Enter to reexecute the command. Initially, you can access the last 20 commands. If you want dBASE to save more or fewer commands, type *SET HISTORY = nn*, where *nn* is the number of commands you want saved (up to a maximum of 65,536).

If dBASE IV detects an error in a command you issue, an error window appears, showing the erroneous command with a message from dBASE IV about what was wrong. You can cancel the command, get help, or edit the command. If you choose Edit, the cursor returns to the dot prompt at the end of the erroneous command, ready for editing.

If you are using the mouse, when an error box appears, you can click Edit, and then click a character in the command line to reposition the cursor where you want to begin typing your correction.

## Editing and Reusing a Previous Command

Before reexecuting a command, you can edit it by using standard dBASE IV editing features. The newly edited command is placed at the end of the command stack on the screen; the original command is left in place, unaltered.

As you learn dBASE IV from the Control Center, you may never find a need to enter a command string at the dot prompt. As you become more accomplished, however, you may find that the speed of entering commands at the dot prompt makes this method of accomplishing tasks an attractive alternative.

# Using the dBASE IV Programming Language

You don't have to learn to program to use dBASE IV. Having reached this point in this book, you know how to use most of dBASE IV's power—and you haven't had to program yet. However, programming in dBASE IV can help you do things quickly and easily.

If you want to gain some programming skills, the dBASE IV programming language is a good place to start because it is quite easy to learn and use. By learning some of the basics of the dBASE IV programming language, you can automate some dBASE IV tasks that views and macros cannot perform.

Programs you can create with the dBASE IV programming language can range from a series of simple commands (much like a DOS batch file) to enormously complicated systems. Chapter 16 covers the basics of programming in dBASE IV; in this chapter you learn the fundamentals of creating and running a dBASE IV program to automate some dBASE IV tasks.

The most basic dBASE IV programs are simply series of commands that a user enters at the dot prompt. A common series of actions in dBASE IV, for example, may be the following steps:

1. Open a database file and its related index file in the work area.
2. Edit the database file.
3. Close the database.

Executing this sequence from the Control Center requires a number of keystrokes; highlighting the file, pressing Enter, choosing Use File, pressing F2, and so on. If you work from the dot prompt, you issue these three commands to execute the steps that follow:

- USE *customer* ORDER *cust_num*
- EDIT
- USE

You can create a simple dBASE IV program that performs the three commands when you enter *DO CUSTEDIT*. To create this program, follow these steps:

1. Move to the Applications panel of the Control Center and select <create>.
2. Choose dBASE Program from the selection box that appears.
3. The text-editing window opens. Enter the program, which may be nothing more than a series of dBASE IV dot prompt commands. For example, type:

```
USE CUSTOMER ORDER CUST_NUM
EDIT
USE
```

4. When you finish typing the program, press Ctrl-End and type a name for the program (in this case, *CUSTEDIT*). dBASE IV automatically appends the extension PRG, which marks the file as a dBASE IV program file.
5. When the Control Center returns, you see the name of the program you just created in the Applications panel. You can run the program by highlighting it, pressing Enter, and choosing Run Application from the menu. If you are working from the dot prompt, you can execute this program by entering *DO CUSTEDIT*.

# Summary

For all its ease and user friendliness, dBASE IV is an exceedingly complex program. As you become more expert with it, you may want to customize dBASE IV to suit your preferences. You also may want to use some of the short cuts that are available.

In this chapter, you learned how the SET commands control the dBASE IV environment and the three ways you can set SET commands: from the Settings option of the Tools menu; by using DBSETUP from the DOS prompt; and from the dot prompt command line of dBASE IV.

You also saw how using macros can speed up your database operations by storing and executing long sequences of keystrokes. Another time-saver is entering dBASE IV commands from the dot prompt. Both these techniques can reduce the amount of time you spend performing your dBASE IV work.

You're now an accomplished dBASE IV Control Center user. Working from the dot prompt gave you an insight into the next step in your dBASE IV education: programming. If you stored those dot prompt commands into a file, you can execute them by telling dBASE IV to DO that file, or by choosing the file from the Applications panel of the Control Center. Part IV of this book teaches you more about the many dot prompt commands and how to create more complicated and intricate programs to automate your dBASE IV work.

# Solving Information Problems with dBASE IV Programming

16

CHAPTER

# Getting Started with dBASE IV Programming

Now that you have spent some time exploring the dBASE IV Control Center and the various ways you can use dBASE IV as an ad hoc database management system, you are ready to dig into the real power of the program. This power is hidden behind front ends, such as the Control Center, automatic screen, report and label generators, and the Applications Generator. But to control and manipulate the power of dBASE, you need to learn a bit about programming and the dBASE language.

You can use the programming tools in dBASE IV in two ways. The first is to fine-tune applications, reports, screens, and labels created by the automatic programming features. The second is to create your own applications from scratch. The next few chapters explore both methods, and also scratch the surface of the Applications Generator and the SQL commands available with dBASE IV. Before you get too involved in the details, however, you learn the answers to a few basic questions about programming in general and dBASE IV dot prompt programming in particular.

# Writing Programs: Why Do It?

Many users find that they can use the Control Center to do everything they want to do with a database. The Control Center is an improvement over its predecessor, the Assistant, and also is a step ahead of anything else currently available. But you can do just so much from a structured set of menus that enable you to execute only one command at a time. Writing your own database applications is more efficient. When you have a repetitive task to perform, such as accounting, customer maintenance, or inventory control, you do not need to perform the task one step at a time from the Control Center.

Among high-level programming languages for data manipulation purposes, dBASE is superior. What that means to you, as a future dBASE application developer, is that you have in dBASE IV all the power of a "real" programming language like C or Pascal, along with a comprehensive toolbox of commands and functions designed for use in a database environment.

Automating your database processes by writing applications is the natural next step after you become comfortable with the Control Center and, perhaps, the Applications Generator. Before you start the programming process, however, you need to develop a programming frame of mind. When you develop an application, you need to think a little differently than when you work from the Control Center.

When you work from the Control Center, you perform each step as you need to. For example, you set up your database and enter data. Then you query it, write a report, or print labels. But some things you cannot do automatically. You cannot make repeated similar queries without entering the whole query over and over again. You cannot automatically use the results of one query to formulate the next. In short, you must perform every step, one step at a time, manually. And to repeat the same steps with different data, you must start all over again.

When you write a program, you should think in terms of just two things: tasks and data. *Tasks* are those functions you want the program to perform, and *data* is the information you need to give to, and get from, the program. When you think of tasks as they apply to your application, you need to break them down into individual actions that, together, make up the task. The smaller and more independent you can make those actions, the more smoothly your tasks (and, therefore, your application) will flow. This technique is called *structured programming*, and the individual actions are called *program modules*.

# Programming from the Top Down

Good programmers view a total application as a large task composed of several smaller tasks, which are made up of program modules. These modules are, in turn, broken up into program segments called *procedures*. As you progress from the largest task to the smallest module, you progress from the general to the specific.

For example, think through an accounting program. An accounting program keeps track of cash receipts and expenditures. That's the big picture. You can break down the function of the program into two broad tasks: keeping track of money coming in and keeping track of money going out. Each of those tasks breaks down further. Keeping track of money coming in, for example, may include keeping track of cash sales, accounts receivable (money owed to you), and money paid against receivables.

Keeping track of money going out may break down into cash outlays (petty cash, for example), credit purchases (accounts payable), and cash payments on credit purchases. Other tasks may include keeping track of sales taxes collected and paid, payroll, interest charged and paid, and many other accounting tasks. Each of those individual tasks should be programmed as a single module, designed to do one thing and one thing only. When the program needs to perform that particular task, it calls the module. In a dBASE language program, each of those modules, if created correctly, is a single program file with the file extension PRG.

To simplify the creation of program modules, some programmers build a library of procedures. Procedures are program fragments that do a particular thing, such as calculate the interest on a loan. When the programmer wants a module to perform that calculation, he can direct the module to use the procedure, instead of writing new code in the module to perform the calculation. That way, no matter how many times the program must calculate loan interest, the programmer writes the code only once.

This kind of programming has three benefits. The first, and most obvious, is that writing the program takes less time. The second is that the program code is shorter, which leads to the third benefit: speed. If the program is smaller, it runs faster.

When you plan a program, you follow this top-down approach by creating a cascading series of PRG files. The first file generally carries the name of your application. If you call your accounting program dAccount, for example, your top module would be named DACCOUNT.PRG. DACCOUNT.PRG might display a Welcome screen, perform some type of security tasks if you want to make sure that the user is authorized to use the accounting system, or perform other general start-up tasks. Then your top module would start the next module, which usually presents some type of main menu.

Depending on how you create your menu system, the second module probably presents the screen that you return to whenever your program completes a task. When you make a menu selection from this main work surface, you actually move down the tree to the program module that performs the task you select.

If you choose to work on accounts receivable, for example, you would make that selection from your main menu or work surface. In all probability, because a number of smaller tasks, or *subtasks*, come under the general heading of accounts receivable, the module invoked by your selection would present another work surface or menu with choices that relate to only accounts receivable. When you select a task from this second work surface, you go one more level down the tree and select a module that performs the specific accounts receivable task you want.

How you display these choices is up to you. With dBASE IV, you have a variety of menu types that enable you to create custom work surfaces. You can use a very simple box menu with numbered selections, or you can go up a step and add a bar menu. If you really want a nice screen, you can build a desktop menu with selections across the top of your screen, each of which can "drop down" bar menus for subtasks. No matter how you choose to present your application, the menu choices you create are used to invoke a module you have designed to perform that single function, and no more.

Remember, when you plan your application, start with the big picture and progress to the specific. Never let a single module perform more than one task, and make sure that all modules return to the work surface when they have finished their respective tasks. Your program then will operate in an orderly manner in which modules execute and then complete themselves, leaving nothing hanging to come back and disrupt the program later. You move from a central point to a task and back again.

Many years ago, a bright entrepreneur wrote a college thesis. His theory was that an air freight company which sent all its planes out from a central point each evening to all of the cities in North America, picked up freight, and returned to the central point where the freight was redistributed and sent to its destination, could operate more smoothly and economically than one that tried to go point to point. No one agreed with the thesis, because the method of the day was to route freight from shipping city to receiving city directly. "No," the entrepreneur said. "That causes too much redundancy in shipping routes and too many chances to lose packages." The result of that thesis was Federal Express, one of today's largest and most efficient freight companies.

Writing dBASE programs is similar to shipping via Federal Express. You should always work from a central module in your program, and always return to that module. The main module should do two things. First, it should route the user to the module that performs the task the user wants performed. Second, it should clean up after the user by clearing memory variables, closing databases, and performing other housekeeping functions. This cleanup ensures that when the user makes the next menu choice, all the data is ready for use, and only the required files are open. Without housekeeping and logical routing of your program flow, you risk losing or corrupting data, and you create situations in which you could lock up the computer in program nightmares, such as endless loops.

A couple of situations exist in which you would not, in all probability, generate program code from scratch: when you want to modify older dBASE programs to take advantage of increased functionality in dBASE IV; and when you want to *tweak* (modify and enhance) dBASE IV code created by the Applications Generator or other automated processes, such as automatic report generation.

In the first case, although you can use much of what you have generated with dBASE III Plus (and virtually all of what you generated with dBASE IV 1.0 and 1.1), you will find that you will want to redesign many of your modules from scratch to get the full benefit of new features in the later releases. Even with dBASE IV code generated by the Applications Generator, you discover that in many ways you can improve on the generated code to increase execution speed and improve the looks of your application. The Applications Generator, however, is a great way to create the bulk of your application, after which you can do the fine-tuning.

**For Related Information...**

▸▸ "Working with the Data File," p. 434.

**FROM HERE...**

# Getting Down to Business

Now that you have a better understanding of why you would want to write a dBASE IV program in the first place, you can begin to write commands from the dot prompt. The first stop on this programming odyssey is a brief introduction to the fundamental building blocks of dBASE programming: commands and functions.

*Commands* cause an action to occur. They do something, they tell the program flow to change, or they manipulate data directly. When you want to get data from a database, for example, you issue the USE command. USE is the command that tells dBASE to open a database and go to the first record. If you want to pause the execution of your program, use the WAIT command. If you want to execute another program module, use the DO command and tell dBASE which module to execute. The SAVE command saves data to special files, STORE puts information in memory variables, and GO takes you to a specific record number. These are commands. They implement a direct action.

*Functions* are much different. They also perform actions, but they do it differently. Functions always perform their task and return a result. You can spot a function by the presence of two parentheses as part of the function name. Between the parentheses is the object on which the function operates. With certain functions, you can put nothing between the parentheses. In such cases, the object is predetermined by the function itself.

Several kinds of functions exist, generally grouped by task. Some of these include functions for operating on text strings or for converting data from one type to another, such as converting dates to character data. Some functions manipulate numbers. Some functions, such as DATE( ), simply return a system or program variable and don't operate on anything. The function DATE( ), for example, returns the system date. If you want to store the system date in a memory variable called *Today*, you could use the STORE command and the DATE( ) function as follows:

```
STORE DATE( ) TO Today
```

If you prefer to use the date as text, add the Date-to-Character function, DTOC( ), to change the date to a character type. In the example that follows, the result is stored in a new memory variable called *Today1*. Notice that you can *nest*, or embed, one function inside another:

```
STORE DTOC(DATE( )) TO Today1
```

To sum up simply, commands cause some type of program execution or data flow control; functions act directly on data and return a result you can use in your program.

Two of the more important actions performed by dBASE commands—program flow control and program data control—tend to be confusing.

Commands for program flow control are among the things that can make dBASE programs more powerful than the Control Center. Program flow commands tell the program where to go next in its execution. Remember that a program works by executing the commands you give it, one at a time. The program executes the first command, then the second, and so on. The program cannot back up or go to another module or make a decision unless you give the program a command to interrupt its linear flow and do something else. Those commands that tell your program to "do something else" are called *program flow commands*. Consider the following example using the conditional command IF:

```
IF <memvar1> = 0
   ? <memvar2>
   USE <database>
   GO <top>
   LOCATE FOR field1 = <memvar2>
   DO <otherpgm>
ENDIF
```

Notice the command `DO <otherpgm>`. This command sends the program off to execute another module (*otherpgm*). The example is a dual example of program flow control. The first instance of flow control is the use of the IF command. The program either executes the commands between IF and ENDIF or it doesn't, depending on whether the IF condition is met. The second example of program flow control is the DO command. The program departs from the linear execution of commands and moves processing to a completely different module.

Unlike the flow control commands, *program data control commands* deal strictly with data. These commands have nothing to do with the way the program executes. They relate to databases, memory variables, and other types of data used by your program.

An example of this type of command is the STORE command. When you use STORE <*value*> TO <*memvar*>, you place data (*value*) in a memory variable (*memvar*) for subsequent use. This command has nothing to do with the order in which other commands are executed. It deals with data only.

# dBugging Your dBASE Application

*Debugging* (finding and fixing program flaws) your programs can be the most frustrating of programming activities. Because it is among the most important, however, take a moment at the start to learn a few tips. You can debug easily or with difficulty. But the most foolproof also is the simplest.

The first time you run an application should never be when the total application is finished. Each module should be tested and debugged individually. That way, when the application is complete, the only bugs you find are most likely the result of interaction between modules.

When you start the debugging process, your first step should be to run the program. When you run a dBASE IV program, dBASE automatically compiles the PRG file. *Compiling* makes your program run faster and more smoothly, among other things. Assuming that your code is not perfect, at some point in execution you will experience an anomaly, ranging from a screen that you don't like to a total disruption of program execution. If you simply have a wrong screen or incorrect menu text, go back to the program module and correct the error. The next time you execute the module, dBASE compares the file creation times on the compiled and uncompiled files and recompiles if the source code (PRG file) is newer than the existing compiled version.

If the program goes astray without any real indication of why, however, your debugging skills are then brought into play. First, you get a lot of help from the dBASE IV compiler. If you have made a syntax or spelling error, the compiler spots the error and stops compiling. Then you have a chance to fix the error and continue. Other common types of bugs exist, such as those that occur when you fail to close off a conditional command. When you use the conditional command IF, for example, you must use ENDIF at the end of the code string involved, as follows:

```
IF <memvar1> = 0
   ? <memvar2>
   USE <database>
   GO <top>
   LOCATE FOR <field1 = memvar2>
   DO <otherpgm>
ENDIF
```

If the condition `<memvar1> = 0` is true, the next lines of code perform their actions: display another memory variable, open a database, go to the first record, and locate the record that contains the contents of the second variable in the field named `field1`. Then your program executes another module, `DO <otherpgm>`.

You must be sure to close the IF statement with the ENDIF command. Suppose that the condition had not been met (*memvar1* was not equal to 0). The program would bypass the code between the IF and the ENDIF without performing any of the actions listed. The program would not begin to execute commands until the command following ENDIF. If you forget to include ENDIF, your program keeps running through your code, ignoring all your commands, until it finds an ENDIF. That's why "closing off" is important for certain commands. Other commands that require closing off are DO WHILE, PRINTJOB, DO CASE, and SCAN.

Failing to close off a command is one of the most common bugs in dBASE programming. Such failures generally are caught by the compiler. When a bug is caught by the compiler, you can fix it and proceed. But when you have a bug that the compiler doesn't catch, you have to find the bug. One of the best ways to do that is with break points. A *break point* is a pause placed in a program that causes the program to stop executing.

The dBASE IV 1.5 debugger screen enables you to set break points in your program. For details on using the debugger, see Chapter 20.

Suppose that you have a program which seems to execute perfectly, except that when you look for the data in the database, you find it isn't there. You know that you saved the information, but you cannot figure out why your program didn't properly append the new record to your database. You do know roughly where in your program the saving and appending was supposed to take place, so you place WAIT commands at several points in your code around the place where you suspect the problem lies.

When you run the program, it pauses when it encounters a WAIT command. At the pause, you can stop program execution by pressing the Esc key to suspend the program. When you suspend execution of a dBASE program, everything stays as it was at the moment you suspended, so you can resume execution from that point. If you cancel the program execution instead of suspending, the files in use are closed, memory variables are released, and the program simply quits.

Both suspend and cancel have their benefits. If you cancel, you get an error message, if appropriate, or simply a notification that you interrupted the program. If you suspend, you can look at the appropriate memory variables and databases to see what has happened to this point in the program. Suppose that you check the memory variables and find everything correct, so you run the program again. This time, when you get to the first WAIT, you press Enter and the program continues to execute until it reaches the next break point. You suspend again and check the databases. This time you find that the data is not where it's supposed to be, so you return to the program code and examine what happened between the two break points.

You suspect that you accidentally used the wrong memory variable when appending the database. So you move the break points to either side of where you think the error is and run the two tests again, this time with the break points closer together. You have narrowed the area of possible trouble down to a few instructions. When you run the program and check the variables, you find that your suspicion is correct. You repair the offending command, remove the break points, and run the module again. This time it executes correctly. You have debugged your code by using break points.

FROM HERE...

**For Related Information...**

▸▸ "Using Advanced Testing with the dBASE Debugger," p. 571.

▸▸ "DEBUG," p. 699.

▸▸ "WAIT," p. 772.

# Editing Code

You can use two ways to write and edit your dBASE code. You can use any ASCII text editor (or any word processor that features an option to save ASCII text files, sometimes called simply *DOS text files*), or you can use the built-in program editor. The benefit of the program editor, at least for beginners, is that you can easily write your code, compile it, run it, and debug it without ever leaving dBASE IV.

The program editor is very basic and easy to use. You invoke the program editor from the dot prompt by typing the following:

MODIFY COMMAND <*filename*>

*Filename* is the name of the program (PRG) file you want to create or edit. You don't need to type the file extension. You also can use the program editor to modify screen (FMT) and text (TXT) files with MODIFY COMMAND <*filename.FMT*> or MODIFY COMMAND <*filename.TXT*>. When you specify no file extension, however, dBASE assumes PRG, the default.

You also can use your favorite text editor in one of two ways. The first is to start and use it outside of dBASE IV, just as if you didn't own dBASE. That's the more difficult of the two ways, because you have to quit dBASE IV, edit the file, and then reload dBASE IV. The other way is to include a command in your CONFIG.DB file called TEDIT. To use TEDIT, simply add the following command to your CONFIG.DB file:

TEDIT=<*d:[directory]myed*>

*Myed* is the command you use to invoke your text editor; *d:[directory]* is the drive and directory (path) where your text editor resides. This command replaces dBASE's built-in program editor with your editor.

The program editor checks the compiled (DBO) program file before execution to ensure that it is the most recent version of your program; your text editor doesn't do this for you. Therefore, be sure that SET DEVELOPMENT is set to ON (the default setting) before you start to make changes with your text editor to ensure that dBASE IV checks the relative date and time stamps on PRG and DBO files and recompiles if you have changed the PRG file since the last compile.

You may want to use your own editor if you have experience with it. You should be aware, however, that dBASE IV occupies a great deal of memory. Your text editor may simply require too much memory to be used from within dBASE IV. For beginners, the dBASE program editor is the best bet.

**For Related Information...**

▸▸ "Creating and Modifying Program Files," p. 440.

# Setting Up Your Environment

You must consider two environments when using dBASE IV. The first is the environment you set for yourself as you begin programming and that was created when you installed dBASE IV. The second is the one you set for your users. Start by configuring your own environment. For the most part, your environment is determined by the CONFIG.DB file. This file is a simple ASCII file containing commands that determine the configuration of dBASE IV at start-up. The following is a typical CONFIG.DB file:

```
BELL = OFF
CLOCK = ON
COLOR = ON
```

```
AUTOSAVE = ON
COLOR OF NORMAL = W/B
COLOR OF TITLES = W/GR+
COLOR OF MESSAGES = R/BG
COLOR OF BOX = N/RB
COLOR OF INFORMATION = N/BG
COLOR OF HIGHLIGHT = BG/RB
COLOR OF FIELDS = GR/W
```

These commands determine such things as the color of your displays, whether the beep (bell) sounds on errors, and whether the clock is displayed in the upper right corner of your screen. (For more on CONFIG.DB, see the "dBASE IV Reference Guide " later in this book.)

The other group of environmental commands is used to set up the environment for your application's users (this environment normally is set through the application's main program file). The SET commands set up the display and a number of other things that affect the way your application looks and feels to the user. You may want the user to see things differently from the way you see them when you are working on the program. While you're writing the program, for example, you probably want to see such things as help, a display of the program code being executed, and several other messages dBASE provides.

When you prepare an application for your users, however, you want it to look as much like a "real" program as possible. You don't want dBASE intruding with its own messages. As part of the housekeeping in your root program module, then, you may want to add the following code:

```
SET TALK OFF
SET ECHO OFF
SET SCOREBOARD OFF
SET STATUS OFF
SET HELP OFF
```

SET ECHO displays program code lines as your program executes. SET TALK echoes the results of various commands to the screen. You want to turn TALK off because you want your application to process the results of your commands and display them the way you want them displayed. (In some cases, you don't display them at all; you simply use the results elsewhere in your program.)

The *scoreboard* (SET SCOREBOARD) is dBASE IV's way of communicating messages to the user when the status bar is off. You may want to hide these messages in your application by setting the scoreboard to OFF—although these messages are important to you as you develop and test your program. Setting SCOREBOARD OFF, however, will not allow the user to see such things as the Caps or Ins status. Many users want to see this. SET STATUS OFF hides the dBASE IV status bar at the bottom of the screen. Because you provide your own help in your application, set HELP to OFF to prevent the dBASE help from appearing to users.

The look of your user environment is a good indication of the professionalism of your programming. Remember that although you do most of your environment housekeeping at the start of your application, you can use the SET commands at any point in your application to modify or customize the work surface or the way dBASE IV handles your data. Remember, also, that when you change a SET command within a program, the command remains the way you put it until you change it again. If you want to make a temporary change to an environmental parameter, be sure to do your housekeeping by resetting the parameter to your application's default value when the program returns to the main menu.

**For Related Information...**

◂◂ "Configuring Settings," p. 63.

▸▸ "SET COLOR," p. 858.

FROM HERE...

# Developing Multiuser Programs

Although this book does not go into detail about network applications, you should know about some of the issues you will encounter if you begin developing multiuser (network) programs. You can use dBASE IV to develop multiuser systems for small and medium-sized applications. But when you get into very large multiuser systems, you generally will encounter some form of database server technology.

A large number of users accessing the database frequently causes a number of network performance anomalies. *Database server* or *client-server* technology solves those problems by moving the actual database manipulation to one computer, the server, while the controlling application resides on the connected workstation, or client. Two issues that become very important in client-server environments are concurrency control and database integrity. In dBASE IV, you find ways to deal with both of these issues.

*Concurrency control* refers to the management of a database record when more than one user wants access to it at the same time. Suppose that user A is reading or browsing a record in a database on a local-area network. User B, unaware that user A is browsing the record, accesses it and makes a change. User A, unaware of the change being made, decides to make a change as well. The first change to hit the record is made, and the other user never knows that the change was made or that his or her change wasn't.

The way dBASE IV prevents this problem is by exercising concurrency control in the form of *record locking*. If the record became locked when user B made the change, user A would have been informed that the change could not be made because the record was locked. You can lock records when they're actually being changed (written to) and leave them unlocked during reading or browsing. That way, anyone can browse a record, but only one user can update it at a time. Fortunately, dBASE IV handles most record-locking tasks automatically.

The second issue, *data integrity*, concerns the number and correctness of database records. As a rule, having more than one copy of a database record is unwise because you never know which one is accurate. When you perform certain *relational functions* (procedures that use two or more databases to produce a combined, or result, *dataset*), however, you create a second copy of some records. In this situation, dBASE IV prevents data integrity problems by building a *virtual result dataset*, a temporary database in which the data exists in memory only for the time that you are using it. If you alter a record in the result, you must update the original database or lose the change. When the procedure is over, you have no chance to keep several copies of the record and risk future confusion.

Another data integrity problem occurs during transaction processing. *Transaction processing* is a procedure that allows users to update records one at a time. Each update, whether it is to an entire record (such as adding a record to a database) or simply to a field in a record (such as changing an address or phone number in a personnel record) is considered a single transaction. (The opposite of transaction processing is *batch processing*, in which hundreds of records might be added to a database at one time.) If the process is interrupted (by a power failure, for example) during transaction processing, only part of the record may be correct. In dBASE IV multiuser databases (and single-user databases, as well), you can control the update process through BEGIN TRANSACTION...END TRANSACTION and ROLLBACK commands.

When you use the BEGIN TRANSACTION command, you automatically create a transaction log. This log contains every action that occurs until the program encounters the END TRANSACTION command. If your update is interrupted, you can use the ROLLBACK command to backtrack to the point just before the aborted transaction began, based on the information in the transaction log. This system prevents your database from being corrupted because of a hardware or software failure during a database update.

**For Related Information...**

▸▸ "Networking Commands," p. 649.

▸▸ "Networking Functions," p. 780.

# Summary

In this chapter, you learned about basic programming concepts and were introduced to several dBASE commands and functions. You learned why you may want to use the dBASE programming language to create database applications, what a program is, and how to plan your application. You also discovered program modules and program flow, debugging techniques, and the program editor. Finally, you learned how to set up variables to get your application started with the right look and feel.

In Chapter 17, you begin working with commands and functions in the context of actually building an application. You use files of various kinds, including databases, programs, screens, and reports. You also manipulate data with indexes and discover conditional commands such as IF, DO WHILE, and DO CASE.

17

CHAPTER

# Understanding the Mechanics of Custom Applications

In Chapter 16, you learned the basic concepts of dBASE programming and applications development. You explored some of the building blocks of an application: top-down program structure, program modules, and commands and functions. Now you're ready to start building your first application.

You begin by learning about the types of files dBASE IV uses. Then you learn how to create databases with CREATE and change program files with MODIFY. You manipulate data with SORT, INDEX, LOCATE, LIST, and DISPLAY. You also learn how to import, export, and copy data. Then you begin to work with multiple databases, using *relational* commands to select data from several sources and bring it together for output.

After that, this chapter introduces you to conditional commands, such as DO WHILE and DO CASE, and to program loops and error trapping. Finally, you are introduced to the last of the basic building blocks you use in your dBASE IV applications: *memory variables*, or *memvars*. You learn what memory variables are and how you put data in them, take data out of them, and manipulate them.

# Understanding File Structure

Like any program, dBASE IV has several file types it uses to accomplish various tasks. Broadly speaking, these tasks are programming, data storage, indexing, memos, report generation, screen generation, label generation, queries, and macros. To keep the tasks separate and to accommodate the different file structures required for the different tasks, dBASE IV adds different file extensions to file names. The file-name extension alone, of course, does not determine the file structure. But the extension is a handy way for you to recognize the type of file with which you are working. As you work, dBASE often recognizes the appropriate file type for a particular task and appends the correct extension to your file automatically, unless you tell it to do otherwise.

When you use the CREATE command to build a database called Mydata, for example, dBASE actually creates a file called MYDATA.DBF because DBF is the default extension for database files. You can use any file extension you want for any file you want, but you must tell dBASE IV specifically what you are doing every time you do it. For simplicity and consistency, avoid using anything but the default extensions unless you have a compelling reason to depart from the standard. Many of the most common dBASE IV file types appear in table 17.1. (dBASE IV has other file extensions. For a complete list, see "The System Configuration File" section of the "dBASE IV Reference Guide," later in this book.)

**Table 17.1 File Types and Extensions for dBASE**

| File type | Extension |
|---|---|
| Database file | DBF |
| Program source | PRG |
| Compiled program code | DBO |
| Catalog of related files | CAT |

| File type | Extension |
|---|---|
| Database memo files | DBT |
| Format source code files | FMT |
| Compiled format files | FMO |
| Index files | NDX |
| Multiple-index files | MDX |
| Label files | LBL |
| Compiled label files | LBO |
| Label source code | LBG |
| Memory files | MEM |
| Query files | QBE |
| Compiled query files | QBO |
| Report forms | FRM |
| Compiled report forms | FRO |
| Report form source code | FRG |
| Screen form files | SCR |
| Text files | TXT |
| View files | VUE |

You can read and modify some of these files directly with an ASCII text editor or with the dBASE IV program editor. Others you cannot edit. Any of the *source code* files—such as those with the extensions PRG, FRG, or FMT—contain ASCII program code. You can modify that code directly. The files with *compiled code* (also called *object code*) have been transformed by dBASE IV's compiler to run more efficiently. They cannot be viewed or edited directly.

Several commands enable you to manipulate some of the dBASE IV file types. You can, for example, use CREATE to build a new database. If you decide that you want to change the organization of the database structure, you can use the MODIFY STRUCTURE command. Similarly, you can use the MODIFY COMMAND command to build a new program (PRG) file or to change an existing one. Other source code files can be modified in the same manner. You can generate a report form using dBASE's automatic features and then modify or fine-tune it manually.

# Working with the Data File

Defining the data file is the first step in writing an application. All database applications begin with data. The only thing you use the surrounding application for is to add to, or edit, the data or manipulate it into reports, labels, or some other output. Before you can begin to define the data files (there may be more than one, depending on the complexity of your application), you must define what you want your program to do. As you can see in figure 17.1, the steps you use to define and write your applications fall into five broad categories.

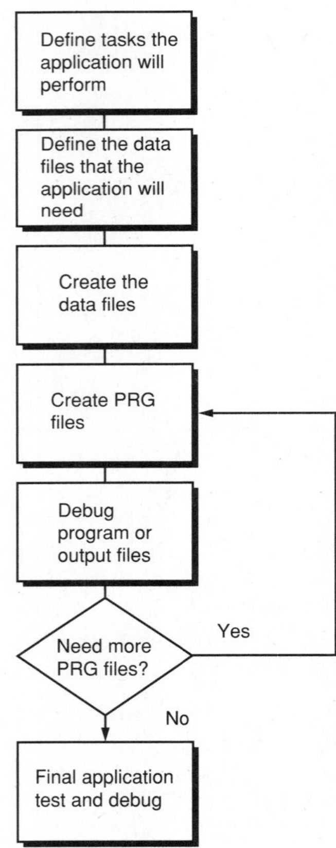


FIG. 17.1

The steps in application development.

First you define the task your application is to perform. Then you define the data files you need. Next you start writing the application, beginning with the data files and proceeding with program and reporting functions. Finally, you debug and test.

After you define the task you want your application to perform, you begin the process of data file creation by defining what you want in the data file. You can do this two different ways, depending on the uses you plan for the data in the database.

Consider the easy case first: Suppose that you are developing a simple mailing list application. You probably want only one database. The information in that database will, most likely, be the information you need in your mailing list, and nothing more. The following is a list of information you probably would want in such an application:

Customer

Contact

Address Line 1

Address Line 2

City, State, ZIP Code

Telephone Number, Extension

FAX Number

To convert this list of required data to a database file, start by choosing a name for the database: Maillist. Then use the CREATE command at the dBASE IV dot prompt to create the file:

```
CREATE Maillist
```

This command creates a file called MAILLIST.DBF and presents you with the screen shown in figure 17.2.

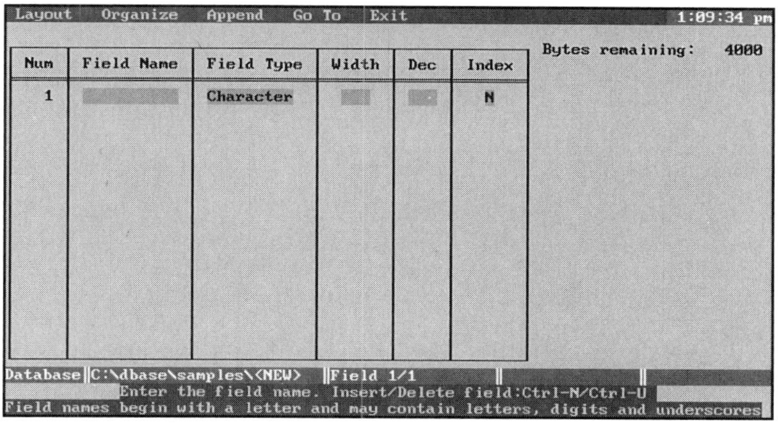

```
Layout  Organize  Append  Go To  Exit                              1:09:34 pm
                                                   Bytes remaining:   4000
Num  Field Name  Field Type  Width  Dec  Index
  1              Character                N

Database C:\dbase\samples\<NEW>  Field 1/1
         Enter the field name. Insert/Delete field:Ctrl-N/Ctrl-U
Field names begin with a letter and may contain letters, digits and underscores
```

FIG. 17.2

Creating a database.

When you see this screen, you can add the field names just as if you had accessed the screen from the Control Center. Notice in figure 17.3 how the various required pieces of information can be divided into convenient fields.

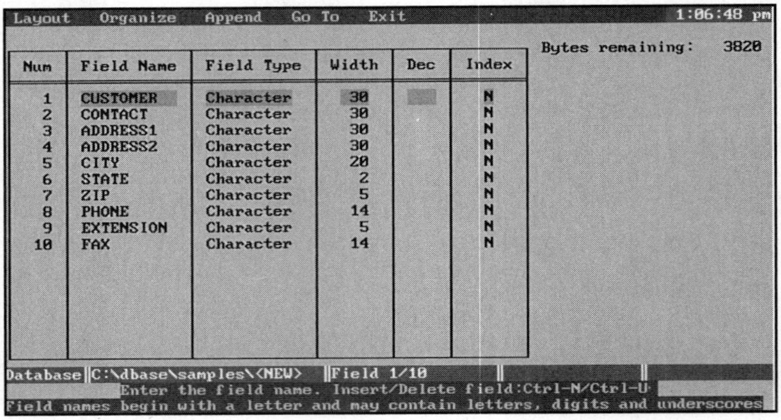

```
Layout   Organize   Append   Go To   Exit                          1:06:48 pm
                                                        Bytes remaining:   3820
```

| Num | Field Name | Field Type | Width | Dec | Index |
|---|---|---|---|---|---|
| 1 | CUSTOMER | Character | 30 | | N |
| 2 | CONTACT | Character | 30 | | N |
| 3 | ADDRESS1 | Character | 30 | | N |
| 4 | ADDRESS2 | Character | 30 | | N |
| 5 | CITY | Character | 20 | | N |
| 6 | STATE | Character | 2 | | N |
| 7 | ZIP | Character | 5 | | N |
| 8 | PHONE | Character | 14 | | N |
| 9 | EXTENSION | Character | 5 | | N |
| 10 | FAX | Character | 14 | | N |

```
Database ║C:\dbase\samples\<NEW>  ║Field 1/10
          Enter the field name. Insert/Delete field:Ctrl-N/Ctrl-U
Field names begin with a letter and may contain letters, digits and underscores
```

FIG. 17.3

Fields in the Maillist database.

**T I P** After creating a database structure, don't forget to save your work. If using the mouse, click on Exit in the menu bar, then click on Save Changes and Exit.

Changing the structure of the database is very easy. Three commands control the structure of your database. The two commands that show you the current structure are LIST STRUCTURE and DISPLAY STRUCTURE. The only difference between the two is that when you use DISPLAY STRUCTURE, the display pauses at each screenful of the listing. LIST STRUCTURE simply scrolls through all of the information without pausing. Figure 17.4 shows the result of the DISPLAY STRUCTURE command on your Maillist database.

The third command, MODIFY STRUCTURE, is used to change the structure of your database. When you use MODIFY STRUCTURE to change the structure of a database that has data in it, dBASE IV prevents data corruption by following three rules:

- If only one field is renamed, the data is copied by position, so no data is lost.
- Data is copied always from the common field names, so multiple fields can be deleted without risking data corruption.

- If multiple fields are renamed, dBASE does not return the data for those fields.

```
.  USE Maillist
.  DISPLAY STRUCTURE
Structure for database:  C:\MAILLIST.DBF
Number of data records:   0
Date of last update:   09/14/92
Field  Field Name    Type         Width  Dec    Index
1      CUSTOMER      Character    30            Y
2      CONTACT       Character    30            N
3      ADDRESS1      Character    30            N
4      ADDRESS2      Character    30            N
5      CITY          Character    20            N
6      STATE         Character    2             N
7      ZIP           Character    5             N
8      PHONE         Character    14            N
9      EXTENSION     Character    5             N
10     FAX           Character    14            N
       ** Total **          181
```

FIG. 17.4

Using DISPLAY STRUCTURE.

As the second rule stipulates, only the fields with matching field names are returned. If you change a field name, you run the risk of losing the data that was in that field. If you change the field size to a larger size, the original data is returned intact. If you reduce the size, dBASE IV *truncates* (cuts the end off of) the data to make it fit. Do not change field types this way—if you do, you cannot return the original data into the fields. Figure 17.5 shows commands for modifying the structure of a database that contains data.

```
. USE Maillist
. COPY TO Temp
     25 records copied
. MODIFY STRUCTURE
     ...
```

*Modify the structure as necessary, saving changes when finished.*

```
     ...
. DISPLAY ALL
...
```

*Check records to make sure no necessary data was lost. If all records are ok, then issue the following command.*

```
        ...
. DELETE FILE TEMP.DBF
```

FIG. 17.5

Using MODIFY STRUCTURE.

The first two commands, USE and COPY TO, open the database and make a copy of it in a file called TEMP.DBF. The next command, MODIFY STRUCTURE, modifies the structure of MAILLIST.DBF. In figure 17.6, notice that the field name CUSTOMER has been changed to COMPANY. To save the changes, select Exit, then Save Changes And Exit. You see the message `Should data be COPIED from backup for all fields?`, to which you should respond Yes. You then are asked whether you want to save the changes made to the structure of the database, to which you also should reply Y. The new structure is saved, and you see a message telling you that the records are being copied. If you have assigned any indexes, you see a message that the indexes are being re-created.

After the changes have been recorded, look at the records to make sure that all necessary information was copied correctly. The DISPLAY ALL command is used for this. If you discover any problems, you still have your original database saved as TEMP.DBF file. If all records were copied correctly, you may delete the temporary database file.

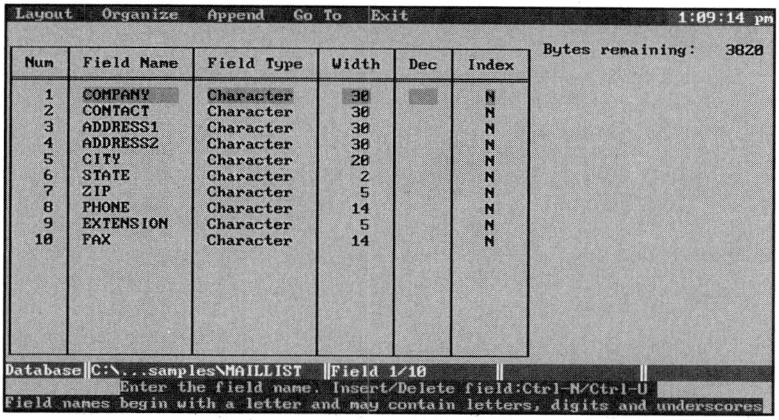

```
Layout  Organize  Append  Go To  Exit                                1:09:14 pm
                                                   Bytes remaining:    3820
Num  Field Name   Field Type  Width  Dec  Index
  1  COMPANY      Character     30          N
  2  CONTACT      Character     30          N
  3  ADDRESS1     Character     30          N
  4  ADDRESS2     Character     30          N
  5  CITY         Character     20          N
  6  STATE        Character      2          N
  7  ZIP          Character      5          N
  8  PHONE        Character     14          N
  9  EXTENSION    Character      5          N
 10  FAX          Character     14          N
Database C:\...samples\MAILLIST  Field 1/10
         Enter the field name. Insert/Delete field:Ctrl-N/Ctrl-U
Field names begin with a letter and may contain letters, digits and underscores
```

FIG. 17.6

Using MODIFY STRUCTURE to change the name of the CUSTOMER field.

**NOTE** When you use COPY TO to make a copy of a database, the entire database (structure and records) is copied to the named file. If you want to copy the corresponding multiple index file as well, include the WITH PRODUCTION option in the COPY TO command line.

You were warned against deleting fields or changing field names because the data in those fields would be lost. But you may want to use this procedure in certain cases. Suppose that someone needs a copy of your database, but doesn't need all of the fields. That person, for example, may want only customer, contact, telephone number, extension, and FAX number fields (no address, city, state, or ZIP fields). Suppose that the person also wants to add a field: Job title.

You begin by opening the Maillist database with USE MAILLIST and then copying it to a new database—FONLIST.DBF. Then you open Fonlist with USE FONLIST and modify the structure to delete the unwanted fields and add the new Job Title field. The new field containing the job title is empty, of course, because the Maillist database has no data for it. Now you can simply add that information to your Fonlist database.

When you write a program, be sure to insert comments into your program file. These comments explain what the code does. The code you write seems to require no explanation now, but your comments are an invaluable guide when you return to modify the code several months from now. If your code must be modified by someone else, your comments are essential to that person.

You can enter comments in two ways. First, you may use an entire line for the comment by placing an asterisk (*) in front of the line. Double ampersands are the second way to leave a comment in a program file. When you use &&, the comment may reside on the same line as a program statement. The following program shows examples of both ways.

```
* This program is used to search for a record
USE Maillist                  && Open the database
SET ORDER TO TAG Customer     && Set the index tag
SEEK "John Smith"             && Search for John Smith
RETURN                        && Return to calling program
```

The first line of the program starts with an asterisk and is used to remind you of the purpose of the program code. Double ampersands (&&) follow commands on subsequent lines. Whether you use an asterisk and a whole line or && and a partial line, dBASE ignores comments.

FROM HERE...

**For Related Information...**

◂◂ "Defining the Database Structure," p. 131.

# Creating and Modifying Program Files

You have created and modified databases. Now you can start on program files. You're not done with the database files completely, however. After you finish with the basics of writing a small program, you return to databases to manipulate the data in several interesting ways.

You have two ways to perform dBASE commands. One way is to enter your commands interactively from the dBASE IV dot prompt. The other way is to create a program file that contains all the commands to execute.

When you write your commands interactively, you cannot do certain things. The program flow commands that return you to different points in your program, for example, do not work at the dot prompt because dBASE processes dot prompt commands one at a time. In addition, if you perform repetitive tasks (such as opening a database and searching for records), you must type the same commands over and over again.

**NOTE** Most of the commands described in this chapter and the rest of this book can be entered either at the dot prompt or from within a program file. Because most examples deal directly with program files, however, examples do not show the dot prompt itself. Keep in mind that whether you enter commands at the dot prompt or in a program file, you do not type the dot, so the examples from here on show precisely what you type.

When you put your commands into a program, you preserve them in a listing called a *program file*, also called a *PRG file* because of its file extension. From this file, dBASE reads the commands one at a time and processes them. You may use the program flow commands that alter the flow of the program. You also may perform tasks over and over again simply by using the program you created.

**NOTE** Earlier versions of dBASE had commands that could not be executed from within a program. These were called *full-screen editing commands*, and they included such commands as MODIFY STRUCTURE. In dBASE IV, these commands can be executed from within a program file. But you should avoid using them in programs because usually you don't want your users getting inside your database structures. Save those commands for your own use from the dot prompt.

# Using the Program Editor

You can use the dBASE program editor to create program code without leaving dBASE. The program editor is like many word processors; you can type and edit text, search for text, and copy and move blocks of text.

To invoke the program editor, use the MODIFY COMMAND command. To create a program file called Mainmenu, for example, type the following from the dot prompt:

```
MODIFY COMMAND Mainmenu
```

Figure 17.7 shows the program editor screen.

After you are in the program editor, you can simply type the dBASE IV commands, one at a time, one on each line.

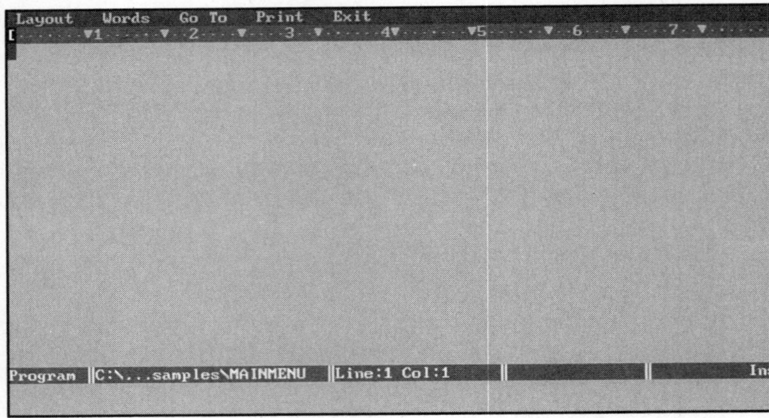


FIG. 17.7

The program editor screen.

When you want to access the program editor pull-down menu bar, press F10. From the menu, you can perform many activities—for example, you can save and test your program without ever leaving the program editor. Virtually every editing function you need is available from the menu bar. You also can use the F1 key for context-sensitive help any time you need it.

Use the mouse to access menu options in the program editor. To test your program from the editor screen, for example, click on Exit in the menu bar, and then click on Run Program (see fig. 17.8). You also can use the mouse to reposition the cursor to edit program lines.

Save the program when you are finished creating it. dBASE automatically adds the extension PRG to the file name MAINMENU. The resulting MAINMENU.PRG file contains your *source code* for that particular program module.

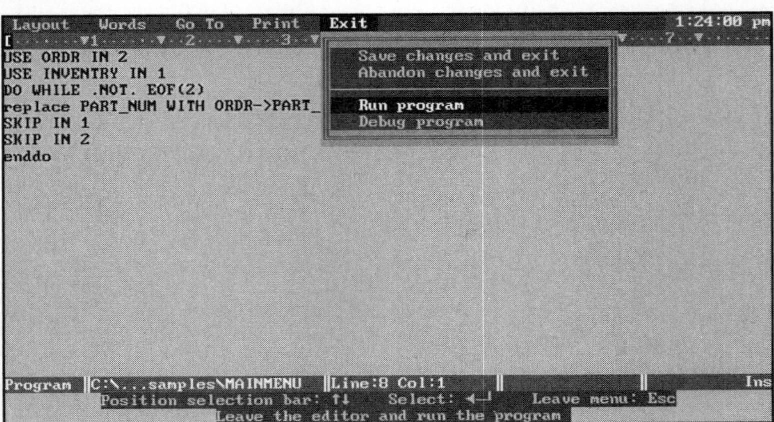


FIG. 17.8

Using the Run Program option in the program editor.

**For Related Information...**

◂◂ "Editing Code," p. 424.

# Manipulating Data

Now you can begin manipulating your data. In this section, you use various techniques to locate records rapidly, display data in your database, and move data between databases. You start with two methods of controlling the order of the data for easy record retrieval: SORT and INDEX.

## Putting Your Database in Order

You can use two methods to control the order of your data. The first way to control data order, SORT, physically changes the order of the data and stores it in a new database with the natural record order based on the sort order. The second method, INDEX, produces a virtual (non-physical) ordering of data. Both have their uses, although INDEX is the more useful of the two.

When you use SORT, dBASE must copy the rearranged data to a new database. The data in the original database is not altered. You would receive an error message for attempting an "illegal" sort if you tried to make SORT alter data in the original database with commands such as the following:

```
USE Mydata

SORT ON Field1 TO Mydata
```

The SORT command always is used after you open the database with USE. The syntax for the SORT command follows:

```
SORT TO <filename> ON <field1> [/A] [/C] [/D]
      [,<field2> [/A] [/C] [/D] ...] [ASCENDING]/
      [DESCENDING] [<scope>] [FOR <condition>]
   [WHILE <condition>]
```

In this syntax, /A sorts in ascending order, /C sorts by uppercase and lowercase, and /D sorts in descending order. The syntax of the SORT command introduces three new terms: *<scope>*, FOR, and WHILE. FOR and WHILE both require *conditions*. You see these modifiers in many dBASE commands.

When you specify a <scope>, you actually specify the number of records for a command to act on. If you want to sort only the next 15 records from the database Mydata using the Name field as the key, for example, you could enter the following:

```
USE Mydata

SORT TO SortData ON Name NEXT 15
```

In this example, the <scope> is NEXT. NEXT sets the scope to a fixed number of records indicated by the number following NEXT (15 in the example). Other scopes include the following:

| | |
|---|---|
| ALL | All records from the beginning of the database to the end of the database |
| REST | All records from the current record to the end of the database |
| RECORD *x* | Only a single record, where *x* is the record number |

In a way, FOR and WHILE are like a <scope> in that you specify the records to act on. FOR and WHILE use conditions, but each chooses records a different way.

FOR starts at the beginning of the file, searches the entire file, and chooses only the records that match the condition.

WHILE starts at the current record pointer location and searches only while the condition is true. The first record that does not meet the condition stops the search and selection of records.

In working with your Maillist database, for example, suppose that you want a command to operate on the customers only in the state of Ohio. You want to store them in alphabetical order by customer name. To store these names in a new database called OHIO.DBF, you can use the code shown in figure 17.9.

```
* Code fragment for storing a subset of Maillist to
* OHIO.DBF, sorted by Customer Name in ascending order
USE Maillist
SORT ON Customer TO Ohio /A FOR State = "OH"
USE Ohio
LIST
```

FIG. 17.9

Using SORT with a FOR scope.

This code creates a database called OHIO.DBF with the same structure as MAILLIST.DBF but containing only the Ohio customers, arranged alphabetically in customer name order.

**TIP**

Try running the code fragment shown in figure 17.9 two times. The second time you execute the program, watch for the `File already exists` pop-up warning box. Select Overwrite to replace the old file with the new file. Then edit the program and insert the environment SET command SET SAFETY OFF at the start of your code fragment. Save the program, run it again, and see what happens.

Notice that dBASE overwrites the old file without warning you or offering you a chance to stop the process. This is an example of the use of the environment SET commands. If you are using the dot prompt commands interactively, you may want to have the added safety of the overwrite warning. In your applications for other users, however, you don't want pop-ups asking the user questions and expecting a decision. Use SET SAFETY OFF in your applications to make your programs do what you intend.

The WHILE scope limits the execution of a command to a specified duration. To specify, for example, that you want the command to continue as long as the records show a Pay field of less than $50,000, use the scope `WHILE Pay < 50000`.

Using SORT creates a physical copy of all or part of your database (depending on the scope and the use of FOR and WHILE), arranged according to the ON portion of the command. SORT has two major disadvantages. First, if you have a large database, the SORT procedure can take a long time. Second, SORT creates a copy of your database, which means that you double (more or less) the amount of disk space your data files occupy.

INDEX does not create a physical copy of your database. Instead, it creates a second file that tells the dBASE record pointer to move from record to record in a certain order. In other words, INDEX creates a "road map" to locations in your database, based on your instructions. Like SORT, INDEX enables you to order your data based on the contents of a selected field. In the case of INDEX, that field is called the *key field*. The file containing the road map is called the *index file*, or just the *index*.

The syntax for the INDEX command follows:

```
INDEX ON <key expression> TO <.NDX filename>/
      TAG <tag name> [OF <.MDX filename>]
   [FOR <condition>][UNIQUE] [DESCENDING]
```

Notice that INDEX ON, like SORT, enables you to set a condition on the records being indexed. Using FOR enables you to create an index that orders specific records. In the same way you used SORT to create a database of records for STATE="OHIO", you can create an index key that includes records for STATE="OHIO" only.

dBASE IV adds some new parameters here, as well as a few new concepts. An index file is a listing of information dBASE needs to access, in a specified order, the records in a database file. When you use an index, record access is remarkably fast because the record pointer does not have to travel through the entire database until it reaches the sought after record. Instead, dBASE refers to the index, which tells the record pointer where to go. The record pointer then can jump directly to the selected record.

This index file, which carries the file extension NDX, is called a *single-index* file because it contains only the information for indexing on a single key field. When you update a database file by adding or deleting records, the index file is updated automatically, if it is open. But if the NDX file is not open when changes are made, you must reindex. Although you normally do not use NDX files, you should be aware of them. Before dBASE IV, you could use only NDX files. If you modify older dBASE programs, you may run up against NDX files.

You have another, more efficient choice, however: the *multiple-index* file. This file, which carries the extension MDX, contains information for several indexes, on different key fields, for the same database. When writing dBASE IV programs, use MDX files instead of the less efficient NDX files.

You create an index with the INDEX ON command or by entering Y in the Index column of the database structure. The first time you create the index, dBASE builds the file automatically and assigns it the same name as the database file, but with the extension MDX instead of DBF. This is called the *production MDX file*. Each index you create in an MDX file contains a *tag*, a name by which the index is referenced.

One MDX file can contain up to 47 tags. If you need more than 47 tags (a rare case, indeed), you can create a different MDX file and add tags to the new MDX file. To create an index in the production MDX file, use the following command:

```
INDEX ON <expression> TAG <tagname>
```

To create a new MDX file, you may use a command such as this:

```
INDEX ON <expression> TAG <tagname> OF <new .MDX file>
```

You specify the new name of the MDX file by typing the new name in your INDEX command line, following the keyword OF. As long as a database is open and you use legitimate fields when you add tags to a multiple-index file, that file continues to be associated with the database.

You need to learn two other important keywords. The first, UNIQUE, tells dBASE that you want INDEX to ignore duplicate key fields. The second keyword, DESCENDING, tells dBASE IV to build the index in descending order instead of the default ascending order.

To begin exploring INDEX, recall the structure of the Maillist database:

| Field | Field name | Type | Width | Dec | Index |
|---|---|---|---|---|---|
| 1 | CUSTOMER | Character | 30 | | N |
| 2 | CONTACT | Character | 30 | | N |
| 3 | ADDRESS1 | Character | 30 | | N |
| 4 | ADDRESS2 | Character | 30 | | N |
| 5 | CITY | Character | 20 | | N |
| 6 | STATE | Character | 2 | | N |
| 7 | ZIP | Character | 5 | | N |
| 8 | PHONE | Character | 14 | | N |
| 9 | EXTENSION | Character | 5 | | N |
| 10 | FAX | Character | 14 | | N |

Although you do not use a single-index file, you should know how one is created. To create a single index called CUSTOMER.NDX using Customer as the key field, enter the lines shown in figure 17.10.

```
* Code fragment for indexing Maillist on a single
* key field: Customer
*
USE Maillist
INDEX ON Customer TO CUSTOMER
USE
```

FIG. 17.10

Creating a single index.

As mentioned earlier, you use multiple-index (MDX) files rather than single-index (NDX) files in your dBASE IV programming. The advantage is that the multiple-index file may contain many different indexes, each referred to by a tag. Now create three tags for the same database in a multiple-index file. Use Customer, Contact, and City as the key fields, as shown in figure 17.11.

FIG. 17.11

Creating a multiple-index file.

```
* Code fragment illustrating the use of .MDX files
*
USE Maillist
INDEX ON Customer TAG Customer
INDEX ON Contact TAG Contact
INDEX ON City TAG City
USE
```

This code creates an index with the name MAILLIST.MDX, containing the three tags specified. You may decide to start an alternative MDX file with a tag for ZIP Codes and to call the alternative index MAILALT.MDX. Use this command to do so:

```
INDEX ON Zip TAG Zip OF Mailalt
```

Multiple-index files offer other benefits besides ease of use and efficiency. When you use MDX files, every time you update the database by adding or deleting records, you automatically update all the associated indexes.

## Finding What You're Looking For

Now that you understand how to put files in order, you are ready to explore how to get information from a database. LOCATE, the first search command, is the only command that takes no advantage of indexing. The syntax for LOCATE follows:

```
LOCATE [FOR <condition>] [<scope>]
   [WHILE <condition>]
```

LOCATE searches through a database to find a record that matches the specified *<condition>*. When you issue the command, LOCATE begins with the first record in the database and skips from record to record until it finds a record that matches the condition. FOR and WHILE can be used with LOCATE to further restrict the condition.

The use of the scope is exactly the same as with SORT. One useful aspect of LOCATE, in fact, is its use of a search scope. Using LOCATE, you can search the Maillist database for a company called *Widgets Unlimited* in Indiana. After opening the Maillist database with USE Maillist, use the following command:

```
LOCATE FOR Company = "Widgets Unlimited" .AND. ;
State = "IN"
```

Notice the Boolean operator AND with the periods on either side. The good news here is that you can find Widgets Unlimited in Indiana while ignoring the one in Colorado and the one in California. The bad news is, if your database is very large and the record you want is near the bottom of the database, you can probably go out to lunch while LOCATE searches for your record.

SEEK and FIND, the two other search commands, take advantage of indexed files. SEEK evaluates an expression and returns a logical true if it can locate the expression. The result of the evaluation must be in the contents of the active index tag in at least one record in the active database, or dBASE returns a logical false. SEEK looks for the expression only in the active index tag and often is used with the conditional command IF and the function FOUND( ), as shown in figure 17.12.

```
* Code fragment demonstrating SEEK and FOUND()
USE Maillist                 && Open the database
INDEX ON Company TAG Coindex && Build a tag index
SEEK "Widgets Unlimited"     && Look for a specific
                             && record
IF FOUND()                   && Did you find it?
DISPLAY Contact              && Display the contents of
                             && the Contact field for
                             && that record
ENDIF                        && Close off the command
USE                          && Close the database
```

FIG. 17.12

Using SEEK to find a database record.

Notice that SEEK looks for the contents of the key field only, which in this case is Company. If an entry exists in the Company field somewhere in the database for Widgets Unlimited, dBASE finds it. However, dBASE finds only the first occurrence. To find additional listings for Widgets Unlimited, you need to do a bit of *looping* and use the conditional command DO WHILE, which is covered later in this chapter.

FIND is the other search mechanism you can use with indexed files. Like SEEK, FIND is very fast and has the same single-field, first-occurrence, no-scope limitations. FIND, however, does not evaluate an expression and then go into the database to see if it can find the expression. FIND looks for the first occurrence of a *literal* (a text string or number) and then returns the data itself instead of a logical true or false indication.

FIND can search for the partial contents of a field and return the entire contents, or it can return the contents of other fields—the same way the example using SEEK returned the Contact after it located the proper record. In both instances, the command's biggest benefit is its capability to locate a record rapidly and move the record pointer so that you can manipulate the contents of other fields in the record.

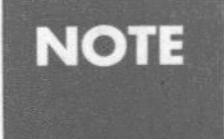

FIND is an old dBASE command, left over from dBASE II. For compatibility reasons, it has been retained in dBASE IV. The SEEK command was added in dBASE III.

SEEK works well with memory variables, and works much better than FIND. FIND works with literal strings, whereas SEEK uses a string in quotation marks. To search for the name *Smith* in the field Lastname, for example, issue this command:

```
FIND Smith
```

or

```
SEEK "Smith"
```

The problem with FIND comes up when "Smith" is stored in a memory variable. Consider the following examples:

| *Example A* | *Example B* |
|---|---|
| STORE "Smith" TO cust | STORE "Smith" TO cust |
| FIND cust | SEEK cust |

In both examples, the memory variable *cust* contains the string Smith. When FIND is executed in example A, dBASE looks for the literal string *cust* rather than the assigned *Smith*. Nothing is found, unless someone's last name is *Cust*. In example B, SEEK uses the contents of *cust—Smith—* and the correct record is found.

If you are using a multiple-index file, you must activate the index tag so that when you use SEEK or FIND, dBASE knows which key field to use. dBASE has a mechanism for indicating which index or key to use: the SET ORDER command. In the multiple-index example shown in figure 17.11, you created an MDX file with tags for Company and Contact. Now, if you want to use SEEK to determine whether an entry for *Joe Jones* exists, you use the index based on the Contact field as the key. You need to put the Contact field in use to control the order of the database. In other words, you want your database to appear to be in Contact order. Use the commands shown in figure 17.13.

```
* Code fragment illustrating SEEK with .MDX file
*
USE Maillist                 && Open the database using the
                             && Maillist.MDX multiple-index
                             && file
SET ORDER TO Contact         && Establish Contact as the tag
                             && which determines the index
                             && and key
SEEK "Joe Jones"             && Locate the desired contents
                             && of the key field
IF FOUND()                   && If you find the record....
DISPLAY                      && Display it
ENDIF                        && Close off the command
USE                          && Close the database and index
```

FIG. 17.13

Using multiple indexes and SET ORDER.

SET ORDER is required any time you open a database with a multiple-index file. SET ORDER also is used if you do not want the database indexed yet want to leave the multiple-index file open. Issuing the command SET ORDER TO without specifying a value puts the database in *natural order*. A database is said to be in natural order when the records are listed in the order in which they were entered.

You have been opening databases with the USE command throughout this chapter. But you have not tried an important option available with USE. The complete syntax for USE follows:

```
USE [<database filename>/?] [IN <work area number>]
   [[INDEX ] <.NDX or .MDX file list>]
   [ORDER <.NDX filename>/<.MDX tag>
   [OF <.MDX filename>]]
   [ALIAS <alias>] [EXCLUSIVE] [NOUPDATE]] [NOLOG]
        [NOSAVE] [AGAIN]
```

Note the keyword IN. When the topic of multiple databases is covered, you learn that you can open several (as many as 40) databases at one time and place them in separate work areas. You use the IN keyword to indicate in which work area you want to open your database. You also can use the SELECT # command (where # is the number or letter of the desired work area) before you open the database, in which case you don't need the IN keyword.

## Showing Your Stuff

After you use LOCATE, SEEK, or FIND to position the record pointer, you want to do something with the data in the record. Sometimes you want to perform further manipulations with the contents of one or more fields. Sometimes, though, you may simply want to display the contents of one or more fields. You have two ways to do that. You can use the question mark (?) or the DISPLAY command. Both work in roughly the same way. Any parameter not in quotation marks is considered a field name or a memory variable. The display shows the contents of the field or the memory variable. If the modifier is enclosed in quotation marks, it is considered to be a literal and is displayed verbatim—word for word. You can display several items by separating them with commas. Figure 17.14 shows an example using ? and DISPLAY.

```
* Code fragment demonstrating two ways to display data
*
USE Maillist                 && Open Maillist
SET ORDER TO Company         && Select the Company index tag
SEEK "Widgets Unlimited"     && Search
? Company, Contact         && Print the contents of the fields
                           && Company and Contact
DISPLAY Company, Contact OFF    && Display the contents
                           && of the fields Company and
                           && Contact, OFF shuts off
                           && the display of record number
USE                        && close Maillist
```

FIG. 17.14

? and DISPLAY used together.

In most cases, if all you want to do is display the contents of a record, ? is the easiest method. If you also want the record number, use DISPLAY.

You can use ? to get the results of a function. If you type *? TIME()*, for example, dBASE responds with the system time.

If you need to send the contents of a field or memory variable to a printer, however, DISPLAY is easier. The syntax for DISPLAY follows:

```
DISPLAY [[FIELDS] <expression list>] [OFF]
   [<scope>] [FOR <condition>]
   [WHILE <condition>] [TO PRINTER/TO FILE <filename>]
```

Notice that you get the advantage of scope as well as the capability to send the field contents to the printer or a file. On the other hand, ?

displays only the data on the screen—a quick and dirty way to get a display if that's all you need.

DISPLAY and ? have a relative called LIST. You encountered LIST when you explored database structures earlier in this chapter. LIST is very much like DISPLAY, both in syntax and usage, with one exception: LIST does not stop when it fills a screen with data. LIST works well with long lists, and DISPLAY with single or few items.

Because you can use LIST to send the list to a file or printer, LIST is good for dumping large amounts of data. LIST also is very good for creating simple reports without any fancy formatting. Use DISPLAY to print a heading line, then find a record and use LIST to send all or some selected records to the printer. LIST prints the field names on the first line, and then each record, making a columnar report.

## Moving Your Data Around

Four commands—IMPORT, EXPORT, COPY TO, and APPEND FROM—enable you to translate files of dissimilar types of data. These commands enable you to adapt data entered into dBASE for use by other programs or adapt data from other programs for use by dBASE.

IMPORT enables you to accept data from PFS:File, Framework, Rapidfile, Lotus 1-2-3, and dBASE II files. EXPORT enables you to send dBASE IV data to Lotus 1-2-3, PFS:File, Framework, Rapidfile, or dBASE II files. COPY enables you to transfer data to dBASE II, comma-delimited, VisiCalc, Framework, Rapidfile, Standard Data Format, Multiplan, and Lotus 1-2-3 files.

Using any of these commands is pretty straightforward. To translate records from the Maillist database to a 1-2-3 worksheet, for example, use this code:

```
USE Maillist                  && Opens Maillist
COPY TO MAILDB TYPE WKS       && Copies records to a WKS file
```

One final command set is used to manipulate the database. It consists of four commands—DELETE, RECALL, PACK, and ZAP—with the first three often used together.

When you use DELETE, you don't actually delete anything. The DELETE command marks a record for deletion. You can unmark it any time. As long as you merely mark the record for deletion, it remains in the database and associated indexes. Deletions become permanent when you use the PACK command.

You can use DELETE on all or some of the records in a database. You mark individual records by using DELETE when the dBASE record pointer is at the record you want to dispose of. You also can use a scope with DELETE to eliminate a range or group of records meeting specified criteria. If you want to empty a database completely, use DELETE ALL.

When you list a database, deleted records still appear, but an asterisk (*) appears before records marked for deletion. If you do not want deleted records to appear when you list a database, use the command SET DELETED ON. This command acts as a filter, displaying only those records that have not been marked for deletion. To view deleted records again, use the command SET DELETED OFF.

After you have deleted records, you can RECALL the records or PACK the database. You use RECALL just as you use DELETE. If you use DELETE NEXT 5 to mark the next five records as deleted, then you may reposition the record pointer and use RECALL NEXT 5. The deletion marks on the five records are removed. To remove records from the database permanently, you must use DELETE to mark the records, and then use PACK.

Another way to empty a database is to use ZAP, which does the same thing as DELETE ALL and PACK in a different way—and much faster. Don't use ZAP unless you are certain that you want to empty the specified database. When you use ZAP, all associated indexes are updated appropriately.

ZAP follows the setting of SET SAFETY. If you have issued the command SET SAFETY ON (which normally is the default setting) and then type *ZAP* to clear the contents of the database, you are prompted with `Are you sure?`, to which you may answer Yes or No. If SET SAFETY is OFF, however, using the ZAP command clears the database without giving you a chance to change your mind.

Now that you know how to create a database and manipulate the data in it, your next task is to learn how to use the data in more than one database at a time. When you use multiple databases, you're using the *relational* capabilities of dBASE IV.

# Using Multiple Databases

dBASE IV is a relational database management system. Think of a *relational database* as one that is basically tabular in format and has unique data locations. A relational database is laid out as a table of data, and no two data locations are the same. You can specify that you want the data at a particular location, and you get that data and only that data. This is not the full definition of a relational database, but it will do for now.

The tabular aspect of dBASE IV is very important to its relational capabilities. If you think of a table of data as a spreadsheet, the rows are the database records and the columns are the database fields. If you want to connect two databases by using a common field (one that is the same in both databases), you would see that the field (column) passes through all the records (rows) in the database. That is what happens when you link two databases together.

Consider the Maillist database:

| Field | Field name | Type | Width | Dec | Index |
|---|---|---|---|---|---|
| 1 | CUSTOMER | Character | 30 | | Y |
| 2 | CONTACT | Character | 30 | | Y |
| 3 | ADDRESS1 | Character | 30 | | N |
| 4 | ADDRESS2 | Character | 30 | | N |
| 5 | CITY | Character | 20 | | N |
| 6 | STATE | Character | 2 | | N |
| 7 | ZIP | Character | 5 | | N |
| 8 | PHONE | Character | 14 | | N |
| 9 | EXTENSION | Character | 5 | | N |
| 10 | FAX | Character | 14 | | N |

Suppose that you want to build a second database that adds fields for job title and date of last contact. You don't need the rest of MAILLIST.DBF for your new database. If you want to get data from both database files, you must have some predictable way of connecting or linking MAILLIST.DBF and your new database. You can call this link a contact log and name it CONTLOG.DBF.

The object is to have two databases from which you can selectively take data. You may want the Company, Contact, and Phone fields from Maillist, for example, and the corresponding Job Title and Last Contact fields from Contlog. The key word here is *corresponding*: You don't want John Jones's record from Maillist jumbled with Jane Smith's record from Contlog.

You need to have one common, or linking, field in both databases. That field has the same name and data in both files. Use the Contact field in this example. Your new database has three fields: Contact, Title, and Lcontact (last contact). By joining the two databases, you can create a virtual result set that contains any combination of fields from both databases. You can build a database with Contact, Phone, and Title, even though two of those fields don't exist in one of the databases.

# Using SET RELATION

When you use SET RELATION to hook up two databases, you are telling dBASE which two databases you want to use and what the linking (key) expression is. The linking expression is more than just a key field because you need to make sure that you have defined the key clearly, which may mean that you need to establish which index in an MDX file is establishing the order. The syntax for the SET RELATION command follows:

```
SET RELATION TO <expression> INTO <alias>
    [,<expression> INTO <alias>]...
```

Notice that you actually can set up multiple relations with the same command if you have opened enough linkable databases.

SET RELATION is never used by itself. Follow this procedure for using SET RELATION with two databases:

1. Select a work area.
2. Open the first database with its proper index.
3. Select a second work area.
4. Open the second database.
5. Issue SET RELATION.

Figure 17.15 shows an example of using Maillist and Contlog together so that related information can be extracted from both databases. After the relation is set, you have a result set that includes all the fields of Maillist and all the fields of Contlog. The files are aligned correctly because they have the Contact field in common.

The following is the result of the code in figure 17.15:

| Record# | Contact | Maillist->Phone | Title |
|---|---|---|---|
| 1 | Joe Jones | (800)555-5555 | VP Sales |
| 2 | Sara Sharp | (800)555-0987 | President |

```
* Code fragment demonstrating setting up a relation
* between two databases whose linking field is Contact
*
SELECT 1                          && Select the work area
                                  && for the first database
USE Maillist ORDER TAG Contact    && Open the first
                                  && database with the
                                  && index tag set to
                                  && Contact
SELECT 2                          && Select the work area
                                  && for the
                                  && second database
   USE Contlog                    && Open the second
                                  && database which has
                                  && only a single-index
                                  && file indexed on
                                  && Contacts as the key
   SET RELATION TO Contact INTO Maillist
                                  && Set the relation
   LIST Contact, Maillist->Phone, Title
                                  && List the contents
                                  && of the result set
                                  && for 3 field
```

FIG. 17.15

Using SET RELATION to join two databases.

In this example, Contlog is the *parent* database, and Maillist is the *child* database.

To use DISPLAY or LIST on records from the result set, you have to tell dBASE which database to search for the field. Note that the virtual result set actually is not a complete database. Instead, it is a set of rules for relating two or more databases to achieve proper record-to-record alignment between the databases.

Notice the arrow (->) in the LIST statement in figure 17.15. Consider this statement:

```
LIST Contact, Maillist->Phone, Title
```

This statement means that you want to list the contents of the Contact field in all the records in the active database (Contlog), the Phone field in the Maillist database (Maillist->Phone), and the Title field in the active database.

Every time you want to refer to a field in a database that is open in a work area other than the active work area, you need to tell dBASE which database you mean. This is known as an *alias* reference. If you are referring to fields in several databases in the same command, use the arrow to tell dBASE which database to act on.

**For Related Information...**

▸▸ "SET RELATION TO," p. 888.

# Working with Conditional Commands

You learned earlier that dBASE evaluates your program code a statement or command at a time, from start to finish. Sometimes, however, you want the program to go off in a different direction, depending on the results of a particular command's execution. This decision-making function and subsequent program flow control is the province of the *conditional commands*. Conditional commands determine the real usefulness of a programming language—and dBASE IV is rich with conditionals.

Before you discover the conditional commands, you need to understand what they do and how they do it. Conditionals help you make decisions. The simplest conditional, IF, enables you to make a decision based on two options, much as the word *if* does in everyday life. Consider the statement, "IF it rains, we will stay inside." The other choice, not staying inside, obviously proceeds from the alternative: it is not raining. You have two choices only: you can stay in or go out. That approach also works if one choice is very specific; the alternative is everything else. In the rain example, suppose that it snows. You still don't have to stay inside, because it is not raining.

You don't have a lot of choices with IF. But you can string many IFs together: IF it rains, we will stay inside; IF it snows, we will go skiing; IF the sun shines, we will go outside; IF the wind blows, we will go sailing; and so on. DO CASE, a dBASE command, makes such multi-condition situations much simpler.

Suppose that you have all these choices, but what you really want to do is lie on the beach. You cannot do that unless it's warm and the sun is shining. Perhaps you know that the sun is out, but you will not go to the beach unless the temperature reaches 80 degrees. You could check the thermometer, and IF it is 80 degrees, off you go. Suppose you check at 7 a.m. and find, not surprisingly, that the temperature is only 60 degrees. Is that the end of your beach plans for the whole day?

What you need is a conditional that enables you to check periodically until the temperature reaches 80 degrees, when you can head for the water. In dBASE, that conditional command is DO WHILE. You can use DO WHILE to execute the same block of code over and over until some predetermined condition is met.

## IF—A Simple Conditional Command

IF provides a way for you to specify one or two possible conditions, let your program test for them, and then continue program execution based on the results of the test. The syntax for the IF command follows:

```
IF <condition>
   <commands>
[ELSE
   <commands>]
ENDIF
```

The IF command has two levels. In simple terms, the IF command says, "IF *x* occurs, do something; otherwise (ELSE), do something different." You always must close off the command with ENDIF. Notice the way IF statements are structured:

IF *x*
  Do something
ELSE
  Do something different
ENDIF

You have two ways to write an IF construct. The first is to put your conditions in the first line. If the conditions are met, dBASE executes the code between the IF and the ENDIF. If the conditions are not met, dBASE "falls through" those instructions without executing them and begins executing program instructions after the ENDIF.

Sometimes, however, you want to have two distinct choices of code to execute before continuing with the rest of your program. To do this, you can *nest* your IF constructs. Nesting is a technique that enables you to execute an IF command, and then, if conditions warrant, execute another from inside the first IF construct (before the ENDIF is reached).

You might say, for example, "IF it doesn't rain, we will go out. ELSE, IF you find a good TV show, we will watch it. If a good TV show is not on, then rest." Now if it rains, you have another decision to make—whether a good show is on TV. Observe how this example is structured in dBASE programming:

```
IF it doesn't rain
   Go out
ELSE
   IF good TV show
         Watch it
   ELSE
         Rest
   ENDIF
ENDIF
```

When you nest IF constructs, you must use the ELSE clause. The other reason for using the ELSE clause is to keep code modules separate and self-contained.

If you choose not to use the ELSE clause, when the IF command tests for your condition and doesn't find it, the program skips all the code within the construct and continues after the ENDIF. If you use the ELSE clause and the IF condition is not met, the program starts executing at the ELSE. When that block of code is completed, program execution continues after ENDIF. IF is really that simple. Figure 17.16 is a brief example of the use of IF.

```
* Code fragment demonstrating IF
USE Maillist ORDER Contact     && Open the database
SEEK "Joe Jones"               && Look for a record
IF FOUND()                     && If you find it
   DO Otherpgm                 && Execute a different
                               && program module
ELSE                           && Otherwise...
   ? "Record Not Found"
ENDIF                          && Close off the command
```

FIG. 17.16

Using IF, including the ELSE clause.

In figure 17.16, the ELSE clause is used because the display of the message `Record Not Found` is an integral part of the IF construct and does not belong outside the ENDIF statement. Even though it would work perfectly well there, after the IF construct has completed successfully, the next command dBASE executes is the one immediately following the ENDIF. If that is the `Record Not Found` message, you see the message whether or not dBASE found your record. This is a case in which you need to keep the entire module inside the IF construct.

You can skip the ELSE if it isn't needed to account for the results of the IF condition when it isn't met. If you simply didn't use the message at all, for example, you would have no reason to use the ELSE clause. Notice the revised program code in figure 17.17.

```
* Code fragment demonstrating IF
*
USE Maillist ORDER Contact      && Open the database
SEEK "Joe Jones"                && Look for a record
IF FOUND()                      && If you find it
   DO Otherpgm                  && Execute a different
                                && program module
ENDIF                           && Close off the command
```

FIG. 17.17

Using IF, excluding the ELSE clause.

## DO CASE—For More Complex Operations

A program often uses a result or user action to change its own behavior. A program, for example, may have the user enter a single number from 1 through 5. For each number the user enters, the program can take a different action.

You could use a string of IF statements to test for each number. But using DO CASE for such tasks is much easier. Observe the syntax of DO CASE.

```
DO CASE
   CASE  <condition>
         <commands>
   [CASE <condition>
         <commands>]
   [OTHERWISE
         <commands>]
ENDCASE
```

You start by opening the command, declaring that you are going to build a DO CASE construct. Then you add as many CASE statements as you need—one for each option you offer. In each instance, you set up for each CASE a condition that, if met, results in the execution of a following block of code. The OTHERWISE clause works in the same way that the ELSE clause does in the IF construct. Don't forget to close off the command with ENDCASE (just as you close an IF construct with ENDIF). Like IF, DO CASE can be nested. Figure 17.18 is an example of the use of DO CASE in a very simple menu.

The DO CASE construct enables you to take the results of a user selection (placed in the memory variable *mchoice* in fig. 17.18) and, based on the selection, execute one of several choices. (When a condition is met, the rest of the choices are skipped.) Of course, DO CASE can be used for many other tasks besides menus, but this example is easy to understand and points out just how the construct is used.

```
* Menu for Maillist Program
*
SET TALK OFF              && housekeeping
SET SCOREBOARD OFF
mchoice = " "             && initialize memvar
CLEAR
TEXT                      && Draw the menu on
                          && the screen
      ======= M A I N  M E N U ==========
               1. Add a Record
               2. Change a Record
               3. Delete a Record
               4. Locate a Record
               5. Quit

ENDTEXT                        && Close off the command
@ 24, 10 SAY "Selection" GET mchoice    && Get the
                               && user's response
   READ                        && Read response
DO CASE                        && Open the command
   CASE mchoice = "1"          && Did the user type 1 ?
      DO Addrec                && Do the Addrec module
   CASE mchoice = "2"          && Did the user type 2 ?
      DO Chngrec               && Do the Chngrec module
   CASE mchoice = "3"          && Did the user type 3 ?
      DO Delrec                && Do the Delrec module
   CASE mchoice = "4"          && Did the user type 4 ?
DO Locrec                      && Do the Locrec module
   CASE mchoice = "5"          && Did the user type 5 ?
      CLEAR                    && Clear the screen
      CANCEL                   && Return to dot prompt
   OTHERWISE                   && If the user types
                               && anything else...
   ? "Invalid Menu Choice"     && Display this message
ENDCASE                        && Close off the DO CASE
```

FIG. 17.18

Using DO CASE in a simple menu.

Notice the OTHERWISE clause in figure 17.18. When you use OTHERWISE, you set up an action to be taken if all other tests fail. Suppose that your user selects the letter Q, for Quit, instead of the number 5. Because the only valid choices are the numerals 1 through 5, the program falls back on the OTHERWISE choice and issues the message shown in the figure. If you do not use the OTHERWISE clause and the user types something other than the choices accounted for in the CASE statements, the program falls through the code and begins executing the code immediately following the ENDCASE command.

DO CASE often is used to evaluate the contents of a memory variable. Where the memory variable obtains its contents from is of no importance to DO CASE. In figure 17.18, you put data into the memory variable *mchoice* by using the READ command to read the results of an @...SAY...GET construct (you learn about those later in this chapter). *mchoice,* however, could contain the results of a database search, the results of a calculation, or any of several other bits of data derived from any of several sources. The important point is that you put data into a memory variable, evaluate it with DO CASE, and direct program flow accordingly.

## DO WHILE—Program Loops

At times you may want to reexecute a block of code over and over until some specified event causes execution to stop or changes program flow. The broad description of this activity is *looping*. In dBASE IV, two commands help you execute program loops: DO WHILE and its subcommand, LOOP. Depending on how you use DO WHILE, you may or may not use both these commands. Look at the syntax of DO WHILE:

```
DO WHILE <condition>
           <commands>
     [LOOP]
     [EXIT]
ENDDO
```

The DO WHILE command is fairly simple to use. First, you set up a condition that dBASE can test. If that condition is true, then dBASE executes the commands after the DO WHILE statement. When ENDDO is reached, dBASE loops back up to the DO WHILE statement and tests the condition. If the condition is still true, then the commands are executed again. If the condition is then false, however, then execution of the program continues with the line following ENDDO.

The LOOP command's syntax is, simply, LOOP. In DO WHILE, you may choose to use LOOP to go back to the DO WHILE condition test before you reach the ENDDO statement. LOOP normally is used in an IF construct so that, if a condition is met, the looping starts again, ignoring the commands after LOOP and before ENDDO.

You also may use EXIT. EXIT enables the program to break out of the loop even if the condition supplied with DO WHILE is true. EXIT causes the program to continue with the line after ENDDO.

Figure 17.19 shows DO WHILE used to execute two program modules (PGM1 and PGM2) repeatedly. The first line that requires the user's response enables PGM1 to operate again. If the user answers Y, then

LOOP is used to return to DO WHILE. If the user answers N, however, then PGM2 begins. When PGM2 is complete, the user again is asked whether the programs should be repeated. No matter what the user answers, when ENDDO is reached, execution goes back to the DO WHILE command. The memory variable *yorn* is tested again, and dBASE determines whether the loop should be run again.

```
* Code fragment demonstrating use of DO WHILE
*
CLEAR                  && housekeeping
yorn = .Y.             && Initialize memvar
DO WHILE yorn          && As long as there is 'Y' in
                       && memvar yorn,
                       && continue DO WHILE
      DO PGM1          && As long as you are in the loop
                       && execute all instructions
@ 10,15 SAY "Do Again? (Y or N)? " GET yorn picture 'Y'
                       && user's response
      READ             && Read the user's response in yorn
      IF yorn          && If the response is 'Y'...
         LOOP          && go back to the top of the
                       && DO WHILE loop
      ENDIF            && Close off the IF
      DO PGM2          && Execute PGM2
@ 10,15 SAY "Do Again? (Y or N)? " GET yorn picture 'Y'
                       && user's response
      READ             && read the user's response in yorn
ENDDO                  && close off the DO WHILE
QUIT                   && close all files and quit
```

FIG. 17.19

A simple DO WHILE loop.

Sometimes the SKIP command is used in a DO WHILE construct, enabling you to perform some operation on record after record. This approach enables you, for example, to set up a filter so that only records that meet a condition are used.

To use the Maillist program to print a mail label for all the people on your list that work at Widgets Unlimited, you could use DO WHILE and SKIP. You would open the database, SEEK the first record, set a filter to all records whose company is Widgets Unlimited, and print a label for each record that matches. Following is a code fragment that shows this use of DO WHILE and SKIP.

```
* Code fragment illustrating DO WHILE and SKIP
*
CLEAR                  && housekeeping and
                       && memvar initialization
CLOSE DATABASES
mname = SPACE(30)
@ 5, 5 SAY "Name of Customer: " GET mname && User inputs
                              && search name
                              && which is stored
                              && in mname
   READ                       && READ the contents of mname
   STORE TRIM(mname) to mname1   && Store the selected
                                 && name enclosed in quotes
                                 && to mname1
   USE Maillist ORDER Customer   && Open the database and
                                 && Set index tag
   SEEK mname1                && SEEK the first record whose
                              && Customer field has the same
                              && contents as the contents of
                              && mname1
   SET FILTER TO Customer=mname   && Set the filter
   DO WHILE .NOT. EOF()       && Do loop
         DO Makelabl          && Print label using
                              && Makelabl module
         SKIP                 && After Makelabl RETURNs,
                              && SKIP to the next record
ENDDO                         && Close off the command
QUIT                          && Close all the
                              && files and return to DOS
```

Now that you have learned about conditionals, one final set of basic program building blocks is left to explore.

# Storing Data in Memory Variables

Throughout this chapter, you have used memory variables in a limited way. Memory variables, however, are among the most useful elements of the dBASE language. Memory variables give you "boxes" to temporarily hold bits of data until you need them again. *Memory variables* are temporary storage places for any type of data you might put in a database field, except for memos. You can have as many as 15,000 memory variables (if your available memory permits), but the default is 500. With good programming practice, 500 should be more than enough for most applications.

To use a memory variable, you must *initialize* it by storing some type of data in it. You can manipulate data in the memory variable, make the memory variable usable by other program modules, or make the memory variable usable only by the program module that initialized it. When you're finished with it, you can remove the memory variable.

**TIP**

When you name memory variables, you may want to precede the variable name with a lowercase letter *m*. You often initialize a memory variable to hold information from, or for, a database field. For convenience's sake, you may give the memory variable the same name as the field. To differentiate the variable from the database field, use the *m* in front of the name. For a database field named Firstname, you may create a memory variable named *mfirstname*.

Another technique that helps you keep your memory variables straight is to use different initial characters to group them. Suppose that you have two variables with the same name: One variable is used for a database field, and the other is used for printing. You may precede one name with a *d* (for database) and the other with a *p* (for print). To make these easier to read, many programmers insert an underscore character between the first letter and the "borrowed" field name—for example, *d_Firstname* and *p_Firstname*.

## Initializing Memory Variables

Initializing memory variables is a simple matter of placing a particular type of data in them. Because you can put four types of data in memory variables (character, numeric, date, and logical), you have four types of memory variables. You can initialize memory variables in two ways. First, you can use the STORE command. To create a memory variable called *mname* that contains the name *John Smith*, use this command:

```
STORE "John Smith" TO mname
```

You also can use the equal sign (=) to initialize a memory variable. To create the same memory variable created in the previous example, enter the following:

```
mname = "John Smith"
```

These different methods work equally well and produce the same result: a new memory variable. When you are writing program code, practice using only one of these methods and then stick to it. You produce more consistent code, which is easier to read, modify, and troubleshoot later on—especially if someone else needs to modify your code.

When you initialize character-type memory variables, place the text assigned to the variable in quotation marks. Using the same technique, you can use numbers as text in a memory variable; for example:

```
STORE "123" TO mHouseNum
```

In this example, the number 123 is treated as character-type data rather than as a numeric value.

When you initialize a memory variable that later is to accept character values, you can initialize it by storing a character value in it or by storing blank spaces in it.

**NOTE** Remember this important, though subtle, point: the contents of any memory variable are treated as data—even blank spaces and the number zero are considered data. Just because a memory variable seems “empty” does not mean that the memory variable has no contents. Because some sort of value—even a space—is required to initialize a memory variable, all active memory variables always contain a value.

Blank spaces can be inserted into a memory variable in two ways. One way is simply to type the number of blank spaces you need between the quotation marks. To store 20 blank spaces in the memory variable *mAccept*, for example, you could enter the following:

```
STORE "                    " TO mAccept
```

or

```
mAccept = "                    "
```

As you can see, you cannot easily tell at a glance exactly how many spaces appear between the quotation marks. A more efficient way to store 20 spaces in the memory variable is to use the SPACE( ) function. Between the parentheses following SPACE, type a number indicating the number of places you want your memory variable to hold. To create the same memory variable created in the previous examples, enter the following:

```
STORE SPACE(20) TO mAccept
```

or

```
mAccept = SPACE(20)
```

To initialize a numeric-type memory variable, simply assign it a numeric value, remembering *not* to include quotation marks, which convert your numeric value to character data. To store the number 100.05 in the memory variable *mCost*, enter the following:

```
STORE 100.05 TO mCost
```

or

```
mCost = 100.05
```

You can initialize a numeric memory variable to any number. Most of the time, however, you use an initial value of zero. Remember, initializing simply means that you are opening the memory variable by putting a value in it. That value can be an actual value that you are about to use, or it can be an "empty" value (zero or spaces) that prepares the memory variable for future use. You cannot refer to a memory variable in your program unless it first has been initialized.

When you initialize a memory variable to accept numbers, initialize the memory variable to zero. You can use the following command:

```
STORE 0 TO mCost
```

Even though you may later use the memory variable to hold a value with two decimal places, for example, you still initialize the memory variable with zero and no decimal places. When you accept the variable (using an @...GET command), you use PICTURE to format the value for the correct number of decimal places. Examine the following code:

```
STORE 0 TO mCost
@ 10,15 SAY"Enter the cost: " GET mCost PICTURE"9999.99"
READ
@ 15,15 SAY "The cost that you entered is " + mCost
```

Although this code initializes `mCost` to `0`, PICTURE formats the variable so that you may enter any value from 0 to 9999.99. The 9's are important because they tell dBASE to accept numbers only, not characters.

Date memory variables are initialized a bit differently from other memory variables. You have three methods for initializing a memory variable for a date: You can store the contents of a date field in a memory variable, use braces ({ and }), or use the character-to-date function, CTOD().

Storing an existing date field in a memory variable is a straightforward operation. If the date field in the database is called *Startdate*, enter the following:

```
STORE Startdate TO mStartdate
```

or

```
mStartdate = Startdate
```

The memory variable *mStartdate* is a date-type memory variable.

If you want to enter the date as a literal character string, however, you may use the following command:

```
STORE {10/15/92} TO mDate
```

or

```
mDate = {10/15/92}
```

In either case, *mDate* is initialized to contain the date October 15, 1990. In the same way that you stored blank spaces to initialize a character memory variable, you may use the braces to store a blank date to initialize a date variable:

```
STORE {} TO mDate
```

or

```
mDate = {}
```

The third way to initialize a date memory variable is to initialize another type of memory variable and then convert it to a date variable. To convert a character memory variable to a date variable, use CTOD(), the character-to-date function. To convert *mDate* (a character variable) to *mStartDate* (a new date variable), enter the following:

```
STORE CTOD(mDate) TO mStartDate
```

or

```
mStartDate = CTOD(mDate)
```

After character, numeric, and date, dBASE IV has one more type of memory variable: *logical*. Logical memory variables have only two possible values: .T. (true) or .F. (false). When you use a logical memory variable to receive input from a user (perhaps as a response to a Yes or No question), however, you don't want to force your user to type *.T.* or

*.F.*—the simpler, more user-friendly response is *Y* or *N*. Fortunately, dBASE accepts .Y. as a substitute for .T., and .N. for .F.. You can, therefore, use Y and N for T and F, as long as you modify the string to become .Y. or .N. before saving it to the logical memory variable. The string becomes .T. or .F. when in the logical memory variable.

You can create many memory variables at once—but don't use that fact as an excuse to become sloppy or inefficient in your programming. Use as many memory variables as you need for a program module, but when you are finished with a memory variable, clear it from memory.

To clear a memory variable, use the RELEASE command. The syntax for RELEASE follows:

```
RELEASE <memvar list>/[ALL [LIKE/EXCEPT<skeleton>]]
```

Notice that RELEASE enables you to clear memory variables in a variety of ways. You can release specific memory variables—for example, to clear *mFirstName* and *mLastName*, enter the following:

```
RELEASE mFirstName, mLastName
```

Using options of the RELEASE command, you can clear groups of memory variables that match certain criteria. To clear all memory variables that start with *p_* (for example, *p_FirstName* and *p_LastName*), enter the following:

```
RELEASE ALL LIKE p_*
```

To release all memory variables, enter this command:

```
RELEASE ALL
```

Be cautious with the ALL option—you accidentally may clear memory variables that you still need.

## Making Memory Variables Public or Private

Memory variables may be public or private. *Public* memory variables are available for use by any program module within your application. Remember, when you put a value into a public memory variable, that value remains until you change it. If you reinitialize the memory variable, perhaps from another module, you wipe out the contents and replace them with the initialization value.

*Private* memory variables are used only by the module in which they were initialized or by modules called by the module that initialized the private memory variable. When you exit a module, you automatically "hide" from use by other program modules all private memory variables initialized by that module. If you return to the private memory variable's module, the memory variable becomes active again and contains the same data it held when you exited from the module.

An easy way to remember the difference between public and private variables is to think of public variables as *global* (available to the entire application) and private variables as *local* (available to the local program module).

Memory variables are declared private or public with the PRIVATE or PUBLIC commands, both of which can be used in two different ways. With the first method, you declare memory variables by name; for example, PUBLIC memvar1, memvar2, memvar3.

In the second method, you use a *skeleton* to declare as public or private all memory variables that fit a certain pattern. PUBLIC ALL LIKE p*, for example, makes public all memory variables that start with the letter *p*. The command PRIVATE ALL LIKE ?????01 makes private all memory variables whose names consist of five characters followed by the number 01, such as *mCost01*, *mBuy_01*, or *mSell01*.

In general, the limitations on memory variable size and contents are the same as the similar limitations on field type and size within a database. Remember to initialize memory variables to the same data type as the data you put in them.

## Using the Data in Your Memory Variables

After you get data into your memory variable, you are able to use, manipulate, and change it. One of the best uses for memory variables is as data-type converters. You learn how to convert data types later in this chapter.

You can use several functions to manipulate data in memory variables. These functions range from functions like STRING(), which enable you to modify a character string, to those like CTOD(), which enable you to change the data type from one kind to another. You also can use math functions, which enable you to perform a calculation on the contents of a memory variable.

In fact, most functions can be used to manipulate the data in a memory variable just as they can be used to alter raw data. Some functions, however, achieve their greatest usefulness when used with memory variables. Following is a list of some of those functions. For more complete information on these functions, including syntax, refer to the "dBase IV Reference Guide," later in this book.

| | | | |
|---|---|---|---|
| ASC() | DMY() | LTRIM() | STUFF() |
| AT() | DOW() | MDY() | SUBSTR() |
| CDOW() | DTOC() | MONTH() | TIME() |
| CHR() | DTOS() | REPLICATE() | TRANSFORM() |
| CMONTH() | LEFT() | RIGHT() | TRIM() |
| CTOD() | LEN() | RTRIM() | UPPER() |
| DATE() | LIKE() | SOUNDEX() | VAL() |
| DAY() | LOOKUP() | SPACE() | YEAR() |
| DIFFERENCE() | LOWER() | STR() | |

Several mathematical functions can be used on numbers or the contents of numeric memory variables. Remember that a function returns a value equal to the results of the function performed on the value within the parentheses. You discovered an easy use of functions when you used the CTOD() function to change a character string into a date string for the purpose of initializing a date memory variable. Another useful function pair is STR() and VAL().

You can use STR() to change the contents of a numeric memory variable to a character string. VAL() performs the opposite function, turning a character string into a number. Suppose that you want to accept the character "1" and use it as the number 1. Character "1" is stored in the memory variable *mChar*. You want to store the contents of *mChar* in the memory variable *mNumber*, and make *mNumber* a numeric memory variable. To do this, you can enter the following:

```
STORE VAL(mChar) TO mNumber
```

This example is typical of the way you can use functions to modify the data in memory variables.

A more sophisticated use of memory variables for data handling is *string manipulation*. When you capture a string of characters in a memory variable, the string sometimes is not set up exactly the way you need it to be. It may have too many characters or unneeded spaces.

The program in figure 17.20 accepts the contents of the Contact field and strips out the first name of the contact for use as the salutation in a letter. This program uses much of what you have learned about conditionals (DO WHILE, in this case), functions, and memory variables.

```
***********************************************************
* Convert.PRG - a program for converting the contents     *
* of the Contact field in MAILLIST.DBF to first name      *
* only and then jumping to PERSLTR.PRG to write a         *
* letter starting with " Dear firstname; ". After         *
* writing the letter, Persltr RETURNs to Convert,skips    *
* to the next name in the database and repeats the        *
* process. The letters are generated in alpha order by    *
* first name, based on the index tag.                     *
***********************************************************

CLEAR                           && Clear the screen
USE Maillist ORDER Contact      && Open the database and
                                && Set index tag
   mfirstname = SPACE(30)       && Initialize the memvar
   PUBLIC mfirstname, mtemp     && Declare it PUBLIC
   mtemp = 0                    && Initialize another memvar
DO WHILE .NOT. EOF()            && Use the whole database
   mtemp = AT(" ",Contact)      && STORE the number
                                && of characters from the
                                && start of the Contact
                                && field to the space
                                && between first and last
                                && name to the memvar
                                && mtemp
      mfirstname = LEFT(Contact,(mtemp[ms]1))
                                && STORE the mtemp[ms]1
                                && number of characters,
                                && starting from the
                                && left, in the Contact
                                && field to the memvar
                                && mfirstname
      DO Persltr             && Call Persltr.prg
      SKIP                   && On RETURN from Persltr,
                             && SKIP to the next record in
                             && the database
ENDDO                        && Close off the command
QUIT                         && Close all files and return
                             && to DOS
```

FIG. 17.20

A program illustrating the conversion of memory variables.

The AT() and LEFT() functions in figure 17.20 enable you to modify the character strings stored in the *mtemp* and *mfirstname* memory variables. You can use AT() to locate a specific character in a field or memory variable. In figure 17.20, AT() is used to locate the space (" ") that separates the first and last names in the Contact field. Then the program stores the number that represents the number of characters from the left of the field to the space in *mtemp*. You need that number when you use the LEFT() function.

LEFT() enables you to capture a specified number of characters in a field or memory variable from the left starting position of the field or memory variable. In figure 17.20, you capture the number of characters, minus 1 in *mfirstname*. (You don't need the space, just the characters before it.) You can do the same thing from another memory variable instead of from a database field.

When Persltr is called (DO Persltr), it can use the data in the public memory variable *mfirstname* in the salutation of the letter to personalize each one. At the end of PERSLTR.PRG, a RETURN command redirects program flow back to CONVERT.PRG. Convert then executes the command immediately following DO Persltr.

Two other functions, LTRIM() and RTRIM(), frequently are used to manipulate data in memory variables. These functions remove unwanted blank spaces preceding or following the value.

LTRIM() removes extra spaces from the left side of a character string. RTRIM(), or simply TRIM(), is used to remove all trailing spaces (those on the right). Figure 17.21 shows examples of LTRIM() and RTRIM().

```
* Program showing the benefit of LTRIM() and RTRIM()
*
mVar1 = "John"
mVar2 = "John "
mVar3 = " John"
mVar4 = " John "
* Test RTRIM(), "John" = "John "
? '"John" = "John " '
?? mVar1 = mVar2
? '"John" = RTRIM("John ") '
?? mVar1 = RTRIM(mVar2)
* Test LTRIM(), "John" = " John"
? '"John" = " John" '
?? mVar1 = mVar3
? '"John" = LTRIM(" John") '
?? mVar1 = LTRIM(mVar3)
* Test LTRIM() and RTRIM(), "John" = " John "
? '"John" = " John " '
?? mVar1 = mVar4
? '"John" = LTRIM(RTRIM(" John ")) '
?? mVar1 = RTRIM(mVar4)
```

FIG. 17.21

LTRIM() and RTRIM().

If you run this program, you see that the original character string ("John") does not equal each of the character strings with the inserted space. When the character string with the space is trimmed, however, it does equal the original character string.

## Making More of Memory Variables with Arrays

You can use memory variables far more efficiently if you want to store a large number of values that are, in some way, related. You want to keep these values together, and you want to avoid using up a lot of memory space by initializing a large number of memory variables.

To do this, you use variable arrays. *Arrays* are like cubbyholes into which you stick values. All the cubbyholes are in the same array, so you deal with the array only. The data in the cubbyholes, however, can be handled as discrete data, following all the same rules as memory variables. Each cubbyhole is called an *array element.*

If you want to use 40 different memory variables, all of which hold data relating to the Maillist program, for example, you can build an array that looks like figure 17.22.

The array in figure 17.22 is a *two-dimensional array*, which means that the array has both length and width greater than one element. In this case, the length is 10 elements and the width is 4. If the width was only 1 element, the array would be one-dimensional. From the standpoint of how you use arrays, there is very little difference between the two.

Initializing an array is simple. Use DECLARE to name the array and indicate its *matrix structure* (the number of rows and columns). The syntax of the DECLARE command is

```
DECLARE array[R,C]
```

In this syntax, *array* is the name of the array, *R* is the number of rows, and *C* is the number of columns. The elements of an array can be any data type. You can, in fact, have all the various data types present in a single array. When you store data in an element of an array, you set the data type for that element. The array as a whole, however, has no assigned data type.

You use STORE to place data in an array in the same way you place data in a memory variable, except you must give the coordinates of the element into which you want to store the information. If you want to store the contents of the fields in the Maillist database in an array called *a_maillist*, you can do it as shown in figure 17.23.

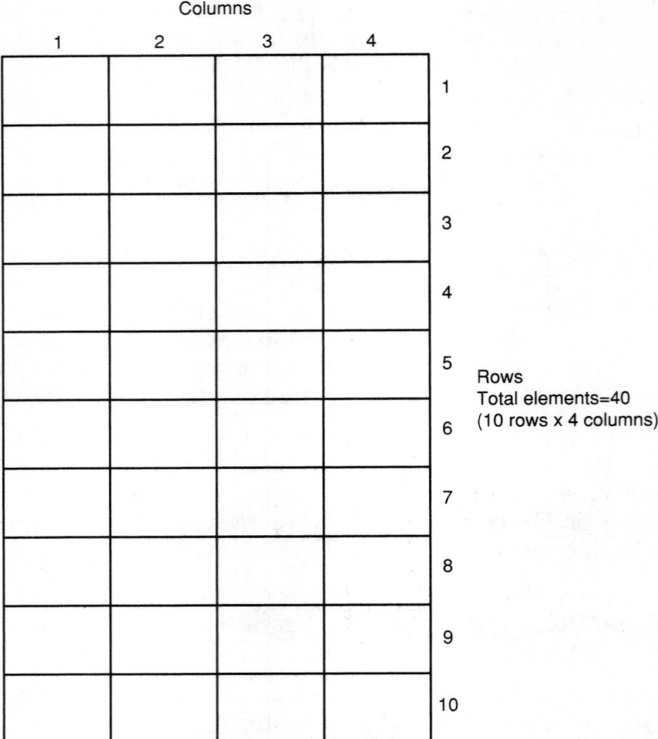


FIG. 17.22

A 10-by-4, two-dimensional array containing 40 elements.

In the program shown in figure 17.23, notice that you first assign the field names to the first column of the array. Then, using a DO loop, you begin assigning fields to the second column of the array. The first time through the loop, *mCount* equals 1. In essence, the command in the DO loop reads as follows:

```
a_maillist[1,2] = &a_maillist[1,1]
```

The variable *mCount* is incremented by 1 to equal 2. The command becomes the following on the second time through the loop:

```
a_maillist[2,2] = &a_maillist[2,1]
```

Notice the use of the ampersand (&), the *macro substitution character.* The macro substitution character tells dBASE to use the contents of the memory variable as a literal, rather than using the memory variable. The first time through the loop, for example, `a_maillist[1,1]` contains the string `Customer`. The use of & makes the command read like this:

```
a_maillist[1,2] = Customer
```

```
* Code fragment illustrating array use
*
DECLARE a_maillist[10,2]        && DECLARE a 10 element,
                                && 2-dimensional array
USE Maillist ORDER Customer     && Open the database and
                                && Set index tag
a_maillist[1,1] = "Customer"    && Store the field names
                                && to the array,
a_maillist[2,1] = "Contact"     && Customer to 1,1, Contact
a_maillist[3,1] = "Address1"    && to 2,1 and so on.
a_maillist[4,1] = "Address2"
a_maillist[5,1] = "City"
a_maillist[6,1] = "State"
a_maillist[7,1] = "Zip"
a_maillist[8,1] = "Phone"
a_maillist[9,1] = "Extension"
a_maillist[10,1] = "Fax"          && until the array is
                                  && full
* Use a DO..ENDDO loop to fill the second dimension of the
* array with data from the records.
   mCount = 1
DO WHILE mCount < 11
   a_maillist[mCount,2] = &a_maillist[mCount,1]
   mCount = mCount + 1
ENDDO
* Use a DO...ENDDO loop to display the data from the array
   mCount = 1
DO WHILE mCount < 11
   ? a_maillist[mCount,1]
   ?? SPACE(10)
   ?? a_maillist[mCount,2]
   mCount = mCount + 1
ENDDO
USE             && Close Maillist
RETURN          && Return to the calling program
                && or the dot prompt
```

FIG. 17.23

Using arrays.

Because Customer is the name of a field, the contents of the Customer field are stored in `a_maillist[1,2]`.

When *mCount* equals 11, it no longer meets the condition of the DO WHILE statement (DO WHILE mCount < 11), and the DO loop ends. All fields from the current record have been assigned to the second column of the array, and another DO loop starts. This loop is used to display the contents of the entire array on-screen, one row at a time.

After the entire array has been displayed, the database is closed, and the program ends.

Any time you need to keep data together in one place and normally would consider using several memory variables to do so, consider using an array instead. The data stays together, you don't have to worry about data types, you can store the contents of one element in another, and you actually use less memory.

> **WARNING:** Never give an array and a memory variable the same name. Memory variables overwrite arrays of the same name.

# Accepting User Input

dBASE can accept user input four basic ways: ACCEPT, INPUT, WAIT, and @...SAY...GET.

ACCEPT and INPUT are the same, except that ACCEPT can accept only character information, whereas INPUT can accept any data type. These commands normally aren't used because they are not nearly as flexible as @...SAY...GET. For example, neither ACCEPT or INPUT enables you to position the prompt where you want it on-screen. The screen location of the prompt is determined by whatever else is on the screen at the time. Just after you clear the screen, for example, the prompt appears at the upper left corner of the screen. The syntax of the two commands follows:

```
ACCEPT/INPUT [<prompt>] TO <memvar>
```

The prompt is optional. In the program shown in figure 17.24, ACCEPT is used to get a word to be used as a scope for the DISPLAY command. ACCEPT waits for the user to type characters and press Enter. When the user does, the program continues, and mScope is assigned a text string. If the user types *QUIT*, the IF test detects this and exits the loop. Anything else that is typed is used as the scope with the DISPLAY command. If the user types *NEXT 10* and presses Enter during the ACCEPT interval, for example, the character string "NEXT 10" is assigned to mScope. The DISPLAY command uses the macro substitution string, so the resulting command is

```
DISPLAY NEXT 10
```

The next 10 records in the database are displayed.

```
* Sample program to enable user to DISPLAY any number of
* records from a database.
USE Maillist ORDER Customer    && Open database and
                               && Set index tag
DO WHILE .T.                   && Start do loop
   CLEAR                       && Clear the screen
   GO TOP                      && Top of database
   ? "How many records would you like to display? "
   ?? "Enter a phrase."
   ACCEPT '"ALL", "NEXT x" (x=a number), "QUIT"' to mScope
   IF TRIM(UPPER(mScope)) = "QUIT"    && Test for QUIT
      EXIT                     && Exit do loop if QUIT
   ENDIF                       && Close IF test
   DISPLAY &mScope             && DISPLAY command with scope
ENDDO                          && Close do loop
USE                            && Close database
RETURN                         && Return to calling program
                               && or dot prompt
```

FIG. 17.24

Sample program using ACCEPT.

WAIT is similar to ACCEPT/INPUT, except that WAIT accepts one character only and does not require Enter to be pressed, whereas ACCEPT/INPUT accepts more than one character and waits for Enter to be pressed. After the user presses one character, WAIT resumes the program. You may find WAIT useful for multiple-choice questions. Figure 17.25 shows an example of WAIT.

In figure 17.25, WAIT is used to accept either E or D to edit or delete the record.

The @...SAY...GET construct is rather complex in that it has many options. To begin with, you need to understand that the basic purpose of the variants of the @ command—whose most common variant is @...SAY...GET—is to enable you to place a prompt at any location on the screen and then accept user keystrokes in response to the prompt.

By using the command options, you can open a window wherever you like on-screen, capture the result of some operation and display it at a location on-screen of your choosing, or print a message anywhere on the screen. The syntax of the @...SAY...GET command is

```
@ <row>,<col> [SAY <expression>
      [PICTURE <expC>] [FUNCTION <function list>]]
   [GET <variable> [[OPEN] WINDOW <window name>]
      [PICTURE <expC>] [FUNCTION <function list>]
      [RANGE [REQUIRED] [<low>],[<high>]]
```

```
          [VALID [REQUIRED] <condition> [ERROR <expC>]]
          [WHEN <condition>] [DEFAULT <expression>]
          [MESSAGE <expC>]]
       [COLOR [<standard>] [,<enhanced>]]
```

Upcoming examples show other @ command options. The major uses, however, are covered in the syntax shown.

An interpretation of the most common use of the command is

@ *screen location* SAY *a prompt for the user* GET the *user's input*

After you get the user's response, you must read it to a memory variable that you previously have initialized to accept the data. The @...SAY...GET command is used most often in a screen format file. Consider the following code:

```
mName = SPACE(30)
@ 08, 10 SAY "Enter your name: " GET mName
READ
? mName
```

```
* A program that demonstrates the use of WAIT
USE Maillist ORDER Customer    && Open database and
                               && Set index tag
ACCEPT "Enter the customer to update. " TO mCustomer
SEEK mCustomer                 && Seek customer from ACCEPT
IF FOUND()                     && Use WAIT for action if
                               && the record is found
   WAIT "<E>dit or <D>elete Customer? " to mAction
   maction = UPPER(MACTION)    && Make uppercase
   DO CASE                     && Actions to perform
      CASE mAction="E"
         DO EDITREC
      CASE mAction="D"
         DO DELREC
      OTHERWISE
         ? "Enter E or D to Edit or Delete customer."
   ENDCASE
ELSE                     && Message if customer not found
   ? "Customer not found."
ENDIF                    && Close if test
USE                      && Close database
RETURN                   && Return to calling program
                         && or to dot prompt
```

FIG. 17.25

Program showing the use of WAIT.

Roughly translated, this code means the following:

1. Store 30 spaces in a memory variable called *mName*.
2. On the eighth line of the screen, 10 characters from the left edge, print the phrase *Enter your name.*
3. Put the user's response into the memory variable *mName*.
4. Read the entry to *mName*.
5. Print the contents of *mName*.

Notice that the command syntax mentions PICTURE. PICTURE is a keyword that enables you to force certain types of data as the acceptable response. Any time you have a GET, a block of spaces opens on-screen. The size of that block, in characters, is determined by the type of data it is expected to accept. If it is accepting data for a numeric memory variable, the space is up to 20 characters wide. If it is accepting character data, it is the size of the string to which the memory variable was initialized.

By using a PICTURE template, you can determine what the GET accepts. You can, for example, force all characters to be uppercase by filling the template with exclamation marks (!). Table 17.2 shows the various kinds of PICTURE templates available.

**Table 17.2 Templates Available with PICTURE**

| Template | Description |
|---|---|
| ! | Converts to all uppercase |
| # | Allows numbers only (including blanks, periods, and signs) |
| $ | Displays the SET CURRENCY string instead of leading zeros |
| * | Displays * instead of leading zeros |
| , | Displays if there are digits to the left of the comma |
| . | Decimal location |
| 9 | Allows numbers only (including signs) |
| A | Allows letters only |
| L | Allows logical data only |
| N | Allows letters, numbers, and underscores |
| X | Allows any character |
| Y | Allows only Y or N; converts lowercase to uppercase, converts to .T. or .F. in the memory variable for storage |

You also have FORMAT functions available that, when used with the PICTURE keyword or the TRANSFORM() function, change the data you input to a different format. Table 17.3 shows the formats available. Note that the formats closely follow the PICTURE templates—and in some cases, such as !, with no difference. If you place a lowercase character in a GET field using PICTURE or FORMAT !, dBASE changes the response to all uppercase characters.

**Table 17.3 FORMAT Options for @...SAY...GET**

| Option | Description |
|---|---|
| ! | Allows any characters—converts letters to uppercase |
| ^ | Shows number in scientific notation |
| $ | Displays numbers as currency ($*nnn.nn*) |
| ( | Encloses negative numbers in parentheses |
| A | Allows alpha characters only |
| B | Aligns numeric data to the left side of a field (@...SAY only) |
| C | Displays CR after a positive number for accounting applications |
| D | Uses the SET DATE format in effect for dates |
| E | Uses the European date format |
| I | Centers text in the field |
| J | Aligns text to the right side of a field |
| L | Displays leading zeros |
| M | Allows a list of choices for a GET |
| R | Displays literals but doesn't enter them |
| S<*n*> | Limits the width in characters of a field to *n* and scrolls within the field if the data is too big to fit |
| T | Trims leading and trailing blanks |
| X | Opposite of C; displays DB after a negative number |
| Z | Displays zero numeric value as a blank string |

The various keyword options available in @...SAY...GET give the command its power. Using the COLOR option enables you to set different colors to highlight your prompt (SAY) and the response field (GET).

Standard color is used for the prompt, and enhanced color is used for the response. Your selections override the settings for the rest of your program for the prompt and the response. You can embed a preset default response in the GET field by using the DEFAULT keyword option. You can test for an acceptable response by specifying an expression that defines a valid response with the VALID keyword and displays your own custom error message (ERROR) if the condition is not met.

If you want to display a message when your program reads the GET statement, you can use the MESSAGE option with any valid character expression. The message appears only if SET STATUS is on. The message then appears centered, on the bottom line of the screen. The WINDOW option enables you to open an editing window on the contents of a memo field. You can specify a range of acceptable numbers with RANGE if your GET memory variable is the numeric data type.

The WHEN keyword is an extremely useful option. WHEN enables you to control when the user can respond. You use WHEN to set a condition that must be met before input is accepted. If the expression that defines the condition returns a logical true (.T.), the GET allows a response. If not, the cursor skips to the next available GET field. Therefore, you can read a response to an earlier GET, test it with an expression, and, based on the results of the test, direct the cursor to the next desired field.

When you use @...SAY...GET to design a data input form, you can use the commands CREATE/MODIFY SCREEN to build your screen. These commands build the @...SAY...GET statements for you.

You have four other uses for @ to explore: @...CLEAR, @...FILL, @...TO, and @...SCROLL. The first, @...CLEAR, is a safe way to clear a screen without clearing any data. The syntax is

```
@ <row1>, <col1> CLEAR [TO <row2>, <col2>]
```

If you want to clear the entire screen without affecting any of the data or memory variables, for example, use the following command:

```
@ 0,0 CLEAR
```

or

```
CLEAR
```

Instead of clearing the entire screen, however, you can clear only a portion of the screen. To clear the only upper half of the screen, use this command:

```
@ 0,0 CLEAR TO 12,0
```

You can clear only the section of the screen used to display a message after the user has finished reviewing the message. For example:

```
IF FOUND()
      DO SomePrgm
ELSE
      @ 20,10 SAY "Record not found."
      WAIT ""
      @ 20,10 CLEAR TO 20,26
ENDIF
```

The @...FILL command works exactly the same way, except that it fills the designated area with the color of your choice. The syntax for the @...FILL command follows:

```
@ <row1>, <col1> FILL TO <row2>, <col2>
      [COLOR <color attribute>]
```

You may find the @...FILL command especially useful for highlighting important information on the screen.

The @...TO command draws a box with a double-line or single-line border, starting with its upper left corner at coordinates specified in *<row1, col1>* and its lower right corner at coordinates *<row2, col2>*, as shown in the following syntax:

```
@ <row1, col1> TO <row2>, <col2>
[DOUBLE/PANEL/<border definition string>]
[COLOR <color attribute>]
```

The PANEL keyword is used to present a solid border with highlight in reverse video.

The @...SCROLL command enables you to move the contents of a certain region of the screen to a new location. The syntax for the @...SCROLL command follows:

```
@ <row1>, <col1> TO <row2>, <col2>
      SCROLL [UP/DOWN/LEFT/RIGHT][BY <expN>][WRAP]
```

If you want to move the section from row 10 to row 15 up 3 lines, for example, you would use the following command:

```
@ 10,79 TO 15,79 SCROLL UP BY 3
```

**For Related Information...**

◂◂ “Using Templates,” p. 205.

◂◂ “Using Picture Functions,” p. 210.

# Summary

You have covered a lot of ground in this chapter. You have developed a grasp of the basic building blocks of dBASE IV programming and started writing simple program code. You discovered the various types of dBASE IV files. You were introduced to the CREATE command so that you could build databases and to the MODIFY commands so that you could build program elements, such as PRG files. Then you began learning about multiple databases and relations. Finally, you explored conditional commands and program loops, memory variables, and accepting user input.

In the next chapter, you modify applications code built by the Applications Generator. You learn how to build menus of several types, you explore windows, and you experiment with updating your database and appending data to your database from within applications. You also are introduced to procedures, procedure files, and libraries.

Also in the next chapter, you learn about creating your own functions. This is a very powerful programming capability that enables you to add a library of custom functions to your library of custom procedures.

18

CHAPTER

# Using Menus, Procedures, and User-Defined Functions

In Chapter 17, you learned about the basic building blocks involved in designing your dBASE application. You learned that the design of your application is centered on a system of user menus. You also learned that these menus direct the way users interact with the data and actions in your application.

In this chapter, you learn how to do the following:

- Create and use windows
- Create and use different menu types
- Use the REPLACE FROM ARRAY command
- Write program modules, using procedures

- Create and use a function
- Access DOS commands from within dBASE
- Create and use keyboard macros

You also examine the kinds of menu styles available in dBASE IV; learn several ways to polish your application; and look at procedures, procedure libraries, and user-defined functions. The chapter concludes with a brief look at running external programs from inside a dBASE IV application and making keyboard macros.

# Designing Your Application

The preceding chapter discussed the general method for designing a database application. In this chapter, you build on this method by developing the menu system around which you build your application. Besides the organization of the data itself, the menu system—or *user interface*—is probably the most important aspect of your application. In dBASE IV, you have two vital tools to help you develop your user interface: menus and windows.

The first tool is the *menu*, which dBASE IV uses in four basic types: horizontal-bar, pull-down, pop-up, and list. Whichever type you select, you need to design the flow of your program carefully. The following are rules of thumb for menu design:

- Never switch between menus on the same level. Provide only menu choices that offer a submenu of that choice or return you to the next higher menu. Switching between menus on the same level produces "spaghetti" code, which can cause endless loops that prevent a user from exiting the menu choice.
- Always provide an escape so that users can return to a higher-level menu if they get into trouble. The escape can be a RETURN TO MAIN MENU command or QUIT TO DOS command, depending on the level of the menu in the overall menu hierarchy. Be sure to close off all files, memory variables, and databases so that you can make this selection.
- Plan your menu hierarchy to flow naturally from one function to the next; the hierarchy should reflect the way users work with the application.
- Keep your main menu selections as broad as possible, based on the main purposes of the application.
- Offer a submenu that provides utilities such as backups, database packing, and reindexing.

The flowchart in Chapter 17 contained a box labeled *Write Program or Output Files*. Your menu system is the first of those files. Figure 18.1 shows the generic block diagram of a typical menu system. You can apply this diagram to virtually any type of menu, including dBASE III Plus list-type menus.

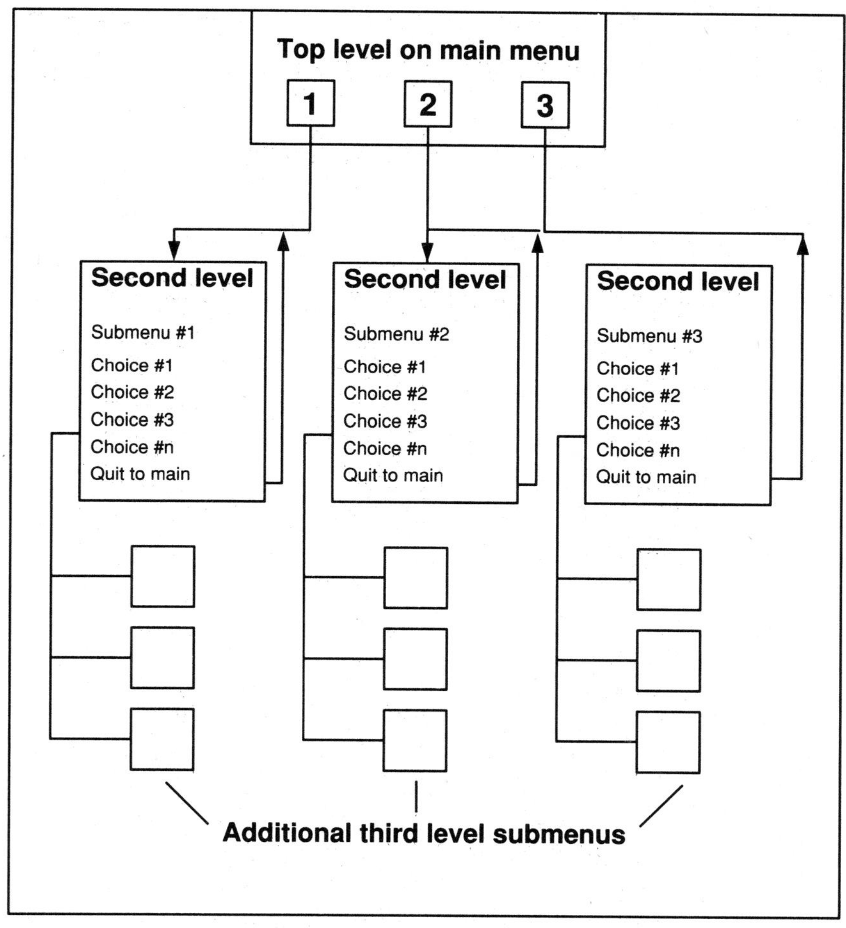


FIG. 18.1

Typical hierarchical menu flow.

The diagram in figure 18.1 shows three levels of menus. First is a *top-level menu* (or *main menu*), with three choices. Each of the three main choices offers a *submenu*, or *second-level menu*, and each second-level submenu offers additional third-level menus. Each second-level submenu includes an *n* choice and a final choice that returns you to the main menu. The *n* choice is the escape. Each third-level submenu also should have an escape to the second-level submenu or the main menu. You may notice that, following the rule of thumb for menu design, none of the choices within a given level sends you to another choice within that level.

The second tool for developing your user interface, the *window*, enables you to carry out different activities in confined portions of the screen. You can use windows, for example, to list data or supply help messages.

A window is just like a small screen on your large screen—it is treated as an entity separate from the screen around it. You may carry out operations in a window without affecting another window or the original dBASE screen.

Memory variables often are used for storing data before you place the data into the database. An *array* is a way to create a memory variable that has slots for storing many memory variables. An array is similar to a database in memory. Therefore, the command APPEND FROM ARRAY can place all the information contained in an array into the database. One row in the array becomes one record in the database.

When you write a program, you find that you can use some code over and over again. You may write code to place error messages on-screen. The same error message may occur during different parts of the program. The error message `Record not found`, for example, may appear when a database is searched and a record not found.

You can place each such error message in a *procedure*, a program file that contains *subprograms*—small, self-contained programs that contribute to the work of a larger program. When an error message occurs, the correct procedure is run from the procedure file. Procedure files perform a function similar to that of the DO CASE...ENDCASE commands. You use procedures when you create menus.

*Functions* are common in dBASE IV programming. LTRIM() and RTRIM(), for example, trim blank spaces from the left or right of a character string, and MAX() determines the maximum value. In addition, dBASE IV enables you to create your own functions, called *user-defined functions*, or UDFs. You can use dBASE commands, for example, to create a UDF to center text on-screen.

With the RUN command, you can access DOS programs and run them from inside dBASE. DOS's BACKUP and RESTORE commands, for example, enable you to back up and restore data from a hard disk.

Finally, keyboard macros are discussed in this chapter. A *keyboard macro* enables you to assign commands to a key so that you or the application user can perform a task simply by pressing a preassigned key.

# Understanding Menus

The four types of menus used in dBASE IV are bar menus, pull-down menus, pop-up menus, and lists. Each type is easy to create and use.

The *bar menu* is similar to Lotus 1-2-3 menus. Menu choices appear across the top of the screen, and you make selections by moving along the list and pressing Enter or by pressing one character highlighted within the choice name. The dBASE IV menu bar contains your top-level, or main menu, choices.

*Pop-up menus* are vertical menus that you can use for main menus, but they are more commonly secondary menus that "pop up" on-screen.

A *pull-down menu* is really just a combination of a bar and pop-up menu. When you move to an option on the bar menu, a pop-up menu appears below the option on the bar menu. You then choose tasks from the pulled-down menu.

The *list* enables you to create a menu of existing data items. You can use data from a database to create a list menu.

# Using Menu Bars and Pull-Down Menus

Before learning about menu bars and pull-down menus, you need to refresh your knowledge of menu design concepts, including the *menu hierarchy*—the system for grouping menus and submenus.

The first step in grouping your menus involves designing the menu contents. You may want to list on a piece of paper all the functions your application will perform. Then collect those functions into logical groups, with each function calling another menu or executing a single program module (PRG file). After you complete this step, draw your menus with the individual choices that execute your plan. Make sure that you include escape choices, a top menu choice for utilities, and a way to exit from the program and return to DOS.

Certain commands are unique to dBASE IV menus. The following are the steps and commands involved in building a bar menu:

| | |
|---|---|
| 1. Name the menu. | DEFINE MENU |
| 2. Name the menu prompts (pads). | DEFINE PAD |
| 3. Designate the action to take when the user selects a choice. | ON SELECTION PAD |
| 4. Open the menu. | ACTIVATE MENU |
| 5. Close the menu. | DEACTIVATE MENU |

A *pad* is a bar menu choice that has four elements: a pad name, a user prompt, a set of location coordinates, and an optional message that appears on the lower line of the screen in the dBASE message area.

**TIP** Enhance your program by defining the pads of your main menu in the order in which you want the highlight bar to access them.

The following are syntax diagrams for commands used to define menus and pads:

```
DEFINE MENU <menu name> [MESSAGE <expC>]
```

and

```
DEFINE PAD <pad name> OF <menu name> PROMPT
<expC> [AT <row>,<col>] [MESSAGE <expC>]
```

After you name the top menu and define the pads that make it up, define the action to take if the user selects a particular pad. You have three choices of action available: you can execute an application module, have the user press Enter to activate a pop-up submenu, or have the submenu pop up automatically when the user moves the highlight bar to the top menu choice. The last two choices create a pull-down menu.

The following commands correspond to each method, beginning with ON SELECTION PAD:

```
ON SELECTION PAD <padname> OF <menuname> [<command>]
```

This command enables the user to move the highlight to the pad and, when the user presses Enter, execute the program code. The code can be a program in a PRG file or in a procedure file.

The next example calls a submenu when the user moves the highlight bar to a pad and presses Enter:

```
ON SELECTION PAD <padname> OF <menuname> ACTIVATE POPUP <nextmenu>
```

Finally, the following example creates a menu that does not require the user to press Enter. Note that you use ON PAD instead of ON SELECTION PAD for this purpose:

```
ON PAD <padname> OF <menuname> ACTIVATE POPUP <nextmenu>
```

To use the menu created in this example, execute the ACTIVATE MENU command. Because you need to name the menu and the optional opening position of the highlight bar, use the following syntax:

```
ACTIVATE MENU <menu name> PAD <pad name>
```

When you finish using a menu, remember to put the menu away and close open files and memory variables. The following command closes a bar menu:

```
DEACTIVATE MENU
```

## Using Pop-Up Menus

Pop-up menus can appear on-screen at any time; however, they normally appear when you make a menu choice from a top-level menu. The pop-up menu is defined much differently from the menu bar. With pop-up menus, you define the appearance of the menu using various menu commands; then you use DO CASE to define the actions to take when you make a selection. Use the following steps and commands to build pop-up menus:

| Step | Command |
|---|---|
| 1. Name the menu. | DEFINE POPUP |
| 2. Define each menu bar. | DEFINE BAR |
| 3. Define the actions each selection will invoke. | ON SELECTION POPUP and DO CASE |
| 4. Open the menu. | ACTIVATE POPUP |
| 5. Close the menu. | DEACTIVATE POPUP |

To make a selection, move the highlight bar to the desired choice and press Enter, or press the first character of the selection. When the choice is made, the number of the bar (as you defined it with the DEFINE BAR statement) is used by the DO CASE command as follows:

```
CASE BAR() = n
      DO <next-program>
```

Notice the use of the BAR() function. This function returns the number you assigned to the bar in the DEFINE BAR statement. You also can invoke the next level of pop-up menu by using the ACTIVATE POPUP command instead of the DO command. Make sure that you do not try to activate a pop-up menu before you have defined it and its bars.

The syntax for defining a pop-up menu follows:

```
DEFINE POPUP <popup name> FROM <row1>,<col1>
   [TO <row2>,<col2>] [PROMPT FIELD <field name>
   /PROMPT FILES [LIKE <skeleton>]/PROMPT
   STRUCTURE] [PROMPT MESSAGE <expC>]
```

To define the option bar on the pop-up, use the following syntax:

```
DEFINE BAR <line number> OF <popup name>
   PROMPT <expC> [MESSAGE <expC>]
      [SKIP [FOR <condition>]]
```

To define a task to perform, use this syntax:

```
ON SELECTION POPUP <popup name>/ALL [BLANK] [<command>]
```

# Sample Menu Programs

The next two program listings show the code needed to create and use a bar menu, pull-down menu, and pop-up menu. Each example is a working menu system. The options on the submenus, however, lack the code necessary to make the options work; when an option is selected, the message `This Choice Is Not Installed` appears.

The first listing, shown here, shows a bar menu with pull-down submenus. Note that the pull-down menu is actually a pop-up menu placed directly below the corresponding option on the bar menu.

```
******************************************************************
* MAINMENU.PRG
* Demonstrates the use of Bar Menus (with pull-downs)
******************************************************************
* General housekeeping commands
CLEAR
SET TALK OFF
SET ECHO OFF
SET STATUS OFF
mLine = REPLICATE('-',25)

* Define the main bar menu
DEFINE MENU mainmenu
   DEFINE PAD exp OF mainmenu PROMPT "EXPENSES" AT 2,4 ;
      MESSAGE "Post, Pay or List Expenses"
   DEFINE PAD rcv OF mainmenu PROMPT "RECEIVABLES" AT 2,22 ;
      MESSAGE "Post, Receive or List Receivables"
   DEFINE PAD prnt OF mainmenu PROMPT "PRINT" AT 2,40 ;
      MESSAGE "Print Utilities, Print Invoices"
```

```
   DEFINE PAD utils OF mainmenu PROMPT "UTILITIES" AT 2,53 ;
      MESSAGE "Application and System Utilities"
   DEFINE PAD getout OF mainmenu PROMPT "EXIT" AT 2,68 ;
      MESSAGE "Close Files, Exit the Application"

* Define the actions to be taken when a selection is made from the
* bar menu. In each case, except Exit, a pull-down menu will be
* shown.
   ON PAD exp OF mainmenu ACTIVATE POPUP exppop
   ON PAD rcv OF mainmenu ACTIVATE POPUP rcvpop
   ON PAD prnt OF mainmenu ACTIVATE POPUP prntpop
   ON PAD utils OF mainmenu ACTIVATE POPUP utilpop
   ON SELECTION PAD getout OF mainmenu DO esc
* When you select EXIT, the procedure esc is executed.
* You must use ON SELECTION PAD rather than ON PAD before a DO
* command.
* Each of the pull-down menus is defined next. Remember, even
* though the menus appear on-screen as a pull-down menu,
* each pull-down is created using a pop-up menu placed below its
* corresponding selection on the bar menu.
DEFINE POPUP exppop FROM 3,4 TO 9,24     && EXPENSES selection
   DEFINE BAR 1 OF exppop PROMPT " EXPENSES" SKIP
   DEFINE BAR 2 OF exppop PROMPT mLine SKIP
   DEFINE BAR 3 OF exppop PROMPT " Post an Expense"
   DEFINE BAR 4 OF exppop PROMPT " Write a Check"
   DEFINE BAR 5 OF exppop PROMPT " List Unpaid Bills"
      ON SELECTION POPUP exppop DO expproc

DEFINE POPUP rcvpop FROM 3,22 TO 9,42    && RECEIVABLES selection
   DEFINE BAR 1 OF rcvpop PROMPT " RECEIVABLES" SKIP
   DEFINE BAR 2 OF rcvpop PROMPT mLine SKIP
   DEFINE BAR 3 OF rcvpop PROMPT " Post Sales"
   DEFINE BAR 4 OF rcvpop PROMPT " Receive a Payment"
   DEFINE BAR 5 OF rcvpop PROMPT " List Receivables"
      ON SELECTION POPUP rcvpop DO expproc

DEFINE POPUP prntpop FROM 3,40 TO 8,60   && PRINT selection
   DEFINE BAR 1 OF prntpop PROMPT " PRINT" SKIP
   DEFINE BAR 2 OF prntpop PROMPT mLine SKIP
   DEFINE BAR 3 OF prntpop PROMPT " Print Utilities"
   DEFINE BAR 4 OF prntpop PROMPT " Print Invoices"
      ON SELECTION POPUP prntpop DO expproc

DEFINE POPUP utilpop FROM 3,53 TO 8,78  && UTILITIES selection
   DEFINE BAR 1 OF utilpop PROMPT " UTILITIES" SKIP
   DEFINE BAR 2 OF utilpop PROMPT mLine SKIP
   DEFINE BAR 3 OF utilpop PROMPT " Application Utilities"
   DEFINE BAR 4 OF utilpop PROMPT " System Utilities"
      ON SELECTION POPUP utilpop DO expproc
```

```
ACTIVATE MENU mainmenu PAD exp       && Activate the bar menu

* This procedure quits the application and returns to DOS when
* EXIT is selected from the bar menu.
PROCEDURE esc
* This procedure is called by each of the pop-up menus. This is only
* done for demonstration purposes. In a normal program, each pop-up
* menu would call a separate procedure. Notice, in this procedure,
* that all of the options have been deactivated.
PROCEDURE expproc

DO CASE
   CASE BAR() = 3
      @ 21,25 SAY "This Choice Is Not Installed"
      WAIT
      @ 21,0 CLEAR
      RETURN
   CASE BAR() = 4
      @ 21,25 SAY "This Choice Is Not Installed"
      WAIT
      @ 21,0 CLEAR
      RETURN
   CASE BAR() = 5
      @ 21,25 SAY "This Choice Is Not Installed"
      WAIT
      @ 21,0 CLEAR
      RETURN

ENDCASE
RETURN                         && Return from the procedure
```

The first five program commands perform general housekeeping tasks such as clearing the screen, shutting off extraneous display to the screen, and shutting off the status bar. Also, 25 hyphens are stored in a memory variable, *mLine*, which creates a dividing line in the menus.

The bar menu is defined next, and has five selections: EXPENSES, RECEIVABLES, PRINT, UTILITIES, and EXIT. Each option is placed in the second row of the screen, at column positions 4, 22, 40, 53, and 68, respectively. Each menu selection displays a different message at the bottom of the screen.

Four ON PAD commands and one ON SELECTION PAD command direct the flow of the program, based on the option the user selects. Notice that the ON PAD commands activate a pop-up menu as soon as the user selects the bar menu option. When EXIT is chosen on the bar menu, ON SELECTION PAD requires that the user press Enter to select this option. When EXIT is chosen, a procedure called *esc* is executed.

The four pop-up menus are defined next, with DEFINE POPUP commands. Along with the definition of the menu itself, each selection from the pop-up menus is defined with the DEFINE BAR commands. Notice that after each menu and its associated selections is an ON SELECTION POPUP command. This command redirects program flow according to the way each menu is designed to call a different part of the application.

The EXPENSES menu, for example, may redirect flow to a program that handles your accounts payable, whereas the RECEIVABLES menu may redirect program flow to a different program—one that manages your accounts receivable. Each ON SELECTION POPUP statement for each pop-up menu should redirect the program to another procedure or program file. For demonstration purposes, each ON SELECTION POPUP command redirects the program flow to one procedure: expproc.

In each pop-up menu definition, two DEFINE BAR commands contain the SKIP option. SKIP causes these bars to be skipped by the cursor when the user presses the arrow keys to move through the menu. This option indicates bars that are menu text, not menu options.

The first skipped item is the pop-up menu title; the title EXPENSES is skipped, for example. The second is the divider line: *mLine*. This line is simply cosmetic—it separates the menu title from the options. Even though this line was initialized with 25 hyphens, only the number of hyphens needed to fill the menu is displayed.

The ACTIVATE MENU command actually displays the main menu onscreen. Notice that the option `PAD exp` appears in this command. This option is included so that the selection EXPENSES is always the selection first highlighted. If the command contained `PAD prnt`, then the PRINT option of the main menu would be the first option highlighted.

At the end of the program is procedure code. Two procedures are included here: `esc` and `expproc`. The procedure `esc` is activated when you select EXIT from the bar menu; `expproc` is activated by any other bar menu selection. Although procedures are used for actions in this example, separate PRG files can just as easily be called from each menu choice.

The next listing shows the same application, but instead of using a combination of a bar menu with pop-up menus, this listing uses all pop-up menus.

```
****************************************************************
* MAINMENU.PRG
* Demonstrates pop-up menus
****************************************************************
* General housekeeping commands
CLEAR
SET TALK OFF
SET ECHO OFF
SET STATUS OFF
mLine = REPLICATE('-',25)

* Define the main pop-up menu
DEFINE POPUP mainmenu FROM 5,25 TO 13,55 ;
   MESSAGE "To select, use arrows and <Enter> or first letter."

      DEFINE BAR 1 OF mainmenu PROMPT "     M A I N   M E N U" SKIP
      DEFINE BAR 2 OF mainmenu PROMPT SPACE(2)+mLine SKIP
      DEFINE BAR 3 OF mainmenu PROMPT "          Expenses"
      DEFINE BAR 4 OF mainmenu PROMPT "         Receivables"
      DEFINE BAR 5 OF mainmenu PROMPT "       Print Utilities"
      DEFINE BAR 6 OF mainmenu PROMPT "          Utilities"
      DEFINE BAR 7 OF mainmenu PROMPT "         Exit to DOS"
         ON SELECTION POPUP mainmenu DO mainproc
* The procedure mainproc contains all of the actions to be
* performed when a selection is made from the main menu.

ACTIVATE POPUP mainmenu        && Activate the main menu

* Each of the pop-up submenus is defined in a separate procedure.
PROCEDURE exppop               && Expenses pop-up

DEFINE POPUP exp FROM 9,35 TO 16,60 ;
   MESSAGE "Post, Pay or List Expenses"
      DEFINE BAR 1 OF exp PROMPT "        EXPENSES" SKIP
      DEFINE BAR 2 OF exp PROMPT mLine SKIP
      DEFINE BAR 3 OF exp PROMPT " Post an Expense"
      DEFINE BAR 4 OF exp PROMPT " Write a Check"
      DEFINE BAR 5 OF exp PROMPT " List Unpaid Bills"
      DEFINE BAR 6 OF exp PROMPT " Return to Main Menu"
         ON SELECTION POPUP exp DO expproc

ACTIVATE POPUP exp
RETURN               && Return from the procedure
*
PROCEDURE rcvpop    && Receivables pop-up

DEFINE POPUP rec FROM 10,35 TO 17,60 ;
   MESSAGE "Post, Receive or List Receivables"
      DEFINE BAR 1 OF rec PROMPT "      RECEIVABLES" SKIP
      DEFINE BAR 2 OF rec PROMPT mLine SKIP
```

```
      DEFINE BAR 3 OF rec PROMPT " Post a Sale"
      DEFINE BAR 4 OF rec PROMPT " Receive a Payment"
      DEFINE BAR 5 OF rec PROMPT " List Receivables"
      DEFINE BAR 6 OF rec PROMPT " Return to Main Menu"
         ON SELECTION POPUP rec DO expproc

ACTIVATE POPUP rec
RETURN                 && Return from the procedure
*
PROCEDURE prntpop      && Print Utilities pop-up

DEFINE POPUP prnt FROM 11,35 TO 18,60 ;
   MESSAGE "Print Utilities, Print Invoices"
      DEFINE BAR 1 OF prnt PROMPT "         PRINT" SKIP
      DEFINE BAR 2 OF prnt PROMPT mLine SKIP
      DEFINE BAR 3 OF prnt PROMPT " Print Utilities"
      DEFINE BAR 4 OF prnt PROMPT " Print Invoices"
      DEFINE BAR 6 OF prnt PROMPT " Return to Main Menu"
         ON SELECTION POPUP prnt DO expproc

ACTIVATE POPUP prnt
RETURN                 && Return from the procedure
*
PROCEDURE utilpop      && Utilities pop-up

DEFINE POPUP util FROM 12,35 TO 19,60 ;
   MESSAGE "Application and System Utilities"
      DEFINE BAR 1 OF util PROMPT "       UTILITIES" SKIP
      DEFINE BAR 2 OF util PROMPT mLine SKIP
      DEFINE BAR 3 OF util PROMPT " Application Utilities"
      DEFINE BAR 4 OF util PROMPT " System Utilities"
      DEFINE BAR 6 OF util PROMPT " Return to Main Menu"
         ON SELECTION POPUP util DO expproc

ACTIVATE POPUP util
RETURN            && Return from the procedure

* This procedure is called when a selection is made from the main
* menu. A DO CASE construct determines which selection from the
* main menu was selected, and executes the correct procedure to
* place the appropriate submenu on-screen.
PROCEDURE mainproc
DO CASE
   CASE BAR() = 3
      DO exppop        && Calls Expenses pop-up

   CASE BAR() = 4
      DO rcvpop        && Calls Receivables pop-up
```

```
   CASE BAR() = 5
      DO prntpop      && Calls Print Utilities pop-up
   CASE BAR() = 6
      DO utilpop      && Calls Utilities pop-up
   CASE BAR() = 7
      DEACTIVATE POPUP
ENDCASE
RETURN          && Return from the procedure
* This procedure is called by each of the pop-up menus. This is done
* only for demonstration purposes. In a normal program, each pop-up
* menu would call a separate procedure. Notice, in this procedure,
* that all of the options have been deactivated.
PROCEDURE expproc
   DO CASE
   CASE BAR() = 3
      @ 21,25 SAY "This Choice Is Not Installed"
      WAIT
      @ 21,0 CLEAR
      RETURN
   CASE BAR() = 4
      @ 21,25 SAY "This Choice Is Not Installed"
      WAIT
      @ 21,0 CLEAR
      RETURN
   CASE BAR() = 5
      @ 21,25 SAY "This Choice Is Not Installed"
      WAIT
      @ 21,0 CLEAR
      RETURN
   CASE BAR() = 6
      DEACTIVATE POPUP
ENDCASE
RETURN
```

Because this program is similar to that of the preceding example, much of the code is similar. The main menu is a pop-up rather than a bar, however, so the code for the main menu is different.

The first five program commands perform general housekeeping such as clearing the screen, shutting off extraneous display, and shutting off the status bar. Also, 25 underscores are stored in a memory variable, *mLine*, which creates a dividing line in the menus.

The main pop-up menu is defined next with the command DEFINE POPUP. Notice that the position of the menu is from row 5, column 25 to row 13, column 55. The column values were chosen to center the menu on-screen and allow enough room in the menu to display each option. The row positions do not precisely center the menu on-screen between the top of the screen and the bottom, but the height is adequate to display each of the options on the menu. One message is displayed at the bottom of the screen, telling the user how to select each option.

The DEFINE BAR commands define each menu option for the pop-up. As with the pop-up menus in the preceding example, two menu selections in each pop-up definition have the optional SKIP command so that they serve as menu text rather than a menu selection, and are skipped by the cursor.

The options that serve as selections are padded with space; the option EXPENSES contains 10 spaces, for example. The spaces are included to center each menu option in the pop-up menu. The menu width is from 25 to 55, or 30 characters wide. Because the menu has a border on each side, 28 positions remain for characters. EXPENSES is eight characters wide, so 20 character positions remain for blank spaces, 10 on each side.

The command ACTIVATE POPUP mainmenu places the main menu on-screen. You may make selections using the arrow keys to highlight an option and press Enter to select the option; or you may press the first letter of the option. When you make a selection from the main menu, the procedure mainproc is activated.

The next four procedures—exppop, rcvpop, prntpop, and utilpop—display pop-up submenus. Each procedure is called by the mainproc procedure, and each contains the commands DEFINE POPUP...MESSAGE, DEFINE BAR, and ON SELECTION POPUP to create the submenu pop-up and menu options and to direct program flow after a selection has been made. As with the preceding example, each menu option leads to a single procedure, expproc. Again, you normally redirect each submenu to a different procedure or program. The single procedure approach appears only for demonstration purposes.

The procedure mainproc is nothing more than a DO CASE...ENDCASE construct. The DO CASE construct redirects program flow to one of the submenu procedures, based on the main menu option you choose. Notice that each CASE in the DO CASE construct tests for the number of the bar that was selected from the main menu.

The final procedure is expproc, which is called by each submenu. No matter which submenu you choose, program flow is redirected to this procedure. As with the mainproc procedure, this procedure uses the DO CASE...ENDCASE construct to determine the selection you have made.

## Enhancing Pop-Up Menus

A few tricks can help you enhance the look of your pop-up menus. One trick is to insert blank lines (bars) between choices for aesthetic reasons when your submenu has only a few choices. You insert blank lines by skipping a number in the <line number> modifier of the DEFINE BAR command. Don't forget that you do this when you write your CASE statements; if you create menu selections on bars 1, 3, 5, and so on, remember to test for these lines (not lines 2, 4, and so on) in your DO CASE construct. Use `BAR() = 1, BAR() = 3, BAR() = 5,` and so on.

You also can insert lines that are not menu choices but are dividers between groups of selections in a long menu, as you saw with the memory variable *mLine*. Instead of just using this memory variable once, however, use it in different bar locations to separate commands.

A second trick enables you to skip a noneffective menu selection; for example, you can skip a menu choice that browses an empty database. The keyword SKIP, along with a FOR condition enables you to avoid selecting that choice. The FOR RECCOUNT() = 0 expression, for example, tests for an empty database. The actual program line would look something like the following:

```
DEFINE BAR 3 OF popmenu PROMPT "Display records"
     SKIP FOR RECCOUNT() = 0
```

**TIP** To invoke a procedure or program from the top-level bar menu, use ON SELECTION PAD.

## Using Pop-Up Lists

Pop-up menus contain fixed information—the text you define with the PROMPT keyword. Lists, however, are pop-ups that can contain information you want to put into them, usually called *variable data*. Examples of variable data include lists of database contents, results of a DIR listing, or results of a listing of active fields in a database. The following listing uses a pop-up menu to show the contents of the Maillist database.

```
*************************************************************
* POPLIST.PRG
* Code fragment that demonstrates a pop-up menu for listing
* the contents of a field of the Maillist database. By using
* the pop-up, you can scroll through the database.
*************************************************************
* Perform housekeeping commands
SET TALK OFF
SET ECHO OFF
CLEAR ALL
CLEAR

* Test for a color display and reset colors
IF ISCOLOR()
         SET COLOR OF BOX TO r/w
         SET COLOR OF MESSAGES TO w/r
         SET COLOR OF HIGHLIGHT TO w/r
ENDIF
USE maillist      && open database
* Define list pop-up using the field customer. Display a message
* at the bottom of the screen to tell user how to exit the list.
DEFINE POPUP fields FROM 2,5 TO 10,50 PROMPT FIELD customer ;
      MESSAGE "Press Esc to close the list"
* When the user makes a selection from the list, redirect
* the program to the procedure DispField
      ON SELECTION POPUP fields DO DispField
ACTIVATE POPUP fields
DEACTIVATE POPUP
CLEAR ALL

PROCEDURE DispField
   STORE PROMPT() TO mSelection    && retrieve selection
   CLEAR
   @ 12,10 SAY "The field you selected is: "+mSelection
   WAIT
RETURN
```

In this program, you see that some of the housekeeping is done first: the screen is cleared, and then special colors are set (for a color monitor). Next, the Maillist database is opened.

The DEFINE POPUP command creates the pop-up menu, but the prompt is set to a field in the database: Customer. When the ACTIVATE POPUP command is executed, a pop-up window appears on-screen, listing all the contents of the Customer field. You may use the arrow keys to scroll through the list of customers.

The ON SELECTION POPUP command redirects the program flow to the procedure DispField after the user has made a selection from the list. When DispField is executed, notice that the selection (PROMPT()) is stored in the memory variable *mSelection*. The procedure simply prints the selection on-screen. You could, however, use the selection as the basis of a SEEK command to find the selected record.

Control is returned from the procedure back to the main part of the program. The pop-up list appears again, and the user may make another selection. If the user presses Esc, the pop-up is deactivated, the database is closed, and memory variables are released.

FROM HERE...

**For Related Information...**

▸▸ "ACTIVATE POPUP," p. 666.

▸▸ "DEFINE MENU," p. 702.

▸▸ "DEFINE POPUP," p. 703.

▸▸ "DO CASE," p. 712.

▸▸ "ON PAD," p. 737.

▸▸ "ON SELECTION PAD," p. 738.

# Creating and Using Windows

Windows are much more than simple on-screen graphic elements. When designed and used properly, windows provide an additional work surface for actions performed by you or by the application. An example of a window for your own actions is one that pops up with context-sensitive help after you press F1. A window that lists database contents in response to a query you make is a window used for the application's actions. In both cases, the action takes place inside the window. If you write your application cleverly, you can open additional windows with additional actions going on within them. You can use up to 20 windows on one screen to display your output, menus, and messages.

You create a window by following these steps:

1. Define and name the window using the DEFINE WINDOW command. This command uses the following syntax:

```
DEFINE WINDOW <window-name>
   FROM <row1>,<col1>
   TO <row2>,<col2>
   [DOUBLE/PANEL/NONE/<border definition string>]
   [COLOR [<standard>]
   [,<enhanced>] [,<frame>]]
```

Use different names in your window definitions. If you use the same name in two window definitions, your system keeps only the last one you defined.

**TIP**

The DEFINE WINDOW command enables you to describe the window location, size, colors, and name. After you define and name a window, you can invoke it at any time with the ACTIVATE WINDOW *<window-name>* command. Remember, if you use the same name in two window definitions, your system keeps only the last one you defined.

2. Activate the window with the ACTIVATE WINDOW command.
3. Write the code for the actions you want to occur inside the window. As long as you have not used DEACTIVATE WINDOW on the window or activated another window on top of it, all the program steps you write between the ACTIVATE WINDOW and DEACTIVATE WINDOW commands execute inside the window.
4. Close the window with the DEACTIVATE WINDOW command. You may want to make sure that you close all open files, databases, and memory variables before you close the active window.

Now you are ready to make a window to list the contents of your Maillist database, as shown in the following example:

```
DEFINE WINDOW Sample FROM 3,5 TO 10,70
USE Maillist
ACTIVATE WINDOW Sample
DISPLAY ALL
USE
DEACTIVATE WINDOW Sample
CLEAR WINDOWS
```

After the window has been activated, all commands and actions take place in the window.

The SCAN command enables you to perform almost the same function as DO...WHILE and SKIP, but with less code. SCAN uses the following syntax:

```
SCAN [<scope>] [FOR <condition>]
   [WHILE <condition>]
   [<commands>]
   [LOOP]
   [EXIT]
ENDSCAN
```

You may notice that you do not need the LOCATE and CONTINUE (or SKIP) commands with SCAN, as you do with DO...WHILE.

The following listing demonstrates a simple dBASE window.

```
****************************************************************
* BROWSER.PRG - A program fragment illustrating the use of
* windows to browse part of a database record by record
****************************************************************
CLEAR ALL                               && Housekeeping
*  Now define the window in which your information will appear
DEFINE WINDOW browser FROM 5,0 TO 12,79 DOUBLE COLOR W+/R,N/RB

ACTIVATE WINDOW browser            && Open the window
   CLEAR                           && Clear the window
@ 0,35 SAY "TELEPHONE LIST"        && Give it a title

mrespons = "  "                    && Initialize the memory
                                   && variable
USE MAILLIST                       && Open the database

SCAN WHILE .NOT. mrespons $ "Qq"   && Scan the database record
                                   && by record until the end
                                   && or the user says to quit
DISPLAY customer, contact, phone OFF     && Display the parts
                                   && of the record you
                                   && want
?                                  && Add a couple of blank lines
?                                  && and prompt the user for a
                                   && response that you read into
                                   && the memvar mrespons

WAIT "Press Q to Quit, Return For Next Name" TO mrespons
CLEAR                              && Clear in preparation for
                                   && the next record if Q was
                                   && not selected
ENDSCAN                            && Close off the SCAN command
USE                                && Close the database
RELEASE mrespons                   && release the memvar
DEACTIVATE WINDOW browser          && Close the window
QUIT                               && Return to DOS
```

You may notice a new operation in the listing. Look at the following line of code:

```
SCAN WHILE .NOT. mrespons $ "Qq"
```

This line uses the $ argument. The dollar symbol here is the relational operator used for substring comparison. It indicates that you are going to compare the contents of the memory variable *mrespons* with the characters that come next. In this case, the next characters are *Q* and *q*. If the *Q* or the *q* is the same as the character stored in *mrespons*, a logical true (.T.) is returned. The line enables you to scan so long as you do not type *Q* or *q*. A rough translation of this code is as follows:

`SCAN` as long as it is `.NOT. true that` mrespons `contains Q or q`

Windows have many uses in dBASE IV applications. One use is to create pop-up error messages using the ON ERROR command. When your program suffers an error, you simply activate the window you defined earlier as your error window, attach appropriate text messages to the error, and then display the text in the error window. You then prompt for a keystroke to clear the window, read the keystroke, deactivate the window, and take appropriate action to correct the error.

Remember, from the time you open a window to the time you close it, programming steps that appear are executed within that window. The window is just like a small version of the display and should be treated as such.

You also can use a window to pop up part of a program for user action. If you want to prompt the user for a response based on some event in your application, for example, you can put that routine into a window. When the event occurs, the window pops up requesting user input and the user responds. At the completion of the action, the application collects the response and closes the window. Using the pop-up window gives your application a professional look and clearly focuses the user's attention on the required action. Such pop-up windows are called *dialog boxes*.

You also can design windows to accept user input into a memo field. Because memo fields are actually 10-character pointers to text in a memo file (FILENAME.DBT), you may want to enable the user to use the dBASE IV text editor (or whatever external editor you have designated) to add or edit memos or notes to database records. To perform this action, you use a special version of the @...SAY...GET command. First, you define a window. Next, you use the following command to open the window and accept user input:

```
@ <x>,<y> [SAY <"message"> [GET <memofield-name> [OPEN]
   WINDOW <window-name>]]
```

This command selects the window you designated in *<window-name>* and, when you press Ctrl-Home or F9, opens the window in the text editor mode. You then can type any message you want or edit the existing message. When you press Ctrl-End, the memo is saved to the DBT file and is available whenever you display the contents of that memo field. If you add the keyword OPEN before WINDOW in this command, the window is opened at once and then replaced with the editing window when you press Ctrl-Home.

You also can use windows to isolate and highlight activities within your application. When an important event takes place, such as an error message or a dialog between user and program, you can place the event in a window to call the user's attention to it, to cover confusing displays (without having to delete them), and to switch program execution temporarily to the immediate work at hand. After the event passes and required user input is collected, you can easily return to normal program execution by closing the window.

FROM HERE...

**For Related Information...**

▸▸ "ACTIVATE WINDOW," p. 665.

▸▸ "DEACTIVATE WINDOW," p. 699.

▸▸ "DEFINE WINDOW," p. 704.

# Putting Text in Windows

You learned previously that you can put text into a window. You can use a window as a help screen, for example, by using a combination of the TEXT command, the various window constructs, and the ON KEY command as follows. First, define the window. The window you define usually should be a generic help window, but the text that appears in the window varies according to the help the user needs. This practice enables you to design context-sensitive help screens. Next, invoke the ON KEY command to trap the F1 key, usually used for help, and place the appropriate text in the window. The following listing shows you how the command works.

```
*************************************************************
* A code fragment that demonstrates a pop-up HELP window.
*************************************************************
CLEAR ALL             && Housekeeping
SET TALK OFF          && Set the environment
SET ECHO OFF
SET BELL OFF
SET STAT OFF
CLEAR

* Now, define the generic window that you will
* continue to use for your HELP screens. Although you
* will use different text for different contexts, this
* will always be the window you invoke.
DEFINE WINDOW helpwin FROM 10,10 TO 20,70 DOUBLE COLOR w/r, n/gr
yorn = .T.                      && Initialize the memvar
USE maillist                    && open a database
ON KEY LABEL F1 DO helpproc     && Define the action to take
                                && if the F1 key is pressed
DO WHILE yorn .AND. .NOT. EOF()
      DISPLAY customer, contact OFF     && Display a record
                                && and ask the user if he
                                && or she wants more.
      @ 23,0 SAY "DO YOU WANT ANOTHER RECORD?" GET yorn PICTURE "Y"
      READ                      && Read the user's response
      SKIP
      CLEAR
ENDDO
* The procedure helpproc displays the help text in the window
* helpwin.
PROCEDURE helpproc              && Name the procedure
ACTIVATE WINDOW helpwin         && Open the help window
TEXT                            && place the following text in the
                                && window

                    H E L P
This is an example of a context-sensitive HELP
window, invoked when the user presses F1. It
pops up in a red window with white text and a
double-line border.

ENDTEXT                         && Close off the TEXT command
WAIT                            && Pause while the user reads
                                && the help message
DEACTIVATE WINDOW helpwin       && Close the help window
RETURN
```

This listing is a generic example of a help window. If you use help windows regularly, you can avoid writing the same code repeatedly by making a library of help procedures that you can call at any time. In this case, by defining the procedure to perform a DO when F1 is pressed, you dictate which help screen pops up in the window. To change to a different help screen at some other point in the program, you call another procedure with the ON KEY command.

# Accepting User Input

In Chapter 17, you learned about arrays and how to accept user input. In this chapter, you learn about three array commands. The first is APPEND FROM ARRAY, which enables you to add the information from an array to the end of the database. REPLACE FROM ARRAY, similar to APPEND FROM ARRAY, enables you to replace a record in the database with the information in the array. The third command, COPY TO ARRAY, enables you to copy information from a record in the database to an array.

> **WARNING:** To avoid damaging your record, do not accept data into the live database until you are satisfied that the data is correct.

Before you use these commands, you must have created an array capable of containing the number of fields that are in each record. Also, with APPEND FROM ARRAY and REPLACE FROM ARRAY, you must make sure that the data in the array is in the same order as the corresponding fields in the database. The data entry procedure shown in the following example uses this technique.

```
****************************************************************
* This code fragment shows how arrays accept user input and
* then edit a record in the Maillist  database.
****************************************************************
*
*
CLEAR ALL                           && Housekeeping
CLEAR
SET BELL OFF
SET TALK OFF
SET ECHO OFF
SET SCOREBOARD OFF
SET STATUS OFF
*
```

```
* First, set up the array to match the fields in your database.
* You use a two-dimensional array with one element for each
* database field. The data must be entered into the array
* elements in the same order as the fields in the database, and
* you must initialize the array for the correct field types and
* sizes.
*
DECLARE mail_aray[1,10]
mail_aray[1,1]=SPACE(30)
mail_aray[1,2]=SPACE(30)
mail_aray[1,3]=SPACE(30)
mail_aray[1,4]=SPACE(30)
mail_aray[1,5]=SPACE(30)
mail_aray[1,6]=SPACE(30)
mail_aray[1,7]=SPACE(30)
mail_aray[1,8]=SPACE(30)
mail_aray[1,9]=SPACE(30)
mail_aray[1,10]=SPACE(30)
*
* Next, set up the user input screen with @..SAY...GET
* where you store the results of the GETs in array elements
* instead of individual memory variables.
*
@ 2,20  SAY "=== MAIL LIST INPUT SCREEN ==="
@ 4,5   SAY "CUSTOMER: " GET mail_aray[1,1]
@ 5,5   SAY "CONTACT : " GET mail_aray[1,2]
@ 6,5   SAY "ADDRESS : " GET mail_aray[1,3]
@ 7,5   SAY "          " GET mail_aray[1,4]
@ 8,5   SAY "CITY    : " GET mail_aray[1,5]
@ 8,35  SAY "STATE: " GET mail_aray[1,6] PICTURE "!!"
@ 8,45  SAY "ZIP: " GET mail_aray[1,7]
@ 10,5  SAY "PHONE   : " GET mail_aray[1,8]
@ 10,45 SAY "EXTENSION:"  GET mail_aray[1,9]
@ 11,5  SAY "FAX NMBR: " GET mail_aray[1,10]

READ

USE maillist                  && Open the database
APPEND FROM ARRAY mail_aray   && Append the record
USE                           && Close the database
*
* Now select a record from the database and edit it.
* First, you need the initialized array. Because you have
* already done that, you won't do it again. In this case, it
* is only necessary to DECLARE the array. You don't need to
* initialize it to the field types because you will be
* storing the contents of a database record, which will have
* the same effect.
*
```

```
                                    && Clear the screen
mcust = SPACE(30)                   && Initialize a memvar
USE maillist                        && Open the database

@ 5,5 SAY "Find Customer Name? " GET mcust
READ
LOCATE FOR customer = mcust
*
* Now store the field contents of the selected record in the array
*
COPY TO ARRAY mail_aray
*
* The next step is to display the array contents as you would
* the screen for fill-in
*
@ 2,20   SAY "=== MAIL LIST INPUT SCREEN ==="
@ 4,5    SAY "CUSTOMER: " GET mail_aray[1,1]
@ 5,5    SAY "CONTACT : " GET mail_aray[1,2]
@ 6,5    SAY "ADDRESS : " GET mail_aray[1,3]
@ 7,5    SAY "          " GET mail_aray[1,4]
@ 8,5    SAY "CITY    : " GET mail_aray[1,5]
@ 8,35   SAY "STATE: " GET mail_aray[1,6] PICTURE "!!"
@ 8,45   SAY "ZIP: " GET mail_aray[1,7]
@ 10,5   SAY "PHONE   : " GET mail_aray[1,8]
@ 10,45  SAY "EXTENSION: " GET mail_aray[1,9]
@ 11,5   SAY "FAX NMBR: " GET mail_aray[1,10]
READ
* The final step is to replace the field contents in the located
* record with the edited ones.
*
REPLACE FROM ARRAY mail_aray
USE                             && Close the database
```

Notice several important features in this procedure. First, the physical layout of the array is the same as the tabular layout of a database. In other words, the horizontal elements (rows) represent the fields of a record, and the vertical elements (columns) represent records. Therefore, if you create an array that is 5 × 10, for example, you can use it to fill in five records in the Maillist database. If you get the rows and columns mixed up (creating a 10 × 1 array instead of a 1 × 10 array, for example), you fill in the first field of each of 10 records instead of each field of only one record.

The second feature comes up when you use DECLARE to declare an array. By default, the array is a *logical* array: each element is only one character and expects a true or a false value. For the array to know that the data types of its elements are different from the logical type, you must initialize the element to the data type you put in it. Using STORE to place data in the element (as you did in the second section of the code fragment) suffices to initialize that element. If you hold the array open and fill in data with @...SAY...GET, however, you need to initialize each element to the correct type of data in advance. In this example, you can use the SPACE() function because all the fields are character fields. You can use `<arrayname>[x,y] = 0` to initialize an element if the data type eventually becomes numeric.

Although you put a data input routine and a data editing routine in the same code fragment, you normally consider these separate procedures. You should realize one important similarity between the two, however: notice that you use the same @...SAY...GET pattern for data entry and editing. By using the same pattern, you avoid confusing the user. Also, because both screens look the same, the application seems to flow correctly. Besides, after you have written the data-entry screen code, which may be a substantial amount for a large application, you can simply copy the code and reuse it as an editing screen.

**For Related Information...**

▸▸ "@...SAY...GET," p. 657.

▸▸ "APPEND FROM ARRAY," p. 669.

▸▸ "DECLARE," p. 700.

▸▸ "REPLACE FROM ARRAY," p. 752.

# Building a Procedure Library

When you write application code, you may find that you repeatedly use the same bits of code. Sometimes you reuse the fragments within the same application; sometimes you use them in several applications. You can preserve frequently used bits of code and reuse them at will by creating a *procedure library*.

You can use the DO command to run chunks of code exactly as if they were separate programs. In earlier examples, you took pieces of code you wanted to run from within a program module and treated them as procedures. But you also can hold many different procedures in a completely separate file, called a *procedure file*. You can access these procedures in three ways:

- Use the SYSPROC = <filename> command in your CONFIG.DB file to specify a procedure file to be used with dBASE.
- Use the SET PROCEDURE TO <filename> command to specify a procedure file for use by your application.

- Use the SET LIBRARY TO <filename> command to access a procedure library file for routines you intend to use with various dBASE applications.

These commands tell your program where to look for procedures. Use the DO command to execute the procedures, just as it would if you ran an external program module.

In dBASE, all programs are treated as procedures, including the active program module. After you have identified the locations of the usable modules or procedures, dBASE knows exactly where to look to run them. Note that dBASE IV looks for procedures in the following order: SYSPROC, then SET PROCEDURE, then SET LIBRARY. You can close a procedure file by using SET PROCEDURE TO without a procedure file name. You should open and close procedure libraries as you need them instead of leaving them open all the time. Because you can have only a single procedure file open at once, you gain the use of other files if you open and close them as needed.

The following is the general format of a procedure file:

```
* Procedure library file Procfile.PRC
*
PROCEDURE proc1
<code for proc1>
RETURN

PROCEDURE proc2
<code for proc2>
RETURN

PROCEDURE procn
<code for procn>
RETURN
```

You may notice that you always start a procedure with `PROCEDURE` *`<procedure name>`* and end with `RETURN`. The PROCEDURE command identifies the procedure, and the RETURN command returns control of program execution to the program that called the procedure. The number of procedures you can have in an open procedure file is limited by memory. You can have as many as 963 procedures in a single file.

Another interesting use for a procedure is to simulate the creation of custom commands. Although you cannot execute a procedure the same way you execute a command, you can program the equivalent of a custom command and execute it with DO <*procedure name*>. When you use a procedure, however, you may want to carry information to it from the module that executes it, and then carry it back again. This flow of information is called *passing parameters*, and dBASE provides several ways to perform this activity.

Storing a value in a public memory variable and then using it later within the procedure is not an efficient way to pass parameters.

You can pass parameters from the DO command to the procedure in a two-step process: identification and initialization. You can pass parameters using memory variables, but this is not the best method. You still use memory variables, however, when you perform your two-step process. No matter how you pass information between programs or procedures, you still need a temporary "holding tank" for the data.

In step one, you identify the parameters you need in a procedure to avoid having to hard-code variables in a program module. Suppose that you have a program module you want to reuse throughout your application, but the module uses different data at different points in the application. You have two choices: hard-code the memory variables in the procedure and duplicate the procedure with different information for each of the uses to which you plan to put it, or set up memory variables as parameters and pass the information to them when you use DO to run the procedure.

When you know the memory variables you want to use as parameters, initialize them in a slightly different way from the usual. Make the first command in the procedure PARAMETERS. This command assigns the parameter names you specify in memory variables as part of the DO command that calls the procedure. Then use DO <*procedure name*> [WITH <*parameters*>]. The parameters you use with the WITH keyword can be any memory variables and need not have the same names as the parameters you specify in the PARAMETERS command. The PARAMETERS command uses the following syntax:

```
PARAMETERS <parameter list>
```

The list may contain up to 50 different memory variables or array elements. Arrays and memory variables are treated differently. A PUBLIC array element can be passed to a procedure, but the array element is not changed by the procedure. A public memory variable, however, is changed if it has been passed as a parameter to a procedure. Parameters passed to the procedure become private memory variables within the procedure and are released when you complete the procedure and use RETURN to return to the program module that called it. To avoid confusion, you may want to use parameter names different from the names of the public memory variables that created the parameters. Although you use different names for the memory variables and the parameters, the parameters are created in the procedure in the order in which you pass them using the WITH keyword in the DO command. Your code appears as follows:

```
DO procedure1 WITH memvar1, memvar2, memvar3
PROCEDURE procedure1
   PARAMETERS parm1, parm2, parm3
   <procedure-code>
RETURN
```

In this example, *memvar1* becomes *parm1*, *memvar2* becomes *parm2*, and so on. Upon the execution of the RETURN command, *parm1*, *parm2*, and *parm3* are released because they are actually private memory variables. Whenever you need the data stored in one of the parameters within the procedure, you should store it to a memvar to avoid altering the original value of the passed variable.

To keep track of the number of parameters that have been passed, use the PCOUNT() function. For example, if after executing the procedure in the preceding code you include the command ? PCOUNT(), the number 3 would be returned, indicating that three parameters had been passed to the procedure.

FROM HERE...

**For Related Information...**


▸▸ "PARAMETERS," p. 740.

▸▸ "PCOUNT()," p. 823.

▸▸ "SET LIBRARY TO," p. 879.

▸▸ "SET PROCEDURE TO," p. 887.

▸▸ "SYSPROC," p. 942.


# Creating User-Defined Functions

Functions are among the dBASE language's most important elements. Among other uses, functions enable you to perform calculations, query the operating system, determine the location of the record pointer, manipulate strings, and change data types. Functions are useful because they accomplish in a single command what often takes an entire procedure to do. Functions also act directly on data and return new data as a result of their actions. Frequently, a function you need doesn't exist in the dBASE language, so dBASE gives you a way to create it.

Functions have three parts: the function name, the data on which they act (the data enclosed in parentheses immediately following the function name), and the result (the modified data) that the function returns. When you create user-defined functions (UDFs), you must take all three aspects into account.

The commands you use in a user-defined function are controlled by the SET DBTRAP setting. To protect the integrity of your database file, if SET DBTRAP is ON (the default setting), commands that may close or alter the structure of the database are blocked. In this case, you cannot use the following commands in a UDF:

USE
CLOSE DATABASE
CONVERT
PACK
MODIFY STRUCTURE
ZAP

In addition, you should avoid using recursive commands (commands that call themselves) in UDFs. For example, don't use BROWSE in a UDF called by a BROWSE command. The following are some commands to avoid when creating a UDF:

ASSIST
BROWSE
CREATE/MODIFY
EDIT
CHANGE
INSERT
APPEND
LIST
DISPLAY

User-defined functions are nothing more than specialized procedures. Nevertheless, remember the rules: you need a function name and a returned result. With that in mind, you can use the general approach of a procedure. First, declare that you are going to define a UDF. In the procedure, you did that with the command PROCEDURE. With UDFs, you do it with the command FUNCTION and the argument *<function-name>*.

After you identify the function and give it a name, you optionally may pass parameters to it with the PARAMETERS command. The parameters are the data in the parentheses immediately following the function name. Following the PARAMETERS command, you need the code that performs the activities of your user-defined function. Finally, you must return a result. You do that with the RETURN command and a memory variable containing the result of the action of your UDF on the data.

Seem confusing? Look at these steps as they may appear in a real program:

```
FUNCTION functionname
   PARAMETERS parm1, parm2, parm3...
   <program code making up UDF>
RETURN m_result
```

Just as you built a library of procedures, you also can build a library of UDFs. You must treat the UDF library in the same way as a library of procedures, however, by invoking the file with the SET PROCEDURE TO command.

You may notice that the RETURN commands in procedures are different from the RETURN commands in UDFs. The RETURN command in a procedure is used alone, to return to the program module that called the procedure. The RETURN in the UDF, however, includes a memory variable containing the value that you are returning. In one case you are transporting a modified piece of data; in the other, you are redirecting program flow.

The following listing shows an actual UDF. This function is used to center text on-screen.

```
*************************************************************
* CENTER.PRG
* Sample program that contains a user-defined function
*************************************************************
* This following code reads text into a memory variable and
* uses the UDF CNTRTEXT to center the text on-screen.
CLEAR
mText = SPACE(75)
@ 10,01 SAY "Enter the text to center on-screen"
@ 11,01 GET mText
        READ
mPhrase = TRIM(mText)

@ 15,CNTRTEXT(mPhrase) SAY mPhrase
* UDF for centering text on-screen.
FUNCTION cntrtext
```

```
PARAMETERS mString
* This function assumes you are using an 80-character-wide screen.
mCntr=LEN(mString)
mCntr=(80-mCntr)/2
RETURN mCntr       && Returns the center position
```

# Running External Programs

You can include non-dBASE language programs in your applications in three ways: by using the RUN command or the RUN() function to run an external program from within the dBASE code; and by using LOAD and then CALL on assembly language modules—a method that requires knowledge of other programming languages.

When you use RUN to run an external program, especially a DOS command, make sure that COMMAND.COM is in the current directory path or that you have used COMSPEC in your AUTOEXEC.BAT file. When you leave your dBASE application to run the DOS command (by using RUN), your computer's operating system must know where to look for the command processor. If you ignore this requirement, you get an error message. When you issue the RUN command with a DOS command, your application leaves dBASE, executes the DOS command, and returns to the dBASE application. It appears to the user that the activity was carried out by the dBASE application. For example, from the dot prompt, type the following command:

```
RUN DIR
```

This command displays a DOS directory of the current subdirectory. This is different from the dBASE DIR command, which does not display all files by default—only database files.

The RUN command also executes an external program. Make sure, however, that you have the memory to run the program and your dBASE application. The memory does not have to cover all the dBASE application, the runtime, and the external program, because most of dBASE departs from your system's memory when you use the RUN command.

Enough of dBASE remains in memory, however, so that when you finish using the external program, your system can return automatically to the same point in your application where you left off. Your system therefore needs enough memory to hold some of dBASE, some of the program you are executing, and COMMAND.COM. Not only does this mean you need sufficient memory, but it also means that when you run a DOS command, dBASE must be able to find COMMAND.COM.

**NOTE** You can use a shorthand notation for RUN—the exclamation point (!). For example, instead of using this command:

```
RUN <program-name/DOS-commands>
```

you can use this command:

```
! <program-name/DOS-commands>
```

Both commands yield the same result.

If the program you want to run uses a considerable amount of memory, you can use the RUN() function instead of the RUN command. This function temporarily reduces the size of dBASE IV 1.5 to only 10K bytes, leaving more room for your other program to run. The syntax of the function follows:

```
RUN([<expL1>,]<expC>[,<expL2>])
```

The expression <*expC*> is a character expression containing your program name. Place quotes around the program name and path, or use a character type variable that contains this information.

The expressions <*expL1*> and <*expL2*> are optional logical expressions. If the first expression is false (.F.) or not specified, dBASE loads the operating system command processor and then your program. When you exit your program, a completion code (usually 0) is returned to dBASE. If you don't want the operating system to load, set the first expression to true (.T.). To reduce the amount of memory used by dBASE IV, set the second logical expression to true (.T.). Otherwise, your program must fit in available memory while dBASE is running.

Remember that RUN() is a function, not a command, so it must be used with a command, such as the ? command. The following example runs the program named MYPROG.EXE, which is located in the \DOS subdirectory on drive C:

```
? RUN(.T.,"C:\DOS\MYPROG.EXE",.T.)
```

**WARNING:** Do not use RUN or RUN() to execute memory-resident programs.

Another way to use external programs is with the CALL construct. You can write a program module in assembly language, for example, and execute it from within your dBASE application by following three rules. First, you must have the assembly code module in *binary* format, in a file with a BIN extension (you do not need to include the extension in your CALL statement). Second, you pass parameters in the form of a character expression, a memory variable, or an element of an array. The data type doesn't matter, except for memo types, which aren't allowed. Third, you must use LOAD to place the module into memory before you can call it. You can have up to 16 such modules, of up to 64K each, in memory at one time.

When do you use RUN and CALL? Each has slightly different uses, depending on the application. RUN takes excellent advantage of small third-party programs or utilities that can enhance your application. By using other programs, you don't have to write the program yourself. Also, your application may take advantage of data in another application or enable the user to switch back and forth between applications. You may want to enable your users to execute Lotus 1-2-3 from within your dBASE IV application.

CALL has a different benefit. Often you need to perform some function for which dBASE is not designed, such as using communications or controlling I/O ports. If you program in assembly language, however, you can build excellent routines for managing these low-level computer functions. You can include advanced features in your dBASE applications by coding them in assembly language, compiling them to a binary file, and then calling them from your dBASE application.

**For Related Information...**

▸▸ "CALL," p. 677.

▸▸ "RUN," p. 759.

▸▸ "RUN()," p. 832.

# Using Keyboard Macros

You can use *keyboard macros* to store small, useful routines and execute them from the keyboard or from within a program module. (Do not confuse the keyboard macro with the macro substitution function, &.)

Three commands are associated with keyboard macros: SAVE MACRO, RESTORE MACRO, and PLAY MACRO.

When do you use a keyboard macro? Suppose that you have a series of keystrokes you want to save and reuse from time to time. Perhaps you want to enable the user to press a function key to execute these keystrokes, or you want to include the keystrokes in a program module as a subroutine. By recording the keystrokes, saving them to a macro associated with a function key, and then saving the macro to a macro file, you can reuse the keystrokes whenever you want.

You create a keyboard macro through the Control Center by accessing the Tools menu and selecting Macro. When you invoke the choice, you are asked to name the macro. You see a menu of name choices starting with F1 (Alt-F1). If you choose F10 (Alt-F10), you can add any letter of the alphabet to the function key. For example, you may choose Alt-F10-A (hold down Alt and F10 and then press A). You can have up to 36 keyboard macros (F1 through F10 plus the 26 letters of the alphabet). You can save your macros to a single file with a KEY file extension by using the SAVE MACRO command. You then can reload them into memory with the RESTORE MACRO command and use them in your application code with the PLAY MACRO command.

After you name the macro and until you press Shift-F10-E, every keystroke you make is put in the macro. Shift-F10-E ends the macro-recording process. At this point, your macro is in memory but is not permanently saved. As long as you stay in dBASE, the macro is available.

If you want to save the macro permanently, use SAVE MACRO, which saves all the macro definitions currently in memory to whatever file you name. You also can save up to 36 macros by using different files when you use SAVE MACRO. To activate a particular set of macros, you simply use RESTORE MACRO on the file that contains the macros you want. You then can invoke the macro by pressing Alt and the appropriate function key or by inserting PLAY MACRO in your program code.

FROM HERE...

**For Related Information...**

◂◂ "Using Macros," p. 404.

# Summary

In this chapter, you learned how to make menus and how to make and use windows. You built code for windows and explored the various types of menus available for your user interface or work surface.

You learned how to display lists and how to build a library of procedures. You examined user-defined functions, and you learned ways to use external programs and binary modules to add power to your applications. Finally, you learned how to use keyboard macros in your programs.

In the next chapter, you learn how to make custom reports with special layouts, quick lists, and mailing labels.

19

CHAPTER

# Planning and Producing Reports and Labels

Chapter 18 described the techniques you can use to produce your application with its work surface and user interface. The chapter discussed menus, windows, ways to make your application accept user input, and methods for organizing the program modules in your application.

Now that you know how to gather data and organize the application, you need to know how to extract the information in useful ways. That step means learning how to perform such tasks as creating reports and labels. Chapters 10 and 11 discussed how to create reports and labels through dBASE IV's Report and Label design screens. In this chapter, you learn how to create a quick report with LIST, define custom reports, control your printer, and take advantage of the various output features available in dBASE IV.

**TIP** Before you can create a quick report by pressing Shift-F9 from the Control Panel, you must have a database to work with.

Chapter 7 showed you how to create a quick report by pressing Shift-F9 from the Control Panel. In this chapter, you begin designing and printing reports by starting with the simplest type of report: a quick report created from the dot prompt with the LIST command.

# Creating a Quick Report with LIST

Although dBASE IV offers several ways to build complex reports, you may want to produce from the dot prompt a quick list of information. You also may want to use this technique when you don't want to build a report form. The benefit of this approach is that, if you just want to list the contents of some or all the fields from some or all the records in a database, you can do so with a minimum of code. Although the results are not particularly glamorous, the listing is clear and readable, and you get the listing quickly.

Before you get any data from the system, however, you need to organize the data for output. You organize databases for output in much the same way, regardless of what your final output may look like.

You need to keep four considerations in mind when getting data ready for a report: the order in which you want the data to appear; which records you want in your report; which fields you want to appear; and how many columns wide your report must be to accommodate the information in the fields you want displayed.

## Selecting Order

In selecting the order, you have two choices: *natural order* (the order in which the data was entered) or *indexed order* (sorted by a particular field, for example, sorted by first name, last name, ZIP Code, or however you specify).

## Selecting Records

You select the records to include in the report in one of two ways. In the first way, suppose that you are using the Maillist database (the fields in Maillist are CUSTOMER, CONTACT, ADDRESS1, ADDRESS2, CITY, STATE, ZIP, PHONE, EXTENSION, and FAX). You have the database indexed by CUSTOMER. Before printing the report, you can use the SET FILTER TO command to select which records to include in the report.

A *filter* is a procedure that acts like the FOR keyword. You use the following construct:

```
SET FILTER TO [FILE <file-name>/?][<condition>]
```

This command selects the contents of a given field or fields that you want to use to determine which records appear in your report. After you filter the database, you run your report. The following is a sample of how you might use these commands:

```
USE Maillist

SET ORDER TO TAG CUSTOMER

SET FILTER TO ZIP = "46280"

LIST
```

These commands list all records in the database with the ZIP Code equal to 46280. All records that match that filter appear in order by company.

The second way to select records, and keep them indexed, is with the INDEX command itself. By using the INDEX ON command, you can select the records to include in the index with a FOR condition. To perform the same task you did with the SET FILTER TO command, use the following commands:

```
USE Maillist

INDEX ON CUSTOMER TAG CustZip FOR ZIP = "46280"

LIST
```

Both techniques provide the same results. If you are working with a large database, however, creating a new index tag takes more time than using an existing index and setting a filter.

## Using Fields/Columns

The last two considerations—determining which fields to include and the width of the report—are related. As you learn in the upcoming discussion on setting up your printer, the width of your report is limited. If you are going to produce a quick report, also referred to as an *unformatted report*, you have to watch the width carefully. If you exceed the number of columns available, each line of your report breaks, and you have part of each record on one line and part on the next. Depending on where the break occurs, your listing can be difficult or even impossible to read. To avoid this problem, determine the number of available columns you have, and then limit the fields in your report to the number of characters that fill but do not exceed that number. Allow one space (column) between each field.

## Producing Your Report

To produce your quick report, you can use the LIST or DISPLAY command to present data on-screen. Both commands can put the data on paper if you add the keywords TO PRINT. The difference between the commands, you may recall, is that DISPLAY causes the display of data to pause between pages, whereas LIST produces a continuous display. LIST is better suited for quick reports.

**TIP** To improve the readability of your report, skip a line after you enter the column headings.

After you have organized your data for output, select the data you want to print and the printer you want to use to print the data. Remember to put a header on your report page. The header usually consists of a title and column headings. Skip a line after the column headings, to improve readability, and list the selected contents of your database to the printer. That's all there is to it. Your report won't be fancy, but producing it is quick and the report is readable. Figure 19.1 shows program code that uses the Maillist database as the basis for a quick report.

The program in figure 19.1 uses an existing index, so the program is in customer order. The records that print are selected by the SET FILTER TO command, selecting records from the state of IN.

After the heading prints, the fields CUSTOMER, CONTACT, and PHONE are printed. Because only three fields are printed, each record fits on a line. The actual printed report looks like the one shown in figure 19.2.

```
*  Code fragment for printing a quick list (unformatted report)
*
* Housekeeping
CLEAR                      && Clear the screen
SET TALK OFF               && Shut off value display
SET ECHO OFF               && Shut off command display
SET HEADINGS OFF           && Suppress the List column headings
* Ready data to print
USE Maillist               && Open the database
SET ORDER TO TAG CUSTOMER     && Set index tag
SET FILTER TO STATE = "IN"    && Set filter
SET PRINTER ON             && Turn on the printer
*
*  Next you need to give the report a title and some column
*  headings.
*  When you use the SET PRINTER ON command, the ? is
*  directed to the printer
*
* Print the report header
? " =========================== P H O N E   L I S T ============================"
? " "
? "        CUSTOMER                     CONTACT PHONE"
? " ————————————————————————————————————————————————"
? " "
* Print the data
LIST customer, contact, phone OFF TO PRINT   && Print the listing
???
* Housekeeping
SET PRINTER OFF          && Turn off the printer
SET FILTER TO            && Close filter
USE                      && Close database
RETURN                   && Return to the dot prompt
```

FIG. 19.1

A code fragment for creating a quick report.

```
===================== P H O N E   LIST ================

    CUSTOMER             CONTACT              PHONE

________________________________________________________

Burns Match Company   Alice McMiller     (317) 642-0328

Burns Match Company   I. T. Burns        (317) 545-3339

Miller's Farms        Sarah Adams        (812) 443-0099

Partners In Grime     Brenda Stanley     (317) 858-3751

Partners In Grime     Melissa Coleman    (317) 575-6209

Sheeba Pet Store      Charles Shmidt     (317) 443-1232

Williams Company      John Williams      (317) 848-1019
```

FIG. 19.2

The printed report.

FROM HERE...

**For Related Information...**

◂◂ "Using Quick Report," p. 224.

▸▸ "SET FILTER TO," p. 872.

▸▸ "SET PRINTER," p. 886.

## Working with Printers and Printing

If you plan to use your dBASE IV application to print reports—in most cases, you will—you need to prepare dBASE for printing. Preparation can mean various things in various printing environments. For simple, generic printers, you usually don't need to do much. And for simple reports, like the one you saw in the code fragment in figure 19.1, you don't need any special commands in the report file.

**TIP** You can have up to four separate printer drivers in the CONFIG.DB file, and each printer can have as many as five different fonts.

When you first install dBASE IV, you also install the printer drivers for the printers that you use. Each time dBASE IV starts, it reads the CONFIG.DB file (the file that contains the printer driver(s) installed, among other start-up parameters). You can have up to four separate printer drivers in the CONFIG.DB file, and each printer driver can have as many as five different fonts.

To switch among the printers that you have installed, use the _pdriver variable in conjunction with the SET PRINTER TO command from within the program. The _pdriver variable is one of a group of variables called *system memory variables*. These variables are special memory variables recognized by dBASE IV as containing information that modifies its configuration from within a program. System variables affect much more than printing, but this discussion focuses on those variables that enable you to configure print functions. The SET PRINTER TO command tells dBASE which port the printer is connected to, such as LPT1, LPT2, COM1, and so on. Remember, you use _pdriver and SET PRINTER TO only if you have more than one printer.

Using these commands is easy. If you want to make sure that the quick report shown in figure 19.2 always prints to the Epson LQ-1500 printer attached to port LPT2, for example, you would change the program as shown in figure 19.3.

```
* Code fragment for printing a quick list (unformatted report)
*
* Housekeeping
CLEAR                          && Clear the screen
SET TALK OFF                   && Shut off value display
SET ECHO OFF                   && Shut off command display
SET HEADINGS OFF               && Suppress the List column headings
******************************************************
* Select the printer driver and printer port to use. *
******************************************************
SET PRINTER TO LPT2
_pdriver = "LQ1500.PR2"
******************************************************
* Ready data to print
USE Maillist                   && Open the database
SET ORDER TO TAG CUSTOMER      && Set index tag
SET FILTER TO STATE = "IN"     && Set filter
SET PRINTER ON                 && Turn on the printer
*
*  Next you need to give the report a title and some column
*  headings.
*  When you use the SET PRINTER ON command, the ? is
*  directed to the printer.
*
* Print the report header
? " =========================== P H O N E   L I S T ============================"
? " "
? "         CUSTOMER                      CONTACT PHONE"
? " ________________________________"
? " "
* Print the data
LIST customer, contact, phone OFF TO PRINT    && Print the listing
???
* Housekeeping
SET PRINTER OFF                && Turn off the printer
SET PRINTER TO                 && Reset printer port
SET FILTER TO                  && Close filter
USE                            && Close database
RETURN                         && Return to the dot prompt
```

FIG. 19.3

Code showing the quick report print instructions.

Configuring dBASE IV to print reports can take a variety of forms. You may be concerned only with configuring your printer with the _pdriver variable. Or you may want to set up for your report a custom format that includes multiple fonts, indented blocks of text, and so forth. The system variables (such as _pdriver) that set the print environment enable you to do all that. These variables should always be in the area of your program module reserved for housekeeping tasks—at the very beginning of the program or module. The use of system memory variables follows the same structure and general syntax as the use of any other variable, as shown in the following example:

```
memvar = contents
```

or

```
STORE contents TO memvar
```

System memory variables differ from other memory variables in that dBASE expects system variable contents to be specifically defined keywords intended for the particular system variable. You can find those intended keywords in the "dBASE IV Reference Guide" in the back of this book. Table 19.1 lists specific system variables you can use for printing.

**Table 19.1 System Memory Variables Used for Printing**

| Variable | Function |
|---|---|
| _alignment | Specifies alignment relative to margins (left, right, center) |
| _box | Specifies if a box will be drawn |
| _indent | Specifies indentation of first line of a paragraph |
| _lmargin | Defines the left margin of a page |
| _padvance | Indicates page advance (line feed or form feed) |
| _pageno | Sets the current page number |
| _pbpage | Indicates beginning page for a print job |
| _pcolno | Determines starting column position |
| _pcopies | Indicates how many copies to print of a print job |
| _pdriver | Sets the printer driver |
| _pecode | Sets the ending printer codes for the print job |
| _peject | Indicates when to eject a page |
| _pepage | Sets the last page of the print job |

| Variable | Function |
|---|---|
| _pform | Sets the current print form |
| _plength | Sets the page length |
| _plineno | Indicates which line to start on |
| _ploffset | Sets left offset |
| _ppitch | Sets or determines printer pitch |
| _pquality | Sets draft or quality mode |
| _pscode | Sets the starting codes for the print job |
| _pspacing | Sets line spacing to 1, 2, or 3 |
| _pwait | Indicates whether to pause after each page |
| _rmargin | Sets right margin |
| _tabs | Sets tabs |
| _wrap | Indicates whether to turn on word wrap |

As the table indicates, you can set up sophisticated custom reports. Later in this chapter, you learn how some of these variables are used. For now, it's enough to know that you can override the settings in CONFIG.DB by setting up your own custom printing environment on a report-by-report basis, resetting any of the values of the system memory variables.

Other elements besides system memory variables affect your printed report, the most important of which is the type of output you want. Most dBASE IV data is sent to the printer as *streaming output*, which is a stream of characters positioned on the page by the printer. A streaming output is created, for example, with the ? and ?? commands sending the contents of a memory variable or a character string to the printer. Some of the other commands that create streaming output are as follows:

| | | |
|---|---|---|
| DIR | LABEL FORM | TEXT...ENDTEXT |
| DISPLAY | LIST | TYPE |
| EJECT PAGE | REPORT FORM | |

These commands send a stream of data to all available output devices, which means that you can print or save to a file or display data on-screen. Some of the commands, such as LIST, offer keywords such as TO PRINT for directing your output to the appropriate device. Otherwise, using the command SET PRINT ON enables dBASE to send streams of characters to the printer as well as to the screen.

If you are using a dBASE command that produces nonstreaming output, however, you must enable the appropriate output device. With the @...SAY...GET command, for example, you use SET DEVICE TO PRINTER to send the output to the printer; output then is directed to the printer only. Therefore, you need to issue the command SET DEVICE TO SCREEN when you complete the print job.

Another print command that may prove useful to you is the ??? command. The difference between ??? and other printing commands is that ??? sends output directly to the printer and bypasses the printer driver. That process means that the command sends any type of characters directly to the printer. The system memory variable _pscode, for example, may contain a printer code that changes the print on your printer. To send _pscode directly to the printer, use the following command:

```
??? _pscode
```

# Controlling Your Print Quality

Before you print a report, you may want to change the type of print your printer is using. You may want some text to be printed in a letter-quality font, for example, or you may want to boldface or italicize certain text. You may want to condense the print to make it fit more columns of text on a page. Making such changes is easy with dBASE IV.

You have several different ways to change the printer type style. By using the following part of the quick report, you can see how to change the style of printing:

```
? " ================ P H O N E  L I S T ==============="
? " "
? "        CUSTOMER                          CONTACT PHONE"
? " ------------------------------------------------"
```

For effect, you may want to print the PHONE LIST heading in bold print, and print the rest of the report in normal print. You can do this by using ?'s STYLE option, and the following command:

```
? " =========== P H O N E  L I S T ===========" STYLE "B"
? " "
? "        CUSTOMER                          CONTACT PHONE"
? " -----------------------------------------------------"
```

Notice type option STYLE "B". This option instructs dBASE to print only the one line in boldface, and the rest of the report in normal characters. The STYLE option also offers other letters, such as I (italic), U (underline), R (raised), and L (lowered). The STYLE option of the ? and ?? commands changes the style of only the single line. If you installed fonts when you were installing your printer drivers, then you can change fonts in the same manner, by using STYLE. To change the PHONE LIST heading to the second font, for example, use the following command:

```
? " =========== P H O N E  L I S T ===========" STYLE "2"
```

You often may need to print more information on a page, but the page is not wide enough. In this case, you can condense the printing by using the _ppitch system memory variable. To condense the printing, use the following command at the beginning of the report:

```
_ppitch = "CONDENSED"
```

This system memory variable uses the printer driver and condenses the printing of the report so that about 17 characters are printed per inch (depending on the type of printer you are using). Therefore, you can print 136 characters on an 8-inch wide page, rather than just 80 characters. To switch back to regular pica printing, use the following command:

```
_ppitch = "PICA"
```

Besides pica and condensed, one other parameter you can use is elite, which prints 12 characters per inch.

Many dot-matrix printers have a letter-quality mode in addition to draft-quality mode. If you want to print the heading for the quick report in letter-quality mode and the rest of the report in draft mode, for example, use the following program code:

```
* Turn letter quality mode on

_pquality = .T.

? " ============ P H O N E  L I S T ===========" STYLE "B"

? " "

? "         CUSTOMER                            CONTACT PHONE"

? "-----------------------------------------------------"

* Turn letter quality mode off

_pquality = .F.
```

Some of the system memory variables require that you provide printer codes to tell the printer what feature you want to use. The memory variables are _pecode and _pscode. These codes should enable printer features other than the ones dBASE controls. Remember, the features that dBASE controls are boldface, italic, letter-quality, underlined, raised, and lowered. When installing dBASE, or using DBSETUP to reconfigure dBASE, you can select codes to change fonts.

Your printer manual contains all the codes you need for different printing styles or modes. When you look up the printer codes, you see the ASCII values to select the mode and the decimal value equivalents. To select prestige elite font on a Toshiba P351 printer, for example, use one of the following codes:

ASCII - Esc, *, 1

DECIMAL - 27, 42, 49

To assign the print code, you can use any of the following:

"{ESC}*1"

"{27}*1"

"{27}{42}{49}"

CHR(27)+"*1"

Each of the four print codes produces the same results. Assigning one of the codes to the system memory variable _pscode looks like the following:

```
_pscode = "{ESC}*1}"
```

Remember that when using these codes, capital letters must be distinguished from lowercase letters.

The PostScript language, much like dBASE, consists of a series of commands and statements. These commands and statements (as opposed to the control codes used with other printers, including Hewlett-Packard LaserJets and "workalikes") define the makeup of a page to be printed on a PostScript printer. The makeup covers character size, page size and orientation, the font, and all other aspects of printing a full page. The specification of the page makeup is transmitted along with the rest of the page definition through the PostScript commands.

A report is embedded into this PostScript command file and is sent to the printer, preceded by the PostScript preamble. The *preamble* describes the page, the fonts, and all those other items discussed in the preceding paragraph. After the report comes the PostScript command SHOWPAGE. At that point, the printer knows that it's got everything it needs to define and print a page. The printer keeps printing until it sees the command SHOWPAGE and the characters which indicate that the job is complete. If the printer doesn't get that information, it keeps printing until it has no more to print; the printer then stops, waiting for the command SHOWPAGE and the end-of-job indication.

When you start dBASE IV, the first thing the program looks for is the CONFIG.DB file. CONFIG.DB contains initial settings, including the printer driver you installed with dBASE IV. This file loads the printer drivers into the printer and continues to load dBASE. In addition, the PostScript driver automatically loads into the printer's memory a standard PostScript preamble file called POSTSCRI.DLD. That file also must be in the printer's memory because the file contains the important SHOWPAGE command. If your PostScript printer clears its memory, you won't be able to print a partial page because the printer won't know that the job is finished. To ensure that the PostScript driver and its accompanying preamble file are in the printer's memory, you must load them as part of the print job. You can load them by including the following line:

```
_pdriver = "POSTSCRI.PR3"
```

At the end of the report, the PostScript printer needs to receive an indication that the job is done. Do that by using the following command:

```
??? "FF "
```

This command sends the characters "FF" (the characters FF followed by a space), which tells PostScript that the job is done. As soon as the printer receives the "FF", the printer returns to the preamble, finds the command SHOWPAGE, and ejects the last page of the report. If you don't include the environmental variable and the command ???, your PostScript printer stops at the last page of your listing and does nothing more.

# Setting Up a Print Form File

When using the report or label generator to produce a report or labels, you may find that by creating a print form file you can format your report or labels. This form file contains print settings that can be included in a report or with labels, such as the pitch and quality of print. When you save a print form file, it is saved with the extension PRF.

# Creating a Print Form File

You make a print form file while creating a custom report or label with the dBASE report or label generator. For example, from the dot prompt, first activate a database. Then type *CREATE REPORT* and the name of the report to create. You can design the report as explained in Chapter 10. Choose the Print menu, shown in figure 19.4. You can select the submenus Destination, Control Of Printer, Output Options, and Page Dimensions.

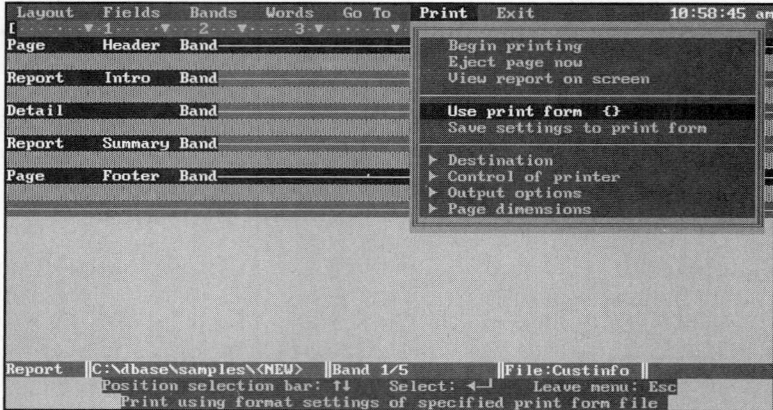


FIG. 19.4

The Print menu.

One of the options you may want to change is Printer Model from the Destination menu. With this option, you can select the printer to print the report to, if you have more than one printer. From the Control of Printer menu, you select Text Pitch to switch among Pica, Elite, or Condensed pitch. Or you may decide that a New Page should come before the report, or be issued after the report. From the Control of Printer menu, you also can set the Starting and Ending Control Codes, enabling you to change your printer's setup through control codes. In the Number Of Copies section of the Output options menu, you can elect to print two copies of each report, rather than a single copy. Finally, you can select double Spacing Of Lines from the Page Dimensions menu.

You may notice that the settings in the previous paragraph correspond to system memory variables. Changing the Printer Model option, for example, corresponds to _pdriver. Selecting the Text Pitch corresponds to _ppitch. Selecting when a New Page should be issued corresponds to _peject. Starting and Ending Control Codes are the same as _pscode and _pecode, respectively. When you decide to print two copies, you alter _pcopies. Finally, selecting double-spacing corresponds to the system memory variable _pspacing. Actually, when the print form is active, each of the system memory variables is reset with the values as assigned in the print form file.

After you have made the appropriate print settings, select Save Settings To Print Form from the Print menu. You can name the file now so that you can recall these settings later.

## Using the Print Form File

Putting the print form file in use is easy. All you have to do is assign the name of the file to the system memory variable _pform. If the print form file is called CON-REPT.PRF, for example, then use the following command:

```
_pform = "CON-REPT.PRF"
```

or

```
STORE "CON-REPT.PRF" TO _pform
```

When you issue this command, all the necessary values are stored to the appropriate system memory variables. The report, then, reflects the settings to the system memory variables.

To place these settings in an actual report, add one of the preceding lines to the housekeeping section of a report program. In figure 19.5, for example, notice how the settings are added to a fragment of the quick report shown earlier in the chapter.

```
*  Code fragment for printing a quick list (unformatted report)
*
* Housekeeping
CLEAR                         && Clear the screen
SET TALK OFF                  && Shut off command display
SET ECHO OFF                  && Shut off value display
SET HEADINGS OFF              && Suppress the List column headings
* Ready data to print
USE Maillist                  && Open the database
SET ORDER TO TAG CUSTOMER     && Set index tag
SET FILTER TO STATE = "IN"    && Set filter

**********
* Add the print form file here
**********
_pform = "CON-REPT.PRF"
**********

SET PRINTER ON                && Turn on the printer
*
*  The report continues ...
      ...
      ...
```

FIG. 19.5

The settings added to a fragment of the quick report.

The advantage in using the print form settings is that you do not have to make all the settings individually. All the settings are changed by using the print form file. As the report progresses, however, you can alter the individual system memory variables to change the appearance of the report. You may have set the print form file, for example, for single spacing. You can change the setting of _pspacing to double-spacing, and then you can set _pspacing back to single spacing as it once was.

# Adding a Print Form File to a Generated Report or Label File

When you create a report or label by using one of the built-in generators, the generator sets up the environment. For example, notice the code fragment taken from a generated-report file as shown in figure 19.6.

```
...
_plineno=0                     && set lines to zero
*- NOEJECT parameter
IF gl_noeject
   IF _peject= "BEFORE"
      _peject="NONE"
   ENDIF
   IF _peject="BOTH"
      _peject="AFTER"
   ENDIF
ENDIF

*- Set-up environment
ON ESCAPE DO Prnabort
IF SET("TALK")"ON"
   SET TALK OFF
   gc_talk"ON"
ELSE
   gc_talk"OFF"
ENDIF
gc_space=SET("SPACE")
SET SPACE OFF
gc_time=TIME()                 && system time for predefined field
gd_date=DATE()                 && system date "    "    "    "
gl_fandl=.F.                   && first and last page flag
gl_prntflg=.T.                 && Continue printing flag
gl_widow=.T.                   && flag for checking widow bands
gn_length=LEN(gc_heading)      && store length of the HEADING
gn_level=2                     && current band being processed
gn_page=_pageno                && grab current page number
gn_pspace=_pspacing            && get current print spacing
   ...
```

FIG. 19.6

A code fragment taken from a generated-report file.

As you look through the code, you may notice that several of the system memory variables are used (the ones that start with _p). You can modify a generated report file to make custom changes to the report, and the same can be done to a generated label file. You can add a print form file, for example, to the report. Notice in figure 19.7 the new copy of the code fragment with the CON-REPT.PRF print form file added.

```
...
_plineno=0                      && set lines to zero
_pform = "CON-REPT.PRF"
*- NOEJECT parameter
IF gl_noeject
   IF _peject="BEFORE"
      _peject="NONE"
   ENDIF
   IF _peject="BOTH"
      _peject="AFTER"
   ENDIF
ENDIF

*- Set-up environment
ON ESCAPE DO Prnabort
*****
* Adding a Print Form File
*****
IF SET("TALK")="ON"
   SET TALK OFF
   gc_talk="ON"
ELSE
gc_talk="OFF"
ENDIF
   gc_space=SET("SPACE")
SET SPACE OFF
gc_time=TIME()                  && system time for predefined field
gd_date=DATE()                  && system date  "    "    "    "
gl_fandl=.F.                    && first and last page flag
gl_prntflg=.T.                  && Continue printing flag
gl_widow=.T.                    && flag for checking widow bands
gn_length=LEN(gc_heading)       && store length of the HEADING
gn_level=2                      && current band being processed
gn_page=_pageno                 && grab current page number
gn_pspace=_pspacing             && get current print spacing
```

FIG. 19.7

The code fragment with the print form file added.

You add the print form file to the beginning of the report file as one of the first steps in setting up the environment. Then, any of the system memory variables used by the report reflect the settings of the print form file.

## For Related Information...

◂◂ "Printing the Report," p. 255.

## Summary

This chapter examined some of the ways you can get information out of the database and onto a printed page. You saw how to create a quick report, also called an unformatted report. You explored ways to set up your printer from within your application program by using system memory variables as part of your housekeeping.

Then, you were introduced to the dBASE IV report generator and ways that you can customize report forms created by the generator. You also learned how you can create a print form file and include the file in any of your reports.

In the next chapter, you learn a shortcut for building your applications: the dBASE IV application generator. You find that you can generate the bulk of your dBASE code with the application generator, and then modify and fine-tune the code by using the skills you have learned so far in this section.

20

CHAPTER

# Using the Applications Generator and the Compiler

In this chapter, you learn how to use the dBASE IV Applications Generator, what types of applications you can develop from scratch, how to polish your applications, and how to customize your applications by adding code.

You also learn more about the debugging process by using the dBASE IV debugger. Finally, you learn how to compile your applications and prepare them for distribution by using dBASE IV's RunTime option.

# Building Applications for Other Users

You need to consider two important factors when you build programs for other users. First, you will not always be around to support the application, so the application must work cleanly (be bug-free) and be understood easily by its users. Second, many users on occasion may misuse the program, so the application must be designed to prevent misuse and to keep the user from damaging data.

If you are getting the idea that building a dBASE IV application involves more than manipulating the database, you're right. Your application must include such vital elements as error trapping, testing user input, housekeeping, and maintaining data integrity. You also must provide program documentation so that users and technical support people can figure out what to do if something goes wrong. All this extra work takes time and experience. One of the best ways to reduce the time involved and to increase your experience is to use the dBASE IV Applications Generator.

The Applications Generator, or *Ap Gen*, enables you to build complex, well-documented dBASE code. You work with the Ap Gen through a pull-down menu system similar to the Control Center. Unlike the dBASE III Plus Ap Gen, dBASE IV includes the generator as part of the main dBASE IV program, which means that you don't need to invoke an external program. New users draw great benefit from using the dBASE IV Ap Gen. The generator is a state-of-the-art program that considers housekeeping, error tracking, and other nuances that separate the amateur applications from the professional.

As professional and advanced as the Ap Gen is, however, remember that the more complex the application, the more potential for error. Also, the types of errors you encounter are tougher to find. Syntax errors are common in human-generated code, but rare in machine-generated code. Also rare are open-ended constructs, such as DO WHILE or IF, which need commands to close them off. You may need to use all your debugging tools to find errors. Fortunately, one of the benefits of using the Ap Gen is its excellent set of debugging tools.

Another benefit of using the Applications Generator is the substantial time you save when coding complex, but repetitive and common, sections of the application. Code for a complex set of menus can run to hundreds of lines and take days to write, check, and document. The Applications Generator enables the developer to produce the code in a few hours or so and leaves time to add the polish that marks the professional application. In other words, you can use the Applications

Generator to do your "grunt work" even if you are an experienced dBASE IV user. Before you start, however, you should learn a few things.

# Planning Programs for the Applications Generator

Thorough planning before you start your program can save you headaches and time. Preplanning takes on a whole new meaning when you are working through a series of pull-down menus. The Applications Generator does not make it convenient for you to check your code along the way and test it module by module as you would when you develop an application manually. Certainly, you can generate, test, modify, and test again, but you limit the need for that if you take time to plan before you start.

The first step is to plan with great care the data flow, the program flow, and the menu structure. You may want to build program modules before you run the Ap Gen. Some of the modules may be report forms, label forms, special help windows, and other external or special modules you learn about later. You need these modules because your application uses them and the Ap Gen asks you about them as you design the structure of your application. Building your application only to find that you need to make another report is frustrating.

Equally important is the layout of your databases. Examine your application and decide how many and what kind of databases you need. Keep the user input in mind and create the databases in advance. The Ap Gen uses your databases exactly as you tell it to, including relational operations among multiple databases. As you progress, you learn how to take advantage of most of dBASE IV's features from within the Applications Generator.

You should follow a special order when you plan your application. If you plan according to this order without backing out to build some missing piece, your plan develops smoothly. In general terms, you need to prepare the following items before you start building your application with the Ap Gen:

Reports
Labels
Data input forms
Databases
Indexes

You may think that by putting reports and labels before databases, the list is backward. When you develop a system, however, you must determine what reports you need first. From the information you include in the reports, you can tell what fields you need in a database or databases.

The order in which the Applications Generator expects you to develop your application is different from the order in which you plan the application. Plan your order according to the following steps:

1. Prepare the files you need to use during the application generation process.
2. Start the Applications Generator.
3. Create the welcome screen.
4. Create the main menu.
5. Create each of the submenus.
6. Create other objects, such as lists or batches.
7. Attach the actions of each object or menu to its object.
8. Generate the menus.
9. Generate the documentation.
10. Generate the application code.
11. Print the documentation.
12. Add any outside modifications to the program and insert them in the PRG files created by the Applications Generator. (Do not include those additional modules you add from within the Ap Gen process by using the Embed Code option.)
13. Run the application and debug.

In simple terms, then, you prepare external files, build the menu system, designate the actions of the menu choices, add your modifications, and debug. By using the Applications Generator, you can cut your coding time by 70 to 80 percent. Remember, however, that you may spend about 60 percent of your time writing and debugging 95 percent of your application. The last 5 percent of your program can consume 40 percent of the total time it takes you to produce a finished program. When you get the application written and it works, for the most part, you still have a good way to go before you finish the job. The benefit in using the Applications Generator is that it can reduce the 95 percent even further and make the overall debugging job easier by eliminating hard-to-find errors.

# Planning the Mailer Application

This section shows you how to create the Mailer application. This application enables you to input, edit, and delete records for a mailing list, as well as print a report and mailing labels. You see the report that is used, the labels, the screen form, and how each is created. Finally, after you see the report, labels, and screen format, you see the database and index to use for this application. The application design follows the design order listed previously.

The database to be used with this application is the MAILLIST database file described in Chapter 17. To create the database file, from the dot prompt, type the following:

```
CREATE MAILLIST
```

When creating the database structure, specify *Y* in the Index column for the CUSTOMER field to create an index tag for this field.

Before using the Applications Generator, you need to design your report and label formats, and your data-entry screen form. (Refer to Chapters 9, 10, and 11 for specific details on designing and creating reports and labels.)

The report for the Mailer application is a simple columnar report. The fields displayed in the report are CUSTOMER, CONTACT, ADDRESS1, ADDRESS2, CITY, STATE, ZIP, PHONE, EXTENSION, and FAX. Figure 20.1 shows the report format used.

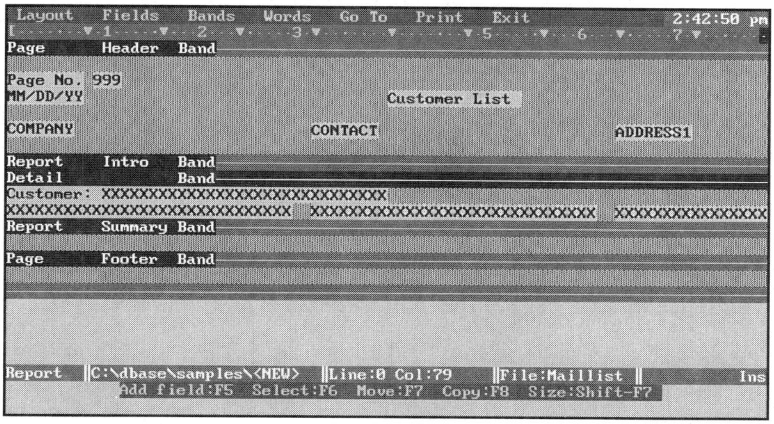

**FIG. 20.1**
The report format used to print the records in the database.

When you are ready to create a report, you can use the Quick Layouts option from the Layout menu. In the report, an extra line is added to the Detail band, and the CUSTOMER field is moved up, with the title, `Customer:`, before the field. The report heading `Customer List` is centered at the top of the report. To create the report from the dot prompt, type the following:

CREATE REPORT MAILCUST

The labels you create are 1-up labels (only one label across). The label is made up of the following fields:

CUSTOMER

ADDRESS1

ADDRESS2

CITY, STATE ZIP

CONTACT

The word *ATTN:* is typed as text. When creating the label, use the Add Field option from the Fields menu. This option enables you to place each field on the label. To create the labels, use the following command:

CREATE LABEL MAILLBLS

You can create a form to add, edit, and browse the data in the database. The form you create looks like the one shown in figure 20.2.

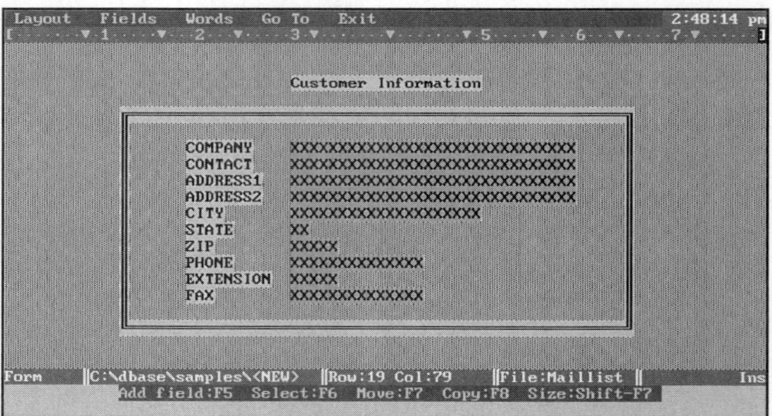


FIG. 20.2

The screen format used to input and edit records in the database.

As with the report, you can use Quick Layouts from the Fields menu to place the fields on-screen. The fields are moved down the screen by inserting blank lines (move the field CUSTOMER to row 5). The fields are centered by selecting the fields and titles with F6 and selecting Words, Position, Center from the menu. A box is drawn around the fields from row 4, column 20, to row 15, column 60. Finally, the text on the screen is added by typing at rows 2, 18, and 19, and then centering the text. You can create the screen format by typing the following:

CREATE SCREEN MAILFORM

When you finish creating and saving the screen form, you are ready to use the Applications Generator.

**For Related Information...**

▸▸ "CREATE/MODIFY LABEL," p. 693.

▸▸ "CREATE/MODIFY REPORT," p. 694.

▸▸ "CREATE/MODIFY SCREEN," p. 695.

# Getting Started with the Applications Generator

Now that you have planned your application and created the files you need in advance, you need to start the Applications Generator. You can start the Ap Gen from the Control Center or the dot prompt. From the Control Center, move to the last panel, Applications. You can select <create> under that panel, or, if you want to modify an existing application, select that application. The other way to select the Ap Gen is to use the command CREATE APPLICATION (or MODIFY APPLICATION if you want to work on an existing application).

## Creating the Mailer Application

From the dot prompt, type the following command:

CREATE APPLICATION MAILER

In response to your command, you see the Application Definition screen (see fig. 20.3).

You use this screen to enter basic information about your application. First, you must name your application. The name you choose should be the same one you used to open the Applications Generator. Second, you must give your top menu a name and specify an opening database. The choice of whether to fill in the remaining fields is up to you. The entries you should make are shown in the following list:

Application name: *MAILER*

Description: *Mail list manager*

Main menu type: *BAR*

Main menu name: *MAINMENU*

Database/view: *MAILLIST.DBF*

ORDER: *CUSTOMER*

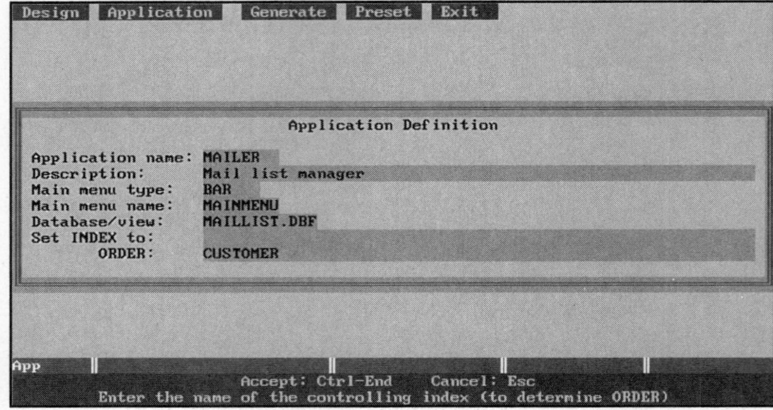


FIG. 20.3

The Application Definition screen.

Because you will be using the default multiple-index file, you can leave Set INDEX to: blank.

You can use the mouse to select options in the Application Definition screen. Select the menu type by clicking on the input field to cycle through available menu types. To select a Database/view or Index file, press Shift-F1 in the appropriate input field to display a pick list, then click on the desired item to select it.

After you have filled in the form, save it by using Ctrl-End. (You use this strange save command throughout the Ap Gen.)

After you fill in the opening screen and save it, you see the work surface, which looks like the one shown in figure 20.4.

Notice the large box on the work surface. You can use that box as a welcome screen for your application. First, you need to remove the existing text with Ctrl-Y. Then you can enter any text you want for your opening screen. Edit the box so that it looks like the one in figure 20.5.

This figure represents what dBASE IV calls an *application object*. Objects can be anything from a welcome screen, such as this, to a menu or a batch procedure. Anything you create or use in the Applications Generator that becomes part of your finished program is an application object.

FIG. 20.4

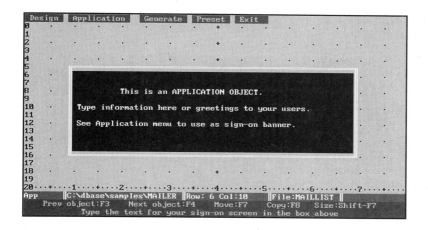

The Applications Generator work surface.

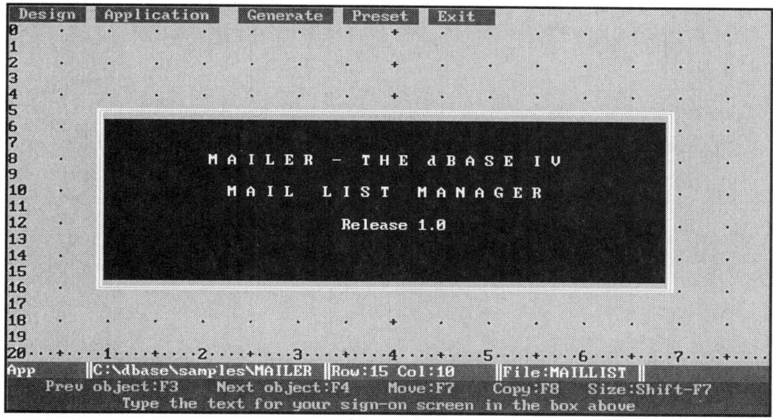


FIG. 20.5

The welcome box with new text.

# Learning the Work Surface

You need to know a few rules for moving around in the work surface. First, you can move an object around the work surface by pressing F7 and using your arrow keys. When you have the object positioned where you want it, press Enter. You also can change the vertical and horizontal size of an object by pressing Shift-F7, and then using your arrows to make the box larger or smaller in either direction. Finally, press F10 to display the menu bar. The choices along the top menu bar change as you enter the menu from different points in your application-generating process. If you run into trouble and need help, press F1.

You can use the mouse to access menu options. Click the menu name in the menu bar, and then click the option to select it. For example, click Application, Display Sign-on Banner, and then Yes to choose that option. To close a menu, click outside the menu area.

## Designing the Menu

Before you get too far in designing this application, you must learn to save your work often. To save, press F10 for the menu, select the Application menu, and then select the option Save Current Application Definition.

You may want to set up the welcome box so that it appears each time you start the application. You can do this in two steps:

1. Press F10 to invoke the menu and select the Application menu.
2. Select Display Sign-on Banner and, from the dialog box, select Yes.

Each time you start the application, this welcome box appears onscreen and identifies for the user the chosen application.

You now should create the application's main menu. The main menu is created from the Ap Gen's Design menu, shown in figure 20.6.

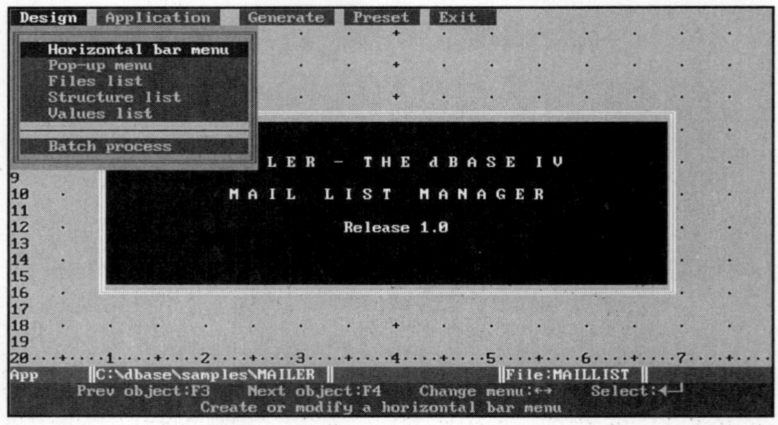


FIG. 20.6

The pull-down Design menu.

Notice that this menu enables you to design horizontal bar menus, popup menus, file lists, structure lists, values lists, and batch processes. Follow these steps to create the main menu:

1. From the Design menu, select Horizontal Bar Menu.
2. When a list box appears on-screen, select <create>.

3. Fill in the menu dialog box that appears, as shown in figure 20.7. Press Ctrl-End when complete.

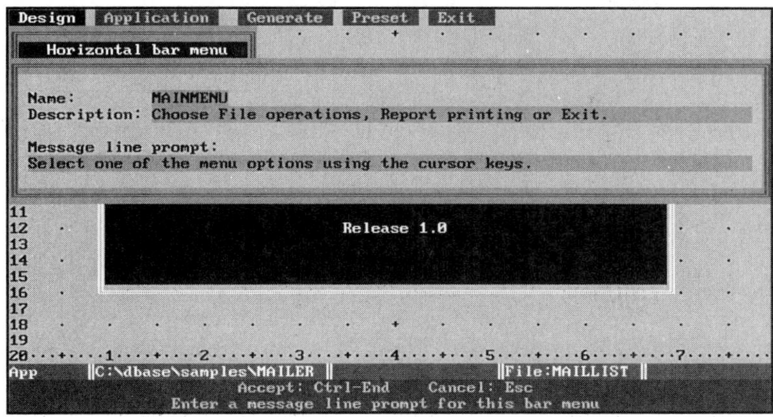


FIG. 20.7

The dialog box containing the main menu name, description, and message.

After you save the information in the dialog box, a double-line box appears across the top of your screen. This box is the bar menu in which you can place the top menu choices.

At this point, you are just creating a graphic. Menus created from this Ap Gen choice are incapable of doing anything at this moment. You attach actions to them later. When you add text to the menu, you first must press F5. Pressing F5 enables you to type menu items in the menu. To add your menu choices to the top menu bar, follow these steps:

1. With the cursor in the menu box, press F5, type *FILES*, and press F5 again.
2. Move the cursor to column 30, press F5, type *REPORTS*, and press F5 again.
3. Move the cursor to column 60, press F5, type *EXIT*, and press F5 one final time.

Figure 20.8 shows the top menu of the Mailer application that will use the database you created earlier. Three choices are available in this example. First, FILES enables the user to add, delete, and change database records in the Maillist database. Second, REPORTS enables the user to print the phone list and mailing labels. Third, EXIT enables the user to exit to the dot prompt or to DOS.

To save the work you have done on the menu, press F10, select the Menu menu, and then select the option Save Current Menu.

FIG. 20.8

The Mailer application top menu bar.

## Using Pull-Down and Pop-Up Menus

Now that you have built your top menu, you need to build the pull-down menus from which the user selects one of several choices along the bar menu. Do you remember the difference between pull-down and pop-up menus that you learned in Chapter 19? dBASE IV's Applications Generator treats all vertical moving bar menus as pop ups. If the pop up is invoked by a horizontal bar menu, it is treated in the application as a pull-down menu. The menus in this exercise are treated as pull-down menus. To create pull-down menus, however, you select Pop-up Menu. Again, you are creating a cosmetic screen at this point. Actions are attached later.

You need to create two pop-up menus and name them according to the items they will be attached to on the main menu; the pop-up menus are named FILES and REPORTS. Follow these steps to create the FILES menu:

1. Press F10 and select Pop-up Menu from the Design menu. Select <create>.
2. When the pop-up information box appears on-screen, fill in the blanks with the information shown in figure 20.9.
3. Press Ctrl-End to save, and an empty pop-up menu box appears on-screen.

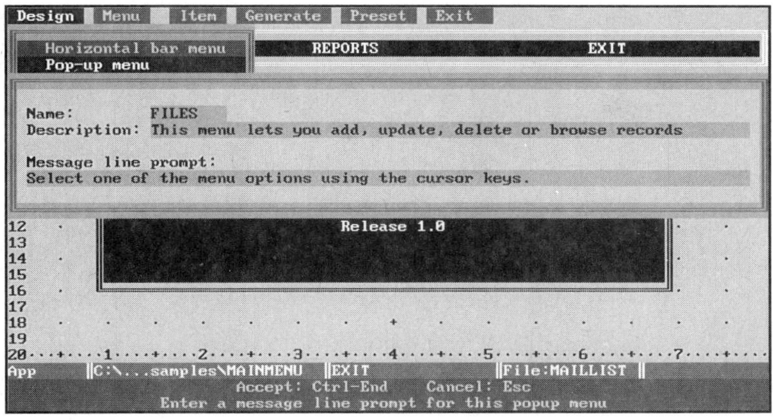


FIG. 20.9

The name box for the FILES menu.

4. Type each menu option, pressing Enter after each:

   Add A Record

   Delete A Record

   Modify A Record

   Browse All Records

5. Press Shift-F7 to size the menu box. Press the up-arrow key four times, and then press Enter.
6. Press F7 to move the menu. Choose Entire Frame from the menu that appears.
7. Use the cursor keys to move the menu to row 2, column 0, and then press Enter.
8. Press F10, select Save Current Menu from the Menu menu, and then select Put Away Current Menu.

Follow these steps to create the REPORTS menu:

1. Press F10 and select Pop-up Menu from the Design menu. Select <create>.
2. When the pop-up information box appears on-screen, fill in the blanks with the information shown in figure 20.10.
3. Press Ctrl-End to save, and an empty pop-up menu box appears on-screen.

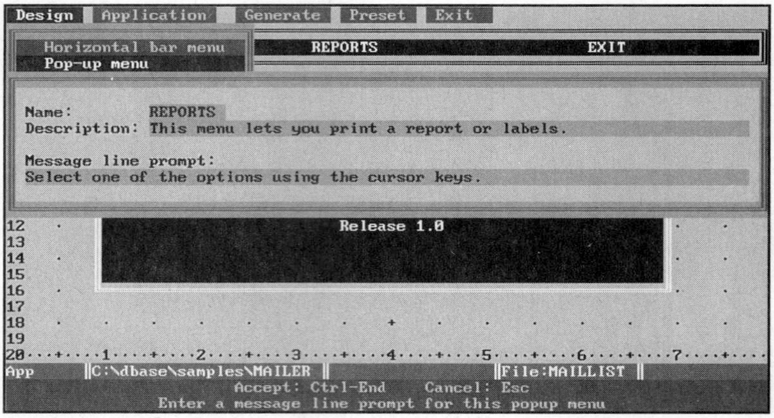

```
Design  Application  Generate  Preset  Exit
 Horizontal bar menu     REPORTS                          EXIT
 Pop-up menu

 Name:          REPORTS
 Description:   This menu lets you print a report or labels.

 Message line prompt:
 Select one of the options using the cursor keys.

12                          Release 1.0
13
14
15
16
17
18
19
20····+····1····+····2····+····3····+····4····+····5····+····6····+····7····+····
App    ||C:\dbase\samples\MAILER ||          ||File:MAILLIST ||
                    Accept: Ctrl-End    Cancel: Esc
               Enter a message line prompt for this popup menu
```

FIG. 20.10

The name box for the REPORTS menu.

4. Type each menu option, pressing Enter after each:

   Print Customer List

   Print Labels

5. Press Shift-F7 to size the menu box. Press the up-arrow key six times, and then press Enter.

6. Press F7 to move the menu. Choose Entire Frame from the menu that appears.

7. Use the cursor keys to move the menu to row 2, column 29, and then press Enter.

8. Press F10, select Save Current Menu from the Menu menu, and then select Put Away Current Menu.

Figure 20.11 shows the pull-down menu created for the first choice on the top menu bar, FILES. Figure 20.12 shows the REPORTS pull-down menu.

You now attach the pop-ups to the main bar menu. To attach a pop-up menu to the Main menu, make sure that the bar menu is in view. Then highlight the menu option to which you attach the pop-up. Make sure that you have the Main menu on-screen. If you have no menus on-screen, select the Design menu, select Horizontal Bar Menu, and then from the list box select MAINMENU. If all your menus are displayed, you can put away the pop-up menus. To do so, press F3 or F4 to make one of the pop-up menus the current object. Then press F10, select the Menu menu, and select the option Put Away Current Menu. To attach the pop-ups, perform the following steps:

1. With the Main menu on-screen, press F3 or F4 until the bar menu is the current object. Move the cursor until FILES is highlighted.

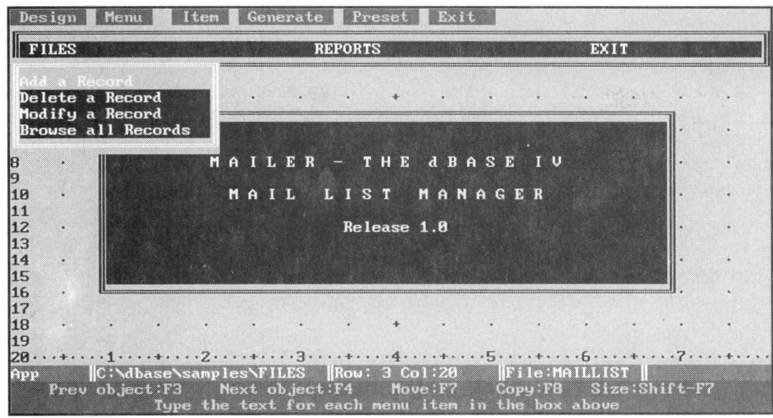


FIG. 20.11 The FILES pop-up menu for the Mailer application.

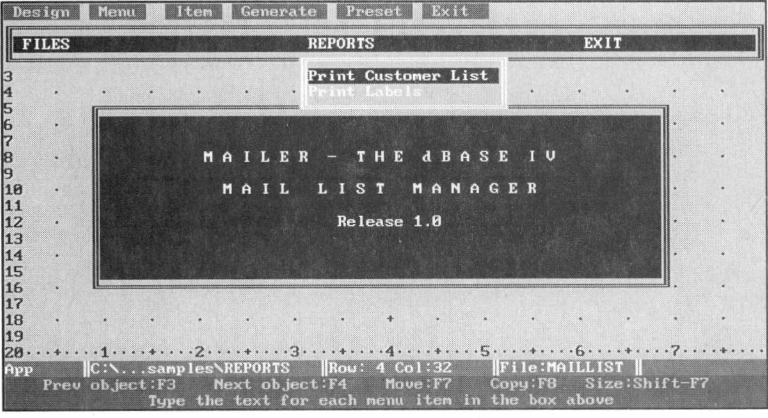


FIG. 20.12 The REPORTS pop-up menu for the Mailer application.

An easy way to select an object or item is to use the mouse. Click an object, such as a menu, on the work surface to make it the currently active object. Likewise, click an item in a menu to highlight that item.

2. Press F10 to invoke the dBASE IV Ap Gen top menu bar. Select Menu.

3. Select Attach Pull-down Menus. (Remember, pop-up menus can be used as pull-down menus.) You are asked whether you want the menu that you are attaching to carry the top menu's attributes and drop automatically. Answering Yes causes the pull-down to appear when you select the main menu option. Answering No means that the user must select with Enter to pull down the menu. Select Yes.

4. Select the Item menu and Change Action. Another menu appears that enables you to make changes to the FILES menu item.
5. Select Open A Menu. A form appears on-screen so that you may specify which menu is to be activated. Fill in the form with the following, and press Ctrl-End when finished:

   Menu type: *POP-UP*

   Menu name: *FILES*

   To select the menu type, press the space bar until `POP-UP` appears, or press P. Press Esc to exit from the Applications Generator menu.

   Use the mouse to select menu specifications. Click the Menu type input field to cycle through the available menu types. At the Menu name field, press Shift-F1 to display a pick list of available menu files, and then click the menu name you want to select. Click the Ctrl-End label in the navigation line to accept your entry.

6. Use the cursor arrows to move to the next choice on the menu—REPORTS. Repeat steps 2 through 5, substituting REPORTS for FILES when specifying the pop-up menu name.
7. When you are finished, use the cursor arrows to move to the EXIT choice on the Main menu.

**TIP** To move to the next menu item without having to exit the Item menu, press the PgDn key.

8. Press F10, select the Item menu, and then select Change Action. From the Change Action submenu, select Quit. You can have your application quit to DOS or return to the dot prompt.
9. Select Return To Calling Program, read the message that appears, and then select OK.
10. While the Ap Gen's menu is still active, select Menu, then select Save Current Menu to save the changes made to the MAINMENU bar menu.
11. From the Menu menu, select Put Away Current Menu.
12. Press F10, and from the Application menu, select Save Current Application Definition to save the latest changes to the application.

At this point in your application, the only things that work are the pull-down menus. The choices on those menus, however, are not activated; that's the next step. You must attach actions to each of the pull-down menus' options. Work on the FILES menu first, and then the REPORTS menu. Follow these steps to attach actions to the pull-down menu options for the FILES menu:

1. Select the FILES menu by pressing F10. Select the Design menu, select Pop-up Menus, and from the list of menus, select the FILES menu. The FILES menu appears on your work surface.
2. Use the arrow key to select the first choice on the menu—Add A Record.
3. Press F10, select the Items menu, and then select Change Action.
4. Select Edit Form (Add, Delete, Edit). Because your first FILES menu choice is Add A Record, use Edit Form in the append mode to begin adding records.
5. A form appears on-screen so that you can customize Edit Form (see fig. 20.13). Fill out the form as shown in the figure, using the format file MAILFORM.

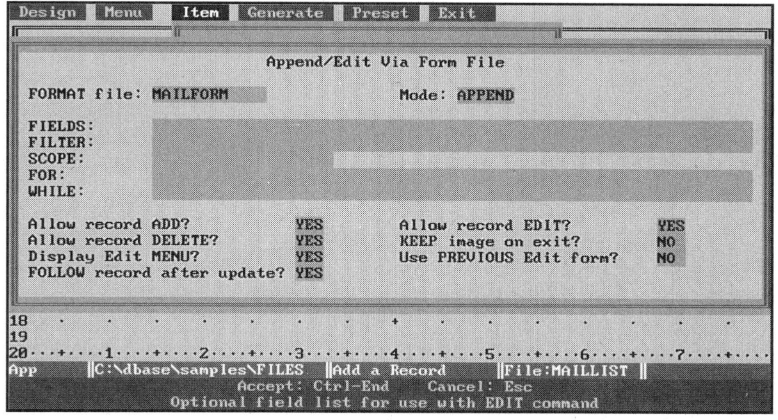


FIG. 20.13

Specifying actions for the Add a Record item.

6. When you have filled out the form as shown in figure 20.13, press Ctrl-End to save your changes. Press Ctrl-End again.
7. Use the arrow key to select the second choice on the menu—Delete A Record.
8. Press F10, select the Items menu, and then select Change Action.

9. Select Edit Form (Add, Delete, Edit). Because your FILES menu choice is Delete A Record, use Edit Form in the edit mode to begin deleting records.
10. A form appears on-screen so that you can customize Edit Form (see fig. 20.14). Fill out the form as shown in the figure, using the format file MAILFORM, and only allowing for deletion from the database.
11. When you have filled the form as shown in figure 20.14, press Ctrl-End to save your changes. Press Ctrl-End again.
12. Use the arrow key to select the third choice on the menu—Modify A Record.

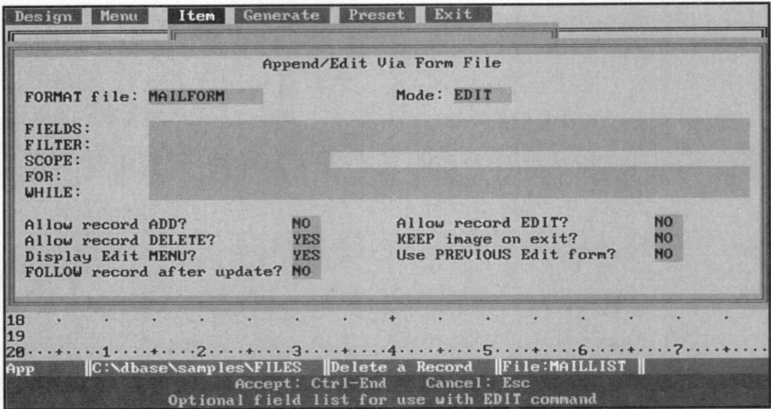


FIG. 20.14

Specifying actions for the Delete a Record item.

13. Press F10, select the Items menu, then select Change Action.
14. Select Edit Form (Add, Delete, Edit). Because your FILES menu choice is Modify A Record, use Edit Form in the edit mode to begin editing records.
15. A form appears on-screen so that you can customize Edit Form (see fig. 20.15). Fill out the form as shown in the figure, using the format file MAILFORM, and only allowing for editing to the database.
16. When you have filled out the form as shown in figure 20.15, press Ctrl-End to save your changes. Press Ctrl-End again.
17. Use the arrow key to select the fourth choice on the menu—Browse All Records.
18. Press F10, select the Items menu, and then select Change Action.

```
Design  Menu  Item  Generate  Preset  Exit

                    Append/Edit Via Form File

FORMAT file: MAILFORM                    Mode: EDIT

FIELDS:
FILTER:
SCOPE:
FOR:
WHILE:

Allow record ADD?             NO         Allow record EDIT?          YES
Allow record DELETE?          NO         KEEP image on exit?         NO
Display Edit MENU?            YES        Use PREVIOUS Edit form?     NO
FOLLOW record after update?   NO

18
19
20
App   ||C:\dbase\samples\FILES ||Modify a Record ||File:MAILLIST ||
                 Accept: Ctrl-End     Cancel: Esc
             Optional field list for use with EDIT command
```

**FIG. 20.15**

Specifying actions for the Modify a Record item.

19. Select Browse (Add, Delete, Edit). Because your FILES menu choice is Browse All Records, you use Browse to be able to view your records in a column format.

20. A form appears on-screen so that you can customize the Browse form (see fig. 20.16). Fill out the form as shown in the figure, using the format file MAILFORM, and not allowing addition, deletion, or editing to the database.

    Toggle between Yes and No choices when setting options for an Edit or Browse operation by clicking the option with the mouse. At the `Allow record ADD?` prompt, for example, click No or Yes to switch the setting of that option. Click the Ctrl-End label in the navigation line to accept your entries.

```
Design  Menu  Item  Generate  Preset  Exit
 FILES            Show item information                 EXIT

                   Browse a Database file or View

FIELDS:
FILTER:

Fields to LOCK onscreen:    0          FREEZE edit for field:
Maximum column WIDTH:       0          FORMAT file:

Allow record ADD?             NO       Allow record EDIT?           NO
Allow record DELETE?          NO       KEEP image on exit?          NO
Display Browse MENU?          YES      Use PREVIOUS Browse table?   NO
FOLLOW record after update?   NO       COMPRESS display?            NO

17
18
19
20
App   ||C:\dbase\samples\FILES ||Browse all Record||File:MAILLIST ||
                 Accept: Ctrl-End     Cancel: Esc
                   Optional field list for Browse
```

**FIG. 20.16**

Specifying actions for the Browse all Records item.

21. When you have filled out the form as shown in figure 20.16, press Ctrl-End to save your changes.

22. Select the Menu menu and the option Save Current Menu. All changes to the FILES menu are saved. Finally, select Put Away Current Menu.

At this point, you have created a welcome screen, top bar menu, and two pull-down menus. You have attached both pull-down menus (FILES and REPORTS) to your menu bar, which you named MAINMENU. You also have selected actions for the choices in your FILES pull-down menus.

Now you add choices to the second menu, the REPORTS menu. You see a slight difference here, although the basic procedure is the same. Because the Applications Generator does not create report forms, you had to do that yourself earlier. Now, you use those two forms. One is the customer listing report (MAILCUST) and the other is the mail label form (MAILLBLS). Although you can run these forms from the dot prompt with the REPORT FORM or LABEL FORM commands, you use them here instead.

Before you can add actions to the options on the REPORTS menu, you must display the REPORTS menu. To display the menu, press F10, select the Design menu, and select Pop-up Menu. From the list of menus, select REPORTS and then press Enter.

To attach actions to the options of the REPORTS menu, you go through the same basic procedure with REPORTS as you did with FILES. Now, however, you use the Display Or Print option on the Change Action choice of the Item menu (you used Browse for the FILES submenu you just created). When you select Display Or Print, you see a menu like the one shown in figure 20.17.

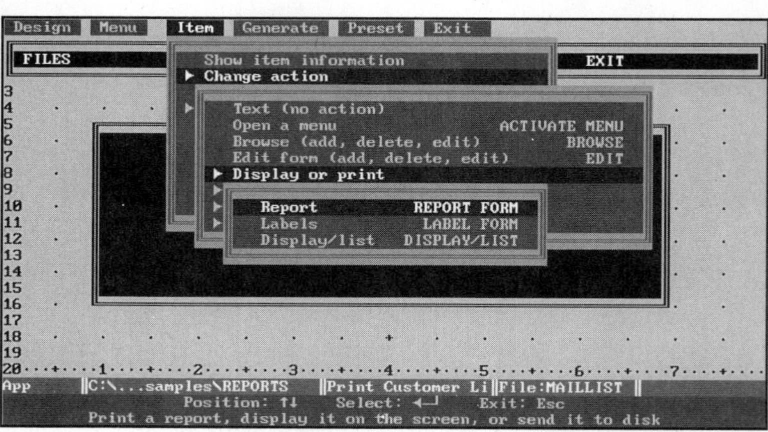


FIG. 20.17

The Display Or Print option for adding reports to your application.

Follow these steps to attach the report and mailing labels to the options:

1. Use the arrow keys to select the first choice on the menu—Print Customer List.
2. Press F10, select the Items menu, then select Change Action.
3. Select Display Or Print. From the Display Or Print menu, select Report.
4. A form appears on-screen so that you can specify the report to print and the options for the report (see fig. 20.18). Fill out the form as shown in the figure.

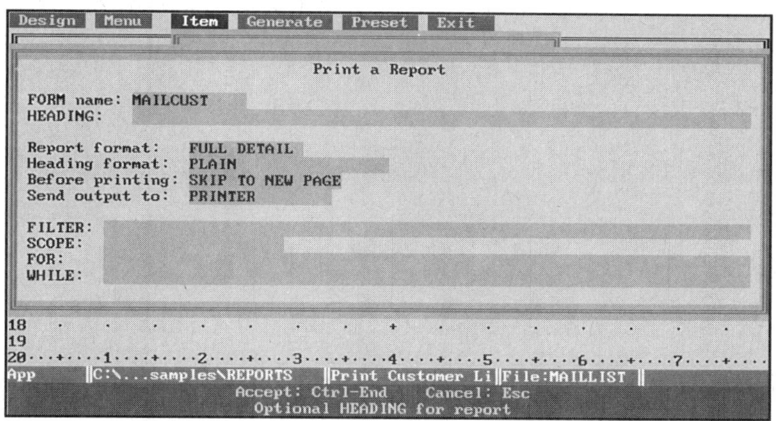

Design Menu Item Generate Preset Exit

Print a Report

FORM name: MAILCUST
HEADING:

Report format: FULL DETAIL
Heading format: PLAIN
Before printing: SKIP TO NEW PAGE
Send output to: PRINTER

FILTER:
SCOPE:
FOR:
WHILE:

App ║C:\...samples\REPORTS ║Print Customer Li║File:MAILLIST ║
Accept: Ctrl-End Cancel: Esc
Optional HEADING for report

FIG. 20.18

The form to specify the report to print.

5. When you have filled out the form as shown in figure 20.18, press Ctrl-End to save your changes. Press Ctrl-End again.
6. Use the arrow keys to select the second choice on the menu—Print Labels.
7. Press F10, select the Items menu, then select Change Action.
8. Select Display Or Print. From the Display Or Print menu, select Labels.
9. A form appears on-screen so that you can specify the labels to print and the options for the labels (see fig. 20.19). Fill out the form as shown in the figure.
10. When you have filled out the form as shown in figure 20.19, press Ctrl-End to save your changes.
11. Select the Menu menu and the option Save Current Menu. All changes to the FILES menu are saved. Finally, select Put Away Current Menu.

You have gone through all the steps required to design a simple application. Before you can use the application, however, you must generate the actual program code. The next section describes generating code for your application.

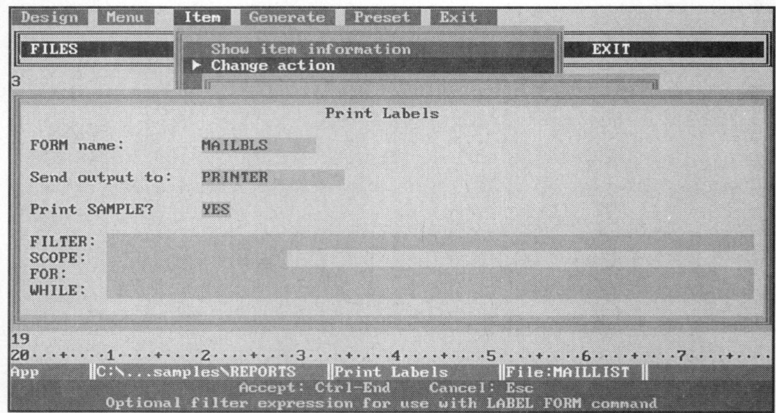


FIG. 20.19

The form to specify the labels to print.

# Generating Code for Your Application

By this time, you may have noticed that many of the choices on the Applications Generator menus have dBASE IV commands written next to them in uppercase letters. Those commands are the ones that the Applications Generator uses to build the code for the choices you make. After you are familiar with the dBASE language, you can anticipate the ways in which the Applications Generator uses these commands. That knowledge may help you get the most out of the Applications Generator. As you develop your application, keep track of enhancements suggested by the structure and flow of your application and the commands used by the Applications Generator. As you continue to polish your program, you can insert small refinements into the code. Later in this chapter, you learn how to perform simple enhancements to Applications Generator code.

After you have built your application, you get to make basic changes. Some of these changes include the dBASE environment, sign-on defaults, and display options. You set up these changes with the Preset menu any time during the development of your application.

The Preset menu enables you to make changes in four areas: Sign-on defaults, Display options, Environment settings, and Application drive/path. These options enable you to change the sign-on defaults (information in the welcome box), change the colors on the screen, change the options in the environment (SET commands), and change the drive and path used for the application.

After all changes have been made and you are ready to generate code, save all changes made to the application. To save, press F10, select the Application menu, and then select the option Save Current Application Definition. Then, follow these steps to generate program code:

1. If the Ap Gen menu is not selected, press F10. Select the Generate menu.
2. Select the option Begin Generation.

   The hard disk begins working, and you see many messages on-screen. After a few minutes, you see the message `Generation is complete. Press any key.`
3. Press Enter.
4. Select the Exit menu.
5. Select Save All Changes And Exit. dBASE returns to the dot prompt.

When program generation is finished, you have two program files: the main menu file (MAINMENU.PRG), and the rest of the application (MAILER.PRG). Several other non-program files also are created at the same time, which dBASE IV uses to generate your final application.

The two program files are full of procedures; each function of the application is created as a procedure. The application then calls each procedure when you make a selection from the menu.

This process differs from the way many programmers write dBASE programs. When writing a program without the aid of the Applications Generator, a programmer would probably create a separate program file for each function. Doing so makes testing and debugging easy. However, with only two files of procedures, the program is faster.

## Generating Documentation about the Application

With the Applications Generator, you not only can generate program code, but you also can generate documentation about the application. This documentation is not something that can be given to a user to learn how to use the application. Rather, it is documentation about the aspects of the application. The following is an excerpt from a documentation file that was created for the Mailer application:

```
Display Application Sign-On Banner: Yes

Screen Image:
0         10        20        30        40        50        60        70
>.....+....|....+....|....+....|....+....|....+....|....+....|....+....|.....+.
00:
01:
02:
03:
04:
05:         #============================================================#
06:         "  "
07:         "  "
08:         "          M A I L E R  -  T H E   d B A S E   I V "
09:         "  "
10:         "             M A I L   L I S T   M A N A G E R "
11:         "  "
12:         "                         Release 1.0 "
13:         "  "
14:         "  "
15:         "  "
16:         #============================================================#
17:
18:
19:
20:
21:
22:
23:
24:
>.....+....|....+....|....+....|....+....|....+....|....+....|....+....|.....+.
Main Menu to Open after Sign-On: MAINMENU.BAR
Sets for Application:
----------------
   Bell         ON
   Carry        OFF
   Centry       OFF
   Confirm      OFF
   Delimiters   OFF
   Display Size 25 lines
   Drive
   Escape       ON
   Path
   Safety       ON

Starting Colors for Application:
--------------
```

```
    Color Settings:
       Text            : W+/B
       Heading         : W/B
       Highlight       : GR+/BG
Page: 2  Date: 3-1-92  5:38p
   Box             : GR+/BG
   Messages        : W+/N
   Information     : B/W
   Fields          : N/BG
Database/View: MAILLIST
Index File(s): MAILLIST
Index Order: CUSTOMER
====================================================================

Menu/Picklist definitions follow:
------------------------
Page: 3  Date: 3-1-92

Layout Report for Horizontal Bar Menu: MAINMENU
------------------------
```

Notice that the excerpt generates specifics about the application: menus, what appears on-screen, databases and index, and the purpose of each menu option. You may find this documentation helpful for creating user documentation.

To create program documentation, press F10, select the Generate menu, and then select the option Select Template. You are asked for a template name. The following names may be used:

| | |
|---|---|
| DOCUMENT.GEN | Used to generate program documentation |
| MENU.GEN | Used to generate an application |
| QUICKAPP.GEN | Used to generate a single-menu application |

When you are generating the application, use MENU.GEN. When generating the preceding documentation, however, use the file DOCUMENT.GEN. When your application has only a single menu, use QUICKAPP.GEN. If you create an application that uses layers of menus, as does Mailer, you must use MENU.GEN as the template. You must set the template before choosing Begin Generation from the Generate menu.

# Running the Mailer Application

After you have created the application and generated the code, you can run the application easily. You may start the application in one of three ways: from the DOS prompt as you start dBASE, from the Control Center, or from the dot prompt.

To start the application from DOS, change to the directory that contains the application and type *DBASE MAILER* and press Enter. dBASE loads into memory, and in turn, loads and executes Mailer.

To start from the Control Center requires a second step. First, switch to the directory containing Mailer. Next, type *dBASE* and press Enter to start dBASE. When the Control Center appears on-screen, move the pointer to the Applications panel, highlight MAILER, and press Enter. You are asked whether you want to Run Application or Modify Application. Select Run Application.

To start from the dot prompt, you first must be in the correct directory and have started dBASE. Type *DO MAILER* and press Enter, and the application starts.

When you select Exit, you return to one of two screens. You return to the dot prompt if you started from DOS or from the dot prompt. If you started from the Control Center, however, you return to the Control Center.

# Managing Memory and Temporary Files

You may find that as you develop more complex applications, your program files become increasingly larger. This growth is particularly true when you use the Applications Generator, which creates only two files rather than many files. Not only does dBASE use memory for applications, but your data also uses memory.

As you run these large applications, dBASE creates temporary files on your hard disk. These files are created when more room is needed in memory than is actually contained in your computer. dBASE normally places these temporary files in your dBASE program directory. Your system's speed slows down when you use the temporary files because dBASE is reading the files from the hard disk, rather than using memory.

If you have enough memory (at least 1.5M of RAM), you can create a RAM disk (at least 512K) and reassign the temporary files to that disk. A RAM disk is quick because it is a disk drive created in memory. DOS comes with a RAM disk called VDISK.SYS or RAMDRIVE.SYS. You install the RAM disk in your CONFIG.SYS file by using the following command:

```
DEVICE=C:\DOS\VDISK.SYS 512
```

or

```
DEVICE=C:\DOS\RAMDRIVE.SYS 512
```

You use this command if the RAM disk program is in the \DOS directory on drive C. The RAM disk is assigned a letter, just as any disk drive is assigned a letter. If you have one hard disk, drive C, the RAM drive is assigned as drive D. If you already have drives C and D, however, then the RAM drive is assigned as drive E.

In your AUTOEXEC.BAT file, add the following line:

```
SET TMP=D:\
```

You add this line if your RAM disk is drive D. TMP is a DOS environment variable. dBASE looks for this variable and uses its contents to know where temporary files are to be stored (in the example, the root directory of drive D). Sometimes, other programs may use the variable name TMP. In this case, substitute the variable DBTMP and add the following command to AUTOEXEC.BAT:

```
SET DBTMP=D:\
```

Another way to balance your memory allocation is to use the SET DBHEAP command. You use this command before you start dBASE IV from the DOS prompt, or you can set DBHEAP from your AUTOEXEC.BAT file. DBHEAP balances the memory between that which dBASE uses for its own overlay files and the memory used by your application.

Setting DBHEAP requires a value. This value is actually a percentage, so that value is from 1 to 100. You specify the percentage of available memory that dBASE should allot to itself. If you are using a large application, you may want to allot less memory to data. A low DBHEAP gives more memory to dBASE, and it runs faster. A high DBHEAP gives more memory to your programs. Adding the following command to your AUTOEXEC.BAT file, for example, allots 40 percent of available memory to data and 60 percent of available memory to the application:

```
SET DBHEAP=40
```

Finally, dBASE IV has a utility called DBCACHE. This utility can help improve performance by providing disk caching specific to the database requirements of a database management application. To use DBCACHE, you must have 1.5M of either expanded or extended memory.

To install the cache, run DBSETUP from the DOS prompt. Access the Reconfigure menu and select the option to install caching. An option to uninstall caching also is available if you choose not to use disk caching.

**WARNING:** Do *not* install DBCACHE if you already are using another disk cache program (such as SmartDrive or PC-Kwik) on your system. Using more than one cache program causes memory conflicts.

FROM HERE...

**For Related Information...**

▸▸ "CREATE/MODIFY APPLICATION," p. 693.

# Learning Additional Capabilities of the Applications Generator

Five additional capabilities are available in the Applications Generator: batch process, file list, structure list, values list, and quick Applications Generator.

The *batch process* enables you to directly program several functions, which your application performs on its own without user intervention. Even though the user may initiate the batch process by making a menu selection, the various components or activities contained in the batch execute under program control.

An example of a batch process is a Maintenance menu that gives you the options of Copy The Database, Pack The Database, and Reindex The Database. Another option on the menu may be Perform All. Each of the menu options performs a dBASE command. Perform All, however, calls a batch process that copies, packs, and reindexes the database all at once.

Creating a batch process is similar to creating a pop-up menu. You enter the process names as you do menu items, you attach actions to the process names, and you attach the batch process to a menu option. Activating the batch process is no different from activating any menu option.

The *files list* enables you to tell users what they may do, and then provides the users with a list of files from which they select. A good example of this process is a reports menu that enables the user to select to print a report, and then offers a list of available reports. The list is created from the file names on the disk.

The *structure list* takes the files list a step further by allowing users to select for use specific fields within a database. For example, perhaps you are offering your users a menu choice for browsing a database. You also may want to let them select which fields they want in the display. With practice, you can even add program code that enables them to index on one of the selected fields to show the browse display in order based on a particular key field.

Taking this progression of lists still another step further, you can use the *values list* to narrow the scope of the file search. This step is achieved by assigning values or a range of values for the database in use. The purpose behind these lists is to give the user a way to narrow the scope of a database under scrutiny.

The fifth additional capability is the *quick Applications Generator*. This process enables you to create a simple one-menu application that enables users to work with a single database. To use this capability, select the option Generate Quick Application from the Application menu.

# Using Advanced Testing with the dBASE Debugger

Earlier in this book, you learned of several simple ways to debug your application. Simple methods do not work, however, for complex applications. Your sample mail list application created with the Applications Generator, for example, is well over 1,000 lines of code. That is not a simple application. If you add to or change the program created by the Applications Generator, your application may misbehave when you first run it. To prevent this problem, you need to use the debugging tools included in the dBASE IV debugger.

The *debugger* is a full-screen program that you access in one of three ways. If your program hits a serious snag, such as a syntax error or open construct (an IF without an ENDIF) during the compile process, the debugger pops up automatically. You can issue the command SET TRAP ON from the dot prompt, and the debugger also pops up on execution errors. These accesses are fine for hard errors, but you need a better way to get at the soft errors that cause your application to wander off into hyperspace for no apparent reason. *Soft errors* are the most common errors you encounter when you generate code with the Applications Generator. To start a debugging session that didn't start itself, type *DEBUG <apname>* at the dot prompt. For example, to debug the application created in this chapter, type *DEBUG MAILER*. dBASE IV loads your application into the debugger and displays the debugger screen with your application's code in the edit window.

**NOTE**

There is nothing wrong with using the Applications Generator to generate application code. Earlier in this book, you were encouraged to use the Ap Gen to make code, and that encouragement bears repeating. Most professional programmers use code generators of one type or another to get the bulk of their code written quickly and with minimal errors. Using a code generator, however, does not guarantee error-free code. Rather, the types of errors you end up with are the toughest to find because they are subtle.

The debugger gives you horsepower by enabling you to set *breakpoints* (temporary pauses in program execution that enable you to view the program's progress and look for errors), edit lines of code, display error messages, trace program execution a step at a time or as executed, trace procedure calls and possible open constructs, and use a variety of other tricks to zero in on the source of an error. The basic debugger screen and debugger commands are shown in figure 20.20.

```
C:\DBASE\SAMPLES\MAILER.PRG
10   *-- Setup environment                      --- Debug Commands ---
11   SET CONSOLE OFF
12   IF TYPE("gn_ApGen")="U"        B      - Change Breakpoint entries
13     CLEAR WINDOWS                D      - Change Display entries
14     CLEAR ALL                    E      - Edit program file
15     CLOSE ALL                    L      - Continue from given line
16     CLOSE PROCEDURE              [n]N   - As 'S' but on same or above level
17     gn_ApGen=1                   P      - Show program traceback info
18   ELSE                           Q      - Quit debugger
19     gn_ApGen=gn_ApGen+1          R      - Run until interrupt or error
20     IF gn_ApGen > 4              [n]S   - Execute next statement
                                    U      - Suspend program & go to dot prompt
DISPLAY                             [n]←┘  - Repeat last step or next
                         :          [n]↑   - Show previous line
                         :          [n]↓   - Show next line
                         :          F1     - Toggle Command Help On/Off
                         :          F9     - Show user screen

DEBUGGER
Work Area: 1      Database file:              Program file: mailer.prg
Record:  0        Master Index:               Procedure:    MAILER
ACTION:                                       Current line: 13

Stopped for step.
```

**FIG. 20.20**

The dBASE IV full-screen debugger and debugger commands.

As shown in figure 20.20, the full-screen debugger carries the following list of commands:

| Debug Commands | |
|---|---|
| B | Change Breakpoint entries |
| D | Change Display entries |
| E | Edit program file |
| L | Continue from given line |

| | |
|---|---|
| [n]N | As 'S' but on same or above level |
| P | Show program traceback info |
| Q | Quit debugger |
| R | Run until interrupt or error |
| [n]S | Execute next statement |
| U | Suspend program and go to dot prompt |
| [n]↵ | Repeat last step or next |
| [n]↑ | Show previous line |
| [n]↓ | Show next line |
| F1 | Toggle Command Help On/Off |
| F9 | Show user screen |

You execute debugger commands from the window along the bottom of the screen. When searching for errors in your program, the debugger gives you two choices: run the program and halt at errors or breakpoints, or run the program a step at a time and observe the reaction of the application as each line of code executes.

If you select the second choice, that is where early application planning pays off. If you carefully planned your application, you know exactly what is supposed to happen as it executes. Admittedly, you may have a few surprises if you didn't write all the code involved (code that was created by the Applications Generator), but you still should have a good idea of the general program flow. When the debugger starts running your application, it continues until it makes an error. You then stop program execution, insert breakpoints by using the breakpoint window in the debugger, and execute again. At this point, the debugging may seem like the elementary debugging you did earlier in this book; however, here's where it gets more complex. You can execute one of two options to trace the wanderings of your program's procedures: single-step through the program and observe the results of executing each line of code, or trace procedure calls.

When you trace procedure calls, you find many of your tougher problems—problems that make your program suddenly perform a task it isn't supposed to perform. Another problem is finding data you didn't expect in a location where it doesn't belong. Both problems are symptoms of an incorrect procedure call or faulty program loop. By stepping through the application one instruction at a time, and tracing execution, you get closer to locating and solving the problem. By using the trace command, P, you get a list of what calls what. Before you attempt your first debugging session on a large application, make sure that you have a printout of all the code the Applications Generator created. A simple way to do that is to print the program code by using the TYPE command with the program names. The NUMBER command numbers the program lines. For example, type the following command:

```
TYPE MAILER.PRG TO PRINTER NUMBER

TYPE MAINMENU.PRG TO PRINTER NUMBER
```

You may notice that dBASE has added many useful comments to the code listing. This feature is called *program documentation* and is crucial if future users must determine what you and the Applications Generator did when you wrote the code. (Do not confuse this with the documentation you can generate when you create the program.)

**TIP** When you add your own modifications to the application, don't forget the program documentation.

With the program listing in front of you, plan the locations for your breakpoints, the correct procedure calls, and proper program execution. Then, run the program—or single-step it—and observe the results. As you get closer to the specific incorrect command or commands, watch your program listing and the edit window of the debugger. Because you can edit your code and re-execute it from inside the debugger, you can try modifications and test them to see whether they give you the results you expect. The debugger numbers each line of code, and you can back up or jump ahead to any point in your application to begin execution. Any time you forget a debugger command, press F1, and help provides a list, descriptions, and correct syntax.

**For Related Information...**

▸▸ "DEBUG," p. 699.

▸▸ "TYPE," p. 769.

# Changing the Applications Generator Code

Although the Applications Generator helps you perform the basic steps involved in creating your application, at times you may want to make minor changes in your program code. Because the Applications Generator generates dBASE program files (PRG files), you can edit the program the same way you would edit dBASE programs you had written yourself—by using the dBASE program editor.

For the MAILER application, dBASE created two program files: MAILER.PRG and MAINMENU.PRG. To edit either of these files, use the MODIFY COMMAND statement from the dot prompt to invoke the program editor (as described in Chapter 17). To edit the MAINMENU file, for example, type:

MODIFY COMMAND MAINMENU.PRG

The program code will appear on-screen, as shown in figure 20.21.

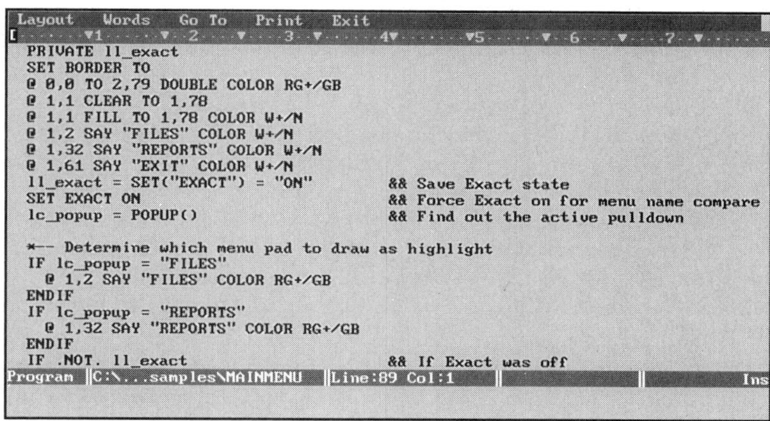


**FIG. 20.21**

Changing code created by the Applications Generator.

> **WARNING:** Be careful when making changes to generated code. If you change even one element in a line of code, such as an index tag name or variable name, that element may reappear elsewhere in the program. Your alteration then may affect how other sections or modules of the program perform.

You may want to "borrow" sections of code from the generated code to include in the programs that you write yourself. Some programmers, for example, use the Applications Generator to design a menu structure, then they delete everything else from the code and add their own modules to be executed when various menu items are selected.

FROM HERE...

**For Related Information...**

◂◂ "Creating and Modifying Program Files," p. 440.

# Using RunTime

Now that your application is finished and debugged, you may want to distribute it. You can distribute a dBASE IV application several different ways. The easiest way, if all your users have copies of dBASE IV, or if you are on a local area network with dBASE IV shared among several users, is to distribute the compiled versions of your code. These versions include the reports, labels, format, and program files. The files are *object code files*, which means that dBASE IV has stripped out the comments and unnecessary spaces, parsed the commands, and produced a binary file that dBASE runs directly. Although in this case dBASE is an interpreter (your application files must be interpreted—they cannot run by themselves), files executed in this manner run faster than source code files and have the benefit of being unreadable by your users. Because the files are unreadable, they also are unchangeable. This feature prevents users from getting inside your complicated application to make changes or to accidentally wipe out data.

RunTime, on the other hand, does not require users to have a copy of dBASE IV. Instead, you create an application and, along with special files (RunTime), give it to the users so that they can use the application without dBASE IV on their computer systems.

# Getting Ready for RunTime

Before you can use RunTime, you need to prepare your application. You also must follow several rules when you use any type of RunTime application. If you don't follow the rules, your application will not run correctly, no matter how well you debugged it. Start out by making sure that you have built your application to run consistently from the correct directories. When you are using an application with full copies of dBASE IV, you most likely installed it. When you did, you may have customized it to operate in preselected subdirectories. If you did, how will your users know where to put the application when they receive it in the mail? To prevent such a problem, you should always produce an installation program. That program, often just a simple DOS batch file, creates the proper subdirectories and copies program, RunTime, and data files to their proper places.

Do not create an application that runs from the root directory. Instead, always create a special subdirectory to keep these files separate from any other files on your user's hard drive.

Another rule you need to follow scrupulously concerns debugging. Before you attempt to compile your application for RunTime distribution, make sure that it's completely debugged. If you don't, users who do not have access to you may not know how to handle your application's "quirks."

Make sure that all program, report, label, and format files referenced in the application are together in the same directory. The best way to ensure that is to create a subdirectory just for preparing RunTime versions of your applications.

You need to distribute some other files with your application and, when you initially write your application, you have to avoid using some dBASE commands. The following commands are not supported by RunTime:

| | | |
|---|---|---|
| ASSIST | COMPILE | CREATE/MODIFY FILE |
| CREATE/MODIFY LABEL | DEBUG | HELP |
| CREATE/MODIFY QUERY | HISTORY | SET DEBUG |
| RESUME | SET DOHISTORY | CREATE/MODIFY SCREEN |
| HISTORY | SET INSTRUCT | CREATE/MODIFY |
| CREATE/MODIFY VIEW | MENU DRIVEN SET | CREATE/MODIFY REPORT |
| MODIFY COMMAND/FILE | SET SQL | SET STEP |
| SET TRAP | SUSPEND | SET ECHO |
| CREATE/MODIFY STRUCTURE | SET HISTORY | LIST/DISPLAY HISTORY |

Besides these commands, the macro substitution (&) character cannot be used to substitute for command verbs. When your application is complete, you place it, the appropriate data files and indexes, and several RunTime files onto your distribution disk. RunTime files are all those that begin with *RunTime* (RUNTIME.OVL, RUNTIME.CAC, RUNTIME.RES, RUNTIME.EXE). Also include RPROTECT.OVL. As pointed out earlier, you should include a batch file for installing your application.

## Using Your Application

Starting the application is easy. Change to the directory that contains the files you just generated—for example \DBASE\MAILER. When you check your directory, you may notice that you have these files:

```
MAILER.DBO
MAILLIST.DBF
MAILLIST.MDX
RUNTIME.EXE
RUNTIME.RES
RUNTIME.OVL
RPROTECT.OVL
```

To start the Mailer application, type the following command and press Enter:

```
RUNTIME MAILER
```

The application operates just as if you had started it from dBASE IV.

## Producing an Application for Distribution

If you are producing an application for distribution, you should copy the files onto master distribution disks, and create an installation program and place it on the distribution disks. Then, as a final predistribution test, install and run your application from the distribution disks. If all goes well and the application installs and runs correctly, use that set of disks as masters for duplicating and producing distribution sets for your users. The master disks you have created are called *gold disks*. From the gold set, you should make another set that you actually use in the physical duplication of the production disks for distribution. This working set is called the *silver set*. Put the gold set in a safe place. Always use DISKCOPY when creating copies of your disks for distribution. Never use the DOS COPY command.

Make sure that you have created adequate documentation for your application. Solid documentation gives users a source from which to learn about the application, how to use it, and what to do if they get lost.

One final word about distribution: You should establish a release-numbering system so that you know what release of your application users have. The release numbers change as you add enhancements or fix the inevitable bugs that crop up. You never want to lose track of which set of disks has bugs on it and which has the bugs fixed.

# Summary

In this chapter, you learned the basics of professional application development. You learned about the Applications Generator, advanced debugging techniques, and the methods used to generate RunTime versions of your applications.

In the next chapter, you learn about one of the most powerful capabilities of dBASE IV—the SQL system. dBASE IV SQL and its multiuser capability make the system among the most powerful of the file-server type databases.

21

CHAPTER

# Using dBASE IV SQL

dBASE IV includes the powerful data-handling capabilities of dBASE IV SQL. Before you dig too deeply into dBASE IV SQL, you need to understand some of the whys and hows of this excellent database management facility. This chapter begins with a discussion of SQL as a database management tool. First you learn what advantages SQL has over native dBASE databases. Then you learn about the structure of dBASE SQL databases and data tables.

You get an introduction to how to use SQL in dBASE IV, both interactively and from within your dBASE IV applications. Next, you take a tour of the SQL command syntax, which includes fewer than 30 commands. After you understand SQL structure and commands, you are ready to delve deeper into SQL as an adjunct to your dBASE IV application development tasks. Finally, you learn about the power of dBASE IV SQL as a multiuser, transaction-oriented database management tool in conjunction with the powerful dBASE procedural language.

## Understanding SQL

Structured Query Language (SQL) is a *nonprocedural language*, which means that you cannot write an SQL program with looping constructs, conditionals, and other program-flow structures. SQL is designed to do just one task: manage data. The language is used to create databases, place data in them, modify the data, and retrieve data from the database. SQL also provides controls on the use of the data, methods for browsing the database, and a few data-handling utilities.

For a data-handling language like SQL to be useful, you must be able to use it interactively or from within an application. The language must have the capability to merge data from several sources, and it must work well in a multiuser environment. Most important, the data-handling language must be specialized (optimized) for data handling only. It also must coexist comfortably with a procedural language (like dBASE IV) so that full applications can be built. The combination of dBASE and SQL fulfills all these requirements.

Because SQL is designed strictly as a data-handling language, it greatly simplifies the management of data. Data-retrieval processes that take many lines of code in dBASE take only a single statement in SQL. Admittedly, the data management statements in SQL are far more complex than those in dBASE. Even given that complexity, however, SQL statements are simpler and more straightforward than the many lines of code and iterative processes required to extract groups of records from a dBASE database. As you discover in this chapter, SQL uses a combination of statements, verbs, predicates, and clauses to build a single SQL command. If that sounds to you like the tools for building a sentence in English, you have picked up on one of SQL's strengths. When you read an SQL command, it sounds like a plain English sentence. This English-like structure adds to SQL's ease of use.

When you compare the ways SQL and dBASE manage data, you see some differences and some similarities. The two are similar—though not identical—in the way they store data. SQL and dBASE are quite different in the commands they use to retrieve data. Because of this, certain commands in the dBASE language cannot coexist with SQL. As a general rule, you cannot use these "disallowed" dBASE commands anywhere you plan to use SQL commands. If you create a program file that contains both dBASE and SQL commands, you cannot use a user-defined function (UDF) that contains disallowed commands, even though you can use UDFs in SQL files. For a complete list of disallowed commands, refer to the dBASE IV manual.

## Using SQL Two Ways

You can use dBASE IV SQL interactively from the special SQL dot prompt, or you can create special program files with a file extension PRS instead of the regular dBASE PRG extension. PRS files can contain both SQL and dBASE IV commands as long as you don't use any disallowed commands. You must have designated an SQLHOME directory path, however, in your CONFIG.DB file. The easiest way to set up an SQL path in CONFIG.DB is to use DBSETUP. You must use SET SQL ON from the dot prompt in order to get the SQL prompt, and you cannot use SQL commands from the dBASE mode—the regular dBASE dot prompt. You can enter SQL commands directly from the SQL prompt the same way you do dBASE commands, or you can use the SQL editor.

You invoke the SQL editor by pressing Ctrl-Home. The SQL editor is similar to the dBASE full-screen editor, except you use it to formulate a single SQL command. Although you can enter an SQL command from the SQL prompt, SQL commands can become quite long and can have several lines in a single command by the time you add all the additional clauses. In this case, creating your command in the SQL editor and then saving it is much easier. After you save the command, you can exit the SQL editor. The command appears on the dBASE command line following the SQL prompt. Figure 21.1 shows the SQL editor work surface.

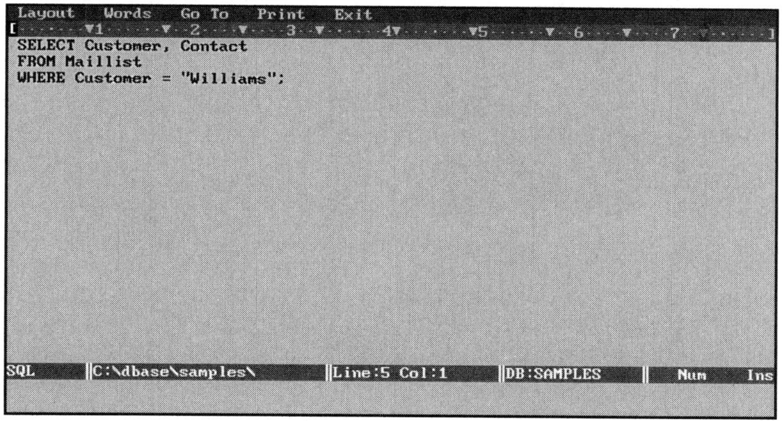


FIG. 21.1

The SQL editor.

When creating an SQL command, you have a major difference between the way you write the SQL command and the way you write a dBASE command. If a dBASE command is too long for the command line, you can break the command with a semicolon (;). If an SQL command is too long for a single command line, however, simply press the Enter key and continue typing your command. You can do this because the SQL editor does not interpret Enter as the end of the command, as dBASE does. When you finish an SQL command, close the command with a semicolon.

SQL commands often are several lines long. Good programming practice actually dictates that you break certain commands, such as

SELECT, for each new clause to improve readability as you scan your code. The following is an example of such a command:

```
SELECT Company, Contact
   FROM Maillist
   WHERE Phone = "212";
```

Notice that the FROM and WHERE clauses are indented to improve readability further and that the whole command ends with a semicolon.

As you progress in this chapter, you learn more about using dBASE IV SQL in your applications. First, however, you need to know more about the structure of SQL databases and tables, as well as the structure and syntax of the SQL language.

# Working with SQL Databases and Tables

In dBASE IV, SQL follows most of the same conventions that large mainframe databases follow. To maintain compatibility with these and other industry-standard SQL databases, dBASE IV SQL must follow certain guidelines in two important areas. The first is the *syntax* of the language, which you learn more about later in this chapter. The second is the *structure* of databases and tables.

dBASE terminology and SQL terminology are quite different. When you speak of a database in dBASE, you mean a single collection of data, stored in tabular form. When you speak of a database in SQL, you refer to a collection of such tables and a data dictionary that describes the tables, their contents, and the database structure (see fig. 21.2). In dBASE IV, dBASE SQL uses all these concepts and all this terminology, except that data dictionaries in dBASE IV SQL are called *catalogs*.

Another terminology difference is in the way you refer to fields and records. In a dBASE database, the data is laid out in tables, just as in the SQL database. A few differences exist in the structure of the two tables, but you may consider them pretty much the same. The records of the dBASE database are the rows of the table, and the fields are the columns. SQL keeps the terminology simple. Rows are rows and columns are columns. The relationships, however, are the same: SQL rows are the same as dBASE records, and SQL columns are the same as dBASE fields.

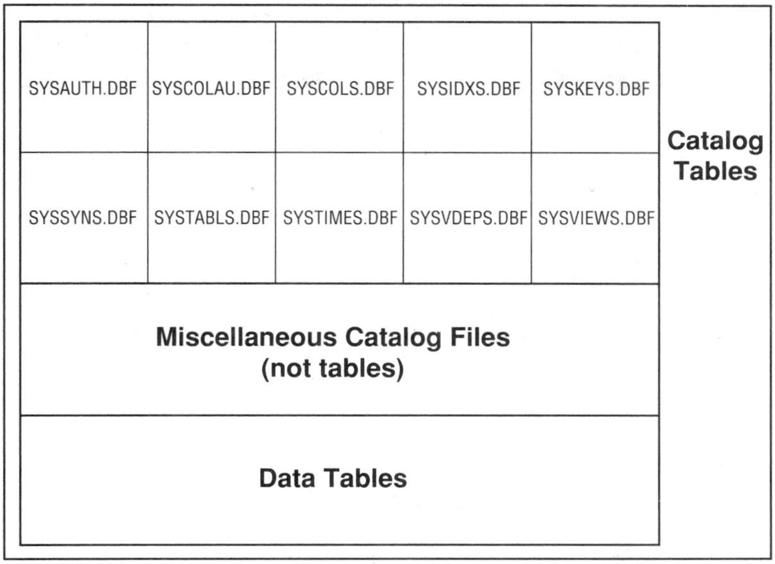

| SYSAUTH.DBF | SYSCOLAU.DBF | SYSCOLS.DBF | SYSIDXS.DBF | SYSKEYS.DBF | Catalog Tables |
|---|---|---|---|---|---|
| SYSSYNS.DBF | SYSTABLS.DBF | SYSTIMES.DBF | SYSVDEPS.DBF | SYSVIEWS.DBF | |

**Miscellaneous Catalog Files (not tables)**

**Data Tables**

FIG. 21.2

An SQL database.

You may have heard implications that much more is involved in gaining access to SQL data than to dBASE data. That's both true and not true. It is true that you must open the database before you can use a table. But after you open the database, access to any table within the database is automatic with the execution of any of the data manipulation statements. When you build an application with dBASE IV SQL, you generally start with CREATE DATABASE and then use CREATE TABLE to create all the tables you need in that application.

The database and its associated tables usually reside in a single subdirectory whose name is the same as the name of the database. After the database is open, any table you create is included automatically in the database. At the same time, the database's catalog is updated. Don't confuse the SQL catalog with the dBASE catalog—they are very different.

You use five SQL commands in manipulating databases and nine commands in manipulating tables. This chapter doesn't deal with the detailed usage of all these commands because they are fairly straightforward. (For the complete syntax of SQL commands, see "SQL Commands" in Part V, "dBASE IV Reference Guide," later in this book.)

The following commands are used in databases:

| Command | Description |
|---|---|
| CREATE DATABASE | Creates a database directory and associated files |
| SHOW DATABASE | Lists databases |
| START DATABASE | Opens a database |
| STOP DATABASE | Closes a database |
| DROP DATABASE | Deletes a database and all its associated files and tables |

The following commands are used in tables:

| Command | Description |
|---|---|
| CREATE TABLE | Creates a new table |
| ALTER TABLE | Adds a column to an existing table |
| CREATE VIEW | Creates a result table |
| CREATE SYNONYM | Defines an alias for a table or view |
| CREATE INDEX | Creates an index for a table or view |
| DROP TABLE | Deletes a table |
| DROP VIEW | Deletes a view |
| DROP SYNONYM | Deletes a synonym, but leaves the table |
| DROP INDEX | Deletes an index |

When you use SQL for the first time, you must begin by creating a database with the CREATE DATABASE command. This command uses the following syntax:

```
CREATE DATABASE [<path>]<database name>;
```

When you create a database, dBASE IV builds under the dBASE directory a subdirectory with the database name as its name. In that directory are several files. Table 21.1 shows an example of the table files making up an SQL database.

**Table 21.1 Tables in a dBASE IV SQL Catalog**

| Table | Description |
|---|---|
| MAILLIST.DBF | The Maillist table |
| SYSAUTH.DBF | The table of authorized table users |
| SYSCOLAU.DBF | The table of authorized column users and their UPDATE privileges |
| SYSCOLS.DBF | The table of column names for all tables in this database |
| SYSIDXS.DBF | The table of all indexes in this database |
| SYSKEYS.DBF | The table of index keys for this database |
| SYSSYNS.DBF | The table of synonyms used in this database |
| SYSTABLS.DBF | The table of tables in this database |
| SYSTIME.MEM | A memory variable file associated with SYSTIMES.DBF |
| SYSTIMES.DBF | The table of creation dates/times for all the tables in this database for use in a multiuser environment |
| SYSVDEPS.DBF | The table of tables for which a view is defined |
| SYSVIEWS.DBF | The table of views |

One file in table 21.1 is not part of the catalog but is listed here for your information. The catalog normally is not considered to contain any actual user-created tables. It contains only those tables created and maintained by dBASE IV. For illustrative purposes, however, the MAILLIST.DBF table is included. When you look at the directory containing the catalog for a given database, you also see all the associated tables in that directory.

Creating an SQL table (CREATE TABLE) is a bit more complex than creating a database. The CREATE TABLE command uses the following syntax:

```
CREATE TABLE <table name>
   (<column name> <data type>
   [,<column name> <data type>...]);
```

You must list each of the columns you want in the new data table, and you must give each column a name and a size. If you intend to import data from one or more columns of another data table into your new table, you must give one of the columns in the new table the same name, data type, and size as the source column in the source table. The data types you may use are shown in table 21.2.

**Table 21.2 Data Types for CREATE TABLE**

| Type | Description |
|---|---|
| SMALLINT | Integer with 6 or fewer digits |
| INTEGER | Integer with up to 11 digits |
| FLOAT (x,y) | A signed floating point number with *x* total digits and *y* decimal places |
| DECIMAL (x,y) | A signed fixed decimal number with *x* total digits and *y* decimal places |
| NUMERIC (x,y) | A signed fixed decimal number with *x* total digits and *y* decimal places, whose precision is set using SET PRECISION |
| CHAR (n) | A character string containing up to *n* characters |
| LOGICAL | A logical true (.T.) or false (.F.) |
| DATE | A date in the format specified by SET DATE and SET CENTURY. (The dBASE date manipulation functions such as CTOD( ) may be used in dBASE IV SQL.) |

When you are using dBASE IV in dBASE mode, you create relationships between databases with the SET RELATION TO command and a few others that enable you to build up a view of the databases involved. This is a crude, but effective, relational operation. With dBASE this process takes several lines of code. With SQL it takes only one command. With SQL, the view capability is truly relational, and such issues as data integrity are handled automatically.

The following example of a VIEW connects two tables (MAILLIST.DBF and MAILINGS.DBF) by using the linking column Customer. The Maillist database has been converted to a table by the DBDEFINE command, and a new table called Mailings has been created with the CREATE TABLE command. The Mailings table has the columns Customer and Lastcont (last contact date, a character data-type column). The contents of the Customer column are the same as the contents of the Customer column in the Maillist table.

```
CREATE VIEW Contacts
(Customer, Contact, Lastcont)
AS SELECT Maillist.Customer, Maillist.Contact,
```

```
    Mailings.Lastcont
    FROM Maillist, Mailings
    WHERE Maillist.Customer = Mailings.Customer;
```

Notice that you must create the relationship between the two data tables by setting the linking columns as equal to one another (Maillist.Customer = Mailings.Customer). The view has three fields only: Customer, Contact, and Lastcont. Notice also that when you use more than one data table, you must indicate both table name and column name, separated by a period (.). Therefore, the customer column of the Maillist table is indicated as `Maillist.Customer`, with the table name first and the column name second. You also need to tell dBASE IV SQL which tables you are using by listing them in the FROM clause, separated by commas (,).

You can use CREATE VIEW to create a view of a single table. The purpose is to build a temporary table that is a subset of a real table. Remember that views are not real tables. They don't exist except as a set of instructions in the SYSVIEWS.DBF table in the database's catalog. When you use a view, dBASE IV SQL temporarily creates the basis of the view as a virtual table in your computer's memory. If you query the view by using the SELECT statement, dBASE IV SQL uses those instructions to retrieve the information you requested and then displays it or stores it to whatever file or real table you choose. After you STOP the database (exit it), the view and its description are gone. When you restart the database, however, you can still access the previously created view by issuing the SELECT command, which is described in the section "Handling Data," later in this chapter.

# Building SQL Statements

Earlier in this chapter, you learned that one of the differences between SQL commands and dBASE commands is that SQL commands always end with a semicolon (;). Other differences also exist. SQL commands use a combination of commands and clauses called *statements* and *predicates*, respectively. Experienced SQL users sometimes refer to commands as *verbs*. The predicate is a special condition that modifies another clause, usually a WHERE clause. Typical predicates are BETWEEN, IN, and FOR. In simple terms, an SQL statement has the following structure:

VERB <*object*>

CLAUSE1 PREDICATE

CLAUSE2

CLAUSEn...;

This structure appeared in the CREATE VIEW example in the preceding section. In this statement, the verb is CREATE VIEW, and its object is Contacts. The first clause is the AS SELECT clause, whose objects are Maillist.Customer, Maillist.Contact, and Mailings.Lastcont. Next is the FROM clause, followed by the WHERE clause, each with its own objects. All SQL statements are built in this manner, either with or without one or more clauses attached. You are ready now to explore the first, and probably the most important, SQL command: SELECT.

# Handling Data

After the tables have been built, four SQL commands deal specifically with the manipulation of data in tables. These commands put data into, get data out of, delete data from, or change data in a data table. The first and potentially most complex of these is the SELECT command.

## SELECT

SQL as a query language owes most of its power to the SELECT command. SELECT, with its clauses and predicates, is the way that you can go to one or more tables of virtually any size or complexity and extract only the particular rows or parts of rows you want. SELECT appears quite simple at first, but it can grow rapidly in complexity as you put more demands on it. The two biggest advantages of SQL as a query language—power and the simplicity of English language-like syntax—are embodied in SELECT. The syntax of the SELECT command follows:

```
SELECT <clause>
[INTO <clause>]
FROM <clause>
[WHERE <clause>]
[GROUP BY <clause>]
[HAVING [NOT] <clause> [AND/OR [NOT] <clause>]]
[UNION <SELECT command...>];
[ORDER BY <clause>/FOR UPDATE OF <clause>]
[SAVE TO TEMP <clause>];
```

The simplest form of SELECT is this: SELECT *<column list>* FROM *<table list>*. Using the Maillist table, you can get a listing of the customers and contacts this way:

```
SELECT Customer, Contact
FROM Maillist;
```

To see all the columns in all the rows, use a wild card:

```
SELECT *
FROM Maillist;
```

If you want to see the customers, contacts, and phone numbers from the companies in New York (area code 212) only, use the WHERE clause to narrow the scope of your search:

```
SELECT customer, contact, phone
FROM Maillist
WHERE phone = "212";
```

This is similar to using the FOR keyword in regular dBASE programming. As with FOR, you can use comparison operators like =, >, and < to set up conditions. You can use the Boolean operators AND, OR, and NOT. (Notice that you don't need the periods on either side of the operator as you do in regular dBASE programming.) Most dBASE functions available with FOR in dBASE may be used in an SQL WHERE clause. You also may use five special functions in dBASE IV SQL. These aggregate functions are as follows:

| | |
|---|---|
| AVG( ) | Average the values in a numeric column |
| COUNT( ) | Count selected rows |
| MAX( ) | Maximum value in a column |
| MIN( ) | Minimum value in a column |
| SUM( ) | Total of values in a numeric column |

Like dBASE functions, these SQL functions return a value that you may use as part of your SQL statement or save to a temporary location (memory variable), using the INTO clause. When used with the SELECT statement, they also can be used to perform a function and return a value. If you want to know the number of companies in the Maillist table, for example, you can use SELECT with DISTINCT and the aggregate function COUNT( ):

```
SELECT DISTINCT COUNT(Company)
FROM Maillist;
```

This statement SELECTs only the first occurrence of each company, and the COUNT( ) function returns a number representing how many times SELECT found such an entry in the Maillist table.

As you can see, the trick is to build your SQL statement by adding conditions that narrow the scope of your search. These conditions enable you to group rows (GROUP), order rows (ORDER), and perform several other very specific manipulations.

The first of these modifiers that enable you to perform specific manipulations is DISTINCT. As shown in the previous example, DISTINCT enables you to avoid duplication in the rows you select with SELECT. Suppose that you have several contacts at a particular company in your version of Maillist. You want to build a list of companies, but you don't want the same company mentioned several times (once for each entry in the table if you have multiple contacts). If you use the following command, every row is displayed:

```
SELECT Company
FROM Maillist;0
```

But if you use this command, you see only the first occurrence of each entry:

```
SELECT DISTINCT Company
FROM Maillist;
```

No matter how many entries (rows) you have for XYZ Corporation, the listing generated by the SQL statement above shows only the first one. You may use DISTINCT only once in any query, even if the statement uses nested queries. When you use nested queries, you must apply DISTINCT to only the first column mentioned in the statement.

You can further format your selected information with GROUP or ORDER or with the UNION clause. These clauses enable you to perform some of the same tasks you can perform with indexes or relational functions from a single, albeit complex, SELECT command.

The GROUP BY clause enables you to collect all the rows that have some column in common. You can use the GROUP BY clause with the Maillist table, for example, to group all the records that have the same company. That way, no matter what the natural order of the table is, all the same company rows are together. This has the effect of showing the contacts in each company together. You also can use the GROUP BY clause to bring together all of the companies in each city or state.

You can add a bit more selection to the GROUP BY clause by including the HAVING clause. HAVING is somewhat like WHERE in SQL or FOR in dBASE, except you use it specifically with GROUP BY. The usual structure is this: GROUP BY <*column*> HAVING <*condition*>. To collect all of the New York companies together by city, for example, you group by city those rows having phone numbers that begin with 212. The SQL statement for doing just that is

```
SELECT Company, Contact, Phone
FROM Maillist
GROUP BY City HAVING Phone = "212";
```

This statement gives you a list of all the rows in the Maillist table showing the company, contact, and telephone number, collected by city for all entries in the 212 area code. Notice that you can use a partial match (just the area code portion of the phone number) unless SET EXACT is ON.

If you also want to show the entries in alphabetical order by company, you can insert *ORDER BY Company* before the GROUP BY CLAUSE. Your command would read as follows:

```
SELECT Company, Contact, Phone
FROM Maillist
ORDER BY Company
GROUP BY City HAVING Phone = "212";
```

You can, of course, use ORDER BY on more than one column. To list the New York contacts in alphabetical order, use this command:

```
SELECT Company, Contact, Phone
FROM Maillist
ORDER BY Company, Contact
GROUP BY City HAVING Phone = "212";
```

You can order by ascending or descending order, but naturally you cannot do both in the same statement.

To get information in your virtual result table without using a legitimate join (you learn about SQL *joins* later in this chapter), use the UNION clause. Unlike other relational commands, UNION does not require a linking column with the same name in each table being used. It does, however, require the same data type and the same column size.

In a UNION clause, you do not see any relationships between the data attached to the column on which you build your UNION. In other words, simply because two tables yield the same state names from a UNION of the tables doesn't necessarily mean that the companies in those states are the same. In a relational operation, it is assumed that the columns in each table are the same and that, when the relation is complete, the two tables line up side by side, row to row. If you did a UNION of SELECTS on two different tables—Maillist and Mailings, for example—you can get a list of all of the cities or companies represented, even if the two tables have no records in common. To use UNION, all you need to do is perform a series of SELECT statements with each complete statement separated by UNION. The general structure is

```
SELECT <column1>
FROM <table1>
UNION
SELECT <column2>
FROM <table2>
UNION
SELECT <column_n>
FROM <table_n>;
```

Earlier in this chapter, you discovered an SQL structure called a *predicate*. The three simplest predicates used with SELECT are BETWEEN, IN, and LIKE. BETWEEN simply means that you narrow the scope of your query to all the values *between* two independent variables. In other words, you can test a column for all of the entries BETWEEN *x* and *y*. The resulting table contains only those rows that meet the criteria. IN enables you to do the same thing, but in this case you test for all of the entries in a column that fit IN a list that makes part of the clause. You use IN with the WHERE clause for tasks like the following:

```
SELECT Customer, Contact
FROM Maillist
WHERE phone IN ("212", "313");
```

This statement gives you a list of all of the companies and contacts for companies located in New York (area code 212) or Michigan (area code 313).

Finally, you can use the LIKE predicate with the WHERE clause to create a skeleton (including the wild cards _ and %) that lets you SELECT based on partial entries. You can do the same thing to a certain extent simply by using the first portion of a character string. The examples in this chapter have been doing that with area codes—actually stripping the area code out of the phone number. If you want to strip a string out of the inside of a column's contents, you have to use the LIKE predicate and wild cards. The benefit of this approach is that you can be quite specific about which characters must be in the string and which are represented by wild-card characters.

To increase your ability to hit the data you want with rifle-shot accuracy, you need to learn about joins. *Joins* are the hallmark of relational database management systems. Joins take advantage of all the benefits of the relational algebra that is the foundation of relation database management system theory. The ability to perform complex multiple-table (multitable) queries depends on the database's capability to perform joins properly. Ironically, SQL has no join command. In SQL, joins are simply actions that certain SQL commands perform when they act on multiple tables. In order to understand how to use multitable joins, you also need to understand how to nest queries within a SELECT statement.

Nested queries within a SELECT statement are called *subqueries*. With dBASE IV SQL, you actually have a choice of using joins or subqueries. For every statement containing subqueries, you can build a statement by using joins that perform the same task. The decision of which to use depends on the complexity of the query. For very complex queries, subqueries are easier to construct and more efficient to execute.

An example of a fairly simple join appeared in a CREATE VIEW example earlier in this chapter. The SELECT portion of that example follows:

```
SELECT Maillist.Customer, Maillist.Contact,
Mailings.Lastcont
FROM Maillist, Mailings
WHERE Maillist.Customer = Mailings.Customer
```

Notice that you connect the column name with the table name in the SELECT clause and that you list the tables in the FROM clause. Finally, you must have the linking column (in this case, the Customer column) that is the same in both tables. In this example, the Customer column has been used to join the Maillist table with the Mailings table. The virtual result table built in the join contains all the data in both smaller tables. Called a *natural join*, this excludes all rows from the result table that don't meet the WHERE clause's condition. Another kind of join is called a *forced join*. Forced joins do not use a WHERE condition and a linking column; every row in one table is joined to every row in the other.

In complex multitable queries that create joins, you can use any of the techniques available for simple queries. You can build several conditions into your query or use functions to narrow your selection criteria. You also can join as many tables (within reason) as you want. Remember, however, that dBASE has to optimize the query; the more complex you make the query, the longer it takes to optimize and execute.

**NOTE**

Several factors affect dBASE IV performance. Performance, in simple terms, means the speed with which dBASE IV reacts to your query and returns an answer. The first, and most important factor, is your hardware platform. No matter how efficient dBASE IV SQL is, it cannot make up for poor hardware performance. When you use dBASE IV SQL in a network environment, you do not experience the high performance in normal ad hoc queries that you do in a database server environment.

Don't expect dBASE IV SQL to bring you blazing speed beyond dBASE database management just because it's SQL. The trick is knowing when to use SQL to improve database performance. If your database is very large and you are using multiple data sets, you benefit a lot by putting all your data management into dBASE IV SQL. If you use single databases and they tend to be fairly small (a few hundred records at most), stick with dBASE. If you are on a local-area network (LAN), however, you probably can benefit by using SQL because SQL sends just the results of your query—not the whole database—through the network. That keeps traffic down somewhat on the LAN.

This is not to say that you get database server performance. Database servers do all their database management from the server, which means that only the specific results of your query return to the workstation. Because all data is handled by the database server, an even smaller amount of data comes back to the workstation than in a LAN environment. That approach is much faster than any file server database system. In dBASE IV SQL, some data must return to the workstation for further manipulation within the query. That means you have far more data traveling on the network "wire" than with a database server, but quite a bit less than with dBASE.

Performance also is affected by database query optimization, which dBASE IV SQL does automatically. You can help dBASE IV SQL optimize your queries even more. When you create a complex query, plan the query carefully so that you can nest the subqueries in a logical order. Don't force dBASE IV to jump back and forth between tables to execute your query. Later in this chapter, you learn about inner and outer subqueries. The order in which you build these subqueries can affect your application's performance significantly.

Finally, when you build your application, take advantage of transaction-processing techniques whenever possible. If you have several queries in a given transaction, set them all up and then execute them all at once by using the BEGIN TRANSACTION command. That way you avoid constantly bringing data back and forth to your workstation. You complete the query and perform any necessary updates all at once.

Remember, in a network environment, dBASE IV SQL provides all the necessary locks on tables and rows in use to avoid loss of data integrity and to enforce concurrent control. If you are holding tables open with a series of queries that depend on user input, you are making the overall system far less efficient because other users are contending for the use of the same tables. If you set up the transaction without actually performing the pieces of it and then perform the whole thing at once with a BEGIN TRANSACTION, you operate at machine speed instead of user speed, and the tables are out of service for a much shorter time.

Subqueries really are quite simple. You nest queries within a single SELECT statement. The nested query is called an *inner query*, and the query in which it is nested is the *outer query*. The nesting occurs inside the WHERE clause of the outer query, and you place the inner query in parentheses.

dBASE IV SQL has two kinds of subqueries: *simple subqueries* and *correlated subqueries*. Simple subqueries work like simple algebraic statements. You (and dBASE IV SQL) evaluate them from the inside out, starting with the subquery nested the deepest in the total statement.

After evaluating the deepest subquery, dBASE IV uses the rows that result to evaluate the next query, and so on. dBASE starts with a fairly large result table and shrinks it as it whittles away at the available rows until it reaches the outermost outer query. At that point you have your final result table, which may have only one or two rows in it. Logically speaking, you have the potential for the most complex queries if your tables are large and you have several of them involved in the query.

Keep one caveat in mind when you are nesting queries. Make sure that the WHERE clause which makes up an outer query can handle the results the inner query returns. Because this means that it often must handle several rows, be sure that you use an appropriate predicate or clause capable of accepting more than one row. As far as syntax is concerned, using a nested SELECT statement as an inner query is no different from using a SELECT statement as a stand-alone query.

Remember that each time dBASE IV SQL evaluates a nested query, it returns rows in a result table just as if that query were by itself. In turn, the next level of the query must deal with that result table. The process is similar to performing a simple query, saving the results in a view, and then performing another query on the view. The difference is that using subqueries is far more efficient and elegant.

The second type of subquery, the correlated subquery, is a bit more complicated. Whereas the simple subquery produces a result table independent of any outer query, the correlated subquery uses values returned by an outer query. The difference between this and a simple subquery is subtle, but important. The outer query must return values for all the rows that the inner query uses. Then the inner query is evaluated for each value. This doesn't mean that the rule of evaluating the inner query first is violated. It means that the total query statement must be performed several times, once for each set of outer query results. The actual last step in the overall query is to correlate the information in the outer query with the information in the inner query to obtain a final result table.

No single format dictates the steps you perform to build a simple or correlated subquery. You must examine the steps your query performs as it evaluates the nested queries and build your query in a logical fashion. A well-structured query yields the best performance.

Keep in mind that anything you can do with subqueries you can do with joins. With a join, you perform a simple query with no nesting. You produce that query by using several tables and then save the results of the query to a result table. When you use joins as an alternative to subqueries, you often need Boolean operators (AND, OR, NOT) to perform the same query. Using nested subqueries, however, is more efficient for dBASE IV SQL to evaluate and results in better performance, especially with large tables.

If your inner and outer queries are directed at the same table, you need to assign aliases to keep the queries separate. When you do this, dBASE IV SQL treats the table as two separate tables. You can use the CREATE SYNONYM statement for this task.

# INSERT

The INSERT statement enables you to add data to an existing table. INSERT is similar to the dBASE APPEND command, but you do not get a data input screen with INSERT. You must build the statement like any other SQL statement.

INSERT has two basic syntax diagrams. With the first syntax diagram, you can add a row with specific values in each column. Those values may be any legitimate dBASE value, including strings, numbers, dates, or the contents of memory variables. Using memory variables, you can produce a data input screen for your users and then use INSERT to put the contents of the memory variables you use in the screen to capture user input. When you insert a literal, remember that dates start out as character strings and must be converted to date format with the CTOD( ) function. If you use INSERT to insert dates from date memory variables, however, they are already in the date data types and require no conversion. Don't forget to use quotation marks if your literal is a character string.

The syntax for using INSERT follows:

```
INSERT INTO <table name> [(<column list>)]
   VALUES (<value list>);
```

To use INSERT in this manner, state the *<table name>* of the table for which you intend to insert data. Then list the names of each column where you want to put new values. (You do not need to list columns that remain empty or unchanged.) Finally, list the values that go into the columns in the same order in which you listed the columns. Remember that essentially you are appending a row onto the data table. In this format, you supply each of the values that go into each column of this new row.

You can use INSERT another way to add rows to a table. If you want to copy the contents of certain rows of a table onto another table (thus appending rows that are only partially filled to the second table), you can use the second form of INSERT. The main use for this second method is to create a second table that you eventually join to the first. In this case, you probably want at least one column in the new table that is identical to a column in the old table. You eventually use that as the linking column in the join.

A similar use might be in an application in which you update one table from user input and several others from the original table. Don't confuse this use of update with the UPDATE command, however. In this context, updating means appending entire rows to the table. The syntax for the second use of INSERT follows:

```
INSERT INTO <table name> [(<column list>)]
   <SELECT command>;
```

Notice that in this case, in place of the VALUES clause, you have a variation on the SELECT command used as a clause. That means you can use SELECT to gather rows from a source table to insert into the target table. All the rules that apply to the stand-alone use of SELECT apply here as well. Make sure that the columns in your column list match the corresponding columns returned as a result of the SELECT statement.

# UPDATE

If you want to change the information in an existing row of a table, you need the UPDATE command. UPDATE enables you to specify a row and columns within that row and then change the data in those locations. The syntax for the UPDATE command follows:

```
UPDATE <table name>/<view name>
   SET <column name> = <new value>
   [,<column name> = <new value>...]
   [<WHERE clause>];
```

Use the WHERE clause to locate the correct row; use the SET clause to change the values in one or more columns. You can use this form of UPDATE interactively or from within a program. You can use the second form of UPDATE, however, only in a program. The syntax of the alternative form of UPDATE follows:

```
UPDATE <table name>
   SET <column name> = <new value>
   [,<column name> = <new value>...]
   WHERE CURRENT OF <SQL cursor name>;
```

This use of UPDATE requires an understanding of cursors, explained later in this chapter. For now, be aware that in this alternative UPDATE, the WHERE clause is replaced by the WHERE CURRENT OF clause to locate the correct row. In simple terms, WHERE CURRENT OF tells SQL to go to the row where a pointer currently is located. The pointer, called a *cursor*, is similar in purpose to the dBASE record pointer. All else about this form of UPDATE is the same as in the other form of the command. Remember that you can use this form only from within a program file.

## DELETE

The last of the data-handling commands in dBASE IV SQL is DELETE. DELETE enables you to remove a row from a data table. In one very dangerous case, it actually lets you remove all the rows from the table. Unlike the dBASE DELETE command, the SQL version actually removes the data in a single step. You are not required to pack the database (using PACK) to erase information physically.

> **WARNING:** Be careful when you use the SQL DELETE command. Your actions are irrevocable. If you use DELETE without specifying the row to DELETE, you erase all the rows in the table. In other words, if you leave out the WHERE clause, DELETE wipes out all your data.

Like UPDATE, DELETE has two forms. The first is for use interactively or from within a program. The second is for use in program files only. The syntaxes for both forms follows:

**Form 1:**

```
DELETE FROM <table name> [<alias name>]
   [<WHERE clause>];
```

**Form 2:**

```
DELETE FROM <table name>
   WHERE CURRENT OF <SQL cursor name>;
```

Notice that the second form—program file use only—uses the same WHERE CURRENT OF clause as the UPDATE command. The reason is that both commands act on a full row of a table. When you specify that row, your specification must point dBASE IV SQL to one and only one row. Using a cursor in an embedded procedure is the most precise way to do that. The one-row rule has two exceptions: using UPDATE to update more than one row in an identical manner, and using DELETE to delete more than one row at a time.

In those two cases, the only way to indicate the desired rows is with the WHERE clause.

# Using Other SQL Commands

You need to know about two other classes of commands before you learn about embedding SQL in dBASE applications. These two classes of commands provide data access security and utilities to simplify your use of SQL with other, non-SQL data. These classes of commands are described in the following sections.

## Controlling Security with SQL

Security, from the perspective of dBASE IV, is the process by which users gain access, first to dBASE IV, and then to various SQL databases and tables. The first layer of security in dBASE IV is the general access security determined by the PROTECT command/utility. PROTECT, when used from the dot prompt or the SQL dot prompt, invokes a full-screen utility that enables you to set a variety of security constraints. Among these constraints are file access, generalized access to dBASE IV, and a set of user IDs and passwords. To benefit from the special security available with dBASE IV SQL, you first must establish, at the least, minimum dBASE IV security with PROTECT.

That minimum security consists of assigning IDs to all users who require SQL privileges. The use of PROTECT usually is reserved for the database administrator (DBA). If the DBA has not assigned an ID to a dBASE IV user and security has been applied to the SQL tables, that user has no access to files in the SQL application.

When the DBA uses PROTECT to set up a security environment, dBASE IV makes encrypted entries in two environmental files: DBSYSTEM.DB and DBSYSTEM.SQL. After a user has gotten past the login process for dBASE IV and into the SQL application, all access to SQL tables is governed by the use of two security commands in SQL. The commands,

GRANT and REVOKE, are used by the DBA, either interactively or from within an application. The syntax for GRANT, the first of these commands, follows:

```
GRANT ALL [PRIVILEGES]/<privilege list> ON
[TABLE] <table list> TO PUBLIC/<user list>
[WITH GRANT OPTION];
```

The first thing you notice about GRANT is the need for a privilege list unless you are granting all privileges. The privilege list is a subset of the following list:

| | |
|---|---|
| ALTER | Use the ALTER command |
| DELETE | Use the DELETE command |
| INDEX | Create an index for a table |
| INSERT | Use the INSERT command to add rows to a table |
| SELECT | Use the SELECT command |
| UPDATE | Use the UPDATE command |

Be careful about how you use these privileges in a program; you might restrict a user from performing tasks built into the application that user is running. In most cases, you need a routine in the application that lets the DBA assign privilege levels to various users, consistent with the way the application is written. In an accounting application, for example, you may want to give a certain class of user the capability to browse salary data but not to modify the tables that go into creating it. You use GRANT to give that group of users the capability to use SELECT but not to use ALTER, DELETE, UPDATE, or INSERT on any of the tables involved.

Even though the commands to perform those processes may be available to the users through a menu system, attempts to execute the menu choices are futile unless the user has the proper privilege level.

If you are using the PUBLIC keyword, all the selected privileges are assigned to all users. GRANT has a special clause that enables users to grant privileges to other users as long as the PUBLIC keyword is not used. The WITH GRANT OPTION clause enables any user to grant his privileges to any other user. The granting user cannot grant privileges he or she doesn't have, of course, but within those guidelines, WITH GRANT OPTION enables users to pass privileges on to other users. When the granting user loses a privilege, the users to whom the user has granted the privilege lose it as well. Remember, you must use the same user IDs in the TO clause as appear in the user lists produced by PROTECT.

If you can grant user privileges in dBASE IV SQL, you also can revoke them. The REVOKE command is exactly the opposite of the GRANT command in that it takes away the privileges assigned by GRANT. In fact, the syntax is essentially the same:

```
REVOKE ALL [PRIVILEGES]/<privileges list>
   ON [TABLE] <table list>
   FROM PUBLIC/<user list>;
```

Again, be careful how you use this command so that you avoid revoking some of the privileges needed by a user of an application while leaving other privileges in such a way that the user can perform only part of a preprogrammed process.

When you build an application for local-area networks accessed by many users, you may want to build security into the application even though the LAN has security capabilities. The reason for this is that users may have application-specific knowledge or requirements that have nothing at all to do with their needs on the LAN.

Security is most useful for simply keeping users out of areas they have no need to use or have not been trained to use. The idea that security is necessary only if you want to keep intruders out is just partially correct. Most damage to or loss of data is caused by well-meaning users who simply don't belong in areas of the application for which they have not been trained. The judicious use of security measures can help keep those users within the boundaries you or the DBA deem appropriate.

# Using SQL Utility Commands

Six utility commands are used to deal with non-SQL data and to keep your application running smoothly. Those commands are DBCHECK, DBDEFINE, LOAD, RUNSTATS, ROLLBACK, and UNLOAD. Of these, three commands (DBDEFINE, LOAD, and UNLOAD) are data-specific; the others deal with tables in the catalog.

## DBDEFINE

DBDEFINE enables you to take a dBASE IV database and convert it to an SQL table. The syntax for the DBDEFINE command follows:

```
DBDEFINE [<filename>];
```

As you can see, the file name is optional, meaning that you can use the DBDEFINE command alone to convert all the DBF files in the current database to SQL tables. That brings up the first rule: Any DBF file you want to convert to an SQL file must be in the directory that contains the database to which the table is to be attached. When you use DBDEFINE on a dBASE database, you convert it to an SQL table and update the catalog in the active SQL database. The DBF file-name extension does not change, but the format of the file does. Because of the file structure of dBASE data files, the changes are not extensive. Both files, in fact, are the same size. The first byte of the file header, however, is different.

dBASE IV and dBASE IV SQL can read the SQL table. But to use the dBASE database with dBASE IV SQL commands, you must convert it to an SQL table and ensure that you have the proper entries in the SQL catalog. Another benefit of DBDEFINE is that it converts all production index files (MDX) to the appropriate SQL indexes automatically.

## LOAD

LOAD enables you to bring data from a non-SQL file into a dBASE IV SQL table. That includes dBASE database files from any level of dBASE. The use of the command follows the same file formats as the dBASE APPEND FROM command. If you don't specify a file type, LOAD assumes that the type is dBASE. The syntax for the LOAD command follows:

```
LOAD DATA FROM [path]<filename>
   INTO TABLE <table name>
      [[TYPE] SDF/DIF/WKS/SYLK/FW2/RPD/dBASEII/
      DELIMITED [WITH BLANK/WITH <delimiter>]];
```

Unlike DBDEFINE, LOAD does not care where the source data is located, as long as you specify the exact path to it. Again, unlike DBDEFINE, the data in the source file is not altered. In other words, DBDEFINE converts the file format of a dBASE IV database to an SQL table and updates the catalog. LOAD takes non-SQL data and copies it to an existing SQL table, in the process converting it to a format acceptable by that table.

## UNLOAD

If REVOKE is the opposite of GRANT in the security commands, UNLOAD is the opposite of LOAD in the utilities. Using UNLOAD on SQL data puts it into another, non-SQL format, in a destination file of your choosing. The syntax for the REVOKE command follows:

```
UNLOAD DATA TO [path]<filename>
   FROM TABLE <table name>
      [[TYPE] SDF/DIF/WKS/SYLK/FW2/RPD/dBASEII
      /DELIMITED [WITH BLANK/WITH<delimiter>]];
```

Notice that LOAD and UNLOAD enable you to work with ASCII, delimited data files. That can be very useful for importing and exporting data from mainframes or databases that are not directly supported.

## DBCHECK

DBCHECK is a housekeeping utility normally used by the DBA only. It checks the catalog for the currently active database to ensure that all the proper entries are present for the table specified in the command. The following is the simple syntax for the DBCHECK command:

```
DBCHECK [<tablename>];
```

If you issue the command without supplying the argument *tablename*, DBCHECK checks all the database and index files in the database catalog. The purpose of the test is to ensure that you have correctly converted the dBASE database and production index files to SQL before you make entries in the catalog. The dBASE database files may be in the SQL database, for example, and you may be attempting to treat them as tables. If the file fails the DBCHECK test, copy the database and index files out of the SQL directory to a temporary directory. Use DROP to remove their entries from the catalog, then put them back in the database directory. Finally, run DBDEFINE to convert the database and index files properly and reinstate their entries in the catalog tables.

## RUNSTATS

Earlier you learned a little bit about tuning the performance of your dBASE application when you use dBASE IV SQL. At the time, you read that dBASE IV SQL optimizes the query to get the best performance: dBASE looks at the command and the tables involved and decides the best way to execute the command. But where does dBASE IV SQL get the raw data it needs to make that optimization decision? Supplying that data is one of the uses of the catalog. The catalog itself, however, must be updated from time to time so that the entries in its tables are a current representation of the actual tables that make up the database. Updating that information—called *database statistics*—is the job of RUNSTATS.

The syntax for RUNSTATS follows:

```
RUNSTATS [<tablename>];
```

If you don't specify a table name, RUNSTATS updates the catalog table entries for all the tables in the current database.

## ROLLBACK

ROLLBACK is a very special command that can mean the difference between data integrity and the potential for corrupting data in one or more tables. You always use ROLLBACK with the dBASE command BEGIN TRANSACTION. The syntax for ROLLBACK follows:

```
ROLLBACK [WORK];
```

The optional WORK keyword is for compatibility with other SQL syntaxes that require it—IBM DB/2 SQL, for example.

The idea behind the ROLLBACK command is that in transaction processing (covered later under "Using SQL for Transaction Processing"), you set up a transaction consisting of a series of commands or processes without actually executing the commands. When the transaction is ready to complete, you can give the user an opportunity to change any information. When the transaction is ready to perform, you commit it, which means that you perform all the tasks in the transaction at the same time. The actual transaction takes a very short time. Only during the transaction are any tables used in the transaction open. When the transaction is complete, all data is updated, and the application awaits the next transaction.

If the transaction is interrupted by a failure of some sort, however, you need a way to ensure that the processes in it are not partially complete. If you had a transaction that, upon completion, updated several tables with new data, and that transaction was prematurely terminated, some tables would be updated, and some would not be. The result could be a discrepancy between tables that should be in agreement. In an accounting application, for example, such a situation could result in an out-of-balance condition. ROLLBACK is the dBASE IV SQL solution.

ROLLBACK wipes out all of the actions appearing between the dBASE BEGIN TRANSACTION and END TRANSACTION commands that immediately precede and follow the transaction. If you use ROLLBACK on a transaction, you take all the data tables involved back to the state that they were in prior to beginning the transaction. The best way to use ROLLBACK is to place it in a procedure called by the dBASE ON ERROR or ON ESCAPE commands.

The following SQL commands cannot be used between BEGIN TRANSACTION and END TRANSACTION in a dBASE transaction:

ALTER
CREATE
DBCHECK

DBDEFINE
GRANT
REVOKE
DROP

This doesn't mean that you cannot use them just before BEGIN TRANSACTION. Actions of these commands, however, cannot be undone by ROLLBACK in the event of an error.

Now that you understand the basics of dBASE IV SQL and the use of the various SQL commands (with a few exceptions), you are ready to progress to the use of SQL within dBASE IV programs and applications. Notice that a few SQL commands have not yet been covered. Those commands are specific to embedded SQL, which is the next subject.

# Using SQL in Program Code

You need to know a few things before you discover techniques for using embedded SQL. First, you learn about the special SQL commands that you use only when you are embedding SQL code in dBASE code. Next, you are introduced to the rules and techniques basic to producing dBASE applications that use SQL to handle the data. You then discover transaction processing techniques, and finally you learn about using dBASE IV SQL and transaction techniques in a multiuser environment.

# Keeping Track of Table Rows: Cursors

The concept of SQL cursors is a bit tricky unless you remember two things: First, the *cursor* really is a row pointer that works in much the same way as the dBASE record pointer. Second, cursors work on result tables only. In other words, you cannot use DECLARE CURSOR for a real SQL table; you must use DECLARE CURSOR for the result of a query. Four SQL statements are associated with dBASE IV SQL cursors:

| | |
|---|---|
| DECLARE CURSOR | Defines a cursor |
| OPEN | Executes an embedded SELECT |
| FETCH INTO | Moves the cursor and transfers row values to memory variables |
| CLOSE | Closes the cursor |

The following sections explain how you use each of these commands.

## DECLARE CURSOR

The first step in using dBASE IV SQL in a program is learning how cursors work. The first step in using a cursor is understanding the DECLARE CURSOR statement. DECLARE CURSOR does two things: it names a row pointer called a cursor; and it defines a result table to be generated with the cursor located before the first row. The cursor is before the first row (or at the end, if the result table is empty) because the FETCH command always advances the cursor one row. The statement uses an embedded SELECT statement to generate the result table. At the time you execute the DECLARE CURSOR statement, however, the action does not take place. All you are doing at this point is setting up what will happen when you actually execute the action with the OPEN command. The syntax for the DECLARE CURSOR statement follows:

```
DECLARE <cursor name> CURSOR
FOR <SELECT command>
[FOR UPDATE OF<column list>/<ORDER BY clause>];
```

You can use the DECLARE CURSOR command in a variety of ways, one of which is to set the stage for updating a table with UPDATE. As you see, using cursors and embedding commands in dBASE IV applications can improve your application's data handling. Cursors also are important because they offer the only easy way to collect the values of multiple rows and return them to your dBASE application's memory variables. Later in this chapter, under "Using Cursors," you see how all four of the cursor statements produce useful data from an SQL table.

## OPEN

The OPEN statement actually executes the process defined by the DECLARE CURSOR statement. The syntax is fairly simple:

```
OPEN <cursor name>;
```

When you issue the OPEN command, all the steps you set up in the DECLARE CURSOR statement associated with the OPEN command execute. The SELECT command creates the result table, and the cursor is positioned just ahead of the first row in the result table. You then are ready to begin collecting data and storing it in memory variables using the FETCH command.

# FETCH

FETCH performs two functions: the first is positioning the cursor, and the second is collecting and storing the data in the row to which the cursor is pointing. FETCH always moves the cursor ahead one row in the result table. When the cursor comes to rest on that row, it collects the data and stores it in memory variables. The memory variables should have the same names as the column names, perhaps with an *m* in front to keep column names visually separate from memory variables.

You must have the same number of memory variables as you have columns in the SELECT clause. The column contents are stored in the memory variables in the order in which you list the columns in the SELECT clause. In other words, the first column after SELECT goes into the first memory variable, the second columns into the second memory variable, and so on.

After you have stored the values of the columns in the row to which the cursor is pointing, you can use that data elsewhere in the application. When you reissue the FETCH, the cursor moves ahead to the next row and performs the same set of tasks. The syntax of the FETCH command follows:

```
FETCH <cursor name>
   INTO <memory variable list>;
```

A similarity here to the series of dBASE commands enables you to loop through a dBASE IV database by using DO WHILE and SKIP to advance the dBASE record pointer through a database. You can see, however, that SQL is far more efficient because the result table usually is much smaller and contains only those rows with data that meets the criteria of the SELECT used to declare the cursor. To do this with dBASE, you need to go through an entire database.

Suppose that you have a database with 10,000 records. In that database are 100 records for which you are searching. You want to update the contents of those—and only those—100 records. Using dBASE, you must advance through every one of the 10,000 records. Using SQL and an index, you can create a result table that contains only the 100 rows and then update them. Searching the data is a slower process than updating the data.

**NOTE**

SQL can improve the search time greatly in a single-user environment and even more in a well-written multiuser application. A dBASE query of a 3,100-record database, for example, took over one minute to perform in a test environment. An SQL query that yielded the same data from the same table took only 14 seconds. But the real benefit is in the update process. Returning to the example of the 10,000-record database, the SQL update would work on 100 rows only instead of being attempted on 10,000 records.

On a network, SQL performs its manipulations and then returns to the work station only the rows meeting the query criteria, greatly reducing network traffic and improving performance. A regular dBASE query must return the entire database as it scans for records meeting a search's criterion.

## CLOSE

The last of the cursor-handling commands is CLOSE. Its purpose is to close the cursor and release any associated memory. If you open the cursor again with OPEN, however, you reexecute the same SELECT statement that the cursor executed originally. This action produces a new result table.

The syntax for the CLOSE command follows:

```
CLOSE <SQL cursor name>;
```

# Using Cursors

The following is the general pattern for using cursors:

```
DECLARE CURSOR
OPEN
FETCH
...... dBASE Processing
CLOSE
```

You can embed certain SQL processes in SQL cursor commands to help narrow the range of data in your result table. You also can use UPDATE and DELETE to update and delete data in an SQL table.

Remember, the more you manipulate your data with SQL, the more efficient your application is. As a rule of thumb, you should handle all data within tables with the dBASE IV SQL commands whenever possible. After you have removed selected data from the table, you can use dBASE commands. By following this two-part method, you are taking advantage of the relative strengths of the two languages: dBASE for program control and operating on selected data and SQL for manipulating tables and selecting data for use by dBASE.

## Using UPDATE with DECLARE CURSOR

The first technique for embedding SQL processes within a cursor command is using UPDATE with DECLARE CURSOR. In this case, UPDATE is embedded within the DECLARE CURSOR command. Later in this procedure, you use UPDATE in the form of UPDATE WHERE CURRENT OF. Remember the second form of the UPDATE command? You use this form with DECLARE CURSOR...FOR UPDATE OF. To refresh your memory, the following is the second form of the UPDATE command:

```
UPDATE <table name>
   SET <column name> = <new value>
   [,<column name> = <new value>...]
   WHERE CURRENT OF <SQL cursor name>;
```

This example shows how you might use these two commands in an application:

```
DECLARE Cursorname CURSOR FOR
SELECT Column1, Column2, Column3
FROM Tablename
FOR UPDATE OF Column3;

OPEN Cursorname;
DO WHILE .T.
FETCH Cursorname INTO Mcolumn1, Mcolumn2, Mcolumn3;
DO Procedure WITH Mcolumn1, Mcolumn2, Mcolumn3
UPDATE Tablename
WHERE CURRENT OF Cursorname;
ENDDO
CLOSE Cursorname;
```

First you create the cursor, give it a name, create the result table with SELECT, and designate the column (Column3, in this case) on which you eventually perform an UPDATE. Next, use OPEN to open the cursor. Doing so executes the SELECT specified in the DECLARE CURSOR statement. After you have opened the cursor, get the data in the first row and put it into the appropriate memory variables. You use the FETCH command for this, placing it inside a dBASE DO WHILE construct so that you can continue to loop through the table until the cursor is at the end. At that point, your dBASE procedure can signal to the DO WHILE that there are no more rows to scan.

After this process is complete, use DO to perform a dBASE procedure that uses the memory variables you filled with the FETCH. During that dBASE procedure or after it, you perform the UPDATE you indicated you were going to perform in the DECLARE CURSOR statement. The UPDATE uses the data in the memory variables (which, presumably, you changed in the dBASE procedure) to put updated information back into the columns at the cursor location, which hasn't moved because of the WHERE CURRENT OF clause in the UPDATE statement. Finally, you use CLOSE to close the cursor when you have looped through all the rows in the affected table and passed beyond the DO WHILE.

## Using DELETE with DECLARE CURSOR

In the preceding example, you saw how UPDATE can be used with DECLARE CURSOR to update a row in a table, based on some action in a dBASE IV procedure. You may have noticed that the UPDATE was part of the DECLARE CURSOR statement, as well as a separate statement later on. In the case of DELETE, however, the DELETE is not part of the DECLARE CURSOR statement. To DELETE the row where the cursor is pointing, you just use the form of the DELETE statement that contains the WHERE CURRENT OF clause. That syntax follows:

```
DELETE FROM <table name>
   WHERE CURRENT OF <SQL cursor name>;
```

> **WARNING:** Be careful when you use this command. Be sure you have done everything you need to do with the row to which the cursor is pointing. When you execute the DELETE using the above syntax, that row is lost irretrievably.

You also can use the INSERT statement as part of a procedure, but it has no special relationship to the cursor because INSERT adds a row to a table. The new row is appended to the table regardless of where the cursor is pointing.

# Embedding SQL Code in dBASE Applications

Now that you are familiar with using SQL as part of a procedure, you are ready to take the final step. In the examples, you have seen simple cases of the use of SQL and dBASE commands together. You learned that you handle the data with SQL and the program execution with dBASE. You learned about the SQL cursor and how it enables you to deal with subsets of an entire table. Now you can put that theory into practice.

The first example is fairly straightforward. It uses a new data table called BIGLIST.DBF. Biglist is a 3,000-row table of names, addresses, and phone numbers and is similar to the Maillist table you have been using up until now. BIGLIST.DBF, however, not only has more rows, but also has several more columns. The data structure is shown in figure 21.3.

```
   Structure for database: C:\DBASE\DB4BOOK\BIGLIST.DBF
   Number of data records: 3119
   Date of last update : 05/24/90
Field     Field Name    Type        Width    Dec    Index
   1      CON           Character    30               N
   2      COM           Character    30               N
   3      AD1           Character    30               N
   4      AD2           Character    30               N
   5      CIT           Character    30               N
   6      STA           Character    2                N
   7      ZIP           Character    10               N
   8      CTY           Character    20               N
   9      TL1           Character    20               N
  10      TL2           Character    20               N
  11      US1           Character    20               N
  12      US2           Character    20               N
  13      US3           Character    20               N
  14      US4           Character    20               N
  15      US5           Character    20               N
  16      US6           Character    20               N
  17      US7           Character    20               N
          ** Total **               363
```

FIG. 21.3

Database structure for BIGLIST.DBF.

The following pages show sample code for retrieving information, adding information, and updating and deleting rows. Rather than include all the menus and other surrounding code, this example simply shows the individual procedures for each of these processes.

```
*****************************************************************
* Bigap.prs - a sample procedure file for querying BIGLIST.DBF, *
* inserting rows, updating rows and deleting rows.              *
*                                                               *
* Bigap.prs must be used from within another application with   *
* DO procedurename                                              *
*****************************************************************
*
******************************************************
* QUERY -                                            *
*                                                    *
*                                                    *
* This procedure allows query only                   *
******************************************************
*
*
PROCEDURE query

CLEAR                && Housekeeping
SET ECHO OFF
SET TALK OFF
SET SCOREBOARD OFF

START DATABASE db4book;     && Start the database that contains
                            && the table biglist
m_comp = SPACE(30)          && Initialize memory variables
m_con = SPACE(30)
m_com = SPACE(30)
m_tl1 = SPACE(20)
*
* Now, ask the user for the company that will be the subject of
* the search. When the user's input is captured, use the TRIM
* function to embed the user's response between two % symbols.
* The % symbol is the SQL wild card for a group of characters, just
* as the * symbol is the DOS wild card. The SQL symbol for a single
* character wild card is the underscore _. The reason for embedding
* the user response in wild cards is to allow the user to enter any
* portion of the company name under search. The LIKE predicate
* will then find all rows in which the com column contains the
* fragment entered by the user. The result table will contain
* all company names that either start with or contain the fragment.
*
@ 5,5 SAY "Enter all or part of the company name: " GET m_comp
READ
```

```
m_comp = "%" + TRIM(m_comp) + "%"      && Embed the user's response
DECLARE comp CURSOR FOR       && Name the cursor (comp)
SELECT con, com, tl1          && Formulate the query (SELECT)
FROM biglist
WHERE com LIKE m_comp;        && Locate rows where the com column
                              && contains the fragment entered
                              && by the user
OPEN comp;                    && Open the cursor and execute
                              && the query

DO WHILE .T.         && Continue the following procedure
                     && until you reach the end of the table.
*
* Collect the contents of the columns that you designated in the
* SELECT statement when you DECLAREd the cursor. Store the contents
* to the memory variables m_con, m_com and m_tl1. You only need enough
* memory variables to account for the number of columns you SELECTed
* in the DECLARE CURSOR statement. The memory variables will be loaded
* in the order you designated the columns in the SELECT statement.
*
FETCH comp INTO m_con, m_com, m_tl1;
IF sqlcode = 0    && If the system memory variable sqlcode returns
                  && 0 (search successful) do the following
CLEAR
@ 0,0 SAY "Here is an entry for the company: " + m_comp
@ 2,0 SAY "CONTACT COMPANY PHONE"
@ 3,0 SAY m_con + m_com + m_tl1
@ 5,0 SAY ""
WAIT
ELSE             && If sqlcode did not = 0 (search not
                 && successful)....
CLEAR
@ 5,25 SAY "Sorry, your record not found..."
WAIT
CLEAR
EXIT                 && Exit from this procedure
ENDIF                && Close of the IF
ENDDO                && Close off the DO WHILE
CLOSE comp;          && Close the cursor
STOP DATABASE;       && Close the database
RETURN               && Return to the calling program

* EOP query
**********************************************************************
* APPENDER -                                                         *
* This procedure will let you append rows to the biglist table, but, *
* for the sake of space, only the basic columns containing the       *
* company name, address1, address2, city, state, zip, main phone     *
```

```
* number and contact name will be filled in. You can use an UPDATE   *
* statement, specifying the columns to update if you wish to fill in *
* the other columns. Refer to the data structure above and use       *
* UPDATE interactively from the SQL dot prompt.                      *
*                                                                    *
**********************************************************************
*
PROCEDURE appender
CLEAR                           && Housekeeping
SET ECHO OFF
SET TALK OFF
SET SCOREBOARD OFF
mrespons = SPACE(1)             && Initialize memvars
mcon = SPACE(30)
mcom = SPACE(30)
mad1 = SPACE(30)
mad2 = SPACE(30)
mcit = SPACE(30)
msta = SPACE(2)
mzip = SPACE(10)
mtl1 = SPACE(20)
START DATABASE db4book;         && Start the database that contains
                                && the table biglist
*
* The first task is to collect the data which will go into the columns
* in memvars from user input.
*
@ 1,5 SAY "Do You Wish to Add a Record to Biglist? " GET mrespons
PICTURE "!"
READ
DO WHILE mrespons = "Y"             && Start the procedure
@ 0,0 CLEAR                         && Clear the screen
@ 2,2 SAY "Enter the CONTACT Name: " GET mcon
@ 3,2 SAY "Enter the COMPANY Name: " GET mcom
@ 4,2 SAY "Enter the 1st ADDRESS : " GET mad1
@ 5,2 SAY "Enter the 2nd ADDRESS : " GET mad2
@ 6,2 SAY "Enter the CITY : " GET mcit
@ 7,2 SAY "Enter the STATE : " GET msta PICTURE "!!"
@ 8,2 SAY "Enter the Zip Code : " GET mzip
@ 9,2 SAY "Enter the PHONE NUMBER: " GET mtl1
READ
IF mcon = SPACE(30)                 && Test for no entry
EXIT
ENDIF                               && Close the IF and add the row
INSERT INTO biglist
(con, com, ad1, ad2, cit, sta, zip, tl1)
```

```
VALUES (mcon, mcom, mad1, mad2, mcit, msta, mzip, mtl1);
@ 15,2 SAY "Do You Wish to Add Another Record? " GET mrespons PICTURE "!"
READ
*
* If the response is [Y]es, go back and do it again. If it is anything
* else, fall through and close out the procedure
*
ENDDO                  && Close off the DO WHILE
CLEAR                  && Clear
STOP DATABASE;         && Close the database
RETURN                 && Return to the calling program
* EOP - appender
*******************************************************************
* UPDATER -                                                       *
*                                                                 *
* This procedure lets you update a row. For the sake of this      *
* example, only the phone number will be updated. You could       *
* easily expand the code in this procedure to allow the user      *
* to select the column for updating.                              *
*******************************************************************
PROCEDURE updater

CLEAR                         && Housekeeping
SET ECHO OFF
SET TALK OFF
SET SCOREBOARD OFF

START DATABASE db4book;       && Start the database that contains
                              && the table biglist
mrespons = SPACE(1)           && Initialize memvars
m_phone = SPACE(20)
m_tl1 = SPACE(20)
m_comp = SPACE(30)
m_com = SPACE(30)
m_cont = SPACE(30)
m_con = SPACE(30)
newfone = SPACE(20)

* As in the procedure "query", ask the user for the company that
* will be updated. This part of the procedure finds the company
* to be updated and stores enough information to allow the next
* part of the procedure to select exactly the correct company.
* Without giving the user the ability to designate exactly which
* row will be updated, you could allow an update to the wrong
* record. The information stored includes the full contents
* of the com, tl1 and con columns
*
```

```
@ 5,5 SAY "Enter all or part of the company name: " GET m_comp
READ
m_comp = "%" + TRIM(m_comp) + "%"    && Embed the user's response
DECLARE comp CURSOR FOR              && Name the cursor (comp)
SELECT con, com, tl1                 && Formulate the query (SELECT)
FROM biglist
WHERE com LIKE m_comp;         && Locate rows where the com column
                               && contains the fragment entered
                               && by the user
OPEN comp;                     && Open the cursor and execute
                               && the query
DO WHILE .T.                   && Continue the following procedure
                               && until you reach the end of the table
                               && or until the user selects a company
*
* Collect the contents of the columns that you designated in the
* SELECT statement when you DECLAREd the cursor. Store the contents
* to the memvars m_con, m_com and m_tl1.
*
* Next, ask the user if this is the correct record. If no, (or anything
* except [Y]es) continue until the correct one is found or you reach
* the end of the table. If [Y]es, store the values that were in the
* memory variables filled by the FETCH and end this part of the procedure.
*
FETCH comp INTO m_con, m_com, m_tl1;
IF sqlcode = 0          && If the system memory variable sqlcode returns
                        && 0 (search successful) do the following
CLEAR
@ 0,0 SAY "Here is an entry for the company: " + m_comp
@ 2,0 SAY "CONTACT COMPANY PHONE"
@ 3,0 SAY m_con + m_com + m_tl1
@ 5,0 SAY "Is this the one you want? " GET mrespons PICTURE "!"
READ
IF mrespons = "Y"
STORE m_com TO m_comp
STORE m_con TO m_cont
STORE m_tl1 TO m_phone
EXIT
ENDIF
ELSE                && If sqlcode did not = 0 (search not
                    && successful)....
```

```
EXIT               && Exit from this procedure
ENDIF              && Close off the IF
ENDDO              && Close off the DO WHILE
CLOSE comp;        && Close the cursor and proceed to the
                   && next part of the procedure
DECLARE updtr CURSOR FOR       && Declare a new cursor for update of
SELECT con, com, tl1           && the tl1 column
FROM biglist
WHERE con = m_cont AND com = m_comp AND tl1 = m_phone
FOR UPDATE of tl1;
@ 7,0 SAY "Enter the new phone number: " GET newfone  && Get the new
READ                          && phone number

@ 0,0 CLEAR                   && Clear the screen
OPEN updtr;                   && Open the new cursor
FETCH updtr INTO m_con, m_com, m_tl1;    && Collect the information
                                         && for updating
IF sqlcode = 0                && Test for successful search
UPDATE biglist                && Update the table with the
SET tl1 = newfone             && contents of newfone
WHERE CURRENT OF updtr;
@ 10,15 SAY "Your Record Has Been Updated With " + newfone
ELSE                          && If the search was not a success
@ 10,25 SAY "Sorry, Your Record Not Found"

ENDIF                    && Close off the IF
CLOSE updtr;             && Close the cursor
STOP DATABASE;           && Close the database
RETURN                   && Return to the calling program

* EOP updater

*****************************************************************
* DELETER -                                                     *
                                                                *
* This procedure allows you to delete a row from the table. It  *
* uses the same code as UPDATER to locate the specific row      *
* before deleting                                               *
*****************************************************************
*
PROCEDURE deleter

CLEAR                         && Housekeeping
SET ECHO OFF
SET TALK OFF
SET SCOREBOARD OFF

START DATABASE db4book;       && Start the database that contains
                              && the table biglist
```

```
mrespons = SPACE(1)         && Initialize memory variables
m_phone = SPACE(20)
m_tl1 = SPACE(20)
m_comp = SPACE(30)
m_com  = SPACE(30)
m_cont = SPACE(30)
m_con = SPACE(30)
newfone = SPACE(20)

@ 5,5 SAY "Enter all or part of the company name: " GET m_comp
READ
m_comp = "%" + TRIM(m_comp) + "%"     && Embed the user's response

DECLARE comp CURSOR FOR               && Name the cursor (comp)
SELECT con, com, tl1                  && Formulate the query (SELECT)
FROM biglist
WHERE com LIKE m_comp;            && Locate rows where the com column
                                  && contains the fragment entered
                                  && by the user
OPEN comp;                        && Open the cursor and execute
                                  && the query

DO WHILE .T.             && Continue the following procedure
                         && until you reach the end of the table
                         && or until the user selects a company
*
* Collect the contents of the columns that you designated in the
* SELECT statement when you DECLAREd the cursor. Store the contents
* to the memory variables m_con, m_com and m_tl1.
*
* Next, ask the user if this is the correct record. If no, (or anything
* except [Y]es) continue until the correct one is found or you reach
* the end of the table. If [Y]es, store the values that were in the
* memory variables filled by the FETCH and end this part of the procedure.
*
FETCH comp INTO m_con, m_com, m_tl1;
If sqlcode = 0    && If the system memory variable sqlcode returns
                  && 0 (search successful) do the following
CLEAR
@ 0,0 SAY "Here is an entry for the company: " + m_comp
@ 2,0 SAY "CONTACT COMPANY PHONE"
@ 3,0 SAY m_con + m_com + m_tl1 @ 5,0 SAY "======= CAUTION - IF YOU DELETE
THIS RECORD, YOU CAN NOT RETRIEVE IT!! ======="
@ 6,0 SAY "Is this the one you want? " GET mrespons PICTURE "!"
READ
IF mrespons = "Y"
STORE m_com TO m_comp
```

```
STORE m_con TO m_cont
STORE m_tl1 TO m_phone
EXIT
ENDIF
ELSE                     && If sqlcode did not = 0 (search not
                         && successful)....
EXIT                     && Exit from this procedure

ENDIF                    && Close off the IF
ENDDO                    && Close off the DO WHILE
CLOSE comp;              && Close the cursor and proceed to the
                         && next part of the procedure

DECLARE dltr CURSOR FOR       && Declare a new cursor for deleting
SELECT con, com, tl1          && the selected row
FROM biglist
WHERE con = m_cont AND com = m_comp AND tl1 = m_phone;

@ 0,0 CLEAR                  && Clear the screen

OPEN dltr;                   && Open the new cursor

FETCH dltr INTO m_con, m_com, m_tl1;    && Collect the information
                                        && for updating
IF sqlcode = 0                          && Test for successful search
DELETE FROM biglist
WHERE CURRENT OF dltr;

@ 10,15 SAY "Your Record Has Been Deleted "

ELSE               && If the search was not a success

@ 10,25 SAY "Sorry, Your Record Not Found"

ENDIF              && Close off the IF

CLOSE dltr;        && Close the cursor
STOP DATABASE;     && Close the database
RETURN             && Return to the calling program

* EOP deleter
```

Most of the preceding example is either self-explanatory or explained in the accompanying comments. Certain points, however, need to be emphasized. First, the database used—DB4BOOK—was the database in which this application was written. In other words, the Biglist table was part of the DB4BOOK database. If you choose to duplicate this application, either you need to re-create the DB4BOOK database by using CREATE on it and its accompanying catalog tables, or you need to substitute whatever database you do create in the example code.

The compiler for dBASE IV SQL does not know how to use multiple databases unless you create them separately and then handle them and their tables individually. When you distribute your application, remember that you need to build the correct directories for each database you use and then place the appropriate data and catalog tables in them. Be sure to distribute the catalog tables with your application.

Another aspect of distributing your application is that dBASE IV optimizes queries, based on the entries in the catalog tables. The optimization is performed at compile time. Therefore, you should recompile your application from time to time.

You can use multiple databases, but you should attempt to put all your tables into a single database. If you cannot, one way to keep information straight is to treat each process as a separate transaction. dBASE IV SQL, however, cannot work with tables in multiple databases within a single query. Whereas multitable joins are quite simple, multi-database joins are impossible, and dBASE IV is incapable of managing distributed databases.

# Recovering from Errors

The preceding example did not include error trapping or other niceties that make the difference between a professional application and one that is just thrown together. In your applications, however, be sure to include appropriate help screens and error messages as well as ways to recover from errors. The example did not include those additions for the sake of clarity while demonstrating the use of SQL embedded in dBASE programs. The ability to include error trapping and recovery is enhanced if you treat your application as a series of transactions. Remember that when you encounter an error that aborts a transaction, you can recover from it and put your data back in order with the ROLLBACK command. Later in this chapter, you see exactly how to do that.

Before you get to transactions, however, you need to understand a bit about how you might build an error recovery routine. As you learned at the beginning of Part IV, you should organize your application in terms of the modules required by the various choices in your menus. Later on, you learned about procedure libraries, and the preceding example demonstrated how you can create a procedure file with individual procedures for querying, appending to, deleting from, and updating an SQL table.

When you create a procedure library for your application, be sure to include a procedure for error recovery. Putting the error recovery procedure in the library is a better choice than trying to include it in each program module. Be careful, though. You must ensure that the procedure file is open whenever you perform a programming task. Otherwise, an error results in a second error because the recovery procedure cannot be found. In this case, the results are quite unpredictable. Finally, you need to allow for graceful recovery from errors on the part of your users, hardware or software failure, and intentional aborts through the Esc key.

In general, good error recovery requires that you stop program execution (the error usually does that for you), notify the user of the error and its nature, and offer a graceful recovery that does not jeopardize your application's data. Several kinds of errors can occur. Some you can trap; others, such as hardware failures, you cannot.

When you are working with multiple data tables on a multiuser system, you really must use transaction-processing techniques to be able to recover from a hardware failure. Rolling back the transaction is the only way to put several interrelated tables in balance after an interruption during an UPDATE or INSERT.

Errors that occur because the user made an incorrect entry are a bit easier to deal with. The first step in minimizing those errors is to ensure that you confine the acceptable input into a user field to the data type and value range appropriate for the module and table in use. You can do that with a combination of picture templates and the RANGE and VALID keywords in the @...SAY...GET construct. These also enable you to trap a user error and execute an error recovery procedure. The errors you encounter in user input situations are called *soft errors*. They rarely require anything more than an error message and automatic return to the input field for another try.

*Hard errors*, however, require careful consideration and carefully prepared recovery techniques. Remember that if you notify your user that an error has occurred, you also must offer a way out (which may be automatic or under user control). You also need to notify the user of the recovery's success or lack thereof. Often, your user has nobody to turn to when an error occurs, and you must figure out from the user's computer screen what has happened.

In addition, you must avoid forward references to database objects in your programs when you use SQL to manage your data. You must define all database objects at the beginning of any program module that contains SQL commands. Unlike dBASE, dBASE IV SQL cannot look ahead.

Finally, you cannot create two SQL objects with the same name. That may not seem like much of a problem, but if you are using a conditional, such as IF, and you attempt to create the same object in both the IF and the ELSE portions of the construct, the dBASE compiler responds with an error. You get the error even though you know that only one of the objects can ever exist at any one time because the IF forces a choice. The compiler, however, doesn't know that. It only knows that you tried to create two objects with the same name, and thus it reports an error.

# Using SQL for Transaction Processing

You have been hearing about transaction processing for the last two chapters, and now you're ready to dig into this technique for maintaining data integrity and concurrent control. As you learned earlier, when you use transaction processing, the only time the data table is locked is between the BEGIN TRANSACTION and END TRANSACTION commands. The following rules apply when using transaction processing:

- The following SQL commands are *not allowed* in transactions:

  ALTER
  CREATE
  DBCHECK
  DBDEFINE

- If you use DELETE to delete a row, the row is not actually deleted until the transaction is completed (END TRANSACTION). If you use the DELETE...WHERE CURRENT OF command, the row is not deleted until the transaction ends and the cursor is closed with CLOSE.
- Inserts and updates (done with INSERT and UPDATE) don't actually occur until the transaction ends.

In general, you can insert almost any data-handling procedure in a transaction construct. The following rules of thumb apply:

- Place everything that prepares for the data handling—including the ON ERROR or ON ESCAPE commands—before the BEGIN TRANSACTION command.
- Before you start the actual transaction, insert a command that tells the transaction how many times to try before giving up.
- Put inside the transaction construct everything that has anything to do with access to a database and data tables.
- Stop the database (STOP DATABASE) before you exit the transaction.

- Place in memory variables any data that you need after the database is closed, and then work on it after the transaction ends.

One of the rules says that you need to specify a number of retries before the transaction code begins. To do this, you use the SET REPROCESS command. SET REPROCESS dictates the number of times dBASE attempts to get data from a table.

In any multiuser environment, a variety of things can stop your application from accessing data. Another user may be using the table, the network may be overloaded, or an error may have occurred. By setting the number of retries (reprocesses), you tell dBASE that you want it to attempt a reasonable number of times to complete the transaction. The result of all of those retries failing is called a *timeout*. Placing the SET REPROCESS command just outside the transaction construct tells dBASE to retry the transaction however many times you designate.

The following sample code shows the Updater procedure as a transaction.

```
*****************************************************************
* UPDATER -                                                     *
*                                                               *
* This procedure lets you update a row. For the sake of this    *
* example, only the phone number will be updated. You could     *
* easily expand the code in this procedure to allow the user    *
* to select the column for updating.                            *
* Unlike the version of UPDATER included in the Bigap procedure *
* file, this version uses transaction processing techniques     *
*****************************************************************

CLEAR                         && Housekeeping
SET ECHO OFF
SET TALK OFF
SET SCOREBOARD OFF

mrespons = SPACE(1)           && Initialize memory variables
m_phone = SPACE(20)
m_tl1 = SPACE(20)
m_comp = SPACE(30)
m_com = SPACE(30)
m_cont = SPACE(30)
m_con = SPACE(30)
newfone = SPACE(20)

@ 5,5 SAY "Enter all or part of the company name: " GET m_comp
READ
m_comp = "%" + TRIM(m_comp) + "%"    && Embed the user's response
```

```
* Here is where the ON ERROR command would go. Since there is
* no error recovery procedure in this example, we simply indicate
* the location of the command. It should read,
* ON ERROR DO recoveryprocedure
*
SET REPROCESS TO 10    && Set the number of retries
                       && You only need this command once since
                       && all of the attempts to access tables
                       && will be controlled by it until you
                       && turn it off

START DATABASE db4book;     && Start the database that contains
                            && the table biglist

BEGIN TRANSACTION           && Start the transaction
DECLARE comp CURSOR FOR     && Name the cursor (comp)
SELECT con, com, tl1        && Formulate the query (SELECT)
FROM biglist
WHERE com LIKE m_comp;      && Locate rows where the com column
                            && contains the fragment entered
                            && by the user
OPEN comp;                  && Open the cursor and execute
                            && the query

DO WHILE .T.      && Continue the following procedure
                  && until you reach the end of the table
                  && or until the user selects a company
FETCH comp INTO m_con, m_com, m_tl1;
IF sqlcode = 0    && If the system memory variable sqlcode returns
                  && 0 (search successful) do the following
CLEAR
@ 0,0 SAY "Here is an entry for the company: " + m_comp
@ 2,0 SAY "CONTACT COMPANY PHONE"
@ 3,0 SAY m_con + m_com + m_tl1
@ 5,0 SAY "Is this the one you want? " GET mrespons PICTURE "!"
READ
IF mrespons = "Y"
STORE m_com TO m_comp
STORE m_con TO m_cont
STORE m_tl1 TO m_phone
EXIT
ENDIF
ELSE             && If sqlcode did not = 0 (search not
                 && successful)....
EXIT             && Exit from this procedure
ENDIF               && Close off the IF
ENDDO               && Close off the DO WHILE
CLOSE comp;         && Close the cursor and proceed to the
                    && next part of the procedure
END TRANSACTION     && Stop the transaction
```

```
STOP DATABASE;           && Close the database

@ 7,0 SAY "Enter the new phone number: " GET newfone
                         && Get the new
READ                     && phone number
@ 0,0 CLEAR              && Clear the screen

START DATABASE db4book;     && Start the database that contains
                            && the table biglist

BEGIN TRANSACTION           && Start another transaction
DECLARE updtr CURSOR FOR    && Declare a new cursor for update of
SELECT con, com, tl1        && the tl1 column
FROM biglist
WHERE con = m_cont AND com = m_comp AND tl1 = m_phone
FOR UPDATE of tl1;

OPEN updtr;                 && Open the new cursor

FETCH updtr INTO m_con, m_com, m_tl1;    && Collect the information
                                         && for updating
IF sqlcode = 0              && Test for successful search
UPDATE biglist              && Update the table with the
SET tl1 = newfone           && contents of newfone
WHERE CURRENT OF updtr;
@ 10,15 SAY "Your Record Has Been Updated With " + newfone

ELSE            && If the search was not a success

@ 10,25 SAY "Sorry, Your Record Not Found"

ENDIF                 && Close off the IF
CLOSE updtr;          && Close the cursor
END TRANSACTION       && Stop the transaction
STOP DATABASE;        && Close the database

SET REPROCESS TO 0    && Turn off retries

* EOP updater
```

The main thing to notice about this rewrite of the procedure is that the data tables are open for significantly less time than they are in the Bigap procedure file. In the original example, the database and its tables are open for the entire procedure. If a user is slow to enter the new phone number, the table is locked and unavailable for use by other users on a network.

In this latest example, the tables are locked only while the user acknowledges that the correct row has been found (or dBASE IV continues the search). From that point on, all operations on the data table are carried out by the program at program speed. Another point to notice is that the database must be started and stopped outside of the transaction construct. In order to limit the time that you have control of the database, place these commands immediately before and after the transaction. This example may have been overzealous for the sake of illustration. With two transactions so close together, the database could have been left open for both; it didn't have to be closed between the transactions.

Note that this example does not have an error-handling procedure. If you try this program without such a procedure, you get another error, as you learned earlier. The location and commands for the error control are indicated in the example as comments.

## Summary

In this chapter, you learned about the purpose and benefits of SQL and how to use the various SQL commands. You learned how to build an SQL statement. You saw the strength of the SELECT command, which is the heart of the structured query language. You learned the difference between a procedural language, such as dBASE, and a nonprocedural language, such as SQL.

Finally, you worked with examples of embedded SQL in dBASE procedure files and program files. You saw how to use the two languages together to manage data and program flow efficiently, and you were introduced to SQL error trapping and transaction processing.

Part V of this book, the "dBASE IV Reference Guide," describes and shows the syntax of the commands and functions in the dBASE language. Because Part IV was intended to show programming techniques, not all commands were covered in detail. Use the "dBASE IV Reference Guide" to add more commands to your bag of dBASE tricks.

# dBASE IV Reference Guide

# Introduction to the dBASE IV Reference Guide

The dBASE IV commands enable you to duplicate many of the functions of the Control Center. Some commands are used in programs you can write yourself using the dBASE IV programming language. This powerful language enables you to create simple, short programs or complex applications.

Part V, "dBASE IV Reference Guide," includes the following sections:

Using dBASE IV Commands
Using Functions
Using SET Commands
Using SQL Commands
Using System Memory Variables

Using the Mouse
Using the System Configuration File
ASCII Table

# Understanding Command Syntax

As with any language, you must follow certain rules when you enter dBASE commands. Each command has its own *syntax*, or rules governing how you type in the command. When you fail to follow proper command syntax, commands don't work properly, and you may receive a "syntax error" message on your screen.

In this Reference Guide, commands are shown with their available *options* enclosed in brackets ([ ]). Options are command parts that you may or may not use, depending on what you want the command to do. Some bracketed options have several *parameters*, which are shown in italic type, between angle brackets (< >). The italic word inside the angle brackets is not meant to be typed—it stands for a value you must supply. For example, where a syntax diagram shows <*filename.EXT*>, you would type a valid file name and extension.

The LIST command, for example, has the following syntax:

```
LIST [[FIELDS] <field list>] [OFF] [<scope>]
   [FOR <condition>] [WHILE <condition>]
   [TO PRINTER/TO FILE <filename>]
```

That may look a bit confusing at first glance, but if you separate the command into its various components, it becomes a bit easier to understand. Throughout this Reference Guide, you will see examples that help you understand the command syntax. Table R.1 shows how to break down each section of the syntax for the LIST command.

Note in all the examples that the brackets and slashes are not in the actual command. The following example combines many of the options of the LIST command:

```
LIST FIELDS LASTNAME, CITY, ZIPCODE FOR ZIPCODE < 90000 ;
   TO PRINTER
```

This command prints a list of the Lastname, City, and ZIPcode fields for those records whose ZIP Code value is less than 9,000.

**Table R.1 Breakdown of LIST Syntax**

| Command item | Description |
|---|---|
| LIST | The LIST command (sometimes called a "verb"), which enables you to list the contents of a database. |
| [[FIELDS] <*field list*>] | The FIELDS option. If you want to list only a few of the fields in a database, specify those fields after you type FIELDS. For example, you could specify FIELDS Lastname, Firstname, City. |
| [OFF] | The OFF option. This prevents the printing of record numbers. |
| [<*scope*>] | The <*scope*> option. This enables you to limit the range of records to include on the list. You could list only the next 25 records by using a scope of NEXT 25. |
| [FOR <*condition*>] | The FOR option. This is similar to a scope but enables you to list only those records that meet the <*condition*>. For example, FOR CITY = "Newcastle" would restrict the list to records whose CITY field contained "Newcastle." |
| [WHILE <*condition*>] | The WHILE option. This will continue adding records to the list until the <*condition*> is no longer true. WHILE RECNO() < 100 would list only those records whose record numbers are under 100. |
| [TO PRINTER/TO FILE <*filename*>] | The TO PRINTER and TO FILE options. The slash indicates that you can choose from either portion of the command. TO PRINTER prints the list; TO FILE CITYLIST.TXT sends the list to the indicated file. |

**NOTE** Some command examples in this book are too long to fit on one line. They are shown with a semicolon (;) at the end of the first line to indicate that the command continues on the next line. The LIST FIELDS example illustrates this practice.

This Reference Guide contains examples for every dBASE IV command but does not show every possible variation of options. A little experimentation at your dot prompt will show you how each command is used. Take the time to try out the examples, and you will discover that command programming is not as complicated as it looks. Be sure to read Part IV of this book to learn about programming in dBASE IV.

# Understanding File Names

File names in dBASE IV follow the same rules as in DOS (see Chapter 3). A valid name for a file consists of the file name (up to eight characters), a period (.), and the file extension (three characters). You are better to use only alphabetic or numeric characters in a file name, although some other characters (_, -, and $) can be used. Using letters and numbers is also easier on the eyes and fingers. Use meaningful file names; for a customer database file, CUSTOMER.DBF is better than CST1299.DBF.

Many common file-name extensions are used in dBASE IV. For example, a file extension of DBF indicates a dBASE IV database file. You are not required to use the DBF extension for your databases, but doing so is recommended. When you use another extension for a database file, you have to remember to include that extension every time you use that database name. If your database is called CUSTOMER.DAT, then you must use the command USE CUSTOMER.DAT to access that database. If your database is called CUSTOMER.DBF, you need only type *USE CUSTOMER*.

# Indirect File Names

You can instruct dBASE IV to create file names out of memory variables. The memory variable is enclosed in parentheses as the *<filename>* portion of the command. If the memory variable *mfile* is equal to "Customer", then the command

```
USE (mfile)
```

does the same thing as the command

```
USE CUSTOMER
```

Indirect file names can be very useful because you can add to a file name:

```
Fileone = "PARTS"            && PARTS database
Filetwo = Fileone + "EXP"    && PARTS EXPlosion database
SELECT 1                     && work area one
USE (fileone)                && same as USE PARTS
SELECT 2                     && work area two
USE (filetwo)                && same as USE PARTSEXP
                             && or: USE (fileone)+"EXP"
```

**NOTE**

Use * and && to indicate comment text that is not meant to be read as program code by dBASE IV. The * is used at the beginning of a program line. The && must be used if any commands are part of the program line. All text past the * or && on the line is ignored.

Comments are useful for documenting the purpose of a command. Using comments helps others understand the program flow and can help you when you return to a program file weeks or months later.

Using indirect file names results in much faster operations than using macro substitution. The USE (fileone) command, for example, runs more quickly than the equivalent USE &fileone command.

## Drive and Directory Names

Like DOS, dBASE IV assumes that a file is in the current subdirectory unless told otherwise. If the current drive and directory is C:\ACCOUNTS, then these two commands are equivalent:

```
USE CUSTOMER

USE C:\ACCOUNTS\CUSTOMER
```

The current directory can be overridden by the SET PATH TO command. This command, similar to the DOS PATH command, specifies the search path that dBASE IV uses when a file name is specified. If the file name is not found in the current directory, the directories in the SET PATH TO command are searched until the file is found.

## Aliases

Aliases are alternatives to actual file names. The alias can be the file name, the alias specified when the database file was opened with USE, the work area letter, or the work area number. Work area numbers are 1 through 40; work area letters are A through J, representing the first ten work areas.

If you have opened a database with the command

```
SELECT 1
USE CUST_ID ALIAS CUSTOMER
```

each of these commands can reference the Company field in the Cust_ID file:

```
CUSTOMER->COMPANY          && using the alias name
A->COMPANY                 && using the alias letter
CUST_ID->COMPANY           && using the actual DBF name
```

The -> is used by dBASE IV to indicate a field name in the database: *database->fieldname*. The -> is made up of two characters: the hyphen (-) and the greater-than symbol (>). For that reason, you shouldn't use the hyphen (-) character in a file name.

# Working with Programs and Procedures

A program is a file that contains a series of dot prompt commands that work together to perform a task. Programs are used for simple tasks like opening a group of database files or setting colors, or for complex applications like keeping track of all of your customer orders. Each command in the program is executed just as if you typed it at the dot prompt. Program files usually have a file extension of PRG and are executed with the DO *<program>* command. When you use DO, dBASE IV compiles the PRG file into an object code file (with a file extension of DBO), which will execute faster than the original PRG file.

A procedure file is a special program file that contains a group of commands or procedures. These procedures typically perform a short, basic task, such as centering a message on-screen. Procedures can be called from other programs with the command DO *<procedure name>*. Procedure files generally have a file extension of PRG and are activated by SET PROCEDURE TO *<filename>*. You can have up to 963 procedures per file, up to the amount of available system memory.

# Using Data Types

You can use the following data types in dBASE IV:

**Character.** Letters and numbers, enclosed in quotes when used in program lines. You can use single quotes (') or double quotes ("), but they must match at both ends of the character string. Examples are "Pork and Beans" and '4122 Rocky Ridge Drive'.

**Numeric.** Number values, either type N (binary-coded decimal) or type F (floating-point numbers). A binary-coded decimal (BCD) value and floating-point binary numeric types are used in dBASE IV. (All numeric values are floating-point values in dBASE III.) Floating-point numbers are used when dealing with very large numbers BCD numbers generally are more accurate and therefore are often used for accounting purposes. Numbers are expressed as whole numbers (1422) or decimal numbers (4.223). You also can have numbers with scientific notation, as in 12E3, which is $12.4^3$ or (12.4 * 10 * 10 * 10).

**Date.** Calendar dates. To convert a character date ("8/28/84") to a date variable, you need to use the CTOD function or enclose the date in braces—for example, {8/28/84}. Using braces for date conversion is easier than using the CTOD function. A blank date can be specified in four ways:

```
{}              && fastest method
{ / / }         && fast method
CTOD("")        && slow method
CTOD(" / / ")   && slow method
```

You can perform date arithmetic with date-type variables.

**Logical.** Expressions that yield a true (.T.) or false (.F.) result. To indicate a true value, you can use .T., .t., .Y., or .y. (notice that the letter is surrounded by periods). For false values, .F., .F., .N., and .n. are used.

**Memo.** Memo fields, which are large amounts of text stored in a separate DBT memo file. You can use memo fields for notes, comments, and other nonstructured data.

# Working with Operators

Several different types of operators are available for mathematical, relational, or logical operations or for controlling string values.

---

## Operator Types

In dBASE IV, you will find four types of operators: mathematical, relational, logical, and string. Mathematical operators are used to perform simple math on numbers. Relational operators are used to define the relationship of one variable to another, such as less than or greater than. Logical operators are used on logical true (.T.) or false (.F.) variables. String operators are used to combine two or more character variables into one character variable.

The following is a list of the mathematical operators:

| Operator | Description |
|---|---|
| + | Addition, unary positive |
| – | Subtraction, unary negative |
| * | Multiplication |
| / | Division |
| ** or ^ | Exponential |
| ( ) | Parentheses for grouping |

The following is a list of the relational operators:

| Operator | Description |
|---|---|
| > | Greater than |
| < | Less than |
| = | Equal to |
| <= | Less than or equal to |
| => | Greater than or equal to |
| <> or # | Not equal to |
| $ | Substring comparison |

The $ symbol used for substring comparison is usually in a statement such as *<expression 1>* $ *<expression 2>*. Think of this statement as meaning "Is expression 1 contained in expression 2?"

The following is a list of the logical operators:

| Operator | Description |
|---|---|
| .AND. | Logical AND |
| .OR. | Logical OR |
| .NOT. | Logical NOT |
| = | Equal to |
| <> or # | Not equal to |
| ( ) | Parentheses used for grouping |

The logical operators are used for expressions that result in a true or false logical data type. The results of a logical expression can be shown in a Boolean table, where 0 = false and 1 = true:

| *A* | *B* | *AND* | *OR* |
|---|---|---|---|
| 0 | 0 | .F. | .F. |
| 0 | 1 | .F. | .T. |
| 1 | 0 | .F. | .T. |
| 1 | 1 | .T. | .T. |

The following is a list of the string operators:

| Operator | Description |
|---|---|
| + | Trailing spaces are left intact when strings are joined |
| – | The first expression's trailing spaces are moved to the end of the second expression's string |
| ( ) | Parentheses used for grouping |

# Precedence of Operators

The set of rules governing the order in which an operation is performed is called the *order of precedence*. For mathematical operations, the order of precedence is this:

1. Expressions contained in parentheses
2. Unary positive (+) and unary negative (–) signs
3. Exponential
4. Multiplication and division
5. Addition and subtraction

The order of precedence can have an unanticipated effect on the result of a mathematical equation. For example, the result of the following equation is 14, not 20:

```
2 + 3 * 4
```

The result is 14 because the order of precedence rules that multiplication must be performed before addition. (According to the rules, the equation works like this: 4 * 3 = 12, then 12 + 2 = 14.) Parentheses can ensure the proper result: (2 + 3) * 4 = 20.

The order of precedence for logical operators is as follows (note that the logical operators are surrounded by periods):

1. .NOT.
2. .AND.
3. .OR.

As with mathematical operators, parentheses in logical operations ensure the desired (and anticipated) result.

If you have several types of operators in a complex expression, the order of precedence is as follows:

1. Mathematical or string operation
2. Relational operations
3. Logical operations

For operations with the same precedence level, the calculation is performed from left to right.

# Using Macro Substitution

Using & as the first character of a memory variable invokes *macro substitution*. When this is used with a command, dBASE IV retrieves the contents of the memory variable, not the memory variable. The following is an example of a command line that invokes macro substitution:

```
whichpart = "Partnum > 14000"
LIST FOR &whichpart
```

Macro substitution is a useful tool, but keep in mind that it can slow down a compiled program.

# Using dBASE IV Commands

dBASE IV is a very flexible database management system. dBASE IV offers many commands that enable you to manage data, and create and modify reports, forms, and menus. Using the commands in dBASE IV, you can create custom applications.

dBASE IV has many different commands, and the commands serve different purposes. You can use most of the commands in applications, and you can use many of the commands from the Dot prompt. Some commands were meant only for applications, however, and some commands you can use only from the dot prompt.

"Using dBASE IV Commands" is divided into two sections. The first section, "dBASE IV Command Categories," lists the commands by category. The second section, "dBASE IV Commands," lists the commands alphabetically.

## dBASE IV Command Categories

Many different dBASE IV commands are available for your use. While some of the most used commands may be easy for you to remember, you may find that you cannot recall some of the commands by name.

This section helps you by grouping commands by function. For example, if you know that you want to perform a calculation, but aren't exactly sure which command to use, you can look under the section "Calculation Commands." After you have determined the command to use, you can look in the section "dBASE IV Commands" to find the syntax and other information for that command. The commands are listed alphabetically in the "dBASE IV Commands" section.

## Array Commands

Array commands are used to create and manage arrays—memory variables that can store columns and rows of information. Using these three commands, you can create an array in memory, restore information to the array from a file on disk, or save the contents of the array to a file in disk.

DECLARE
RESTORE FROM
SAVE TO

## Record and Field Commands

These commands are used to look at and change the data in a database. You also can use these commands to add blank records and move text into a memo field.

| | | |
|---|---|---|
| APPEND | APPEND MEMO | CHANGE/EDIT |
| APPEND FROM | BLANK | INSERT |
| APPEND FROM ARRAY | BROWSE | READ |

## Database Commands

Database commands enable you to use and modify database files. With this group of commands, you can open and close databases, index and sort the data, search for specific records, add and change field data, and import and export your database data.

| | | | |
|---|---|---|---|
| CLOSE | DELETE | JOIN WITH | RENAME |
| COPY TO | DELETE FILE | LIST/DISPLAY | REPLACE |
| COPY FILE | DIRECTORY/DIR | LIST/DISPLAY FILES | REPLACE FROM ARRAY |
| COPY MEMO | DISPLAY | LIST/DISPLAY STRUCTURE | SELECT |
| COPY STRUCTURE | ERASE/DELETE FILE | MODIFY STRUCTURE | SORT TO |
| COPY TO | EXPORT TO | PACK | UPDATE ON |
| CREATE FROM | GO/GOTO | PROTECT | USE |
| CREATE/MODIFY STRUCTURE | IMPORT FROM | RECALL | ZAP |

## Exiting Command

Using this command, you exit dBASE IV and return to the DOS prompt. Any open files will be closed before returning to DOS.

QUIT

## Search Commands

This group of commands enables you to look for specific records in the current database. You can look for records by indexed fields (FIND or SEEK) or for any data in any field in the database (LOCATE). Because FIND and SEEK use indexes, these commands are much faster than the LOCATE command. Use FIND and SEEK for often-searched data and create indexes for those data fields. Use LOCATE for seldom-searched items.

| | |
|---|---|
| CONTINUE | SEEK |
| FIND | SKIP |
| LOCATE | |

## Help Commands

The two Help commands are used to get help on a specific dBASE IV command or to search the available help screens. (You also can get help by accessing the dBASE IV Control Center from the dot prompt.) The help screens are useful when you are entering commands; the screens help ensure that you are using the proper syntax of commands and provide help on the various command options.

ASSIST
HELP

---

## Index Commands

This series of commands is used to create indexes, activate an index for a database, and update any indexes. You also can use these commands to copy or delete index tags from an MDX file or to create an MDX file from a series of NDX files.

COPY INDEXES
COPY TAG
DELETE TAG
INDEX ON
REINDEX

---

## Commands That Ask the User for Data

This group of commands enables the user to enter data from the keyboard.

@...SAY...GET
ACCEPT
INPUT
KEYBOARD

**TIP** Commands that ask the user for data have no Control Center equivalents.

---

## Label Commands

Label commands are used to create label format (LBL) files that can be used with databases. You can create different types of labels for mailing, inventory tags, file folders, or any other use.

CREATE/MODIFY LABEL
LABEL FORM
MODIFY LABEL

## Macro Commands

These commands are used to create, store, and play back macro commands. A macro is a series of saved keystrokes that can be played back, just like a tape recording. Suppose that you have a series of keystrokes you use to open a database, update information, and print a report. You have to type this same sequence each day. If you record those keystrokes in a macro, you can play back the keystrokes with the press of just one or two keys, performing your daily routine much more quickly.

You also can use macros in a programming environment. Suppose that you have a list of three things which need to be done to a file. You could place a list of the three items on the screen and ask the user to choose one item. Based on the choice, you could play back a series of keystrokes that perform the desired function.

You can create macros from the Control Center with the Tools menu or by pressing Alt-T. Macros are stored in macro libraries. You can have multiple macro libraries, but only one can be active at a time.

PLAY MACRO
RESTORE MACROS
SAVE MACROS TO

## Calculation Commands

This series of commands is used to calculate mathematical values from a series of variables or array elements.

**NOTE** Calculation commands have no Control Center equivalents.

AVERAGE
CALCULATE
COUNT TO
SUM
TOTAL ON

# Memory Variable Commands

This series of commands is used to create, store, display, or change memory variables or memory variable arrays. You also can declare variables as either public (usable by other programs) or private (usable only by the current program).

**NOTE** Memory variable commands have no Control Center equivalents.

COPY TO
DECLARE
DISPLAY/LIST MEMORY
PRIVATE/PRIVATE ALL
PUBLIC
RELEASE
RESTORE FROM
SAVE TO
STORE

# Menu and Pop-Up Commands

This series of commands enables you to define, activate, deactivate, and use dBASE IV menu bars. Menu bars are lists of choices from which you make a selection by pressing the Alt key and the first letter of the choice, or by moving the cursor to the choice and pressing Enter. Menu bars can be horizontal and can include pull-down menus and pop-up menus like those in the Control Center.

**NOTE** Menu and pop-up commands have no Control Center equivalents.

ACTIVATE MENU
ACTIVATE POPUP
DEACTIVATE MENU
DEACTIVATE POPUP
DEFINE BAR
DEFINE MENU
DEFINE PAD
DEFINE POPUP
DEFINE WINDOW
ON PAD
ON SELECTION PAD
ON SELECTION POPUP
SHOW MENU
SHOW POPUP

## Networking Commands

Used for dBASE IV network installations, these commands enable you to convert a database for network use, control file and record locking, and control network security. Some commands require exclusive use of the database. For these, you must open the database with the USE <*database*> ... EXCLUSIVE command.

Networking commands have no Control Center equivalents.

CONVERT
DISPLAY/LIST USERS
LOGOUT
UNLOCK

## Printing Commands

Printing commands enable you to send data to the printer to create labels, reports, or any other printed output. These commands also are used to create label forms and report forms.

Many commands covered elsewhere in this "dBASE IV Reference Guide," such as LIST MEMORY TO PRINT, also have options for sending information to the printer.

?/??
???
CREATE/MODIFY REPORT
DEFINE BOX FROM
EJECT
EJECT PAGE
ON PAGE
PRINTJOB...ENDPRINTJOB
REPORT FORM

## Program File Commands

These commands most commonly are used to manipulate dBASE IV program files. Commands in this group help you document, compile, and create programs; set procedures; run DOS commands; scan the database; and perform several other functions.

*/&&
CALL
CANCEL
COMPILE
CREATE/MODIFY APPLICATION
DEBUG
DEXPORT
DISPLAY/LIST HISTORY
DISPLAY/LIST STATUS
DO
DO CASE
DO WHILE
FUNCTION
IF
LIST HISTORY
LIST STATUS
LOAD
MODIFY APPLICATION
MODIFY COMMAND/FILE
NOTE
ON ERROR/ESCAPE/KEY
PARAMETERS
PROCEDURE
RETRY
RETURN
RUN
SCAN
SUSPEND
WAIT

---

## Query and View Commands

These commands are used to create and modify database queries and views of the environment. Queries and views also can be created from the Control Center.

CREATE/MODIFY QUERY
CREATE/MODIFY VIEW
MODIFY QUERY
MODIFY VIEW

---

## Screen Control Commands

These commands are used to place text and messages on-screen, draw boxes and windows, and save and restore screens to and from disk.

?/??
@ SAY...GET
@...CLEAR
@...FILL TO
@...
@...SCROLL
ACTIVATE SCREEN
ACTIVATE WINDOW
CLEAR
CREATE/MODIFY SCREEN
DEACTIVATE WINDOW
DEFINE WINDOW
MODIFY SCREEN
MOVE WINDOW
ON READERROR
RELEASE SCREENS
RESTORE SCREEN FROM
RESTORE WINDOW
SAVE SCREEN TO
SAVE WINDOW
TEXT
TYPE

## Transaction Processing Commands

Transaction processing with error checking helps you ensure that all data modifications are completed properly.

BEGIN TRANSACTION
RESET
ROLLBACK

# dBASE IV Commands

In this section commands are listed alphabetically, and examples and other information are shown for each command. Where available, the equivalent Control Center commands also are shown.

When instructed to press F10 to access the Control Center menus, you can alternatively click on the menu name with the mouse, and then click on the menu option you need to use.

## */&&

### Syntax

```
*/&& (program comment)
```

### Control Center Procedure

None.

### Purpose

Places a comment or nonexecutable text in the program. You use comments to document the function of a command or a series of commands. Documenting, or *commenting*, your program helps you keep track of what each part of your program is intended to accomplish and helps others understand what the program is doing (or will do) at any point. Comments appear in many of the code examples in this book.

The * must be the first nonspace character on the line; otherwise, dBASE interprets the character as a multiplication symbol. For example, if you enter

USE Clients * use the clients database

you receive an error message. Use && to add comments to a line that contains a command. Any characters in the rest of the line following * or && are ignored when the program is run or compiled.

### Example

```
* This is an example of a comment. Notice that the asterisk
* character is the first nonspace character on the line.
USE CLIENTS         && these are comments that are ignored
```

## ?/??

### Syntax

```
?/??
   [<expression 1>
      [PICTURE <character expression>]
      [FUNCTION <function list>]
      [AT <numeric value>]
      [STYLE <font number>]]
   [<expression 2> ...]
   [,]
```

### Control Center Procedure

None.

### Purpose

Sends the *<expression>* to the screen or to the printer if you use SET PRINTER ON. Use ? to print the expression on a new line; use ?? to print the expression at the current position. The comma (,) option delays printing the expression until dBASE encounters a ?/?? command that does not end with the trailing comma. You can use the trailing-comma technique to print complex expressions that are longer than the available 1024-character command line.

Use the PICTURE, FUNCTION, AT, and STYLE options to format the appearance of the output on the printer. The PICTURE commands are shown in the @...SAY...GET command.

In addition to the values listed in @...SAY...GET commands, the FUNCTION command has three possible values:

| | |
|---|---|
| V <*number*> | Causes expressions that are displayed in a column to be <*number*> characters wide. You can use this option to print the contents of a memo field; for example, a <*number*> of 0 causes the memo field to be printed as it was stored in the memo editor. |
| H <*number*> | Is used in conjunction with the system variable _wrap set to true. This arrangement causes word wrapping to be controlled by the _lmargin and _rmargin system variables. This value is used only with memo fields. |
| ; | Causes the text to wrap when a semicolon (;) is found in the text. The semicolon is not printed. |

When an expression may not fill in the PICTURE template, you can use four other functions to format the text:

| | |
|---|---|
| @B | Left-justifies data in the template |
| @I | Centers the data in the template |
| @J | Right-justifies data in the template |
| @T | Used with the other functions. Trims off blank spaces before the text is aligned with one of the other functions. |

You can use two other functions for numbers:

| | |
|---|---|
| $ | Displays the floating currency symbol before or after the amount, depending on the SET CURRENCY parameter |
| L | Displays leading zeros to fill out the field width |

The AT <*numeric value*> specifies the starting column number of the expression.

The STYLE option displays the text with various text attributes:

| | |
|---|---|
| B | Bold |
| I | Italic |
| U | Underline |
| R | Raised (superscript) |
| L | Lowered (subscript) |

To use STYLE to specify the typeface (font) to use for printing, use the numbers 1 through 5, which correspond to the user-defined fonts specified in the CONFIG.DB file. You can make lines overstrike each other by setting the _wrap option to false.

### Example

```
* Send column headings to printer
SET PRINTER ON
?? "Column 1" AT 0,
?? "Column 2" AT 10,
?? "Column 3" AT 20
* Now print some text and numbers under each column
?? "Corn" AT 0 PICTURE "!!!!!!!!" FUNCTION "L",
?? 12.33 AT 10 PICTURE "99.99" FUNCTION "$",
?? "per case" AT 30 PICTURE "!!!!!!!!!" FUNCTION "I"
?? "Tamales" AT 0 PICTURE "!!!!!!!!" FUNCTION "J",
?? 1.19 AT 10 PICTURE "99.99" FUNCTION "L",
?? "per can" PICTURE "!!!!!!!!!" AT 30 FUNCTION "R"
?? DATE()-10,                    && 10 days ago
?? SPACE(10) + DTOC(DATE())      && current date
```

## ?/??

### Syntax

```
?/?? [<expression 1>
       [PICTURE <character expression>]
       [FUNCTION <function list>]
       [AT <numeric value>]
       [STYLE <font number>]]
    [<expression 2> ...]
    [,]
```

### Control Center Procedure

None.

### Purpose

Displays the *<expression>* on-screen. Use ? to place the expression on a separate line; use ?? to display at the current screen position. The comma (,) option delays displaying the expression until a ?/?? command that does not end with the trailing comma is reached. You can use the comma option to output complex expressions that are longer than the available 1,024-character command line. Use the PICTURE, FUNCTION, AT, and STYLE options to format the appearance of the output on-screen. The PICTURE commands are shown in the @...SAY...GET command.

The FUNCTION command has three possible values:

| | |
|---|---|
| V <*number*> | Causes expressions that are displayed in a column to be <*number*> characters wide. You can use this value to display the contents of a memo field; for example, a <*number*> of 0 causes the memo field to be displayed as it was stored in the memo editor. |
| H <*number*> | Used in conjunction with the system variable _wrap set to true. This arrangement causes word wrapping to be controlled by the _lmargin and _rmargin system variables. This value is used only with memo fields. |
| ; | Causes the text to wrap when a semicolon (;) is found in the text. The semicolons are not displayed. |

When an expression may not fill in the PICTURE template, you can use four other functions to format the text:

| | |
|---|---|
| @B | Left-justifies data in the template |
| @I | Centers the data in the template |
| @J | Right-justifies data in the template |
| @T | Used with the other functions; trims off blank spaces before the text is aligned with one of the other functions |

You can use two other functions for numbers:

| | |
|---|---|
| $ | Displays the floating currency symbol before or after the amount, depending on the SET CURRENCY parameter |
| L | Displays leading zeros to fill out the field width |

The AT <*numeric expression*> specifies the starting column number of the expression.

You can use the STYLE option to display the text with various text attributes (some monitors are not able to display some styles):

| | |
|---|---|
| B | Bold |
| I | Italic |
| U | Underline |

R Raised (superscript)

L Lowered (subscript)

The STYLE option with a *<font number>* from 1 through 5 selects a user-defined font specified in the CONFIG.SYS file. This option affects only the printed appearance of the text, not the on-screen appearance.

You may want to use the @...SAY command to position text on-screen because this command gives you more precise control over the placement of the text.

### Example

```
* Display a message at the beginning of the next line
? "Are you ready to continue? "
```

## ???

### Syntax

```
??? <character expression>
```

### Control Center Procedure

None.

### Purpose

Sends characters directly to the printer without using any installed printer driver. This command is used most often to send printer control codes.

**TIP**

Use the ?/?? command with the STYLE option to change the printed appearance of an individual item—for example, to print one line in a different font. Use the ??? command to change the printed appearance of larger sections of text. You can use the _pscode and _pecode system variables to set the principal font to use for the printed document.

### Example

```
* Send LaserJet reset code
??? "{27}E"
```

# @ SAY...GET

### Syntax

```
@ <row>, <col>
   SAY <expression>
      [PICTURE <character expression>]
         [FUNCTION <function list>]
   GET <variable>
      [[OPEN] WINDOW <window name>]
      [PICTURE <character expression>]
      [FUNCTION <function list>]
      [RANGE [REQUIRED] [<low value>] [,<high value>]]
      [VALID [REQUIRED] <condition>
         [ERROR <character expression>]]
      [WHEN <condition>]
      [DEFAULT <expression>]
      [MESSAGE <character expression>]
      COLOR [<standard> [,<enhanced>]]
```

### Control Center Procedure

None.

### Purpose

Creates a custom form for input and output of data. The form is displayed at the specified *<row>* and *<column>* screen coordinates. If you used SET DEVICE TO PRINTER, the form is printed on the printer. The row and column values are relative to the upper left corner of the screen or the upper left corner of the active window. The *<row>* value can range from 0 to the maximum number of lines on the display or from 0 to 32,767 for a printer. The *<column>* value can range from 0 to 79 on-screen and from 0 to 255 for a printer. (Your printer may not be able to print all 255 characters on one line.) If you used SET STATUS ON, the status line appears on line 22. The SET SCOREBOARD ON command reserves line 0. To use lines 0 and 22, set these parameters to OFF.

The SAY option shows the information on-screen but doesn't allow it to be changed. Use the GET option to display the information and make it available for editing. You can use multiple @...GET commands to show all information on-screen and then use the READ command to enable full-screen editing mode.

### Example

```
* Show two fields on the screen, and then READ the data
firstname = space(10)
lastname = space(10)
@ 12,10 SAY "First Name " GET firstname
@ 13,10SAY " Last Name " GET lastname
   READ
```

The @ SAY...GET command has many available options. You usually can combine these options to determine exactly how the information will be shown and to control the type of information that the user can enter. @ SAY...GET options are shown here. An example is given for each option.

COLOR — Defines the colors to be used for the variable areas. The <*standard*> color is used for SAY commands, and the <*enhanced*> color is used for GET commands. See the SET COLOR command for color values. You can use the default colors by not specifying the colors.

```
COLOR B/BG      && blue on cyan
```

DEFAULT — Places the preset value in the variable area during APPEND operation. The user can press the Enter key to accept the value or type another value. The default value type must match the variable type used in the @ expression.

```
DEFAULT "CA"   && default character value
DEFAULT 39.17  && default numeric value
```

ERROR — Displays the <*character string*> if the user inputs a value that doesn't meet the requirements specified with VALID. This option overrides dBASE IV's error message `Editing condition is not satisfied`.

```
ERROR "Not within valid range"
```

FUNCTION — Similar to the PICTURE option, but FUNCTION applies to the entire data item, whereas PICTURE is used for only a portion of the entry.

```
FUNCTION "!"       && uppercase the entry
```

MESSAGE

Displays a help message, centered at the bottom of the screen, when the cursor is placed on the entry field. You can set the position of the message with the SET MESSAGE...AT command.

```
MESSAGE "dollar amount of order"
```

WINDOW

Opens a separate editing window if the variable is a memo field. The window enables you to edit memo fields in a window instead of using the full screen. The <*window name*> must be the name of a previously defined window. The <*row*> and <*column*> parameters of the @ command specify the relative positions in the editing window.

```
WINDOW memo_wind
```

OPEN WINDOW

Enables you to open and close the <*window name*> as a default window name.

```
OPEN WINDOW memo_wind
```

PICTURE

Restricts the input data to certain types of data and formats the data. The <*character expression*> can be a function, such as @! to force all uppercase characters. The @ symbol indicates that the format should apply to the entire width of the input variable. (See the table of PICTURE functions following these option descriptions.)

```
* Force entry to uppercase characters
PICTURE "@!"
* a phone number with area code
PICTURE "@(999) 999-9999"
```

RANGE

Defines the lowest and highest value allowed in the input field. You define ranges for character, numeric, and date values for fields of their respective data type. You can use the REQUIRED option to require entry of the variable.

```
RANGE 1,10          && 1-10 inclusive
RANGE 100           && 100 or above
RANGE ,55           && 55 or below
* any date in 1992
RANGE {1/1/92},{12/31/92}
```

| | |
|---|---|
| VALID | Provides a condition that must be met before data is accepted. If the input data does not meet the <*condition*>, an Editing condition not satisfied message or ERROR <*message*> appears. You can use the REQUIRED option to force a validity check every time you enter the field, whether the data is changed or not. |

```
* Tax is the input variable
VALID STATE="CA"
```

| | |
|---|---|
| WHEN | Prevents the user from placing the cursor on the input field when the <*condition*> is false. If the <*condition*> is false, the input field is skipped. |

```
* Allow editing only if the user has an
* access level of 9 or higher
* (Access is the memory variable used for
* the user's authority level)
WHEN access >=9
```

Table R.2 lists the format functions for the FORMAT and PICTURE parameters.

**Table R.2 Format Functions for FORMAT and PICTURE**

| Function | Action |
|---|---|
| ! | Allows any character but converts it to uppercase |
| ^ | Shows numbers in scientific notation |
| $ | Shows numbers in currency format |
| ( | Puts negative numbers in parentheses |
| A | Allows alphabetic characters only |
| B | Left-justifies text (for @...SAY command only) |
| C | Displays "CR" (credit) after any positive number |
| D | Uses current date format (set with SET DATE) |
| E | Uses European date format |
| I | Centers text (for @...SAY command only) |
| J | Right-justifies text (for @...SAY only) |

| Function | Action |
|---|---|
| L | Displays leading zeros |
| M | Allows a list of choices for the GET input variable—for example, M$L for dollar format with leading zeros |
| R | Displays the allowable characters in the input field but doesn't save them with the input data |
| S <*number*> | Limits field width to <*number*> characters. The field data is scrolled horizontally as needed. Must be a positive number, without a space, such as "S20". |
| T | Trims leading and trailing blanks from a field |
| X | Displays "DB" (debit) after a negative number |
| Z | Displays zeros as a blank string, rather than as zero characters (0) |

Some functions can be used together, and some are for specific field types only.

Templates are used to format a single character in the input field. Table R.3 shows the various available template symbols.

When you use a picture template for a decimal number, make sure that you include a decimal point in the template. You also need at least one digit to the left of the decimal point and another position for the sign (+ or –). To allow positive or negative numbers from .99 to 99.99, for example, use the template 999.99 to allow for the plus or minus sign.

**Table R.3 Template Symbols**

| Template | Description |
|---|---|
| ! | Converts letters to uppercase characters; allows other characters, such as numbers or punctuation |
| # | Allows only numbers, blanks, and signs (+ or –) |
| $ | Displays the SET CURRENCY string in place of leading zeros |
| * | Displays asterisks in place of leading zeros |

*continues*

**Table R.3 Continued**

| Template | Description |
|---|---|
| , | Displays commas if there are digits to the left of the comma position |
| . | Sets decimal point position |
| 9 | Allows only numbers for character data, or numbers and signs (+ or –) for numeric data |
| A | Allows letters only |
| N | Allows alphabetic or numeric characters, including the underscore; no spaces or punctuation |
| L | Allows only logical data entries (Y/N, .T./.F.) |
| X | Allows any character |
| Y | Allows logical Y/y/N/n; converts to uppercase (Y/N) |

## @...TO

### Syntax

```
@ <row 1>, <col 1> TO [TO <row 2>, <col 2>]
    [DOUBLE / PANEL / <border definition string>]
    [COLOR <color attribute>]
```

### Control Center Procedure

None.

### Purpose

Draws a box on-screen with a single-line border. Specify DOUBLE to get a double-lined box; PANEL to display a solid, highlighted border; or *<border definition string>* to use any characters you specify as the border. The *<border definition string>* follows the rules of the SET BORDER command. The COLOR codes follow the rules of the SET COLOR command.

You can draw a horizontal line by specifying the same row coordinates, or a vertical line by specifying the same column coordinates.

### Example

```
* Draw a double-line box in the center of the screen
* Make the colors inside the box Red/White
@ 8,20 TO 12,60 DOUBLE COLOR R/W
```

# @...CLEAR

### Syntax

```
@ <row 1>, <col 1> CLEAR [TO <row 2>, <col 2>]
```

### Control Center Procedure

None.

### Purpose

Clears part of the current screen or active window. The specified row and column are relative to the upper left corner of the active screen or window. If you don't specify the TO row and column, the active screen or window is cleared to the lower right corner.

### Example

```
* Clear all of row 12
@ 12,0
* Clear a portion of row 15
@ 15,20 CLEAR TO 15,60
* Clear a rectangular area
@ 10,0 CLEAR TO 15,79
```

# @...FILL TO

### Syntax

```
@ <row 1>, <col 1> FILL TO [<row 2>, <col 2>]
[COLOR <color attribute>]
```

### Control Center Procedure

None.

### Purpose

Changes the color of an area of the screen. The row 1/column 1 parameters are the upper left corner of the active screen or window. The color attributes are the same values used in SET COLOR. Any text in the FILL area is not erased, unless you don't specify a COLOR.

### Example

```
* Place a red background and white foreground
* in the center of the screen
@ 8,20 FILL TO 12,60 COLOR R/W
```

# @...SAY...GET

### Syntax

```
@ <row>, <col>
  SAY <expression> [PICTURE <character expression>]
  [FUNCTION <function list>]
  GET <variable>
     [[OPEN] WINDOW <window name>]
     [PICTURE <character expression>]
     [FUNCTION <function list>]
     [RANGE [<low value>] [,<high value>]] [REQUIRED]
     [VALID [REQUIRED] <condition>
        [ERROR <character expression>]]
     [WHEN <condition>]
     [DEFAULT <expression>]
     [MESSAGE <character expression>]
  COLOR [<standard> [,<enhanced>]]
```

### Control Center Procedure

None.

### Purpose

Creates a custom form for input and output of data. The form is displayed at the specified row and column screen coordinates. If you used SET DEVICE TO PRINTER, the form is printed. The row and column values are relative to the upper left corner of the screen or to the upper left corner of the active window. The *<row>* value can range from 0 to the maximum number of lines on the display, or up to 32,767 for a printer. The *<column>* value can range from 0 to 79 on-screen, and from 0 to 255 on the printer.

See the @...SAY command for examples and a complete discussion of all the options.

# @...SCROLL

### Syntax

```
@ <row-1>,<col-1> TO <row-2>,<col-2> SCROLL
[UP/DOWN/LEFT/RIGHT] [BY <expN>] [WRAP]
```

### Control Center Procedure

None.

### Purpose

Shifts the contents of areas on the screen. Use this technique to shift a block up, down, left, or right on the display.

### Example

```
* Move a block of text to the right 3 spaces.
@ 3,3 TO 5,10 SCROLL RIGHT BY 3
```

## ACCEPT

### Syntax

```
ACCEPT [<prompt>] TO <memory variable>
```

### Purpose

Asks the user for an answer to a question and creates a character-type variable from the user entry. The *<prompt>* can be a character string ("Enter your name") or a memory variable. The user can enter up to 254 characters. If you don't use a prompt, dBASE IV places a question mark on-screen in the spot where the user enters the data.

The ACCEPT command usually is used in dBASE IV command files or programs. If you need to ask the user for a numeric variable, you can use the INPUT command or convert the ACCEPT character memory variable to a numeric data type.

> **TIP**
>
> If the user presses the Esc key when your program is using ACCEPT to collect input, your program might be terminated. You may want to use the SET ESCAPE OFF command just before the ACCEPT command to prevent program termination.

### Example

```
* Ask the user's name
* Store it as the username memory variable
@ 10,0          && clear the line
ACCEPT "Please Enter your User ID" TO username
```

## ACTIVATE MENU

### Syntax

```
ACTIVATE MENU <menu name> [PAD <pad name>]
```

### Purpose

Activates a menu bar that was defined with the DEFINE MENU command and displays the menu bar on-screen. The PAD option highlights the specified pad name. Only one menu bar can be active at one time; all others are temporarily suspended until the current menu is deactivated.

### Example

```
* Activate the mainprog menu bar,
* highlighting the Print choice as default
ACTIVATE MENU mainprog PAD print
```

## ACTIVATE POPUP

### Syntax

```
ACTIVATE POPUP <pop-up name>
```

### Purpose

Activates a previously defined pop-up menu on-screen. (Pop-ups already must have been defined with the DEFINE POPUP command.) Only one pop-up menu can be active at a time, but previously activated pop-ups remain on-screen until they are deactivated.

### Example

```
* Deactivate the previous pop-up and activate the new one
DEACTIVATE POPUP          && whichever pop-up last activated
ACTIVATE POPUP pop3b
```

## ACTIVATE SCREEN

### Syntax

```
ACTIVATE SCREEN
```

### Control Center Procedure

None.

### Purpose

Enables access to the entire screen rather than to the currently active window. Windows and pop-up menus remain on-screen, but the user can overwrite the window or pop-up area. When you deactivate the screen by activating a window, the pop-ups and windows are reactivated.

### Example

```
* Restore access to the whole screen
ACTIVATE SCREEN
```

## ACTIVATE WINDOW

### Syntax

```
ACTIVATE WINDOW <window name list> / ALL
```

### Control Center Procedure

None.

### Purpose

Activates and displays windows from memory. You direct all screen output to the window, not the full screen. Windows are created with the CREATE/MODIFY WINDOW command. The ALL option enables you to restore all of the windows in memory. The windows are displayed in the order they are defined.

### Example

```
* Activate the help_05 window just to see how it looks
ACTIVATE WINDOW help_05
```

## APPEND

### Syntax

```
APPEND [BLANK]/[NOORGANIZE]
```

### Control Center Procedure

From the Control Center, highlight the database file, press F2 and then F10, highlight Records, and highlight Add New Records.

### Purpose

Used to add records to the current database. APPEND displays all the fields of the current record, and you can add data to each field. If you have more than one screenful of fields, use the PgUp and PgDn keys to move from one screen to another. After you enter data in the last field, pressing Enter adds a new record. The PgDn key also adds new records to the database. You can use Ctrl-End to complete a record. Pressing Esc cancels any changes to the current record.

While you are entering data, you can use the PgUp key to display the preceding record. You can use the PgDn key to display the next screenful of fields if you have too many fields for one screen, or use PgUp to see the previous screenful of fields. If you are at the end of the database, you can use the PgDn key to add another blank record.

If the database contains a memo field, move the cursor to the memo field and then use Ctrl-Home to enter the dBASE IV editor for the memo field. After you enter the desired text, use Ctrl-End to save the information or press Esc to cancel any changes to the memo information. Use the NOORGANIZE option to prevent the user from accessing the ORGANIZE menu.

### Examples

```
USE CUSTOMER    && open the database
APPEND          && add a record, entering data
```

The BLANK option adds a blank record at the end of the database but does not show the field on-screen for entry. This option usually is used in programs that read values or memory variables from the screen. The following example illustrates the use of APPEND BLANK:

```
* Read two fields from the screen
* adding the information to the STATES database.
* Structure of STATE database
* Field Name   Type          Length    Dec
* STATE        Character     2
* ZIP          Numeric       5         0
*
* Set up database and memory variables
USE STATES
mstate = SPACE(2)          && character variable
mzip = 0                   && numeric variable
* Read values from screen
@10,15 SAY "STATE " GET mstate PICTURE "!!"
@11,15 SAY " ZIP  " GET mzip PICTURE "99999"
READ
* Store variables to database
APPEND BLANK
REPLACE STATE WITH mstate, ZIP with mzip
```

## APPEND FROM

### Syntax

```
APPEND FROM <filename>
   [[TYPE] <file type>] [REINDEX]
   [FOR <condition>]
```

### Control Center Procedure

From the Control Center, highlight the database file, press Shift-F2 and then F10, highlight Append, and highlight Append Records from dBASE File.

### Purpose

Copies data from one file into another database, adding the new records at the end of the target database. Also used to import data from nondatabase-type files.

This command has two main functions: to add the records from one database into another and to import data from nondatabase files, such as a Lotus 1-2-3 version 1A worksheet (WKS) file. (Use the IMPORT command to convert 1-2-3 version 2.x files.)

For you to use APPEND FROM to add data from another database, both databases must have similar structures, but they don't have to be identical. Only data from the same named fields is added to the target database.

### Examples

If you have two customer databases and want to combine them into one database, you can use the following code:

```
USE CUST2                    && second database
APPEND FROM CUST1            && Adds CUST1 data to
                             && CUST2 database
```

The following code creates a database from a comma-delimited (nondatabase) file:

```
APPEND FROM ORDERS.TXT TYPE DELIMITED
```

## APPEND FROM ARRAY

### Syntax

```
APPEND FROM ARRAY <array name> [REINDEX]
   [FOR <condition>]
```

### Control Center Procedure

None.

### Purpose

Used to add records to a database file from a memory array. Memory array variables are stored like rows and columns of data in a spreadsheet. The first column of data in the first row is called data element [1,1], the second column is called [1,2], and so on. The [1,1] array element is entered into the first database field, the [1,2] array element is entered into the second database field, and so on.

If more array elements than fields are in the database, the excess elements are ignored. The [2,1] array element is entered into the next record's first database. The array types and database field types must match.

### Example

If you have a three-element array and five array values, you can enter the following:

```
DECLARE PARTNUM[5,3]          && sizes the array
...                           && array values assigned
USE PARTS
APPEND FROM ARRAY PARTNUM     && Adds 5 records to database
```

# APPEND MEMO

### Syntax

```
APPEND MEMO <memo field name>
   FROM <filename>
   [OVERWRITE]
```

### Control Center Procedure

None.

### Purpose

Imports text from a text file into the memo field of the current record.

You must specify the name of the target memo field. If you don't specify the OVERWRITE parameter, text is added to existing memo data. If you use OVERWRITE, the text replaces existing memo data.

### Example

```
* Add text to the NOTES memo field
USE CLIENT                && the NOTES field is a memo type
GOTO 48                   && position to record number 48
* Append the text to existing memo data
APPEND MEMO NOTES FROM SMITH.TXT
```

# ASSIST

### Syntax

```
ASSIST
```

### Control Center Procedure

None.

### Purpose

Accesses the Control Center from the dot prompt. You also can use the command in a program, but you may not want to enable a user to access other files and functions. From the Control Center, you can exit back to the dot prompt by pressing the Esc key. You also can press Alt-E to open the Exit menu and then choose the Exit To Dot Prompt option.

# AVERAGE

### Syntax

```
AVERAGE [<numeric expression list>]
   [<scope>]
   [FOR <condition>]
   [WHILE <condition>]
   [TO <memory variable list> / TO ARRAY <array name>]
```

### Purpose

Calculates the arithmetic mean of a series of numeric variables. All records are used to calculate the average unless you use a scope, FOR, or WHILE. The average is displayed on-screen unless you use TO or TO ARRAY to store the average in a specified memory variable or array.

You can use the AVERAGE command to calculate the average of series of data variables.

You may want to exclude records whose numeric fields are 0 by using the FOR option, as in

```
AVERAGE cost FOR .NOT. ISBLANK (cost)
```

### Example

```
* Find the average of two data variables, storing the result
* in the COST_AVG and SEE_AVG memvars
USE STOCKS
AVERAGE COST, SELL TO COST_AVG, SELL_AVG
```

# BEGIN TRANSACTION

### Syntax

```
BEGIN TRANSACTION [<path name>]
   <transaction commands>
END TRANSACTION
```

### Control Center Procedure

None.

### Purpose

Defines the beginning and ending points of a series of commands that are part of a single transaction. With transaction processing, you can make sure that the entire process is completed properly. If the transaction doesn't complete properly, you can change the data back to its original form.

During transaction processing, a transaction log file is created in the current directory or under the specified *<path name>*. On a stand-alone system, the file is called TRANSLOG.LOG. On a network system, the file is called *<computer name>*.LOG, where *<computer name>* is the network name of the computer that started the transaction.

You can use two functions, COMPLETED() and ROLLBACK(), to test whether the transaction or rollback completed without errors. If COMPLETED() is true, the transaction completed properly. If ROLLBACK() is true, the ROLLBACK command completed properly.

### Example

```
* Update the database with transaction processing
* Set up a transaction error trap program
ON ERROR DO trantrap
BEGIN TRANSACTION
USE SALES INDEX SALES
   DO update1           && a program that changes data
   DO update2           && another program
END TRANSACTION
IF ROLLBACK()
   @ 22,20 SAY "Data restored to original state."
ELSE
   @ 22,20 SAY "Transaction rollback unsuccessful."
   @ 23,20 SAY "Restore data from a current backup."
ENDIF
ON ERROR            && clear transaction error trap
RETURN
* This is the trantrap procedure
PROCEDURE TRANTRAP
@ 20,20 SAY "Error occurred during transaction."
@ 21,20 SAY "Removing changes from data files."
ROLLBACK            && roll back the changes
RETURN
```

# BLANK

### Syntax

```
BLANK [FIELDS <field-list>/LIKE/EXCEPT <skeleton>]
[REINDEX] [<scope>] [FOR <condition>] [WHILE <condition>]
```

### Control Center Procedure

From the Edit or Browse screens, select Blank Record from the Records menu to blank the current record.

### Purpose

Fills records or fields with blanks. Using the BLANK command, you can blank an entire record, a set of records, or just selected fields in records. Fields that are designated as read-only cannot be blanked.

### Example

```
* Blank the NAME field in records where the city is Chicago
BLANK FIELDS NAME FOR CITY="Chicago"
```

# BROWSE

### Syntax

```
BROWSE
   [NOINIT]
   [NOFOLLOW]
   [NOAPPEND]
   [NOMENU]
   [NOEDIT]
   [NODELETE]
   [NOCLEAR]
   [NOORGANIZE]
   [COMPRESS]
   [FORMAT]
   [LOCK <number>]
   [WIDTH <number>]
   [FREEZE <field name>]
   [WINDOW <window name>]
   [FIELDS <field name1> /R /<column width>]
      /<calculated field name 1> = <expression 1>
      [,<field name2>[/R ][/<column width>]
      /<calculated field name 2> = <expression 2>] ...]
```

### Control Center Procedure

From the Control Center, highlight the database file and press F2.

### Purpose

Enables you to view and edit records in your database. (If a database is not currently in use, dBASE IV will ask for the database.) Fields are shown in the order of the structure of the database, unless you specify the fields you want by using the FIELDS option. You can scroll through records with the PgUp and PgDn keys. You can use the left- and right-arrow keys to view fields that are not displayed on-screen.

While in BROWSE mode, you can add records (unless the NOAPPEND option is used) by moving to the last record and pressing the down-arrow key. dBASE IV asks whether you want to add records to the database. To say that you do, press Y. You can press the F10 key to activate the BROWSE menu bar, unless the NOMENU option is specified. You can change to the EDIT mode by pressing the F2 key.

If the database file is protected, you can read and edit only those fields allowed by your access level.

Options for BROWSE are described in table R.4.

**Table R.4 BROWSE Options**

| Option | Description |
|---|---|
| NOINIT | Uses the command line options you specified with the previous BROWSE command |
| NOFOLLOW | When you are using an indexed file, this option doesn't reposition the record if you make a change to a field that is part of the index. If you omit this command, a change to an index field in a record will cause the screen to redisplay. |
| NOAPPEND | Prevents you from appending records to the database if you move past the last record |
| NOMENU | Prevents the display of the menu bar |
| NOEDIT | Prevents you from changing any field |
| NODELETE | Prevents you from deleting records |
| NOCLEAR | Keeps the BROWSE table on-screen when you finish browsing. Omitting this option clears the screen after you exit BROWSE. |

| Option | Description |
|---|---|
| NOORGANIZE | Prevents use of the Organize menu |
| COMPRESS | Displays more lines on-screen (two more in 25-line mode) by placing the column headings at the top line and not displaying a line separating the headings and data. |
| FORMAT | Uses the active screen format (FMT) file. The fields still are placed on the same row, but the formatting options specified by the @...GET commands are used (@...SAY commands are ignored). Any fields specified by the FIELDS option are ignored; fields are displayed according to the specification of the format file. |
| LOCK <*number*> | Enables you to specify the number of fields that will not move when you use the arrow keys to move other fields to the display. Use the F3 or F4 key to scroll left or right, respectively. The LOCK option is ignored if you are in EDIT mode. |
| WIDTH <*number*> | Limits the width of any fields to the value you specify. While you edit a field, the data scrolls in the field when you use the arrow keys. Memo fields always show a width of 4. If you set the width to 5 and the numeric field is eight characters wide, the field data is displayed with asterisks. |
| FREEZE <*fieldname*> | Enables you to edit only the field specified. All other fields are displayed. If you switch to EDIT mode, FREEZE is disabled. |
| WINDOW <*window name*> | Enables you to use a window definition to determine the area that will be used by the BROWSE command. The window is closed automatically when you exit BROWSE. |
| FIELDS ... | Specifies the fields that you want to be displayed during the BROWSE. The /R option to FIELDS enables you to designate a field as read-only. Use <*column width*> to limit the width of one field. |

### Examples

With the FIELDS option, you can construct calculated fields, as in this example:

```
BROWSE FIELDS COST = QUANTITY*UNIT_PRICE
```

COST will be used as the column heading. Each field can have a column width assigned to it; for example, the code

```
BROWSE FIELDS LASTNAME/8
```

causes the Lastname field to be shortened to eight characters.

```
USE CUSTOMERS                    && open the database
* Look only at the specified fields, allowing editing of data:
* Limit the company field to 10 characters,
* other fields to 20 characters
* Don't allow changing the credit limit field
* Don't allow deleting or adding records
BROWSE NODELETE NOAPPEND FIELDS LASTNAME, COMPANY/10,;
   CRED_LIM /R, SALESMAN WIDTH 20
```

## CALCULATE

### Syntax

```
CALCULATE [<scope>] <option list>
   [FOR <condition>]
   [WHILE <condition>]
   [TO <memory variable list> /TO ARRAY <array name>]
```

### Purpose

Computes various financial and statistical functions from the data fields in your database. The functions available as *<option list>* are shown in table R.5.

You can limit the set of figures used to obtain the average by specifying a FOR or WHILE *<condition>*. The calculated values are displayed on-screen (if SET TALK is in its default setting, ON) or stored in the memory variable or array if you use the TO/TO ARRAY option.

### Example

```
* Determine the average cost and show the number of items
USE STOCKS
CALCULATE AVG(COST), CNT() TO COST_AVG, NUM_RECS
```

**Table R.5 CALCULATE Options**

| Option | Action |
|---|---|
| AVG(<*numeric expression*>) | Calculates the arithmetic average of the values in the numeric field |
| CNT( ) | Counts the number of records that meet the FOR <*condition*> |
| MAX(<*expression*>) | Returns the largest value in the database field. The database field can be a numeric, date, or character field. |
| MIN(<*expression*>) | Returns the smallest value in the database field. The database field can be a numeric, date, or character field. |
| NPV(<*rate*>, <*flows*>, <*initial*>) | Calculates the net present value of the database field. The <*rate*> is the discount rate as a decimal number, as in `.10` for 10%. The <*flows*> are a series of signed periodic cash flow values. The <*initial*> parameter is the initial investment. |
| STD(<*expression*>) | Calculates the standard deviation of the values in the database field. The standard deviation is the square root of the variance. |
| SUM(<*numeric expression*>) | Returns the sum of the values in the database field for the records specified by the FOR <*condition*> |
| VAR(<*numeric expression*>) | Determines the population variance of the values in the database field |

# CALL

## Syntax

```
CALL <module name> [WITH <expression list>]
```

### Control Center Procedure

None.

### Purpose

Executes a binary file program module that has been loaded into memory with the LOAD command. Such files are generally assembly language programs that perform some special function. You can load up to 16 binary program files at once, and each file can be up to 64K long.

Some binary program files require an <*expression list*> of variables to be passed to and from the program. The data supplied in the <*expression list*> must be in the form expected by the called program.

### Example

```
* Call the FINDFILE.BIN assembly language program
* The BIN file has been previously loaded with LOAD.
filename = "CUSTOMER.INF"     && find this file
foundfile = 0                 && will be 1 if file found
CALL findfile WITH filename, foundfile
IF foundfile = 1
   ? "Found the file!"
ELSE
   ? "Didn't find the file!"
ENDIF
```

## CANCEL

### Syntax

```
CANCEL
```

### Control Center Procedure

None.

### Purpose

Stops the currently executing program, closes all files, and returns you to the dot prompt. (Procedure files are not closed.) Use this command to stop everything when you test and debug your programs.

### Example

```
* Ask whether OK to cancel program
answer = .F.
   @ 24,25 SAY "Cancel program? (Y/N) " ;
   GET answer PICTURE "Y"
   READ
```

```
IF answer
   CLOSE PROCEDURE       && needed because CANCEL
                         && doesn't close procedure
   CANCEL
ENDIF
```

# CHANGE/EDIT

### Syntax

```
CHANGE/EDIT
   [NOINIT]
   [NOFOLLOW]
   [NOAPPEND]
   [NOMENU]
   [NOEDIT]
   [NODELETE]
   [NOCLEAR]
   [NOORGANIZE]
   [<record number>]
   [FIELDS <field list>]
   [<scope>]
   [FOR <condition>]
   [WHILE <condition>]
```

### Control Center Procedure

From the Control Center, highlight the database file and press F2. If you see the Browse screen, press F2 again to see the Edit screen.

### Purpose

Enables you to edit and change the contents of records in the current database or view. CHANGE and EDIT commands are identical. If you don't use FOR, WHILE, or a scope, all records are accessible with the PgUp and PgDn keys.

You can change between BROWSE and EDIT mode by using the F2 key, unless the FOR, WHILE, or *<scope>* option is specified.

You can use the arrow keys to move from field to field in the record. You can use the PgUp and PgDn keys to move to the preceding record or the next record. You can use Ctrl-End to save all changes and Esc to save all changes except those changes made to the current record. Use Ctrl-Home (or F9) to edit a memo field, and press Ctrl-Home again when you have finished with the memo field.

If you use PgDn when you are at the last record, you can append records to the database, unless you use the NOAPPEND option. If you are using dBASE IV on a network, the current record is LOCKED when you make a change, along with any related records, but the EDIT/CHANGE command is active.

Options for the CHANGE and EDIT commands are described in table R.6.

**Table R.6 CHANGE/EDIT Options**

| Option | Description |
|---|---|
| NOINIT | Uses the command line options that you specified with the previous CHANGE/ EDIT command |
| NOFOLLOW | When you use an indexed file, this option doesn't reposition the record if you make a change to a field that is part of the index. If you omit this command, a change to an index field in a record causes the screen to redisplay. |
| NOAPPEND | Prevents you from appending records to the database if you move past the last record |
| NOMENU | Prevents the display of the menu bar |
| NOEDIT | Prevents you from making changes to any field |
| NODELETE | Prevents you from deleting records |
| NOCLEAR | Keeps the CHANGE/EDIT form on-screen when you finish editing. Omitting this option clears the screen after you exit. |
| NOORGANIZE | Prevents use of the Organize menu |
| *<record number>* | Enables you to edit a specific record, rather than the current record |
| FIELDS *<field list>* | Enables you to specify which fields will be edited or changed |
| *<scope>* | Enables you to specify the number of records used. NEXT 12 would limit you to the next 12 records. |

| Option | Description |
|---|---|
| FOR <*condition*> | Enables changes only to those records that meet the condition. `FOR STATE = "CA"` would permit changes to records whose two-character STATE field contains "CA." |
| WHILE <*condition*> | Is similar to FOR <*condition*> but begins with the current record and continues as long as the condition is true. `WHILE COST < 1000` enables you to edit or change records until a record is found that has a COST of 1000 or more. |

### Example

```
* Go to record 15, edit the indicated fields in the record
* Don't allow appending or deleting records
USE INVOICE                  && open the database
GOTO 15                      && goto record 15
EDIT NOAPPEND NODELETE FIELDS CUSTOMER, ITEM, QUANTITY, COST
```

## CLEAR

### Syntax

```
CLEAR [ALL/FIELDS/GETS/MEMORY/MENUS/
   POPUPS/TYPEAHEAD/WINDOWS/SCREENS]
```

### Control Center Procedure

None.

### Purpose

Clears the current screen or window and releases any active GET statements. You can specify only one CLEAR action per command.

The ALL option closes all open databases and their associated index, format, and memo files. It also releases all memory variables and closes any active catalog file. The FIELDS option releases the field list you set with SET FIELDS. The GETS option clears any open @...GET statements.

The MEMORY option releases any memory variables and performs the same function as RELEASE ALL used at the dot prompt.

The MENUS option clears all user menus from the screen and erases them from memory. The POPUPS option does the same for pop-up menus. The TYPEAHEAD option clears any pending keystrokes in the keyboard buffer. The WINDOWS option clears all windows from the screen and deletes them from memory. CLEAR SCREEN clears all screen memory variables.

### Example

```
* Clear any waiting keystrokes
CLEAR TYPEAHEAD
* Clear the current SET FIELDS list
CLEAR FIELDS
```

## CLOSE

### Syntax

```
CLOSE ALL
CLOSE ALTERNATE
CLOSE DATABASES
CLOSE FORMAT
CLOSE INDEXES
CLOSE PRINTER
CLOSE PROCEDURE
```

### Control Center Procedure

CLOSE ALL, CLOSE ALTERNATE, CLOSE PRINTER, CLOSE PROCEDURE: None.

CLOSE DATABASES, CLOSE FORMAT: From the database display, press F10 and select Exit. From the Control Center, highlight the database file, press Enter, and select Close File.

CLOSE INDEXES: From the Data Entry screen, press F10 and select Organize, Order Records By Index, and Natural Order.

### Purpose

Closes any open files. Closing database files with CLOSE DATABASES also closes the database's index, memo, and format files. Properly closing a file ensures that the data is written to disk. The CLOSE ALL command closes all types of files.

### Example

```
CLOSE ALL                && close all files
CLOSE PROCEDURE          && close the procedure file
CLOSE DATABASES          && close DBF DBT NDX MDX FMT files
* Use these two commands to close the DBF file
* without closing the other files
SELECT 1                 && work area 1
USE                      && closes just the DBF
```

# COMPILE

### Syntax

```
COMPILE <filename> [RUNTIME]
```

### Control Center Procedure

None.

### Purpose

Reads the dBASE IV program *<filename>* and compiles it into an executable object code file. These executable files run much more quickly than the nonexecutable program files in dBASE III. The RUNTIME option lists as errors any commands not allowed by the dBASE IV run-time version.

When you run a program from the dot prompt, you use DO *<PRG filename>*; dBASE IV then compiles the program into an executable file and runs the program. The COMPILE command compiles the program file without running the program. During the compilation process, each command line in the program is checked for proper syntax, and errors are reported. You should recompile programs created in earlier versions of dBASE IV before running them under dBASE IV 1.5.

> **WARNING:** Make sure that all your program files have different file names. If you have a CUSTLIST.PRG and CUSTLIST.PRC file, compiling one may overwrite the other.

### Example

```
* Compile the MAINPROG.PRG program
* (This command is usually used from the dot prompt,
* not from within programs)
COMPILE mainprog
```

# CONTINUE

### Syntax

```
CONTINUE
```

### Control Center Procedure

None.

### Purpose

Searches for the next record that matches the condition specified by the most recent LOCATE command. The LOCATE command finds the first record in the database that matches a specified condition. You then can determine whether that record is the record you want. If it is not, use CONTINUE to look for the next match. You can repeat the CONTINUE command until the end of the LOCATE scope or the end of the file.

### Example

```
* Find a record dated before April 1, 1991.
* Display the name and address and ask whether the user
* wants to delete this record, then continue searching
* to the end of the file.
USE MEMBERS
DO WHILE .NOT. EOF()
   mYes = .F.
   LOCATE FOR DATE < {04/01/91}
   @ 10,10 SAY FIRSTNAME + " " + LASTNAME
   @ 11,10 SAY ADDRESS
   @ 12,10 SAY CITY + " " + ZIPCODE
   @ 14,10 SAY "Delete this record? Y/N:"
   @ 14,35 GET mYes PICTURE "Y"
   READ
      IF mYes
         DELETE
      ENDIF
   CONTINUE
ENDDO
```

## CONVERT

### Syntax

```
CONVERT [TO <numeric value>]
```

### Purpose

Adds to the database a special field for holding information about whether a record currently is being used by another user. The added field, called _dBASElock, is a numeric field with a default length of 16.

TO <*numeric value*> changes the field length. Allowable lengths are 8 through 24.

The _dBASElock field has space for the following values:

| | |
|---|---|
| Count | A two-byte hexadecimal number used by CHANGE() |
| Time | A three-byte hexadecimal number containing the time the lock was placed on the record |

| | |
|---|---|
| Date | A three-byte hexadecimal number containing the date the lock was placed on the record |
| Name | A 0- to 16-character representation of the log-in name of the user who is using the record |

Every time a record is changed, the count value increases. You can use the CHANGE() function to determine whether the record has been changed. Repositioning the record pointer with the GOTO command sets CHANGE() to false, unless another user has made a change to the record. The LKSYS() function retrieves the _dBASElock information.

### Example

```
* Change a single-user DBF file to a multiuser file
USE CUSTOMER EXCLUSIVE
CONVERT
```

## COPY FILE

### Syntax

```
COPY FILE <filename> TO <filename>
```

### Control Center Procedure

From the Control Center, press F10 and select Tools, DOS Utilities, Operations, Copy, Single file.

### Purpose

Is similar to the COPY command in MS-DOS. COPY FILE creates a duplicate of any file. Specify the complete file name and extension for each file to copy.

You must close any open file before you can use this command. If you use the COPY command to copy a database (DBF) file, you also must copy any associated memo (DBT) and index (NDX, MDX) files with a separate copy command.

### Example

```
* Make a backup copy of the CUSTOMER database on
* the A: floppy drive
COPY FILE CUSTOMER.DBF TO A:CUSTOMER.DBF
* Don't forget to copy the memo file
COPY FILE CUSTOMER.DBT TO A:CUSTOMER.DBT
```

## COPY INDEXES

### Syntax

```
COPY INDEXES <NDX file list>
   [TO <MDX filename>]
```

### Control Center Procedure

None.

### Purpose

Transforms a list of single-index (NDX) files into index tags contained in a single multiple-index (MDX) file. This capability converts dBASE III index files into MDX files. The TO option enables you to specify the name of the MDX file; if the name is not specified, the files are placed in the current MDX file. If the MDX file does not exist, it is created. The NDX files must be in use before you use the COPY INDEXES command.

### Example

```
* Copy the old index files into the MEMBERS.MDX file
USE MEMBERS INDEX LASTNAME, CITY, MEMNUM
COPY INDEXES LASTNAME, CITY, MEMNUM TO MEMBERS
* Make the MDX file active, closing old index files
SET INDEX TO MEMBERS
```

## COPY MEMO

### Syntax

```
COPY MEMO <memo field name> TO <filename>
   [ADDITIVE]
```

### Control Center Procedure

None.

### Purpose

Copies the information from the memo field of the current record to a text (TXT) file. The ADDITIVE option adds the data to the *<filename>* if it exists; otherwise, the file name is overwritten. If the file name exists, it can be overwritten with SET SAFETY OFF. If you used SET SAFETY ON, dBASE IV prompts you for verification before overwriting the file.

### Example

```
USE CLIENTS                    && open the database
GOTO 12                        && record 12
* Copy record 12's NOTES memo data to the
* CLIENT.TXT file, adding to existing data
COPY MEMO NOTES TO CLIENTS.TXT ADDITIVE
```

## COPY STRUCTURE

### Syntax

```
COPY STRUCTURE TO <filename>
   [FIELDS <field list>] [WITH PRODUCTION]
```

### Control Center Procedure
None.

### Purpose
Copies the structure of the current database to a new DBF file but does not copy any data. This action creates an empty database (and associated memo file if needed) from the current database. Use the FIELDS option to specify a list of fields; otherwise, the command affects all the fields in the current database. If PROTECT currently is in use, only those fields authorized to the current user are copied to the new file.

### Example
```
* Create a new database structure from the CLIENTS list
USE CLIENTS
COPY STRUCTURE TO REGION10
```

## COPY TAG

### Syntax
```
COPY TAG <tag name> [OF <MDX filename>] TO <NDX filename>
```

### Control Center Procedure
None.

### Purpose
Converts dBASE IV multiple-index files (MDX) into single-index (NDX) files. You can use COPY TAG to convert dBASE IV indexes into dBASE III indexes or to create an NDX file for use by a dBASE IV database. To use the command, you must have a database active. Only one index tag can be created at a time.

### Example
```
* Create a LASTNAME.NDX file from the current database
* The MEMBERS database has an MDX file called MEMBERS.MDX
* There are two index tag fields in
* MEMBERS: LASTNAME and CITY,
* so two COPY TAG commands are needed to create the
* MEMLAST.NDX and MEMCITY.NDX index files
USE MEMBERS INDEX MEMBERS
COPY TAG LASTNAME TO MEMLAST
COPY TAG CITY TO MEMCITY
```

# COPY TO

### Syntax

```
COPY TO <filename>
    [[TYPE] <file type>]
    [FIELDS <field list>]
    [<scope>]
    [FOR <condition>]
    [WHILE <condition>]
    [WITH PRODUCTION]
```

### Control Center Procedure

COPY TO TYPE: From the Control Center, highlight the database file, press F10, and select Tools and Export.

COPY TO another dBASE IV file: From the Control Center, press Shift-F2 on the data file and then choose `Layout: Save this database file structure`. Enter a name for the new file.

### Purpose

Copies all or part of the currently active database into a new file. COPY TO also exports data for use by other programs. All records are copied, including records that were marked for deletion. (Use SET DELETED ON to prevent copying of records marked for deletion.) You can limit the records being copied by using a scope or by using the FOR and WHILE options. If you need only some of the fields in the new file, use the FIELDS option. The WITH PRODUCTION option copies the production index if you are creating a dBASE IV file.

The TYPE option enables you to copy to non-dBASE IV file formats. Table R.7 lists the options and the file types they create.

**Table R.7 TYPE *<file type>* Options**

| Option | Description |
|---|---|
| DELIMITED | Comma-delimited ASCII file. All fields are separated by commas, and character field data is surrounded by double quotes. Each record is placed on a separate line. Most programs have an option that lets them import comma-delimited files. Creates a TXT file. |
| DELIMITED WITH *<delimiter>* | Similar to a delimited file, but character fields are surrounded by the character you specify in *<delimiter>*. Creates a TXT file. |

| Option | Description |
|---|---|
| DELIMITED WITH BLANK | A delimited file in which character fields are separated by a space character. Creates a TXT file. |
| SDF | System Data Format ASCII file. A fixed-length file in which each field has the width of the record in the DBF file. A character field of 10 characters will always have 10 characters in it, even if any or all of the positions are blank. Creates a TXT file. |
| DBASEII | Exports data into a dBASE II (DB2) file. You need to rename the file with a DBF file extension before the file can be used in dBASE II. |
| DBMEMO3 | Exports a dBASE IV database that contains a memo field into database (DBF) and memo (DBT) files usable by dBASE III. You must use this option to export to dBASE III a dBASE IV database that has a memo field. Note that dBASE IV can use and modify dBASE III DBF/DBT files, but you need to use COPY...DB3MEMO to make dBASE IV files usable by dBASE III. |
| RPD | RapidFile RPD file format. |
| FW2 | Framework II (FW2) database format. |
| SYLK | A Multiplan spreadsheet formula file. Each record is converted to a Multiplan row, and fields are converted to columns in the row. The database field names are used as the headings for each column in the spreadsheet file. |
| DIF | VisiCalc version 1 (DIF) format. Each record is converted to a VisiCalc row, and fields are converted to columns in the row. The database field names are used as the headings for each column in the spreadsheet file. |
| WKS | Lotus 1-2-3 release 1A (WKS) format. Each record is converted to a row, and fields are converted to columns in the row. The database field names are used as the headings for each column in the spreadsheet file. |

When specifying a file name, do not use the single letters A through J, or M. You can specify a file name such as AA, or other double-letter combinations.

You can use indirect file names as the <*filename*>, which is much faster than using macro substitution file names. If fields in the database were protected with PROTECT, only those fields for which the user has privileges are copied to the new file.

### Example

```
USE CUSTOMERS                     && open the database
* Create a WKS file with these fields
COPY TO CUSTOMER TYPE WKS FIELDS COMPANY, CRED_AMT, PAST_DUE
* Create a delimited text file for records
* whose PAST_DUE field is greater than 1000
outfile = "PASTDUE"               && use indirect reference
COPY TO (outfile) TYPE DELIMITED FOR PAST_DUE < 1000
```

## COPY TO...STRUCTURE EXTENDED

### Syntax

```
COPY TO <filename> STRUCTURE EXTENDED
```

### Control Center Procedure

None.

### Purpose

Creates a new file whose records describe the structure of the current file. The new file is organized as follows:

| | |
|---|---|
| FIELD_NAME | Field name |
| FIELD_TYPE | Field type (Character, Numeric, and so on) |
| FIELD_LEN | Field Length |
| FIELD_DEC | Number of decimal places (Numeric or Floating field type only) |
| FIELD_IDX | Index flag |

You can use this command to document the structure of your database files. You then can use these structure files to re-create missing database files or temporary database files needed by your program. You also can use COPY TO to create database structures based on user input (see the example for CREATE FROM).

### Example

```
* Create a STR structure database from the current database
* the CUSTOMER.DBF's structure file is called CUSTOMER.STR
USE CUSTOMER
COPY TO CUSTOMER.STR STRUCTURE EXTENDED
```

## COPY TO ARRAY

### Syntax

```
COPY TO ARRAY <array name> [FIELDS <field list>]
   [<scope>]
   [FOR <condition>]
   [WHILE <condition>]
```

### Purpose

Takes the contents of one or more records from the current database and fills an existing array. The array must already have been created with DECLARE. Make sure that the array is big enough to hold the data from the database.

Field data from the first record is stored in the first column of the array; the second data field is stored in the second column, and so on. The next record is stored in the next row of the array. The array is filled within any restrictions you impose with scope, FOR, or WHILE, until all array elements are filled. The data types of the array elements are the same as the data types in the fields you specify.

### Example

```
* Fill up the CUST_ARRAY array with data from
* the customer data file
USE CUSTOMER
NUM_RECS = RECCOUNT()                && number of records
DECLARE CUST_ARRAY[num_recs, 3]      && make the array
COPY TO ARRAY CUST_ARRAY FIELDS CUST_NUM, PAYMENT, PAYDATE
```

## COUNT

### Syntax

```
COUNT [TO <memory variable>]
   [<scope>]
   [FOR <condition>]
   [WHILE <condition>]
```

### Purpose

Counts the number of records in the database that meet the scope, FOR, or WHILE condition. The count can be stored in a memory variable with the TO option. In a network, the database is locked for the user until the count is completed. If you are on a network and used SET LOCK OFF, the database is not locked, but you may not get an accurate count if another user also is using the database.

### Example

```
* Find the number of stocks that cost more than $50/share
USE STOCKS
COUNT FOR COST > 50 TO counter
? "Items found: ", counter
```

## CREATE FROM

### Syntax

```
CREATE <filename> FROM <structure extended file>
```

### Control Center Procedure

None.

### Purpose

Creates a database file from the structure specified in the parameter *<structure extended file>*. CREATE FROM can be used to create databases with a structure defined by the user. When the database file is created, it becomes the active file in the current work area. If the structure extended file has a Y in the FIELD_IDX field, a production MDX file is created for the new database.

### Example

```
* Create an empty structure file that can be used for
* creating a database based on user input.
* Assume that the user has specified the following fields
* for the ORDERS database by answering
* on-screen questions
* FIELD NAME     TYPE       LENGTH     DEC      IDX
* LASTNAME       Character    15                  Y
* PAID           Numeric       5        2
USE CUSTOMER           && any database file is OK
COPY TO ORDERS.STR STRUCTURE EXTENDED
* Use the new structure database
USE ORDERS.STR
ZAP                    && empty it
* Create the record for the first field (NAME)
APPEND BLANK
REPLACE FIELD_NAME WITH "LASTNAME", FIELD_TYPE WITH "C", ;
   FIELD_LEN WITH 15
* Create the record for the PAID field
```

```
APPEND BLANK
REPLACE FIELD_NAME WITH "PAID", FIELD_TYPE WITH "N", ;
   FIELD_LEN WITH 5, FIELD_DEC WITH 2
USE                 && close the database
* Now create the ORDERS.DBF from the structure file
CREATE ORDERS FROM ORDERS.STR
```

# CREATE/MODIFY APPLICATION

### Syntax

```
CREATE APPLICATION <filename>/?
MODIFY APPLICATION <filename>/?
```

### Control Center Procedure

CREATE APPLICATION: From the Control Center, highlight <create> in the Applications panel, select Applications Generator, and press Enter.

MODIFY APPLICATION: From the Control Center, highlight the application name, press Enter, select Modify Application, and press Enter.

### Purpose

Starts the dBASE IV Applications Generator. The Applications Generator creates or modifies the programming code for a complete application, including all the code required for accessing data, printing reports, displaying menus, responding to user selections, and so on. You also can start the Applications Generator from the Control Center.

### Example

```
* Create the Payables application
* (This command is normally used
* at the dot prompt, not in programs)
CREATE APPLICATION payables
```

# CREATE/MODIFY LABEL

### Syntax

```
CREATE LABEL <filename>
```

### Control Center Procedure

CREATE LABEL: From the Control Center, highlight Label Create and press Enter.

### Purpose

Causes the labels design screen to appear. You then can design new label formats that are stored in the label (LBL) file. The label file is added to the current catalog. The labels design screen is interactive, just like the Control Center.

After you create the label, save it and then use LABEL FORM to print the database data in the label format. When you create labels, dBASE IV also creates an LBG file that contains the program commands for printing the label. You can look at or change this file with MODIFY COMMAND *<label filename>*. Changes you make to the LBG file, however, are not reflected in the LBL file.

### Example

```
USE CUSTLIST
CREATE LABEL Custmail
```

## CREATE/MODIFY QUERY

### Syntax

```
CREATE/MODIFY QUERY <filename>/?
```

### Control Center Procedure

CREATE QUERY: From the Control Center, highlight <create> under Queries and press Enter.

MODIFY QUERY: From the Control Center, highlight the query name and press Shift-F2.

### Purpose

Accesses the queries design screen to create a new query or modify an existing query. A query extracts records that meet the defined query conditions. You also can use a query to modify records in your database. If you use the ? parameter, dBASE IV shows you a list of available queries. On this list, you can highlight the query you want to use and then press Enter. The query is added to the current catalog.

See Chapter 13 for information on how to use the queries design screen.

### Example

```
* Modify the FINDCUST query
* (This command is normally used at the
* dot prompt, not in a program)
MODIFY QUERY FINDCUST
```

## CREATE/MODIFY REPORT

### Syntax

```
CREATE REPORT <filename>/?
MODIFY REPORT <filename>/?
```

### Control Center Procedure

CREATE REPORT: From the Control Center, highlight <create> in the Reports panel and press Enter.

MODIFY REPORT: From the Control Center, highlight the report name and press Shift-F2.

### Purpose

Brings up the dBASE IV Reports design screen, which enables you to create or modify report forms (FRM files). The Reports design screen enables you to make simple or complex reports based on the active database and any related databases. If you have a catalog open and you have SET CATALOG ON, the report form is added to the catalog. If you use the ? parameter instead of the *<filename>*, dBASE IV shows a list of all report form files in the current drive/directory. You also can access the Reports design screen from the dBASE IV Control Center.

After you save the report form file, a generated report form (FRG) file is created. This file contains the dBASE IV commands required to print the report. You can use MODIFY COMMAND or a text editor to change the FRG file, but changes you make to the FRG file do not affect the FRM file.

When you use dBASE IV to modify a report form created in dBASE III, the form is saved in a dBASE IV format and is no longer usable in dBASE III.

### Example

```
* Change the report form
MODIFY REPORT sales
```

## CREATE/MODIFY SCREEN

### Syntax

```
CREATE/MODIFY SCREEN <filename>/?
```

### Control Center Procedure

Highlight <create> in the Forms column and press Enter to enter the Forms design screen.

### Purpose

Accesses the Forms design screen to create custom screen forms that specify the placement of text and data input fields. CREATE creates a new screen. MODIFY changes existing screen files. Use the ? parameter to choose from a list of screens. See Chapter 9 for more information on screen creation.

### Example

```
* Change the INV_EDIT screen format
* (This command is normally used at the
* dot prompt, not within programs)
MODIFY SCREEN INV_EDIT
```

## CREATE/MODIFY STRUCTURE

### Syntax

```
CREATE <filename>

MODIFY STRUCTURE
```

### Control Center Procedure

CREATE: From the Control Center, highlight <create> and press Shift-F2 or Enter.

### Purpose

Takes you to the database file design screen to create a file or to modify the structure of the existing file. You specify the field names, types, lengths, and the presence of an MDX tag for each field in your database. The database file is created in the current drive and directory, unless you specify another drive or directory. If a catalog is active, the created database is added to the current catalog. The *<filename>* parameter can be an indirect file name.

The structure of all database files is shown in table R.8.

**Table R.8 Database Structure**

| Item | Description |
|---|---|
| FIELD NAME | The name of the field, up to 10 characters long. Use letters, numbers, and the underline (_) character. Spaces and other punctuation marks are not allowed, and the first character of the field name must be a letter. Press Enter to finish the field name. |
| TYPE | The type of field, specified by the first letter of the allowed types. Field types are Character, Numeric (Binary Coded Decimal), Floating point numeric, Logical (.T./.F., Y/N), Date, and Memo. You also can press the space bar until the desired field type is displayed. Press Enter to finish. |

| Item | Description |
|---|---|
| WIDTH | The width of the field. For character fields, the width is the maximum number (up to 254) of characters allowed in the field. Numeric fields can be up to 20 digits, including the decimal point and sign. |
| DECIMAL PLACES | For numeric fields, the number of decimal places allowed. |
| MEMO | A memo field. Memo fields show as `memo` on-screen (when the associated memo DBT file is empty) or as `MEMO` if the DBT file has data. |
| LOGICAL | One-character fields that hold a T (true) or F (false), or Y (Yes) or N (No). |
| DATE | A date field, normally displayed as MM/DD/YYYY. |
| INDEX TAG | If set to Yes or true, a tag is added to the production MDX file, and a production index file is created and updated. |

A database can have up to 255 fields, with up to 4,000 bytes per record. A record size counter is shown on-screen. Instructions and error messages appear at the bottom of the screen. The pull-down menus at the top of the screen also can be used.

When you use the MODIFY STRUCTURE command, you should change names and insert or delete fields in two separate operations, or some data may be lost. You can convert field types from one type to another, but be sure to keep a backup copy of your database until you are sure that the data was converted properly. A backup copy of the database (named <*database*>.DBK) is kept automatically by dBASE IV, but the copy is overwritten with the next MODIFY STRUCTURE command.

If you are a network user, the database file must not be in use by others when you use the MODIFY STRUCTURE command unless you have exclusive use of the data file.

## CREATE/MODIFY VIEW

### Syntax

```
CREATE VIEW <view filename> /? FROM ENVIRONMENT
MODIFY VIEW <filename>
```

### Control Center Procedure

None.

### Purpose

Builds (CREATE) or changes (MODIFY) a view (VUE) file for use with dBASE III Plus. Use the ? parameter to choose from a list of VUE files in the current catalog. The VUE file contains information about all open database files, indexes, and work areas; relations between open database files; the current work area number; active field lists; open format (FMT) files; and any filter conditions that are in effect. Use SET VIEW TO to activate a VUE file.

FROM ENVIRONMENT creates the view file from the dBASE IV environment.

### Example

```
* Create the ADDITEMS view for dBASE III users
CREATE VIEW ADDITEMS FROM ENVIRONMENT
```

## DEACTIVATE MENU

### Syntax

```
DEACTIVATE MENU
```

### Purpose

Deactivates the active menu bar and removes it from the screen, but keeps the menu bar in memory for later use. Because this command always acts on the current menu, you don't need to specify a menu name.

### Example

```
* Deactivate the current menu
DEACTIVATE MENU
```

## DEACTIVATE POPUP

### Syntax

```
DEACTIVATE POPUP
```

### Purpose

Removes the current pop-up from the screen but leaves the pop-up in memory for later use. Any text that was concealed by the pop-up is redisplayed. This command can be used in a program only because a pop-up must be on-screen for it to be deactivated.

### Example

```
* Deactivate the current pop-up
DEACTIVATE POPUP
```

## DEACTIVATE WINDOW

### Syntax

```
DEACTIVATE WINDOW <window name list> / ALL
```

### Control Center Procedure

None.

### Purpose

Clears the windows from the screen but does not delete them from memory. You can redisplay the windows with the ACTIVATE WINDOW command. Any text that was "behind" the window is redisplayed. You can specify a <*window name list*> or use ALL to clear all windows from the screen.

### Example

```
* Clear these two previously loaded windows
DEACTIVATE WINDOW EDIT_WIN, HELP_WIN
```

## DEBUG

### Syntax

```
DEBUG <filename> / <procedure name> [WITH <parameter list>]
```

### Control Center Procedure

None.

### Purpose

Starts the dBASE IV program debugger so that you can see the commands as they execute. You can edit the program or procedure, display the values of expressions, and set breakpoints or stopping points for the program.

The debugger divides the screen into four windows: an edit window, a debug window, a breakpoint window, and a display window.

### Example

```
* Debug the CUSTEDIT program
* (The command is normally used from
* the dot prompt, not in programs)
DEBUG custedit
```

# DECLARE

### Syntax

```
DECLARE <array name 1>
        [{<number of rows>,} <number of columns>]
    {,<array name 2>
        [{<number of rows>,} <number of columns>]
...}
```

### Control Center Procedure

None.

### Purpose

Creates one- or two-dimensional arrays of memory variables. Note that an entry in brackets ([]) is required in an array definition, as in `DECLARE readings[20,3]`. Array names can be up to 10 characters long and can contain letters, numbers, or underscores (_), but the names *must* start with a letter. If only one number is specified, the array is one-dimensional. The maximum size of an array (number of rows * number of columns) is 1170.

### Example

```
* Create the parts and costs array
DECLARE arr_parts[100,2]
DECLARE arr_cost[100]
```

# DEFINE BAR

### Syntax

```
DEFINE BAR <line number> OF <pop-up name>
    PROMPT <character expression>
    [MESSAGE <character expression>]
    [SKIP [FOR <condition>]]
```

### Purpose

Defines a single option (bar) in a pop-up menu. One DEFINE BAR command is needed for each choice in the pop-up. The <*line number*> specifies where the pop-up bar appears. If the line number exceeds the number of lines available in the pop-up window, the user can scroll choices in the pop-up to reach the option.

PROMPT specifies the text to appear on the bar. Any specified line of text that exceeds the width of the bar is truncated to fit. A minimum of one bar is needed for each pop-up.

MESSAGE enables you to display a message, usually on the last line of the screen (message placement can be changed with the SET MESSAGE AT command). MESSAGE normally provides additional information about the pop-up choice (such as a description) and is limited to 79 characters. The SKIP option displays the bar and its text but prevents the user from selecting the option. SKIP FOR displays the bar at all times but allows its selection only if the <*condition*> is met.

### Example

```
* Define two pop-up bars
DEFINE BAR 12 OF PRINTBAR PROMPT "Choice 1"
DEFINE BAR 13 OF PRINTBAR PROMPT "Choice 2"
* Redefine the second choice so that it can't be selected
bar13 = .F.
DEFINE BAR 13 OF PRINTBAR PROMPT "Choice 2";
   SKIP FOR .NOT. bar13
```

## DEFINE BOX FROM

### Syntax

```
DEFINE BOX FROM <print column> TO <print column>
       HEIGHT <number of rows>
   [AT LINE <print line>]
   [SINGLE/DOUBLE/<border definition string>]
```

### Control Center Procedure

None.

### Purpose

Defines the size and style of a box to be printed around lines of text. The left and right edges of the box are defined by the FROM...TO parameters. The HEIGHT parameter specifies the height of the box. Use AT LINE to specify the beginning line number for the top edge of the box; if you don't use AT LINE, the current print line is used.

The box can be made up of single or double lines (SINGLE or DOUBLE), or the characters specified in the <*border definition string*>, which follows the rules of the SET BORDER command.

The _BOX system variable must be set to true for the box to be printed. You use the ?/?? command to specify which text to print in the box.

### Example

```
* Print a box around the title block
DEFINE BOX FROM 20 TO 80 HEIGHT 5 DOUBLE
?    && blank line
? space(40) + "SALES REPORT"
? space(44) + DATE()
```

## DEFINE MENU

### Syntax

```
DEFINE MENU <menu name> [MESSAGE <character text>]
```

### Purpose

Used with the DEFINE PAD command to create a menu bar. Using DEFINE MENU is the first step in creating a menu bar. The command assigns a name to the menu bar. The optional MESSAGE parameter displays a message of up to 79 characters at the bottom of the screen. Any message assigned by the DEFINE PAD command overwrites the MENU message, unless you relocate the message with the SET MESSAGE AT command.

### Example

```
* Define the MAINMENU menu bar
DEFINE MENU mainmenu
```

## DEFINE PAD

### Syntax

```
DEFINE PAD <pad name> OF <menu name>
PROMPT <character expression>
   [AT <row>, <col>]
   [MESSAGE <character expression>]
```

### Purpose

Defines a single pad of a menu bar. A *pad* is a choice that is selected from the main menu. Use DEFINE PAD to specify all of the pads of a menu. You must use the DEFINE MENU command to define the menu name before you define the pad for that menu.

The PROMPT text is displayed inside the menu pad. Each prompt gets one blank space added to the prompt text. The line AT *<row>*, *<column>* defines the starting location of the prompt text; if this information is not specified, the text is displayed in the upper left corner of the screen. You may need to use the SET SCOREBOARD OFF command to prevent the scoreboard from overwriting any pad text on the first line (line 0) of the screen.

When the menu is displayed on-screen, the left- and right-arrow keys are used to move from one pad prompt to another. For each pad, an optional MESSAGE can be displayed at the bottom of the screen; the message can be up to 79 characters long.

### Example

```
* Define a menu
DEFINE MENU print
* Define the four pads of the print menu
DEFINE PAD print1 OF print PROMPT "to printer 1"
DEFINE PAD print2 OF print PROMPT "to printer 2"
DEFINE PAD screen OF print PROMPT "to screen"
DEFINE PAD file OF print PROMPT "to file"
```

## DEFINE POPUP

### Syntax

```
DEFINE POPUP <pop-up name> FROM <row 1>, <col 1>
      [TO <row 2>, <col 2>]
   [PROMPT FIELD <fieldname>]
      / PROMPT FILES [LIKE <skeleton>
      / PROMPT STRUCTURE]
      [MESSAGE <character expression>]
```

### Purpose

Defines a pop-up menu that contains special fields, messages, and a border. The *<pop-up name>* is the name used when you activate the pop-up or use the ON SELECTION POPUP command. The FROM and TO values are coordinates defining the upper left and lower right corners of the pop-up window. The pop-up menu covers any text on-screen within those coordinates. When the pop-up is deactivated, the hidden text is redisplayed.

If you omit the TO coordinates, dBASE IV automatically sizes the pop-up for the longest field and maximum number of lines: the last column will be 79, and the bottom line number will be the line above the status bar (22). If the status bar was turned off with SET STATUS OFF, the number of the last line will be one line less than the maximum number of lines on-screen. The minimum window size is 1 row and 1 column. Any prompt lines that don't fit in the pop-up window can be scrolled as the user moves the cursor through the choices.

Use PROMPT FIELD, PROMPT FILES, or PROMPT STRUCTURE if you don't want to use the DEFINE BAR command to create the menu choices for your pop-up menu. PROMPT FIELD places the contents of the named field for each record in the database in the pop-up window (memo fields are not displayed). The PROMPT FILES command displays the catalog file name in the pop-up window. (The LIKE parameter displays only those catalog files that match the *<skeleton>*.) The PROMPT STRUCTURE option displays the fields of the database, or the fields defined by the SET FIELDS list if you used SET FIELDS ON.

The MESSAGE text appears centered at the bottom of the screen, overwriting any other text in that position, including any SET MESSAGE TO text.

### Example

```
* Define the popups
DEFINE POPUP edit_pop from 3,4 TO 10,10
DEFINE POPUP show_pop from 3,15 TO 12,23
DEFINE POPUP prnt_pop from 3,30 TO 8,41
```

## DEFINE WINDOW

### Syntax

```
DEFINE WINDOW <window name> FROM <row 1>, <col 1>
      TO <row 2>, <col 2>
   [DOUBLE/PANEL/NONE/<border definition string>]
   [COLOR [<standard>] [, <enhanced>] [,<frame>]]
```

### Purpose

Defines a window's name, placement, borders, and screen colors. The FROM parameter determines the upper left corner of the window, and the TO parameter sets the lower right corner. The default border is a single-line box; you can specify DOUBLE for a double-line box or NONE for no lines around the border. The *<border definition string>* follows the rules of the SET BORDER command. Don't use characters 7, 8, 10, 12, 13, 27, or 127 in the border definition string, because these characters can cause printing problems.

The COLOR option enables you to specify the foreground and background colors used for standard and enhanced characters, and the foreground and background colors used for the frame. Colors are specified in the same way they are with SET COLOR TO. Windows you create with the DEFINE WINDOW command are displayed with the ACTIVATE WINDOW command.

### Example

```
* Define a double-line window
DEFINE WINDOW edit_win FROM 3,10 TO 12,70 DOUBLE
```

# DEFINE WINDOW

### Syntax

```
DEFINE WINDOW <window name> FROM <row 1>, <col 1> TO <row 2>, <col 2>
   [DOUBLE/PANEL/NONE/<border definition string>]
   [COLOR [<standard>] [,<enhanced>] [,<frame>]]
```

### Control Center Procedure

None.

### Purpose

Defines screen windows, borders, and colors. See the DEFINE WINDOW command for an example and a complete discussion of the options.

# DELETE

### Syntax

```
DELETE
   [<scope>]
   [FOR <condition>]
   [WHILE <condition>]
```

### Control Center Procedure

From the Control Center, highlight the database file and press Shift-F2. Then select Mark Record For Deletion from the Records menu.

### Purpose

Marks records for deletion in the current database. The records are not removed from the database until you use the PACK command. Records marked for deletion can be unmarked with the RECALL command (see RECALL).

The DISPLAY and LIST commands show marked records with an asterisk (*) in the first column. If the status bar is on-screen (SET STATUS ON), `Del` is displayed on the status bar to indicate marked records. Use Ctrl-U to alternately mark or recall records. To mark groups of records for deletion, use the scope, FOR *<condition>*, or WHILE *<condition>*.

DELETE only marks records for deletion. To delete files, use the ERASE command (*see ERASE*).

### Example

```
* Remove all inactive customers
* (Make sure that the date is set correctly!)
USE CUSTOMERS             && open the database
* Mark all records whose last order was more than
* one year ago
DELETE FOR YEAR(Last_ord) < Year(Date())
* Recall customers with no order date, since
* these are probably new customers
RECALL FOR ISBLANK (Last_ord)
* Permanently delete marked records
PACK
```

## DELETE FILE

### Syntax

```
DELETE FILE <filename> / ?
```

### Control Center Procedure

From the Control Center, press F10, select Tools and DOS Utilities, highlight the file, press F10, and select Delete, Single File from the Operations menu.

### Purpose

Deletes files from disk. The ? parameter displays a list of files that you can select for deletion (*see ERASE*).

### Example

```
* Remove temporary database
DELETE FILE TEMP.DBF
```

## DELETE TAG

### Syntax

```
DELETE TAG
   <tag name 1> [OF <MDX filename>]
   [,<tag name 2> [OF <MDX filename>]
   ...]
```

### Control Center Procedure

From the Control Center, highlight the database file, press F2 and then F10, select Organize, and select Remove Unwanted Index Tag.

### Purpose

Removes index tags from multiple-index (MDX) files if you specify tag names. If you specify index file names, the specified indexes are deleted but not closed. This command enables you to remove from the MDX file any index tags that will not be needed. This may speed up operations that move through the database, such as DISPLAY or LIST.

You also can use DELETE TAG if you are approaching the limit of 47 tags per single MDX file.

You can specify more than one index tag name to be deleted from the MDX file. If you delete all index tags from an MDX file, the MDX file also is deleted.

### Example

```
* Remove the CITY tag from the MEMBER.MDX file
USE MEMBER INDEX MEMBER.MDX
DELETE TAG CITY OF MEMBER.MDX
```

## DEXPORT

### Syntax

```
DEXPORT SCREEN/REPORT/LABEL <filename> [TO <BNL filename>]
```

### Control Center Procedure

None.

### Purpose

Creates a Binary Named List (BNL) file from a screen, report, or label design file that can be used with the DGEN() function to generate dBASE code. dBASE IV uses the following file extensions for BNL files:

| | |
|---|---|
| Screens | .snl |
| Reports | .fnl |
| Labels | .lnl |

### Example

```
DEXPORT SCREEN MYFORM.SCR TO MYFORM.BNL
```

## DIRECTORY/DIR

### Syntax

```
DIRECTORY/DIR
   [[ON] <drive>:]
   [[LIKE] [<path>] <skeleton>]
```

### Control Center Procedure

From the Control Center, press F10 and select Tools and DOS Utilities.

### Purpose

Shows a list of files that match the optional <*skeleton*>; this command is similar to the DOS DIR command. If you don't specify a file skeleton, only database files are listed. For database files, the file name, number of records, file size (in bytes), and amount of remaining space on the disk are shown. A DIR listing of other files shows only the file names. (The file information may not be current unless SET AUTOSAVE is ON. See SET AUTOSAVE.)

### Example

```
DIR                   && show all DBF files in current directory
DIR *.FMT             && show only the format files in
                      && current directory
DIR CL*               && show only DBF files starting with CL
DIR D:\DBASE4\DATA    && show DBF files in D:\DBASE4\DATA\
```

## DISPLAY

### Syntax

```
DISPLAY
DISPLAY FILES
DISPLAY HISTORY
DISPLAY MEMORY
DISPLAY STATUS
DISPLAY STRUCTURE
DISPLAY USERS
```

### Control Center Procedure

From the Control Center, highlight a database file and press Enter, select Display Data, and press Enter.

### Purpose

These commands are similar to their LIST equivalents but show only one screenful at a time. A prompt reminds you to press a key to continue with the display. See the equivalent LIST command for a detailed discussion of the DISPLAY commands.

## DISPLAY/LIST HISTORY

### Syntax

```
DISPLAY/LIST HISTORY
   [LAST <number>]
   [TO PRINTER/TO FILE <filename>]
```

### Control Center Procedure

None.

### Purpose

Shows a history of the commands that were entered from the dot prompt. The history buffer normally contains the last 20 commands, but you can change the number of commands to record with the SET HISTORY command.

LIST HISTORY scrolls through the contents of the history buffer without pausing until it reaches the end of the list. DISPLAY HISTORY produces a pause at each screenful of history.

### Example

```
* List last 15 commands to printer
LIST HISTORY LAST 15
EJECT     && send out formfeed
```

## DISPLAY/LIST MEMORY

### Syntax

```
DISPLAY MEMORY [TO PRINTER / TO FILE <filename>]
LIST MEMORY [TO PRINTER / TO FILE <filename>]
```

### Purpose

Shows on-screen the names, contents, and other information of all memory variables. DISPLAY pauses at each screenful of the display, LIST continues until all memory variables are displayed (or until you press the Esc key). You can send the memory variables to the printer with TO PRINTER or to a file with TO FILE *<filename>*.

The LIST/DISPLAY MEMORY command shows the following information: variable name, values, whether the memory variable is public or private, the program that created the memory variable, the number of memory variables used, and the number available.

You can use this command to show the contents of memory variables at various moments during program execution. You also can store the data in a file for viewing at a later time when troubleshooting a program.

### Example

```
* Store the contents of memvars in a file
Name = "Wayne Ash"
City = "Auburn"
Sales = 1625.22
When = "Before changes"
LIST MEMORY TO FILE BEFORE.TXT
Name = "Greg Thorsell"
```

```
City = "Roseville"
Sales = 448.28
When = "After changes"
LIST MEMORY TO FILE AFTER.TXT
```

## DISPLAY/LIST STATUS

### Syntax

```
DISPLAY/LIST STATUS [TO PRINTER/TO FILE <filename>]
```

### Control Center Procedure

None.

### Purpose

Gives you detailed information about the current status of your dBASE IV session. DISPLAY pauses with each screenful of data; LIST scrolls to the end of the status listing without pausing. You can send the information to the printer with TO PRINTER or to a file with TO FILE *<filename>*. You will find this command very useful when you debug programs.

The status report includes information on each open database file: the current work area number, database drive/path/file name, read-only status, open index files (NDX and MDX), file names of memo files, filter formulas, database relations, and format files. You also see the current file search path, the default disk drive, print destination, any loaded binary program modules, the currently selected work area, printer left-margin setting, and the current procedures file. Also listed are the reprocess and refresh count, settings for devices, currency symbols, delimiter symbols, the number of open files, ON command settings, most SET command settings, and function key assignments. If low-level files are being used, information about these files also is displayed. (See the section, "Using Functions," for a list of low-level file functions.)

### Example

```
* Save the current status to a file for later viewing
LIST STATUS TO FILE STATUS01.TXT
```

## DISPLAY/LIST USERS

### Syntax

```
DISPLAY USERS
LIST USERS
```

### Purpose

Shows a list of network users who are logged on. The DISPLAY command produces a pause after each screenful of user names; the LIST command scrolls through the list until it reaches the end. If two users log in under the same name, that name appears only once on the list.

### Example

```
* Show list of current users
@ 12,10 SAY "Current User List"
DISPLAY USERS
```

## DO

### Syntax

```
DO <program filename> / <procedure name>
   [WITH <parameter list>]
```

### Control Center Procedure

From the Control Center, highlight the application name, press Enter, and select Run Application.

### Purpose

Runs a program file or procedure. The DO command compiles the program specified in *<program filename>* (if the program is not compiled already), saves it as a DBO file, and then runs the DBO file. The compiled program runs faster than an equivalent, noncompiled program, such as those programs created in dBASE III.

WITH *<parameter list>* enables you to pass parameter variables to a procedure. The procedure must have a PARAMETERS statement, and the types of variables used in the DO and PARAMETERS command must match. You can use the DO command at the dot prompt or from a program file.

In most cases, if the program you specify in a DO command is a dBASE III program, DO compiles and saves it as a dBASE IV program.

### Example

```
* Run the CENTER MESSAGE procedure, passing the message
* text as the first parameter and the line number as
* the second.
* The procedure was loaded with the
* SET PROCEDURE TO command.
```

```
MESSAGE = "Please wait while data is accessed..."
DO CENTER WITH MESSAGE, 12
* This is the Center procedure, which does the actual work
* This is contained in the procedure file
PROCEDURE Center
PARAMETERS Message, line_num
* Figure out where the starting point should be
* The ABS function makes sure that it is positive
startpos = INT (ABS((80-LEN(message))/2))
@line_num, startpos SAY message
RETURN
```

## DO CASE

### Syntax

```
DO CASE
   CASE <condition>
      <commands>
   [CASE <condition>
      <commands>]
   ...
   [OTHERWISE
      <commands>]
ENDCASE
```

### Control Center Procedure

None.

### Purpose

Performs actions based on the available alternatives. The first match for a condition is the one accessed by the program, even if other CASE <*conditions*> could have been applied. The OTHERWISE action is used if none of the CASE <*conditions*> is true. (For more information about DO CASE, see the example for IF.)

### Example

```
* Ask the user to choose items 1-4 or Q (Quit)
* DO the program that matches the choice
DO WHILE .T.              && loop to get choice
   answer = " "
   @ 12,15 SAY "Please enter your choice (1/2/3/4/Q) "
   @ 12, col() GET answer PICTURE "!"
   READ
   * Run the selected program
         DO CASE
            CASE answer = "1"
               DO program1
            CASE answer = "2"
```

```
         DO program2
      CASE answer = "3"
         DO program3
      CASE answer = "4"
         DO program4
      CASE answer = "Q"
         EXIT      && exits DO loop
      OTHERWISE
         @ 13,15 SAY "Please choose 1-2-3-4 or Q to quit"
   ENDCASE
ENDDO
```

## DO WHILE

### Syntax

```
DO WHILE <condition>
   <commands>
   [LOOP]
   [EXIT]
ENDDO
```

### Control Center Procedure

None.

### Purpose

Repeats a series of commands as long as the <*condition*> is true or until an EXIT command is executed. The LOOP option enables you to restart the loop at any point. The SCAN/ENDSCAN command also runs a series of commands while processing a series of records (*see SCAN*).

### Example

```
* Ask a question, and allow only the desired answer
answer = " "
DO WHILE .NOT. answer $ "YN"
   * Ask the question. Note that the question includes
   * the desired answers
   @ 23,15 SAY "Edit another record? (Y/N)"
   @ 23,col() GET answer PICTURE "!"
   READ
   DO CASE
      CASE answer = "Y"
         DO editrec          && editing procedure
           CASE answer = "N"
              EXIT                 && exit DO loop
      ENDCASE
   ENDDO
   RETURN
```

# EJECT

### Syntax

```
EJECT
```

### Control Center Procedure

Highlight a Report or Label form in the Control Center and press Enter. Select Print. Select Eject Page Now from the Print menu.

### Purpose

Sends a form-feed character to the printer (or line-feeds if _padvance = "LINE FEEDS"), advancing the paper to the top of the next page (top of form). The EJECT command sets the prow() and pcol() values to zero.

**TIP**

Make sure that you position the paper in your printer correctly. If you use a dot-matrix printer and continuous (fanfold) paper, position the paper so that the perforated edge is above the print head and then turn on the printer. Some printers automatically feed the paper to the proper position. If you have a laser printer, make sure that the form-feed light is not on.

You can use the PRINTSTATUS() function to make sure that the printer is turned on and ready before you issue an EJECT or other printing command.

### Example

```
* Print contents of memory variables
LIST MEMORY TO PRINT
* Send a form-feed
EJECT
```

# EJECT PAGE

### Syntax

```
EJECT PAGE
```

### Control Center Procedure

None.

### Purpose

Tells the ON PAGE handler to advance the paper to the next page by sending the correct number of line feed commands to the printer. EJECT PAGE also performs any other functions defined by the ON PAGE command, such as printing page headers or footers. This command increases the page number system variable (_pageno) and sets the _plineno and _pcolno variables to zero.

### Example

```
* Send a page eject, using the page handler
* previously defined with ON PAGE
EJECT PAGE
```

## ERASE/DELETE FILE

### Syntax

```
ERASE <filename> / ?
DELETE FILE <filename> / ?
```

### Control Center Procedure

From the Control Center, press F10, select Tools and DOS Utilities, highlight the file, press F10, and select Delete, Single File from the Operations menu.

### Purpose

Removes a file from disk. These commands are equivalent to the DELETE or ERASE commands in MS-DOS. The *<filename>* parameter must include the file extension. The ? parameter shows you a menu of files. If you erase a database (DBF) file, you also may need to erase the associated memo (DBT) and multiple-index (MDX) files. You cannot use wild cards (*, ?) with the ERASE/DELETE command. The *<filename>* must be closed before you can delete it.

### Example

```
* Delete the CUSTTEMP.DBF file and its memo file
ERASE CUSTTEMP.DBF        && assumes file is not in use
ERASE CUSTTEMP.DBT        && delete the memo file
ERASE CUSTTEMP.MDX        && and the multiple-index file
```

## EXPORT TO

### Syntax

```
EXPORT TO <filename>
   [TYPE] PFS/DBASEII/FW2/FW3/FW4/RPD/WK1
   [FIELD <field list>]
   [<scope>]
   [FOR <condition>]
   [WHILE <condition>]
```

### Control Center Procedure

From the Control Center, highlight the database file, press F10, and select Tools and Export.

### Purpose

Creates files that other programs can use. PFS:File, dBASE II, Framework, Lotus 1-2-3, and RapidFile file types are supported. For other file types, use the COPY command (see COPY). If an index is in use, the records are exported in index order.

If the *<filename>* already exists, it is overwritten without warning unless you used SET SAFETY ON. You can specify individual fields with the FIELD option. You can export parts of the database by using the scope, FOR, or WHILE options.

### Example

```
* Export the indicated fields to a RapidFile database
* Use the order specified by the CL_ZIP (Client ZIP Code) index
USE CLIENTS ORDER CL_ZIP
EXPORT TO CLIENTS TYPE RPD FIELDS CUSTOMER, CITY,;
   STATE, ZIP_CODE
```

## FIND

### Syntax

```
FIND <literal key>
```

### Control Center Procedure

From the Control Center, highlight the database file, press F2 and then F10, select Go To, and select Index Key Search.

### Purpose

Finds the first record in an indexed file that matches the *<literal key>*. The index key type must match the literal key type. FIND is a fast way to get to a specific record because it looks up the record in the index file instead of looking at each record's data. FIND is similar to SEEK. FIND can search only for a character or numeric string; SEEK can search for an expression.

FIND and SEEK use an index (NDX) or multiple-index (MDX) file. In a multiple-index file, the controlling or master index matches the literal key. You can specify a specific index tag or file by using the SET ORDER TO command (*see SEEK, SET ORDER TO*).

FIND looks in the master index for an exact match of the literal key, unless you used SET EXACT OFF. (See the following example.) FIND ignores records marked for deletion if you used SET DELETED ON. Any records not part of the SET FILTER command also are ignored.

SET NEAR ON gets the record that is the nearest match for the literal key in case an exact match is not found. With SET NEAR OFF, an unsuccessful FIND results in the placement of the record pointer at EOF().

Note that with the FIND command, you don't need to use quotes around the literal key as you do with the SEEK command.

### Example

```
* Find a record where CITY="FORT WORTH"
USE CLIENT ORDER CITY
SET EXACT ON
FIND "FORT WORTH"    && finds only "FORT WORTH"
* Equivalent SEEK command, note quotes in command
SET EXACT OFF
FIND "FORT"          && will find "FORT WORTH", or
                     && "FORT MYERS", or "FORT COLLINS", and so on.
```

## FUNCTION

### Syntax

```
FUNCTION <procedure name>
```

### Control Center Procedure

None.

### Purpose

Inserted to indicate a user-defined function (UDF). UDFs perform processes that may not be available among the existing dBASE IV functions. Functions can be stored in the currently executing file, a procedure file, or any other object code file. Functions cannot contain any SQL commands, but you can use functions with non-SQL commands in an SQL program file.

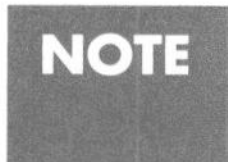


In every DBO file, dBASE IV maintains a list of functions. You may want to keep all functions in one file to eliminate possible duplicate function definitions.

### Example

```
* Function to compute the total cost of an item
* less any discount
FUNCTION total_cost
PARAMETERS listprice, quantity, discount
* extended cost
ext_cost = (listprice * quantity)
```

```
* Determine a discount amount
disc_amt = 0
IF discount > 0
   disc_amt = ext_cost * discount
ENDIF
* total cost including discount
total_cost = ext_cost - disc_amt
* Return the total cost value
RETURN(total_cost)
```

# GO/GOTO

### Syntax

```
GO/GOTO BOTTOM/TOP [IN <alias>]
```

or

```
GO/GOTO [RECORD] <record number> [IN <alias>]
```

or

```
<record number> [IN <alias>]
```

### Control Center Procedure

From the Control Center, highlight the database file, press F2 and F10, and select Go To, the Record number.

### Purpose

Positions the record pointer on a specific record in a database. BOTTOM and TOP are used to go to the last and first record. If an index is active, TOP goes to the first record according to the index, which may not be record number 1. BOTTOM goes to the end of the database, according to the index. You can go to a specific record number with the RECORD option.

The short version of the command is to simply specify a *<record number>* parameter. The IN *<alias>* option enables you to position the record pointer in another work area. You can use the numbers 1 through 40 or the letters A through J as the *<alias>*, or you can use a file alias.

### Example

```
SELECT 1                      && work area 1
USE INVOICE                   && open the database
GOTO 12                       && to record 12
SELECT 2                      && work area 2
USE CLIENTS ORDER COMPANY     && open database with an index
* If CLIENTS contains 4 records indexed on LASTNAME Field
```

```
* Record #        LASTNAME
*     1           Appleby
*     4           Duncan
*     5           Jones
*     3           Smith
*     2           Zimmerman
GOTO BOTTOM                    && positions to record 2
* Go to a specific record in another work area
recpoint = 32
GOTO recpoint IN INVOICE       && record # 32 in INVOICE.DBF
```

# HELP

### Syntax

```
HELP <dBASE IV keyword or command>
```

### Control Center Procedure

From any screen, press F1.

### Purpose

Enables you to get help on any dBASE IV command. If you specify a dBASE IV keyword or command, you are given information about that command. Issuing the HELP command without a keyword brings you to the main Help menu. You also can press the F1 key to access the Help menu.

Press Esc when you want to exit Help. The Help text you last consulted remains on-screen so that you can refer to it as you type the command. When you press Enter, the Help text disappears.

# IF

### Syntax

```
IF <condition>
   <commands>
ELSE
   <commands>
ENDIF
```

### Control Center Procedure

None.

### Purpose

Executes a command or series of commands, depending on whether the given *<condition>* is true or false. You can use the IF command only in a program, not at the dot prompt. You can nest several IF statements together, but CASE accomplishes the same effect and is easier to understand.

### Example

```
* Add a discount to the purchase if more than $1000
IF purchase > 1000
   discount = .10           && 10% discount
ELSE
   discount = .02           && 2% discount
ENDIF
* alternative if more than two choices available
* Note that as soon as a condition is true, the discount
* is applied. If the purchase is $700, only the 5% discount
* is used, even though 700 < 5000
DO CASE
   CASE purchase < 500
      discount = 0
   CASE purchase < 1000
      discount = .05
   CASE purchase < 5000
      discount = .10
   OTHERWISE
      discount = .15
END CASE
```

## IMPORT FROM

### Syntax

IMPORT FROM *<filename>* [TYPE] PFS/DBASEII/FW2FW3/FW4/
RPD/WK1/WKS

### Control Center Procedure

From the Control Center, highlight the database file, press F10, and select Tools and Import.

### Purpose

Imports data from non-dBASE IV files to create a dBASE IV database. IMPORT creates dBASE IV files from dBASE II, Framework, RapidFile, PFS:File, and Lotus 1-2-3 files. You must specify the complete file name, including the extension, for each type of file. If you are importing from a dBASE II file, you need to rename the dBASE II file something other than *<filename>*.DBF, such as *<filename>*.DB2. The new dBASE IV file is called *<filename>*.DBF.

A maximum of 255 fields can be created in the dBASE IV file, with up to 254 characters per field. If you import data from a PFS:File database, IMPORT creates the dBASE IV database (DBF), format file (FMT), and compiled format file (FMO), with the same file name but with their respective extensions.

### Example

```
* Import data from a Lotus 1-2-3 release 2.x WK1 file
IMPORT FROM SALES.WK1 TYPE WK1
```

## INDEX ON

### Syntax

```
INDEX [ON <key expression>] [TO <NDX filename>]
   [UNIQUE]
```

or

```
INDEX [ON <key expression>]
   [TAG <tag name>] [OF <MDX filename>]
   [FOR <condition>] [DESCENDING] [UNIQUE]
```

### Control Center Procedure

From the Control Center, highlight the database file, press F2 and then F10, select Organize, and then select Create New Index or Modify Existing Index.

### Purpose

Creates an index to a database to enable fast access to desired records. Indexing does not rearrange the records in the database; it creates a file containing a sorted order of record pointers to the database.

You can index on any type of field except logical or memo fields. You may need to convert one type of data to another if your *<key expression>* includes multiple fields. The resulting index file is stored in the current drive/directory unless you specify otherwise. If the index file already exists, you are asked whether you want to overwrite the existing file, unless you specified SET SAFETY OFF.

If you use the INDEX command without options or keywords, dBASE prompts you for the index expression. The TAG option enables you to specify the name of the MDX file; if you don't use the TAG option, the tag is placed in the current MDX file.

You can use the FOR option to create an index of only the records matching the condition specified with FOR. The UNIQUE option creates an index of just the unique records, rather than all the records. Indexing is done in ascending order, unless you use the DESCENDING option.

Use FOR as an alternative to SET FILTER TO. FOR gives you much faster operation because the condition is evaluated only if the record is changed. If you use SET FILTER TO, the condition is evaluated every time you move the record pointer. The FOR option may not always be useful if you need to create multiple INDEX...FOR commands every time you want to work with just part of the database.

You can use numeric fields in an index. If you use several numeric fields as part of the index, however, the index is based on the sum of the values. You should use an index that converts the numbers to character strings, as shown in the following example.

If the indexes are not current, use the REINDEX command.

### Example

```
* Index on FIRSTNAME + LASTNAME
USE CLIENTS
INDEX ON FIRSTNAME + LASTNAME TAG NAMES
* Index only records where the state is Texas
INDEX ON STATE TAG TEX FOR STATE="TX"
```

## INPUT

### Syntax

```
INPUT [<prompt>] TO <memory variable>
```

### Purpose

Asks the user to enter characters from the keyboard, which are assigned to the *<memory variable>*. The type of *<memory variable>* created depends on the type of data entered. If the user enters characters, a character variable is created. Numeric entry creates a numeric variable. Date entry creates a date variable. (With a date entry, you must tell the user to use braces [{}] around the date value.) If the memory variable already exists, the new data replaces the old variable data.

**TIP**

INPUT creates character, numeric, or date values, based on user entry. ACCEPT creates only character values. You then can use a conversion function to convert the character value to a numeric or date value. Using ACCEPT might make it easier for the user to enter date values, for example, because the user does not have to remember to place braces ({}) around the date.

### Example

```
* Ask the user for a number, then verify that it is a number
INPUT "Enter a number " TO numval
DO CASE
   CASE TYPE(numval) = "C"        && convert it
      ? "That was a character!"
      numval = val(numval)
   CASE TYPE(numval) = "D"
      numval = dow(numval)
      ? "That was a date! Here's the day number: "
      ?? numval
   CASE TYPE(numval) = "F"
      ? "That was a floating point number!"
   CASE TYPE(numval) = "U"
      ? "You didn't enter anything!"
ENDCASE
*
* This way is actually faster
ACCEPT "Enter a number" TO numval
numval = val(numval)
```

## INSERT

### Syntax

```
INSERT [BEFORE] [BLANK]/[NORGANIZE]
```

### Control Center Procedure

None.

### Purpose

Creates a new blank record. INSERT is similar to the APPEND command, except that records are placed at the current record location, rather than at the end of the database. If the current pointer location is record 48, INSERT creates a new record number 49, with the old record 49 renumbered as record 50. All succeeding records will be renumbered: record 50 is now record 51, 51 becomes 52, and so on.

When a new record is inserted, the empty record is displayed on-screen, and you can enter data. If a format file is active, it displays the record on-screen. Now you can enter data only into the new record; you cannot move to another record. If the record has a memo field, move the cursor to the memo field and press Ctrl-Home to add memo data. After typing your memo data, press Ctrl-End to save the memo data or Esc to escape without saving the memo data. You can use the F1 key to display the various editing keys.

Using the BLANK option creates the record at the current position, but the empty record is not displayed on-screen for editing. Use BROWSE, CHANGE, EDIT, or REPLACE to edit the new record. The BEFORE option creates a record just before the current record. If the current record is record number 84, for example, INSERT BEFORE creates a new record 84.

If you want to have data from the preceding record placed in the new record's fields, use the SET CARRY ON command before the INSERT command (see SET CARRY ON). If you are on a network, you must have exclusive use of the database file before you can use the INSERT command.

The NORGANIZE option prevents using the Organize menu.

The INSERT command usually isn't needed if your files are indexed because an index makes a record appear to be in a position other than its physical record location in the database file. Because INSERT requires records to be physically moved in the database file to make room for the insertion, this command should be avoided when working with large database files.

### Example

```
* Insert a record just before record number 59
USE INVOICE
GOTO 59
INSERT BEFORE
```

## JOIN WITH

### Syntax

```
JOIN WITH <alias> TO <filename>
   FOR <condition>
   [FIELDS <field list>]
```

### Control Center Procedure

None.

### Purpose

Creates a new database file by combining the records and fields from two open databases. Specify the entire drive and directory along with the file name if you want the new database to be placed in a specific drive and directory.

The FIELDS option specifies the fields to be used from each database. If the two source databases have the same field name, you must precede the field name with the alias name, such as CLIENT->STATE. You can join fields of any type (except memo) to the new database. If you forget to exclude memo field types, you will get an error message. You can use the SET FIELDS command before JOIN as an alternative to the FIELD option.

If you want to extract only part of the source database records, use the FOR <*condition*> option.

During the JOIN operation, the record pointer is positioned on the first record in the active database. Then the second database is scanned to see whether it meets the FOR <*condition*>. If the condition is true, a record is added to the new file. The data from all fields (or the fields specified by the FIELDS option or SET FIELDS TO) is added to the new database. After all records from the second database are scanned, the record pointer in the active file is set to the second record. This process continues until the join is complete.

If either of the files is large, the JOIN operation can take a long time. The JOIN command also can create very large files: if the two databases each have 200 records, for example, and the condition is always true, you end up with 40,000 records (200*200).

To build a relationship between two files, use the SET RELATION command instead of the slow, disk-intensive JOIN command.

### Example

```
* Extract all past due accounts (date in PASTDUE
* field older than 30 days) from the SALES database
* into a new OVERDUE.DBF
* Make sure that the CUST_ID field data matches for
* each JOIN operation
SELECT 2              && work area 2
USE SALES
SELECT 1              && work area 1 (active area during JOIN)
USE CUSTOMER
* Alternative is to :
* USE SALES IN 2               && work area 2
* USE CUSTOMER IN 1            && work area 1
* SELECT 1
* These fields will be added to the new database
SET FIELDS TO A->CUST_ID, B->PASTDUE, B->LASTPAY
SET TALK ON           && to see the current record number during JOIN
* Perform the JOIN command for the <condition>
JOIN WITH SALES TO OVERDUE FOR ;
   SALES->PASTDUE < DATE()-30 .AND. ;
   CUSTOMER->CUST_ID = SALES->CUST_ID
```

# KEYBOARD

### Syntax

```
KEYBOARD <character expression> [CLEAR]
```

### Purpose

Places a series of characters into the keyboard buffer. dBASE IV then reads the characters as if the user had typed them. You can place characters into the keyboard buffer up to the limit of the typeahead buffer. The default is 20 characters, unless you use the SET TYPEAHEAD TO command to change the typeahead buffer value.

You can place any of the 255 IBM characters (ASCII values 1 through 255) in the keyboard buffer. You also can use the CHR() function, key labels ("{TAB}"), and numeric ASCII values ({[89]}).

The CLEAR option clears the keyboard buffer. Use CLEAR if you want to clear out, in anticipation of the next keyboard input, any characters the user typed.

### Example

```
* Place the user name in the keyboard buffer
* so that it is input in the next keyboard input command
KEYBOARD CLEAR  && clear the keyboard buffer
username = "JASON"
KEYBOARD username
ACCEPT "Your user name is " TO thisuser
```

# LABEL FORM

### Syntax

```
LABEL FORM <label filename> / ?
   [<scope>]
   [FOR <condition>]
   [WHILE <condition>]
   [SAMPLE]
   [TO PRINTER / TO FILE <filename>]
```

### Control Center Procedure

LABEL FORM: From the Control Center, highlight the label name, press Enter, and select Print Labels.

LABEL FORM...TO PRINT: From the Control Center, highlight the label name, press Enter, and select Print Label.

### Purpose

Uses the *<label filename>* created or modified with the CREATE/ MODIFY LABEL command. All data in the current database is displayed, printed, or sent to a file, based on the design of the label. You can limit the number of labels printed by using a scope, FOR, or WHILE clause. Any active filter (SET FILTER TO) also limits the labels to be created.

If any indexes are active, they determine the order of the printed labels. If the LBL file was created in dBASE III, the dBASE III label engine prints the labels. For labels created with dBASE IV, the LABEL FORM command compiles the label definition into a label object (LBO) file and then processes the labels. A new LBO file is created only if the date and time of the LBG are later than any existing LBO file (unless you used SET DEVELOPMENT OFF).

The SAMPLE option prints a test label on the printer to make sure that the labels are aligned properly. A single row of labels is printed, and a message is displayed asking whether you want more test labels. If the labels did not align properly, adjust the label blanks in the printer, answer Y, and try again until the samples align properly.

The TO FILE option sends the label output to a disk file in the label format. The text file contains any printer codes required by your printer so that you can print labels later by sending this file directly to your printer. The ? option shows you a list of label files from which you can choose.

### Example

```
* Print some mailing labels. Use SAMPLE to align the labels
USE MAILLIST ORDER ZIPCODE
@ 10,20 SAY "A test pattern will print. Align the forms"
@ 11,20 SAY "Press Y to print another label sample, or "
@ 12,20 SAY "Press N to print the mailing labels."
LABEL FORM AV6062 SAMPLE TO PRINT
```

## LIST HISTORY

*See* DISPLAY HISTORY.

## LIST STATUS

*See* DISPLAY STATUS.

## LIST/DISPLAY

### Syntax

```
LIST/DISPLAY
   [[FIELDS] <expression list>]
   [OFF]
```

```
[<scope>]
[FOR <condition>]
[WHILE <condition>]
[TO PRINTER/TO FILE <filename>]
```

### Control Center Procedure

From the Control Center, select the report (or create a new one), press Shift-F2 and F10, and then select either Begin Printing or View Report On Screen from the Print menu.

### Purpose

Shows the contents of the current database on-screen. The DISPLAY command produces a pause at each screenful of data; LIST scrolls all data until the command is completed. You can pause the LIST display by pressing Ctrl-S; press any key to continue. You can press the Esc key to abort LIST or DISPLAY unless you used SET ESCAPE OFF, in which case the Esc key is ignored (*see SET ESCAPE OFF*).

All fields are displayed unless you used the FIELDS option to specify the desired fields. If the combined width of the fields is wider than your display, the rest of the field information is displayed on subsequent screen lines. Memo fields normally are not displayed unless specified in the FIELDS list. If the memo field is empty, `memo` is displayed. If the memo field has data, `MEMO` is displayed. You can use the SET MEMOWIDTH command to limit the width of the memo field when displayed (*see SET MEMOWIDTH*).

You can limit the number of records listed with the scope, FOR, or WHILE options. Use TO PRINTER to print the list; use TO FILE <*filename*> to place the list in a file. The record numbers are displayed unless you use the OFF option.

The field names are shown at the top of the list if SET HEADING is ON (*see SET HEADING ON*).

### Example

```
* Display all records of the ORDERS file that show
* orders on back order (SHIPDATE date field is blank).
* Suppress record numbers from the display.
* All fields will be shown.
USE ORDERS
DISPLAY OFF FOR ISBLANK(SHIPDATE)
* Repeat command, sending list to the printer
* but showing only ITEM, QUANTITY, and SHIPDATE fields
DISPLAY OFF FIELDS ITEM, QUANTITY, SHIPDATE ;
FOR ISBLANK(shipdate)
```

## LIST/DISPLAY FILES

### Syntax

```
LIST/DISPLAY FILES [LIKE <skeleton>]
   [TO PRINTER/FILE <filename>]
```

### Control Center Procedure

From the Control Center, press F10 and select Tools and DOS Utilities.

### Purpose

Shows a list of all files matching the file name shown in *<skeleton>*. LIST/DISPLAY FILES is similar to the DIR command, except that LIST/DISPLAY FILES also enables you to send the files to the printer or to a disk file. The *<skeleton>* parameter specifies a set of files, such as `*.PRG` for all PRG files, or `CUST*.DBF` for all database files starting with "CUST." If you don't specify a file extension, only dBASE IV database (DBF) files are displayed. The DISPLAY FILES command is similar to LIST FILES, except that the former pauses at each screenful of data.

The file name, the number of records (if a DBF file), and the date and time the file was last updated are shown. The total file size and number of files, along with the remaining unused space on the disk, are shown at the end of the list.

### Example

```
* Examples of LIST
LIST FILES     && same as DIR; shows all database files
* Show all format files, one screenful at a time
DISPLAY FILES LIKE *.FMT
* Show all index files (NDX or MDX), plus any file whose
* extension ends with "DX"
LIST FILES LIKE *.?DX
* Create a file containing a list of all DBF files
LIST FILES TO FILE DBFLIST.TXT
```

## LIST/DISPLAY STRUCTURE

### Syntax

```
LIST/DISPLAY STRUCTURE
   [IN <alias>]
   [TO PRINTER/TO FILE <filename>]
```

### Control Center Procedure

From the Control Center, highlight the database file, press Shift-F2 and F10, and select Layout and Print Database Structure.

### Purpose

Shows the structure of the database. The DISPLAY command produces a pause at each screenful of data; LIST scrolls all data until the end of the structure is reached. You can pause the LIST display with Ctrl-S and then press any key to continue. The Esc key aborts the LIST or DISPLAY, unless you used SET ESCAPE OFF, in which case Esc is ignored (*see SET ESCAPE OFF*).

The following information is shown: the database file name, number of records, date and time of the last change, complete information on each field (field name, type, size, index tags), and the total number of bytes per record. The size of one record is the sum of all field widths plus one. The extra byte indicates whether the record is marked for deletion (*see DELETE*).

Normally, the structure of the database in the current work area is displayed. Use the IN *<alias>* option to specify a database in another work area. Use the TO PRINTER option to send the database structure list to the printer. The TO FILE option places the database structure in the specified *<filename>*.

### Example

```
* Display the DBF structure on-screen,
* pausing at each screenful
USE CLIENTS
DISPLAY STRUCTURE
* Send the DBF structure to the printer
DISPLAY STRUCTURE TO PRINTER
* Store the DBF structure in a text file
* (great for database documentation)
LIST STRUCTURE TO FILE CLIENTS.TXT
```

## LOAD

### Syntax

```
LOAD <binary filename>
```

### Control Center Procedure

None.

### Purpose

Loads binary program files into memory. The binary files usually used with this command are assembly language programs that perform low-level functions not available among the dBASE IV or

MS-DOS commands. You can load up to 16 binary files in memory at one time, and each binary file can be up to 64K in size. The LIST/DISPLAY STATUS command shows you which binary files currently are loaded. After loading, binary files are accessed with the CALL command (*see CALL*).

### Example

```
* Load binary file DOSCALLS.BIN
LOAD DOSCALLS
```

## LOCATE

### Syntax

```
LOCATE [FOR] <condition> [<scope>]
   [WHILE <condition>]
```

### Control Center Procedure

From the Control Center, highlight the database file, press F2 and then F10, select Go To, and select Forward or Backward Search.

### Purpose

Searches the current database file for the record that matches the *<condition>*. This operation is a sequential search of the file and therefore can be quite slow compared to an indexed SEEK or FIND. If a match is not found, the record pointer will hold at the end of the file. After a match is found, use the CONTINUE command to look for the next match (*see CONTINUE*). You can use the WHILE option to restrict LOCATE.

When a match is found, the pointer is positioned at the matching record number, and FOUND() is true (*see FOUND*).

### Example

```
* Find the first record that contains "Merger talks" in the
* NOTES memo field. This will be a slow search.
USE WORKDATA
* show number of records
? RECCOUNT()
* show record numbers during LOCATE command
SET TALK ON
LOCATE FOR UPPER(NOTES) = "MERGER TALKS"
* and the results are these:
IF FOUND()
   ? "Found record number ", RECNO()
ELSE
   ? "No match found"
ENDIF
```

# LOGOUT

### Syntax

```
LOGOUT
```

### Purpose

Logs out the current user and establishes a new log-in screen when used with the PROTECT command. The current user is immediately logged out; dBASE IV then prompts for a new group name, log-in name, and password. The LOGOUT command terminates all program files and closes all open databases and their associated files. LOGOUT does not log you out of the network.

### Example

```
* Logoff current user and get new user name
LOGOUT
```

# MODIFY APPLICATION

*See* CREATE/MODIFY APPLICATION.

# MODIFY COMMAND/FILE

### Syntax

```
MODIFY COMMAND/FILE <filename>
   [WINDOW <window name>]
```

### Control Center Procedure

From the Control Center, highlight the application name, press Enter, and select Modify Application.

### Purpose

Activates the dBASE IV program editor and enables you to edit command files (programs), format files, or any text file. The program editor also is available from the Control Center. You can use the optional WINDOW parameter to edit the file in a window (<*window name*>) rather than the one in the active window (if any) or on the full screen (if no window is active). Files can be any size up to the limit of available disk space. Each text line can be up to 1,024 characters long. After you issue the MODIFY COMMAND/FILE command, a menu offering various editing commands appears at the top of the screen.

To use your own word processor to edit files from within dBASE IV, specify the name of the file that starts up your word processor with the TEDIT command in the CONFIG.DB file.

### Example

```
* Edit the CUSTEDIT.PRG program
* (This command is normally used at the
* dot prompt, not in programs)
MODIFY COMMAND custedit
```

## MODIFY LABEL

### Syntax

```
MODIFY LABEL <filename>
```

### Control Center Procedure

MODIFY LABEL: From the Control Center, highlight the label name and press Shift-F2.

### Purpose

Enables you to make changes to an existing label file. Any changes to the label file cause a new label program (LBG) file to be created from the changed label definition. You can use the MODIFY COMMAND <*label filename*> command to change the format of the label. Any changes you make to the LBG file, however, are not reflected in the LBL file.

### Example

```
USE PARTS
MODIFY LABEL BINLABEL
```

## MODIFY QUERY

*See* CREATE/MODIFY QUERY.

## MODIFY SCREEN

### Syntax

```
MODIFY SCREEN
```

*See* CHANGE/MODIFY SCREEN.

## MODIFY STRUCTURE

### Syntax

```
MODIFY STRUCTURE
```

### Control Center Procedure

From the Control Center, highlight the database file and press Shift-F2.

### Purpose

Enables you to change the structure of the current database (*see CREATE/MODIFY STRUCTURE*).

### Example

```
* Change structure of database
USE CLIENTS
MODIFY STRUCTURE
```

## MODIFY VIEW

*See* CREATE/MODIFY VIEW.

## MOVE WINDOW

### Syntax

```
MOVE WINDOW <window name>
   TO <row>, <column> / BY <delta row>, <delta column>
```

### Control Center Procedure

None.

### Purpose

Moves a window to a new screen location. You can move a window by specifying a new location with the TO option, or you can use the BY option to move it relative to its current position. If the window does not fit in its new location, an error message is shown, and the window is not moved. You can use a negative amount to move a window up or to the left of its current position.

### Example

```
* Move the window
MOVE WINDOW edit_win TO 12,3
* Move a window two rows and three columns from current position
MOVE WINDOW edit_win BY 2,3
* Move window up two rows, left 10 rows
MOVE WINDOW edit_win BY -2,-10
```

## NOTE

### Syntax

```
NOTE/* <text>
```

or

```
[<command>] && <text>
```

### Control Center Procedure

None.

### Purpose

Indicates comments or nonexecutable text or lines in a program. (*See* */&&.)

## ON ERROR/ESCAPE/KEY

### Syntax

```
ON ERROR <command>
ON ESCAPE <command>
ON KEY [LABEL <key label name>] [<command>]
```

### Control Center Procedure

None.

### Purpose

Specifies an action to take if an error occurs (ON ERROR), the Esc key is pressed (ON ESCAPE), or a key is pressed (ON KEY). These commands usually are placed at the beginning of the program (although they can be placed anywhere) to change the actions to take.

These commands set a trap that waits for the condition to occur; when it does, the *<command>* is executed. If the specified *<command>* is the name of another program, the commands in that program are executed. If the subprogram contains RETURN, execution of the main program picks up at the line following the statement that sprang the trap. You can cancel the trap by using this command without specifying any action to take (*<command>*), as in ON ERROR.

The ON ERROR command traps only dBASE IV errors, not errors at the operating-system level (such as the `drive not ready` error in MS-DOS). ON ERROR usually is used to trap programming errors. Table R.9 shows the *<key label names>* for the keys that can spring the ON KEY trap.

**Table R.9 Key Label Names**

| Key | Name |
|---|---|
| F1 to F10 | F1, F2, F3... |
| Ctrl-F1 to Ctrl-F10 | CTRL-F1, CTRL-F2, CTRL-F3... |
| Shift-F1 to Shift-F9 | SHIFT-F1, SHIFT-F2, SHIFT-F3... |

*continues*

**Table R.9 Continued**

| Key | Name |
|---|---|
| Alt-0 to Alt-9 | ALT-0, ALT-1, ALT-2... |
| Alt-A to Alt-Z | ALT-A, ALT-B, ALT-C... |
| Ctrl-A to Ctrl-Z | CTRL-A, CTRL-B, CTRL-C... |
| Left arrow | LEFTARROW |
| Right arrow | RIGHTARROW |
| Up arrow | UPARROW |
| Down arrow | DOWNARROW |
| Home | HOME |
| End | END |
| PgUp | PGUP |
| PgDn | PGDN |
| Del | DEL |
| Backspace | BACKSPACE |
| Ctrl-<*left arrow*> | CTRL-LEFTARROW |
| Ctrl-<*right arrow*> | CTRL-RIGHTARROW |
| Ctrl-End | CTRL-END |
| Ctrl-Home | CTRL-HOME |
| Ctrl-PgUp | CTRL-PGUP |
| Ctrl-PgDn | CTRL-PGDN |
| Ins | INS |
| TAB | TAB |
| Back-Tab (Shift-Tab) | BACKTAB |
| Return/Enter | CTRL-M (on most keyboards) |

### Example

```
* Set up error trapping
ON ERROR DO err_trap
* This error trapping program (ERR_TRAP.PRG) or
* procedure code (PROCEDURE ERR_TRAP)
* saves various program information
```

```
PROCEDURE ERR_TRAP
LIST HISTORY TO history.err
LIST STATUS TO status.err
LIST MEMORY TO memory.err
* Close everything
CLOSE ALL
* Print a message
@ 24,0          && clears a line
@ 24,5 say "Error found. Program status saved.
Contact programmer."
WAIT " "     && wait for keystroke before quitting
QUIT
RETURN
```

# ON PAD

## Syntax

```
ON PAD <pad name> OF <menu name>
   [ACTIVATE POPUP <pop-up name>]
```

## Purpose

Associates a pop-up menu with the pad of a menu. When the cursor is placed on the pad of the menu bar, the pop-up menu is displayed. The menus that appear in the dBASE IV Control Center are pop-up menus. When you move the cursor left and right along the menu options (pads) at the top of the screen, the pop-up menus are displayed. The pop-up must be enabled with the ACTIVATE POPUP command; otherwise, the prompt pad is disabled.

# ON PAGE

## Syntax

```
ON PAGE [AT LINE <number> <command>]
```

## Control Center Procedure

None.

## Purpose

Specifies a command program (page handler) to be executed when the print job comes to the specified line *<number>*. (The *<command>* program also is run when the EJECT PAGE command is executed.) The _plineno system variable keeps track of the current printed line number. When this value equals the *<number>* specified after AT LINE, the *<command>* is executed.

The *<command>*, or page handler, typically is a procedure that prints a footer or header on each page before the print job can continue. See the PRINTJOB...ENDPRINTJOB command for an example of the ON PAGE command.

### Example

```
* Before starting report program, set up page handling
* Page break occurs at line 60
* NEW_PAGE is a procedure that does page headings
ON PAGE AT LINE 60 DO new_page
```

## ON READERROR

### Syntax

```
ON READERROR <command>
```

### Control Center Procedure

None.

### Purpose

Specifies the commands to be executed if an error occurs during full-screen editing. These errors include basic errors (such as invalid dates) or user-defined errors (such as input that fails a VALID condition). The *<command>* usually is specified as DO *<command file>*, which recovers from the error or shows a help message for the user. You can disable READERROR by issuing ON READERROR without specifying a *<command>*.

### Example

```
* Activate error trapping for the editing program
ON READERROR DO edit_err
DO editdata          && editing program
ON READERROR         && disable error trapping
```

## ON SELECTION PAD

### Syntax

```
ON SELECTION PAD <pad name> OF <menu name>
   [<command>]
```

### Purpose

Associates a command with a menu bar pad. When you select the pad, the *<command>* is entered. The *<command>* can be a single command, a program file, or a procedure file.

### Example

```
* List some database fields to the printer
* when the pad is selected
ON SELECTION PAD print_pad OF showdata ;
LIST NAME, ADDRESS, CITY TO PRINTER FOR STATE = "AZ"
```

## ON SELECTION POPUP

### Syntax

```
ON SELECTION POPUP <pop-up name> / ALL
[BLANK][<command>]
```

### Purpose

When a pop-up selection is made, the *<command>* is executed. The *<command>* can be a single command, a program file, or a procedure file. The ALL option specifies that the *<command>* will be executed for all the active pop-ups.

### Example

```
* Show a list of database files
* when the pop-up is chosen
ON SELECTION POPUP dirlist DIR
```

## PACK

### Syntax

```
PACK
```

### Control Center Procedure

From the Control Center, highlight the database file, press F2 and F10, and select Organize and Erase Marked Records.

### Purpose

Removes any records that are marked for deletion in the current database. If any indexes are open, the database is automatically reindexed.

The DELETE command marks records for deletion. The records are not actually deleted from the file, however, until you use the PACK command. You can unmark a record with the RECALL command if you do so before you use PACK (*see DELETE, RECALL*).

If any NDX indexes are associated with the file, make sure that they are activated with the USE...INDEX *<index names>* command or the SET INDEX TO command to ensure that the indexes are kept up-to-date. (MDX files updated automatically.) If the files are not active during the PACK command, you may have problems accessing the data. A quick REINDEX, however, cures that problem.

### Example

```
* Remove deleted records, reindex
* CLIENTS.MDX is the multiple-index file
USE CLIENTS INDEX CLIENTS
```

```
PACK
* ZIP and NAME are NDX files
USE NAMELIST INDEX ZIP,NAME
PACK
```

## PARAMETERS

### Syntax

```
PARAMETERS <parameter list>
```

### Control Center Procedure

None.

### Purpose

Assigns local variable names to a list of variables passed from a calling program. This command usually is used in procedures or functions because variables that are public are available to called programs. The local variables are released when the procedure or function is completed. The variables in the *<parameter list>* can be changed and returned to the calling program. See examples under PROCEDURE and FUNCTION.

## PLAY MACRO

### Syntax

```
PLAY MACRO <macro name>
```

### Control Center Procedure

From the Control Center, press F10 and select Tools, Macros, and Play.

### Purpose

Plays back the macro commands assigned to *<macro name>* that are contained in the current macro library. Use the RESTORE MACROS command to load a macro library file. Macros are identified by their macro key, which is assigned when the macro is created. You can assign macro keys as Alt-F1 through Alt-F9, or Alt-F10 followed by a letter (A through Z). Each macro library file can contain up to 35 unique macros.

### Example

```
* Load a macro file, play the DATA_IN macro
RESTORE MACROS FROM DATAMAC
PLAY MACRO DATA_IN
```

## PRINTJOB...ENDPRINTJOB

### Syntax

```
PRINTJOB
<commands>
ENDPRINTJOB
```

### Control Center Procedure

None.

### Purpose

Sends a series of programming commands to the printer as part of a print job. Any print job-related settings (such as _pbpage, the beginning printer page) or commands (such as ON PAGE), should be included as part of the print job. See "Using System Variables" elsewhere in this "dBASE IV Reference Guide" for information about print job-related settings.

The PRINTJOB...ENDPRINTJOB command can be used in a program only, not from the dot prompt. Print jobs cannot be nested; only one print job can be active at a time.

### Example

```
* Print a quick list of the inventory
USE INVENTRY ORDER INVENTRY
_peject = "AFTER"        && eject the last page
SET PRINT ON
PRINTJOB
* At the end of the page, do the
* pagehead program or procedure
ON PAGE AT LINE _plength-1 do pagehead
SCAN
   * print the field information for each record
   ? item_num, item_name, instock, backorder
ENDSCAN
ENDPRINTJOB
SET PRINT OFF
RETURN
* end of program fragment
*
* This is the pagehead procedure, contained in
* the procedure file enabled with SET PROCEDURE TO
PROCEDURE pagehead
EJECT PAGE
? "Run Date", DATE(), TIME(), "Page " AT 65, ;
     _pageno PICTURE "999" AT 70
?
?
RETURN
* End of pagehead procedure
```

# PRIVATE/PRIVATE ALL

### Syntax

```
PRIVATE ALL [LIKE / EXCEPT <skeleton>]
PRIVATE <memory variable list>
```

### Purpose

Creates a local memory variable that can be different from a memory variable with the same name if that memory variable was created in a higher-level program. You can use PRIVATE on a single memory variable or on a list of memory variables. A <*skeleton*> enables you to specify memory variables with similar names. The skeleton "sum*", for example, could be used to make private all memory variables that start with sum.

The public availability of memory variables becomes important when one program executes another, as often occurs in common structured programming (see Part IV). Suppose that program A executes, or *calls*, program B. Because memory variables in program B are local by default, they are available only to program B. When program B finishes, program A continues, and any private variables in program B are cleared. If you want to share program B's variables with program A, program B's variables must be declared as public.

### Example

```
* Declare some memvars as private
PRIVATE ALL LIKE b_*
PRIVATE username
* These are all explicitly private variables
b_item1 = "Hard disk"
b_item2 = "Monitor"
b_item3 = 155.33
username = "Jason"
* This is implicitly private to this program ordernum = 52338
```

# PROCEDURE

### Syntax

```
PROCEDURE <procedure name>
```

### Control Center Procedure

None.

### Purpose

Marks the beginning of a subroutine. Most frequently used procedures are short subroutines that perform actions which can be used by many calling programs. You can store procedures in the file currently executing or combine them with other procedures in a procedure file. The SET PROCEDURE command enables procedure files.

Procedures can have parameters passed through them. Parameters can be explicitly passed with a DO...WITH command, or they can be implied with public variables. You can have up to 963 procedures per file. All procedure code segments must start with PROCEDURE and end with RETURN. Procedure names are up to nine characters long and can contain letters, numbers, or underscores (_). Procedure names must begin with a letter. (Actually, procedure names are of unlimited length, but only the first nine characters are used by dBASE.)

Procedures execute faster than separate files because they are preloaded into memory.

### Example

```
* Procedure to center a message at the indicated line
PROCEDURE center
PARAMETERS message, line_num   && passed from calling program
*
* Figure out where the starting point should be
* The ABS function makes sure that it is positive
startpos = INT(ABS((80-LEN(message))/2))
@line_num, startpos SAY message
RETURN
* end of center procedure
```

## PROTECT

### Syntax

```
PROTECT
```

### Control Center Procedure

From the Control Center, highlight the database file, press F10, and select Tools and Protect Data.

### Purpose

Creates and maintains security for dBASE IV files. This menu-driven process is issued by the database administrator. When you issue the PROTECT command, you are asked for the administrator password. (If a password does not exist, you create one at this time.)

> **WARNING:** The administrator password is important. You cannot access the security system without supplying the password. You can change the password only if you enter the correct password when you invoke PROTECT. If you forget the password, you cannot retrieve it from the system, and any files protected by the password are unavailable. You should write the password down on paper, but keep the paper in a secure area (under lock and key—not taped to the computer).

The following list describes the three types of database protection:

- *Log-in security*. Prevents access to the database by unauthorized persons.
- *Field and file security*. Can prevent access to certain fields in a database or certain files.
- *Data encryption*. Encrypts dBASE IV files so that they cannot be read.

## PUBLIC

### Syntax

```
PUBLIC <memory variable list> / ARRAY
<array name 1> [{<number of rows>,} <number of columns>]
{, <array name 2> [{<number of rows>,} <number of columns>
  ] ...}
```

### Purpose

Makes selected memory variables available to all programs. Note that if you use array names, you should use brackets for the number of array elements, as in `my_array[4,12]`. You must declare a variable as public before you can assign a value to it. Memory variables created from the dot prompt are made public automatically. Memory variables created by a program file are normally private, unless you first declare them as public.

If you declared a memory variable public, subprograms can change the values, and the changed values are kept for the main program. Public variables start as logical type variables until you assign a value to them. You can use the LIST/DISPLAY MEMORY command to show whether a memory variable is public or private.

### Example

```
* Declare some memvars as public
PUBLIC item1, item2
? TYPE(item1)   && returns "L" for Logical type
item1 = "Wayne"
item2 = 4920
? TYPE(item1), TYPE(item2)&& returns "C" and "N" (Character, Numeric)
```

## QUIT

### Syntax

```
QUIT [WITH <expN>]
```

### Control Center Procedure

From the Control Center, press F10 and select Quit to DOS from the Exit menu.

### Purpose

Ends the current dBASE IV session. Any open files are closed, and you are returned to the DOS prompt (or your menuing system). The optional WITH clause specifies a value to be returned by dBASE to the calling program or operating system.

> **WARNING:** Using QUIT is the only way that you should exit dBASE IV. If you just turn off your computer or press the reset button, any open data or other files may be damaged, resulting in data loss.

### Example

```
* Ask user whether it's OK to QUIT to DOS prompt
"answer = .F."
   @ 24,15 SAY "Quit to DOS Prompt?";
      GET ANSWER picture "Y"
   READ
IF ANSWER
   QUIT
ELSE
   RETURN
ENDIF
```

## READ

### Syntax

```
READ [SAVE]
```

### *Control Center Procedure*

None.

### *Purpose*

Enables you to enter data in a field or memory variable. READ usually is used in dBASE IV programs to enable full-screen editing or input of record data or multiple memory variables. Several @...GET commands are used to position the input areas on-screen; then the READ command enables you to enter data in fields by typing in those input areas.

The READ command clears the effects of all @...GET commands after completion, unless you use the SAVE option. If you use the SAVE option, make sure that you use the CLEAR GETS command before you do another series of @...GET commands. You also should close any screen format (FMT) files before using the READ command; otherwise, the format file may overwrite part of the screen.

### *Example*

```
* This displays a centered message at line 10 and
* then asks the user to input the information
* The DO loop allows the user to correct the data
* Note that the "answer" loop only allows input
* of the YNQ keys
*
* Initialize the needed variables
mname = SPACE(20)
maddress = SPACE(20)
mcity = SPACE(16)
mstate = SPACE(2)
mphone = SPACE(12)
* center the message on line 10
message = "Please enter information"
@ 10, INT((80-LEN(message))/2) SAY message
* get the information until user says it is OK
DO WHILE .T.
   * display prompts and blank memory variables
   @ 11,20 SAY "Name " GET mname FUNCTION "!"
   @ 12,20 SAY "Addr " GET maddress FUNCTION "!"
   @ 13,20 SAY "City " GET mcity FUNCTION "!"
   @ 13,46 SAY ", "    GET mstate FUNCTION "!"
   @ 14,20 SAY " Tel " GET mphone PICTURE "999-999-9999"
   * Read the data
   READ
   * Ask if all information is correct
   message = "All information OK? (Y/N/Q)"
```

```
    answer = " "   && set up variable for answer
    * Exit this next loop only if answer contains YNQ
    DO WHILE .NOT. answer $ "YNQ"
       * Center message, GET answer
       @ 16, INT((80-LEN(message)/2)) SAY message ;
          GET answer PICTURE "!"
       READ
    ENDDO
    * Exit loop if data OK (answer = "Y")
    * Allow for exit if user wants to quit (answer = "Q")
    * Otherwise loop back to get the information again
    IF answer $ "YQ"
       EXIT
    ENDIF
ENDDO                  && while .T.
IF answer = "Q"
   RETURN              && exit this subprogram
ENDIF
```

# RECALL

### Syntax

```
RECALL
   [<scope>]
   [FOR <condition>]
   [WHILE <condition>]
```

### Control Center Procedure

From the Control Center, highlight the database file, press F2, highlight the marked record, press F10, and select Records and Clear Deletion Mark.

### Purpose

Unmarks records that were marked for deletion with the DELETE command (see DELETE). Only the current record is recalled, unless you specify a scope, FOR, or WHILE clause. You can recall a specific record by using a scope of `RECORD` *<n>*, where *n* is the record number.

> **WARNING:** After the ZAP or the PACK command are used on the database, the records cannot be recalled by dBASE IV and cannot be unerased with an unerasing program.
>
> Be careful if you are using a scope, FOR, or WHILE. You can test your condition or scope by using the LIST/DISPLAY commands (with SET DELETED OFF) to show those records that match the condition. Look carefully at the displayed records to ensure that you are not recalling the wrong records.

Note that SET DELETED must be set to OFF for RECALL to work, unless you specify the record to recall using GOTO or RECALL RECORD <*record number*>.

### Example

```
* Recall the current record
USE INVOICE
GOTO 44
RECALL
* An alternative
USE INVOICE
RECALL RECORD 44
* Recall all records
RECALL ALL
```

## REINDEX

### Syntax

```
REINDEX
```

### Control Center Procedure

From the Control Center, highlight the database file, press F2 and then F10, select Organize, select Modify Existing Index, highlight the index, and press Ctrl-End. (This updates a single index tag only.)

### Purpose

Rebuilds all the single-index (NDX) and multiple-index (MDX) files for the current work area. The tags inside the production MDX file also are updated. If any indexes were created with the UNIQUE option, the rebuilt index still is unique, even if you have SET UNIQUE OFF. In a network, you must have exclusive use of the database file before you can use the REINDEX command. Indexes automatically are updated (if active) during a PACK command.

### Example

```
* Update the index file
USE INVENTORY INDEX INVINDEX
REINDEX
```

## RELEASE

### Syntax

```
RELEASE <memory variable list>
RELEASE ALL [LIKE/EXCEPT <skeleton>]
RELEASE MODULES [<module name list>]
   /MENUS [<menu name list>]
```

```
/POPUPS [<pop-up name list>]
/SCREENS [<screen name list>]
/WINDOWS [<window name list>]
```

### Purpose

Removes memory variables or program modules, menus, pop-ups, screens, or windows. This command enables the memory space used by the variables or modules to be used for other purposes. You can specify a list of specific memory variables (ITEM1, ITEM2), or a skeleton (ITEM*).

In a subprogram, RELEASE ALL deletes all memory variables created in the subprogram or any of its subprograms. Memory variables of higher-level programs are not affected. Using the RELEASE ALL command at the dot prompt deletes all memory variables except system variables.

RELEASE MODULES removes specified program modules (which were loaded into memory with the LOAD command) from memory; do not specify the BIN file name extension. RELEASE MENUS removes the listed menus from the screen and memory, along with any ON SELECTION and ON PAD commands associated with the listed menus. RELEASE POPUPS, RELEASE SCREENS, and RELEASE WINDOWS do the same thing to pop-ups, screens, and windows, respectively.

> **WARNING:** Use the memory variable skeleton pattern carefully. If you use a line like RELEASE ALL LIKE HMEM*, you might delete some needed memory variables. Assign memory variables carefully, or let the end of a subprogram release any private memory variables when it finishes.

### Example

```
* Declare some variables as public
PUBLIC qmem1, qmem2, qmem10, username
STORE 0 to qmem1, qmem2, qmem10
username = "Elizabeth"
* release the qmem1, qmem2, and username variables
* but not the qmem10 variable
RELEASE ALL LIKE qmem?
RELEASE username
```

## RELEASE SCREENS

### Syntax

```
RELEASE SCREENS <screen name list>
```

### Control Center Procedure
None.

### Purpose
Removes a screen from memory. The screen must have been saved previously with the SAVE SCREEN command.

### Example
```
* Release the edit_scrn screen
RELEASE SCREEN edit_scrn
```

## RENAME

### Syntax
```
RENAME <old filename> TO <new filename>
```

### Control Center Procedure
From the Control Center, press F10, select Tools and DOS Utilities, highlight the file, press F10, and select Operations and Rename Single File.

### Purpose
Changes the name of a file from *<old filename>* to *<new filename>*. The complete file name must be specified in both parameters. This command is similar to the RENAME command in MS-DOS.

If you rename a database file, make sure that you also rename any memo or other associated files, such as indexes. When renaming a database file, you can use the MODIFY STRUCTURE command to save the file with the new name. Using the MODIFY STRUCTURE command also saves any associated files with the new name.

### Example
```
* Rename a program file
RENAME CLIENT.PRG TO DATAENT.PRG
```

## REPLACE

### Syntax
```
REPLACE <field> WITH <expression> [ADDITIVE]
   [, <field> WITH <expression> [ADDITIVE] ...]
   [<scope>] [REINDEX]
   [FOR <condition>]
   [WHILE <condition>]
```

### Control Center Procedure

None.

### Purpose

Replaces the contents of the specified field in the current database with the <*expression*>. Only the current record's data is replaced, unless you specify a scope, FOR, or WHILE. The <*fieldname*> and the <*expression*> must be the same type of data. When you put memo data into a character field, the memo data is truncated (shortened) to fit the width of the field. The ADDITIVE option adds the <*expression*> to the data in a memo field. The REINDEX option updates the index file after all the replacements are made.

If the replaced field is part of the active index, the record moves to its new position in the file, which can cause problems if you use a scope, FOR, or WHILE. If you use REPLACE ALL, the REPLACE starts with the first record, according to the index. Because the field changed was part of the index, the record pointer moved past some records.

Suppose that you want to replace a Customer ID field with "CN" plus the old customer ID. You would use a REPLACE ALL command, and the first record would be changed. The record then moves to a new position in the index. The next REPLACE works on the record after the first record's new position—the command will not work on the record that previously followed the first record. To prevent this problem, use SET ORDER TO to place the database in its record number (natural) order before using REPLACE. After the REPLACE is finished, you can use SET ORDER TO <*tag name*> to reactivate the index order.

The REPLACE command starts at the current record position. If you are at the end of the file, no data is replaced unless you specify a scope, FOR, or WHILE.

### Example

```
* Replace data in the current record
USE ORDERS
GOTO 58
* Puts current date in SHIPDATE field
REPLACE SHIPDATE WITH DATE()
* Change all STATE fields in the database to uppercase
USE CUSTOMER
REPLACE ALL STATE WITH UPPER(STATE)
```

# REPLACE FROM ARRAY

### Syntax

```
REPLACE FROM ARRAY <array name>
    [FIELDS <field list>]
    [<scope>]
    [FOR <condition>]
    [WHILE <condition>]
    [REINDEX]
```

### Control Center Procedure

None.

### Purpose

Places data from an array into the fields of the current database. *Arrays* are groups of variables arranged like records in a database. A column in an array is similar in function to a field in a database. Rows of arrays are like records in a database. The REPLACE FROM ARRAY command takes a row of array data and places it in the current record. The data from the first array element is placed into the first field of the database, the second array element into the second field, and so on until there are no more array elements or database fields.

If a SET FIELDS statement is active, those fields are used by the REPLACE FROM ARRAY command. You also can use the FIELDS option to specify which database fields should be replaced with array elements.

Array elements are placed into the fields in the order specified by the FIELDS option. If you specify scope, FOR, or WHILE, the database fields that meet the condition are replaced by array elements until all of the array elements are used. If additional array elements are available, additional records are used that meet the condition specified with scope, FOR, or WHILE. The REINDEX option updates the index file after all the replacements are made.

### Example

```
* Replace the indicated fields with values
* from the READDATA() array
* Each row of the array has four elements:
* meter readings 1-4, all numeric
* The target fields in the READINGS database are
* also numeric fields
* The array was defined with the DECLARE readdata (10,4) command
USE READINGS
* Make sure that there's a value in the first array element
* indicating that there are reading values in the rest of
```

```
* that element row
IF READDATA [1,1] <> 0
   APPEND BLANK
   REPLACE FROM ARRAY readdata
ENDIF
```

## REPORT FORM

### Syntax

```
REPORT FORM <report form filename>/?
   [PLAIN]
   [HEADING <character expression>]
   [NOEJECT]
   [SUMMARY]
   [<scope>]
   [FOR <condition>]
   [WHILE <condition>]
   [TO PRINTER/TO FILE <filename>]
```

### Control Center Procedure

REPORT FORM: From the Control Center, highlight the report name, press Enter, and select Print Report.

REPORT FORM ... TO PRINT: From the Control Center, highlight the report name, press Enter, and select Print Report.

### Purpose

Prints data from the current database or view, using the report form created by the CREATE/MODIFY REPORT command. The report can be sent to the screen, to the printer (with TO PRINTER), or to a file (with TO FILE *<filename>*). The report form (FRM) file is converted to the form program file (FRG) and then compiled to the form object file (FRO). The FRO file is run to print the report.

The ? option shows a list of reports that can be selected. The PLAIN option prints the report with headers or footers printed on the first page only. The HEADING option specifies an extra heading to be printed on each page. NOEJECT cancels the first form feed so that the report starts printing on the current page. The SUMMARY option prints only the subtotals and totals of the report.

Use a scope, TO, or WHILE to limit the report to part of the database. In a network environment, the database file is locked for exclusive use by the report form. If another user used the FLOCK() or RLOCK() parameters, dBASE IV displays the message `File is in use by another` when you try to print. If you receive this message, you can copy the database to a temporary file and run the report from that file, or just SET LOCK OFF.

### Example

```
* Print a report of the customers in Nevada
USE CUSTOMERS ORDER CUSTOMERS
REPORT FORM custlist FOR STATE = "NV" TO PRINTER
```

## RESET

### Syntax

```
RESET [IN <alias>]
```

### Control Center Procedure

None.

### Purpose

Removes the integrity tag from a file. The integrity tag indicates that a file was a part of a BEGIN TRANSACTION. The integrity tag normally stays with the file until the transaction or ROLLBACK command completes successfully, or until the RESET command is used. This command affects the current database unless you use the IN <*alias*> option.

> **WARNING:** This command should not be used in a program file. It should be used at the DOT prompt to correct an unusual situation or during the development of a program.

### Example

```
RESET IN 2          && reset work area 2
```

## RESTORE FROM

### Syntax

```
RESTORE FROM <filename>
   [ADDITIVE]
```

### Purpose

Retrieves saved memory variables and arrays from a memory variable file. This command can be used to save needed memory variables from one dBASE IV session for use in another. The ADDITIVE option adds the saved memory variables to any existing memory variables; without ADDITIVE, all existing memory variables are cleared before the saved memory variables are loaded. You can load up to 25,000 memory variables at one time. (You can adjust that number by modifying your CONFIG.DB file.)

The restored variables are declared as private variable types, unless you first declare the memory variables public and then use RESTORE with the ADDITIVE option. Memory variables are saved to a memory file through the SAVE command.

### Example

```
* Create some memvars
STORE 0 to qmem1, qmem2,       && private variables
PUBLIC username                && declare it public
username = "Elizabeth"         && give it a value
LIST MEMORY                    && show them on screen
SAVE TO SAVEMEM                && save them to the memory file
RELEASE ALL                    && clear all memvars
RESTORE FROM SAVEMEM           && load them from disk
* Show the restored memvars, note that all are private
LIST MEMORY
```

## RESTORE MACROS

### Syntax

```
RESTORE MACROS FROM <macro library file>
```

### Control Center Procedure

From the Control Center, press F10 and select Tools, Macros, and Load Library.

### Purpose

Restores or loads macros from the specified macro library file (KEY). Macro library files are created from the Control Center and saved with the SAVE MACROS command. The library file contains macro keystrokes assigned to the macro key. If the macro library contains a macro key that was loaded previously from another macro library, the old macro command is overwritten by the new one.

### Example

```
* Load a macro file, play the DATA_IN macro
RESTORE MACROS FROM DATAMAC
PLAY MACRO DATA_IN
```

## RESTORE SCREEN FROM

### Syntax

```
RESTORE SCREEN FROM <screen name>
```

### Control Center Procedure

None.

### Purpose

Displays a screen that was saved with a SAVE SCREEN command. The RELEASE SCREEN command removes the screen from memory.

### Example

```
* Restore the screens
RESTORE SCREEN FROM OLDSCRN
```

## RESTORE WINDOW

### Syntax

RESTORE WINDOW <*window name list*> /ALL FROM <*filename*>

### Control Center Procedure

None.

### Purpose

Restores specific window definitions from a disk file. Use the ALL parameter to restore all of the window definitions from the disk file. If the window definition already exists in memory, it is overwritten with the definition from the disk file.

### Example

```
* Save the current windows
SAVE WINDOWS ALL TO wind042
CLEAR                       && clear the screen
@ 15,20 say "Updating user file, please wait"
DO userupdt                 && updating program
CLEAR
RESTORE WINDOW ALL FROM wind042
```

## RESUME

### Syntax

```
RESUME
```

### Control Center Procedure

None.

### Purpose

Resumes the execution of a program that was stopped with the SUSPEND command. You usually use RESUME during program debugging. You may want to use the CLEAR command to clear the screen before you use RESUME to restart the program. If you used the ROLLBACK command while the program was suspended, the

RESUME command restarts the program with the command that appears after the END TRANSACTION statement in the program. (RESUME is used from the dot prompt only, not in programs.)

### Example

```
RESUME
```

## RETRY

### Syntax

```
RETRY
```

### Control Center Procedure

None.

### Purpose

Reexecutes a command that caused an error. Using the RETRY command with the ON ERROR command can help you determine which command caused an error. You also can find the error with the ERROR() function, correct the error, and then use RETRY to repeat the command that caused the error.

### Example

```
* Recover from a printer error. This code fragment is
* part of the ERR_TRAP.PRG program called by the
* ON ERROR DO ERR_TRAP command, and contains code that traps
* many different kinds of errors
*
err_found = ERROR()
DO CASE
   CASE err_found = 126
      ? "Printer not connected or turned on."
   CASE err_found = 127
      ? "Printer not ready."
   * CASE statements for other errors
ENDCASE
? "Please correct the error; then press a key."
WAIT ""                  && wait for the user to press a key
RETRY
RETURN
```

## RETURN

### Syntax

RETURN [<*expression*> / TO MASTER / TO <*procedure name*>]

### Control Center Procedure

None.

### Purpose

Returns control to the calling program, to the Control Center, or to the dot prompt. In the calling program, the command following the calling command (DO <*program*>) is executed next.

In a FUNCTION, the RETURN command returns the computed value of the user-defined function. If you want RETURN to return you to the master (main) program, use TO MASTER. Use TO <*procedure name*> to return control to an active procedure.

You must put a RETURN command at the end of a procedure. At the end of a program, RETURN happens automatically, even if you do not include RETURN in the code.

RETURN releases any private memory variables that were defined in the called program, but it does not release public memory variables. RETURN also clears any ERROR() value.

### Example

```
* Ask user whether it's OK to cancel out of current subprogram
answer = .F.
   @ 24,20 SAY "Cancel this subprogram? (Y/N) " ;
      GET answer PICTURE "Y"
   READ
* return to calling program; otherwise continue
IF answer
   RETURN
ENDIF
```

## ROLLBACK

### Syntax

```
ROLLBACK [<database filename>]
```

### Control Center Procedure

None.

### Purpose

Restores the database and index files to the state they were in before the transaction started and then stops the transaction. Any transaction commands not yet executed are ignored, and the program continues, starting with the command following the END TRANSACTION statement. The ROLLBACK command helps to ensure that a series of commands (the transaction) is completed properly. If an error prevents the transaction from completing, you can use the ROLLBACK command to put the data back in its original state, as if the transaction had never begun.

When the ROLLBACK command successfully completes, the ROLLBACK() function is set to true. The ROLLBACK can fail if a record's pre- and post-transactional contents are inconsistent or if the transaction log file is unreadable.

See the BEGIN TRANSACTION example for a sample ROLLBACK process.

> **WARNING:** ROLLBACK cannot be used in dBASE IV version 1.5 with a transaction log file from a previous version of dBASE. Be sure the transaction log file was created with the current version.

# RUN

### Syntax

```
RUN / ! <DOS command>
```

### Control Center Procedure

From the Control Center, press F10, select Tools and then DOS Utilities, press F10, select DOS, and select Perform DOS command.

### Purpose

Performs a DOS command within a dBASE IV program or at the DOS prompt. You must have enough memory available to load the COMMAND.COM file (the DOS command processor), or the message `Insufficient memory` is displayed. You can pass any variables to the DOS command by using macro substitution, as shown in the example.

If you run a program that will use a considerable amount of memory, use the RUN() function, described in the "Using Functions" section elsewhere in this "dBASE IV Reference Guide."

### Example

```
* Reset the DOS time to noon
time = "12:00"
RUN TIME &time
* Run the CHKDSK program
RUN chkdsk C:
```

# SAVE MACROS TO

### Syntax

```
SAVE MACROS TO <macro library file>
```

### Control Center Procedure

From the Control Center, press F10 and select Tools, Macros, and Save Library.

### Purpose

Saves the currently defined macros in a disk file. You then can use RESTORE MACROS to load the macros during another dBASE IV session. You can create macros and assign them to macro keys from the Tools menu in the Control Center or by pressing Alt-T from the ASSIST screen.

If the macro library file already exists, you are asked for permission to overwrite the old macro library file (unless you specified SET SAFETY OFF).

### Example

```
* Save the currently defined macros
SAVE MACROS TO datamac
```

## SAVE SCREEN TO

### Syntax

```
SAVE SCREEN TO <screen name>
```

### Control Center Procedure

None.

### Purpose

Saves the current screen image to memory. You then can clear the screen and recall the screen with the RESTORE SCREEN command.

### Example

```
* Save the current screen
SAVE SCREEN TO scrn012
CLEAR
@ 12,15 say "Please wait while database is updated"
DO DATAUPDT    && program to update the database
* Redisplay the screen
RESTORE SCREEN FROM scrn012
```

## SAVE TO

### Syntax

```
SAVE TO <filename> [ALL LIKE/EXCEPT <skeleton>]
```

### Purpose

Saves all or some of the memory and array variables to a disk file so that they can be restored later in the current session (with the RESTORE command) or during another dBASE IV session. The memory file usually has the extension MEM and is stored on the current drive/directory unless you specify otherwise. All memory and array variables are stored, unless you use the ALL LIKE or EXCEPT options.

See RESTORE for an example of using SAVE TO.

## SAVE WINDOW

### Syntax

```
SAVE WINDOW <window name list> / ALL TO <filename>
```

### Control Center Procedure

None.

### Purpose

Saves window definitions to a disk file. The window definitions can be restored from disk with the RESTORE WINDOW command. (*See RESTORE WINDOW.*)

### Example

```
* Save current window definitions
SAVE WINDOW ALL TO WINDFILE
```

## SCAN

### Syntax

```
SCAN [<scope>]
   [FOR <condition>]
   [WHILE <condition>]
      [<commands>]
      [LOOP]
      [EXIT]
ENDSCAN
```

### Control Center Procedure

None.

### Purpose

Performs the commands in the SCAN/ENDSCAN construct for all records in the current database. This construct is an alternative to the DO WHILE command. You can scan only some records by using a scope, FOR, or WHILE. The LOOP command in SCAN/ENDSCAN goes to the beginning of the command sequence. The EXIT command terminates the SCAN and enables the command after ENDSCAN to be executed.

### Example

```
* Look for unentered zip codes
* If found, do the procedure to determine
* the correct zip code
USE CUSTOMER
SCAN FOR ZIPCODE = 0
   DO find_zip    && procedure to determine zip code
ENDSCAN
*
* equivalent code
USE CUSTOMER
DO WHILE .NOT. EOF()
   IF ZIPCODE = 0
      DO find_zip
   ENDIF
   SKIP
ENDDO
```

## SEEK

### Syntax

```
SEEK <expression>
```

### Control Center Procedure

From the Control Center, highlight the database file, press F2 and then F10, select Go To, and select Index Key Search.

### Purpose

Searches for a record in the current database whose indexed key is equal to *<expression>*. The SEEK command searches quickly because it uses the current index look for data instead of searching through every record.

The expression specified can be a memory variable but must be of the same data type as the key index field. An exact match must be found for the SEEK to be successful, unless you used SET EXACT OFF. Records marked for deletion are ignored if SET DELETED is ON. Also records are excluded according to any SET FILTER command (*see SET DELETED, SET FILTER*).

If the search is successful, FOUND() is set to true (.T.), and the record pointer is positioned on the found record. If the search is unsuccessful, FOUND() is false (.F.), and the record pointer is positioned at the end of the file (EOF). If you specified SET NEAR ON, an unsuccessful SEEK causes the record pointer to land on the nearest match.

### Example

```
* Find the record with the closest match
* to "Tabasco" in the ITEMS database
* The index key is UPPER(ITEM_NAME)
USE ITEMS ORDER INAME
* Allow for something close
SET EXACT OFF
SEEK "TABASCO"
```

An alternative procedure:

```
SET NEAR ON
searchfor = "Tabasco"
SEEK UPPER(searchfor)
* and the results are these:
IF FOUND()                  && found a match
   ? "Found record number ", recno()
ELSE
   IF EOF()          && not even a close match found
      ? "No match found, at end of file"
   ELSE                     && found a close match
      ? "Closest match is record ", recno()
   ENDIF
ENDIF
```

## SELECT

### Syntax

```
SELECT <work area/alias>
```

### Control Center Procedure

None.

### Purpose

Selects a database work area or database as the active database. Work area 1 (or A) always starts as the active area. You can have up to 40 work areas active, designated by the numbers 1 through 40. You can designate the first 10 work areas by the letters A through J.

A work area consists of the active database plus any associated indexes, queries, or format files. You can specify the current work area by the number, letter, or alias associated with the file. You also can use a variable as an explicit expression, such as *(thisone)*, if the variable *thisone* equals 1.

In addition, you can use a numeric expression as the work area, as shown in the example.

### Example

```
* Display the number of records in each open database
counter = 1
DO WHILE counter < 40
   SELECT counter
   IF ""<>DBF()           && test for an open database
      * Show work area number, database name, # of records
      ? counter, DBF(), reccount()
   ENDIF
   counter = counter + 1
ENDDO
```

## SHOW MENU

### Syntax

```
SHOW MENU <menu name> [PAD <pad name>]
```

### Purpose

Displays a menu bar without activating it. During your development work on a program, you can use this command to display menus without activating them so that you can see how the menu will appear. When you have displayed a menu this way, you cannot use the arrow keys to move through the menu pads.

### Example

```
* Show the menu bar, just so you can look at it
SHOW MENU main_menu
```

## SHOW POPUP

### Syntax

```
SHOW POPUP <pop-up name>
```

### Purpose

Displays a pop-up bar without activating it. During your development work on a program, you can use this command to display pop-ups without activating them so that you can see how the pop-up will appear. When you have displayed a pop-up this way, you cannot use the arrow keys to move through the options, and no messages are displayed.

### Example

```
* Show the popup, just to see how it looks
SHOP POPUP edit_pop
```

# SKIP

### Syntax

```
SKIP [<number value>] [IN <alias>]
```

### Control Center Procedure

From the Control Center, highlight the database file, press F2 and then F10, select Go To, and select Skip.

### Purpose

Moves the record pointer in the database file. A positive *<number value>* moves the pointer forward in the database, and a negative value moves the pointer backward. If the database is indexed, SKIP moves forward or backward according to the index. Any filter set with SET FILTER is observed. You cannot skip past the beginning or end of the file. Use the IN option to skip records in a different work area.

### Example

```
* Move forward 5 records
SKIP 5
* Move back 2 records
SKIP -2
```

# SORT TO

### Syntax

```
SORT TO <filename> ON <field1> [/A] [/C] [/D]
   [, <field2> [/A] [/C] [/D] ...]
      [ASCENDING] / [DESCENDING]
   [<scope>]
   [FOR <condition>]
   [WHILE <condition>]
```

### Control Center Procedure

From the Control Center, highlight the database file, press F2 and F10, and select Organize and Sort Database On Field List.

### Purpose

Creates a new database from the current database, with the data in the new database sorted by the order of the specified fields. Sorting is done in ascending order (/A) unless you specify descending with /D. You can add the /C option to ascending (/A /C) or descending (/D /C) sorts to specify that dBASE IV ignore uppercase or lowercase characters. The /A or /D option is required for each field used in the sort. The ASCENDING or DESCENDING options affect all fields that do not have a /A or /D parameter. You can use a scope, FOR, or WHILE to extract a selected part of a database.

The SORT command works much like the INDEX command, but SORT creates a separate database file, and INDEX creates an index file for the current database. Using the SORT command reorders the data in the new database according to the sort fields. The INDEX command does not actually reorder the data—it enables you to work with the data as if it had been reordered. SORT also works with individual fields, not field expressions.

### Example

```
* Sort the customer file by last, first, and company names
* into a TEMPCUST.DBF file. Extract only those records
* where the TOTALBUY field is > 10,000.
USE CUSTOMER
SORT TO TEMPCUST ON LASTNAME, FIRSTNAME, COMPANY ;
FOR TOTALBUY > 10000
```

## STORE

### Syntax

```
STORE <expression> TO <memory variable list> /
   <array element list>
<memory variable>/<array element> = <expression>
```

### Purpose

Stores values in memory variables or arrays. The STORE command enables you to assign a single value to many memory variables. The alternative syntax stores one value in one variable. The *<expression>* used determines the type of memory variable created. If the memory variable already exists, it is overwritten with the new value.

Memory variables can contain letters, numbers, or underscores but must start with a letter. Memory variables can be up to 10 characters long. You should not use the single letters A through J, and M, because database aliases may use these letters. Memory variables with the same names as database fields are permitted, but they can cause confusion in some situations and should be avoided. If you need a memory variable with the same name as a database field, use a variable name such as `mqty`.

### Example

```
* These two commands are equivalent
STORE "Christine" to username
username = "Christine"
```

# SUM

### Syntax

```
SUM [<numeric expression list>]
   [TO <memory variable list> / TO ARRAY <array name>]
   [<scope>]
   [FOR <condition>]
   [WHILE <condition>]
```

### Purpose

Calculates the sum of a numeric expression and stores the sum in a memory variable or array if you specify TO; otherwise, the sum is displayed on-screen. All numeric fields are summed unless you specify a <*numeric field list*>. All records are used unless you specify a scope, FOR, or WHILE.

### Example

```
* Determine the total sales and commissions for January 1992
USE STOCK
SUM SALES, COMM TO sales_sum, comm_sum ;
   FOR SELLDATE >= {1/1/92} .AND. SELLDATE <= {1/31/92}
```

# SUSPEND

### Syntax

```
SUSPEND
```

### Control Center Procedure

None.

### Purpose

Stops the current program and returns you to the dot prompt. When you are at the dot prompt, you can perform any dot prompt command and then use RESUME to restart the program where you left off, or use CANCEL to cancel all programs. You can use SUSPEND during debugging.

While your program is suspended, you can start other programs with the DO command. Be careful, however, not to start too many programs or to restart the current program. Memory variables created at the dot prompt while a program is suspended are private to the suspended program.

### Example

```
* Suspend the program
SUSPEND
```

# TEXT

### Syntax

```
TEXT
<text>
ENDTEXT
```

### Control Center Procedure

None.

### Purpose

Sends blocks of *<text>* to the screen. Use this command to print quick blocks of messages to the screen without worrying about specific placement of the text. You can use this command in program files only.

### Example

```
* Display some text on the screen
TEXT
The Monthly Status report has been selected.
Please make sure that the printer is ready
and that the proper paper is loaded.
Press a key when you are ready to start the report.
ENDTEXT
```

# TOTAL ON

### Syntax

```
TOTAL ON <key field> TO <filename>
   [FIELDS <fields list>]
   [<scope>]
   [FOR <condition>]
   [WHILE <condition>]
```

### Purpose

Totals the numeric fields of the current database and then creates a second database that contains the total of the fields in the current database. One record is created for each group of records that have the same *<key field>* data. The structure of the TO database is the same as that of the current database, except for any memo fields.

The numeric field size must be large enough to hold the sum of all the numeric data. If a field is not large enough, asterisks are placed in that field in the created database. You can use the MODIFY STRUCTURE command to increase the size of the fields in the source database.

### Example

```
* Summarize the sales of all stock items into a summary DBF
* Extract only 1991 sales
* The primary index is based on the Stock Number field
USE SALES ORDER STOCK_NUM
TOTAL ON STOCK_NUM TO SALES91 FOR YEAR(SELL_DATE) = 1991
```

## TYPE

### Syntax

```
TYPE <filename> [TO PRINTER / TO FILE <filename> / [NUMBER]
```

### Control Center Procedure

From the Control Center, press F10, select Tools and then DOS Utilities, highlight the file, and select Operations and then View, Single File.

### Purpose

Displays the contents of an ASCII text file. The text file usually is displayed on-screen, but it can be sent to the printer with TO PRINTER or to a file with TO FILE <*filename*>. The NUMBER option prints line numbers for each line. If you used SET HEADING ON, the SET HEADING TO page heading is printed on each page. The SET DATE ON command prints the current date in the SET DATE format. Page numbers are displayed on the right side of the page.

### Example

```
* Send the contents of a short help text file to screen
* This could be an alternative to the TEXT/ENDTEXT command
* Make sure the text file is not longer than a screen,
* or part of the file will be scrolled off the screen
TYPE help042.TXT
```

## UNLOCK

### Syntax

```
UNLOCK [ALL/IN <alias>]
```

### Purpose

Releases the record and file locks that were placed on a database so that other users can modify the data. When a user is changing a record on a network, that record is *locked* so that other users cannot change the data. Other users can look at the record. (Entire files can be locked with the USE <*database*> ... EXCLUSIVE command or the FLOCK() function.) The UNLOCK command unlocks the record or file lock for the current work area, another work area (the IN <*alias*> option), or all databases (the ALL option). Any files that are related to the file you unlock are unlocked also.

### Example

```
* Increase the price on record 15
USE PARTS
GOTO 15                && get to record 15
IF RLOCK()
   REPLACE cost with cost * 1.1)
ENDIF
```

## UPDATE ON

### Syntax

```
UPDATE ON <key field> FROM <alias>
   REPLACE <fieldname 1> WITH <expression 1>
   [, <fieldname 2> WITH <expression 2> ...]
   [RANDOM] [REINDEX]
```

### Control Center Procedure

From the Control Center, highlight a query name or <create> in the Query panel, press Shift-F2 and F10, and select Update.

### Purpose

Takes data from another database into the fields of the current database. The key field matches data from different databases that have that field in common. If the target (current) database has several records with a matching key field, only the first record receives the values from the source database.

Both databases must have current indexes that match the key field. If you use RANDOM, only the target (current) database needs to have an index that matches the current field. You do not need to specify the key field name as one of the field names to be replaced, although such a specification is allowed. To take data from the source database, you must use the work area as part of the <*expression*>, as shown in the example. The REINDEX option updates the index file after all the replacements are made.

### Example

```
* Update data in the ORDERS database
* from the TEMPORDR database
* The key field is the customer number; the total cost
* is taken from the TEMPORDR database and used to
* update the ORDERS year-to-date values in the ORDERS
* database. The current date is placed in
```

```
* the LASTDATE field.
USE ORDERS ORDER CUST_NUM
USE TEMPORDA ORDER CUST_NUM IN 2
UPDATE ON CUST_NUM FROM TEMPORDR ;
REPLACE YEARSALES WITH YEARSALES + TEMPORDR->SELLPRICE *
TEMPORDR->QUANTITY;
YEARQTY WITH YEARQTY + TEMPORD->QTY, LASTDATE WITH DATE()
```

## USE

### Syntax

```
USE [<database filename>/?] [IN <work area number>]
   [[INDEX <.ndx or .mdx file list>]
   [ORDER <.ndx filename>/[TAG] <.mdx tag>
   [OF <.mdx filename>]]
   [ALIAS <alias>] [EXCLUSIVE] [NOUPDATE]] [NOLOG]
      [NOSAVE] [AGAIN]
```

### Control Center Procedure

From the Control Center, highlight the database file and press F2.

### Purpose

Opens a database file (and an associated memo file, if the database has a memo field). USE can open MDX and NDX index files optionally. When you use USE without any options, it closes the database file and associated index and memo files in the current work area. USE ? displays a list of the databases in the current catalog or of all databases in the current directory.

The <*database filename*> can be a specific file name, such as CLIENTS, or an indirect reference for a file name, such as (currdata). The IN option enables you to specify the work area number (1 through 40). The area number does not have to be the current area.

The INDEX option enables you to open any associated index files (NDX) or multiple-index files (MDX). The multiple-index file contains fields that were defined as index tags. Each tag is similar to an NDX file, but the tag index pointers are contained in one MDX file. An MDX file can have up to 47 index tags, but the MDX file uses only one DOS *file handle*. (DOS allows only a certain number of files to be open at any one time. The maximum number of file handles available is specified by the FILES parameter in your CONFIG.SYS file. For you to use dBASE IV, your CONFIG.SYS file should specify `FILES = 99`.)

The ORDER option determines which index sets the order of the database. This controlling index then is used for order by any

SEEK or FIND commands. The ORDER...OF parameter specifies the name of the MDX file. ORDER TAG LASTNAME OF CLIENTS, for example, indicates using the tagged LASTNAME field that is part of the CLIENTS.MDX file. If you have multiple indexes active, you can use the SET ORDER command to change the controlling index. The ALIAS option specifies the database alias that can be used in other commands. If an ALIAS is not specified, the database file name is assigned as the alias.

The EXCLUSIVE option is used in networks to indicate that the current user only has access to the database, so that the file is not shared by other users on the network. In a nonnetwork environment, the database is opened as EXCLUSIVE automatically, and the EXCLUSIVE option is ignored. The NOUPDATE option makes the database file read-only so that you cannot make any changes to it.

The NOLOG command can be used to open or close files during a transaction without them being part of the transaction log file. NOSAVE opens a database file as a temporary file, which is erased when you close it. Using the AGAIN command, you can open a database file in more than one work area.

### Example

```
* Open the CLIENTS database in work area 1 and
* LETTERS database in work area 2, using the
* ZIP index tag
USE CLIENTS IN 1 ORDER ZIP
USE LETTERS IN 2 ORDER ZIP
```

## WAIT

### Syntax

```
WAIT [<prompt>] [TO <memory variable>]
```

### Control Center Procedure

None.

### Purpose

Pauses the currently running program until a key is pressed. You can store the keystroke in the *<memory variable>*, but you may want instead to use ACCEPT or INPUT to store the value. You can specify your own message with the *<prompt>* or use the default “Press any key to continue” by not specifying a *<prompt>*.

### Example

```
* Wait for the printer to be set up
? "Please make sure the printer is ready, then"
WAIT           && use the default message
```

# ZAP

### Syntax

```
ZAP
```

### Control Center Procedure

None.

### Purpose

Removes all records from the current database. This command is the same as a DELETE ALL and PACK command used together but removes the records more quickly. If SET SAFETY ON was enabled (the default), dBASE IV asks for verification before the file is cleared. If you respond Yes, the file is cleared of all data, but the structure of the file is retained. Any associated index files are reindexed, and any associated memo file is emptied also. On a network, you must have exclusive use of the database before you can use the ZAP command.

> **WARNING:** The ZAP command erases all data in a database file. Make sure that you have current backups of the data before you use this command. After ZAP is used on a database, dBASE IV cannot recover the data that had been marked for deletion.

### Example

```
* Clear out the CUSTTEMP database
USE CUSTTEMP
ZAP
```

# Using Functions

Functions give dBASE the capability to perform many different operations. You can use functions to convert from character information to numeric and vice versa. You also may select specific information from a character string. Some functions return a true or false answer, performing a test on information. Still other functions enable you to perform mathematical functions.

Many functions require arguments—information you provide so that the function can be performed. A few functions, however, require no arguments. The VERSION() function, for example, returns the version of the operating system, without giving an argument. All functions must be used with a command, even if the command is the question mark (?), which simply places the result of the function on-screen.

"Using Functions" is divided into two main sections. The first section, "Categorizing Functions," briefly groups the functions by categories. The second section, "Functions," lists all functions alphabetically.

## Categorizing Functions

This section lists functions by categories. Sometimes, you will want to find information on a function, but may not be able to remember the exact name of the function. Using this section, you may look for the function by category. For example, look under the category "Date and Time Functions" to find date and time functions. After you locate the correct function, you can get more information on the function by looking in the alphabetic list.

## Character Variable Functions

This group of functions is used with character variables. These functions enable you to find characters in a string, find upper- or lowercase variables, strip off blanks from the beginning and end of a character string, replace characters, and perform searches based on the spoken sound of a word.

The character string in each function can be an actual character string ("Smith & Jones") or a character variable. In each of the examples given in the alphabetical listing, the result of the function is shown.

| | | |
|---|---|---|
| AT() | LEN() | SOUNDEX() |
| DIFFERENCE() | LIKE() | SPACE() |
| ISALPHA() | LOWER() | STUFF() |
| ISBLANK() | LTRIM() | SUBSTR() |
| ISLOWER() | REPLICATE() | TRANSFORM() |
| ISUPPER() | RIGHT() | TRIM |
| LEFT() | RTRIM/TRIM() | UPPER() |

## Data-Type Conversion Functions

This group of functions enables you to convert memory variables or data from one type of variable to another. Included in this group are date-to-character, string-to-numeric, number-to-character, and character-to-date functions.

| | |
|---|---|
| ASC() | DTOC() |
| CHR() | STR() |
| CTOD() | VAL() |

## Database Status Functions

This group of functions tells you the status of databases you are using. You can determine whether you are at the beginning or end of the database, the last time the database was updated, and the number of records in a database along with the current record and record size. Most of these functions enable you to work with a database in another work area by specifying the database's <*alias*> name.

| | | |
|---|---|---|
| ALIAS() | FIELD() | MEMLINES() |
| BOF() | FLDCOUNT() | MLINE() |
| DBF() | FSIZE() | RECCOUNT() |
| DELETED() | FTIME() | RECNO() |
| EOF() | LUPDATE() | RECSIZE() |
| FDATE() | | |

## Keyboard Functions

This group of functions is used to get information relating to the keyboard. You can determine the assignment of the function keys, wait for a user to press a key, determine the last key pressed, or find the key last used to exit a menu.

FKLABEL()
FKMAX()
INKEY()
LASTKEY()
READKEY()

## Date and Time Functions

This group of functions is used with date and time variables. You can use these functions to determine the day of the week, the month name, day or month numbers, or the current date or time.

| | |
|---|---|
| CDOW() | DTOS() |
| CMONTH() | MDY() |
| DATE() | MONTH() |
| DAY() | TIME() |
| DMY() | YEAR() |
| DOW() | |

## Environment Functions

This group of functions is used to retrieve information about the current operating environment. You can determine the amount of disk space on a disk, whether or not a file exists, the operating system in use, and other information.

| | |
|---|---|
| CATALOG() | MEMORY() |
| DISKSPACE() | OS() |
| FILE() | SET() |
| GETENV() | VERSION() |

## Database Search Functions

This group of functions is used with commands that search for data, such as SEEK and LOCATE. These functions often are used to determine whether a search was successful.

FOUND()
LOOKUP()
SEEK()

## Help Display Functions

This function is used when you create context-sensitive help screens.

VARREAD()

## Index Functions

This group of functions is used with dBASE IV indexes and index tags. These functions can tell you the key expression used for the index and the index file names and can make another index or index tag active.

| | |
|---|---|
| DESCENDING() | ORDER() |
| FOR() | TAG() |

KEY()
MDX()
NDX()
TAGCOUNT()
TAGNO()
UNIQUE()

## Mathematical Functions

This group of functions is used to return various mathematical calculations. You can determine minimum or maximum values, determine absolute values, perform *modulo* arithmetic (a division process that returns the remainder), round off numbers, or determine a numbers sign.

ABS()
CEILING()
EXP()
FIXED()
FLOAT()
FLOOR()
INT()
MAX()
MIN()
MOD()
RAND()
ROUND()
SIGN()
SQRT()

## Financial Functions

This group of functions is used in financial calculations. You can use these functions to determine such things as present value, future value, or payment required.

FV()
PAYMENT()
PV()

## Trigonometric Functions

This group of functions performs various trigonometric calculations, such as sine, cosine, tangent, logarithms, and the value of pi. In each of the examples, SET DECIMAL TO 2 (the default value) is in effect.

ACOS()
ASIN()
ATAN()
ATN2()
COS()
DTOR()
LOG()
LOG10()
PI()
RTOD()
SIN()
TAN()

## Menu Functions

This group of functions is used to get information about bar and pop-up menus that have been defined in a program.

BAR()
MENU()
PAD()
POPUP()
PROMPT()

## Networking Functions

This group of functions is used to return information about databases running on a networked system. You can determine who has changed the database, whether a field or record is locked, the name and security level of the current user, and when the database was last changed.

ACCESS()
CHANGE()
FLOCK()
ID()
ISMARKED()
LKSYS()
LOCK()
NETWORK()
RLOCK()
USER()

## Printer Functions

This group of functions is used to determine the current status of the printer or the current row or column location of the printing position.

PCOL()
PRINTSTATUS()
PROW()

## Programming Environment Functions

This group of functions is used to execute binary programs or to determine information about the currently executing program.

Also included are error-trapping functions.

CALL()
CERROR()
DGEN()
ERROR()
HOME()
IIF()
LINENO()
MESSAGE()
PCOUNT()
PROGRAM()
RUN()
SELECT()

## Screen Functions

This group of functions returns information about the active screen, such as the current row or column position of the cursor, or whether the monitor is attached to a color video adapter.

COL()
ISCOLOR()
ROW()
WINDOW()

## Transaction-Processing Functions

These two functions are used to determine the status of transaction processing or whether a transaction-processing rollback was successful.

COMPLETED()
ROLLBACK()

## Macro Substitution/ Variable-Type Functions

These two functions are used to perform macro substitution, where the contents of a variable are placed at the macro variable name. The TYPE() function returns the type of variable.

&
TYPE()

## Low-Level File I/O Functions

dBASE IV 1.5 provides special functions for manipulating binary files at the operating system level. These functions are intended for use by experienced programmers with an expert knowledge of the operating system and of using C language type functions with data stream files.

| | | |
|---|---|---|
| FCREATE() | FFLUSH() | FREAD() |
| FCLOSE() | FGETS() | FSEEK() |
| FEOF() | FOPEN() | FWRITE() |
| FERROR() | FPUTS() | |

# Functions

In this section functions are listed alphabetically, and examples and other information are shown for each function.

## &

### Syntax

```
&
```

### Purpose

The macro substitution function. The contents of the memory variable, such as &Username, are placed inside the variable expression.

### Example

```
Name = "Christine"
* These two statements will display the same message
@ 12,20 SAY "Current user is &name."
@ 13,20 SAY "Current user is " + name.
* The two statements following the USE
* statement are also equivalent
USE CUSTOMER ORDER Firstname
SEEK Name
SEEK "&Name"
```

## ABS()

### Syntax

```
ABS(<numeric expression>)
```

### Purpose

Returns the absolute value of the <*numeric expression*>, or the positive value of the <*numeric expression*>. You can use the ABS function to determine the number of days between two dates, without worrying about getting a negative value.

### Example

```
? ABS(1433)                         && returns 1433
? ABS(-792)                         && returns 792
? ABS(-392) > 300                   && returns .T.

(392 > 300)
? ABS({11/25/91} - {12/04/91})      && returns 9
```

## ACCESS()

### Syntax

```
ACCESS( )
```

### Purpose

Returns the current user's access level. You then can use the level with the PROTECT command to limit user access to certain fields or databases. Only if the DBSYSTEM.DB file is accessed by dBASE IV when the program is started will the log-in screen be shown. If a user has an access level of 0, that user cannot access encrypted databases. In a non-networked system, ACCESS() will return a 0.

### Example

```
@ 12,15 SAY "Your access level is " + STR(ACCESS())
```

## ACOS()

### Syntax

```
ACOS(<cosine value>)
```

### Purpose

Returns the angle size in radians for any given <*cosine value*>. The <*cosine value*> must be from –1 to +1. Use SET DECIMALS and SET PRECISION to fix the number of decimal places and accuracy returned.

### Example

```
? ACOS(.224)        && returns 1.34
```

## ALIAS()

### Syntax

```
ALIAS ([<alias>])
```

### Purpose

Returns the alias name of the current work area or of the work area specified as the optional *<alias>*. The *<alias>* is a number between 1 and 40.

### Example

```
SELECT 3                          && work area 3
USE CLIENTS ORDER CLIENTS         && open a database
SELECT 1                          && work area 1
USE ORDERS ORDER ORDNUM
* Alias for current work area (1)
? ALIAS()                         && returns "ORDERS"
* Alias for work area 3
? ALIAS(3)                        && returns "CLIENTS"
```

## ASC()

### Syntax

```
ASC(<character expression>)
```

### Purpose

Returns the ASCII code of the first character of the *<character expression>*, which can be a character string or a string variable. See the ASCII table at the end of this "dBASE IV Reference Guide" for all the ASCII characters and their decimal values.

### Example

```
? ASC("A")          && returns 65
Stockloc = 55C12
? ASC(Stockloc)     && returns 53, since ASC("5") = 53
```

## ASIN()

### Syntax

```
ASIN(<sine value>)
```

### Purpose

Returns the angle size in radians for the *<sine value>*. The *<sine value>* must be from –1 to +1. Use SET DECIMALS and SET PRECISION to fix the number of decimal places and accuracy returned.

### Example

```
? ASIN(.492)        && returns 0.51
```

# AT()

### Syntax

```
AT(<character string 1>,<character string 2>/<memo field name>)
```

### Purpose

Looks for *<character string 1>* in *<character string 2>* or in the *<memo field>*. If *<character string 1>* is found, the starting position number is returned. If *<character string 1>* is not found in *<character string 2>*, 0 is returned.

### Example

```
* Look for "beans"
Lookfor = "BEANS"
Lookin = "String Beans"
* Force Lookin uppercase for exact match
? AT(Lookfor, upper(Lookin))       && prints 8
? AT("BEANS", "STRING BEANS")      && prints 8
```

# ATAN()

### Syntax

```
ATAN(<tangent value>)
```

### Purpose

Returns the angle size in radians for the *<tangent value>*. The *<tangent value>* must be between $-\pi/2$ and $+\pi/2$. Use SET DECIMALS and SET PRECISION to fix the number of decimal places and accuracy returned.

### Example

```
? ATAN(1.00)          && returns 0.79
```

# ATN2()

### Syntax

```
ATN2(<sine angle>, <cosine angle>)
```

### Purpose

Returns the angle size in radians for the *<sine>* and *<cosine>* of the same angle. The *<sine>* and *<cosine>* values must be between $-\pi/2$ and $+\pi/2$. Use SET DECIMALS and SET PRECISION to fix the number of decimal places and accuracy returned.

### Example

```
? ATN2(.50, .80)          && returns 0.56
```

# BAR()

### Syntax

```
BAR()
```

### Purpose

Returns the number of the most recently selected bar from a pop-up menu. This function returns a 0 if there is no active pop-up menu, no pop-up menus have been defined, or the Esc key was used to deactivate the active pop-up menu.

### Example

```
* Determine which bar was pressed
* The pop-up menu was previously defined
@ 12,15 SAY "You selected bar number " + STR(BAR())
```

# BOF()

### Syntax

```
BOF([<alias>])
```

### Purpose

If BOF is true, the record pointer is at the beginning of the file. The optional *<alias>* can be used to indicate an active database in another work area. This function is used often to make sure that the record pointer is not moved past the beginning of the file.

### Example

```
* If record pointer is not at beginning of the file,
* move to previous record
USE ORDERS ORDERS ORDNUM       && the ORDNUM index is active
GOTO 12                       && go to record 12
IF .NOT. BOF()
   SKIP -1
ENDIF
```

# CALL()

### Syntax

```
CALL(<binary filename> [, <expression list>])
```

### Purpose

Executes a binary program module, such as those written in assembly language or C. The module first must be loaded with the LOAD command before it can be executed. The *<expression list>* is an option list of values that is expected by the program module, in the same way a procedure expects parameters. Up to seven expressions can be passed to the module. Only one value (the first expression) is returned to dBASE IV after the module has finished.

### Example

```
* The "MONTYPE" binary module determines the type of monitor
LOAD MONTYPE                 && loads the module
@ 12,15 SAY "Current monitor is " + CALL(MONTYPE, VIDCARD)
```

## CATALOG()

### Syntax

```
CATALOG()
```

### Purpose

Returns the name of the catalog file currently in use.

### Example

```
SET CATALOG TO SAMPLES
? CATALOG()
C:SAMPLES.CAT
```

## CDOW()

### Syntax

```
CDOW(<date variable>)
```

### Purpose

Returns the day name for the *<date variable>*, which can be a date-type memory variable, field, or any function that returns a date-type variable.

### Example

```
* On what day were you born?
Whatdate = {}                && makes an empty date variable
@ 12,15 SAY "What is your birthday? " ;
GET Whatdate PICTURE "@D"
READ
@ 13,15 SAY "You were born on a " + CDOW(Whatdate)
```

## CEILING()

### Syntax

```
CEILING(<numeric expression>)
```

### Purpose

Returns the smallest integer that is greater than or equal to the *<numeric expression>*.

### Example

```
?CEILING(14.0001)        && returns 15
```

## CERROR()

### Syntax

```
CERROR()
```

### Purpose

Returns the number of the last compiler error message. The *dBASE IV Language Reference* manual contains a list of all compiler error messages.

### Example

```
* Compile a dBASE IV program
* Ask user for program name
Progname = space(20)
@ 12,15 SAY "Enter program to compile " ;
   GET prog_name PICTURE "@!"
READ
* Make sure that file exists
IF FILE(Prog_name)             && file does exist
   @ 13,15 SAY "Compiling program, please wait."
   * If an error occurs, print error number and message
   ON ERROR ? ERROR(), MESSAGE()
   * Compile the program
   COMPILE Prog_name
   * Set up normal error-trapping procedure
   ON ERROR DO errtrap
   * Determine whether a compiling error occurred
   IF CERROR() > 0
      @ 20,15 SAY "Your program did not compile."
   ELSE
      @ 20,15 SAY "Program compiled OK."
   ENDIF
ELSE                           && the program doesn't exist
   @ 13,15 SAY "That program doesn't exist."
ENDIF
```

## CHANGE()

### Syntax

```
CHANGE([<alias>])
```

### Purpose

Returns a logical true (.T.) if another user has changed a record since it was read from the database. Only databases that have been converted to network database files with the CONVERT command can use the CHANGE() function. You can force the CHANGE() value to false by using a GOTO RECNO() command or any command that repositions the record pointer. Use the optional *<alias>* parameter to check the CHANGE() in another work area.

### Example

```
IF CHANGE()
   @ 12,15 SAY "Record has been changed."
ELSE
   @ 12,15 SAY "Record has not been changed."
ENDIF
```

## CHR()

### Syntax

```
CHR(<numeric expression>)
```

### Purpose

Converts a *<numeric expression>* to a character expression. You can use this function to send control characters (escape sequences) or to send a line-drawing character to your printer. Use a number from 0 to 255. Note that some printers may not be able to print line-drawing characters.

### Example

```
SET PRINT ON                 && send "?" output to printer
? CHR(12)                    && sends form feed, works like
EJECT SET PRINT OFF          && sets output back to screen
* Beeps the speaker and prints the message
? CHR(7) + "Printer at top of form"
```

## CMONTH()

### Syntax

```
CMONTH(<date variable>)
```

### Purpose

Returns the month name for the *<date variable>*, which can be a date-type memory variable, field, or function.

### Example

```
* What month is that?
Whatmonth = {}                  && makes an empty date variable
@ 15,15 SAY "Enter any date " ;
   GET Whatmonth PICTURE "@D"
```

```
READ
@ 16,15 SAY "The month name is " + CMONTH(Whatmonth)
```

## COL()

### Syntax

```
COL()
```

### Purpose

Returns the current column position of the cursor.

### Example

```
* Place a message at the current column position
@ 12,col() SAY "Please wait."
```

## COMPLETED()

### Syntax

```
COMPLETED()
```

### Purpose

Returns a logical true (.T.) if the BEGIN...END TRANSACTION was completed properly. COMPLETED() is set to false with the BEGIN TRANSACTION command and set to true with the END TRANSACTION command. COMPLETED() often is used with the ROLLBACK() function.

### Example

```
* Determine whether the transaction completed properly
IF COMPLETED()
   @ 22,30 SAY "Transaction completed OK."
ELSE
   @ 22,30 SAY "Warning! Transaction did not complete!"
ENDIF
```

## COS()

### Syntax

```
COS(<radian angle>)
```

### Purpose

Returns the cosine value of the *<radian angle>*. Use SET DECIMALS and SET PRECISION to fix the number of decimal places and accuracy returned.

### Example

```
? COS(.822)                 && returns 0.68
```

# CTOD()

### Syntax

```
CTOD(<character expression>)
```

### Purpose

Converts a <*character expression*> to a date variable. (Remember this function as an abbreviation of "Character TO Date.") The <*character expression*> is formatted as MM/DD/YY, unless you have changed the date format with SET DATE and SET CENTURY. A year in the 20th century is assumed if you specify only two characters as "yy."

An alternative is to use braces ({ }) to convert character text to a date format.

### Example

```
Birthdate = "05/06/78"
Datetype = CTOD(Birthdate)          && converts to date variable
Datetype = {05/06/78}               && alternative
```

# DATE()

### Syntax

```
DATE()
```

### Purpose

Returns the current system date in the form MM/DD/YY. You can change the format of the date by using the SET CENTURY, SET DATE, or SET MARK command. The current date is whatever date DOS understands the current date to be, as set by the DOS DATE command or your computer's automatic clock/calendar. If the date is not correct, then you must change it at the DOS prompt or by using a RUN DATE command at the dBASE IV dot prompt. You can add or subtract values from the DATE() value.

### Example

```
* Make sure that the date is current
IF DATE() = {1/1/80}     && wrong system date
   RUN DATE              && run DOS DATE command
ENDIF
* Determine next payment due date
Duedate = DATE() + 30    && adds 30 days to the current date
```

# DAY()

### Syntax

```
DAY(<date variable)>
```

### Purpose

Returns the numeric value of the day of the month of the *<date variable>*, which can be a memory variable, date field, or any function that returns a date-type variable.

**NOTE** DAY() returns the day number of the month. DOW() returns the day number of the week.

### Example

```
* Extract the day of the month number
Duedate = {1/31/92}
? DAY(Duedate)              && returns 31
```

## DBF()

### Syntax

```
DBF([<alias>])
```

### Purpose

Returns the name of the database in the current work area or in the work area specified by the optional *<alias>*. If no database is open, a null string is returned.

### Example

```
CLOSE ALL               && close all databases
IF "" = DBF()           && if no database in use, open CUSTOMER.DBF
   USE CUSTOMER
ENDIF
```

## DELETED()

### Syntax

```
DELETED([<alias>])
```

### Purpose

Returns a logical true (.T.) if the current record has been marked for deletion; otherwise, DELETED() returns a logical false (.F.). The current work area is used, unless you specify another work area with the *<alias>* option.

### Example

```
* Delete the current record
* Undelete if record is already deleted
* Ask the question, only accept Y or N
```

```
Answer = .F.
   * Set up the message text
   IF DELETED()
      Message = "Already deleted, undelete?"
   ELSE
      Message = "Delete this record?"
   ENDIF
   @ 22,30 SAY Message + " (Y/N) " GET answer PICTURE "Y"
   READ
ENDDO
IF answer = "Y"          && OK to change it
   IF DELETED()
      RECALL    && unmark deletion
   ELSE
      DELETE    && mark for deletion
   ENDIF
ENDIF
```

## DESCENDING()

### Syntax

```
DESCENDING([[<multiple index file>,] <numeric expression> [,<alias>]])
```

### Purpose

Returns a true (.T.) value if the specified MDX tag was created using the DESCENDING option, or false (.F.) if it was not. The *<numeric expression>* specifies the tag number, and the optional *<multiple index file>* and *<alias>* expressions specify the index and database files if other than the current files.

### Example

```
USE CUSTOMER
INDEX ON CITY TAG REVCITY DESCENDING
? TAGNO("REVCITY")
   6
? DESCENDING(6)
.T.
```

## DGEN()

### Syntax

```
DGEN(<character expression>[,<character expression>])
```

### Purpose

Runs the dBASE IV Template Language interpreter from within dBASE to create dBASE programs from template (GEN) files. The first <*character expression*> is the name of the GEN file, and the optional second expression provides an argument to pass to the template program.

### Example

```
* Create a program from ENTERDAT.SCR screen form
DEXPORT SCREEN ENTERDAT
APROGRAM=DGEN("FORM.GEN","ENTERDAT.SNL")
```

## DIFFERENCE()

### Syntax

```
DIFFERENCE(<char 1>, <char 2>)
```

### Purpose

Determines the difference between two character strings by converting the strings to a SOUNDEX() code (see SOUNDEX) and then subtracting the two values. A number from 0 to 4 is returned, with 4 representing a close match. If the strings have no letters in common, 0 is returned. One letter in common returns 1.

### Example

```
* Compare the difference between two strings
?DIFFERENCE("SMITH", "SMYTHE")          && returns 4
?DIFFERENCE("SMITH", "JONES")           && returns 2
?DIFFERENCE("Janssen", "Jones")         && returns 3
String1 = "Fred" String2 = "Frank"
?DIFFERENCE(String1, String2)           && returns 2
```

## DISKSPACE()

### Syntax

```
DISKSPACE()
```

### Purpose

Returns the number of bytes available on the current drive. You can use this information to find out, for example, whether enough room is on the disk to copy the current database.

### Example

```
PROCEDURE SPACEON_A
PARAMETER Space_ok       && returned to caller
* Make sure that there is enough room on A: for the file
* If Space_ok is true, there's enough room
USE ORDERS
* Determine how big the file is
Filesize = (RECCOUNT() + RECSIZE()) + 2000
* Determine available space on A:
```

```
SET DEFAULT TO A:
Spaceon = DISKSPACE()
SET DEFAULT TO C:
IF Spaceon < Filesize
   ? "Not enough room on the A: drive"
   Space_ok = .F.
ELSE
   Space_ok = .T.
ENDIF
RETURN                        && back to calling program
```

## DMY()

### Syntax

```
DMY(<date variable>)
```

### Purpose

Converts the <*date variable*> to the form *dd monthname yy*. If SET CENTURY is ON, the year value is converted to YYYY. The <*date variable*> can be a date-type memory variable, a date field, or any function that returns a date-type variable.

### Example

```
Pastdue = {4/1/92}
? DMY(Pastdue)           && returns "1 April 92"
SET CENTURY ON
? DMY({11/25/51})        && returns "25 November 1951"
```

## DOW()

### Syntax

```
DOW(<date variable>)
```

### Purpose

Returns a number corresponding to the day of the week, with Sunday as day number 1, Monday as day number 2, and so on. The <*date variable*> can be a date memory variable, field, or any function that returns a date variable.

### Example

```
?DOW({10/31/92})         && returns 7 (Saturday)
```

## DTOC()

### Syntax

```
DTOC(<date variable>)
```

### Purpose

Converts a date-type variable into a character string. (Remember this function as an abbreviation of "Date TO Character.")

### Example

```
Date1 = "01/03/80"        && character variable
Date2 = CTOD(Date1)       && converted to date variable
Date3 = DTOC(Date2)       && back to character variable
```

## DTOR()

### Syntax

```
DTOR(<angle degrees>)
```

### Purpose

Converts <*angle degrees*> to radians. If the angle has minutes or seconds values, convert them to decimal fractions before using DTOR().

### Example

```
? DTOR(60.525)        && returns 1.06
```

## DTOS()

### Syntax

```
DTOS(<date variable>)
```

### Purpose

Converts the <*date variable*> into a string variable. The date is converted to a YYYYMMDD character string, even if you have used SET CENTURY or SET DATE to change the date to another form. This function is useful if you want to have an index that includes a date variable.

### Example

```
* Set up an index of back ordered parts
* Backdate is a date field
* Partnum is a character field
USE ORDERS
INDEX ON DTOS(backdate)+partnum TAG BACKORDR
```

## EOF()

### Syntax

```
EOF(<alias>)
```

### Purpose

Returns a logical true (.T.) if the record pointer is at the end of a file; otherwise, returns a logical false (.F.). When EOF() is true, the current record number is RECCOUNT() + 1. The current work area is used unless you specify the optional <*alias*>. A logical false is also returned if no database is in use in the current or specified work area.

### Example

```
USE ORDERS
GO BOTTOM
? EOF()         && returns .F.
SKIP 1
? EOF()         && returns .T.
```

## ERROR()

### Syntax

```
ERROR()
```

### Purpose

Returns the error number of the last ON ERROR condition. You need to use the ON ERROR command to trap errors. When an error occurs, you can use the RETRY command to try the command again or RETURN to return to the calling program. The *dBASE IV Language Reference* manual contains a list of all error codes and messages.

### Example

```
PROCEDURE Err_trap
PARAMETER fatal, errorcnt
* This is the error-trapping procedure, which was
* enabled with a "ON ERROR DO Err_trap" command
* Fatal = if error is catastrophic, cancel the program
DO CASE
   CASE ERROR() = 125
      @ 22,20 say "Printer not ready, please correct."
      Fatal = .F.                 && not a fatal error
   CASE ERROR() = 21
      @ 22,20 SAY "Out of memory, program cancel
      Fatal = .T.
   * Other CASE statements to handle other errors
END CASE
* Determine whether a fatal error occurred
IF Fatal                         && Fatal is .T.
   CANCEL                        && Fatal error, cancel program
```

```
ELSE                                    && Fatal is .F.
   RETRY                                && Try same command again
ENDIF
RETURN
```

## EXP()

### Syntax

```
EXP(<numeric expression>)
```

### Purpose

Returns the value *x* from the equation `y = ex`. The returned value is always a real number, with SET DECIMALS determining the accuracy of the displayed answer.

### Example

```
SET DECIMALS TO 4
? EXP(12)             && returns 162754.7914
```

## FCLOSE()

### Syntax

```
FCLOSE(<file handle>)
```

### Purpose

Closes a low-level file.

## FCREATE()

### Syntax

```
FCREATE(<filename>[,<privilege>])
```

### Purpose

Creates a low-level file and returns the file handle number.

## FDATE()

### Syntax

```
FDATE(<character expression>)
```

### Purpose

Returns the date that a file was last modified. The *<character expression>* contains the file name. The FDATE() function does not support wild-card characters for the file name.

### Example

```
? FDATE("C:\DOS\MYTEXT.TXT")
02/22/92
```

# FEOF()

### Syntax

```
FEOF(<file handle>)
```

### Purpose

Returns true (.T.) if at the end of a low-level file.

# FERROR()

### Syntax

```
FERROR()
```

### Purpose

Returns the error status of a low-level file operation.

# FFLUSH()

### Syntax

```
FFLUSH(<file handle>)
```

### Purpose

Writes the system buffer of a low-level file to disk.

# FGETS()

### Syntax

```
FGETS((<file handle>[,<bytes to read>][,<end of line character>])
```

### Purpose

Reads a character string from a low-level file.

# FIELD()

### Syntax

```
FIELD(<numeric expression> [,<alias>])
```

### Purpose

Returns the name of the specified field in the current database. The returned field name is all uppercase characters. The *<number expression>* refers to the field number as shown with LIST/DISPLAY STRUCTURE. If the field number is not defined in the database structure or is not a number from 1 to 255, a null string (" ") is returned. The current work area is assumed unless you specify the *<alias>* of database open in another work area.

### Example

```
* Structure of NAMES.DBF is:
* NAME
* ADDRESS
* CITY
* STATE
USE NAMES
? FIELD(3)          && returns "CITY"
```

## FILE()

### Syntax

```
FILE("<filename>")
```

### Purpose

Determines whether the *<filename>* exists. The *<filename>* must include the complete file name and extension, plus the drive/directory name if needed, and must be enclosed in quotation marks. FILE() uses dBASE's PATH when searching for the existence of the file.

### Example

```
* Check for the memory file that contains the check number
* If found, load the Checknum variable
* If not found, start with check number 100
IF FILE("CHECKNUM.MEM")
   RESTORE FROM CHECKNUM ADDITIVE
ELSE
   Checknum = 100
   * Create the Checknum.mem memory file
   SAVE TO CHECKNUM ALL LIKE Checknum
ENDIF
```

## FIXED()

### Syntax

```
FIXED(<numeric expression>)
```

### Purpose

Transforms long, real floating-point numbers into binary-coded decimal (BCD) numbers. You may lose some accuracy of the number during the translation. The allowable range is from $10^{308}$ to $10^{-308}$.

### Example

```
SET DECIMALS TO 5
Afloat = PI()
Bfixed = FIXED(Afloat)
```

# FKLABEL()

### Syntax

```
FKLABEL(<numeric value>)
```

### Purpose

Returns the name of the function key denoted by the <*numeric value*>. See the SET FUNCTION command for a list of all programmable function keys. The <*numeric value*> can be from 1 to 28.

### Example

```
? FKLABEL(8)          && returns "F9"
```

# FKMAX()

### Syntax

```
FKMAX()
```

### Purpose

Returns the number of programmable function keys available in dBASE IV. The F2 through F10 keys, Shift-F1 through Shift-F10, and Ctrl-F1 through Ctrl-F10 are available for use by dBASE IV. F1 is reserved for the Help key, and F11 and F12 are not available.

### Example

```
? FKMAX()             && returns 28
```

# FLDCOUNT()

### Syntax

```
FLDCOUNT([<alias>])
```

### Purpose

Returns the number of fields in the structure of the specified database file. If no alias is specified, the function returns the number of fields in the database in use in the current work area.

### Example

```
USE CUSTOMER IN 2
? FLDCOUNT(2)
12
```

# FLOAT()

### Syntax

```
FLOAT(<numeric expression>)
```

#### Purpose
Converts binary-coded decimal (BCD) numbers to long, real, floating-point numbers.

#### Example
```
Afixed = 14.2254
FLOAT(Afixed)
```

## FLOCK()

#### Syntax
```
FLOCK([<alias>])
```

#### Purpose
Locks the database to prevent multiple users from updating the same file. If the database is locked, a logical true (.T.) is returned. If the database is not being used in a network, a logical false (.F.) is returned. All records are locked in the database, which is useful for operations that need to work on the entire file. To lock individual records, use RLOCK(). Although other users can't change the data, they can have read-only access to the database. Any database that has been related to the current database also is locked. Use the optional *<alias>* to check the file-locking status of a database in another work area.

#### Example
```
IF FLOCK()
   @ 12,15 SAY "Database is locked, please wait"
ENDIF
```

## FLOOR()

#### Syntax
```
FLOOR(<numeric expression>)
```

#### Purpose
Returns the largest integer that is less than or equal to the *<numeric expression>*.

#### Example
```
?FLOOR(18.839)             && returns 18
```

## FOPEN()

#### Syntax
```
FOPEN(<filename>[,<privilege>])
```

#### Purpose

Opens an existing low-level file and sets the specified privilege level.

## FOR()

#### Syntax

```
FOR([[<multiple index file>,]<numeric expression>[,<alias>]])
```

#### Purpose

Returns a true (.T.) value if the specified MDX tag was created using the FOR clause to make a conditional index, or false (.F.) if it was not. The *<numeric expression>* specifies the tag number, and the optional *<multiple index file>* and *<alias>* expressions specify the index and database files if other than the current files.

#### Example

```
USE CUSTOMER
INDEX ON CITY TAG ZIPCITY FOR ZIP > "44559"
? TAGNO("ZIPCITY")
7
? FOR(7)
.T.
```

## FOUND()

#### Syntax

```
FOUND([<alias>])
```

#### Purpose

Returns a logical true (.T.) if the desired record was found with the FIND, LOCATE, SEEK, or CONTINUE command. Each work area has one FOUND(); use the *<alias>* option to determine whether a record was found in another work area.

#### Example

```
USE INVENTRY ORDER PARTNUM
SEEK "WIDGETS"
IF FOUND()
   @ 12,15 SAY "Found record number " + RECNO()
ELSE
   @ 12,15 SAY "Couldn't find it."
ENDIF
```

## FPUTS()

#### Syntax

```
FPUTS(<file handle>,<character expression>[,<number
of characters to write>][,<end of line character>])
```

### Purpose
Writes a character string to a low-level file.

## FREAD()

### Syntax
```
FREAD(<file handle>,<number of bytes to read>)
```

### Purpose
Reads a specified number of bytes from a low-level file.

## FSEEK()

### Syntax
```
FSEEK(<file handle>,<number of bytes to move>[,start position>])
```

### Purpose
Moves the file pointer in a low-level file.

## FSIZE()

### Syntax
```
FSIZE(<character expression>)
```

### Purpose
Returns the size in bytes of the specified file. The *<character expression>* contains the file name, which cannot contain wild-card characters.

### Example
```
? FSIZE("C:\DOS\MYTEXT.TXT")
12800
```

## FTIME()

### Syntax
```
FTIME(<character expression>)
```

### Purpose
Returns the time that the specified file was last modified. The *<character expression>* contains the file name and cannot include wild-card characters.

### Example
```
? FTIME("C:\DOS\MYTEXT.TXT")
11:13:09
```

# FV()

### Syntax

```
FV(<payment>, <rate>, <periods>)
```

### Purpose

Calculates the future value based on equal regular deposits (<*payment*>) into an investment yielding a fixed interest rate (<*rate*>) over a number of time periods (<*periods*>). The <*payment*> can be negative or positive. The <*rate*> is the interest rate per period; if the interest rate is yearly, the <*rate*> is the yearly interest rate divided by 12. The <*period*> is the number of payments. The result of the FV function is the total deposits plus the generated (and compounded) interest.

Make sure that you enter the interest value as a decimal number: 14 percent interest should be entered as 0.14. The interest rate should be the interest rate per period: if you are making monthly payments at 14 percent interest, the interest rate is 0.14 / 12.

### Example

```
* determine total of all payments
* (principal plus interest paid)
Monthpay = 320.44              && monthly payment
Numperiod = 36                 && three year loan (36 months)
Int_rate = 0.1433 / 12         && monthly interest rate
Total_pay = FV(Monthpay, Int_rate, Numperiod)
? Total_pay                    && returns 14307.62
```

# FWRITE()

### Syntax

```
FWRITE(<file handle>,<character expression>[,<number of bytes>])
```

### Purpose

Writes characters to a low-level file.

# GETENV()

### Syntax

```
GETENV(<"DOS environmental variable name">)
```

### Purpose

Returns the contents of a DOS environmental system variable such as PATH. You can see the current system variables with the

RUN SET command at the dot prompt. Your DOS operating system manual contains a list of environment variables. You also can set environmental variables at the DOS prompt with the SET command. The <*DOS environmental variable name*> must be a character string enclosed in quotation marks.

**Example**

```
* Get the COMSPEC variable
Comspec = GETENV("COMSPEC")
* Will return "C:\COMMAND.COM" on most non-networked systems
```

## HOME()

**Syntax**

```
HOME()
```

**Purpose**

Returns the directory path from which dBASE IV was run.

**Example**

```
? HOME()
C:\DBASE\
```

## ID()

**Syntax**

```
ID()
```

**Purpose**

Returns the name of the current user on a multiuser system.

**Example**

```
mString="The current user is: "
? mString + ID()
The current user is: Johnson
```

## IIF()

**Syntax**

```
IIF(<condition>, <expression 1>, <expression 2>)
```

**Purpose**

The immediate IF function, a shortcut to the IF...ENDIF command. If the <*condition*> evaluates to a logical true (.T.), <*expression 1*> is returned. If the <*condition*> evaluates to a logical false (.F.), <*expression 2*> is returned. The two expressions must be the same type: character, numeric, logical, or date.

### Example

```
* Determine whether the item is on back order
* {} indicates a blank date
Message = IIF(ISBLANK(Backdate), "Order completed.",;
   "Items on back order.")
@ 12,15 SAY Message
* Equivalent to:
IF ISBLANK(Backdate)
   Message = "Order completed."
ELSE
   Message = "Items on back order."
ENDIF
@ 12,15 SAY message
```

## INKEY()

### Syntax

```
INKEY([<number of seconds to wait>])
```

### Purpose

Returns an integer value that represents the last key pressed by the user. It does not wait for a keystroke, and the program continues. If no key has been pressed, a value of 0 is returned. You can use the INKEY function in a DO WHILE loop to wait for a key. The optional <*number of seconds to wait*> will cause the program to delay for that number of seconds. A value of 0 will cause an infinite wait for the user to press a key.

If the keyboard buffer contains characters that have not been processed, INKEY() will return the value of the first character in the buffer. You can use CLEAR TYPEAHEAD to clear the keyboard buffer.

Table R.10 shows values returned by the INKEY function.

**Table R.10 Values Returned by INKEY**

| Key | Name | Decimal value | Key | Name | Decimal value |
|---|---|---|---|---|---|
| Ctrl-A | Ctrl-left arrow | 1 | Shift-F2 | | –21 |
| Ctrl-B | End | 2 | Shift-F3 | | –22 |
| Ctrl-C | PgDn | 3 | Shift-F4 | | –23 |
| Ctrl-D | Right arrow | 4 | Shift-F5 | | –24 |
| Ctrl-E | Up arrow | 5 | Shift-F6 | | –25 |

*continues*

**Table R.10 Continued**

| Key | Name | Decimal value | Key | Name | Decimal value |
|---|---|---|---|---|---|
| Ctrl-F | Ctrl-right arrow | 6 | Shift-F7 | | –26 |
| Ctrl-G | Del | 7 | Shift-F8 | | –27 |
| Ctrl-H | | 8 | Shift-F9 | | –28 |
| Ctrl-I | Tab | 9 | Alt-a | | –435 |
| Ctrl-J | | 10 | Alt-b | | –434 |
| Ctrl-K | | 11 | Alt-c | | –433 |
| Ctrl-L | | 12 | Alt-d | | –432 |
| Ctrl-M | | 13 | Alt-e | | –431 |
| Ctrl-N | | 14 | Alt-f | | –430 |
| Ctrl-O | | 15 | Alt-g | | –429 |
| Ctrl-P | | 16 | Alt-h | | –428 |
| Ctrl-Q | | 17 | Alt-i | | –427 |
| Ctrl-R | PgUp | 18 | Alt-j | | –426 |
| Ctrl-S | Left arrow | 19 | Alt-k | | –425 |
| Ctrl-T | | 20 | Alt-l | | –424 |
| Ctrl-U | | 21 | Alt-m | | –423 |
| Ctrl-V | Ins | 22 | Alt-n | | –422 |
| Ctrl-W | Ctrl-End | 23 | Alt-o | | –421 |
| Ctrl-X | Down arrow | 24 | Alt-p | | –420 |
| Ctrl-Y | | 25 | Alt-q | | –419 |
| Ctrl-Z | Home | 26 | Alt-r | | –418 |
| Esc | Ctrl-[ | 27 | Alt-s | | –417 |
| F1 | Ctrl-\ | 28 | Alt-t | | –416 |
| Ctrl-] | Ctrl-Home | 29 | Alt-u | | –415 |
| Ctrl-^ | Ctrl-PgDn | 30 | Alt-v | | –414 |
| Ctrl-PgUp | | 31 | Alt-w | | –413 |
| Space bar | | 32 | Alt-x | | –412 |
| Backspace | | 127 | Alt-y | | –411 |
| Backtab | Shift-Tab | –400 | Alt-z | | –410 |

| Key | Name | Decimal value | Key | Name | Decimal value |
|---|---|---|---|---|---|
| Ctrl-Backspace | | –401 | Alt-1 | | –451 |
| Ctrl-Enter | | –402 | Alt-2 | | –450 |
| F2 | | –1 | Alt-3 | | –449 |
| F3 | | –2 | Alt-4 | | –448 |
| F4 | | –3 | Alt-5 | | –447 |
| F5 | | –4 | Alt-6 | | –446 |
| F6 | | –5 | Alt-7 | | –445 |
| F7 | | –6 | Alt-8 | | –444 |
| F8 | | –7 | Alt-9 | | –443 |
| F9 | | –8 | Alt-0 | | –452 |
| F10 | | –9 | Ctrl-0 | | –404 |
| Ctrl-F1 | | –10 | Ctrl-1 | | –404 |
| Ctrl-F2 | | –11 | Ctrl-2 | | –404 |
| Ctrl-F3 | | –12 | Ctrl-3 | | –404 |
| Ctrl-F4 | | –13 | Ctrl-4 | | –404 |
| Ctrl-F5 | | –14 | Ctrl-5 | | –404 |
| Ctrl-F6 | | –15 | Ctrl-6 | | 30 |
| Ctrl-F7 | | –16 | Ctrl-7 | | –404 |
| Ctrl-F8 | | –17 | Ctrl-8 | | –404 |
| Ctrl-F9 | | –18 | Ctrl-9 | | –404 |
| Ctrl-F10 | | –19 | Ctrl— | | –403 |
| Shift-F1 | | –20 | | | |

*Note: Alt-key values are used by Macro Handler only.*

### Example

```
* Wait for the user to press any key before continuing
@ 24,20 SAY "Press a key to continue"
DO WHILE INKEY() = 0
ENDDO
```

## INT()

### Syntax

```
INT(<numeric expression>)
```

### Purpose

Truncates the <*numeric expression*> to an integer. All decimal places in the number are discarded.

### Example

```
? INT(49.293)            && returns 49
```

## ISALPHA()

### Syntax

```
ISALPHA(<string>)
```

### Purpose

Tests whether the first character of <*string*> is alphabetic. A logical true (.T.) is returned if the first character is alphabetic. A logical false (.F.) is returned if the first character is not alphabetic.

### Example

```
?ISALPHA("Tom")                  && returns true
?ISALPHA("100 Forest Lane")      && returns false
```

## ISBLANK()

### Syntax

```
ISBLANK(<expression>)
```

### Purpose

Tests an expression to see whether it contains a blank value. Returns true (.T.) if the expression is blank; returns false (.F.) if it is not blank.

### Example

```
? ISBLANK(" ")
.T.
? ISBLANK("Carl")
.F.
```

## ISCOLOR()

### Syntax

```
ISCOLOR()
```

### Purpose

Returns a logical true (.T.) if a color video adapter card is installed in your system. You then can use COLOR statements that are appropriate for your monitor/card setup.

### Example

```
* Set up proper colors for the monitor
IF ISCOLOR()
   Front = "w/b"
   Back = "bg/b"
ELSE
   Front = "w/n"
   Back = "n/w"
ENDIF
SET COLOR TO &Front, &Back
```

## ISLOWER()

### Syntax

ISLOWER(<*string*>)

### Purpose

Determines whether the first character of the <*string*> is a lowercase character. A logical true (.T.) is returned if the first character is lowercase; a logical false (.F.) is returned if the first character is uppercase or a numeric character.

### Example

```
? ISLOWER("Thomas Hardy")          && returns false
? ISLOWER("corn on the cob")       && returns true
? ISLOWER("4129 Creek Road")       && returns false
```

## ISMARKED()

### Syntax

ISMARKED([<*alias*>])

### Purpose

Returns a logical true (.T.) if dBASE IV has placed a marker in the database file indicating that the file is in a state of change. Otherwise, a logical false (.F.) is returned. Use the optional <*alias*> to specify another active work area.

### Example

```
IF ISMARKED()
   @ 12,15 SAY "Record has been changed."
ENDIF
```

## ISUPPER()

### Syntax

```
ISUPPER(<string>)
```

### Purpose

Determines whether the first character of the *<string>* is uppercase. If it is, true (.T.) is returned. If the first character is lowercase or a numeric character, then false (.F.) is returned.

### Example

```
? ISUPPER("Wuthering Heights")          && returns true
? ISUPPER("cocker spaniel")             && returns false
? ISUPPER("12 cases")                   && returns false
```

## KEY()

### Syntax

```
KEY( [<character expression>,] <numeric expression> [, <alias>])
```

### Purpose

Returns the expression used to create the index. If multiple indexes are active, the *<numeric expression>* is the index number. The current database is used unless an *<alias>* is specified. If there is not an active index, a null string (" ") is returned.

### Example

```
USE CUSTOMER INDEX Cust_id, Cust_name
* Cust_id index = Custid
* Cust_name index = UPPER(Custname)
? KEY(2)            && returns "UPPER(custname)"
```

## LASTKEY()

### Syntax

```
LASTKEY()
```

### Purpose

Returns the ASCII value of the last key used to exit a full-screen command. Values returned are the same as for INKEY() (see table R.10).

### Example

```
* Wait for user to press F10 key
DO WHILE .T.
   @ 24,20 SAY "Press F10 when ready"
   READ
   IF LASTKEY() = -9
```

```
        DO ENTRDATA
     ENDIF
  ENDDO
```

## LEFT()

### Syntax

```
LEFT(<string>/<memo field name>,<number>)
```

### Purpose

Returns the left <*number*> characters of the character string or of the contents of the memo field. If the <*number*> is 0, a null string (" ") is returned; if the <*number*> is greater than the length of the string, the entire string is returned.

### Example

```
* Will return "The whole truth"
? LEFT("The whole truth and nothing but",15)
```

## LEN()

### Syntax

```
LEN(<string> / <memo field name>)
```

### Purpose

Returns the length of the <*string*> or the number of characters in the specified memo field. The length of the entire string, including any spaces, is returned. Use the TRIM() function to trim off trailing spaces.

### Example

```
* The string has four trailing spaces
?LEN("1495 Arcadia    ")                 && returns 16
?LEN(TRIM("1495 Arcadia    ")            && returns 12
Item_desc = "New Hebrides"
?LEN(Item_desc)                          && returns 12
```

## LIKE()

### Syntax

```
LIKE(<search pattern>, <string>)
```

### Purpose

Compares the <*search pattern*> with the <*string*> and returns a logical true (.T.) if the pattern is found in the string. The search pattern usually contains a wild card—the asterisk (*), which stands for any number of characters, or the question mark (?), which stands for any character in that position.

### Example

```
? LIKE("Smith*","Smithereens")      && returns .T.
? LIKE("*son", "Johnson")           && returns .T.
? LIKE("Smith","Smythe")            && returns .F.
? LIKE("J?n", "Jan")                && returns .T.
```

## LINENO()

### Syntax

```
LINENO()
```

### Purpose

Returns the line number of the next command in a program that will be executed. Usually used during debugging.

### Example

```
* In the error-trapping procedure,
* what line number caused the error
@ 24,1 SAY "Error at command before line # " + STR(LINENO())
```

## LKSYS()

### Syntax

```
LKSYS(<n>)
```

### Purpose

Returns information about when a record was locked or updated and who performed the action. Values of <*n*> are shown in table R.11.

**Table R.11 Values for *n* in LKSYS**

| Value | Meaning |
|---|---|
| 0 | Time when lock was placed |
| 1 | Date when locked was placed |
| 2 | Log-in name of user who locked the record |
| 3 | Time of the last update or lock |
| 4 | Date of the last update or lock |
| 5 | Log-in name of the user who last updated or locked the record or database |

The database must have been changed previously with the CONVERT command to create a hidden field containing the user name and other information (see CONVERT). A null string (“ ”) is returned if the database was not converted.

### Example

```
* Display data and time a record
* was locked.
? "Record was locked " + LKSYS(4) + " " + LKSYS(3)
```

## LOCK()

*See* RLOCK.

## LOG()

### Syntax

```
LOG(<numeric variable>)
```

### Purpose

Returns the natural logarithm of the *<numeric variable>*. The logarithm is *x*, where *<numeric variable>* = *ex*. The logarithmic value returned is a type F (floating-point) number.

### Example

```
?LOG(2.33)                  && returns 0.85
```

## LOG10()

### Syntax

```
LOG10(<numeric variable>)
```

### Purpose

Returns the base 10 logarithm of the *<numeric variable>*. The LOG10 function returns *y*, where *<numeric variable>* = LOG10(*<numeric variable>*).

### Example

```
? LOG10(3)                  && returns 0.48
```

## LOOKUP()

### Syntax

```
LOOKUP(<return field>, <look-for expression>, <look-in field>)
```

### Purpose

Looks at the *<look-in field>* for the *<look-for expression>*. If the expression is found, LOOKUP returns the *<return field>* value. Use this function to return a value from a record when searching a database.

### Example

```
* Using LOOKUP() function
USE PARTS ORDER Partname        && part name index is active
* Find the "Brake Pads" record, return number on back order
? LOOKUP(backordr, "Brake Pads", Partname)
* Equivalent function using SEEK
SEEK "Brake Pads"
IF FOUND()
   ? backordr
ENDIF    .
```

## LOWER()

### Syntax

```
LOWER(<string>)
```

### Purpose

Changes the <*string*> to all lowercase characters. To use text from a memo field, first use the MLINE() function (*see MLINE()*).

### Example

```
Bankname = "FIRST TRUST BANK"
? LOWER(Bankname)              && returns "first trust bank"
? LOWER("Acme Painting")       && returns "acme painting"
```

## LTRIM()

### Syntax

```
LTRIM(<string>)
```

### Purpose

Removes leading blanks from the <*string*>. This is useful in conjunction with the LEN() function to determine the number of characters in a character field.

### Example

```
* There are two spaces at the beginning of the string in quotes,
* below Item_desc = "  Playing cards"
? LTRIM(Item_desc)       && returns "Playing Cards" without
                         && spaces at beginning
? LEN(LTRIM(Item_desc))  && returns 13
```

# LUPDATE()

### Syntax

```
LUPDATE([<alias>])
```

### Purpose

Returns the date that the database was last changed. If no database is in use, a blank date is returned. The current work area is assumed unless you specify the *<alias>* of a database open in another work area.

### Example

```
* Determine whether the inventory database was updated today
USE INVENTRY
IF LUPDATE < DATE()
   ? "Inventory database not updated today"
ENDIF
```

# MAX()

### Syntax

```
MAX(<expression 1>, <expression 2>)
```

### Purpose

Returns the greater value of the two expressions, which can be numeric, date, or character types. The greater number, or the later date, is returned.

### Example

```
? MAX(15,33)                     && returns 33
? MAX("Oranges", "Apples")       && returns "Oranges"
? MAX({07/04/92}, {01/25/92})    && returns date type
                                 && 07/04/92
```

# MDX()

### Syntax

```
MDX(<numeric expression> [, <alias>])
```

### Purpose

Returns the name of the multiple-index (MDX) file indicated by the *<numeric expression>*. The current database is used, unless the optional *<alias>* parameter is specified. If no MDX file is active, or if no MDX files are associated with the database, a null string (“”) is returned.

### Example

```
* PARTS.DBF has a PARTS.MDX multiple-index file
USE PARTS
? MDX(1)              && returns "PARTS.MDX"
```

## MDY()

### Syntax

```
MDY(<date variable>)
```

### Purpose

Converts a <*date variable*> to the form "month, day, year." The "month" is the full name of the month, "day" is the two-digit day value, and "year" is the two-digit year value. If you have used SET CENTURY ON, four digits will be displayed as the year.

### Example

```
Date1 = {10/10/75}
SET CENTURY OFF
? MDY(Date1)          && returns "October 10, 75"
SET CENTURY ON
? MDY(Date1)          && returns "October 10, 1975"
```

## MEMLINES()

### Syntax

```
MEMLINES(<memo field name>)
```

### Purpose

Returns the number of word-wrapped lines in the <*memo field name*> of the current database.

### Example

```
USE CLIENTS
GOTO 43
IF MEMLINES("Notes") > 0
   ? "No comments found in the Notes memo field"
ELSE
   ? "Total lines in Notes memo field is " + ;
     STR(MEMLINES("Notes"))
ENDIF
```

## MEMORY()

### Syntax

```
MEMORY()
```

### Purpose

Returns the amount of system RAM (in kilobytes) that is not in use.

### Example

```
* Display available memory
? "Unused memory = " + STR(Memory()) + "Kbytes."
```

## MENU()

### Syntax

```
MENU()
```

### Purpose

Returns the name of the most recently selected menu. If no menu is active, then a null string ("") is returned.

### Example

```
@ 12,15 SAY "Last menu selected was " + MENU()
```

## MESSAGE()

### Syntax

```
MESSAGE()
```

### Purpose

Returns the error message of the last error. The *dBASE IV Language Reference* contains a list of all the error messages on a single-user system. The *Networking with dBASE IV* manual contains a list of network error messages.

### Example

```
* In the error-trapping procedure
@ 23,1 SAY "Last error " + STR(ERROR())
@ 24,1 SAY "Error msg  " + MESSAGE()
```

## MIN()

### Syntax

```
MIN(<expression 1>, <expression 2>)
```

### Purpose

Returns the smaller value of the two expressions, which can be numeric, date, or character types. The smaller number, or the earlier date, is returned.

### Example

```
? MIN(15,33)                      && returns 15
? MIN("Oranges", "Apples")        && returns "Apples"
? MIN({07/04/92}, {01/25/92})     && returns date type 1/25/92
```

## MLINE()

### Syntax

MLINE(*<memo field name>*, *<numeric expression>*)

### Purpose

Extracts the *<numeric expression>* line number from the *<memo field>* in the current database.

### Example

```
* Extract the first and last line of the Notes memo field
USE CLIENTS
GOTO 18
? "First line is " + MLINE("Notes",1)
? "Last line is " + MLINE("Notes",MEMLINES("Notes"))
```

## MOD()

### Syntax

MOD(*<numeric expression 1>*, *<numeric expression 2>*)

### Purpose

Returns the remainder of dividing *<numeric expression 1>* by *<numeric expression 2>*.

### Example

```
? MOD(13, 4)        && returns 1
```

## MONTH()

### Syntax

MONTH(*<date variable>*)

### Purpose

Returns the month number of the *<date variable>*, which can be a date memory variable, a date field, or a function that returns a date-type variable.

### Example

```
Date2 = {7/4/91}
? MONTH(date2)      && returns 7
```

## NDX()

### Syntax

```
NDX(<numeric expression> [, <alias>]
```

### Purpose

Returns the name of the index (NDX) file for the current database or the index file for the optional *<alias>* database. The index can be specified with the USE...INDEX command or with the SET INDEX TO command. If no index is associated with the *<numeric expression>* that indicates the index number, a null string is returned.

### Example

```
USE MEMBERS INDEX Name, City, Memnum
? NDX(2)            && returns "CITY.NDX"
```

## NETWORK()

### Syntax

```
NETWORK()
```

### Purpose

Returns a logical true (.T.) if the system is running on a network. If not, a logical false (.F.) is returned.

### Example

```
* Do some file or record locking command
* if running on a network
IF NETWORK()
   * file or record locking commands
ENDIF
```

## ORDER()

### Syntax

```
ORDER([<alias>])
```

### Purpose

Returns the name of the primary-order index (NDX) file or multiple-index (MDX) tag. The index file name, but not its extension, is returned in uppercase characters. The current database is used, unless you specify the optional *<alias>*.

### Example

```
USE CLIENTS
SET INDEX TO Lastname, Company, City
? ORDER()     && returns "LASTNAME", the primary index
```

```
SET ORDER TO 2
? ORDER()     && returns "COMPANY", now the primary index
```

## OS()

### Syntax

```
OS()
```

### Purpose

Returns the name of the operating system installed on your computer.

### Example

```
* If your computer's operating system is DOS 3.3
? OS()                      && returns "DOS 3.30"
```

## PAD()

### Syntax

```
PAD()
```

### Purpose

Returns the name of the last pad selected from the active menu. You select a menu pad by highlighting the desired pad and pressing the Enter key. The menu pad name is not cleared by the DEACTIVATE MENU or DEACTIVATE POPUP command.

### Example

```
@ 12,15 SAY "Last pad selected was " + PAD()
```

## PAYMENT()

### Syntax

```
PAYMENT(<principal>, <rate>, <periods>)
```

### Purpose

Returns the payment required, given the *<principal>*, *<rate>*, and *<periods>*. The *<principal>* can be a positive or negative value and is the principal value of the loan. The *<rate>* is the interest rate per *<periods>*; if the interest rate is a yearly value, you will need to divide the annual interest rate by 12. The *<periods>* parameter represents the number of payment periods of the loan.

Make sure that you enter the interest value as a decimal number: 14 percent interest should be entered as 0.14. The interest rate should be the interest rate per period: if you are making monthly payments at 14 percent interest, the interest rate is 0.14/12.

### Example

```
* Determines payment for a loan
Prin_bal = 250000                  && loan amount
Num_pays = 360                     && 30 year loan (360 months)
Int_rate = 0.1175/12               && monthly interest rate
Monthpay = PAYMENT(Prin_bal, Int_rate, Num_pay)
? Monthpay                         && returns 2523.52
```

## PCOL()

### Syntax

```
PCOL()
```

### Purpose

Returns the current column position (relative to _ploffset) of the printer. In @...SAY and @...GET commands, you can use the dollar symbol ($) to get the column position for the screen or the printer, whereas PCOL() is used only with the printer.

### Example

```
@ 20,15 SAY "Current printing column is " + STR(PCOL())
```

## PCOUNT()

### Syntax

```
PCOUNT()
```

### Purpose

Returns the number of parameters that are passed to a procedure or user-defined function.

### Example

```
PROCEDURE ADDRESS
PARAMETERS P1,P2
MYADD=P1+"  "+P2
? MYADD
? PCOUNT()
RETURN
DO ADDRESS WITH "Dallas, TX","75299"
Dallas, TX 75299
2
```

## PI()

### Syntax

```
PI()
```

### Purpose

Returns 3.14159 as the π value. Use SET DECIMALS and SET PRECISION to change the accuracy of the displayed value.

### Example

```
? PI()          && returns 3.1416, with SET DECIMALS TO 4
```

## POPUP()

### Syntax

```
POPUP()
```

### Purpose

Returns the name of the currently active pop-up menu. If no pop-up menu is active, a null string ("") is returned. If no pop-up menus are defined, dBASE IV returns the error message `POPUP has not been defined.`

### Example

```
? 12,15 SAY "Current pop-up menu name is " + POPUP()
```

## PRINTSTATUS()

### Syntax

```
PRINTSTATUS()
```

### Purpose

Returns a logical true (.T.) if the printer is on-line and ready.

> **WARNING:** Some printers will not support this command, and networked printers or printers with a printer buffer may return an inaccurate response.

### Example

```
IF .NOT. PRINTSTATUS()
   @ 15,20 SAY "Please make sure printer is ready."
ENDIF
```

## PROGRAM()

### Syntax

```
PROGRAM()
```

### Purpose

Returns the name of the program or procedure that was running when an error occurred. Can be used during debugging a program in conjunction with the Breakpoint window. The program name returned does not include its file-name extension.

### Example

```
* Simple error trapping
ON ERROR ? "Error ", ERROR(), " in ", ;
   PROGRAM(), "at line", LINENO()
```

## PROMPT()

### Syntax

```
PROMPT()
```

### Purpose

Returns the character string associated with the last selected pop-up or menu option. If no pop-ups or menus are in memory (even if they have been deactivated), or if the Esc key was used to exit a pop-up or menu, a null string (“”) is returned.

### Example

```
@ 12,15 SAY "You selected the " + PROMPT() + " choice."
```

## PROW()

### Syntax

```
PROW()
```

### Purpose

Returns the current printing row on the printer. The printing row is set to 0 after an EJECT command.

### Example

```
* Eject paper to top of form before continuing
IF PROW() <> 0
   EJECT
ENDIF
```

## PV()

### Syntax

```
PV(<payment>, <rate>, <periods>)
```

### Purpose

Returns the present value of equal regular *<payments>* at a constant interest *<rate>* for the *<periods>*. If the interest is compounded daily, use a *<rate>* of the annual interest rate divided by 365. If the interest is compounded monthly, use a *<rate>* of the annual interest rate divided by 12.

Make sure that you enter the interest value as a decimal number: 14 percent interest should be entered as 0.14. The interest rate should be the interest rate per period: if you are making monthly payments at 14 percent interest, the interest rate is 0.14 / 12.

### Example

```
* How much has been saved over five years?
Monthpay = 150              && amount saved each month
Int_rate = 0.0822/12        && annual interest compounded monthly
Num_pays = 60               && five years (60 months)
Amt_saved = PV(Monthpay, Int_rate, Num_pays)
? Amt_saved                 && returns 7359.49
```

## RAND()

### Syntax

```
RAND([<numeric expression>])
```

### Purpose

Returns a random number. The optional *<numeric expression>* is the random number seed used to generate the number. If the *<numeric expression>* is a negative number, the seed is taken from the system clock. A seed value of 100001 is the default value. The number returned is from 0 to 0.999999.

### Example

```
* Returns first random number, based on a seed of 14
? RAND(14)
* Compute the next random number using the same seed
? RAND()
```

## READKEY()

### Syntax

```
READKEY()
```

### Purpose

Returns an integer value for the key used to exit a full-screen command. The value returned is different if data was changed on the screen. Table R.12 shows the values returned.

**Table R.12 Values Returned by READKEY**

| Data changed | # Change | Key pressed |
|---|---|---|
| 0 | 256 | Ctrl-S, left arrow, Ctrl-H |
| (none) | 256 | Backspace |
| 1 | 257 | Ctrl-D, right arrow, Ctrl-L |
| 2 | 258 | Ctrl-A, Ctrl, left arrow |
| 4 | 260 | Ctrl-E, up arrow, Ctrl-K |
| 5 | 261 | Ctrl-J, down arrow, Ctrl-X |
| 3 | 259 | Ctrl-F, Ctrl, right arrow |
| 6 | 262 | Ctrl-R, PgUp |
| 7 | 263 | Ctrl-C, PgDn |
| 12 | (none) | Ctrl-Q, Esc |
| (none) | 270 | Ctrl-W, Ctrl-End |
| 15 | 271 | Enter, Ctrl-M (fill last record) |
| 16 | (none) | Enter, Ctrl-M (at beginning of record in APPEND) |
| 33 | 289 | Ctrl-Home |
| 34 | 290 | Ctrl-PgUp |
| 35 | 291 | Ctrl-PgDn |
| 36 | 292 | F1 (Help function key) |

### Example

```
* Save the data only if changed
* This saves time over saving unchanged data
DO inputdata                        && data input routine
IF READKEY() >= 256
   DO savedata                      && save data routine
ENDIF
```

## RECCOUNT()

### Syntax

```
RECCOUNT([<alias>])
```

### Purpose

Returns the number of records in the database. All records are included, even those excluded by a SET FILTER or SET DELETED ON command. The current database is used, unless you specify the optional <*alias*> of another active database.

### Example

```
* CLIENTS.DBF has 138 records
USE CLIENTS
? RECCOUNT()          && returns 138
```

## RECNO()

### Syntax

```
RECNO([<alias>])
```

### Purpose

Returns the current record number of the database in the current work area or in another open database specified by <*alias*>. If a database is empty, or the current record pointer is at BOF(), RECNO() returns 1. If no database is in use, RECNO() returns 0. If the current record pointer is at EOF(), RECNO() will return RECCOUNT() + 1.

### Example

```
* ORDERS.DBF has 382 records
USE ORDERS
? RECCOUNT()          && returns 382
GOTO 322
? RECNO()             && returns 322
GOTO BOTTOM
? RECNO()             && returns 382
SKIP 1
? RECNO()             && returns 383
```

## RECSIZE()

### Syntax

```
RECSIZE([<alias>])
```

### Purpose

Returns the size in bytes of one record of the current database, or of an open database in another area if you use the <*alias*> option. You then can determine the size of the database, which is computed with the formula (32*<*number of fields*>)+34.

### Example

```
USE ORDERS
? RECSIZE()         && returns size of one record
```

## REPLICATE()

### Syntax

REPLICATE(<*string*>, <*number of times to repeat*>)

### Purpose

Repeats the <*string*> the specified number of times. This function is useful for drawing lines in reports or for creating simple bar charts based on numeric variables.

### Example

```
? REPLICATE("E",4)              && returns "EEEE"
* These are values corresponding to test scores
Grade_a = 3
Grade_b = 10
Grade_c = 15
Grade_d = 8
Grade_f = 2
?"A = " + REPLICATE("A",grade_a)
?"B = " + REPLICATE("B",grade_b)
?"C = " + REPLICATE("C",grade_c)
?"D = " + REPLICATE("D",grade_d)
?"F = " + REPLICATE("F",grade_f)
```

This example displays the following on the screen:

```
A = AAA
B = BBBBBBBBBB
C = CCCCCCCCCCCCCCC
D = DDDDDDDD
F = FF
```

## RIGHT()

### Syntax

RIGHT (<*string*> / <*variable*> , <*number*>)

### Purpose

Returns the <*number*> of characters from the string, counting from the last character of the string. You may want to use the TRIM() function to remove any trailing spaces.

### Example

```
* There are four spaces at the end of "Lunch    "
? RIGHT ("Out to Lunch    ",9)       && returns "Lunch    "
? RIGHT (TRIM("Out to Lunch    "),5)  && returns "Lunch"
```

## RLOCK()

### Syntax

```
RLOCK([<character string list of record numbers>, <alias>]/
    [<alias>]
```

### Purpose

Used to lock multiple records, where the *<character string list of record numbers>* indicates the records to be locked. The LOCK() function is exactly like RLOCK(). The records in the current database are locked, unless you specify another work area with the optional *<alias>* parameter. The maximum number of records that can be locked is 50. After a record is locked, other users can access the record information only in read-only mode.

When all the records are locked successfully, a logical true (.T.) is returned. If the record locking is unsuccessful, a logical false (.F.) is returned. Records are unlocked when you use the UNLOCK command, when the database is closed, or when you quit dBASE IV.

### Example

```
* Lock record 15 of the CLIENTS.DBF database
USE CLIENTS
IF RLOCK("15")
   @ 12,15 SAY "Record 15 is locked."
ELSE
   @ 12,15 SAY "Couldn't lock record 15."
ENDIF
```

## ROLLBACK()

### Syntax

```
ROLLBACK()
```

### Purpose

Returns a logical true (.T.) if the ROLLBACK command was successful. A logical false (.F.) is returned if the ROLLBACK was unsuccessful.

### Example

```
* Rollback the transaction if not completed
IF .NOT. COMPLETED()
```

```
    ROLLBACK
    IF ROLLBACK()
       @ 22,30 SAY "Transaction rolled back OK."
    ELSE
       @ 22,20 SAY "Transaction rollback failed."
       @ 23,20 SAY "Restore data from backup!"
    ENDIF
ENDIF
```

## ROUND()

### Syntax

ROUND(<*numeric expression*>, <*number of decimal places*>)

### Purpose

Rounds the <*numeric expression*> to the specified <*number of decimal places*>. If you specify a negative number of decimal places, the number is rounded to whole numbers of 10 * *x*, where *x* is the negative <*number of decimal places*>.

### Example

```
SET DECIMAL TO 2
?ROUND(14.3972,1)        && returns 14.4
?ROUND(14.3972,0)        && returns 14
?ROUND(14.3972,-1)       && returns 10
```

## ROW()

### Syntax

ROW()

### Purpose

Returns the current row number of the cursor.

### Example

```
* Print a message at the current row
@ ROW(), 35 SAY "Please wait."
```

## RTOD()

### Syntax

RTOD(<*radian value*>)

### Purpose

Converts the <*radian value*> to degrees.

### Example

```
? RTOD(3.22)        && returns 184.49
```

## RTRIM/TRIM()

### Syntax

```
RTRIM/TRIM (<string>)
```

### Purpose

Removes trailing blanks from the <*string*>. RTRIM() and TRIM() are equivalent. These commands are useful for removing excess spaces from data fields.

### Example

```
* There are five spaces at the end of each string
? RTRIM("Pinion Rings     ")       && returns "Pinion Rings"
Username = "Cathy Hill     "
? TRIM(Username)                   && returns "Cathy Hill"
```

## RUN()

### Syntax

```
RUN([<logical expression>,]<character expression>[,
     <logical expression>])
```

### Purpose

Run a DOS command or other external program from within dBASE IV. Returns a completion code from the program or operating system. The <*character expression*> is the program name. The first optional <*logical expression*> is to be set true (.T.) if the command or program name is to be passed directly to the operating system. Otherwise, a copy of the operating system's command interpreter (COMMAND.COM) is loaded. If the second optional <*logical expression*> is true (.T.), dBASE IV is rolled out of memory to make room for the program being run. The amount of memory used by dBASE IV is reduced to as little as 10K bytes in this case.

> **WARNING:** The DOS commands PRINT and ASSIGN are TSR programs.

### Example

```
? RUN(.T.,"C:\ACCESS\ACCESS.COM",.T.)
0
```

## SEEK()

### Syntax

```
SEEK(<expression> [, <alias>])
```

### Purpose

Searches the currently active database (or another opened database by using <*alias*>) for the <*expression*>. If the <*expression*> is found, a logical true (.T.) is returned; if not found, a logical false (.F.) is returned.

### Example

```
USE CUSTOMERS INDEX Cust_id
* Look for customer id SM1002
IF SEEK("SM1002")
   @ 12,15 SAY "Found the customer!"
ELSE
   @ 12,15 SAY "Didn't find the customer!"
ENDIF
* This does the same thing, but moves to the found record
USE CUSTOMERS ORDER cust_id
SEEK "SM1002"
IF FOUND()
   @ 12,15 say "Found it!"
ELSE
   @ 12,15 say "Didn't find it!"
ENDIF
```

## SELECT()

### Syntax

```
SELECT([<alias>])
```

### Purpose

Returns the number of the next available work area, or the work area corresponding to the alias specified. dBASE IV 1.5 allows up to 40 work areas.

### Example

```
CLOSE ALL
USE MYLIST ORDER STREET
USE ADDRESS IN 2 ORDER STREET
? SELECT()
3
? SELECT("ADDRESS")
2
```

## SET()

### Syntax

```
SET("<character expression>")
```

### Purpose

Returns the status of a SET command, where <*character expression*> is one of the valid SET keywords, surrounded by quotation marks. See “Using SET Commands” elsewhere in this “dBASE IV Reference Guide” for the valid SET keywords.

### Example

```
* Make sure that database encryption is set on
IF SET("ENCRYPTION") <> "ON"
   SET ENCRYPTION ON
ENDIF
```

## SIGN()

### Syntax

```
SIGN(<numeric expression>)
```

### Purpose

Returns a number for the sign of the <*numeric expression*>. If <*numeric expression*> is negative, a –1 is returned; if it is positive, a 1 is returned; if it is zero, a 0 is returned.

### Example

```
? SIGN(13)              && returns 1
? SIGN(-14.22)          && returns -1
? SIGN(0)               && returns 0
```

## SIN()

### Syntax

```
SIN(<angle value in radians>)
```

### Purpose

Returns the sine of the <*angle value in radians*>. The value returned is a type F (floating-point) number and varies from –1 to +1. Use SET DECIMALS and SET PRECISION to change the accuracy of the displayed value.

### Example

```
? SIN(PI()/2)        && returns 1
```

## SOUNDEX()

### Syntax

```
SOUNDEX (<string>)
```

### Purpose

Converts a <*string*> to a four-digit code indicating its phonetic value. The following logic is followed by SOUNDEX in dBASE IV:

- The code's first character is the first character of the string.
- All occurrences of the letters *a, e, h, i, o, u, w,* and *y,* are removed from the string, except for the first character of the string.
- The remaining letters are assigned a number, as follows:

  1 = *b, f, p, v*
  2 = *c, g, j, k, q, s, x, z*
  3 = *d, t*
  4 = *l*
  5 = *m, n*
  6 = *r*

- Excess repeating letters, as the second *e* in *teeth*, are dropped (the first *e* in *teeth* is retained).
- The code is in the form *letter digit digit digit*, with trailing zeros added if there are fewer than three digits. Any digits after *letter digit digit digit* are dropped.
- Code conversion stops at the first nonalphabetic character.
- Leading blanks are skipped.
- If the first nonblank character is nonalphabetic, a 0000 code is returned.

The result is a sound-alike code that can be used for searching.

### Example

```
? SOUNDEX("Smithsonian")    && returns S532
* Set up a soundex index
USE FOODDATA
INDEX ON SOUNDEX(Item_name) TAG FSOUND
SEEK SOUNDEX("Beens")       && will find Item_name "Beans"
```

## SPACE()

### Syntax

```
SPACE (<number>)
```

### Purpose

Creates a character string with the specified <*number*> of space characters.

### Example

```
? SPACE(8)                      && returns 8 space characters
? LEN(SPACE(10))                && returns 10
```

## SQRT()

### Syntax

```
SQRT(<numeric expression>)
```

### Purpose

Returns the square root of the *<numeric expression>*. The returned value is always a type F (floating-point) value, even if the *<numeric expression>* is a type F or N. The SET DECIMALS value determines how many decimals are displayed by the result of this function.

### Example

```
? SQRT(16)                  && returns 4
SET DECIMALS TO 4
? SQRT(2)                   && returns 1.4142
```

## STR()

### Syntax

```
STR(<numeric expression>[,<length>] [,<decimals>]
```

### Purpose

Converts a number to a character string, with a default *<length>* of 10 characters and no *<decimals>*. The *<length>* value includes the decimal point, if any. If you specify fewer decimal places than are in the numeric expression, the value is rounded off to the number of *<decimals>*. If you specify a *<length>* that is smaller than the number of digits to the left of the decimal, asterisks are returned in place of the number.

### Example

```
Number1 = 1423.8374
? STR(Number1)              && returns "1424"
? STR(Number1,7,2)          && returns "1423.84"
```

## STUFF()

### Syntax

```
STUFF (<char 1>, <number 1>, <number 2>, <char 2>)
```

### Purpose

Replaces part of the *<char 1>* string with the *<char 2>* string. The *<number 1>* is used as the starting point for the replacement. The

*<number 2>* value is used to determine the number of characters in the *<char 2>* string to replace into the *<char 1>* string. STUFF() does not work in memo fields.

### Example

```
* Change all phone numbers in CUSTOMER
* from "xxx xxxx" to "xxx-xxxx
USE CUSTOMER
REPLACE ALL PHONE WITH STUFF(PHONE,4,"-")
```

## SUBSTR()

### Syntax

```
SUBSTR (<string>/<memo field name>,<start position>,[<number of characters>]
```

### Purpose

Extracts part of the *<string>*. The extracted string starts with the character at *<start position>* and continues for the *<number of characters>*. The starting position number must be a positive number.

### Example

```
Note_name = "Do Re Mi Fa Sol La Ti Do"
? SUBSTR(Note_name, 7,2)      && returns "Mi"
```

## TAG()

### Syntax

```
TAG([<.MDX filename>,] <numeric expression> [, <alias>])
```

### Purpose

Returns the name of the multiple-index (MDX) tag for the index specified by the *<numeric expression>*. The current database is used, unless you use the optional *<alias>* parameter to indicate another open database. If there is no tag name, a null string ("") is returned.

### Example

```
* The inventory database has the following fields tagged
* Part_num, Part_name, Last_ord, Supplier
* The index tags are contained in the INVENTRY.MDX file
USE INVENTRY
? TAG(3)            && returns "INVENTRY"
```

## TAGCOUNT()

### Syntax

```
TAGCOUNT([<multiple index file>[,<alias>]])
```

### Purpose

Returns the number of indexes that are currently active. If a multiple index file is not specified, the number of active indexes in the current work area or work area specified by the alias are returned, including any active NDX files.

### Example

```
USE CUSTOMER IN 2
? TAGCOUNT(2)
6
```

## TAGNO()

### Syntax

```
TAGNO(<index tag or NDX file>[,<MDX file>[,<alias>]])
```

### Purpose

Returns the index number for the specified index tag or NDX file order. If you do not specify an alias, the function assumes the currently active work area.

### Example

```
USE CUSTOMER ORDER ZIP
TAGNO("ZIP")
4
```

## TAN()

### Syntax

```
TAN(<angle size in radians>)
```

### Purpose

Returns the tangent of the *<angle size in radians>*. Use SET DECIMALS and SET PRECISION to change the accuracy of the displayed value.

### Example

```
? TAN(PI())                  && returns 0
```

## TIME()

### Syntax

```
TIME()
```

### Purpose

Converts the system time into a character string in the format HH:MM:SS. The time is always returned in a 24-hour format. If you need to use the system time in a mathematical calculation, use SUBSTR() and VAL().

**NOTE** The system time must be set properly in order for this function to return the current time.

### Example

```
* If the current time is 1:44:00 PM
? TIME()         && returns the character string "13:44:00"
```

## TRANSFORM()

### Syntax

```
TRANSFORM(<variable expression>, <PICTURE format>)
```

### Purpose

Applies a PICTURE format to a variable without requiring that you use an @...SAY command. The TRANSFORM() function always returns a character-type variable for any variable used. See the @...SAY command in the section "Using dBASE Commands" elsewhere in this "dBASE IV Reference Guide" for complete details of the PICTURE parameters.

### Example

```
Unitcost = 4882.33
? TRANSFORM(unitcost, "@$ C")
* Results in "$4,882.33 CR"
```

## TRIM()

### Syntax

```
TRIM(<string>)
```

### Purpose

Removes trailing spaces; see RTRIM().

## TYPE()

### Syntax

```
TYPE(<variable name>)
```

### Purpose

Determines the type of the *<variable name>*. Possible types are the following:

| Type | Meaning |
|---|---|
| C | Character |
| N | Numeric |
| L | Logical |
| M | Memo |
| D | Date |
| F | Floating point number |
| U | Undefined |

### Example

```
* Has a user logged in yet?
IF TYPE("user") = "U"
   DO Loguser  && no user logged in, do log-in program
ENDIF
Logdate = DATE()
? TYPE("Logdate")        && returns "D"
Counter = 12
? TYPE("Counter")        && returns "N"
```

## UNIQUE()

### Syntax

UNIQUE([[*<character expression>*,]*<numeric expression>*[,*<alias>*]])

### Purpose

Returns a true (.T.) value if the specified index tag was created using the UNIQUE option to eliminate duplicate records, or false (.F.) if it was not. The *<numeric expression>* specifies the index number, and the optional *<character expression>* and *<alias>* expressions specify the index and database files if other than the current files.

### Example

```
USE CUSTOMER INDEX ON ADDRESS1 TO ADDRINDX UNIQUE
? TAGNO("ADDRINDX")
   8
? UNIQUE(8)
.T.
```

## UPPER()

### Syntax

UPPER(*<string/variable>*)

### Purpose

Converts all characters in the <*string/variable*> to uppercase. You must use the MLINE() function to extract data from memo fields and then use UPPER() to uppercase the variable.

### Example

```
* Convert all the LASTNAME field data to uppercase
USE CLIENTS
REPLACE ALL LASTNAME WITH UPPER(LASTNAME)
```

## USER()

### Syntax

```
USER()
```

### Purpose

Returns the name of the logged-in user on a protected system. A null string ("") is returned if the database is not protected.

### Example

```
IF LEN(USER()) > 0
   @ 20,20 SAY "Current user is " + USER()
ELSE
   @ 20,20 SAY "No user logged in."
ENDIF
```

## VAL()

### Syntax

```
VAL(<character expression>)
```

### Purpose

Converts character-type data made up of numerals into numeric data. If the <*character expression*> includes a non-number character, 0 is returned. The number of decimals displayed is determined by the SET DECIMAL value. Text is converted from left to right until a non-number character or blank is encountered.

### Example

```
Thisaddr = "4933 Magnolia Street"
? VAL(Thisaddr) + 2     && returns the number 4935 (4933+2)
Thisaddr = "PO Box 1085"
VAL(Thisaddr)           && returns 0
```

## VARREAD()

### Syntax

```
VARREAD()
```

### Purpose

In conjunction with @..SAY..GET commands used with full-screen editing, this function returns the name of the field currently being edited. The field name is returned as all uppercase characters. Use the ON KEY command to set up a help screen.

### Example

```
* Set up the F1 key as the help key
* Showhelp is the help screen procedure
ON KEY LABEL F1 DO showhelp
DO Scrn_input              && screen input program
* Program continues... *
*
*
* The showhelp procedure
PROCEDURE Showhelp
* Shows help based on the field being edited
CLEAR TYPEAHEAD  && clear any keystrokes in the buffer
DO CASE
CASE VARREAD() = "CONTACT"
   @ 24,10 SAY "Enter customer contact name"
CASE VARREAD() = "ADDRESS"
   @ 24,10 SAY "Enter business address"
OTHERWISE                  && any other field
   @ 24,10 SAY "Enter value"
END CASE
RETURN
```

## VERSION()

### Syntax

```
VERSION()
```

### Purpose

Returns the dBASE IV version number, which can be useful for other applications that are version-specific.

### Example

```
* If you are using dBASE version 1.5
? VERSION()                 && returns "dBASE IV 1.5"
```

## WINDOW()

### Syntax

```
WINDOW()
```

### Purpose

Returns the name of the currently active window.

### Example

```
ACTIVATE WINDOW DATAENT
? "The current window is: " + WINDOW()
The current window is: DATAENT
```

## YEAR()

### Syntax

```
YEAR(<date variable>)
```

### Purpose

Returns the year as a numeric value from the *<date variable>*, which can be a date memory variable, a date field, or a function that returns a date-type variable.

### Example

```
* If the current date is 1/3/92
? YEAR(DATE())      && returns 1992
```

# Using SET Commands

The SET commands enable you to change many of the default values of dBASE IV. You can specify screen colors, for example, or the type of display you are using. Other SET commands enable you to change the format of the date, change the number of decimals to display, change the current disk drive and directory, and program the function keys to perform dBASE IV operations.

You access the various SET commands by typing *SET* at the dot prompt or by using Tools/Settings from the Control Center. Each of the SET options also can be used in your program with any of the various SET...TO commands covered in this section.

When you change any of the SET options at the dot prompt or Control Center, they affect only the current dBASE IV session. When you exit dBASE IV, the options revert to their defaults. To make permanent changes to the SET options, you must change the CONFIG.DB file (see "Using the System Configuration File" elsewhere in this "dBASE IV Reference Guide").

The SET() function returns the settings of many of the SET commands (see the "Using Functions" section in this "dBASE IV Reference Guide").

In the section "SET Commands," the SET commands are grouped alphabetically. The default value is shown in uppercase letters, and optional values are shown in lowercase letters.

The actions of the SET commands also can be performed through the Tools/Settings screen in the Control Center.

# Categorizing the SET Commands

How often have you thought of a restaraunt that serves food you like but cannot remember the name of the restaurant so that you can make reservations? You may find that this happens with the SET commands. You know what you want the command to do, but cannot remember exactly which SET command you need.

This section lists the SET commands by category. Look for the category of the SET command. For example, you may want a SET command to change a network setting. Look under the category "Network SET Commands." When you find the command that you want, look for the syntax in the alphabetical listing in the "SET Commands" section.

---

## Output Redirection Commands

These two commands are used to capture screen output and save it in a text file on disk.

SET ALTERNATE
SET ALTERNATE TO

---

## Database SET Commands

This group of commands affects the current database by limiting the records being accessed and setting up multiple file relations and other functions.

SET AUTOSAVE
SET CARRY
SET CARRY TO
SET CONFIRM
SET DELETED
SET FIELDS
SET FIELDS TO
SET FIELDS TO ALL
SET FILTER TO
SET INDEX TO
SET KEY TO
SET NEAR
SET ORDER TO
SET RELATION TO
SET SAFETY
SET SKIP TO()
SET UNIQUE
SET VIEW TO

## Date and Time SET Commands

This group of commands controls the displayed format of dates and times.

SET CENTURY
SET CLOCK
SET CLOCK TO
SET DATE
SET HOURS TO
SET MARK TO

## Database Encryption SET Command

This command enables you to encrypt your databases so that only authorized users can access them. Be careful with this command; if you forget your log-in name, the database cannot be unencrypted.

SET ENCRYPTION

## Environment SET Commands

These commands are used to change the environment while you are using dBASE IV. You can set up a catalog, change the default drive and directory, assign function keys, control whether commands are stored in the history file, and set the path to be used to access files.

SET CATALOG ON
SET CATALOG TO
SET DBTRAP
SET DEFAULT TO
SET DIRECTORY TO
SET FULLPATH
SET FUNCTION
SET HISTORY
SET HISTORY TO
SET PATH TO

## Help Message Display SET Commands

These two commands are used to determine how help messages are displayed if incorrect commands are entered, or to control the display of program code as the program is generated by dBASE IV.

SET HELP
SET INSTRUCT

## Memo Field SET Commands

These commands change the minimum size of dBASE IV memo files or the width of memo field output.

SET BLOCKSIZE TO
SET MEMOWIDTH
SET WINDOW OF MEMO TO

## Network SET Commands

This series of SET commands is used on network installations. These commands enable you to set the exclusive use of a database, lock records for single-user use, and set the reprocess and refresh rates.

SET EXCLUSIVE
SET LOCK
SET REFRESH TO
SET REPROCESS TO

## Printing SET Commands

These SET commands are used with commands that send data to the printer. You can route screen display commands to the printer, set the margins, specify the printer driver to be used, and turn the printed output on and off.

SET DEVICE TO PRINTER
SET MARGIN TO
SET PRINTER
SET PRINTER TO

## Program File SET Commands

This series of commands is used while you create, use, or debug program files. A program file contains a series of dBASE IV commands. You can specify the current procedure file, determine whether commands and the settings of variables will be echoed to the screen, enable or prevent access to the design mode, and change various program debugging settings.

SET DEBUG
SET DESIGN
SET DEVELOPMENT ON
SET DOHISTORY
SET ECHO
SET ESCAPE
SET LIBRARY TO
SET PROCEDURE TO
SET STEP
SET TRAP
SET TYPEAHEAD TO

## Screen Display SET Commands

This series of SET commands controls the appearance of the screen. You can set screen colors, choose the characters used for menu borders, control whether the cursor is displayed, specify the field delimiters, choose screen format files, control screen message display, and control other settings.

SET BORDER TO
SET COLOR
SET COLOR OF NORMAL
SET COLOR TO
SET CONSOLE
SET CURSOR
SET DELIMITERS
SET DELIMITERS TO
SET DEVICE TO SCREEN
SET DISPLAY TO
SET FORMAT TO
SET HEADINGS
SET INTENSITY
SET MESSAGE TO
SET MENU
SET ODOMETER TO
SET SCOREBOARD
SET SPACE
SET STATUS
SET TALK
SET TITLE

## Sound SET Commands

These commands control the sound of the bell or turn it on or off. Single tones of any frequency and duration can be specified with these commands.

SET BELL
SET BELL TO

## SQL SET Commands

These two commands control the display of SQL queries.

SET PAUSE
SET SQL

## Number Display SET Commands

These commands affect how numeric variables appear on-screen and the accuracy of string comparisons. You can set the number of decimal points, the precision used in mathematical calculations, and the thousands separator character.

| | |
|---|---|
| SET CURRENCY | SET FIXED |
| SET CURRENCY TO | SET POINT TO |
| SET DECIMALS TO | SET PRECISION TO |
| SET EXACT | SET SEPARATOR TO |

# SET Commands

## SET ALTERNATE

### Syntax

```
SET ALTERNATE on/OFF
```

### Purpose

Starts (SET ALTERNATE ON) and stops (SET ALTERNATE OFF) the recording of screen output to store in the alternate file. The alternate file is specified by the SET ALTERNATE TO command. Using the OFF parameter file does not close the output file; you can add to the currently open file by using the SET ALTERNATE ON command. See the SET ALTERNATE TO command for an example.

## SET ALTERNATE TO

### Syntax

```
SET ALTERNATE TO [<filename> [ADDITIVE]]
```

### Purpose

Creates the text file <*filename*> that will contain the recorded output. The file name has a default extension of TXT and is created in the current directory unless you specify otherwise. The ADDITIVE option enables you to add data to an existing file. If the <*filename*> exists, it is overwritten. Use SET ALTERNATE TO or CLOSE ALTERNATE to close the output file. To stop recording screen output in the text file temporarily, use SET ALTERNATE OFF. When you want to resume sending output to the file, use SET ALTERNATE ON.

Any text or data that is displayed on-screen also is stored in the alternate file. Only @...SAY, EDIT, BROWSE, and APPEND operations are not stored in the alternate file. You can use the ? and ?? commands to store text in a file, along with such other commands as REPORT FORM and LIST. Use the ?? command at the beginning of output recording to eliminate a blank line at the top of the file. The ? command first outputs a carriage return and line feed, which causes a blank line if ? is the first command after the SET ALTERNATE command is used.

### Example

```
* Store the contents of certain records
* to a text file
USE ORDERS ORDER Partnum
SET HEADINGS ON               && field names at top of list
SET ALTERNATE TO backordr.txt
? SPACE(20) + "BACKORDERD ITEMS - " + DTOC(DATE())
? ""                          && a blank line
* List all back-ordered items older than 30 days
LIST PARTNUM, PARTNAME, ONHAND, BACKORD, BACKDATE ;
   FOR BACKDATE < DATE() - 30
SET ALTERNATE OFF
```

# SET AUTOSAVE

### Syntax

```
SET AUTOSAVE on/OFF
```

### Purpose

Determines whether each record is saved to disk immediately or is stored in a disk buffer. SET AUTOSAVE ON saves each record immediately; SET AUTOSAVE OFF stores data in the disk buffer until the buffer is full, and then updates the records on disk. The default setting is OFF.

### Example

```
* Turn on AUTOSAVE
* Note: will slow database operations a bit
SET AUTOSAVE ON
```

# SET BELL

### Syntax

```
SET BELL ON/Off
```

### Purpose

Controls whether the bell is sounded when you arrive at the end of a field or when an error occurs. The bell normally is on and has a frequency of 512 hertz and 2 clock ticks (each clock tick is about 0.0549 seconds). You can change the frequency and duration of the bell with the SET BELL TO command. You can sound the bell in your program with a ?CHR(7) command. See SET BELL TO for an example.

# SET BELL TO

### Syntax

```
SET BELL TO [<frequency>, <duration>]
```

### Purpose

Sets the frequency (pitch) and duration (length) of the bell. The frequency range is from 19 to 10,000 cycles per second (hertz). For low-pitched sounds, use a frequency between 20 and 550. For a high pitch, use a value from 550 to 5,500. Frequencies above 5,500 might not be audible to all users. The duration can be between 2 and 19 ticks; each tick is about 0.0549 seconds. The bell is sounded when the cursor encounters the end of a data entry field or when an error occurs (if SET BELL is ON). Use SET BELL TO without parameters to return to the default values.

You may want to choose a less strident sound for data-entry purposes, and a more forceful sound for your error-trapping routines. Some people find the end-of-field bell used with data entry screens annoying.

### Example

```
* Enable the bell during error traps only
* The normal mode is SET BELL OFF
* This is the err_trap procedure, enabled with
* ON ERROR DO err_trap
PROCEDURE err_trap
SET BELL TO 1000, 5
SET BELL ON                    && enable the bell
? CHR(7)                       && sound the alarm
SET BELL OFF                   && disable the bell
@ 23,25 SAY "ERROR, PLEASE CORRECT AND PRESS ENTER KEY"
WAIT ""                        && wait for Enter key
RETURN
```

## SET BLOCKSIZE TO

### Syntax

SET BLOCKSIZE TO <*number of 512-byte blocks*>

### Purpose

Changes the default block size of the memo field database and multiple-index files. To remain compatible with dBASE III files, the default size is one 512-byte block. A memo field file and index file use up file space in groups of *blocksize*. Larger blocksize values enable faster string manipulation, as when you are searching for data in a memo, but may slow down other I/O processing. Smaller values cause slower string manipulation but also can offer better performance.

### Example

```
* Ensure that you're using dBASE III memo block size
* This is the default value
SET BLOCKSIZE TO 1
```

# SET BORDER TO

### Syntax

```
SET BORDER TO [SINGLE/DOUBLE/PANEL/NONE/<border
     definition string>]
```

### Purpose

Changes the default border of menus, windows, and @...SAY and @...TO commands from a single line to other border types. Use SINGLE to return to the default value, DOUBLE for double lines, and PANEL for inverse video boxes using ASCII character 219 ([bf]). The *<border definition string>* contains values for the eight side and corner positions in a box. Eight values must be specified in the *<border definition string>*. Indicate default values by inserting commas with no values.

Table R.13 shows the order and positions used for the eight side and corner positions on the border.

**Table R.13 Border Positions**

| Border number | Position | Border number | Position |
|---|---|---|---|
| 1 | Top line | 5 | Top left corner |
| 2 | Bottom line | 6 | Top right corner |
| 3 | Left line | 7 | Bottom left corner |
| 4 | Right line | 8 | Bottom right corner |

### Example

```
SET BORDERS TO ,,179,179,213,184,212,190
```

In the example, border positions 1 and 2 use the default values.

# SET CARRY

### Syntax

```
SET CARRY on/OFF
```

### Purpose

Determines whether data fields are brought forward to new records when you use the APPEND and INSERT commands. A new record normally contains blank fields. With SET CARRY ON, field data from the previous record is placed in the new, blank record. You can use the SET CARRY TO command to determine which fields in the record are carried forward. See SET CARRY TO for an example.

### Example

```
* Turn on carry during data input routine
SET CARRY ON
DO data_in                && data input routine
SET CARRY OFF             && reset to default
```

## SET CARRY TO

### Syntax

```
SET CARRY TO [<field list> [ADDITIVE]]
```

### Purpose

Specifies which fields will be carried forward to new records if you used the SET CARRY ON command. The ADDITIVE option adds the *<field list>* to the previous SET CARRY field list. If you need to specify all fields after you use a *<field list>*, use the SET CARRY TO command without a list of fields.

### Example

```
* Add records, assume that Areacode and ZIPcode
* fields are the same as the previous record
USE CUSTOMERS
SET CARRY TO AREACODE, ZIPCODE
SET CARRY ON
APPEND BLANK
SET CARRY OFF
```

## SET CATALOG ON

### Syntax

```
SET CATALOG on/OFF
```

### Purpose

Determines whether files that you use or create are added to the current catalog. SET CATALOG ON adds these files to the current catalog (set with SET CATALOG TO); SET CATALOG OFF does not add files to the current catalog.

### Example

```
* Don't add new files to current catalog
SET CATALOG OFF
```

## SET CATALOG TO

### Syntax

```
SET CATALOG TO [<filename> / ?]
```

### Purpose

Determines the *<filename>* of the active catalog file, which is assumed to have a CAT file-name extension and is stored in the current directory. The SET CATALOG TO command automatically performs a SET CATALOG ON command. Use the ? parameter to select the catalog from a list.

The master catalog file, CATALOG.CAT, contains a list of the other catalogs. The catalog files are standard DBF files with the file structure shown in table R.14.

To close a catalog, use the SET CATALOG TO command without parameters.

**Table R.14 Catalog File Structure**

| Field | Field name | Type | Width | Description |
|---|---|---|---|---|
| 1 | Path | Character | 70 | Drive and directory name. |
| 2 | File_Name | Character | 12 | File name, including extension. |
| 3 | Alias | Character | 8 | Alias file name. |
| 4 | Type | Character | 3 | The default file extension of the type of file. |
| 5 | Title | Character | 80 | An optional description of the catalog. If SET TITLE is ON, you are prompted for a description each time you create a catalog. |
| 6 | Code | Numeric | 3 | The number dBASE IV assigns to each database file that is used. Program files are assigned 0, and each new database file gets the next higher number. Index, format, label, query, report form, screen, and view files are assigned the same number as the database file they are used with. |
| 7 | Tag | Character | 4 | Not used. |

### Example

```
* Set up new catalog
SET CATALOG TO Custcat.CAT
SET CATALOG ON
```

## SET CENTURY

### Syntax

```
SET CENTURY on/OFF
```

### Purpose

Determines the display and input of the century prefixes of the years in dates. SET CENTURY ON shows all four digits of the year portion of the date—for example, 1992. SET CENTURY OFF (the default) shows only the last two digits of the year portion of a date—for example, 92. With SET CENTURY OFF, all dates are assumed to be in the 1900-to-1999 date range (the 20th century).

### Example

```
SET CENTURY OFF
? {10/10/92}        && displays "10/10/92"
SET CENTURY ON
? {10/10/92}        && displays "10/10/1992"
```

## SET CLOCK

### Syntax

```
SET CLOCK on/OFF
```

### Purpose

Turns the on-screen display of the time ON or OFF (default). The clock normally is displayed at row 0, column 68, unless you have used the SET CLOCK TO command. See SET CLOCK TO for an example.

## SET CLOCK TO

### Syntax

```
SET CLOCK TO [<row>, <column>]
```

### Purpose

Determines the position of the time display if SET CLOCK ON is enabled. If you use SET CLOCK TO without the *<row>* and *<column>* parameters, the time is displayed at row 0, column 68.

### Example

```
* Display the clock at the bottom left corner of the screen
SET CLOCK TO 24,0
SET CLOCK ON
```

## SET COLOR

### Syntax

```
SET COLOR ON/OFF
```

### Purpose

Switches between color and monochrome screen display on systems that have both types of monitors. SET COLOR ON enables color display; SET COLOR OFF enables monochrome display. Monochrome display adapters default to OFF; all others default to ON.

### Example

```
* Sets color on/off according to previously
* defined variable NEEDMONO
IF needmono
   SET COLOR OFF
ENDIF
```

## SET COLOR OF NORMAL

### Syntax

```
SET COLOR OF NORMAL / MESSAGES / TITLES / BOX / HIGHLIGHT /
   INFORMATION / FIELDS TO [<color attribute>]
```

### Purpose

Enables you to set the indicated area to the *<color attribute>* value. Tables R.x and R.x in the SET COLOR TO section show the colors and the attribute group names.

## SET COLOR TO

### Syntax

```
SET COLOR TO [[<standard>] [,[<enhanced>][,[<perimeter>][,
   [<background>]]]]]
```

### *Purpose*

Enables you to set the color values used for each of the parameters. Each parameter can have a foreground/background color pair; for example, BG/B indicates cyan letters on a blue background. With some monitors (such as EGA-type displays), the *<perimeter>* parameter cannot be set. You can change only one of the color values by specifying that parameter only. A color value of ",R" sets the *<enhanced>* color to red, leaving the *<standard>* color unchanged. If you don't specify one of the colors in a foreground/background pair, that color is set to black. A color pair of /N+ is the same as N/N+.

Use the plus sign (+) with the color value (for example, R+) to indicate a high-intensity color. (You cannot set high-intensity background colors on an EGA monitor.) An asterisk (*) added to the color value causes that color to blink; for example, R* indicates blinking red. Use a blank (X) as either the foreground or background color for times when you don't want to see the characters, as in password entry. Monochrome monitors can use the U color for underline and I for inverse video instead of color values. Other color values on monochrome displays can be hard to read on some monochrome screens.

Table R.15 shows the various color values, and table R.16 shows the attribute groups available in dBASE IV.

**Table R.15 Color Table**

| Color | Letter code | Color | Letter code |
|---|---|---|---|
| Black | N or blank | Magenta | RB |
| Blue | B | Brown | GR |
| Green | G | Yellow | GR+ |
| Cyan | BG | White | W |
| Blank | X | *<color>*+ | Bright color |
| Grey | N+ | *<color>** | Blinking color |
| Red | R | *<color>**+ | Bright, blinking color |

**Table R.16 Color Attribute Groups**

| Group name | Partial example |
|---|---|
| NORMAL | @...SAY output, unselected BROWSE fields |
| MESSAGES | Message line, error box interiors, prompt box interiors |
| TITLES | List headings, browse field names headings, ruler line |
| BOX | Menu borders, list borders, prompt box borders |
| HIGHLIGHT | Highlighted menu and list choices, selected box |
| INFORMATION | Clock, error box borders, status line |
| FIELDS | Editable fields in BROWSE or @...GET |

(A complete list appears in *dBASE IV Language Reference.*)

## SET CONFIRM

### Syntax

```
SET CONFIRM on/OFF
```

### Purpose

Determines whether the cursor automatically moves to the next field (SET CONFIRM OFF) when the last character of the field has been entered, or whether the user must press Enter before the cursor moves to the next field (SET CONFIRM ON). Some users are accustomed to pressing Enter, as they would with an adding machine; using SET CONFIRM ON makes sure that the cursor is in the proper field when you enter a group of numbers.

### Example

```
* Turn on confirm during data entry program
SET CONFIRM ON
DO data_in                    && data input routine
SET CONFIRM OFF               && reset to default
```

## SET CONSOLE

### Syntax

```
SET CONSOLE ON/off
```

### Purpose

Turns the screen display on and off. SET CONSOLE OFF prevents reports and programs that are sent to the printer from being displayed on-screen. SET CONSOLE ON sends the reports and programs to the screen and to the printer. This command is available from within programs only, not at the dot prompt.

### Example

```
* Don't show the report while it's printing
@ 12,15 SAY "Report printing..."
SET CONSOLE OFF
REPORT FORM custlist TO PRINT
SET CONSOLE ON
@ 13,15 SAY "Report finished!"
```

## SET CURRENCY

### Syntax

```
SET CURRENCY LEFT/RIGHT
```

### Purpose

Determines the position of the currency character. The currency character normally is placed on the left (SET CURRENCY LEFT) but can be changed to the end of the currency string (SET CURRENCY RIGHT). If you change the position of the currency character, you also may need to change the thousands separator character (SET SEPARATOR) and the character used for the decimal point (SET POINT). See SET CURRENCY TO for an example.

## SET CURRENCY TO

### Syntax

```
SET CURRENCY TO [<currency unit character>]
```

### Purpose

Changes the symbol that is used in the display of currency values. The *<currency unit character>* can be any alphabetic character and defaults to the dollar sign ($). If you change the currency symbol, you also may need to change the thousands separator character (SET SEPARATOR) and the character used for the decimal point (SET POINT).

### Example

```
* Use DM for currency displays
MTOT = 123456.78
SET CURRENCY TO "DM"
SET CURRENCY RIGHT
SET POINT TO "."
SET SEPARATOR TO ","
* Displays "123,456.78 DM"
@ 5,10 SAY MTOT PICTURE "@$"
```

## SET CURSOR

### Syntax

```
SET CURSOR ON/off
```

### Purpose

Determines whether the cursor is displayed. SET CURSOR OFF hides the cursor; SET CURSOR ON redisplays the cursor.

### Example

```
* Turn off cursor while getting the password
password = space(8)
SET CURSOR OFF
@ 12,15 SAY "Enter Password " ;
GET password PICTURE "@!" COLOR N/N
READ
SET CURSOR ON
```

## SET DATE

### Syntax

```
SET DATE [TO]
   AMERICAN / ANSI / BRITISH / FRENCH / GERMAN /
   ITALIAN / JAPAN / USA / MDY / DMY / YMD
```

### Purpose

Determines the displayed format of the date. The number of digits for the year value is determined by the SET CENTURY setting. The available formats are shown in table R.17.

**Table R.17 SET DATE Formats**

| Format name | Result | Examples using January 3, 1992 | |
|---|---|---|---|
| | | SET CENTURY ON | SET CENTURY OFF |
| AMERICAN | mm/dd/yy | 01/03/92 | 01/03/1992 |
| ANSI | yy.mm.dd | 92.01.03 | 1992.01.03 |
| BRITISH | dd/mm/yy | 03/01/92 | 03/01/1992 |
| FRENCH | dd/mm/yy | 03/01/92 | 03/01/1992 |
| GERMAN | dd.mm.yy | 03.01.92 | 03.01.1992 |
| ITALIAN | dd-mm-yy | 03-01-92 | 03-01-1992 |
| JAPAN | yy/mm/dd | 92/01/03 | 1992/01/03 |

| Format name | Result | Examples using January 3, 1992 | |
|---|---|---|---|
| USA | mm-dd-yy | 01-03-92 | 01-03-1992 |
| MDY | mm/dd/yy | 01-03-92 | 01-03-1992 |
| DMY | dd/mm/yy | 03/01/92 | 03/01/1992 |
| YMD | yy/mm/dd | 92/01/03 | 1992/01/03 |

## SET DBTRAP

### Syntax

```
SET DBTRAP ON/off
```

### Purpose

Determines whether errors are trapped when a dBASE command is interrupted when another command is executed. The default is ON.

### Example

```
* Turn on error trapping
SET DBTRAP ON
```

## SET DEBUG

### Syntax

```
SET DEBUG on/OFF
```

### Purpose

Determines whether output from the SET ECHO command is sent to the printer (SET DEBUG ON) or the screen (SET DEBUG OFF). This command is useful during program debugging because you can see the assignment of variables and other functions while the program is running.

### Example

```
* Turn on debug for the CUSTEDIT program
SET DEBUG ON
DO custedit
SET DEBUG OFF        && resets debug back to normal
```

## SET DECIMALS TO

### Syntax

```
SET DECIMALS TO <number of decimal places>
```

### Purpose

Determines the number of decimal places that are displayed for numeric fields. The <*number of decimal places*> can be from 0 to 18. Because any decimal number less than 1 includes a "0." before it, there can be up to 20 numbers in a decimal value.

### Example

```
SET DECIMALS TO 2
? 3 / 5                    && displays 0.60
SET DECIMALS TO 18         && maximum allowed
? 3 / 5                    && displays
0.600000000000000000
```

## SET DEFAULT TO

### Syntax

```
SET DEFAULT TO <drive>[:]
```

### Purpose

Specifies the default drive for all operations and file storage. The default is the drive that was in use when you started dBASE IV; the default can be changed with an entry in the CONFIG.DB file. The default directory is the one in use on the new default drive. Use the SET DIRECTORY command to change the default drive and directory in one step. See the example given for SET DIRECTORY TO.

## SET DELETED

### Syntax

```
SET DELETED on/OFF
```

### Purpose

Determines whether records marked for deletion are ignored by other dBASE IV commands. If this command is set ON, marked records are not shown by commands such as LIST and DISPLAY. If this command is set OFF (the default), marked records are shown. The INDEX and REINDEX commands always include marked records, whether SET DELETED is on or off. This command applies to the current work area only, not to any other open or related files.

If you need to recall (unmark) records marked for deletion, use SET DELETED OFF so that the RECALL ALL command can access marked records.

### Example

```
* Don't show deleted records during LIST
USE custlist
SET DELETED ON
LIST TO PRINT
SET DELETED OFF
```

## SET DELIMITERS

### Syntax

```
SET DELIMITERS on/OFF
```

### Purpose

Determines whether the field delimiters (usually colons) are displayed around entry fields. SET DELIMITERS ON displays the entry field delimiters; SET DELIMITERS OFF (the default) does not display the delimiters. You can change the delimiter characters with the SET DELIMITERS TO command.

### Example

```
* Don't want delimiters around input fields
SET DELIMITERS OFF
```

## SET DELIMITERS TO

### Syntax

```
SET DELIMITERS TO <delimiter characters> / DEFAULT
```

### Purpose

Defines the characters used to delimit entry fields if SET DELIMITERS is set to ON. You can specify two characters; the first character is used for the beginning of the field, and the second character is used for the end of the field. You can change back to the default delimiters by issuing SET DELIMITERS TO without a value or by using SET DELIMITERS TO DEFAULT.

### Example

```
* Set up field delimiters
SET DELIMITERS TO "<>"   && will show as "<entry area>"
SET DELIMITERS ON        && must be enabled to use delimiters
```

## SET DESIGN

### Syntax

```
SET DESIGN ON/off
```

### Purpose

Controls access to the design mode, where the user can make changes to the database, report form, label, query, and applications from the Control Center. SET DESIGN OFF prevents design mode access; SET DESIGN ON enables design mode access.

### Example

```
* Don't let user get into design screen
SET DESIGN OFF
```

## SET DEVELOPMENT ON

### Syntax

```
SET DEVELOPMENT ON/off
```

### Purpose

Determines whether dBASE IV checks the creation date and times of the compiled object file with the source code. If the date and times are different, the program is recompiled when SET DEVELOPMENT is ON and you use the DO *<program name>* command. SET DEVELOPMENT ON does the creation date and time checking (the default); SET DEVELOPMENT OFF does not check the creation date and times. The command normally is left ON to prevent using outdated object code files. If you used SET DEVELOPMENT OFF, you need to use COMPILE to compile the program files manually before you use the program.

### Example

```
* Make sure source code has not changed since last COMPILE
SET DEVELOPMENT ON
```

## SET DEVICE TO PRINTER

### Syntax

```
SET DEVICE TO PRINTER
```

### Purpose

Sends all @...SAY output to the printer rather than the screen. Any @...GET commands are ignored. If an @...SAY command specifies a row and column location that is above the current printer column and row, a page eject occurs. Output to the printer is canceled with the SET DEVICE TO SCREEN/FILE command.

### Example

```
* Ask whether user wants hard copy of current record
answer = .F.
```

```
      @ 24,15 SAY "Print hard copy of this record? (Y/N) ";
         GET answer PICTURE "Y"
      READ
   IF answer
      SET PRINT ON
      * Showdata routines displays screen data using @...SAYS
      DO showdata
      SET PRINT OFF
   ENDIF
```

# SET DEVICE TO SCREEN

### Syntax

```
SET DEVICE TO SCREEN
```

### Purpose

Sends @...SAY commands to the screen rather than to the printer (SET DEVICE TO printer) or a file (SET DEVICE TO FILE <*filename*>). This command normally sends @...SAY commands back to the screen after a SET DEVICE TO printer/FILE command.

### Example

```
* Send a simple report to the printer
USE ORDERS
@ 11,35 SAY "Report printing"
SET DEVICE TO PRINTER
@ 2,35 SAY "BACK ORDER REPORT"&& report title
@ 3,35 SAY DATE(), TIME()
@ 5,0                          && skip to line 5
LIST CUSTOMER, PARTNUM, PARTDESC, BACKDATE ;
   FOR BACKDATE < DATE()-30
SET DEVICE TO SCREEN           && @...SAYs back to screen
EJECT                          && form feed
@ 12,35 SAY "REPORT FINISHED"
```

# SET DIRECTORY TO

### Syntax

```
SET DIRECTORY TO [[<drive>:][<path>]]
```

### Purpose

Changes the current working drive and directory for all operations and storage of files. The <*drive*> parameter is optional, but if used it must include the colon (:). There should be no spaces between the <*drive*> and <*path*> parameters. SET DIRECTORY TO without parameters restores the drive and directory that were in use when you first started dBASE IV.

The SET DIRECTORY command is equivalent to the RUN CD <*path*> command. You can use the SET DIRECTORY command to change the default drive and directory in one command.

### Example

```
* Change to the D:\CLIENT\DATA directory
SET DIRECTORY TO D:\CLIENT\DATA
* Equivalent to:
SET DEFAULT TO D:
SET DIRECTORY TO \CLIENT\DATA
* dBASE III equivalent:
SET DEFAULT TO D:
RUN D:
RUN CD \CLIENT\DATA
```

## SET DISPLAY TO

### Syntax

```
SET DISPLAY TO MONO / COLOR / EGA25 / EGA43 / MONO43
```

### Purpose

Selects a monochrome or color display, or sets the number of lines on EGA or VGA displays. If you SET DISPLAY to a display type that is not installed on your computer, the command is ignored and an error message is shown on-screen.

### Example

```
* Set up 43-line screen, then mono or color
* according to previously defined variable NEEDMONO
IF NEEDMONO
   SET DISPLAY TO MONO43
ELSE
   SET DISPLAY TO EGA43
ENDIF
```

## SET DOHISTORY

### Syntax

```
SET DOHISTORY on/OFF
```

### Purpose

Maintains compatibility with dBASE III programs. This command is ignored in dBASE IV programs.

## SET ECHO

### Syntax

```
SET ECHO on/OFF
```

### Purpose

Determines whether commands from dBASE IV programs are displayed on-screen (or printer, if SET DEBUG is ON) during execution. SET ECHO ON will display or print the commands; SET ECHO OFF (the default) will not display or print the commands. This command is useful during debugging but can clutter the screen. Place SET ECHO ON and SET ECHO OFF around a block of program commands that are causing problems so that you will see only those commands when program execution reaches that point in your code.

### Example

```
* Check this area of the program for problems
SET DEBUG ON          && send commands to printer, not screen
SET ECHO ON           && start output
* Problem program block here
SET ECHO OFF          && stop output
SET DEBUG OFF         && reset debug status
```

## SET ENCRYPTION

### Syntax

```
SET ENCRYPTION ON/off
```

### Purpose

Determines whether copied files—such as those created with COPY, JOIN, and TOTAL—are stored as encrypted files. Use SET ENCRYPTION OFF to copy a file to an unencrypted file. You must have successfully logged on with the PROTECT command to access an encrypted file.

### Example

```
* Set encryption off for now
SET ENCRYPTION OFF
```

## SET ESCAPE

### Syntax

```
SET ESCAPE ON/off
```

### Purpose

Determines whether pressing the Esc key halts the execution of a program or stops screen output. If SET ESCAPE is set to OFF, the Esc key is ignored, unless you are using Esc for INKEY() functions. The default ON setting enables the program to respond to Esc.

When Esc is pressed during a dBASE IV program, you will see an error box with three options: Cancel, Ignore, Suspend.

You then have the option of canceling the current program, ignoring the pressing of Esc and resuming the program, or suspending the program. A suspended program can be continued with the RESUME command.

> **WARNING:** Make sure that the program is operating properly before you use the SET ESCAPE OFF command. With Esc disabled, you will not be able to stop programs that are stuck in endless loops. The only way to stop the program is to reboot your computer, which may cause data damage or loss. Test the program completely before using the SET ESCAPE OFF command. You may want to use the ON ESCAPE command to trap the Esc key.

## SET EXACT

### Syntax

```
SET EXACT on/OFF
```

### Purpose

Determines whether the length of two compared character strings must be exactly the same. If SET EXACT is OFF, the second string is compared to the first string until the last character of the second string is reached. If SET EXACT is ON, the strings must compare exactly, including trailing blanks.

### Example

```
* Compare two strings
firstone = "Smithsonian"
secondone = "Smith"
SET EXACT OFF
? firstone = secondone          && returns .T.
SET EXACT ON
? firstone = secondone          && returns .F.
```

# SET EXCLUSIVE

### Syntax

```
SET EXCLUSIVE on/OFF
```

### Purpose

Enables a user or program to open a database for exclusive use (SET EXCLUSIVE ON). This command prevents other users on a network from being able to access the database until SET EXCLUSIVE is set to OFF. If you use the CREATE and SAVE commands, EXCLUSIVE is set to ON.

### Example

```
* Make sure that exclusive is ON
SET EXCLUSIVE ON
```

# SET FIELDS

### Syntax

```
SET FIELDS on/OFF
```

### Purpose

Determines whether the fields list specified in the SET FIELDS TO command is used. If SET FIELDS is OFF, all fields in the current database are available for use.

### Example

```
USE INVENTORY
SET FIELDS TO PART,DESC
LIST TO PRINT       && only PART and DESC are listed
SET FIELDS OFF
LIST TO PRINT       && all fields are listed.
```

# SET FIELDS TO

## Syntax

```
SET FIELDS TO [<field> [/R] /<calculated field id> ...]
    [,<field> [/R] /<calculated field id> ...]
```

### Purpose

Determines the fields that are used as defaults when you use commands such as LIST and DISPLAY. The /R parameter sets the read-only flag for database fields. You can specify calculated fields, such as QTY_ORD * UNITPRICE. Use SET FIELDS TO without parameters to clear the field list. The SET FIELDS TO command is additive; specifying additional commands adds to the field list.

### Example

```
* Specify active fields
SET FIELDS TO ID_CODE, ITEMDESC
```

## SET FIELDS TO ALL

### Syntax

```
SET FIELDS TO ALL [LIKE/EXCEPT <skeleton>]
```

### Purpose

Enables you to specify similarly named fields to the field list. The <*skeleton*> can include the ? wild card, which indicates any match in that character position, and the * wild card, which indicates any match for multiple character positions.

### Example

```
* Add to the current field list
* Adds CUSTNUM, CUSTNAME, CUSTADDR, CUSTCITY, etc.
SET FIELDS TO ALL LIKE CUST*
```

## SET FILTER TO

### Syntax

```
SET FILTER TO [FILE <filename>/?] [<condition>]
```

### Purpose

Causes only those records that meet the <*condition*> to be accessed by other dBASE IV commands. The TO FILE <*filename*> option adds a query file to an open catalog—if SET CATALOG is ON. The FILE ? option displays a list of available query files for the current database.

This command applies to the current work area only. Use a GO TOP or SKIP command to initialize the action of the filter so that subsequent records will meet the filter <*condition*>.

**NOTE** If you have a large database with active indexes, the FILTER command can cause a slower movement through the database with a SKIP command. If you will be using the same filter often in your program, consider using the INDEX FOR command for faster access to that part of your database.

### Example

```
* Limit access to part numbers 14000 - 14999
USE PARTS
SET FILTER TO partnum >= 14000 .AND. partnum < 15000
```

## SET FIXED

### Syntax

```
SET FIXED on/OFF
```

### Purpose

This command is provided to maintain compatibility with dBASE III programs. It is ignored by dBASE IV. Use the SET DECIMALS command in dBASE IV programs.

## SET FORMAT TO

### Syntax

```
SET FORMAT TO [<format filename> / ? ]
```

### Purpose

Enables a predefined screen format (FMT) file to be used for data input with the READ, EDIT, APPEND, INSERT, CHANGE, or BROWSE commands. The format file is created with the CREATE/ MODIFY SCREEN command or from the Control Center. If the compiled format file (FMO) is not found, the FMT file is compiled and used. Use the ? parameter to choose from a list of available format files. Close the format file with a CLOSE FORMAT command or by issuing SET FORMAT TO without parameters.

**NOTE** Use the MODIFY SCREEN command to change a format file. Using the MODIFY COMMAND command produces differences between the FMO and FMT files.

### Example

```
* Use the format file for the entry screen
USE CLIENTS
SET FORMAT TO client
APPEND
```

## SET FULLPATH

### Syntax

```
SET FULLPATH on/OFF
```

### Purpose

Determines whether the full drive and path names are returned with functions such as DBF() and NDX(). SET FULLPATH is not available from the SET menu but can be stored in the CONFIG.DB file.

### Example

```
SET DIRECTORY TO D:\CLIENT\DATA
USE INVOICE
SET FULLPATH OFF
? DBF()          && returns "D:INVOICE.DBF"
SET FULLPATH ON
? DBF()          && returns "D:\CLIENT\DATA\INVOICE.DBF"
```

## SET FUNCTION

### Syntax

```
SET FUNCTION <key number> / <key name> / <key label>
   TO <command string>
```

### Purpose

Assigns the *<command string>* to the function key. You can indicate the function key by its number (1 through 10), by its name (for example, Shift-F10), or by its key label (for example, F10). Use the semicolon (;) to indicate pressing the Enter key. You can assign commands to keys F1 through F10, Shift-F1 through Shift-F9, and Ctrl-F1 through Ctrl-F10. The Alt-F1 through Alt-F10 keys are available for macros only. The F11 and F12 keys are not available for programming.

### Example

```
* Assign current date to F10
SET FUNCTION F10 TO DTOC(DATE())
* Assign current time to Shift-F10
```

```
SET FUNCTION SHIFT-F10 TO TIME()
* Assign "Newcastle", Enter key, "CA" to Ctrl-F3
SET FUNCTION CTRL-F3 TO "Newcastle;CA"
```

# SET HEADINGS

### Syntax

```
SET HEADINGS ON/off
```

### Purpose

Controls whether field headings are shown when you use the DISPLAY, LIST, SUM, or AVERAGE command. If SET HEADINGS is ON (the default), field headings are shown. If SET HEADINGS is OFF, field headings are not shown. When SET HEADINGS is ON, the width of the column is set to the width of the field name or the width of the field, whichever is greater.

The field headings appear in uppercase if you used uppercase field names in LIST or other commands. If the field names are in lowercase, the field name headings are displayed or printed in lowercase.

### Example

```
* Turn on the headings for this quick list
SET HEADINGS ON
USE CUSTLIST
LIST CUSTNAME, CONTACT, PHONE TO PRINT
SET HEADINGS OFF
```

# SET HELP

### Syntax

```
SET HELP ON/off
```

### Purpose

Determines whether the dBASE IV Help box is displayed if an incorrect command is encountered in a program or entered at the dot prompt. The Help box contains three options: Cancel, to cancel the command; Edit, to edit the command and then reexecute it; and Help, to display the dBASE IV help message for that command.

### Example

```
* Disable help box during program
SET HELP OFF
```

# SET HISTORY

### Syntax

```
SET HISTORY ON/off
```

### Purpose

Stores commands typed at the dot prompt in a history buffer. With SET HISTORY set to ON, you can use the up and down arrows to recall previous commands to the current dot prompt. The LIST HISTORY and DISPLAY HISTORY commands also show the contents of the history buffer, which normally contains the last 20 commands executed. The size of the history buffer is specified by the SET HISTORY TO command. See SET HISTORY TO for an example.

# SET HISTORY TO

### Syntax

```
SET HISTORY TO <number of commands>
```

### Purpose

Sets the size of the history buffer, which can be from 0 to 16,000 commands. SET HISTORY TO 0 clears the contents of the history buffer.

> **WARNING:** The number of history commands that can be stored is limited by the amount of memory available while dBASE IV programs run, dBASE IV itself, and memory variables. Setting too large a value can slow down your program or produce an `Insufficient memory` error message.

### Example

```
* Store 50 commands in history buffer
SET HISTORY TO 50
```

# SET HOURS TO

### Syntax

```
SET HOURS TO [12/24]
```

### Purpose

Displays time clock (if SET CLOCK is ON), using a 12- or 24-hour clock; the default is a 12-hour clock. SET HOURS TO without a parameter changes the value to the default, which can be set to either value in the CONFIG.DB file.

### Example

```
* Set up clock display in upper right corner
* Current time is 9:31:44 pm
SET CLOCK ON                && turns on clock display
SET CLOCK TO 12             && clock displays 9:31:44
SET CLOCK TO 24             && clock displays 21:31:44
```

## SET INDEX TO

### Syntax

```
SET INDEX TO ?/<filename list> [ORDER <NDX filename> /
   [TAG] <MDX tag> [OF <MDX filename>]]
```

### Purpose

Opens index files for the current database. The first index file name in the *<filename list>* is the active or controlling index; the other index files are updated but do not control the movement through the file. Both index (NDX) and multiple-index (MDX) files are available. The command attempts first to open an MDX file; if the command cannot find one, it opens an NDX file.

The TAG *<MDX tag>* OF *<MDX filename>* option enables you to specify the tag name contained in the MDX file. The ORDER option enables you to specify a controlling index that is not the first index file in the *<filename list>*. You also can change the controlling index with the SET ORDER TO command. Use SET INDEX TO without any parameters to close the current indexes.

You should keep all indexes up-to-date when you use a database. If the indexes are not current, the `Record not in index` error message may occur, or searching for a record with FIND or SEEK will be unsuccessful.

### Example

```
* Set up index using tag NAMES
USE custlist
SET INDEX TO TAG NAMES
```

## SET INSTRUCT

### Syntax

```
SET INSTRUCT ON/off
```

### Purpose

Determines whether the prompt boxes are displayed or whether the dBASE IV code is shown while reports, labels, and forms are being generated.

### Example

```
* Turn off prompt boxes, etc.
SET INSTRUCT OFF
```

## SET INTENSITY

### Syntax

```
SET INTENSITY ON/off
```

### Purpose

Determines whether the enhanced screen color is used for @...GET commands (@..SAY commands use the standard screen color). Screen colors are set with the SET COLOR TO command.

### Example

```
* Turn on high intensity for this message
SET INTENSITY ON
answer = .F.
   @ 12,20 SAY "Are you sure? (Y/N) " ;
      GET answer PICTURE "Y"
   READ
ENDDO
```

## SET KEY TO

### Syntax

```
SET KEY TO [<match expression>/RANGE <low expression>,
   <high expression>/<low expression>[,]/,<high expression>]
   [IN <alias>]
```

### Purpose

Filters the database to permit the display of only records meeting the conditions specified. Because it operates on an index key, SET KEY requires that a database be in use with an active index. SET KEY TO issued without any of the optional arguments cancels the filtering specified in the previous SET KEY command. Data types for optional expressions should be the same.

### Example

```
USE CUSTOMER ORDER CITY
SET KEY TO "Chicago","Dallas"
```

## SET LIBRARY TO

### Syntax

```
SET LIBRARY TO [<filename>]
```

### Purpose

Enables you to specify a library file that contains procedures and functions that are to be used throughout your dBASE programs.

### Example

```
SET LIBRARY TO libproc
```

## SET LOCK

### Syntax

```
SET LOCK ON/off
```

### Purpose

Determines whether certain dBASE commands will automatically lock database files in a multiuser system. With SETLOCK ON, the commands listed in table R.18 will automatically try to lock a file. Automatic locking is disabled by SET LOCK OFF.

**Table R.18 Commands That Automatically Lock Files**

| Command | Action | Level | SET LOCK OFF Disables LOCK? |
|---|---|---|---|
| @GET/READ | Edit | Record | No |
| APPEND FROM | Update | File | No |
| APPEND [blank] | Update | Record | No |
| AVERAGE | Read only | File | Yes |
| BROWSE | Edit | Record | No |
| CALCULATE | Read only | File | Yes |
| CHANGE/EDIT | Edit | Record | No |
| COPY TAG | Read/write | File | Yes on read/No on write |
| COPY [STRUCTURE] | Read/write | File | Yes on read/No on write |
| COUNT | Read only | File | Yes |

*continues*

**Table R.18 Continued**

| Command | Action | Level | SET LOCK OFF Disables LOCK? |
|---|---|---|---|
| DELETE/RECALL | Update | Record | No |
| DELETE/RECALL | Update | File | No |
| EDIT | Update | Record | No |
| INDEX | Read/write | File | Yes on read/No on write |
| JOIN | Read/write | File | Yes on read/No on write |
| LABEL | Read only | File | Yes |
| REPLACE | Update | Record | No |
| REPLACE [scope] | Update | File | No |
| REPORT | Read only | File | Yes |
| SET CATALOG ON | Catalog | File | No |
| SORT | Read/write | File | Yes on read/No on write |
| SUM | Read only | File | Yes |
| TOTAL | Read/write | File | Yes on read/No on write |
| UPDATE | Update | File | No |

### Example

```
* Enable automatic file locking
SET LOCK ON
* Disable automatic locking
SET LOCK OFF
```

## SET MARGIN TO

### Syntax

```
SET MARGIN TO <number of columns>
```

### Purpose

Sets the left margin value for all printed output. You also can use the _ploffset system memory value to set the left margin. Both commands affect the left margin, but only the last command is used—the two are not additive. The system memory variable _lmargin is added to the SET MARGIN value when _wrap is true (.T.).

### Example

```
* Set the left margin if not correct
IF _ploffset <> 10
   SET MARGIN TO 10
ENDIF
```

## SET MARK TO

### Syntax

```
SET MARK TO [<single character>]
```

### Purpose

Changes the delimiter used in the date display of month/day/year. Any single character can be used. The default is the slash (/), but the delimiter also may be determined by the format selected with the SET DATE command. SET MARK overrides the character specified in SET DATE.

### Example

```
* Change the date delimiter
* Current date is 06/15/92
SET CENTURY OFF
SET DATE TO USA
? DATE()             && displays "06-15-92"
SET DATE TO MDY
? DATE()             && displays "06/15/92"
SET MARK TO "."
? DATE()             && displays "06.15.92"
```

## SET MEMOWIDTH

### Syntax

```
SET MEMOWIDTH TO <number of characters>
```

### Purpose

Determines the width of memo fields when they are sent to the screen or printer. The default value is 50; the range can be from 8 to 255. Word wrap will occur if the system variable _wrap is set to true (.T.). (See the "Using System Memory Variables" section of this "dBASE IV Reference Guide.")

### Example

```
* Set up memo field width of 45
SET MEMOWIDTH TO 45
_wrap = .T.          && make sure that word wrap is enabled
```

## SET MENU

### Syntax

```
SET MENU ON/off
```

### Purpose

This command is provided for compatibility with dBASE III programs. It is ignored by dBASE IV.

## SET MESSAGE TO

### Syntax

```
SET MESSAGE TO [<message text> [AT <row> [,<column>]]]
```

### Purpose

Displays the *<message text>* at the *<row>*, *<column>* location. If the AT *<row>*, *<column>* parameter is not specified, the message is displayed at line 24 (on 25-line screens) or line 42 (on 43-line screens). If the *<column>* parameter is not specified, the message is centered on the *<row>*. If SET STATUS is ON, the message is displayed on the bottom line. If you want a message to appear on line 0 (the top line), first use SET SCOREBOARD OFF.

The SET MESSAGE location also is used for @...SAY...GET commands that have a MESSAGE parameter. Messages are not displayed inside or over window areas.

### Example

```
* Put all data entry messages at the screen bottom
* They will be centered, because no <column> was specified
* The SCRNLINES variable was previously set for the
* number of lines on the screen
SET MESSAGE TO "DATA ENTRY" AT scrnlines
```

## SET NEAR

### Syntax

```
SET NEAR on/OFF
```

### Purpose

When SET NEAR is set to ON, a FIND or SEEK puts the record pointer just after the most likely location of the desired record. You therefore can get close to the desired record even if an exact match cannot be found. With SET NEAR OFF (the default), an unsuccessful FIND or SEEK will place the record pointer at the end of the file.

The SET NEAR command affects the FOUND() and EOF() functions. With SET NEAR ON, FOUND() is true for an exact match and false for a near match, and EOF() is false with a near match. With SET NEAR OFF, FOUND() is false and EOF() is true.

### Example

```
* Set up near matches for the find routine
SET NEAR ON
DO findcust          && find customer program
SET NEAR OFF
```

## SET ODOMETER TO

### Syntax

```
SET ODOMETER TO <record count interval>
```

### Purpose

Determines the update interval for functions that display a record counter. The default value is 1, and the maximum is 200. To remove the record counter from the screen for operations such as COPY, RECALL, and INDEX, use SET TALK OFF.

A low odometer value can slightly degrade the performance of some commands.

### Example

```
* Turn on the record counter for reindexing
USE CLIENTS INDEX CLIENTS
SET ODOMETER TO 20
SET TALK ON          && enable display of odometer
REINDEX
SET TALK OFF         && turn it back off
```

## SET ORDER TO

### Syntax

```
SET ORDER TO
SET ORDER TO <index number>
SET ORDER TO [TAG] <filename> / <MDX tagname> [OF <MDX filename>]
   [NOSAVE]
```

### Purpose

The SET ORDER TO command offers three alternatives:

- The first alternative inactivates any index for the current database. Records are shown in their natural, record-number order. When you plan to use a LOCATE command, you will find the desired record faster if you first use the SET ORDER TO command to inactivate the indexes.
- The second command determines the active NDX index, where <*index number*> is the relative position of the desired index as given in the index list. The <*index number*> can be from 0 to 10 (a value of 0 resets to natural order). This command maintains compatibility with dBASE III NDX index files when there are no open MDX files.
- The third alternative assigns the controlling dBASE IV index files or tags; the order must be specified with the order file name, not its number. The [OF <*MDX filename*>] option is used if an identical tag name appears in two or more open MDX files or when you want to use an index file other than the production MDX file. The NOSAVE option tells dBASE not to save indexes created by a query when the MDX file is closed.

### Example

```
* Place the CUSTLIST file in
* ZIP index order
USE CUSTLIST
SET ORDER TO TAG ZIP
* Put file in natural order
SET ORDER TO
```

## SET PATH TO

### Syntax

```
SET PATH TO <path list>
```

### Purpose

Like the DOS PATH command, SET PATH TO specifies the drive and directories that will be used by dBASE IV to find files (normally program files) that are not in the current directory. The <*path list*> can be up to 60 characters long, and each directory must be separated by a semicolon (;).

NOTE

If you have specified a path with the DOS PATH command, dBASE IV ignores it. To use a path, you must specify it from within dBASE. The Control Center does not use the SET PATH path specification. The DIR command uses the current directory only.

### Example

```
SET PATH TO C:\DBASE4\PROGRAMS;C:\DBASE4
```

## SET PAUSE

### Syntax

```
SET PAUSE on/OFF
```

### Purpose

Determines whether the screen output of SQL SELECT commands is paused with each screenful of data. SET PAUSE ON enables pausing of the display; SET PAUSE OFF (the default) causes the screen output to continue until the command is completed. The SET PAUSE setting is similar to the difference between the LIST and DISPLAY commands: SET PAUSE OFF is like LIST; SET PAUSE ON is like DISPLAY.

### Example

```
* Pause after each screenful of SQL data
SET PAUSE ON
```

## SET POINT TO

### Syntax

```
SET POINT TO <decimal point character>
```

### Purpose

Changes the character used as the decimal point in numbers. The default is a period (.), but this can be changed to a comma (,) for international users. Any single character can be used except a number or a space. To change back to the default value, use SET POINT TO without a parameter value.

### Example

```
* Set up for nomal decimal character
SET POINT TO "."
```

# SET PRECISION TO

### Syntax

```
SET PRECISION TO <number of decimal places>
```

### Purpose

Determines the number of decimal places used by dBASE IV internally in all mathematical calculations of type-N numbers. The default value is 16, but any value from 0 to 20 can be used.

### Example

```
* Set up maximum precision
SET PRECISION TO 20
```

# SET PRINTER

### Syntax

```
SET PRINTER on/OFF
```

### Purpose

Determines whether all screen output (other than @...SAY commands) is sent to the printer (SET PRINTER ON) or sent to the screen (default value of SET PRINTER OFF).

### Example

```
* List system status to printer
* while showing screen message
SET PRINTER ON
CLEAR
@ 12,15 SAY "Printing system status"
LIST STATUS
EJECT
SET PRINTER OFF
```

# SET PRINTER TO

### Syntax

```
SET PRINTER TO <DOS device>
SET PRINTER TO \\<computer name>\<printer name> = <destination>
SET PRINTER TO FILE <filename>
```

### Purpose

The SET PRINTER TO offers three options:

- The first alternative determines the output port for all printed output. The *<DOS device>* normally is set to PRN, but you can change it to any of the three parallel ports (LPT1, LPT2, LPT3) or the serial ports (COM1, COM2, COM3, COM4).

- The second alternative sends output to a shared network printer and tells the network server to print the next print job. The *<computer name>* is the network-assigned name for the network file server. The *<printer name>* is the network-assigned name for the printer on the network. The *<destination>* is the installed shared printer, such as LPT1, LPT2, or LPT3.
- The third alternative sends printer output to the file specified in *<filename>*. The output includes the printer control commands that are used by the currently installed printer driver (as defined by the _pdriver system memory variable). After you use this command, you can use the DOS COPY command at any time to send the printer-formatted file to the printer. All printed output is sent to the *<filename>* until you use a SET PRINTER TO command without parameters.

### Examples

```
* Send output to LPT2:
SET PRINTER TO LPT2
* Send output to the network printer
SET PRINTER TO \\MAINCPU\PRINTER = LPT1
* Send printed output to a file
SET PRINTER TO FILE OUTPUT.TXT
```

## SET PROCEDURE TO

### Syntax

```
SET PROCEDURE TO [<procedure filename>]
```

### Purpose

Opens a procedure file (*<procedure filename>*) that contains a number of routines used by a dBASE IV program. You can have up to 963 procedures in a procedure file, but you are limited to the number of procedures that will fit in available memory (RAM). Most procedure files are short routines. You can close a procedure file with the CLOSE PROCEDURE command or by using SET PROCEDURE TO without a file name parameter.

When you use this command, dBASE assumes that the procedures have been compiled to an object code file with a DBO file extension. If the object code file cannot be found, the source file is compiled to a DBO file. Only one procedure file can be active at one time.

> **WARNING:** Make sure that your procedure program does not have the same file name as any other program. If it does, the compiled procedure will overwrite the other program's compiled file.

### Example

```
* Open the procedure file
SET PROCEDURE TO progproc
```

## SET REFRESH TO

### Syntax

```
SET REFRESH TO <number of seconds>
```

### Purpose

Sets the time interval in *<number of seconds>* when dBASE IV checks a file to determine whether a record being browsed or edited has been changed. The default value is 0, and the value can range from 1 to 3,600 seconds (one hour). When the refresh value expires, dBASE IV checks any files that are in a BROWSE or EDIT mode and updates the screens with any changes that are found.

### Example

```
* Update screen every 15 seconds
SET REFRESH TO 15
```

## SET RELATION TO

### Syntax

```
SET RELATION TO [<key expression> INTO <alias>
   [, <key expression> INTO <alias> ...]]
```

### Purpose

Links two databases together, based on a common *<key expression>*. The *<key expression>* value must match the controlling index of the child database. You can set multiple relations by specifying additional key expressions into *<alias>* parameters. The INTO *<alias>* database must have been previously opened with a USE command. The active (parent) database is linked to the child database with the child database's INTO *<alias>* name. When you move through the active parent database, the child database follows the key expression of the parent database. If there isn't a matching record in the child database, the record pointer is positioned at EOF().

### Example

```
* Link the customer's STATE field with the Salestax
field
SELECT 2                      && child database
USE SALESTAX ORDER STATE      && indexed on STATE field
SELECT 1                      && parent database
USE CUSTOMER
* set the parent-child relation
SET RELATION TO customer->state INTO salestax
* show the customer's state and sales tax rate
LIST customer->state, salestax->state, salestax->rate
```

## SET REPROCESS TO

### Syntax

SET REPROCESS TO [<*number of retries*>]

### Purpose

Determines the number of times that dBASE IV tries a network record or file lock command before returning an error. The default is 0; if you don't specify the ON ERROR command, the message `Please wait, another user has locked this record or file` appears until the record or file is available. The command is retried until the record or file is available or until you press the Esc key. Allowable values are from _1 to 32,000. The _1 value sets up an infinite retry that cannot be canceled with the Esc key.

### Example

```
* Set up 20 tries as maximum
* An err_trap routine will tell the user
* that the record is in use by another
SET REPROCESS TO 20
```

## SET SAFETY

### Syntax

```
SET SAFETY ON/off
```

### Purpose

Prevents existing files from being accidentally overwritten. If SET SAFETY is ON, the message, `File already exists, Overwrite or Cancel` appears when you try to overwrite an existing file. You then must select Overwrite to overwrite the file. Because SET

SAFETY OFF assumes that you want to overwrite an existing file, the message is not displayed.

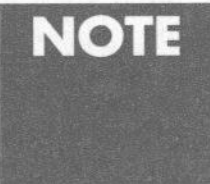


With SET SAFETY OFF, files will be overwritten or erased. Make sure that you are aware of the SET SAFETY status before you use commands that overwrite or erase files.

### *Example*

```
* Reindex the file; automatically overwrite the old
index
USE STUDENTS
SET SAFETY OFF
INDEX ON lastname + firstname TO STUDENTS
* Make sure that user verifies zapping a database
SET SAFETY ON
USE TEMPDATA
ZAP
```

## SET SCOREBOARD

### *Syntax*

```
SET SCOREBOARD ON/off
```

### *Purpose*

Determines whether the keyboard indicators are shown on line 0 of the screen. SET SCOREBOARD ON (along with SET STATUS OFF) displays the keyboard indicators. (If SET STATUS is OFF, the SET SCOREBOARD command is ignored.) The indicators are these: Del to indicate records marked for deletion, Ins for Insert mode, Caps for Caps Lock mode, and Num for Number Lock mode. SET SCOREBOARD OFF disables the keyboard indicators on line 0.

### *Example*

```
* Don't need the scoreboard on
SET SCOREBOARD OFF
```

## SET SEPARATOR TO

### *Syntax*

```
SET SEPARATOR TO [<separator character>]
```

### *Purpose*

Determines the character used as the thousands separator. The default is the comma, but this can be changed to any character. This command is most commonly used with the SET POINT and

SET CURRENCY commands. Only one character is allowed as the separator character. See SET CURRENCY TO for an example.

## SET SKIP TO()

### Syntax

```
SET SKIP TO [<alias> [, <alias> ] ...]
```

### Purpose

When this command is used with the SET RELATION command, it makes all records in the child database accessible as you move the record pointer through the parent database. The *<alias>* activates the SET SKIP command for those *<alias>* databases that you specify. The SKIP list is active until you use a SET SKIP TO command without any parameters; closing the database or relations does not affect the SKIP list.

### Example

```
* Set up the grades and students relationship
* The GRADES database is indexed on the STUDENTID field
* as is the STUDENTS database
USE GRADES IN 2                  && work area 2
USE STUDENTS IN 1                && work area 2
SELECT 1
* Sets up the relation
SET RELATION TO studentid INTO grades
* Make sure that all grade records are used
SET SKIP TO grades
* List all the student's test scores
LIST students->studentid, students->lastname, student-
>firstname,;
grades->testdate, grades->score
```

## SET SPACE

### Syntax

```
SET SPACE ON/off
```

### Purpose

Determines whether a space is printed between variables or data when the ? or ?? parameters are used. If SET SPACE is ON, a space is printed between the characters; SET SPACE OFF prevents printing of the space.

### Example

```
firstname = "Erica"
lastname = "Jean"
SET SPACE ON
? firstname, lastname    && results in "Erica Jean"
SET SPACE OFF
? firstname, lastname    && results in "EricaJean"
```

## SET SQL

### Syntax

```
SET SQL on/OFF
```

### Purpose

Enables the use of SQL commands at the dot prompt. SET SQL ON enables the use of SQL commands; SET SQL OFF disables the use of SQL commands. When the SQL commands are enabled, the SQL prompt is shown in place of the dot prompt. The SET SQL command cannot be used in programs.

### Example

```
SET SQL ON  && Used only at dot prompt, not in programs
```

## SET STATUS

### Syntax

```
SET STATUS ON/off
```

### Purpose

Determines whether the status bar is shown at the bottom of the screen. The status bar contains the current command name, the file in use, the current record number, the total number of records, and the keyboard status information (Del, Caps, Ins, Num) if SET SCOREBOARD is ON. SET STATUS ON (the default) will display this information; SET STATUS OFF will not show the information. The status line is displayed on line 23 of a 25-line screen and on line 41 of a 43-line screen.

### Example

```
* Turn off status bar
SET STATUS OFF
```

## SET STEP

### Syntax

```
SET STEP on/OFF
```

### Purpose

Performs one command at a time, halting between commands. When SET STEP is ON, the message `Press SPACE to Step, S to Suspend, or Esc to Cancel...` is displayed between the execution of each command. You can press the space bar to execute the next command, press S to suspend the program and display the dot prompt, or press Esc to cancel the currently executing program. SET STEP primarily is used during debugging. The default value is OFF.

### Example

```
* Turn step on for problem code area
SET STEP ON
* commands causing problems
SET STEP OFF
```

## SET TALK

### Syntax

```
SET TALK ON/off
```

### Purpose

Determines whether the response to dBASE IV commands is displayed after the command is entered. Programs normally contain a SET TALK OFF command to disable the dBASE IV command response because responses would clutter the screen. Use SET TALK ON (the default) to show the commands.

### Example

```
* Turn off dBASE IV responses
* They just clutter the screen during the program
SET TALK OFF
```

## SET TITLE

### Syntax

```
SET TITLE ON/off
```

### Purpose

Determines whether the catalog file title prompt is displayed. If SET TITLE is ON, creating or adding to a report, label, database, query, form, program, or application produces a prompt for the catalog title. (The catalog file title is shown as the description in these cases.) If SET TITLE is OFF, the catalog title prompt is not displayed.

### Example

```
* Don't need to show the catalog title prompt
SET TITLE OFF
```

## SET TRAP

### Syntax

```
SET TRAP on/OFF
```

### Purpose

Activates the dBASE IV debugger when a program causes an error or when the Esc key is pressed. If SET TRAP is OFF (default), pressing the Esc key displays a message box with three options: Cancel, Ignore, and Suspend.

You have the option of canceling the current program, ignoring the pressing of the Esc key, or suspending the program. A suspended program can be continued with the RESUME command. When SET TRAP is ON, dBASE IV brings up the debugger when an error occurs or when the Esc key is pressed (see DEBUG).

If an ON ERROR command is in effect, SET TRAP is ignored, and the ON ERROR statement is executed.

## SET TYPEAHEAD TO

### Syntax

```
SET TYPEAHEAD TO <number of characters>
```

### Purpose

Specifies the size of the type-ahead buffer. The buffer normally holds 20 characters (keystrokes); allowable values are from 0 to 32,000. During full-screen editing or appending, the keyboard buffer stores 20 characters only, regardless of the SET TYPEAHEAD TO value. You can use the CLEAR TYPEAHEAD command to clear the keyboard buffer.

If you have an error-handling procedure in your program, you may want to set the TYPEAHEAD buffer to 0 to disable the keyboard buffer. Doing so ensures that errors are properly trapped and that the error-handling procedure is not inadvertently bypassed by unprocessed keystrokes in the buffer.

### Example

```
* Disable TYPEAHEAD because the ON ERROR command is used
ON ERROR DO err_trap          && error trapping procedure
SET TYPEAHEAD TO 0
* Clear out any characters in keyboard buffer
CLEAR TYPEAHEAD
```

## SET UNIQUE

### Syntax

```
SET UNIQUE on/OFF
```

### Purpose

Determines whether only records with unique key values are included in the index files (SET UNIQUE ON) or whether all records are included in the index (the default SET UNIQUE OFF).

### Example

```
* Print a list of only the unique city names in the database
USE CUSTLIST
SET UNIQUE ON
INDEX ON city TAG cityuniq   && also activates the new index
LIST CITY TO PRINT
```

## SET VIEW TO

### Syntax

```
SET VIEW TO <query filename> / ?
```

### Purpose

Executes a query (QBO or QBE) that was created with the Control Center or at the dot prompt (with CREATE/MODIFY VIEW). Use the ? parameter to choose from a list of available queries. If a catalog is open and SET CATALOG is ON, the catalog is updated to include the *<query filename>*.

### Example

```
* Set up the customer status query
USE CLIENTS
SET VIEW TO CUSTSTAT
```

include the <*query filename*>.

### Example

```
* Set up the customer status query
USE CLIENTS
SET VIEW TO CUSTSTAT
```

## SET WINDOW OF MEMO TO

### Syntax

```
SET WINDOW OF MEMO TO <window name>
```

### Purpose

Determines the window specification (<*window name*>) that will be used when you edit memo fields with the APPEND, BROWSE, CHANGE, EDIT, or READ command. The <*window name*> must have been previously specified with the DEFINE WINDOW command. You can override this window for an individual memo field by using the WINDOW parameter of an @...GET command.

### Example

```
USE CLIENTS         && has a memo field called NOTES
DEFINE WINDOW memo_wind FROM 15,0 TO 20,79
SET WINDOW OF MEMO TO memo_wind
@ 1,1 GET NOTES     && relative position in memo_wind window
```

# Using SQL Commands

The SQL commands are similar to many of their dBASE IV counterparts. SQL commands work on *tables* or *views*, which are selected records from an SQL database. Table R.19 shows important SQL terms and their equivalent terms in dBASE IV.

**Table R.19 Comparing SQL and dBASE Terms**

| SQL | dBASE |
|---|---|
| Database | Group of related files |
| Table | Database file |
| Row | Record |
| Column | Field |

## SQL Data Types

The SQL language supports eight *data types*, which are similar to the data types used in dBASE IV. Table R.20 shows the different data types.

**Table R.20 SQL Data Types**

| Type | Description |
|---|---|
| SMALLINT | Whole numbers from –99,999 to 999,999. |
| INTEGER | Positive whole numbers up to 11 digits, negative whole numbers up to 10 digits. |
| FLOAT (*x*,*y*) | Exponential numbers from 0.1e-307 to 0.9e+308, where<br>*x* = the total number of digits<br>*y* = number decimal places |
| DECIMAL (*x*,*y*) | Decimal numbers to 19 significant digits (with a negative sign as one digit in negative numbers), where<br>*x* = the total number of digits<br>*y* = number decimal places |
| NUMERIC(*x*,*y*) | Numbers to 20 significant digits (with a negative sign as one digit in negative numbers), where<br>*x* = the total number of digits + 1 for the decimal point<br>*y* = number decimal places |
| DATE | A date in the form mm/dd/yy. |
| CHAR(*n*) | A series of up to 254 characters, enclosed in single or double quotation marks, where *n* represents the number of characters. You can compare character-type columns only to other character-type columns or string constants. |
| LOGICAL | True (.T. or .Y.) or false (.F. or .N.) values. You can compare LOGICAL columns only to other LOGICAL columns or constants. |

Make sure that you are comparing only compatible data types; you cannot, for example, compare character columns with float-type columns. INTEGER, SMALLINT, FLOAT, DECIMAL, and NUMERIC column types are compatible with each other.

# SQL Functions Used in SELECT

The SQL functions that can be used in the SELECT command are shown in table R.21.

When you use SQL functions, the column name is placed within the parentheses, as in SUM(ord_qty), which sums the ORD_QTY column. You also can use the column number, as in SUM(3), which sums the values in column 3 of the table or view. The asterisk (*) is used to apply a function to the entire row (not column) of data, as in AVG(*).

**Table R.21 SQL SELECT Functions**

| Function | Description |
|---|---|
| COUNT() | Counts the number of selected rows. |
| SUM() | Sums the values in a numeric column. |
| MIN() | Determines the minimum value in the column. The column can be a character, date, or numeric column. |
| MAX() | Determines the maximum value in the column. The column can be a character, date, or numeric column. |
| AVG() | Determines the average value in a numeric column. |

# SQL Predicates

SQL predicates are the words BETWEEN, IN, and LIKE used in the WHERE clause. BETWEEN looks for values within the range, IN looks for values in a list, and LIKE compares a character column to a character string. Table R.22 shows examples of each, and an equivalent dBASE IV *<condition>*.

**Table R.22 Comparing SQL Predicates and dBASE IV Conditions**

| SQL Predicate | dBASE IV Condition |
|---|---|
| `WHERE ord_qty BETWEEN 100 and 200;` | `FOR ord_qty >= 100 .AND. ord_qty <= 200` |
| `WHERE unit_type IN ("EA", "CASE", "PALLET");` | `FOR unit_type + "/" $ "EA/CASE/PALLET/"` |
| `WHERE custname LIKE "CH%";` | `FOR LEFT(custname,2) = "CH"` |

The LIKE command permits the following wild cards: an underscore (_), which matches any single character, and the percent symbol (%), which matches any number of characters. You can combine the predicates with the AND, OR, and NOT logical operators.

# dBASE IV Functions and Commands in SQL

You can use some dBASE IV functions and commands in SQL statements. You can, for example, use the DATE() function in a WHERE clause to limit the SQL command to rows with certain date values. Some functions, such as COL(), can be used only in an SQL program, not at the SQL prompt. Many dBASE IV commands can be used in *SQL mode* (entered at the SQL dot prompt or used in an SQL program).

> **WARNING:** Because all SQL commands end with a semicolon (;), make sure that you enter the dBASE IV command on one complete line *without* using a semicolon, whether entered at the SQL prompt or included in an SQL program.

# SQL Security

In dBASE IV, the PROTECT command prevents unauthorized users from accessing specific databases. After a database has been protected, the user must log in with a password to use the database, enter dBASE IV commands, or use ASSIST mode.

The dBASE IV PROTECT command also *encrypts* databases so that they can be used by only authorized users. See the PROTECT command in the "dBASE IV Commands" section elsewhere in this Reference Guide.

To assign privileges to SQL files, use the SQL commands GRANT and REVOKE. These commands grant or revoke various *privileges* that are used to limit access to SQL tables and views.

# SQL Command Descriptions

SQL commands follow the same syntax rules that dBASE IV commands observe. See the introduction to this Reference Guide for information about dBASE IV command syntax and the way it is diagrammed in this book.

Most SQL commands can be entered at the SQL prompt; those commands that can be used in only SQL programs are noted in their descriptions in this chapter.

Remember that all SQL statements end with a semicolon (;). Several of the examples on the following pages show an SQL statement broken into separate lines, for clarity. You can break your SQL statements into several lines, as well—as long as the SQL statement has the semicolon at the end of the command (and nowhere else). This is the opposite of the way dBASE IV works with semicolons. In dBASE IV, a semicolon indicates that the statement continues; in SQL, a semicolon indicates the end of the statement.

The SQL commands that follow are listed alphabetically.

## ALTER TABLE

### Syntax

```
ALTER TABLE <table name> ADD (<column name> <data type>
   [,<column name> <data type>...]);
```

### Purpose

Adds new columns called *<column name>* to the existing *<table name>*. The new table can use any of the SQL data types.

### Example

```
ALTER TABLE parts ADD (newnum CHAR(6));
```

## CLOSE

### Syntax

```
CLOSE <SQL cursor name>;
```

### Purpose

Closes the SQL cursor, releasing the memory used by the cursor. You can reopen the cursor again with an OPEN *<SQL cursor name>* command. This command is used only in SQL program files (PRS files).

### Example

```
CLOSE partscur;
```

## CREATE DATABASE

### Syntax

```
CREATE DATABASE [<path>]<database name>;
```

### Purpose

Creates a new database and the SQL catalog tables that will be used with the new database. The *<path>* can be up to 64 characters long but shouldn't include any space characters. If the *<path>* does not exist, it is created automatically. When the SQL database is created, it becomes the active SQL database.

### Example

```
CREATE DATABASE parts;
```

## CREATE INDEX

### Syntax

```
CREATE [UNIQUE] INDEX <index name> ON <table name>
   (<column name> [ASC/DESC] [,<column name> [ASC/DESC]...]);
```

### Purpose

Creates an index that is based on the columns specified in *<column name>*. The index helps the SELECT commands execute faster. Columns of any data type except logical can be used as the index column. The UNIQUE option creates an index made up of only the unique values in the *<column name>*, to prevent duplicate index key values. Use the ASC option to create ascending indexes; use DESC to create descending indexes.

### Example

```
CREATE INDEX partnum ON parts (partnumbr);
```

# CREATE SYNONYM

### Syntax

```
CREATE SYNONYM <synonym name> FOR <table/view>;
```

### Purpose

Creates an alternative name for a view or table in the current database, enabling you to use a shortened table or view name.

### Example

```
CREATE SYNONYM pn FOR partnumbr;
```

# CREATE TABLE

### Syntax

```
CREATE TABLE <table name> (<column name> <data type>
   [,<column name> <data type>...]);
```

### Purpose

Creates a new SQL table for the current database. The *<table name>* is defined by the *<column name>* and the *<data type>* for each column. Any data type, except memo, can be used. Tables can contain up to 255 columns.

### Example

```
CREATE TABLE parts
(part_num char(8),
part_desc char (20),
unitcost decimal(5,2),
unitby char(3),
vendcode char(9));
```

# CREATE VIEW

### Syntax

```
CREATE VIEW <view name> [(<column name>, <column name>..)]
   AS <subselect> [WITH CHECK OPTION];
```

### Purpose

Creates a table based on the columns defined in other tables or views. After using this command, you can add data to the view, which updates the underlying tables. You can define the *<column name>* for each column of the view; if you don't specify the *<column name>*, the view contains the column names of the underlying tables in the *<subselect>* predicate. Use the WITH CHECK

OPTION parameter to make sure that inserted or updated rows meet the condition of the SELECT...WHERE command that defines the rows of the view.

### Example

```
* Create a view containing back-ordered parts
CREATE VIEW backordr
AS SELECT partnum, partdesc, orddate
FROM orders WHERE shipdate = {};
```

## DBCHECK

### Syntax

```
DBCHECK [<table name>];
```

### Purpose

Looks at the current catalog table for any SQL tables to make sure that the underlying DBF and MDX files are consistent with the catalog tables. If any differences are found, error messages are returned.

### Example

```
* Make sure that the PARTS catalog table is consistent
* with the underlying databases and indexes
DBCHECK parts;
```

## DBDEFINE

### Syntax

```
DBDEFINE [<database file name>];
```

### Purpose

Creates catalog table entries for the <*database file name*> and its associated indexes. If you want to create catalog entries for all databases and indexes in the current SQL database, use the DBDEFINE command without a <*database file name*>. Any memo fields in the database are ignored. If the MDX index was created with the INDEX...UNIQUE command, an SQL database is not created.

### Example

```
* Create SQL catalog for all databases
DBDEFINE;
```

# DECLARE

### Syntax

```
DECLARE <cursor name> CURSOR FOR <SELECT command>
   [FOR UPDATE OF<column list>/ORDER BY <clause>];
```

### Purpose

Defines an SQL *cursor* that acts as a record pointer to SQL data. The cursor points the rows of the result table. The cursor is associated with the *<SELECT command>*, and must be opened with the OPEN *<cursor>* command. Use the FOR UPDATE option if you want the cursor to allow updates. The ORDER BY option enables you to determine the order of the columns.

### Example

```
* Table to show ordered parts
DECLARE partordr CURSOR FOR
SELECT partnum, partdesc, onhand, backqty, ordqty, ordate
FROM parts
WHERE ordqty > 0;
```

# DELETE FROM

### Syntax

```
DELETE FROM <table name> [<alias name>] [WHERE <clause>];
```

### Purpose

Deletes rows from the *<table name>*. All rows are deleted unless you include the WHERE *<clause>*. After rows are deleted, they are erased permanently—there is no UNDELETE command as in dBASE IV. Deleted rows can be recalled only if they are part of a BEGIN...END TRANSACTION command sequence.

> **WARNING:** You may want to use the SELECT...WHERE command to look at the rows that will be deleted. Doing so helps you to make sure that you have used the proper WHERE clause.

### Example

```
* Delete all inactive customers
DELETE FROM custnames WHERE lastdate < DATE() - 400;
```

## DELETE FROM WHERE CURRENT OF

### Syntax

```
DELETE FROM <table name> WHERE CURRENT OF <SQL cursor name>;
```

### Purpose

Deletes the last row that has been fetched by the *<SQL cursor name>* on the *<table name>*. This command is used only in SQL program (PRS) files.

### Example

```
DELETE FROM parts WHERE CURRENT OF partcurs;
```

## DROP DATABASE

### Syntax

```
DROP DATABASE <database name>;
```

### Purpose

Deletes a database by deleting DBF and MDX files in the database directory for which there is a corresponding entry in the Systables and Sysidxs catalog tables. Use the STOP command before you use DROP DATABASE.

### Example

```
* Drop the temp database from the current SQL environment
DROP DATABASE temp;
```

## DROP INDEX

### Syntax

```
DROP INDEX <index name>;
```

### Purpose

Removes the index specified in *<index name>*. Indexes are dropped automatically when the table that defined the index is dropped.

### Example

```
* Drop the temp index but keep the temp database
DROP INDEX temp;
```

# DROP SYNONYM

### Syntax

```
DROP SYNONYM <synonym name>;
```

### Purpose

Removes the *<synonym name>* from the current table or view. Synonyms are created with the CREATE SYNONYM command and are deleted automatically if their associated tables or views are deleted.

### Example

```
* Drop the temp synonym
DROP SYNONYM temp;
```

# DROP TABLE

### Syntax

```
DROP TABLE <table name>;
```

### Purpose

Deletes the *<table name>* from the current view or table. The table was created with the CREATE TABLE command. Any indexes, views, and synonyms that were created from the table also are deleted automatically.

### Example

```
* Delete the temp table and all its related files
DROP TABLE temp;
```

# DROP VIEW

### Syntax

```
DROP VIEW <view name>;
```

### Purpose

Deletes the *<view name>*. No underlying tables are deleted, but any synonyms and views based on the view are deleted.

### Example

```
* Delete the temp view
DROP VIEW temp;
```

# FETCH

### Syntax

```
FETCH <cursor name> INTO <memvar list>;
```

### Purpose

Moves the cursor to the next row of the result table and puts the values from that row into the *<memory variable list>*. The DECLARE...CURSOR and OPEN CURSOR commands must have been used before the FETCH command.

### Example

```
* Move the previously defined cursor to the next row
FETCH partcurs INTO mparts, mdesc, mqty, munitcost;
```

## GRANT

### Syntax

```
GRANT ALL [PRIVILEGES]/<privilege list>
     ON [TABLE] <table list>
     TO PUBLIC/<user list>
     [WITH GRANT OPTION];
```

### Purpose

Gives the current user access to the current database tables and views. The database must have been protected with the dBASE IV PROTECT command, and the user must have logged in to gain access to dBASE IV. Entries for the *<privilege list>* are described in table R.23.

The ALL option grants the user all privileges. The TO PUBLIC option grants all users access to the table and view. The GRANT OPTION parameter grants a user the power to grant privileges to other users.

**Table R.23 GRANT Privileges**

| Privilege | Effect |
|---|---|
| ALTER | User can add columns to a table (not allowed on a view) |
| DELETE | User can delete rows from a view or table |
| INDEX | User can use CREATE INDEX |
| INSERT | User can add rows to a view or table |
| SELECT | User can display rows from a view or table |
| UPDATE | User can update rows in a table or view, or update only specific columns |

### Example

```
* Give the insert privilege to user "Jason"
GRANT ALL INSERT ON TABLE custname TO Jason;
```

## INSERT INTO

### Syntax

```
INSERT INTO <table name> [(<column list>)] VALUES (<value list>);
INSERT INTO <table name> [(<column list>)] <SELECT command>;
```

### Purpose

These commands insert rows in a table or updatable view. The *<column list>* option enables you to specify the order of the columns that are used with the *<value list>*.

The INSERT INTO...VALUES command inserts the *<value list>* data into the row. The *<value list>* can be constants, character strings, memory variables, dBASE IV functions that return a value, or the SQL keyword USER. Separate the values in the *<value list>* with commas, and make sure that each value matches the data type of the corresponding column.

The INSERT INTO...SELECT command inserts rows retrieved by a SELECT command.

### Example

```
* Insert the memory variables into parts table
INSERT INTO parts VALUES (partnum, partdesc, cost, unitsize);
```

## LOAD DATA FROM

### Syntax

```
LOAD DATA FROM [<path>]<file name> INTO TABLE <table name>
   [[TYPE] SDF/DIF/WKS/SYLK/FW2/RPD/dBASEII/
   DELIMITED [WITH BLANK/WITH <delimiter>]];
```

### Purpose

Imports data from another type of file (specified in *<file name>*) and adds it to the existing *<table name>*. Use the complete *<path>* and *<file name>* if the file is not in the current SQL directory. The allowable file *<types>* are listed in table R.24.

**Table R.24 File Types for LOAD DATA FROM**

| Type | Description |
|---|---|
| SDF | System data format ASCII files |
| DIF | VisiCalc files |
| WKS | Lotus 1-2-3 spreadsheet files |
| SYLK | MultiPlan spreadsheet files |
| FW2 | Framework II database and spreadsheet files |
| RPD | RapidFile database files |
| dBASEII | dBASE II files |

Files in dBASE III, dBASE III Plus, and dBASE IV format do not require a TYPE parameter. The DELIMITED option enables you to transfer data from a formatted ASCII text file. For more on importing files, see APPEND FROM in the "dBASE IV Commands" section elsewhere in this Reference Guide.

### Example

```
* Append the data from the PARTS.DBF file into the PARTS
* SQL table
LOAD DATA FROM C:\DBASE4\DATA\PARTS.DBF INTO TABLE parts;
```

## OPEN

### Syntax

```
OPEN <cursor name>;
```

### Purpose

Opens a cursor that was previously defined with the DECLARE CURSOR command. The SELECT command associated with the cursor is executed, and the cursor is placed before the first row in the result table.

### Example

```
* Open the previously defined partcurs cursor
OPEN partcurs;
```

## REVOKE

### Syntax

```
REVOKE ALL [PRIVILEGES]/<privileges list>
   ON [TABLE] <table list> FROM PUBLIC/<user list>;
```

### Purpose

Removes access privileges on the current TABLE or *<table list>*. The privileges were given with the GRANT command. You can revoke all privileges with ALL PRIVILEGES; to revoke just some of the privileges, use the *<privilege list>*. Entries for the *<privilege list>* are described in table R.25.

**Table R.25 REVOKE Privileges**

| Privilege | Effect |
|---|---|
| ALTER | User can add columns to a table (not allowed on a view) |
| DELETE | User can delete rows from a view or table |
| INDEX | User can use CREATE INDEX |
| INSERT | User can add rows to a view or table |
| SELECT | User can display rows from a view or table |
| UPDATE | User can update rows in a table or view, or update only specific columns |

You can revoke privileges from all users by using FROM PUBLIC or revoke privileges from specific users by using the FROM *<user list>* option. Only those privileges granted previously can be revoked. You can revoke privileges from the current table or from a *<table list>*.

### Example

```
* Revoke the DELETE privilege from user Stacy
REVOKE ALL DELETE ON parts FROM Stacy;
```

## ROLLBACK

### Syntax

```
ROLLBACK [WORK];
```

### Purpose

Restores the contents of a view or table to the way they were before you started the BEGIN...END TRANSACTION command block. The WORK option is included to maintain compatibility with IBM's DB2 implementation of the SQL standard. ROLLBACK is most commonly used in programs, accompanied by the dBASE command ON ERROR.

### Example

```
* Rollback the changes to the current custname table
ROLLBACK;
```

## RUNSTATS

### Syntax

```
RUNSTATS [<table name>];
```

### Purpose

Updates the database statistics of the SQL system catalog tables. The statistics are used to help SQL determine the best way to execute the SQL database operations. RUNSTATS often is used after commands that make changes to a table or when data is added to more than 10 percent of the rows in a table. Use the optional *<table name>* to update statistics for a specific table. If you don't specify a table name, all table statistics are updated.

### Example

```
* Update the statistics for the partsnum table
RUNSTATS partsnum;
```

## SELECT

### Syntax

```
SELECT <clause>
   [INTO <clause>]
   [FROM <clause>]
   [WHERE <clause>]
   [GROUP BY <clause>]
   [HAVING <clause>]
   [UNION <subselect>]...
   [ORDER BY <clause>/FOR UPDATE OF <clause>]
   [SAVE TO TEMP <clause>];
```

### Purpose

Produces a result table by selecting rows and columns from a table or group. The result table is used by other SQL commands.

Each clause syntax of the command is detailed in the following entries, along with an example for that clause.

### Syntax—SELECT Clause

```
SELECT [ALL/DISTINCT] <column list> /*
```

### Purpose

The SELECT clause specifies the columns, SQL aggregate functions, or expressions that should be included in the result table. You can use the ALL option to select all columns or use the DISTINCT option to eliminate duplicate rows based on the column list. You can select all columns with the * option or specify a *<column list>*.

### Example

```
* Select these columns...
SELECT ALL parts, desc, cost, vendor, orddate
```

### Syntax—INTO Clause

```
INTO <memory variable 1> [,<memory variable 2>, ...]
```

### Purpose

This clause is used when a SELECT statement would return only a single row. The result values are stored in the memory variables: column 1's result in *<memory variable 1>*, column 2's result in *<memory variable 2>*, and so on. If more than one row is in the result table, only the first row's data is placed in the memory variables. If you specify the INTO clause, you cannot also specify the GROUP BY, HAVING, UNION, ORDER BY, FOR UPDATE OF, or SAVE TO TEMP clause.

### Example

```
* ... store results into memory variables
INTO mpart, mdesc, mcost, mvendor, morddate
```

### Syntax—FROM Clause

```
FROM <table>/<view> [alias] [[, <table>/<view> [<alias>]] ...]
```

### Purpose

The required FROM clause specifies the tables or views that are used to create the result table. You can use an *alias,* which can be up to 10 characters long; it must start with a letter, and is used in the same manner as database aliases. Do not use single-letter aliases of A through J—they are reserved for database alias names.

### Example

```
* ... From the PARTS table
FROM parts
```

### Syntax—WHERE Clause

```
WHERE [NOT] <search condition 1>
   [AND/OR [NOT] <search condition 2> ...]
```

### Purpose

Specifies the search condition used to determine the data that will appear in the result table. You can use any of the comparison operators. (Operators are <, >, <=, >=, =, <>, and #—see "Working with Operators" in the introduction to this Reference Guide.) The search condition can use any valid expression. Include parentheses as needed to achieve the desired result.

### Example

```
* ... for all order quantities 100 or more
WHERE ordqty >= 100
```

### Syntax—GROUP BY Clause

```
GROUP BY <column>[,<column>...]
```

### Purpose

Groups the rows in the result table by columns that have the same values so that each group is reduced to a single row. Each item is separated by a comma.

### Example

```
* Group by the orddate column
GROUP BY orddate
```

### Syntax—HAVING Clause

```
HAVING [NOT] <search condition 1>
[AND/OR [NOT] <search condition 2> ...]
```

### Purpose

Restricts grouped rows that appear in the result table. Groups are specified with the GROUP BY clause. You can combine search conditions with the AND/OR NOT option.

### Example

```
* Only if the quantity is more than 10
HAVING qty > 10
```

### Syntax—UNION Clause

```
<subselect> [UNION <subselect>]...]
   [ORDER BY <clause>/ FOR UPDATE OF <clause>]
   [SAVE TO TEMP <clause>] [KEEP]];
```

### Purpose

Combines the result tables of two or more *<subselect>* entries into a single result table. Duplicate rows are eliminated. Each *<subselect>* must produce the same number of columns, with compatible data types and widths. The ORDER BY option enables you to specify the order of the result union. The SAVE TO TEMP clause creates a temporary table that can be saved as a dBASE IV DBF file if you use the KEEP option.

### Example

```
* Save it to a temporary database
UNION part1 SAVE TO TEMP newparts
```

### Syntax—ORDER BY Clause

```
ORDER BY <column name>/<column number> [ASC/DESC]
[, <column name>/<column number> [ASC/DESC]...];
```

### Purpose

Determines the order of rows in the result table. Data is placed in the rows in ascending (ASC, the default) order or descending (DESC) order. The order of the columns in the result table is determined by the *<column names>* or *<column number>* values.

### Example

```
* Result table in this order
ORDER BY vendor, parts, desc, cost, orddate
```

### Syntax—FOR UPDATE OF Clause

```
FOR UPDATE OF <columns> [, <column> ...]
```

### Purpose

Specifies which columns can be updated when you use the UPDATE WHERE CURRENT OF command. This command is used only in programs and is ignored if entered at the SQL prompt. The columns specified must be in the FROM clause of the SELECT command.

### Example

```
* Update the orddate column only
FOR UPDATE OF ORDDATE
```

### Syntax—SAVE TO TEMP Clause

```
SAVE TO TEMP <table name> [(<column> [,<column>...])] [KEEP]
```

### Purpose

This clause is a dBASE extension to the SQL SELECT command. The clause saves, as a temporary table or as a dBASE file, the result table generated by a SELECT statement. Unless you specify the optional KEEP keyword, the table is available only for the remainder of the SQL session.

### Example

```
* Save the selected tables, partnumber, desc, and
qty
* columns to a DBF data file named parts
SAVE TO TEMP parts (partnumber,desc,qty) KEEP
```

## SET SQL OFF

### Syntax

```
SET SQL OFF
```

### Purpose

Exits SQL mode and returns you to the dBASE IV dot prompt. A semicolon at the end is not required.

### Example

```
* Return to the dBASE IV dot prompt
SET SQL OFF
```

## SET SQL ON

### Syntax

```
SET SQL ON
```

### Purpose

Enters SQL mode from dBASE IV. There is no semicolon at the end.

## SHOW DATABASE

### Syntax

```
SHOW DATABASE;
```

### Purpose

Lists the SQL databases that are available for use. The database name, creator's user ID, creation date, and DOS directory name are shown.

### Example

```
* Show current SQL database list
SHOW DATABASE;
```

## START DATABASE

### Syntax

```
START DATABASE <database name>;
```

### Purpose

Activates a database for use by subsequent SQL commands. START DATABASE is normally the first command used when you enter SQL commands at the SQL prompt. Only one database can be active at any one time. Use STOP DATABASE to finish using a database.

### Example

```
* Start using the PARTS database
START DATABASE parts;
```

## STOP DATABASE

### Syntax

```
STOP DATABASE;
```

### Purpose

Closes the current database. The database must be stopped (closed) before you can start (open) another database. Use this command before you use the DROP DATABASE command.

### Example

```
* Stop using the currently active PARTS database
STOP DATABASE;
```

## UNLOAD DATA TO

### Syntax

```
UNLOAD DATA TO [path]<file name>
   FROM TABLE <table name>
   [[TYPE] SDF/DIF/WKS/SYLK/FW2/RPD/dBASEII/
   DELIMITED [WITH BLANK/WITH<delimiter>]];
```

### Purpose

Exports the SQL table *<table name>* to the *<file name>*. The type of file created defaults to a dBASE IV DBF file, unless you use the TYPE option. The available types are described in table R.26.

**Table R.26 File Types for UNLOAD DATA TO**

| Type | Description |
|---|---|
| SDF | System data format ASCII files |
| DIF | VisiCalc files |
| WKS | Lotus 1-2-3 spreadsheet files |
| SYLK | MultiPlan spreadsheet files |
| FW2 | Framework II database and spreadsheet files |
| RPD | RapidFile database files |
| dBASEII | dBASE II files |

Files in dBASE III, dBASE III Plus, and dBASE IV format do not require a TYPE parameter. The DELIMITED option enables you to transfer data to a formatted ASCII text file.

### Example

```
* Export the CURRORD table data to a Lotus spreadsheet file
UNLOAD DATA TO orders FROM TABLE currord TYPE WKS
```

## UPDATE

### Syntax

```
UPDATE <table name>/<view name>
SET <column name>=<new value>[,<column name>=<new value>...]
   [WHERE <clause>];
UPDATE <table name>
   SET <column name>=<new value>[,<column name>=<new value>...]
   WHERE CURRENT OF <SQL cursor name>;
```

### Purpose

Changes the table or view data in columns for the specified rows. The new value for each column is specified by the SET... parameter.

UPDATE...WHERE is used to select the rows in the table or view that you want to update. The WHERE CURRENT OF clause is used to update only the row currently pointed to by the cursor.

### Example

```
* Add 5 percent to all costs, update the last increase date
* field for all rows where the cost has not increased in
* the last 90 days
UPDATE parts SET cost = cost * 1.05, lastinc = DATE()
WHERE lastinc = DATE() - 90;
```

# Using System Memory Variables

The system memory variables enable you to change various printer parameters to control the appearance of printed output. All system memory variables start with the underline character (_) and have default values when you start dBASE IV. You can change the system memory variables within your program, at the dot prompt, or while in the report generator. The default values in this section are shown in uppercase letters, and alternative values are shown in lowercase letters. You can use uppercase or lowercase characters when you use the system memory variables.

## _Alignment

### Syntax

```
_alignment = "LEFT"/"center"/"right"
```

### Purpose

Determines the alignment of the text printed with the ?/?? commands. The text normally is placed at the left margin but can be centered or right-justified. The _alignment command affects text within the margins, not text that is aligned with the PICTURE functions. The _alignment setting is ignored if the _wrap variable is set to true (.T.).

### Example

```
* Set up left text alignment
_alignment = "LEFT"
```

## _Box

### Syntax

```
_box = <condition>
```

### Purpose

Determines whether the boxes that are defined with the DEFINE BOX command are printed. You can set the *<condition>* to true (.T.) or false (.F.), or to a statement that evaluates as true or false. The _box variable normally is set to true.

### Example

```
* Turn off box printing
_box = .F.
```

## _Indent

### Syntax

```
_indent = <number of columns>
```

### Purpose

Determines the *<number of columns>* to indent the first paragraph of text printed with the ? command when the _wrap variable is set to true (.T.). The _indent value normally is 0. The lowest value is the negative of _lmargin; if _lmargin is 15, _indent can be as low as –15. The highest value is one less than the difference between _rmargin and _lmargin (_rmargin – _lmargin –1). The sum of the _indent and _lmargin values must be less than the _rmargin value. The _indent value is used only if _wrap is set to true.

**NOTE** The _ploffset (page left offset) value also can affect the actual printed position of the text.

### Example

```
* Set up five-character indent
_indent = 5
```

# _Lmargin

### Syntax

```
_lmargin = <left margin column position>
```

### Purpose

Defines the left margin used with the ? command if _wrap is set to true. The _lmargin value defaults to 0 but can be from 0 to 254. If _lmargin is set to 0, the first printed position will be at the left edge of the paper plus any _ploffset (page left offset) value (see "_Ploffset"). The (_lmargin + _indent) value must be less than the _rmargin value.

### Example

```
* Set up eight-character left margin
_lmargin = 8
```

# _Padvance

### Syntax

```
_padvance = "FORMFEED"/"linefeeds"
```

### Purpose

Determines whether dBASE IV advances the paper to the next top of form by using the form feed character or by outputting linefeed commands. The _padvance variable set to LINEFEEDS is useful for printing short forms, such as checks, without having to set the forms length setting on the printer. The _plength variable is then used to set the length of the form.

### Example

```
* Set up for check printing
_padvance = "LINEFEEDS"
```

# _Pageno

### Syntax

```
_pageno = <page number>
```

### Purpose

Sets the current page number. The default value is 1, but it can be set to between 1 and 32,767. You also can use the _pageno value in your report to output the current page number (? _pageno).

### Example

```
* Set up first page number
_pageno = 1
```

# _Pbpage

### Syntax

```
_pbpage = <beginning page number>
```

### Purpose

Determines the beginning page number for a print job. Any page number less than the _pbpage value will not be printed. The _pbpage value defaults to 1 but can be set to between 1 and 32,767. The _pbpage value must be less than or equal to _pepage (print job end page). This command is useful if you want to print just the remaining part of a report after a printer jam.

### Example

```
* Start printing on page 1
_pbpage = 1
```

# _Pcolno

### Syntax

```
_pcolno = <column number>
```

### Purpose

Determines the beginning column number for streaming output or returns the current column number. The _pcolno value can be from 0 to 255.

### Example

```
* Set up column 0
_pcolno = 0
```

# _Pcopies

### Syntax

```
_pcopies = <number of copies>
```

### Purpose

Determines the number of copies to be printed in a print job. The default is 1; you can use values from 1 to 32,767. This command can be used only in a program, because it requires a PRINTJOB/ENDPRINTJOB command.

### Example

```
* Set up two copies of report
_pcopies = 2
```

# _Pdriver

### Syntax

```
_pdriver = "<printer driver file name>"
```

### Purpose

Assigns the desired printer driver or returns the name of the currently active printer driver. The printer driver is assigned when dBASE IV is installed, or you can set the default printer driver in the CONFIG.DB file. The *<printer driver file name>* must include the drive and directory name if the specified PR2 file doesn't exist in the current directory. An ASCII printer driver can be used to produce ASCII text files containing no printer commands.

### Example

```
* Set up a custom printer driver
_pdriver = "CUSTOM3.PR2"
```

# _Pecode

### Syntax

```
_pecode = <control codes>
```

### Purpose

Determines the ending control codes for a print job. The _pecode is sent after the ENDPRINTJOB command in your program. The *<control codes>* can be text or printer control commands, such as {27} for the <escape> character used by most printers. The Hewlett-Packard LaserJet printer reset code could be sent as "{ESC}E", "{27}{69}", or "{27}E" (because "E" = "{69}").

### Example

```
* Set up HP LaserJet reset command
* at print job end
_pecode = "{ESC}E"
```

# _Peject

### Syntax

```
_peject = "BEFORE" / "after" / "both" / "none"
```

### Purpose

Determines whether a page is ejected from the printer before and after the print job. Use the _peject command before the PRINTJOB command.

### Example

```
* Set up page eject before next printjob
_peject = "BEFORE"
```

# _Pepage

### Syntax

```
_pepage = <ending page number>
```

### Purpose

Determines the ending page of a print job, with a default *<ending page number>* value of 32,767. The allowable values are 1 to 32,767. The _pepage variable should not be less than the _pbpage (print beginning page) value. This variable is useful in conjunction with the _pbpage system variable to print a portion of a print job.

### Example

```
* End print job at page 20
_pepage = 20
```

# _Pform

### Syntax

```
_pform = "<print form file name>"
```

### Purpose

Activates the *<print form file name>* or returns the name of the currently active *<print form file name>*. Setting the _pform *<print form file name>* enables you to use the following settings from the print form, instead of the current settings: _padvance, _pageno, _pbpage, _pcopies, _pdriver, _pecode, _peject, _pepage, _plength, _ploffset, _ppitch, _pquality, _pscode, _pspacing, and _pwait.

### Example

```
* Set up our custom print form
_pform = "CUSTOM12.PRF"
```

# _Plength

### Syntax

```
_plength = <paper length in lines>
```

### Purpose

Sets the length of the output page; the default is 66 lines. This is the number of lines on the entire page from the top to bottom of the paper. A value from 1 to 32,767 can be assigned. The _plength value is then used to determine when a _peject and _padvance take place. You can use _plength to set up for short forms, such as checks or invoices.

The number of lines on a page also is affected by the setting of the number of lines per inch. The lines per inch normally is set at 6, but you can set up 8 lines per inch or other values by using a printer control code sequence.

### Example

```
* Set up for legal paper
_plength = 84
```

## _Plineno

### Syntax

```
_plineno = <line number>
```

### Purpose

Assigns the <*line number*> for streaming output or returns the current <*line number*>. The _plineno value can range from 0 (the default) to the current _plength-1.

### Example

```
* Set up line number 12
_plineno = 12
* Show current line number
? _plineno
```

## _Ploffset

### Syntax

```
_ploffset = <column number>
```

### Purpose

Determines the page left offset for printed output, or the number of columns from the left edge of the paper where _lmargin will be set. Use the _ploffset value to adjust text on the printed page. The _ploffset default is 0 but can range from 0 to 254.

### Example

```
* Set up eight-character left margin
_ploffset = 8
```

## _Ppitch

### Syntax

```
_ppitch = "pica"/"elite"/"condensed"/"DEFAULT"
```

### Purpose

Sets the printer pitch (number of characters per inch) or returns the string corresponding to the current printer pitch. The default for _ppitch is "DEFAULT". The current pitch is defined by the current setting on the printer. The _ppitch variable sends the appropriate escape code (defined by the currently active printer driver) to the printer. Pica is 10 characters per inch (cpi), elite is 12 cpi, and condensed is about 17.16 cpi (on most printers).

### Example

```
* Set up condensed print
_ppitch = "condensed"
```

## _Pquality

### Syntax

```
_pquality = <condition>
```

### Purpose

Enables you to select the print quality of the output on printers that can produce several levels of print quality. The default setting is .F.. If _pquality is set to false (.F.), the printer will print in draft mode. If this variable is set to true (.T.), the output is set to near-letter quality. You also can use _pquality to return the current print quality setting as true (near-letter quality) or false (draft).

### Examples

```
* Set printer to near-letter quality
_pquality = .T.
* Report on current setting
IF _pquality = .T.
    ? "Printer set to near-letter quality mode."
ELSE
    ? "Printer set to draft mode."
ENDIF
```

## _Pscode

### Syntax

```
_pscode = <control code>
```

### Purpose

Sends the <*control codes*> string to the printer at the beginning of a print job. (The _pecode is used for the ending control code of a print job.) You can set the _pscode variable at any time. It is sent to the printer by the PRINTJOB command. The <*control code*> can be ASCII text or values; values must be enclosed in braces ({ }). To send the landscape command code for a Hewlett-Packard LaserJet printer, for example, you can use {27}&l1O or "{ESC}dl10" or {27}{38}{108}{49}{79} as the <*control code*>.

### Example

```
* Set starting control code for print job
_pscode = "{ESC}dl1O"
```

## _Pspacing

### Syntax

```
_pspacing = 1 / 2 / 3
```

### Purpose

Determines the line spacing for printed output. The default is single spacing (1).

The _pspacing value will affect the height of a box. If _pspace is 3, then a box that has a defined height of 5 will print as 15 lines high.

### Example

```
* Set up double spacing
_pspacing = 2
```

## _Pwait

### Syntax

```
_pwait = <condition>
```

### Purpose

Determines whether the printer will pause after printing each page to enable you to insert paper. The default is false (.F.). The <*condition*> can be .T. or .F., or a condition that evaluates to true or false. Use a _pwait setting of .T. to print on single-sheet, manually fed paper.

### Example

```
* Set up for continuous paper
_pwait = .F.
```

# _Rmargin

### Syntax

```
_rmargin = <right margin column position>
```

### Purpose

Defines the right margin position for ?/?? output when _wrap is true. The default value is 79. The minimum value is the greater of (_lmargin + 1) and (_lmargin + _indent + 1). The maximum value is 255. If _wrap is set to false, the _rmargin value is ignored.

### Example

```
* Set for wide paper margin
_rmargin = 130
```

# _Tabs

### Syntax

```
_tabs = "<tab stop positions>"
```

### Purpose

Sets the tab stops for screen, printer, or file output with the ?/?? commands. _tabs also sets the default tab stops used within memo fields. The default value is a null string (“”), but the default tab stops are at every eight character positions (_tabs = “8,16,24,32...”).

### Example

```
* Set up tab stops every 10 columns
_tabs = "10,20,30,40,50,60,70,80"
```

# _Wrap

### Syntax

```
_wrap = <condition>
```

### Purpose

Sets word wrapping between the margins on (if *<condition>* is true) or off (if *<condition>* is false). The _alignment, _indent, _lmargin, and _rmargin variables are used only when _wrap is on (true).

### Example

```
* Make sure that word wrap is on
_wrap = .T.
```

# Using the Mouse with dBASE IV 1.5

To use a mouse with dBASE IV 1.5, be sure a mouse driver is loaded into your computer's memory. Normally, this is done by including a DEVICE=MOUSE.SYS command in your CONFIG.SYS file, or by putting a MOUSE.COM command in your AUTOEXEC.BAT file. Consult the manual that came with your mouse for specific instructions on loading your mouse driver.

If a mouse driver is present in memory, dBASE IV 1.5 automatically displays the mouse pointer, which is a small rectangle that looks like a cursor. If your mouse has more than one button, use only the left button with dBASE IV. You use this button in three ways:

1. To *click* on an item, press the button once and release it.
2. To *double-click*, press the button twice in rapid succession.
3. To *drag* an object, hold down the button while moving the mouse, then release the button when the dragging is complete.

# Using the Mouse in Work Surfaces

This section discusses ways the mouse can be used in various work areas of dBASE IV.

---

## Control Center

To highlight or activate a file, click on the file name. To create a new file, double-click on the <create> marker.

---

## Menus

To pull down a menu, click on the menu name in the menu bar. To select an option from the menu, click on that option. To cycle through or toggle available multiple-choice options, click on the item until the desired choice appears. To close a menu, click outside the menu area.

---

## Navigation Line

The navigation line at the bottom of the screen may display key labels, such as `Data:F2` or `Help:F1`. To simulate the keypresses described, click on the key label in the navigation line. For double labels, such as `Prev/Next field:Shift-Tab/Tab`, click on the appropriate keystroke within the label (for example, Tab or Shift-Tab).

## Lists

When dBASE IV presents a list, such as a files list box or the expression builder box, click on an item to highlight it. Click on it again to select it. If the item is not initially highlighted, you can double-click on it to select it. To move up or down a list, click on the top or bottom borders of the box. To close the list box, click outside the box.

## Data Entry Boxes

To open a data entry box, click on the related menu option. Relocate the cursor within the input area by clicking on the new position. To zoom the box to provide a larger input area, double-click on the entry box, then double-click in the zoomed area again to reduce it. To abort the data entry, click outside the box, or click inside the box but outside the input area to accept data.

## Error and Warning Boxes

An error box can ask for a response, such as Cancel, Edit, or Help. Click on the appropriate response word. To abandon an operation and close the box, click outside the box area.

## Help Screens

When presented with help options, such as Contents or Related Topics, click on the option button at the bottom of the Help screen. To select an item from a list, double-click on the item. To scroll up and down a list, click on the top or bottom border of the box, or double-click to move up or down a page at a time. To exit Help, click outside the Help box.

## Browse Screen

To highlight a field, click on the field. To reposition the cursor within a field, click on the new position. To pan right or left, click on the right or left borders of the browse table, or double-click to move to the extreme right or left field. To move the highlight up or down a row, click on the top or bottom borders of the browse table, or double-click to move up or down a page at a time. To size a column, drag the right column border to the right or left. To edit a memo field, double-click on the memo marker.

## Edit and Form Screens

Click on a field to highlight it, or click on a position within a field to relocate the cursor. To edit a memo field, double-click on the memo marker or in the memo window.

## Database Design

Click on a row or field to highlight it, or click on a position within a field to relocate the cursor. Click on the Field Type or Index input fields to cycle through available choices. To add a new field definition row, click below the last row.

## Form, Label, and Report Design

In the design surface, double-click on the position where you want to add a field. Double-click on a field to modify it. To move or copy an item, click on it or drag over it to highlight it, press F6 to select, click on the `Move:F7` or `Copy:F8` labels, and move the item to the new location and click. To create a box or line, select Box or Line from the Layout menu, click on the position to start drawing the box or line, drag the mouse to draw it, and then release the button when finished. To size an item, click on it, click on `Size:Shift-F7`, move the mouse pointer to the size desired and click. In the Report Design screen, double-click on a band border to open or close the band.

## The Dot Prompt and Program Editor

To reposition the cursor, click on the new position. From the dot prompt, double-click on the command line to open an editing window. To select a block of text in the program editor, drag the mouse over the block.

## Queries Design

To highlight a field, click on the field in the file skeleton or the top border of a field in the view skeleton. To move right or left in the file skeleton, click on the Tab or Shift-Tab labels in the navigation line. To pan to see fields that are off the screen, click on the left or right arrowhead symbol in the skeleton. To add or remove a field from the view skeleton, double-click on the field name in the file skeleton. To reposition the cursor, click on the new position within a field. To zoom a field to a larger input area, double-click on the field or input area, then double-click on the zoomed area to reduce it again.

## Applications Generator

To select a design object on the work surface, click on the object. The last menu used with the object is activated. To move an object, click on the top or left border and drag the object to the new location. To size an object, click on the right or bottom border and drag the object to the correct size.

# Using the System Configuration File

The CONFIG.DB file contains the default configuration of your installation of dBASE IV. Created during the installation process, the file contains configuration information, memory allocation parameters, function key definitions, SET command settings, and color settings. You can change the CONFIG.DB file with a program editor, by using the DBSETUP program, or with the command MODIFY COMMAND CONFIG.DB. The CONFIG.DB file normally is stored in the dBASE IV program directory.

The only way to change some configuration parameters is to edit the CONFIG.DB file. Following is a list of the parameters you can change only by editing CONFIG.DB:

| | | |
|---|---|---|
| ASCIISORT | GETS | RESETCRT |
| BUCKET | INDEXBYTES | SQLDATABASE |
| COMMAND | LANGTABLES | SQLHOME |
| EXPSIZE | NOCLOCK | SYSPROC |
| FASTCRT | PRINTER | TEDIT |
| FILES | PROMPT | WP |

In addition, several configuration parameters are related to memory allocation and custom design surfaces that can be specified in your CONFIG.DB file. These also are listed in this section.

**TIP**

To specify a configuration file other than CONFIG.DB, use the optional /C switch when starting dBASE IV. To use a configuration file named MYCONFG.TXT, for example, type:

*DBASE /C C:\DBASE\MYCONFG.TXT*

# Configuration Commands

This series of commands is used in the CONFIG.DB file to control the default configuration of dBASE IV.

## ASCIISORT

### Syntax

```
ASCIISORT = ON/off
```

### Default

```
ASCIISORT = ON
```

### Purpose

Causes sorting to be performed in ASCII order. This option works only if LANGTABLES is set to ON.

# BUCKET

### Syntax

```
BUCKET = <number of 1K memory blocks>
```

### Default

```
BUCKET = 2
```

### Purpose

Specifies the number of 1K memory blocks. Use larger values if you have multiple screens or many PICTURE clauses in a format file. The range is from 1 to 31.

# COMMAND

### Syntax

```
COMMAND = <dBASE IV command or program>
```

### Default

```
COMMAND = ASSIST
```

### Purpose

Specifies a <*dBASE IV command or program*> to execute automatically when dBASE IV is started. For example, to automatically run a program called MAINPROG.PRG whenever you start up dBASE, make sure that `COMMAND = DO MAINPROG` appears in your CONFIG.DB file. The default is `COMMAND = ASSIST`, which brings you immediately to the Control Center. Remove this line if you want to go straight to the dot prompt when you start dBASE IV.

You also can start a program immediately as you start up dBASE by following the DBASE command with the program name. For example, typing *DBASE MAINPROG* at the DOS prompt is equivalent to using *COMMAND = DO MAINPROG* in the CONFIG.DB file.

# EXPSIZE

### Syntax

```
EXPSIZE = <number of 1K bytes>
```

### Default

```
EXPSIZE = 100
```

### Purpose

Specifies the size (in bytes) of the memory buffer that holds expressions during program compilation. If your program uses complex expressions, you may see the error message `EVAL work area overflow`. You can correct this problem by specifying a larger EXPSIZE value. The allowable range is from 100 to 2000.

## FASTCRT

### Syntax

```
FASTCRT = ON/off
```

### Default

```
FASTCRT = ON
```

### Purpose

Controls the use of a fast display option. The default ON setting enables dBASE to display information on color screens more quickly but may cause a "snow" effect on CGA-type video/monitor setups. If you see "snow" on your screen during screen displays, set FASTCRT to OFF in your CONFIG.DB file.

## FILES

### Syntax

```
FILES = <number of files>
```

### Default

```
FILES = 99
```

### Purpose

Controls the number of files dBASE IV can have open at any one time. The allowable range is from 15 to 99.

## GETS

### Syntax

```
GETS = <number of GET statements>
```

### Default

```
GETS = 128
```

### Purpose

Specifies the number of @..GET statements that can be active at any one time. Increase this value (the allowable range is from 35 to 1023) if your input screen has a large number of fields or if you are using multiple input screens.

## INDEXBYTES

### Syntax

```
INDEXBYTES = <number of 1K index file nodes>
```

### Default

```
INDEXBYTES = 2
```

### Purpose

Specifies the number of 1K index file nodes that can be in memory at one time. If your index contains large and complex index key expressions, change the INDEXBYTES value (the range is from 2 to 128).

## LANGTABLES

### Syntax

```
LANGTABLES = OFF/on
```

### Default

```
LANGTABLES = OFF
```

### Purpose

Changes the setting for the language table, allowing foreign language characters, lower and upper case characters to be sorted together. LANGTABLES defaults is OFF if the country code is set to United States; otherwise the default is ON.

## NOCLOCK

### Syntax

```
NOCLOCK = OFF/on
```

### Default

```
NOCLOCK = OFF
```

### Purpose

If set to ON, the clock display is suppressed.

## PDRIVER

### Syntax

```
PDRIVER = <printer driver file name>
```

### Default

The value varies, depending on the printer you use.

#### Purpose

Specifies the default printer driver, which is selected during the installation of dBASE IV. The <*printer driver file name*> must exist in the dBASE IV home directory or in the currently set path. Use the _pdriver system memory variable to change the current printer driver temporarily.

#### Sample Entry

```
PDRIVER = HPDSK150.PRS
```

## PRINTER

#### Syntax

```
PRINTER <printer number> = <filename>
   [NAME <printer name string>] [DEVICE <device>]
```

#### Default

The value varies, depending on the printer(s) you use.

#### Purpose

Enables you to configure up to four different printers. The <*printer number*> is a value of 1 to 4. The <*filename*> is the name of the printer driver file. The <*name string*> defines the printer name that will be shown on the Printer Destination menus. The <*device*> specifies the DOS port to use, such as LPT1 or COM2.

#### Sample Entry

```
PRINTER 1 = HPDSK150.PR2 NAME "HP DeskJet (HP 2276)"
DEVICE LPT1
```

## PRINTER FONT

#### Syntax

```
PRINTER <printer number> FONT <font number> =
   <begin font escape code>, <end font escape code>
   [NAME <font name string>]
```

#### Default

The value varies, depending upon the printer(s) you use.

#### Purpose

Installs or changes the fonts for the <*printer number*> set with the PRINTER command. The <*font number*> specifies a number from 1 to 5 that is used to identify the font. The <*begin font escape code*> is the printer escape code that is used to “turn on” the font. The <*end font escape code*> is the printer escape code that is used to “turn off” the font (normally the command that sets the font back to the printer's default). These escape codes can be found in your printer manual. The *<font name string>* is the text that is displayed on the Words Style menu to describe the font.

### Sample Entry

```
PRINTER 1 FONT 1 =
{27}(10U{27}(s0u0p10h12v0s0b3t2Q,
   {27}{69} NAME "Courier 10/12 pt"
```

## PROMPT

### Syntax

```
PROMPT = "<dBASE IV dot prompt string>"
```

### Default

The dBASE dot prompt (.).

### Purpose

Defines a prompt string to replace the "dot" of the dot prompt. The *<prompt string>* can be up to 19 ASCII characters.

### Sample Entry

```
PROMPT = "<Enter DB4 Command>"
```

## REFRESH

### Syntax

```
REFRESH = <number of seconds>
```

### Default

```
REFRESH = 0
```

### Purpose

Specifies the number of seconds between screen updates when dBASE is used on a network.

## REPROCESS

### Syntax

```
REPROCESS = <number of retries>
```

### Default

```
REPROCESS = 0
```

### Purpose

Specifies the number of retries for executing a command when dBASE is used on a network. A setting of –1 calls for infinite retries.

## RESETCRT

### Syntax

```
RESETCRT = ON/off
```

### Default

```
RESETCRT = ON
```

### Purpose

Resets the display screen to the mode in use before an external program was run.

## SQLDATABASE

### Syntax

```
SQLDATABASE = <SQL database name>
```

### Default

```
SQLDATABASE = SAMPLES
```

### Purpose

The name of the SQL database that is activated when you start dBASE IV. The default is set when you install dBASE IV.

## SQLHOME

### Syntax

```
SQLHOME = <path name>
```

### Default

The DBASE\SQLHOME directory of the drive where you installed dBASE IV.

### Purpose

Sets the drive and directory names that contain your SQL database.

## SYSPROC

### Syntax

```
SYSPROC = <file name>
```

### Purpose

Enables you to specify a file containing procedures to be used by your dBASE programs.

# TABS

### Syntax

```
TABS = <tab setting list>
```

### Default

Every eight columns.

### Purpose

Sets the initial tab stop settings. The default is every eight columns (8, 16, 24...) but can be set to any series of numbers separated by commas.

### Sample Entry

```
TABS = 10,20,30,40,50,60,70,80
```

# TEDIT

### Syntax

```
TEDIT = <ASCII file editor program>
```

### Default

The built-in text editor.

### Purpose

Specifies the program to be used as the text editor for the MODIFY COMMAND command. The text editor should be able to read and write ASCII text files. The command line must include the program name, drive, and directory.

> **WARNING:** You must have enough extra memory available to load the text editor program. Many word processing programs can read and write ASCII text files, but many of these require you to specify saving the file as a text file rather than as a normal word processing file that may contain non-ASCII characters.

### Sample Entry

```
TEDIT = C:\WPLIB\PE
```

# WP

### Syntax

```
WP = <memo field editing program>
```

### Default

The built-in text editor.

### Purpose

Specifies the name of the program to use for editing dBASE IV memo fields. Include the drive and directory of the program.

> **WARNING:** You must have enough extra memory available to load the word processing program.

### Sample Entry

```
WP = C:\WP51\WP
```

# Memory Allocation Commands

This series of CONFIG.DB commands controls the amount of memory used by dBASE IV for memory variables, run-time symbols, and compile-time symbols. You can use the LIST/DISPLAY MEMORY command to get information about the current allocation of memory.

To conserve memory, use small values for MVBLKSIZE and RTBLKSIZE commands. If your system doesn't have enough dynamic memory to maintain the memory variables, you get an error message.

## CTMAXSYSMS

### Syntax

```
CTMAXSYSMS = <number of compile-time symbols, from 1 to 5000>
```

### Default

```
CTMAXSYSMS = 500
```

### Purpose

The maximum number of compile-time symbols allocated to a program or procedure file. These are the names of the user-defined variables, fields, and procedures. Increase this value if you see the message `Exceeded maximum number of compile time symbols` when compiling a file.

## MVARSIZE

This command has been retained from dBASE III for compatibility purposes. It is ignored by dBASE IV.

## MVMAXBLKS/MVBLKSIZE

### Syntax

```
MVMAXBLKS = <number of blocks, from 1 to 150>
MVBLKSIZE = <number of memory variables, from 25 to 100>
```

### Default

```
MVMAXBLKS = 10
MVBLKSIZE = 50
```

### Purpose

MVMAXBLKS sets the maximum number of blocks of dynamic memory available for memory variables. The MVBLKSIZE command sets the number of memory variables for each block. The default values allow for up to 500 memory variables. Each memory variable in a block uses up to 56 bytes of memory, so the default uses a total of 28,000 bytes of memory.

## RTMAXBLKS/RTBLKSIZE

### Syntax

```
RTMAXBLKS = <number of blocks, from 1 to 150>
RTBLKSIZE = <number of memory variables, from 25 to 100>
```

### Default

```
RTMAXBLKS = 10
RTBLKSIZE = 10
```

### Purpose

RTMAXBLKS sets the maximum number of blocks of dynamic memory available for user-defined memory variables and run-time session symbols. RTBLKSIZE is the number of memory variables and symbols for each block. These function in the same way as the MVMAXBLKS and MVBLKSIZE variables.

# Function Key Assignment Commands

In the CONFIG.DB file, you can select the commands to be used when you press the function keys. (Current assignments are displayed by the DISPLAY/LIST STATUS command.) You can define F2 through F10, Shift-F1 through Shift-F9, and Ctrl-F1 through Ctrl-F10. The F1 and Shift-F10 keys, along with the Alt-function key combinations used for macros, are not assignable. These entries are equivalent to the SET FUNCTION command.

## <key label>

### Syntax

```
<key label> = "<command string>"
```

### Default

See table R.27.

### Purpose

The *<key label>* is the name of the key, such as F2, Shift-F8, or Ctrl-F3. The *<command string>* is the command or text assigned to that key, and must be enclosed in quotes. The semicolon is used to indicate the Enter key. Table R.27 shows the default settings of the function keys.

**Table R.27 Default Function Key Settings**

| Key | Setting | Key | Setting |
|---|---|---|---|
| F1 = | "HELP;" | F6 = | "DISPLAY STATUS;" |
| F2 = | "ASSIST;" | F7 = | "DISPLAY MEMORY;" |
| F3 = | "LIST;" | F8 = | "DISPLAY;" |
| F4 = | "DIR;" | F9 = | "APPEND;" |
| F5 = | "DISPLAY STRUCTURE;" | F10 = | "EDIT;" |

***Note:*** *F1 and SHIFT-F10 are not programmable.*

### Sample Entry

```
F3 = "DO HELP;"
```

# SET Commands in CONFIG.DB

The SET commands can be specified at the dot prompt or within the CONFIG.DB file. (See "Using SET Commands" elsewhere in this Reference Guide for information about each of the SET commands.) You also can change the various settings from the SET menu. The SET commands in the CONFIG.DB file are permanent for every dBASE IV session, whereas the SET commands at the dot prompt, within a program, or from the SET menu affect only the current dBASE IV session.

Table R.28 shows the default for each SET command in the CONFIG.DB file.

**Table R.28 CONFIG.DB SET Command Defaults**

| Command | Default |
|---|---|
| ALTERNATE | ON |
| ALTERNATE | *<filename>* |
| AUTOSAVE | OFF |
| BELL | ON |
| BELL | *<frequency, duration>* |
| BLOCKSIZE | 1 |
| BORDER | SINGLE |
| CARRY | OFF |
| CATALOG | OFF |
| CATALOG | *<catalog file name>* |
| CENTURY | OFF |
| CLOCK | OFF |
| CLOCK | 0,69 |
| COLOR | *<on/off>* |
| COLOR | *<color settings>* |
| CONFIRM | OFF |
| CONSOLE | ON |
| CURRENCY | "$" |
| CURRENCY | LEFT |
| CURSOR | ON |
| DATE | AMERICAN |
| DBTRAP | OFF |
| DEBUG | OFF |
| DECIMALS | 2 |
| DEFAULT | *<default drive letter>* |
| DELETED | OFF |
| DELIMITERS | OFF |
| DELIMITERS | "::" |
| DESIGN | ON |
| DEVELOPMENT | ON |
| DEVICE | SCREEN |
| DIRECTORY | *<default directory>* |
| DISPLAY | *<default set during installation>* |

*continues*

**Table R.28 Continued**

| Command | Default |
|---|---|
| ECHO | OFF |
| ENCRYPTION | ON |
| ESCAPE | ON |
| EXACT | OFF |
| EXCLUSIVE | OFF |
| FULLPATH | OFF |
| FUNCTION *<key label>* | *<command>* |
| HEADING | ON |
| HELP | ON |
| HISTORY | ON |
| HISTORY | 20 |
| HOURS | 12 |
| INSTRUCT | ON |
| INTENSITY | ON |
| LIBRARY | *<library file>* |
| LOCK | ON |
| MARGIN | 0 |
| MARK | "/" |
| MEMOWIDTH | 50 |
| MENUS | ON |
| NEAR | OFF |
| ODOMETER | 1 |
| PATH | *<path list, up to 60 characters>* |
| PAUSE | OFF |
| POINT | "." |
| PRECISION | 16 |
| PRINTER | OFF |
| PRINTER | PRN |
| PROCEDURE | *<procedure file>* |
| REFRESH | 0 |
| REPROCESS | 0 |
| SAFETY | ON |
| SCOREBOARD | ON |
| SEPARATOR | "," |
| SPACE | ON |
| SQL | OFF |
| STATUS | OFF |
| STEP | OFF |
| TALK | ON |
| TRAP | OFF |
| TYPEAHEAD | 20 |
| UNIQUE | OFF |
| VIEW | *<query/view filename>* |

# Color Setting Commands

These CONFIG.DB settings enable you to specify the default color settings. The syntax of each *<color setting>* follows:

[*<standard foreground>/<standard background>, <enhanced foreground>/<enhanced background>*]

You also can use the COLOR command to specify the complete color setting (see SET COLOR in the "Using SET Commands" section elsewhere in this Reference Guide for further information and examples).

The following color settings are available in the CONFIG.DB file:

```
COLOR OF NORMAL = <color setting>
COLOR OF TITLES = <color setting>
COLOR OF MESSAGES = <color setting>
COLOR OF BOX = <color setting>
COLOR OF INFORMATION = <color setting>
COLOR OF HIGHLIGHT = <color setting>
COLOR OF FIELDS = <color setting>
```

Table R.29 shows the color letter codes for each color.

**Table R.29 Color Codes**

| Color | Letter code | Color | Letter code |
|---|---|---|---|
| Black | N or blank | Magenta | RB |
| Blue | B | Brown | GR |
| Green | G | Yellow | GR+ |
| Cyan | BG | White | W |
| Blank | X | *<color code>*+ | Bright color |
| Grey | N+ | *<color code>** | Blinking color |
| Red | R | *<color code>**+ | Bright, blinking color |

# Design Surface Programs

dBASE IV 1.5 enables you to specify special programs that will execute when entering, exiting or using various design surfaces.

### *Syntax*

```
KEYWORD = <entry>,<exit>,<layout>,<field>,<execute>
```

The following keywords represent supported program types:

| Keyword | Control Center surface |
|---|---|
| PRGCC | Catalog menu |
| PRGDATA | Database design |
| PRGQUERY | Queries design |
| PRGFORM | Forms design |
| PRGREPORT | Reports design |
| PRGLABEL | Labels design |
| PRGAPPLIC | Applications |
| PRGBROWSE | Browse screen |
| PRGEDIT | Edit screen |

# Default File Extension Settings

In most cases, you can override the default file name extensions by specifying the full *<filename.extension>* as the file name. Table R.30 shows the default file extensions, along with their purpose.

**Table R.30 Default File-Name Extensions**

| Extension | Purpose |
|---|---|
| $$$ | Temporary file |
| ACC | Multiuser access control file |
| APP | Application design object file |
| BAK | Command, procedure, or database backup file |
| BAR | Horizontal bar design object file |
| BCH | Batch process design object file |
| BIN | Binary file |
| CAT | Catalog file |
| CHT | Chartmaster file, used with dBASE/Chartmaster Bridge program |
| COD | Template source file |
| CPT | Encrypted memo file |

| Extension | Purpose |
|---|---|
| CRP | Password information file |
| CVT | Database file with change detection field |
| DB | Configuration file |
| DB2 | Renamed dBASE II file used for import and export |
| DBF | Database file |
| DBK | Backup DBF created when structure was modified |
| DBO | Command and procedure object file |
| DBT | Database memo file |
| DEF | Selector definition file |
| DIF | Data Interchange Format (VisiCalc) file |
| DOC | Documentation file |
| FIL | Files list design object file |
| FMO | Compiled screen form file |
| FMT | Generated screen form file |
| FNL | Report binary name list file |
| FR3 | Renamed dBASE III report form file |
| FRG | Generated report form file |
| FRM | Report form file |
| FRO | Compiled report form file |
| FW2, FW3, FW4 | Framework spreadsheet/database file |
| GEN | Template file |
| KEY | Keystroke macro file |
| LB3 | Renamed dBASE III label form file |
| LBG | Generated label form file |
| LBL | Label form file |
| LBO | Compiled label form file |
| LNL | Label binary name list file |
| LOG | Transaction log file |
| MDK | Backup MDK from when DBF structure was modified |

*continues*

**Table R.30 Continued**

| Extension | Purpose |
|---|---|
| MDX | Multiple-index file |
| MEM | Memory file |
| NDX | Single-index file |
| POP | Popup menu design object file |
| PR2 | Printer driver file |
| PRF | Print form file |
| PRG | dBASE IV command or procedure file |
| PRS | dBASE/SQL command or procedure file |
| PRT | Printer output file |
| QBE | QBE query file |
| QBO | Compiled QBE query file |
| QRY | Query file |
| RES | Resource file |
| RPD | RapidFile database file |
| SC3 | Renamed dBASE III screen file |
| SCR | Screen file |
| SNL | Screen binary name list file |
| STR | Structure list design file |
| T44/W44 | Intermediate work files used by SORT and INDEX |
| TBK | Database memo backup file |
| TXT | ASCII output text file |
| UPD | QBE Update query file |
| UPO | Compiled Update file |
| VAL | Values list design object file |
| VUE | View file |
| WIN | Logical window save file |
| WKS | Lotus 1-2-3 worksheet file |
| WK1 | Lotus 1-2-3 worksheet file |

# ASCII Table

The ASCII table shows the decimal values and characters for each of the characters in the ASCII character set. You can use the ASCII character values in text with the CHR() function. Some commands, such as printer setup commands, use the ASCII codes entered as {<*decimal value*>}.

For example, you can set the printer-ending-code variable (_pecode) for the HP LaserJet as the following:

```
_pecode = "{27}{69}"
```

## ASCII Table

| Decimal Value | ASCII Character |
|---|---|
| 0 | (null) |
| 1 | ☺ |
| 2 | ☻ |
| 3 | ♥ |
| 4 | ♦ |
| 5 | ♣ |
| 6 | ♠ |
| 7 | • (bell) |
| 8 | ◘ (backspace) |
| 9 | ○ (tab) |
| 10 | ◙ (line feed) |
| 11 | ♂ |
| 12 | ♀ (form feed) |
| 13 | ♪ (carriage return) |
| 14 | ♫ |
| 15 | ☼ |
| 16 | ► |
| 17 | ◄ |
| 18 | ↕ |
| 19 | ‼ |
| 20 | ¶ |
| 21 | § |
| 22 | ▬ |
| 23 | ↨ |
| 24 | ↑ |
| 25 | ↓ |

*continues*

## ASCII Table Continued

| Decimal Value | ASCII Character | Decimal Value | ASCII Character |
|---|---|---|---|
| 26 | → | 65 | A |
| 27 | ← (Escape, end of file) | 66 | B |
| 28 | └─ | 67 | C |
| 29 | ↔ | 68 | D |
| 30 | ▲ | 69 | E |
| 31 | ▼ | 70 | F |
| 32 | (space) | 71 | G |
| 33 | ! | 72 | H |
| 34 | " | 73 | I |
| 35 | # | 74 | J |
| 36 | $ | 75 | K |
| 37 | % | 76 | L |
| 38 | & | 77 | M |
| 39 | ' | 78 | N |
| 40 | ( | 79 | O |
| 41 | ) | 80 | P |
| 42 | * | 81 | Q |
| 43 | + | 82 | R |
| 44 | , | 83 | S |
| 45 | - | 84 | T |
| 46 | . | 85 | U |
| 47 | / | 86 | V |
| 48 | 0 | 87 | W |
| 49 | 1 | 88 | X |
| 50 | 2 | 89 | Y |
| 51 | 3 | 90 | Z |
| 52 | 4 | 91 | [ |
| 53 | 5 | 92 | \ |
| 54 | 6 | 93 | ] |
| 55 | 7 | 94 | ^ |
| 56 | 8 | 95 | _ |
| 57 | 9 | 96 | ` |
| 58 | : | 97 | a |
| 59 | ; | 98 | b |
| 60 | < | 99 | c |
| 61 | = | 100 | d |
| 62 | > | 101 | e |
| 63 | ? | 102 | f |
| 64 | @ | 103 | g |

| Decimal Value | ASCII Character | Decimal Value | ASCII Character |
|---|---|---|---|
| 104 | h | 143 | Å |
| 105 | i | 144 | É |
| 106 | j | 145 | æ |
| 107 | k | 146 | Æ |
| 108 | l | 147 | ô |
| 109 | m | 148 | ö |
| 110 | n | 149 | ò |
| 111 | o | 150 | û |
| 112 | p | 151 | ù |
| 113 | q | 152 | ÿ |
| 114 | r | 153 | Ö |
| 115 | s | 154 | Ü |
| 116 | t | 155 | ¢ |
| 117 | u | 156 | £ |
| 118 | v | 157 | ¥ |
| 119 | w | 158 | ₧ |
| 120 | x | 159 | *f* |
| 121 | y | 160 | á |
| 122 | z | 161 | í |
| 123 | { | 162 | ó |
| 124 | \| | 163 | ú |
| 125 | } | 164 | ñ |
| 126 | ~ | 165 | Ñ |
| 127 | Δ | 166 | ª |
| 128 | Ç | 167 | º |
| 129 | ü | 168 | ¿ |
| 130 | é | 169 | ⌐ |
| 131 | â | 170 | ¬ |
| 132 | ä | 171 | ½ |
| 133 | à | 172 | ¼ |
| 134 | å | 173 | ¡ |
| 135 | ç | 174 | « |
| 136 | ê | 175 | » |
| 137 | ë | 176 | ░ |
| 138 | è | 177 | ▒ |
| 139 | ï | 178 | ▓ |
| 140 | î | 179 | │ |
| 141 | ì | 180 | ┤ |
| 142 | Ä | 181 | ╡ |

*continues*

## ASCII Table Continued

| Decimal Value | ASCII Character | Decimal Value | ASCII Character |
|---|---|---|---|
| 182 | ╢ | 219 | █ |
| 183 | ╖ | 220 | ▄ |
| 184 | ╕ | 221 | ▌ |
| 185 | ╣ | 222 | ▐ |
| 186 | ║ | 223 | ▀ |
| 187 | ╗ | 224 | α |
| 188 | ╝ | 225 | β |
| 189 | ╜ | 226 | Γ |
| 190 | ╛ | 227 | π |
| 191 | ┐ | 228 | Σ |
| 192 | └ | 229 | σ |
| 193 | ┴ | 230 | μ |
| 194 | ┬ | 231 | τ |
| 195 | ├ | 232 | Φ |
| 196 | ─ | 233 | Θ |
| 197 | ┼ | 234 | Ω |
| 198 | ╞ | 235 | δ |
| 199 | ╟ | 236 | ∞ |
| 200 | ╚ | 237 | φ |
| 201 | ╔ | 238 | ε |
| 202 | ╩ | 239 | ∩ |
| 203 | ╦ | 240 | ≡ |
| 204 | ╠ | 241 | ± |
| 205 | ═ | 242 | ≥ |
| 206 | ╬ | 243 | ≤ |
| 207 | ╧ | 244 | ⌠ |
| 208 | ╨ | 245 | ⌡ |
| 209 | ╤ | 246 | ÷ |
| 210 | ╥ | 247 | ≈ |
| 211 | ╙ | 248 | ° |
| 212 | ╘ | 249 | • |
| 213 | ╒ | 250 | · |
| 214 | ╓ | 251 | √ |
| 215 | ╫ | 252 | $^{n}$ |
| 216 | ╪ | 253 | $^{2}$ |
| 217 | ┘ | 254 | ■ |
| 218 | ┌ | 255 | (unprintable space) |

# INDEX

## Symbols



## A

## B

## C

## D

## E

## G

## H



## I

## J

## K



## L

## M

## N

## O

## P

## Q

## R

## S

## U

## V



## W

## X-Y-Z

# Personal computing is easy when you're using Que!

**Using 1-2-3 for DOS Release 2.3, Special Edition**
**$29.95 USA**
0-88022-727-8, 584 pp., $7^3/_8$ x $9^1/_4$

**Using 1-2-3 for DOS Release 3.1+, Special Edition**
**$29.95 USA**
0-88022-843-1, 584 pp., $7^3/_8$ x $9^1/_4$

**Using 1-2-3 for Windows**
**$29.95 USA**
0-88022-724-9, 584 pp., $7^3/_8$ x $9^1/_4$

**Using 1-2-3/G**
**$29.95 USA**
0-88022-549-7, 584 pp., $7^3/_8$ x $9^1/_4$

**Using AlphaFOUR**
**$24.95 USA**
0-88022-890-3, 500 pp., $7^3/_8$ x $9^1/_4$

**Using AmiPro**
**$24.95 USA**
0-88022-738-9, 584 pp., $7^3/_8$ x $9^1/_4$

**Using Assembly Language, 3rd Edition**
**$29.95 USA**
0-88022-884-9, 900 pp., $7^3/_8$ x $9^1/_4$

**Using BASIC**
**$24.95 USA**
0-88022-537-8, 584 pp., $7^3/_8$ x $9^1/_4$

**Using Borland C++, 2nd Edition**
**$29.95 USA**
0-88022-901-2, 1,300 pp., $7^3/_8$ x $9^1/_4$

**Using C**
**$29.95 USA**
0-88022-571-8, 950 pp., $7^3/_8$ x $9^1/_4$

**Using Clipper, 3rd Edition**
**$29.95 USA**
0-88022-885-7, 750 pp., $7^3/_8$ x $9^1/_4$

**Using DacEasy, 2nd Edition**
**$24.95 USA**
0-88022-510-6, 584 pp., $7^3/_8$ x $9^1/_4$

**Using DataEase**
**$24.95 USA**
0-88022-465-7, 584 pp., $7^3/_8$ x $9^1/_4$

**Using dBASE IV**
**$24.95 USA**
0-88022-551-3, 584 pp., $7^3/_8$ x $9^1/_4$

**Using Excel 3 for Windows, Special Edition**
**$24.95 USA**
0-88022-685-4, 584 pp., $7^3/_8$ x $9^1/_4$

**Using FoxPro 2**
**$24.95 USA**
0-88022-703-6, 584 pp., $7^3/_8$ x $9^1/_4$

**Using Freelance Plus**
**$24.95 USA**
0-88022-528-9, 584 pp., $7^3/_8$ x $9^1/_4$

**Using GeoWorks Ensemble**
**$24.95 USA**
0-88022-748-6, 584 pp., $7^3/_8$ x $9^1/_4$

**Using Harvard Graphics 3**
**$24.95 USA**
0-88022-735-4, 584 pp., $7^3/_8$ x $9^1/_4$

**Using Harvard Graphics for Windows**
**$24.95 USA**
0-88022-755-9, 700 pp., $7^3/_8$ x $9^1/_4$

**Using LetterPoerfect**
**$24.95 USA**
0-88022-667-6, 584 pp., $7^3/_8$ x $9^1/_4$

**Using Microsoft C**
**$24.95 USA**
0-88022-809-1, 584 pp., $7^3/_8$ x $9^1/_4$

**Using Microsoft Money**
**$19.95 USA**
0-88022-914-4, 400 pp., $7^3/_8$ x $9^1/_4$

**Using Microsoft Publisher**
**$22.95 USA**
0-88022-915-2, 450 pp., $7^3/_8$ x $9^1/_4$

**Using Microsoft Windows 3, 2nd Edition**
**$24.95 USA**
0-88022-509-2, 584 pp., $7^3/_8$ x $9^1/_4$

**Using Microsoft Word 5.5: IBM Version, 2nd Edition**
**$24.95 USA**
0-88022-642-0, 584 pp., $7^3/_8$ x $9^1/_4$

**Using Microsoft Works for Windows, Special Edition**
**$24.95 USA**
0-88022-757-5, 584 pp., $7^3/_8$ x $9^1/_4$

**Using Microsoft Works: IBM Version**
**$24.95 USA**
0-88022-467-3, 584 pp., $7^3/_8$ x $9^1/_4$

**Using MoneyCounts**
**$24.95 USA**
0-88022-696-X, 584 pp., $7^3/_8$ x $9^1/_4$

**Using MS-DOS 5**
**$24.95 USA**
0-88022-668-4, 584 pp., $7^3/_8$ x $9^1/_4$

**Using Norton Utilities 6**
**$24.95 USA**
0-88022-861-X, 584 pp., $7^3/_8$ x $9^1/_4$

**Using Novell NetWare, 2nd Edition**
**$24.95 USA**
0-88022-756-7, 584 pp., $7^3/_8$ x $9^1/_4$

**Using ORACLE**
**$24.95 USA**
0-88022-506-8, 584 pp., $7^3/_8$ x $9^1/_4$

**Using OS/2 2.0**
**$24.95 USA**
0-88022-863-6, 584 pp., $7^3/_8$ x $9^1/_4$

**Using Pacioli 2000**
**$24.95 USA**
0-88022-780-X, 584 pp., $7^3/_8$ x $9^1/_4$

**Using PageMaker 4 for Windows**
**$24.95 USA**
0-88022-607-2, 584 pp., $7^3/_8$ x $9^1/_4$

**Using Paradox 4, Special Edition**
**$29.95 USA**
0-88022-822-9, 900 pp., $7^3/_8$ x $9^1/_4$

**Using Paradox for Windows, Special Edition**
**$29.95 USA**
0-88022-823-7, 750 pp., $7^3/_8$ x $9^1/_4$

**Using PC DOS, 3rd Edition**
**$24.95 USA**
0-88022-409-3, 584 pp., $7^3/_8$ x $9^1/_4$

**Using PC Tools 7**
**$24.95 USA**
0-88022-733-8, 584 pp., $7^3/_8$ x $9^1/_4$

**Using PC-File**
**$24.95 USA**
0-88022-695-1, 584 pp., $7^3/_8$ x $9^1/_4$

**Using PC-Write**
**$24.95 USA**
0-88022-654-4, 584 pp., $7^3/_8$ x $9^1/_4$

**Using PFS: First Choice**
**$24.95 USA**
0-88022-454-1, 584 pp., $7^3/_8$ x $9^1/_4$

**Using PFS: First Publisher, 2nd Edition**
**$24.95 USA**
0-88022-591-2, 584 pp., $7^3/_8$ x $9^1/_4$

**Using PFS: WindowWorks**
**$24.95 USA**
0-88022-751-6, 584 pp., $7^3/_8$ x $9^1/_4$

**Using PowerPoint**
**$24.95 USA**
0-88022-698-6, 584 pp., $7^3/_8$ x $9^1/_4$

**Using Prodigy**
**$24.95 USA**
0-88022-658-7, 584 pp., $7^3/_8$ x $9^1/_4$

**Using Professional Write**
**$24.95 USA**
0-88022-490-8, 584 pp., $7^3/_8$ x $9^1/_4$

**Using Professional Write Plus for Windows**
**$24.95 USA**
0-88022-754-0, 584 pp., $7^3/_8$ x $9^1/_4$

**Using Publish It!**
**$24.95 USA**
0-88022-660-9, 584 pp., $7^3/_8$ x $9^1/_4$

**Using Q&A 4**
**$24.95 USA**
0-88022-643-9, 584 pp., $7^3/_8$ x $9^1/_4$

**Using QBasic**
**$24.95 USA**
0-88022-713-3, 584 pp., $7^3/_8$ x $9^1/_4$

**Using Quattro Pro 3, Special Edition**
**$24.95 USA**
0-88022-721-4, 584 pp., $7^3/_8$ x $9^1/_4$

**Using Quattro Pro for Windows, Special Edition**
**$27.95 USA**
0-88022-889-X, 900 pp., $7^3/_8$ x $9^1/_4$

**Using Quick BASIC 4**
**$24.95 USA**
0-88022-378-2, 713 pp., $7^3/_8$ x $9^1/_4$

**Using QuickC for Windows**
**$29.95 USA**
0-88022-810-5, 584 pp., $7^3/_8$ x $9^1/_4$

**Using Quicken 5**
**$19.95 USA**
0-88022-888-1, 550 pp., $7^3/_8$ x $9^1/_4$

**Using Quicken for Windows**
**$19.95 USA**
0-88022-907-1, 550 pp., $7^3/_8$ x $9^1/_4$

**Using R:BASE**
**$24.95 USA**
0-88022-603-X, 584 pp., $7^3/_8$ x $9^1/_4$

**Using Smart**
**$24.95 USA**
0-88022-229-8, 584 pp., $7^3/_8$ x $9^1/_4$

**Using SuperCalc5, 2nd Edition**
**$24.95 USA**
0-88022-404-5, 584 pp., $7^3/_8$ x $9^1/_4$

**Using TimeLine**
**$24.95 USA**
0-88022-602-1, 584 pp., $7^3/_8$ x $9^1/_4$

**Using Turbo Pascal 6, 2nd Edition**
**$29.95 USA**
0-88022-700-1, 800 pp., $7^3/_8$ x $9^1/_4$

**Using Turbo Pascal for Windows**
**$29.95 USA**
0-88022-806-7, 584 pp., $7^3/_8$ x $9^1/_4$

**Using Turbo Tax: 1992 Edition Tax Advice & Planning**
**$24.95 USA**
0-88022-839-3, 584 pp., $7^3/_8$ x $9^1/_4$

**Using UNIX**
**$29.95 USA**
0-88022-519-X, 584 pp., $7^3/_8$ x $9^1/_4$

**Using Visual Basic**
**$29.95 USA**
0-88022-763-X, 584 pp., $7^3/_8$ x $9^1/_4$

**Using Windows 3.1**
**$27.95 USA**
0-88022-731-1, 584 pp., $7^3/_8$ x $9^1/_4$

**Using Word for Windows 2, Special Edition**
**$27.95 USA**
0-88022-832-6, 584 pp., $7^3/_8$ x $9^1/_4$

**Using WordPerfect 5**
**$27.95 USA**
0-88022-351-0, 584 pp., $7^3/_8$ x $9^1/_4$

**Using WordPerfect 5.1, Special Edition**
**$27.95 USA**
0-88022-554-8, 584 pp., $7^3/_8$ x $9^1/_4$

**Using WordStar 7**
**$19.95 USA**
0-88022-909-8, 550 pp., $7^3/_8$ x $9^1/_4$

**Using Your Hard Disk**
**$29.95 USA**
0-88022-583-1, 584 pp., $7^3/_8$ x $9^1/_4$

# Find It Fast with Que's Quick References!

Que's Quick References are the compact, easy-to-use guides to essential application information. Written for all users, Quick References include vital command information under easy-to-find alphabetical listings. Quick References are a must for anyone who needs command information fast!

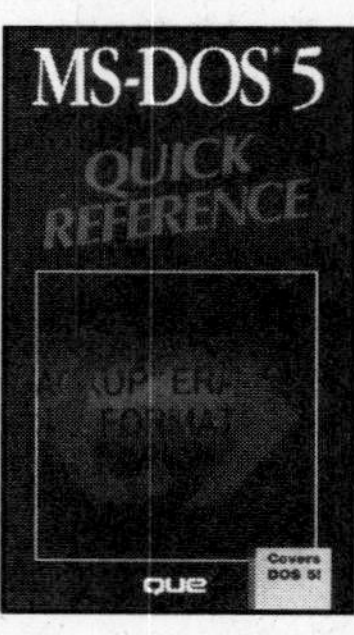


**1-2-3 for DOS Release 2.3 Quick Reference**
*Release 2.3*
**$9.95 USA**
0-88022-725-7, 160 pp., $4\frac{3}{4}$ x 8

**1-2-3 for DOS Release 3.1+ Quick Reference**
*Releases 3 , 3.1, & 3.1+*
**$9.95 USA**
0-88022-845-8, 160 pp., $4\frac{3}{4}$ x 8

**1-2-3 for Windows Quick Reference**
*1-2-3 for Windows*
**$9.95 USA**
0-88022-783-4, 160 pp., $4\frac{3}{4}$ x 8

**AutoCAD Quick Reference, 2nd Edition**
*Releases 10 & 11*
**$8.95 USA**
0-88022-622-6, 160 pp., $4\frac{3}{4}$ x 8

**Batch File and Macros Quick Reference**
*Through DOS 5*
**$9.95 USA**
0-88022-699-4, 160 pp., $4\frac{3}{4}$ x 8

**CorelDRAW! Quick Reference**
*Through Version 2*
**$8.95 USA**
0-88022-597-1, 160 pp., $4\frac{3}{4}$ x 8

**dBASE IV 1.1 Quick Reference**
*Through Version 1.1*
**$9.95 USA**
0-88022-905-5, 160 pp., $4\frac{3}{4}$ x 8

**DR DOS 6Quick Reference**
*Version 6*
**$9.95 USA**
0-88022-827-X, 160 pp., $4\frac{3}{4}$ x 8

**Excel for Windows Quick Reference**
*Excel 3 for Windows*
**$9.95 USA**
0-88022-722-2, 160 pp., $4\frac{3}{4}$ x 8

**Fastback Quick Reference**
*Version 2.1*
**$8.95 USA**
0-88022-650-1, 160 pp., $4\frac{3}{4}$ x 8

**Hard Disk Quick Reference, 1992 Edition**
*Major hard disks & MS-DOS 5*
**$9.95 USA**
0-88022-826-1, 160 pp., $4\frac{3}{4}$ x 8

**Harvard Graphics 3 Quick Reference**
*Version 3*
**$9.95 USA**
0-88022-887-3, 160 pp., $4\frac{3}{4}$ x 8

**Harvard Graphics Quick Reference**
*Version 2.3*
**$8.95 USA**
0-88022-538-6, 160 pp., $4\frac{3}{4}$ x 8

**Laplink III Quick Reference**
*Laplink III*
**$9.95 USA**
0-88022-702-8, 160 pp., $4\frac{3}{4}$ x 8

**Microsoft Word Quick Reference**
*Through Version 5.5*
**$9.95 USA**
0-88022-720-6, 160 pp., $4\frac{3}{4}$ x8

**Microsoft Works Quick Reference**
*Through IBM Version 2.0*
**$9.95 USA**
0-88022-694-3, 160 pp., $4\frac{3}{4}$ x 8

**Paradox 3.5 Quick Reference**
*Version 3.5*
**$9.95 USA**
0-88022-824-5, 160 pp., $4\frac{3}{4}$ x 8

**MS-DOS Quick Reference**
*Through Version 3.3*
**$8.95 USA**
0-88022-369-3, 160 pp., $4\frac{3}{4}$ x 8

**Norton Utilites 6 Quick Reference**
*Version 6*
**$9.95 USA**
0-88022-858-X, 160 pp., $4\frac{3}{4}$ x 8

**PC Tools 7 Quick Reference**
*Through Version 7*
**$9.95 USA**
0-88022-829-6, 160 pp., $4\frac{3}{4}$ x 8

**Q&A 4 Quick Reference**
*Versions 2, 3, & 4*
**$9.95 USA**
0-88022-828-8, 160 pp., $4\frac{3}{4}$ x 8

**Quattro Pro Quick Reference**
*Through Version 3*
**$8.95 USA**
0-88022-692-7, 160 pp., $4\frac{3}{4}$ x 8

**Quicken 5 Quick Reference**
*Versions 4 & 5.0*
**$9.95 USA**
0-88022-900-4, 160 pp., $4\frac{3}{4}$ x 8

**Windows 3 Quick Reference**
*Version 3*
**$8.95 USA**
0-88022-631-5, 160 pp., $4\frac{3}{4}$ x 8

**Windows 3.1 Quick Reference**
*Through Version 3.1*
**$9.95 USA**
0-88022-740-0, 160 pp., $4\frac{3}{4}$ x 8

**WordPerfect 5.1 Quick Reference**
*WordPerfect 5.1*
**$9.95 USA**
0-88022-576-9, 160 pp., $4\frac{3}{4}$ x 8

**WordPerfect Quick Reference**
*WordPerfect 5*
**$8.95 USA**
0-88022-370-7, 160 pp., $4\frac{3}{4}$ x 8

**WordPerfect for Windows Quick Reference**
*WordPerfect 5.1 for Windows*
**$9.95 USA**
0-88022-785-0, 160 pp., $4\frac{3}{4}$ x 8

**To Order, Call: (800) 428-5331**
**OR (317) 573-2500**